NIGHTINGALES

NIGHTINGALES

*The Story of
Florence Nightingale
and her
Remarkable
Family*

GILLIAN GILL

SCEPTRE

NB Throughout the text the family name 'Bonham-Carter' always appears hyphenated. During those parts of Florence Nightingale's life with which this book is mainly concerned, the family generally wrote their name as 'Bonham Carter'; however, at some later point the family added a hyphen, and this version is the generally accepted one at the time of writing.

First published in Great Britain in 2004 by Hodder and Stoughton
A division of Hodder Headline
This paperback edition published in 2005

A Sceptre paperback

1

A CIP catalogue record for this title is available from the British Library

ISBN 0 340 82303 8

Typeset in Adobe Garamond by Palimpsest Book Production Limited,
Polmont, Stirlingshire

Printed and bound in Great Britain by
Mackays of Chatham Ltd, Chatham, Kent

Hodder Headline's policy is to use papers that are natural, renewable and recyclable products
and made from wood grown in sustainable forests. The logging and manufacturing processes
are expected to conform to the environmental regulations of the country of origin

Hodder and Stoughton Ltd
A division of Hodder Headline
338 Euston Road
London NW1 3BH

FOR CHRISTOPHER AND CATHERINE,
who keep me sane and hopeful

CONTENTS

Map ix

Family Tree x

Introduction xiii

1   ENTAILS AND ABOLITIONISTS   1

2   ONE BIG HAPPY FAMILY   24

3   WEN AND FANNY, BEN AND ANNE, SAM AND MAI   46

4   LEA HURST AND EMBLEY   71

5   A PRIVILEGED VICTORIAN CHILDHOOD   87

6   IN FATHER'S LIBRARY   115

7   DOING EUROPE IN STYLE   135

8   COMING OUT   153

9   PROBLEMS WITH THE NICHOLSONS   169

10   MRS. NIGHTINGALE SAYS NO   190

11   FLORENCE NIGHTINGALE IS TEMPTED   205

12   DE PROFUNDIS CLAMAVI DOMINE   233

13   BREAKING FREE   254

14   MANAGING HARLEY STREET   276

15   BRITAIN GOES TO WAR   297

16   STEEPED UP TO OUR NECKS IN BLOOD   323

17   WOMAN TROUBLE   353

18   SPRING AT LAST   370

19   IN THE CRIMEA   385

20   LIVING TO FIGHT THEIR CAUSE   414

21   FAMILY MATTERS   435

      Notes   466

      Acknowledgments   515

      About the Author   519

      Picture Acknowledgments   520

      Index   521

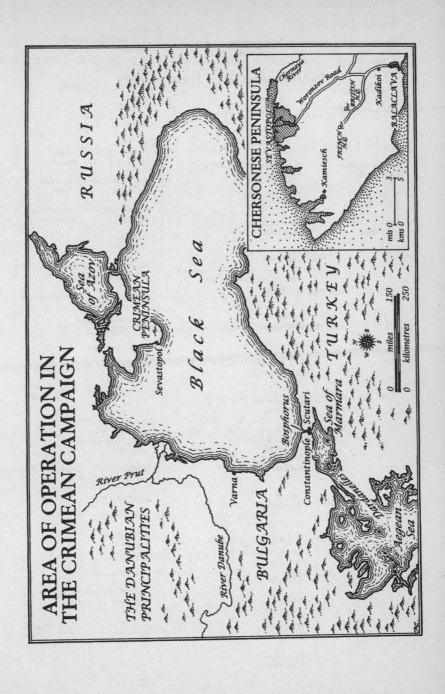

AREA OF OPERATION IN
THE CRIMEAN CAMPAIGN

RUSSIA

Sea
of Azov

CRIMEAN
PENINSULA

Sevastopol

Black Sea

THE DANUBIAN
PRINCIPALITIES

River Prut

River Danube

Varna

BULGARIA

Bosphorus

Constantinople

Scutari

Sea of
Marmara

TURKEY

Dardanelles

Aegean
Sea

miles   150

0   250
kilometres

CHERSONESE PENINSULA

Chernaya River

Woronzov Road

SEVASTOPOL

Kadikoi

BALACLAVA

Kamiesch

FRENCH

BRITISH

mls 0   3
kms 0   5

Nightingale Family

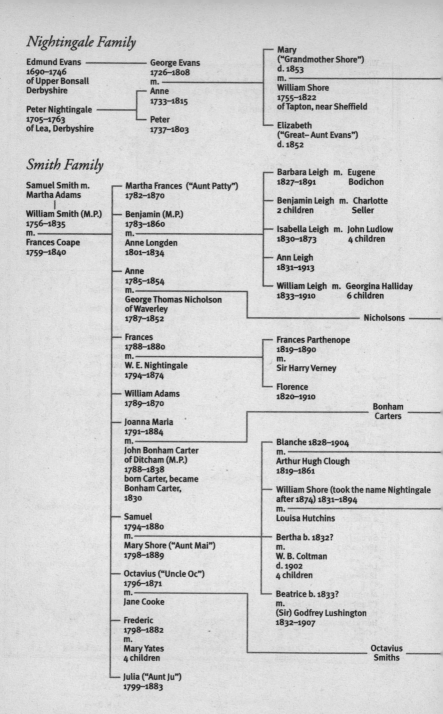

Edmund Evans
1690–1746
of Upper Bonsall
Derbyshire

George Evans
1726–1808
m.
Anne
1733–1815

Peter Nightingale
1705–1763
of Lea, Derbyshire

Peter
1737–1803

Mary
("Grandmother Shore")
d. 1853
m.
William Shore
1755–1822
of Tapton, near Sheffield

Elizabeth
("Great–Aunt Evans")
d. 1852

Smith Family

Samuel Smith m.
Martha Adams
|
William Smith (M.P.)
1756–1835
m.
Frances Coape
1759–1840

Martha Frances ("Aunt Patty")
1782–1870

Benjamin (M.P.)
1783–1860
m.
Anne Longden
1801–1834

Anne
1785–1854
m.
George Thomas Nicholson
of Waverley
1787–1852

Frances
1788–1880
m.
W. E. Nightingale
1794–1874

William Adams
1789–1870

Joanna Maria
1791–1884
m.
John Bonham Carter
of Ditcham (M.P.)
1788–1838
born Carter, became
Bonham Carter,
1830

Samuel
1794–1880
m.
Mary Shore ("Aunt Mai")
1798–1889

Octavius ("Uncle Oc")
1796–1871
m.
Jane Cooke

Frederic
1798–1882
m.
Mary Yates
4 children

Julia ("Aunt Ju")
1799–1883

Barbara Leigh m. Eugene
1827–1891   Bodichon

Benjamin Leigh m. Charlotte
2 children   Seller

Isabella Leigh m. John Ludlow
1830–1873   4 children

Ann Leigh
1831–1913

William Leigh m. Georgina Halliday
1833–1910   6 children

Nicholsons

Frances Parthenope
1819–1890
m.
Sir Harry Verney

Florence
1820–1910

Bonham
Carters

Blanche 1828–1904
m.
Arthur Hugh Clough
1819–1861

William Shore (took the name Nightingale
after 1874) 1831–1894
m.
Louisa Hutchins

Bertha b. 1832?
m.
W. B. Coltman
d. 1902
4 children

Beatrice b. 1833?
m.
(Sir) Godfrey Lushington
1832–1907

Octavius
Smiths

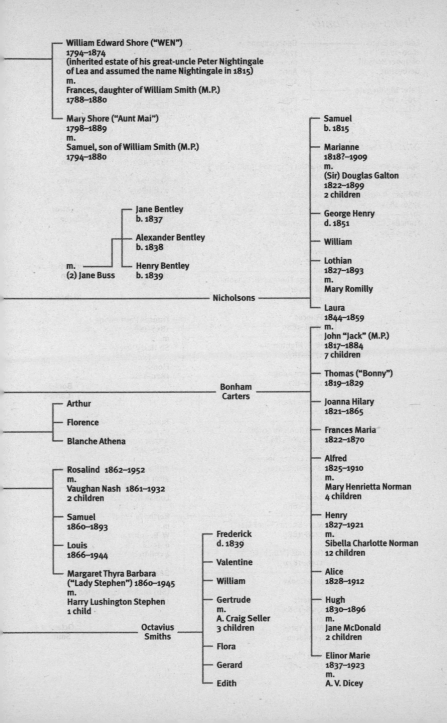

William Edward Shore ("WEN")
1794–1874
(inherited estate of his great-uncle Peter Nightingale
of Lea and assumed the name Nightingale in 1815)
m.
Frances, daughter of William Smith (M.P.)
1788–1880

Mary Shore ("Aunt Mai")
1798–1889
m.
Samuel, son of William Smith (M.P.)
1794–1880

Jane Bentley
b. 1837

Alexander Bentley
b. 1838

Henry Bentley
b. 1839

m.
(2) Jane Buss

Nicholsons

Bonham
Carters

Arthur

Florence

Blanche Athena

Rosalind 1862–1952
m.
Vaughan Nash 1861–1932
2 children

Samuel
1860–1893

Louis
1866–1944

Margaret Thyra Barbara
("Lady Stephen") 1860–1945
m.
Harry Lushington Stephen
1 child

Octavius
Smiths

Frederick
d. 1839

Valentine

William

Gertrude
m.
A. Craig Seller
3 children

Flora

Gerard

Edith

Samuel
b. 1815

Marianne
1818?–1909
m.
(Sir) Douglas Galton
1822–1899
2 children

George Henry
d. 1851

William

Lothian
1827–1893
m.
Mary Romilly

Laura
1844–1859
m.
John "Jack" (M.P.)
1817–1884
7 children

Thomas ("Bonny")
1819–1829

Joanna Hilary
1821–1865

Frances Maria
1822–1870

Alfred
1825–1910
m.
Mary Henrietta Norman
4 children

Henry
1827–1921
m.
Sibella Charlotte Norman
12 children

Alice
1828–1912

Hugh
1830–1896
m.
Jane McDonald
2 children

Elinor Marie
1837–1923
m.
A. V. Dicey

INTRODUCTION

Europe was still in tumult after the great revolutionary uprisings of '48 and threadbare radicals were pouring across the English Channel, but it was domestic sedition, not international anarchy, that led William Edward Nightingale to take refuge in London in the autumn of 1849. WEN, as he was often known, was in such a state his friends barely recognized him. On excellent terms with the foreign secretary, Lord Palmerston, WEN could usually be relied on for some juicy political gossip, and as a founding member of the British Association, he was exceptionally well up on such scientific breakthroughs as the recent discovery of the planet Neptune. But on this occasion all WEN could talk about was Florence, his younger daughter, and her refusal to marry Richard Monckton Milnes. The heinous ingratitude of daughters formed the theme of WEN's remarks, with variations on the fundamental instability of women.

Ever since Monckton Milnes's long and delicate courtship had terminated with a tortured no from Florence, life at the Nightingales' had been bedlam. Fanny Smith Nightingale, WEN's wife, screamed like a cockney fishwife. Parthenope, the elder Nightingale daughter, spent half the day ranting hysterically and the other half prostrate on the red silk damask sofa in the drawing room. And Florence, WEN's darling, the cause of the clamor, paced silently about the house, white and abstracted, for all the world like a Christian facing the lions. It was quite insufferable, and WEN had been obliged to take flight to sympathetic friends in London and the peace of the Athenaeum.

A prudent and peace-minded man, WEN preferred libraries to drawing rooms, uncouth Derbyshire to fashionable Hampshire, and scientific meetings to family visits. WEN's marital strategy was to give the energetic, sociable, ambitious Fanny her head, as long as her expenses were reasonable and her guests did not keep him from enjoying his breakfast. The strategy had worked. Temperamentally, WEN and Fanny were much at odds, but their shared social backgrounds, religious heritage, and intellectual interests made for a successful marriage. Until the problems with Florence began coming to a head, the Nightingales had presented an affectionate and united face to the world, and WEN and his daughters were exceptionally close. In a very unconventional move, WEN had taken on the education of his two clever daughters himself, and this had been a pleasure for all parties. One of the great delights of WEN's life was to find in Florence a mental capacity and a thirst for knowledge that if anything exceeded his own.

But in the fall of 1849 Flo was twenty-nine, and her days of declining Greek nouns and reading political philosophy in her father's library were long past. Everyone knew that intellect did not count for much in a girl's life, and everyone agreed it was time Flo put her remarkable mind to marriage, as her mother had done at about the same age. If Parthe had been able to attract a suitable husband, the pressure would have been off Flo, but, sadly, the elder sister was plain and no suitors had come forward for her.

Several eligible men had danced attendance on Flo, and around 1844 her first cousin Henry Nicholson, whose adoration had been evident for years, had proposed. Marriage between first cousins was quite common in the Nightingales' circle—Laura Nicholson, Henry's younger sister, would eventually marry her first cousin John Bonham Carter, and of course Victoria's marriage to Albert made the whole thing chic. Henry Nicholson was the eldest son, heir to his father's fortune and to the sumptuous Waverley Abbey estate, so the marriage was clearly desirable. All the same, when Florence refused Henry, both Fanny and WEN made no fuss even though Flo's rejection caused a split in Fanny's extended family. Cousin Marianne Nicholson especially, enraged at Flo's treatment of her favorite brother, vowed Flo a hatred as passionate as their former friendship. But even Flo's mother, Fanny, was prepared to weather the Nicholsons' fury, since Richard Monckton Milnes had become a regular visitor at Embley and Lea Hurst and seemed devoted to Flo. It was obvious to all in the large, booming, opinionated Nightingale-Shore-Smith-Nicholson-Carter clan that if a man could have been designed to satisfy a mother's fondest hopes and realize a daughter's secret dreams, Monckton Milnes was the man for Fanny and for Flo.

Richard came from an upper-middle-class Yorkshire family of Dissenter tradition that had been close to the families of WEN and Fanny for several generations. In his youth, Richard had spent several years in Italy, Florence's country of birth, and his manners were full of Mediterranean brio. The Milneses were not at all as wealthy as the Nightingales, but Richard was supremely well connected, his adored mother and sister were both charming women, and his father, by good management, had regained possession of Fryston, the family home in the West Riding. As Mrs. Monckton Milnes, Flo would make a strategic family alliance much desired by both sides and gain a position and an establishment. Her husband would be an intellectual equal, eager to support the philanthropic interests so dear to her. And Flo liked Monckton Milnes. She admitted so herself. In his company she emerged from her shell, talked, laughed, made music, looked young and pretty again. This made her refusal to marry him even more incomprehensible to her father.

As WEN saw it, even if Richard had not been quite such a good match, Flo needed to accept him, for her financial and therefore social situation was far from assured. As the members of the Milnes family were aware, since they had known Florence's family on both sides forever, the greater part of the fortune that enabled the Nightingales to lead such an agreeable life was subject to an odious legal entanglement. During his lifetime WEN had the use and benefit of the Nightingale-related assets that had come to him through his mother and maternal grandmother. However, he was unable to leave the Nightingale estate to his wife or to his children, because both were female. The Nightingale portion of WEN's fortune included the two large estates of Embley Park in Hampshire and Lea Hurst in Derbyshire. On WEN's death, these would pass to his sister, Mai Smith, and after her death to her son, Shore Smith. Thus while WEN was able to support his family in great style and comfort, if he were to die suddenly his widow and daughters would have only the inheritance derived from his own father. WEN was an affectionate and intelligent man, and he worried about what might happen to his wife and to his elder daughter, who, against her wishes, seemed headed for spinsterhood. If Flo married well, much of the other three Nightingales' anxiety would be allayed. As Mrs. Monckton Milnes, Florence would be able to offer an agreeable home to her mother and sister, if they stood in need.

But Florence had said no to Monckton Milnes and, apparently, to marriage in general. For more than six years she had entertained the addresses and toyed with the affections of one of the most popular men in England, only to send him away in the end like a whipped dog. If anything, Flo's refusal left her father even more furious than her mother. It made no sense to him. Flo had always been an especially brilliant young thing, WEN reminded his friends at the club—everyone had been mesmerized by her, men and women, young and old, family and strangers. She had quite put poor Parthe in the shade. WEN had given Flo everything a girl could want, from Parisian frocks to opera tickets to Roman holidays. Even at this moment she was getting ready for a lengthy journey through Greece and Egypt. And all she could do to thank him was act the martyr, chafe at the light domestic duties asked of her, and look down her nose at her father and her home. No wonder Parthe felt hard done by, and Fanny complained that he rewarded Flo for being ungrateful and disagreeable. What would come of the nation, WEN demanded rhetorically, if all loving fathers were held hostage by hard-hearted modern girls like Flo? It was an important question, WEN's friends agreed as they passed the port, and not just for the Nightingale family.

FLORENCE NIGHTINGALE'S refusal of marriage was not merely a whim. It was an individual act of religious dedication and it was an indicator for general social change. The mystic assurance that she had been directly called by God to His service gave Florence the strength to resist the yearnings of her passionate nature for love and companionship, as well as the claims made on her by society to fulfill her natural role as a woman. A spiritual imperative determined her espousal of celibacy, as it had for many exceptional young women over the centuries, even though the brilliant and fashionable Miss Florence Nightingale of Embley Park was not obviously cut in the mold of the virgin anchorite. She was very much the new woman, archetypally English Victorian in her ambition and restless pragmatism, her determination to channel spiritual energies into social reform, just as her friend Lord Shaftesbury did. Her dream was not just to nurse cholera patients, as medieval saints had once kissed lepers, or even to found the modern equivalent of a leprosarium. Florence's dreams were large-scale, suited to a woman born into the ruling class of Great Britain, the hegemonic power of the nineteenth century. She dreamed of becoming a nurse, of developing nursing as a profession for educated, dedicated, capable young women like herself, of making Britain a healthier, safer, happier place for all its citizens, of reassessing and rebuilding the whole system of health care in public institutions. As her sister, Parthe, once remarked of her in admiration and envy, Florence was ambitious, very.

To start with, however, Florence Nightingale simply wanted the freedom to leave the shelter of home and go into the public world of factories, mills, mines, hospitals, poorhouses, law courts, prisons, garrisons, and schools. Given freedom, and a modicum of cash, she could find out what could be done to improve things. Florence Nightingale was quite convinced she had the God-given talent to make a difference, and woe betide her and society if she was forced to bury that talent in the earth. Women, she wrote passionately in her private diaries, had the right to be free and the duty to work, just like men. But it was precisely this right that society at large denied. It was this demand that the three other Nightingales rejected, insisting with all their combined strength that Florence's place was at home, with them. Her first, her essential, her highest duty as a Christian woman, whether or not she married, was to ensure the care of her immediate family.

In its laws, its traditions, its science, its myths, its shibboleths, nineteenth-century society decreed that women were fragile, ethereal beings who belonged in the home, and only there. Women had no place in the public sphere. The most bitter and divisive social crusade was not, in fact, to free the slaves, end discrimination against religious minorities, extend the franchise to the non-propertied classes, or enact a ten-hour working day. These famous campaigns were very long and hard fought, but by the end of the century they had been largely successful in Great Britain. The longest, toughest fight was for equal legal and political rights, financial independence, and personal liberty for women, and the battleground was not so much Parliament or the law courts as individual homes throughout the land.

Girls born in the first part of the nineteenth century in England had remarkably few legal rights, professional opportunities, and personal freedoms even if they were born to families of wealth and privilege. In the year Florence rejected the proposal of Richard Monckton Milnes, Victoria could be queen of England but no lady in the land could vote like her husband, enter Parliament like her father, join the India Office like her brother, preach from the pulpit like her nephew, or serve as justice of the peace like the gentleman farmer she hunted with. Few girls even from elite families received a secondary education, and none could enter the universities, much less gain access to the professions such as medicine, law, or the Church. In this period many women had to work but few could earn a living wage. Only a handful of exceptional women, such as Fanny Trollope, Margaret Oliphant, or Fanny Kemble, could earn enough to offer a decent standard of living to children or other relatives who were dependent on them.

If a woman married well, her chances of financial security significantly improved. This is the reason why the heroine's marriage makes the happy ending for so many of the novels of the period. But once a woman married, her identity legally merged into her husband's, and a wife's civil status as "feme covert" was, as feminist reformer Frances Power Crabbe put it in an 1868 essay, that of a criminal, an idiot, or a child. Unless a father paid to keep his daughter's assets under the control of her male relatives, an English woman who married could own nothing, purchase nothing, contract for nothing, and bequeath nothing without her husband's acquiescence. Everything a married woman inherited, everything she earned, was his to do with as he willed. So was her body. So were her children.

The great majority of English people of the period, women as well as men, saw this manifest inequality as natural and ineluctable. Even those who deprecated the suffering of individual women assumed that this was the price to be paid to keep families strong and intact. An editorial in the *Saturday Review* of 1857 expressed the common view: "Married life is a woman's profession, and to this her training—that of dependence—is modelled. Of course by not getting a husband or by losing him, she may find that she is without resources. All that can be said of her is, she has failed in business, and no social reform can prevent such failure."

For Victorians, the family was the foundation for the whole social edifice. It constituted a refuge from the degrading cares of the marketplace, a still center in the swirling chaos of modern life. Since it was universally agreed that God and nature had made men the superior sex, happy families depended on the successful exercise of power by fathers. The campaign for equal rights for women seemed to strike at the roots of social order, and it was resisted for posing a real and probable threat to the peace of every family in the land.

The seismic shift in social attitudes occasioned by the women's rights movement was registered with peculiar clarity in the Nightingale-Shore-Smith family. Wealth, prominence, education, a tradition of independent thinking in both religion and politics set this family in the vanguard of social change. The ancestors of Florence Nightingale on both sides were Dissenting Protestants, members of the Christian groups who gave the world John Milton, Oliver Cromwell, Isaac Newton, and John Locke, to name but a few. Their coreligionists, the so-called Puritans, had rejected religious constraints and sailed across to America to found colonies in New England. By the late eighteenth century, Nightingale's grandparents on both sides had become "Rational Christians," founding members of the Unitarian movement, which produced Joseph Priestley, Samuel Taylor Coleridge, and Ralph Waldo Emerson, and whose influence on both English and American culture was quite disproportional to its numbers.

Inclined for generations to question received truths, forced by religious prejudices and legal barriers to excel in the socially scorned areas of commerce, industry, science, technology, and education, the Nightingale ancestors came inevitably to political radicalism, and thus in turn to what we now call feminism. The social advances secured by English women during the nineteenth century can be charted precisely in this clan and illustrated by the stories of specific women over four generations.

Elizabeth Evans, Florence Nightingale's paternal great-aunt, born in 1759, was a lonely, strange, vehement autodidact living in a bleak Derbyshire village. Florence deeply loved and revered Miss Evans, but she saw clearly how frustration had twisted her great-aunt's character and caused her endless pain. In the next generation, Martha (Patty) and Julia Smith, Florence's two spinster aunts, were nourished in that brief feminist dawn at the turn of the nineteenth century that produced Mary Wollstonecraft. Informally educated, well read, intensely curious women with few outlets for their talents and energies, the Smith sisters were dependent all their lives on the charity of relatives. Undeterred by poverty, they devoted themselves to such radical causes as the abolition of slavery, independence for Poland, higher education for girls, and the extension of the franchise to women. Aunts Patty and Ju were actually too extreme in their views for their affectionate but censorious Victorian nieces, Florence Nightingale and Barbara Leigh Smith Bodichon, though these two proved to have radical plans of their own. Florence and Barbara received excellent secondary educations but were unable to go on to university or professional school. Each worked, in her different way, to ensure that the next generation of women in the family would at last have the opportunity to train and enter the professions if they wished. By the 1880s, a strong contingent of women from the fourth generation, like Rosalind Nash and Lettice Verney, were able to take their places at Cambridge and Oxford universities alongside their brothers and cousins.

No one on the Nightingale family tree is as famous and achieving as Florence. She was, in all kinds of ways, extraordinary. Nonetheless, the spiritual intensity, the passion for ideas and for facts, the ability to get things done, the concentrated energy for which Florence Nightingale became famous all over the world were all traits waiting for expression in the generations of her mother and grandmothers. Nourished by their wisdom, sheltered by their care, witness to their frustrations, she was motivated to succeed where they had been obliged to fail. In this she is typical of women all over the world today, even as she is quintessentially a Victorian.

HOW, THEN, should we best think about our Nightingales? At first, no doubt, as four strange and compelling individuals. And then perhaps as a rather modern-seeming nuclear family—Fanny, WEN, Parthe, and Flo, two parents and two children, strenuously engaged in the sibling rivalry, intergenerational struggle, and sexual agon now so familiar to us.

The individual strangeness is hard to miss. Florence, of course, virtually ab ovo, was an alien creature, a funny little girl who grew into an oddly intimidating young woman. Who else takes to her bed at the age of thirty-seven for two decades—tortured with pain but working ceaselessly, unable to bear the mere whiff of a close family member on the stairs? Who else reemerges into sociability in her late sixties and finally shuffles off the mortal coil at ninety, after five decades spent fervently waiting for death? Fanny and WEN—charming people, devoted married couple, pillars of society—were both, in different ways, rebels and dreamers. And as for Parthenope, the most fragile of the four, she spent fifty years mixing her own brand of eccentricity—one part artistic sensibility, two parts neurasthenia, three parts chronic ill health—and challenging the other three to love her despite it all.

In some ways, of course, to be odd was to be typically Victorian. Lytton Strachey captures this quality very well in his collection of Eminent Victorians (Henry Manning, Florence Nightingale, Thomas Arnold, Charles George Gordon), but other specimens are in ample supply. The statesmen Melbourne, Palmerston, Gladstone, and Disraeli were all very different, but they were all eccentrics. Dickens, Thackeray, George Eliot, Charlotte Brontë were writers whose lives read stranger than their fiction. Elizabeth Barrett Browning and Dante Gabriel Rossetti were famously weird even in their day, while Tennyson, Emily Brontë, and Christina Rossetti kept their oddness under wraps by meeting as few people as possible. Victoria herself, if only by force of being Queen Empress, grew increasingly odd as her reign continued. And this is not to mention more minor figures like "opium eater" essayist Thomas De Quincey, bohemian novelist Wilkie Collins, or poet, painter, and certified lunatic John Clare. In an age when children drank beer for lunch, gin was mother's milk to many, port flowed by the barrel at gentlemen's clubs, and people took opium, alcohol, arsenic, antimony, and mercury to regain their health, delusion prospered and dementia lurked. It wasn't just the madwoman in the attic but the crazy uncle in the asylum, the brother who committed suicide, and the sister who refused to get out of bed.

Yet to see the Nightingales merely as neurotics or candidates for family therapy misses a crucial aspect of their lived experience—the degree to which they identified themselves as members of a group rather than as isolated individuals. Affluent modern Westerners like to be monads, human billiard balls cheerfully rebounding off the corners of the world. Upper-middle-class English Victorians were more like threads woven into the warp and woof of society. The Nightingales were part of a stiff, sticky, supportive family matrix that kept them short of the adultery, drug addiction, alcoholism, and suicide they saw all around them. The apparently individualizing traits we see in our four Nightingales—their wit and curiosity and drive, their spiky iconoclasm, their refusal to be bored, especially by bores—also made them charter members of a highly specific social caste. We see in these four remarkable people the expression of an achieving family's heritage, the mark of an enlightened religious faith, the shaping of a progressive educational philosophy, and the reflection of a financially and intellectually privileged milieu.

Nightingales is the story of one extraordinary woman's struggle to find an independent role for herself in Victorian England, and of the painful dynamics that her struggle set off in her nuclear and extended family. The struggle took place in Paris, Rome, Frankfurt, Athens, and Cairo, as well as in England's handsomest drawing rooms and gardens. It was observed by some of the most interesting people of the day—writers Elizabeth Gaskell and Harriet Martineau, mathematicians Charles Babbage and Ada Lovelace, philanthropists Lord Shaftesbury and Julia Ward Howe, philosopher John Stuart Mill, medical pioneer Elizabeth Blackwell, classicist Benjamin Jowett. Queen Victoria and Prince Albert have cameo roles in this story.

Florence Nightingale is one of the most remarkable women known to history. She was a bona fide heroine in her time, a nineteenth-century woman who yearned to become a new Teresa of Avila, mystic, religious reformer, saint. She is also one of the best-documented women who has ever lived. We shall be spending a good deal of time with Florence as a child, girl, and young woman, since these were the years when her life was tightly bound up with her family. And no book on the Nightingales could fail to give some account of Florence's extraordinary twenty-one months in Turkey and the Crimea, one of the most famous events in women's history. All the same, this is not a biography of Florence Nightingale. When her health breaks down in 1857 and she moves into seclusion to work all out for health reform, I shall not follow her into the bedroom upstairs or monitor the business she conducts there. Just as she kept beloved family and friends resolutely at bay during her fifteen-odd years of frenzied reform lobbying and continued thereafter to focus her energies on international health care issues, so we too shall hear of Florence's activities after 1858 only insofar as family and friends are involved.

In thousands of autobiographical fragments—journals and diaries and drafts of letters not sent, comments scribbled in the margins of books and on scraps of paper—Florence Nightingale made sure that posterity knew just how hard it was to be her. The sheer volume and vehemence of this record has obscured how difficult it also was to be Florence Nightingale's mother, father, aunt, cousin, friend, and sister. Having a would-be saint in the family is not an unalloyed asset, and living down the street, as her sister and brother-in-law Sir Harry Verney did, from an international icon of the female gender is not all beer and skittles—or, perhaps I should say in this case, champagne and croquet. In this book, we shall see how the Nightingale clan adored and criticized Florence, supported and fought her, empathized with and misunderstood her, defined and were defined by her. No longer an isolated woman in a spotlight, Florence becomes in this book the leading actress in a drama full of meaty roles, part comedy, part tragedy, part epic.

Through the collage of viewpoints afforded us by several generations of this remarkable family we gain insight into the Victorian era. But the Nightingale story is not just a lavish period piece, and the problems the Nightingales experienced were not limited to the elite of one country at one time. *Nightingales* is the story of an influential, functioning, evolving family unit, and how it held strong to meet the challenges of its day.

Chapter 1

ENTAILS AND
ABOLITIONISTS

T o get the measure of our four Nightingales, we need to go back to the time before Victoria became Regina and find the source of their wealth, their class identity, their social confidence, their philanthropic energy, their political influence, and their neuroses. Let us see them first as part of an expansive, tumultuous, brilliant clan that in the course of the nineteenth century included, most prominently, Smiths, Shores, Nicholsons, Bonham-Carters, Leigh Smiths, Cloughs, and Verneys. This clan in turn formed part of the "intellectual aristocracy" chronicled by Noel Annan,[1] members, in Virginia Woolf's words, of the "very communicative, literate, letter-writing, visiting, articulate, late nineteenth century world."[2] This small, closely knit group provided Britain with many of its scientists, theologians, philosophers, sociologists, journalists, university teachers, and writers.[3]

Moving farther out in the circles, both Fanny and WEN's families were by tradition Unitarian, or "Rationalist Christian," and thereby hooked into an international network of believers, small in number but of great influence, especially in New England. Long after most clan members had ceased to attend Unitarian services, this Unitarian heritage was to shape the lives of male and female descendants.[4] Then the Nightingales and their expanding clan were conspicuous members of that larger rising middle class in Britain that stood beneath the "dignified" classes of monarchy, aristocracy, and gentry and above the agricultural and industrial laborers. This was the "efficient" class, which, according to Walter Bagehot, who belonged to it, in fact ruled England and made it work.[5]

Finally, this clan, living in the years when all the world accepted that Britannia ruled the waves, was deeply, self-consciously, triumphantly, but not narrowly, English.

So our story begins in the late eighteenth century in the Midlands, the industrial heartland of England, more specifically in the county of Derbyshire, where Nightingales began the move up the social ladder that in three generations brought them from mere local prominence to international fame.

Nightingale, "singer of the night," began in Middle English as the name of a small, inconspicuous, and not uncommon bird with a singularly sweet song. Greek *filomela,* Persian *bulbul,* just plain American *thrush,* the nightingale has become the bird of poetry par excellence. Across cultures the nightingale is female, a brutally ravished heroine, a caged companion to a lonely Chinese emperor, the Philomel of melody whom Shakespeare summoned to lull Titania in the magic wood. The soldiers who met Florence Nightingale in the Crimea knew her affectionately as "the Bird," and the romantic associations of her surname had their own small part to play in the legend crafted around the woman.[6]

Given the traditional femaleness of nightingales, it seems fitting that WEN, Fanny, Parthenope, and Florence, our four protagonists, came to be Nightingales through the distaff side. In fact, Florence would have been plain, unromantic Miss Shore, whose mother was—oh horrors!—a Smith were it not for a piece of legal sleight of hand.[7] In 1803, the eight-year-old William Edward Shore inherited the lands and estate of his great-uncle Peter Nightingale, squire of Lea Hall in Derbyshire. Peter Nightingale was the brother of young William Edward's maternal grandmother, Anne Nightingale Evans, and the uncle of his mother, Mary Evans Shore. William Edward—the man variously known for sixty years to friends and family as Nightingale, Night, Uncle Night, and WEN (as I shall generally refer to him for convenience)—took the name of Nightingale only in 1815, when he turned twenty-one.[8]

The boy inherited the estate through an entail. Entail provisions were ancient and complex strategies worked into English law whereby the capacity to sell or bequeath real property was restricted so that the family of the original owner kept control. The theory was that a piece of land belonged to a family and that a specific individual might hold it and enjoy its profits during his lifetime but could not sell it or control its disposition after his death. One common entail on the "heirs of the body" sought to ensure that, if an heiress died, her family property would pass to her own children or revert to her own family if she had no children, not to any subsequent wives and children her husband might have.

The primary purpose of land tenure law was to keep a property intact across the generations, and the time-honored way to do this was to give preference to a single male heir. If a man had six daughters and then a son, his real property must by law pass intact to the youngest child. If a man had several sons, the eldest inherited the property. In the worst-case scenario of a man with only daughters, however, his property was equally divided between the daughters. Entails on an heir-male prevented such divisions by dispossessing all the daughters in favor of some distant male relative. In *Pride and Prejudice,* Jane Austen dramatized the dark shadow cast over the lives of Mrs. Bennet and her daughters by an entail on the heir-male that governed the Bennet estate. In the event of Mr. Bennet's death, his wife and children would be cast into penury since his house and fortune would inexorably pass to his male cousin.

Entail provisions were often eccentric, and according to one contemporary witness, this was true of the Nightingale entail. That redoubtable lady Frances Coape Smith, together with her husband William Smith, M.P., visited her old friends the Shores in their Tapton home in 1804 and recorded the following entry in her travel journal: "William Shore, a lad of about ten years of age, has had 100,000 pounds left him by a Mr. Nightingale, with the whimsical prohibition of neither benefiting himself when under age, nor suffering his daughters to inherit. Should he not have a son, it goes to his sister."[9] Mrs. Smith had no way of knowing it in 1804, but the Nightingale entail would turn out to be of immediate importance to her own family. Not only would her daughter Fanny eventually marry the lucky William (Shore) Nightingale, but her son Sam would marry William's sister and heir presumptive, Mary (Mai) Shore.

The medieval law of entail was one of the most arcane of legal specialties, and the further one ventures into the question of the Nightingale entail, the murkier things become. Frances Smith obviously did not understand it since she says the boy WEN inherited a hundred thousand pounds. An entail governs real property, not personal property, so presumably what Frances meant was that WEN inherited real property worth some one hundred thousand pounds. She says that WEN would be unable to benefit from the Nightingale money during his minority, but thereafter she implies that he could do anything he liked with it except leave it to his female children. But things were much more complicated than this. Much of the land surrounding the new house of Lea Hurst and all the Embley Park property were purchased by WEN, and yet they were subject to the Nightingale entail, and so passed on his death to his sister, Mai, and his brother-in-law, Sam Smith. On the other hand, the Nightingale land in Derbyshire proved to have valuable coal deposits, generating revenue that WEN was able to invest. Such investments were not real property, and it was increasingly unclear whether their profits fell under the terms of the Nightingale entail or formed part of WEN's personal estate and could thus pass to his daughters. And so, because he failed to produce a son, WEN was throughout his life accountable to Sam Smith, as husband to Mai, heir under the entail but not a legal entity under the doctrine of "feme covert," and father and trustee to Shore, who, as the only male child, would inherit from his mother.

One thing is clear. Fanny Nightingale and her two daughters were in rather the same position as Jane Austen's fictional Bennet women. They lived in the shadow of an entail, and this created stresses. Most specifically, they all three knew that on WEN's death they would lose their home. The large, expensive, and greatly beloved estates of Embley and Lea Hurst would pass to the Sam Smiths. Property issues smaller than this have been the bane of families throughout history. As we shall see, the Shore-Smith-Nightingale family showed some greatness of spirit in the considerate and civilized way they handled the problems of the Nightingale entail.

WHEN WILLIAM EDWARD inherited from Great-uncle Peter Nightingale in 1803, his grandmother Anne Nightingale Evans was still alive— she died only in 1815—as was his mother, Mary Evans Shore. If my own small son were to inherit a fortune from my uncle, I should probably harbor some bitterness at being passed over. But married women in England around 1800 were obliged to accept the fact that the law hated to trust women with money, so Mrs. Shore is unlikely to have felt any resentment about her son's windfall. In fact, she had the satisfaction of knowing that the Nightingale money would come to her son if she should die young and her husband start a new family. Furthermore, with his only son rich in his own right, William Shore the elder, himself a wealthy man from a wealthy family, would be able to leave his widow more than comfortably off and find a large dowry for his daughter. Mai, as she was always called to distinguish her from her mother, would have excellent marriage prospects. That was about as much as a woman could rationally hope for in England at the turn of the nineteenth century.

The Shores, the family of WEN's father, and the Evanses, the family of his maternal grandfather, made their homes and their livings in the Midlands. This region is only a couple of hundred miles from London and yet, in the view of England's oligarchy from the days of Chaucer well into the nineteenth century, a barbarous place, though not, of course, quite as bad as Scotland. Like many northerners, the Shores and their kin engaged in what the Victorians liked to disparage as "trade"—that is to say, commerce, industrial production, and finance. Their moral tone was high, their thrift and diligence exemplary; they made and mined and banked and became rich. But in custom, and in that crucial class marker in England, language, to an educated English southerner, they were at best provincial, at worst uncouth.

Originally, the Nightingales came out of the same class as the Shores since the origin of the Nightingale fortune was lead. In Derbyshire, the mining of that traditionally ignoble metal goes back many centuries, and a certain Peter Nightingale first came to local prominence as the owner of a lead mine in Wirksworth, Derbyshire. Records of the Nightingales' commercial transactions apparently go back to the seventeenth century, and in the early eighteenth century, they managed to move up the social ladder when the first Peter purchased the Manor of Lea, across the valley from Wirksworth, and became master of Lea Hall. Peter Nightingale had only two children, a daughter, Anne, and a son, Peter, and the son of course inherited all the real property. The second Peter, who never married and thus produced no children who could inherit his real property, moved the family up several more notches. He was born in 1736 and earned the epithet "Mad Peter." Local legend has it that the second Peter was a squire straight out of the novels of Fielding and Sterne, a hard-riding, hard-drinking bachelor.

Peter Nightingale Jr.'s madness did not extend to money. When he was not taking stone walls head-on or falling down dead drunk, Mad Peter seems to have had his wits about him.[10] Far from dissipating his father's fortune, he established a lead-smelting plant on his Lea property, built a mill for cotton spinning on the Lea Brook, and found the money to acquire the adjacent manors of Cromford and Wakebridge. He also modernized Lea Hall, giving it a pillared façade in the new Georgian style.[11] This was more in keeping with the social status of a man who served for a time as high sheriff of Derbyshire. The cotton mill in Lea did not prosper and so, in what proved to be a canny decision, Nightingale turned it over to John Smedley, who changed the Lea mill from cotton to wool and soon began to make a profit. Smedley's factory is still in business today, the oldest mill in continuous production in England. The imposing mill buildings still crowd the narrow sidewalks of Lea. A bridge bearing the company's arms extends over the road like an industrial Bridge of Sighs.

In 1776 Peter Nightingale sold his Cromford property to Richard Arkwright, and this was to prove a most significant deal, not only for the fortunes of the Nightingale family but for the history of Derbyshire. Arkwright, a pioneer in the installation and exploitation of machines for spinning thread, harnessed the Bonsall Brook and the Cromford Sough, a local lead mine drain, and started spinning. Cotton imported from America's slave South was spun and woven into cloth, priced to appeal to ordinary citizens all over the world, then shipped by Britain's merchant navy, and marketed by British merchants. England became rich and slavery, far from withering away as the American founding fathers had piously assumed, brought the slave-owning states not only prosperity but also international legitimacy.[12] All of this intense industrial activity was occurring in what amounted to Peter Nightingale's backyard.

Arkwright was a competent engineer, but his real claim to fame was as an industrial organizer. He pioneered the factory system that not only revolutionized textile manufacture all over the world well into the twentieth century but offered a general model for concentrated, large-scale mass production units. In Cromford, Arkwright and his son built accommodation for their growing workforce on the site and houses for weavers in the village, with a third story to accommodate the looms. Cromford, hitherto a small community of sheep-farming and lead-mining families strung out along a rocky, narrow mountain valley, developed into the prototype of the factory complex. Versions of Cromford were established in Germany and the United States, and Americans from small textile towns in the South would feel at home in the village even today. By 1800 the Lea Brook was harnessed and polluted, the air in the deep valleys was thick with particulates from the lead smelting, and lead had made the ground bare in patches—"bellanded," in the local term.[13]

The Arkwright mills still dominate Cromford today. They are at the heart of the Peak District, one of the wildest and most beautiful parts of England, a mecca for hikers, rock climbers, and mountain bikers.[14] But when Parthe and Flo Nightingale spent their summers at their father's new house, Lea Hurst, the local industry was not tourism. "Dark satanic mills," in the words of William Blake's famous diatribe "Jerusalem," had in all truth spread over the "green and pleasant land" of Derbyshire. The lead mines and smelters, the coal mines, Smedley's woolen mill at Lea, and Arkwright's great cotton mills in Cromford were the source of the Nightingales' wealth and social prominence.

The price of industrialization was clearly visible to the Victorians themselves.[15] The horrors of life in the mills, the mines, and the clay pits, the unparalleled disease and squalor of the slums in England's great cities, were studied and recorded in chilling detail in a series of great governmental reports in the mid-nineteenth century. They were also a major theme for the leading writers of the time. Hood's *The Song of a Shirt,* Elizabeth Barrett's *Cry of the Children,* Carlyle's *Chartism,* Dickens's *Oliver Twist, Hard Times,* and *Bleak House,* Gaskell's *Sylvia* and *North and South,* and Disraeli's *Sybil* all in different ways raised the national consciousness and fueled the engine of social reform. But these writers were in the main not opposed to industry and commerce per se. They saw that industrialization was a powerful force for equality and democracy, that factories offered opportunities for the talented few and a path to a better life, however stony and uphill, for the many.

One of the most revolutionary features of the textile mill system was that it brought together thousands of female workers, gave them communal housing, and paid them something at least approaching a living wage. This led to a new level of sexual equality among working-class young people that some called female emancipation and others female corruption. Everyone agreed it was subversive. Many prominent Victorian women, especially those who had connections with the Midlands and North of England, were fascinated by the phenomenon of the mill girl. In *Adam Bede* George Eliot set up a contrast between her heroine Dinah Morris's industrial village, Snowfield—which was based directly on Cromford—and Hayslope, her hero Adam's rich, warm, traditional agricultural home. At the end of the book Eliot "saves" Dinah by marrying her to Adam and retiring her into traditional domesticity.

Harriet Martineau, though a generation older than George Eliot, was more radical in her views on women workers. Martineau argued that industrialization offered ordinary women opportunities they had never had before. The daughter of a manufacturer, Martineau was not nostalgic for the old England of landlord and tenant. In Martineau's view, where the life of agricultural workers was degraded and stagnant, industrial workers were a dynamic force in society. What the oppressed women of England needed was cheaper bread, better schools, and public libraries, not a move out of the industrial sector into domesticity. Martineau wrote to Richard Monckton Milnes: "I have *seen* the women and girls at Lowell and Waltham [the textile mills in Massachusetts]—fresh and brisk—dancing in the winter evenings, and walking in the summer—playing on the piano, attending Emerson's lectures, reading and writing while working in the mills 70 hours a week."[16]

Florence Nightingale, on her father's side, was a child of the industrial Midlands, and her favorite home, Lea Hurst, was just down the road from Cromford, where the industrial revolution can be said to have started. Her parents and the Martineau family had long been friends and allies. Even as a very small child, Nightingale was outraged by the social chasm between rich and poor that opened up at the end of the Lea Hurst driveway. As she grew up she became deeply involved in her Derbyshire community and for a number of years organized evening classes for the young mill women who lived near her home. In the lives of her students, Florence Nightingale saw poverty and toil, but she also saw strength, self-respect, and independence, qualities singularly lacking in most women of her own class.

DURING WILLIAM EDWARD (SHORE) NIGHTINGALE'S minority, the Nightingale inheritance was in trust and the Derbyshire estates grew notably in value. By his early twenties WEN had an annual income of some seven thousand to eight thousand pounds, perhaps four hundred thousand in today's terms. In an age when men and women tried to feed their families on a few shillings a week, this income made WEN a rich man.

How large a part William Shore Sr. played in the management of his son's inheritance during his minority is not known since Shore is a rather shadowy figure in Nightingale history. Whereas his wife lived to be ninety-five and played an active role in the lives of her grandchildren, William Shore died in 1822, before any of the new generation could know him. Shore was not a man in the public eye and in their adult letters WEN and Mai say little of their father. Nonetheless, the slim evidence we have points to the fact that William was not only intelligent, well educated, and able but a man of high principles, strong religious faith, radical political sympathies, and deep devotion to his family. No one was better suited to the task of serving as his son's trustee and also of educating young William to take on the new opportunities and responsibilities that the Nightingale fortune would entail.

William Shore was a member of an old, respected, and affluent clan of Yorkshire Dissenters or Nonconformists, minority Protestants who refused allegiance to the established Church of England. Dissenters had suffered social, political, and financial discrimination because of their religious views ever since the late seventeenth century. Under the Test and Corporation Acts, Dissenters had no right of public assembly, were barred from holding public office, and could take degrees at Oxford and Cambridge only by abjuring their faith. As a result of the years of discrimination and even persecution they had known, English Dissenters formed a closely knit national community. The Shores intermarried with local coreligionists, and they also maintained strong cultural, commercial, and familial ties with Dissenting families in other parts of the country.

Sheffield, the home of the Shores, was an old Yorkshire industrial city, famous above all for cutlery and silver plate. William Shore and his brothers Samuel and John established the first bank in Sheffield. By the 1780s, William Shore of Sheffield was a wealthy man, but the extraordinary political vicissitudes of the period 1789 to 1815 left him little peace of mind. The political tides had once again turned against the Dissenters, and local yahoos roamed in search of mayhem and loot. The Shores had reason to fear for their homes and businesses. In 1792, anti-Jacobin rioters in Manchester, inflamed by the Anglican clergy and encouraged by local magistrates, attacked the house of Thomas Walker, William Shore's brother-in-law. Walker courageously defended himself against the mob, but then a trumped-up charge of conspiring to overthrow the government was brought against him. Walker's acquittal cost him three thousand pounds, and his business never recovered from the slander. Abuse of this kind led a number of notable Dissenters to emigrate to the United States.[17]

William Shore and his wife and children lived on the moors on the outskirts of Sheffield, in Tapton near the Derbyshire border. The house was about twenty-five miles, or a day's ride on horseback, from Peter Nightingale at Lea Hall. Florence recalled in 1890 that her paternal grandfather, Mr. Shore, "was most charming—he was so kind but he could be very stern—utterly disinterested & his wife too, caring nothing for money—of a racy independent Northern stock, living their lives away from all neighbours." Of her grandmother, whom she had known very well, Nightingale told Lady Margaret Verney that she was "very clever, very original and a thorough lady" but not educated, unable to spell and reading only her Bible and prayer book. "She never did anything because anyone was looking at her, or abstained from doing anything because anyone was looking at her . . . She dressed once for all in the morning said her prayers & came down to breakfast—after her midday dinner she went upstairs knelt down by her bed & prayed aloud, there was no concealment about it . . . we children knew that grandmother went up to say her prayers & we could hear her voice in the passage, speaking to God with such passion & earnestness—as if He were in the room—which He certainly was."[18]

The wild, antisocial attitude that characterized both Mary Evans Shore and her sister, Elizabeth Evans, mirrored the bleak moors and crags of their native country as well as the rough, uncompromising humor of the poorer country people. Anyone who has read Emily Brontë's *Wuther-*

ing Heights or Juliet Barker's superb biography of the Brontës will have a good sense of this. Florence Nightingale felt at home at Lea Hurst, liking Derbyshire because it was considered wild and unfashionable. Even as a teenager she found her father's tenants and the workers from the nearby Cromford cotton mills more interesting than the wealthy families who left cards for her mother at Embley. As Nightingale would recall later: "The greatest delight of those child days was our visits to my dear old Aunt in the valley . . . She lived in the most perfect of the Derbyshire old houses, with its paved terrace and its flight of stone steps overlooking the dashing River—with a Virginia creeper over its roof, which in Autumn was a perfect sheet of fire twisting with a broad-leaved Vine in & out of the old mullioned windows."[19]

Through the Nightingale inheritance William Edward became a country squire. By adopting the name of Nightingale and marrying the charismatic Fanny Smith, WEN became in many ways more of a Smith-Nightingale than a Shore. For the Shores and their Midlands clan, this was no cause for rejoicing. Especially after Parthe and Flo were born, WEN's mother, living in Tapton, and his aunt, in Cromford, would have liked him less wealthy and cosmopolitan, settled year round at Lea, close to them.

Florence noted the disjunction between her father and his past and believed that William Edward would have been happier as a manufacturer or banker Shore than as a gentleman Nightingale. Florence wrote: "My father is a man who has never known what struggle is . . . Effleurez, n'appuyez pas [keep it light, don't bear down hard] has been not the rule but the habit of his life, liberal by instinct not by reflection. But not happy. Why not? He has not enough to do. I see him eating his breakfast as if the destinies of a nation depended upon his getting done, carrying his plate about the room, delighting in being in a hurry, pretending to himself week after week that he is going to Buxton [a market town near Lea Hurst] or elsewhere in order to be in legitimate haste. I say to myself how happy that man would be with a factory under his superintendence with the interests of 2 or 300 men to look after."[20]

This is Florence The Censor, scribbling her most intimate thoughts on a scrap of paper—for herself and for us—and giving vent to harsh judgments of her family that she could not voice otherwise. If he was neither as industrious nor as productive as she would have liked—who

was?—Florence knew as well as anyone else that her father was a singularly lovable man, a singularly good man, and a singularly effective man
to boot. Probity and acumen, idealism and efficiency characterized
WEN's financial affairs throughout his long life. Unlike virtually every
other Victorian of note, in reality and fiction, he seems never to have
been seriously indebted or to have incurred losses that endangered his
lifestyle.[21]

I NOW TURN to the other side of the Nightingale family, Fanny's side,
the more distinguished side—the Smiths.[22] The distinction came from
the public service of Fanny's father. If Florence Nightingale inherited her
talent for mathematics, taste for accounting, and managerial expertise
from her Shore-Nightingale ancestors, from the Smith side she took her
ambition, her charisma, and her political acumen. As a woman, Florence
Nightingale could not be elected to the House of Commons, but to an
astonishing extent she followed her grandfather Smith's example by devoting decades of her life to lobbying Parliament and the British government to enact and implement social reforms.

If his name was common, William Smith (1756–1835) was not.
First elected to Parliament in 1784, William Smith sat in the House of
Commons for forty-six years, an independent voice of principle and reason. An urban, Dissenter, Whig merchant in a parliamentary sea of
landowning, Anglican, Tory aristocrats, Smith was often ostracized and
jeered by his fellow members. They circulated a piece of partisan doggerel about him that the *Dictionary of National Biography* has chosen to
repeat in their entry on Smith. This I see as the English establishment's
enduring snub to a man who refused to toe the line.

> *At length, when the candles burn low in their sockets,*
> *Up gets William Smith with his hands in his pockets,*
> *On a course of morality fearlessly enters,*
> *With all the opinions of all the dissenters.*

A short extract from his published writings gives a sense of what
William Smith said in his hundreds of speeches: "Whatever right over
man may be legitimately exercised by the society to which he belongs; to

whatever privation of liberty he may subject himself, by crime legally proved; though he may forfeit even life itself, yet as long as he remains a rational, moral, accountable creature, it arises out of the essence of his nature that he cannot be the proper object of barter and sale, and be indiscriminately transferred as property from hand to hand—far less that such a right can by any possibility be acquired over his certainly innocent offspring."[23]

The standard biography of William Smith culled from obituaries and nineteenth-century memoirs paints him as a jolly, unexceptional man, a good father and friend, a good clubman and committeeman, an able lieutenant in the abolitionist fight. The most telling thing Sir James Stephen gives us about William Smith was that he never had a day's ill health in his life: a classic put-down. Such accounts are deliberately misleading, good examples of Victorian revisionist historiography.[24] They smooth the radical edges off an unconventional, idiosyncratic life. They make a live wire into a bore, a risk-taker into a middle-of-the-roader, a rebel into a pillaster of the establishment.

William Smith was a survivor, and by the time he died in 1835, many of the political causes he fought for over decades, though not his religious and philosophical ideas, had become middle of the road. The slave trade was abolished in 1806 and slavery itself in British territories in 1833. The Unitarian Act of 1812 (known as William Smith's Bill) made it legal for the first time to preach and advocate non-Trinitarian doctrine. The Test and Corporation Acts were repealed in 1828 and the Catholic Emancipation Act was passed in 1829, placing Dissenting Protestants and Catholics on the same legal and political footing as their Anglican brethren. The first Reform Act was passed in 1832, drafted in large part by William's son-in-law John Bonham-Carter, the first small step toward extending the franchise to all citizens. Blood sports like bullbaiting and cockfighting were banned.

But when Smith entered Parliament in 1784, any man who was a public advocate for such measures was considered a dangerous extremist. After 1789, as the revolution in France took its increasingly bloody course, such a man risked arrest, trial on a count of high treason, imprisonment, fines, or even transportation to Botany Bay, the equivalent of a death sentence.[25] William Smith survived the storm of reaction that came over Britain following the revolutions in the American colonies and

France, but many men he knew fared less well. The radical fringe of the intelligentsia, men like William Godwin, Joseph Priestley, Richard Price, and Horne Took, suffered for their beliefs.[26] These men dared to question the very foundations of British society—government by monarchy and oligarchy, the unequal distribution of wealth and civil rights, a father's despotic power over his wife and children, the sexual double standard, the inerrancy of the Bible.

William Smith also knew women like Mary Wollstonecraft, Amelia Opie, Anna Barbauld, and Helen Maria Williams, whose very existence seemed to many the ultimate threat to nation and family. They dared to assert that liberty and equality applied to both sexes. They lived independent lives, remained single or chose their own mates, published novels, poems, and essays, and sometimes even got paid for them. This was revolution, and the reaction to it would be merciless.

In his library William Smith had a notable collection of subversive literature by contemporaries like Rousseau, Voltaire, Tom Paine, Adam Smith, John Locke, Jeremy Bentham, William Godwin, and Mary Wollstonecraft. He not only read these books but allowed his wife and children, daughters as well as sons, to read them. Worst of all, in the eyes of his contemporaries, William Smith, his wife, Frances, and many of their closest friends were Socinians, Rational Christians, founding members of the new Unitarian sect. This was the smallest and most reviled sect within the small, reviled community of English Protestant Dissenters. In Parliament, William Smith was the principal spokesman for the Dissenting community and the lone voice of Unitarianism.

It is a savage historical irony that the Unitarian background of people like Erasmus Darwin (Charles's grandfather), Joseph Priestley, Richard Price, Ada Lovelace, Charles Babbage, Samuel Taylor Coleridge, and Josiah Wedgwood has so often been either misunderstood or ignored. Unitarians should not be dismissed as tyrannical bigots straight out of the pages of Nathaniel Hawthorne, or more recently the screenplays of Ingmar Bergman. In fact, in the late eighteenth century, religious convictions led a small group of men and women into the intellectual avant-garde and inspired a dogged commitment to improve social conditions for all. For William Smith and his Unitarian friends on both sides of the Atlantic, faith was a spur, not a hobble.

WILLIAM SMITH was intelligent, cultured, energetic—a man of parts, as they liked to say in the eighteenth century—but none of this would have got him into politics if his family had not been wealthy. In the eighteenth century a great deal of money was necessary to succeed if one had not been born Lord This or the Honourable Mr. That.

The Smiths came originally from Newport, Isle of Wight, and they were Presbyterians. The family began its move up the social ladder when Samuel Smith, a young ironmonger and our William Smith's grandfather (Florence Nightingale's great-great-grandfather), saved Elizabeth Leigh from death or injury in a carriage accident. To the chagrin of her rich and prominent family, Miss Leigh fell in love with her rescuer and eloped with him. Samuel and Elizabeth had eleven children. After the early death of their father, three of the sons, William, Benjamin, and Samuel II, left the Isle of Wight and went to London to seek their fortunes in the grocery business.

Their bachelor uncle Joseph Smith was a wholesale grocer who owned the Sugar Loaf in Cannon Street, a shop in the heart of the City specializing in sugar, tea, and spices. These luxury products came to England from her colonial possessions, notably the slave plantations in the West Indies. Our William Smith's youthful uncle (Florence's great-great-uncle), also called William, went out to Antigua, did well, and acquired property but died at twenty-six. In a 1738 letter to his sister Elizabeth Travers, William wrote of his horror at the social conditions he found in Antigua. "I must say I think they [the slaves] are the Most Miserable People on Earth, and that to be a Freeborn Subject is the Greatest Blessing in this Life."[27] William Smith of Antigua's deep revulsion against slavery was to inspire three generations of Smiths to fight for abolition.

After William's tragic death, his uncle Joseph and his brothers Benjamin and Samuel continued the business, soon building up extensive property holdings, not only in the West Indies but in the southern states of what would soon become the United States of America. The Sugar Loaf prospered. The firm was worth some forty-six thousand pounds by 1757 and seventy thousand pounds by 1761, and the partners were making about four thousand pounds a year in income.[28] Even during the

American War of Independence, a very difficult time for English merchants, the Smiths managed to stay afloat and even cheered on the colonists. When the United States became a sovereign nation, the Smiths could afford, as a gesture of solidarity with the new republic, not to pursue their right to legal compensation from the British government for the valuable property rights they owned in Savannah, Georgia. This choice of principle over interest was a matter of pride in the family.[29]

The Smiths' rise to affluence is a nice example of Weber's Protestant ethic at work, but it was not easy, much less inevitable. The Smiths' Presbyterian faith and increasingly radical ideas on religion, economics, and politics set them against the grain of society. In eighteenth-century England governmental legislation rigged the rules of the social and economic game against anyone who was not a member of the established Church of England. To give one example of the abuses possible under the various acts of Parliament directed against Dissenters, the City of London in the mid-eighteenth century had a policy of electing Dissenters to offices that they were barred by law from accepting. The City then fined the Dissenters for refusing to serve or for neglecting their duties, and used the fines to build a magnificent home for its lord mayor.[30] To be an Anglican was, in essence, to hold the key to the door of the professions, the officer class, the universities, and national, local, and colonial government. Even in trade and industry, where Jews and Dissenters were permitted to operate, the path of least resistance for a man intent on success was to be seen regularly at his local church, take communion at Christmas and Easter, put money in the plate, and keep any religious doubts and doctrinal disagreements to himself.

But religious compromise on the basis of materialist self-interest was precisely what Presbyterian intellectuals like the eighteenth-century Smiths could not make. In this they were the direct heirs of the men and women who had sailed on the *Mayflower*. They stubbornly followed the dictates of conscience, attended the religious community of their choice, educated their children in their own beliefs, and accepted that this made their financial aspirations more difficult. Like their Jewish counterparts, they knew that they had to be more amiable, efficient, prudent, and law-abiding than the next man, since a disgruntled competitor, an unhappy client, or a sadistic official could take revenge within a legal system that was unapologetically biased.[31]

THE BENJAMIN AND WILLIAM SMITH who came from the Isle of Wight to join their bachelor uncle Joseph's grocery business never married and had no children. But in 1754 their youngest brother, Samuel, married Martha Adams, daughter of a wealthy London Dissenting family. The Adamses were more distinguished than the Smiths. One member of Miss Adams's family had managed to be both Lord Mayor of London and a zealous Protestant who "founded the Arabic Professorship at Cambridge for the conversion of the Arabs."[32] As his father had with Miss Leigh, Samuel managed to marry for love and for money since his darling Patty (as Martha was always called) brought him a dowry of six thousand pounds, double his stake in the grocery business at that time. More important, she stood to inherit not only from her father but from her wealthy uncle Thomas Halsey, M.P. At the age of twenty-five, Martha Adams Smith died in childbirth along with her baby, and at about the same time an infant daughter was carried off by smallpox. This left the grieving Samuel with one child, his three-year-old son, William. As it turned out, William would inherit not only from his father and his father's bachelor brother, Benjamin, but from his maternal grandfather Adams and great-uncle Halsey. Samuel Smith married again, but he had no other children and the second Mrs. Samuel Smith defied stereotype by proving to be a loving stepmother.

Letters show that Samuel entered with unusual sensitivity into his son's tastes and pleasures. As he wrote to his son at school, from the time of Martha's death William was "the first object of [his] affection." "I think I have always treated you as the Friend as well as Parent." This was an exceptional remark in a century when the philosopher Jean-Jacques Rousseau consigned his newborn children to an orphanage, where they were pretty sure to die, and great ladies, from the queen down, rarely even saw their children. Just as abusive parents tend to produce children who abuse in their turn, so loving fathers tend to produce sons who become loving fathers. By the mid-eighteenth century there was already in the Smith family a tradition of love and loyal commitment between husband and wife and between parent and child, which was to continue, as we shall see, through the nineteenth century and beyond.

Samuel wanted nothing better than that his only son should succeed him at the Sugar Loaf, but he considered the best education to be the best preparation for business and life. Such an attitude was rare in its day, though common within the proto-Unitarian community. The Dissenters had established and financed a number of remarkable academies, and the young William Smith was sent first to Mr. French's school at Ware and then to Daventry, the school that educated many of the most famous and accomplished men of the time, Anglicans as well as Dissenters. Daventry was perennially short of money and it had no towering chapel like Eton, but its teaching was outstanding and its students committed. Daventry, under the benign guidance of the Reverend Caleb Ashworth, encouraged discussion on any issue, political, religious or cultural, the masters did not rely upon the birch to maintain order, and the elder boys were not permitted to prey on the younger. In comparison with the Eton, Winchester, or Charterhouse of the time, Daventry was a beacon of enlightenment.

When William Smith left Daventry, at age sixteen or seventeen, he went into his father's business and worked there for nine years. Though a rich young man with even richer prospects, at this point in his life he did not have a great deal of choice of career. For a Dissenter of his generation, to attend university meant going abroad to Switzerland or the Netherlands, or at least to Edinburgh, and family needs probably made that impossible. Lady Stephen, the most intuitive of the biographical sources, comments that William Smith "was perhaps inclined to take prosperity too much for granted; but with a cultivated mind, quick sympathies and that power of enjoyment which is such a priceless treasure— he was well equipped for the battle of life."[33]

IN 1770 SAMUEL SMITH decided to put two thousand pounds into a new home five miles outside the city of London in the green suburb of Clapham. Samuel continued to spend almost all his time in Cannon Street, but nonetheless the family was now brought into a more distinguished and varied social circle that was to have great consequences for William. In Clapham lived a number of very wealthy London merchants and bankers, in particular several branches of the prominent Thornton family. Several Thornton men were members of Parliament and directors of the East India Company and the Bank of England.

In terms of lifestyle and commercial interests, Samuel Smith and his son, William, had much in common with Clapham neighbors, but they were at different ends of the spectrum of Protestant religious doctrine. The Claphamites were Anglicans but in their theology they were closer to Calvinism or Scottish Presbyterianism than to standard Anglicanism. They were the spiritual fathers of a powerful movement within the Church of England, usually known as Evangelicalism, that would so shape the Victorian era. From the reminiscences of Julia Smith, William's youngest daughter, we get an interesting little vignette that tells us something of what Clapham was like. Of Mr. and Mrs. Henry Thornton, whom she knew as a child, Julia writes: "Something foreboding in Mr. and Mrs. HT something the reverse of indulgent. Marianne [Thornton, Julia's friend] was writing a letter for her mother when somebody came in saying such and such a vessel is sd [said] to be gone down. A family of their friends were in the vessel. M[arianne] dropped her pen Mrs. T[hornton] sd If you can't write that letter M I must do it myself."[34]

In 1781 the twenty-five-year-old William Smith married Frances Coape, and after returning from the honeymoon, his wife pregnant with their first child, William was increasingly intent on leaving the grocery business and going into Parliament. This was an ambitious plan since, as Lady Stephen notes, "A middle class Dissenter, owing his fortune to trade, bearing the plebeian name of Smith, and, worst of all, a Unitarian, needed some courage to enter the House at all."[35]

William Smith's parliamentary career began in April 1784, when he was elected member for Sudbury, perhaps the most notorious of the rotten boroughs.[36] A rotten borough was a community that in ancient times had been given the right to return a member to Parliament and continued to do so even after it had lost most (or in the famous case of Old Sarum, all) of its inhabitants. Even in nonrotten boroughs, voters in Smith's day and for forty years after were few and far between, and easily bought. In fact, until the Reform Act of 1832, only 4.4 percent of the British population could go to the polls and raise their hands or voices in public support of a candidate.

So in 1784 William Smith bought the election at Sudbury for three thousand pounds. Then, as was common at that time, once he had entered Parliament he changed constituency, and soon changed again. First he moved to Camelford, a constituency with seventeen voters, all in the pocket of the local landowner, who accepted a modest two thousand pounds for the seat. At last, in 1802, after he had made a name for himself in the Commons and moved into the reformist circles of Charles James Fox, William Smith became the member for Norwich, "one of the main provincial centres of the reform movement with its own thriving Revolution Society and radical periodical, *The Cabinet.*"[37] Smith continued to represent Norwich until 1830. In 1812, he was eulogized in the *Norwich Chronicle* for his "strength of understanding, simplicity of manners, gentleness of disposition, and uprightness of conduct."

Nonetheless, William Smith owed to Norwich perhaps the greatest disappointment of his political career. In the election of 1806 Norwich voters rejected him, preferring to send in a man who had given unqualified support for a purely local issue—the rejection of a plan to modernize the town's roads.[38] Thus when the great parliamentary debate of 1806 ended with a successful vote to abolish the slave trade, William Smith was forced to watch the historic debate from the gallery, though afterward he hurried over to Wilberforce's house for the celebration party.

No ACCOUNT OF the political life of William Smith would be complete without a discussion of his part in the late-eighteenth-century campaign to prohibit the trade in slaves throughout the British Empire, and ultimately to abolish slavery.

Abolitionism, as it came to be called, was an extremely rare and unpopular stand in the eighteenth century, especially for members of the merchant class, like the Smiths. Though there were relatively few slaves living in England, trade with the West Indies and the American colonies was lucrative. In many cases, slave labor, mainly in the sugar plantations, even the actual trade in human cargo, was the basis of English merchants' fortunes. Most families who made money in the West Indies—the ancestors of both Elizabeth Barrett and Robert Browning, for example—vehemently opposed any government intervention in the way they ran their plantations. James Boswell was typical of his generation in arguing that the slave trade was a good thing. Was it not sanctioned by God in the Bible? Was it not a mainstay of British prosperity and thus a force for progress? Slaves, Boswell and most Englishmen liked to believe, were treated humanely in transit, if for no other reason than that they constituted such valuable merchandise. On the plantations, people liked to say, British slaves lived far better than they had in Africa.

Fortunately, in England and France the economic and cultural forces supporting slavery, though strong, were not as deeply rooted as in the United States. English Quakers in the 1670s were the first to insist that no Christian could in conscience own other human beings, trade in human life, or even acquiesce in a social order where slavery was tolerated. In the eighteenth century, the abolitionist position was strengthened by writers of the French and English Enlightenment who questioned the whole idea of racial inferiority and the legal right of any man to enslave another.

The Smiths signed on to the abolitionist cause at a relatively early period even though abolition posed special concerns for them. The sugar and spices sold in the Sugar Loaf were grown by slaves, and William Smith and his partners stood to incur significant losses if the racial and thus economic balance in the West Indies was disturbed. But the direct contact with slave societies the Smiths had had through their commercial activities reinforced rather than weakened the ethical imperatives they received from their religious communities and their enlightened education.[39]

The acknowledged leader of the English abolitionists, both in the Commons and without, was William Wilberforce, and William Smith was known to be Wilberforce's chief lieutenant in Parliament. A small, slight, ugly man, crooked of body but of great charisma, Wilberforce was born into a family of very wealthy merchants who had abandoned the Dissenting faith of their ancestors for socially acceptable Anglicanism.[40] At Cambridge University Wilberforce's golden tongue and singular charm and tact won him acceptance into a powerful set. A drinker, gambler, and general dilettante, he was the model of the young Regency rake, and he became a close friend of the young William Pitt, a commoner destined to be one of England's greatest prime ministers. Like Pitt, Wilberforce could afford to buy his way into Parliament, and he entered the House of Commons soon after coming down from the university.

Then, at twenty-five, Wilberforce's Dissenter heritage asserted itself. Out of the blue, it seemed, he experienced a religious conversion and changed from prodigal son to crusader. Henceforward Wilberforce devoted his life to making England a more truly Christian, Bible-reading,

and moral nation. Wilberforce was convinced that the way to reform society was to persuade and convert the ruling elite, whose moral corrupt-
ness and irreligious ways easily equaled their power. Wilberforce aimed
to effect reform from the top down. Continuing friendship with men
like Pitt was crucial.

The key issue upon which Wilberforce concentrated at the outset of
his career, and the rock upon which he built his immense moral ascendancy, was slavery. Year after year William Wilberforce rose in the House
of Commons to propose the abolition of the slave trade. Ultimately
Wilberforce's eloquence, persistence, hard work, organizational skills,
and moral authority prevailed.[41]

Wilberforce's antislavery campaign was a model for subsequent reformers. Lord Shaftesbury was to apply Wilberforcian principles of strategy and organization when he began his campaign for reform of factory
working conditions, the Ten Hour Work Day Bill, and so on. Florence
Nightingale, in her turn, sought to secure national sanitation and health
care reforms by lobbying Parliament to enact legislation, using personal
connections to gain the support of the politically powerful, and judiciously mobilizing public opinion through the press.

As the men who funded and led the campaign to abolish slavery,
William Wilberforce and the Clapham Saints earned an important place
in British history, and they also gave rise to a distinguished mandarin caste
in British society. Charles Darwin, Lord Macaulay, Lord Eldon, Octavia
Hill, Virginia Wolf, Vanessa Bell, the Stracheys (Lytton, James, Alix, and
Ray), E. M. Forster, G. M. Trevelyan, John Maynard Keynes, J. S. Hal-
dane, and Naomi Mitchison are among the famous descendants of the
Venns, the Thorntons, the Babingtons, the Macaulays, the Trevelyans, and
the Stephens of Clapham.[42] By contrast, William Smith's lifelong contribution to the abolitionist campaign has received little notice.

This neglect is rooted in both politics and religion. William Smith
worked tirelessly for abolition, but on almost every issue but slavery he
and Wilberforce were on opposite ends of the political spectrum. A wily
politician, Wilberforce balanced his radical stand on slavery with a conservative, even reactionary stand on other matters. In the Commons he
was a loyal Tory and supporter of his old friend Pitt. Furthermore, in the
eyes of Evangelicals, the Unitarian Smith was not a Christian. Wilber-

force to the end longed to convert his heretical friend and save him from hell, but in vain. There is no evidence that William Smith ever tried to convert William Wilberforce to Unitarianism.

Smith remained in the House of Commons until 1825 and had the joy of seeing the wisdom of his ideas confirmed and many political hopes realized at last in the great swell of reform legislation of the early 1800s.

Slavery did not die out in the world when the English Parliament voted to abolish it, and so in 1835 William Smith defied his anxious wife and children by getting out of bed to attend a meeting of the antislavery society. Within days of that meeting he was dead at his son Benjamin's house at Blandford Square. His grieving family had the comfort of knowing that it was because men like their father bothered to get out of their sickbeds to attend meetings that the carapace of greed, ignorance, and indifference that protected the English slave owners was slowly being chipped away.

Chapter 2

ONE BIG
HAPPY FAMILY

Williamlliam Smith and Frances Coape were head over heels in love when they married, and they were very well suited: both were Dissenting Protestants, both had inherited money, both were very handsome. For at least twenty years they were most happy when in each other's company and sharing a bed. Florence Nightingale several times remarked on how beautiful her grandmother was in the last years of her life, so I presume that when she was young Frances Coape Smith was stunning. A little, plump, quick, decisive woman whose smooth, dark hair and small regular features would be passed on to her Nightingale granddaughters, Frances had a vitality and a curiosity that matched William's own. And Frances was healthy as well as beautiful, giving birth to thirteen live children, of whom ten lived to see sixty and beyond. This was a time when many children died young and many women died in childbirth. How relieved Samuel Smith must have been, after the tragedies of his own married life, to see his daughter-in-law so effortlessly fertile.

Miss Coape and her two sisters, Joanna and Maria, lost their parents early on but were tenderly reared by relatives and received by the standards of the day an excellent education.[1] Frances was indeed a "blue"— to use the far from complimentary term her contemporaries had for a learned young woman—but she was also a prig. She accepted William Smith's proposal of marriage only when she had got him to agree that their family would have prayers every day. The learning would get deeper and broader as Frances aged since she had a good mind, but the prig-gishness too would deepen, to the discomfort of her growing family and even of her husband. As he took on the role of M.P., man about town, and member of the intellectual elite, William moved steadily away from the intellectually narrow circles of Nonconformism, where his wife remained most comfortable. Frances's extant letters to her children—so pious, so self-righteous, so lacking in humor and tenderness, so very different from William's—make it easy to caricature her. But in essentials, Frances was at one with her highly unconventional husband, and the legacy she passed on to her children, especially her daughters, was of trained intellect as well as fierce Protestant morality.

William and Frances were married in style on January 6, 1781, and set up house across the common in Clapham from William's father, Samuel Smith, in a property called Eagle House. An independent establishment for newlyweds was somewhat unusual at that time, but William was well able to afford a good wedding and a new house. In 1779 he had inherited a large estate from his dead mother's family. This inheritance also enabled him to retire from participating actively in the Cannon Street business, leaving its direction to his cousins Kemble and Nash. Old Samuel had after all given his son too liberal an education, and though trade made William Smith rich and he certainly enjoyed having money, his heart was not in the countinghouse. The Smith family, especially the unmarried daughters, would finally pay a very heavy price for William's hands-off attitude to moneymaking. Fortunately, two of William's sons, Benjamin and Octavius, inherited grandfather Samuel's taste for business as well as father William's radical politics. They became independently wealthy as young men and kept their parents and sisters from destitution.

After their wedding, William and Frances set off on an exhausting tour of the south and west of England, which of course included a visit to the Smith relatives on the Isle of Wight, notably old Uncle Benjamin, who had retired there after selling his share in the grocery business. The Smith couple traveled in a phaeton, a dashing, light, open carriage perched on four high wheels and drawn by two horses. It was named for the rash charioteer who drove too close to the sun, and was not for the faint of heart. Readers of Georgette Heyer's Regency novels will recall her heroes tooling around in phaetons. With the Smiths, on this as on many future trips, went Frances's sister Maria Coape. Maria, who was eight years younger, remained a spinster and spent the rest of her life living with her married sisters. Maria Coape had a valuable role in her sister Smith's large family, and she was a familiar presence to great-nieces like Florence Nightingale and Hilary Bonham-Carter. In her youth, Miss Maria Coape was an accomplished singer and keyboardist who loved opera, notably the fashionable Handel. She taught her nieces, especially Patty, who was only sixteen years her junior, to play and sing. Florence Nightingale's beautiful singing voice and the passion for opera she developed as an adolescent can be traced back through her aunt Patty to her Coape great-aunt.

LARGE FAMILIES like the Smiths were not rare in any class at this period. What was rare was for fathers to have much to do with their children when they were little. In the affluent classes even mothers often left the care of small children to servants. Women of the high bourgeoisie spent more time at home and were more involved in child rearing than the women of the aristocracy, but a rich merchant or industrialist was probably as distant from his children as a duke or a baronet. William Smith was an exception here, and the tenderness he showed toward his children when they were little earned their lifelong love and respect.

In his domestic life William was in fact more Victorian than Regency, a devoted family man who delighted in the company of his wife and children. With the births of Martha (Patty) in 1782, Benjamin in 1783, Anne in 1785, Frances (Fanny) in 1788, William Adams (Adams) in 1789, Joanna Maria in 1791, Samuel in 1794, Octavius in 1796, Frederic in 1798, and Julia in 1799, William Smith found himself the father of a swarm of children whose talents and exuberance impressed all comers.[2]

The Smiths' unusually hands-on style of parenting can best be seen in their summer activities. From the time of their wedding in 1781 until 1804, when Napoleon kept them closer to home, William and Frances adopted the pattern of touring for several months of every summer and taking the children along. This was exceptional. Eighteenth-century men of means were often away from home, and even women of the period paid frequent visits when they could, but they left the children at home with servants or relatives. But the Smiths wanted to share the excitement of travel and were eager for their children to learn as much of the world as possible at first hand. Usually the Smiths explored different areas of England, Wales, or Scotland but on two occasions they crossed the Channel. In true "blue" fashion, Frances Smith wrote up their tours in extensive travel journals, some accompanied with little sketches. This tradition was handed down to her children and thence to her grandchildren.

The Smiths seem to have had four main aims as tourists—to visit as many cultural sites and beauty spots as possible, to be outdoors most of the day, to visit friends and family, and to go to bed as tired as possible. Simply to get from point A to point B in England in the last quarter of the eighteenth century took time and energy. The roads were bad to terrible, sometimes impassable, and there was also danger from highwaymen. The Coape sisters, in fact, though cultured young ladies of high moral tone, were no sissies. They routinely suffered discomforts and dangers that our young people today can get only from enrolling in organized and expensive extreme sports ventures.

It rained a great deal in those days, and with the rain came mud, deep on the roads and thick on the clothes, a particular problem for women who were expected to be clean and neat but whose clothes and, in particular, shoes, were flimsier than men's. Patty Smith says in her reminiscences that on her mother's four-month trip to Scotland in 1786, Frances Smith had no maid, and, whatever the weather, rode sidesaddle, walked, or drove with William in the famous open phaeton: "My mother's sole dresses were two habits and two hats, with plumes of feathers, one tipped with blue and yellow & one with blue," Patty notes in admiration.[3] Since Frances was pregnant or just recovering from childbirth for the first twenty years of her married life, those riding habits must have had a great deal of room to expand around the abdomen.

Insufficiently exercised by the journey, if there was a mountain, the Smiths climbed up; if a cave, they climbed down.[4] They zealously toured mines or manufactures or mills, and could also be tempted by castles or stately homes. On a visit to the Midlands in 1783 when they stayed with their friends the Shores and the Milneses, Frances climbed Langdale Pike, the first lady known to have done so. Naturally it rained. In Scotland in 1786 they took a five-mile row across Loch Lomond and then went up Ben Lomond. In 1794, on another tour of the Midlands and

Lake District, the Smith family stayed with Lord Muncaster, William's friend and abolitionist ally in the Commons. The Muncaster family dated back to the Norman Conquest, and a tower at the castle was reputedly built at the time of Tacitus's Agricola. For Ben and Patty, who were well advanced in Latin, this visit was an exciting live history lesson. At Whitehaven, Mr. Smith and Ben went down a coal mine, walking a mile underground "by the light of a pitched rope." At Keswick, another beauty spot in the Lake District, it was raining as usual and the steep roads were slippery. The groom fell into a stream with his horse, eleven-year-old Benjamin was thrown over the head of his, and Maria Coape fell off three times. But everyone arrived in one piece, so it was a pretty good day. The family party reached Parndon after three months on the road. On December 13, 1794, Samuel Smith was born, Frances's tenth baby in some thirteen years. As Lady Stephen remarks: "If there were giantesses in those days, Mrs. William Smith was certainly among them."[5]

When the Smiths toured the Continent, they devoted more time to culture than to nature, but the pace was no less exhausting. During their three-month tour in 1788, they covered nearly sixteen hundred miles. Frances, in a Catholic country for the first time, experienced culture shock at Calais when she saw "a crucifix exposed to public view." The statue of the Virgin Mary in Strasbourg, "dressed extremely fine . . . in yellow painted taffety," amazed her. Such religious images were quite foreign to her religious tradition. In Paris, the Smiths drove out to Versailles to attend what would prove to be the last "Fête de Saint Louis," the day when members of the French royal family showed themselves to their subjects. They were able to observe the King and Queen of France at close quarters, first in the chapel and then at the ceremonial lunch—"le grand couvert." Marie Antoinette, Frances noted, ate not a bite.

At the end of her first Continental tour, Frances was a very different woman, a cosmopolitan and a confirmed art lover like her husband, seeing beauty, not sacrilege, in great religious painting. Comparing her journey to the more extended tour that had been recorded by the celebrated Hester Thrale Piozzi, Samuel Johnson's dear friend, Frances wrote: "How I wished to visit the Gallery at Dresden, and see those far famed pictures—the Notte of Correggio, Rembrandt's daughter painted by himself, and inimitable pictures by Ferdinand Bol—and how much do I desire too to see Rome and above all the Pictures in the world, the Transfiguration of Raphael—and above all the Churches in the world, Michael Angelo's Saint Peter's."[6] The love of art, the thirst to see great works for oneself, was one of the many things Frances and William Smith passed on to their children. Their daughter Fanny Smith Nightingale developed a lifelong passion for the plastic arts. On her honeymoon in 1818–20, Fanny realized her mother's dream as well as her own by going to Italy. In 1837–39 she and WEN took their two teenage daughters on a great tour of the Continent to complete their education. Later, when Florence Nightingale visited Rome in 1847–48 with her friends the Bracebridges, she sent back to her family detailed accounts of what she had seen there, notably the Sistine Chapel. On her way home from Egypt in 1850, Florence visited the galleries in Dresden and was not the woman to miss Hester Thrale Piozzi's Rembrandts and Correggios. We can imagine Fanny saying to Parthe as the family at Embley pored over Flo's marvelous letters from abroad, "Oh, how my mother longed to see Dresden and Rome!"

IN 1785, already the father of two with another on the way, William Smith bought a house in the country. Upper House in Little Parndon near Harlow in Essex was a two-hundred-acre property situated about twenty miles from London, and thus an easy day's ride for a vigorous man like William Smith. The estate was very old but the red brick house was new, built in the 1760s. It stood on a small rise and, since Essex is not known for its mountainous terrain, the Smith family humorously called their home the Mount. The large garden at Parndon gave ample scope for the small children's games, and as time went on the growing boys were able to develop their skills in field sports, a passion for them as for most men of the period. The girls, who were not permitted to walk or ride out alone, and only exceptionally took part in field sports, probably preferred London or Clapham. At Parndon they were under their redoubtable mother's thumb and had to rely more for stimulation on their parents' guests.

Though pleasantly rural, Parndon had some cultural amenities, notably the nearby East India Company College of Haileybury. A number of eminent men taught at Haileybury, including the demographer the Reverend Thomas Robert Malthus, who often walked over to the Mount with his family. Malthus aroused great controversy among his contemporaries by arguing that growth in population would always outpace production and that efforts to keep poor people alive were therefore futile. Malthus was a provocative guest at the Mount especially since he was at the opposite end of the political spectrum from William Smith, who was committed to social reform. According to Julia Smith, Patty Smith was the first member of the family to become friendly with the Malthuses. An enthusiastic horsewoman, Patty was able to get farther afield than the other Smith women and to make independent contact with local families.

For all its amenities, Parndon was quickly too small for the Smith family. William and Frances, who so often took advantage of the hospitality of friends when traveling, were embarrassed to be unable to reciprocate. Therefore, between 1797 and 1803, Parndon underwent extensive renovations. The house doubled in size, from twenty to forty rooms, and its style changed from old-fashioned Georgian to newfangled "Italian." William built a magnificent new library to accommodate his impressive collection of books, prints, and maps. Julia Smith remembered what a magical place that library had been for her as a child, and the wonderful talk she had there once with the already legendary William Wilberforce.

By buying Parndon, Smith also bought the right to make appointments to the living at the local Anglican church, a somewhat delicate task for a man who by 1790 was a declared Unitarian and thus an infidel of the blackest dye in the eyes of the Anglican faithful. Fortunately, William Smith was a tolerant as well as a generous man, and so relations with the Anglicans were relatively smooth. When in Parndon, the Smith family worshipped in their designated pew in the village church, though they attended the evening services, which, according to Julia, had less doctrine. William Smith made a point of going through his children's copies of the Prayer Book and excising those portions that they need not subscribe to. When the vicar of the neighboring parish of Great Parndon made a fuss about a little Sunday school for girls that the Smith women started at the Mount, the idea was dropped.[7] Sunday schools for the poor were a very controversial issue at that time and for the vicar at Parndon a Unitarian Sunday school must have seemed a terrifying prospect. He did not understand for a moment that Frances and Patty wanted to teach the local children to read, not undermine their belief in the Holy Trinity.[8]

In 1794 William Smith bought a London townhouse at 6 Park Street (now 16 Queen Anne's Gate). The house still stands and is only a five-minute walk from the House of Commons. For Frances Coape Smith it was a wrench to leave Clapham, where she had many friends, but the new house's proximity to the Commons would allow her to enter more into her husband's professional life, and it was much safer for William. When engaged in one of the regular late-night sessions at the House, the considerate William was inclined to dismiss his servant and horse and walk back to Clapham alone—a risky procedure at a time when travelers were often assaulted and robbed, and one that greatly alarmed his wife.[9] Park Street soon became a center for the Whig elite. Some seventy years later Florence Nightingale would settle upon another house in reasonable proximity to the Houses of Parliament for just the same reasons.

One indication of Smith's rising reputation was that in 1802 he was elected to the exclusive King of Clubs—a group of notable wits, scholars, and men about town. The club was limited to thirty and met once a month for dinner at an inn, mainly to discuss literary and cultural topics. Lord Holland, the Honourable William Lamb (later Lord Melbourne), the poet William Cowper, the scientist Thomas Malthus, and Henry Hallam (father of Tennyson's beloved friend) were among the members of the King of Clubs.[10] In 1806, William Smith was elected a fellow of the Royal Society, and he also became a member of the Linnaean Society and of the Society of Antiquaries. In the next generation, William Edward Nightingale was unable to follow his father-in-law into politics, but he did emulate William Smith in the catholicity of his intellectual tastes. Both men were in touch with the most up-to-date ideas and were eager to pass on what they knew to their families. For intelligent, curious daughters, barred from higher education, such fathers were more precious than gold.

As he became known in the Commons, William Smith was appointed to several governmental bodies. He was deputy chairman of the British Fisheries and in 1803 was one of the three royal commissioners appointed by Parliament to supervise the construction of roads, canals, harbors, and bridges in Scotland and thus open that country to trade and industry. Smith was probably given this job because he was one of the rare members of Parliament who had actually visited Scotland and liked nothing better than a wet day's ride through the heather. William Smith was zealous in his work for the commission and formed surprisingly good relations with the Scottish noblemen who owned most of the land and who stood to gain financially from the new infrastructure. William was given the freedom of six Scottish cities, and the Duchess of Argyll was forced to accept that Mrs. Smith could not be persuaded to break the Sabbath by making a fourth at whist.[11]

PARK STREET AND PARNDON, especially the renovation of Parndon, were delightful but expensive. Patty Smith recorded in her diary that her father's friend Lord Muncaster warned him that buying 6 Park Street had been the ruin of both Lord Apsley and Lord Malmsbury. William Smith, who had never lacked for money in his life, laughed off the warning, sure that he could find the way to meet all his mounting expenses, but Muncaster was on the mark. In 1798 Smith asserted his right to take his father's place as head of the Cannon Street business. This initially brought him another three thousand pounds a year in income but also involved him in business dealings for which he had neither taste nor talent. The fortunes of the Smith parents were beginning to take a decided downturn, and there was a growing pack of young lads to set up in life and young girls to find husbands for.

One reason William Smith was short of money was that he had developed a passion for paintings. William was possessed of both money and taste and lived at a time when impoverished French aristocrats were selling their treasures in England. The three tours of the Continent that Smith took in 1788, 1790, and 1803 were opportunities to visit galleries and art dealers. This was a period when you could get a Poussin for thirty-four pounds, two shillings, and sixpence and a "spirited sketch" by Rubens for five guineas.[12] By about 1810, Smith had put together a personal collection that today would make anyone's mouth water. In his heyday he owned three Rembrandts—"The Mill," "Portrait of a Rabbi," and the now famous "Rembrandt's Mother."[13]

Smith did not just collect Continental old masters. He was one of the founders of the National Gallery, and of the British Institute in Pall Mall that was set up to promote the work of English artists. He was a personal friend of Joshua Reynolds and owned some of his portraits as well as works by Gainsborough and Stubbs. He collected the work of regional artists both in Derbyshire and in his longtime parliamentary constituency of Norwich. Joshua Reynolds was one of the people who visited the Smiths at Park Street. On one occasion Frances, rather incongruously, was anxious for Reynolds to use her two-year-old daughter, Anne, as a model for the infant Hercules. Anne was an unusually stout child and slow to walk. Patty Smith remembered that Sir Joshua "set the poor child down on her feet not knowing she couldn't stand, she was so heavy, she fell back on her head & for a moment we thought she was killed though no one would make much of the alarm before Sir Joshua."[14]

In the eyes of his English contemporaries, William Smith's most important acquisition was the portrait of the great actress Sarah Siddons that Reynolds painted for the Royal Academy. Smith bought this picture for seven hundred pounds, an act of some extravagance given the cheapness of a Rembrandt or Rubens, and it hung over the front drawing room chimneypiece in Park Street after 1794. Patty Smith thought it "the finest female portrait in the world," and apparently Mrs. Siddons thought so too. When the family was away, she would ask the housekeeper to let her into the house and then stand gazing at her own likeness.[15]

WILLIAM AND FRANCES SMITH were excellent parents, intelligently committed to the health, happiness, and prosperity of their children. Well versed in the scientific advances of his time, William decided to have all his children vaccinated against smallpox while they were infants. At this time in England outbreaks of smallpox regularly took thousands of lives and horribly scarred many more. On the other hand, the vaccination then used live cowpox, and some vaccinated patients died. In fact, one Smith daughter, born in 1787, died of cowpox. But ten Smith children lived long and healthy lives and were never a source of infection to others.

In education for their children as in health, the Smiths were in the vanguard. William Smith had received an excellent education, and he determined his sons should have the same. Ben was sent first to Dr. Knox's school near Tunbridge and then to Hackney, where Thomas Belsham, his father's great friend, was principal. Robert and Rodes Milnes (father and uncle of Richard Monckton Milnes) were also at Dr.

Knox's. Adams went to a school in Cheam, and the younger boys attended the establishment of Dr. Cogan, a former tutor at Daventry and a notable scholar. Benjamin Disraeli was also a pupil at Dr. Cogan's school. Unlike their father, Benjamin, Octavius, and Samuel were able to go on from school to Trinity College, Cambridge, though their religious affiliation prevented them from taking a degree.

The Smith girls were educated mainly at home, by their parents, older siblings, governesses, and private tutors. Their greatest advantage was that they were given unusually wide access to books. Julia says that one of her first memories is of reading the inscriptions over the shops in Clapham and of someone remarking on how forward she was. Julia was three at the time and not particularly used to praise.[16] The Smith girls, notably Patty, read widely in their father's library, which had over a thousand volumes. It included not only the great Latin, Greek, and English classics and works on religion but the latest, and often most controversial, poetry, philosophy, science, economics, and political theory, in English and French, which both William and Frances read fluently.[17] Their mother probably exercised as much censorship over the girls' reading as she could, but according to Lady Stephen, Frances Smith herself read not only travel journals, history, memoirs, and religious books with her children, but Mary Wollstonecraft's *A Vindication of the Rights of Woman,* Tom Paine's *The Rights of Man,* and Rousseau's *Emile.* These were the kind of books that Frances's Victorian granddaughters would feel obliged to keep out of the sight of conventional young lady visitors.

The Smith parents were insistent that their children master several languages. William had his daughters tutored in French and Italian by native-speaking émigrés who were common in London at that time. At the Dissenting academies they attended, the Smith sons would have learned Greek and Latin and perhaps Hebrew, and Patty taught herself Latin, using her father's books. As adults, both Patty and Julia became fluent in German and learned enough ancient Greek to be able to tutor their more boneheaded nephews in the vacations. At that time, Greek and German were the keys to high culture, both ancient and modern.

The Smith parents visited their sons at school—a less common practice among parents at the time than one might imagine—and followed their progress closely, too closely perhaps for the second son, Adams. He was the first child born to William and Frances who found it hard to

keep up, not only with his parents but with his almost equally formidable elder sister and brother, Patty and Ben. Even as a lad of ten, Ben kept
pace with his father, but Adams could not. This was obvious on a typically strenuous visit to North Wales that the Smiths took in 1800. The
tale of one day, when the family was trying to reach Llanwrst via Capel
Curig in Snowdonia, illustrates how much was demanded of the Smiths
as young children.

On this occasion, it was decided that William, Ben, and Adams
would go cross-country, making the twenty-odd miles of fairly rugged
terrain on foot. While the older males were walking, eighteen-year-old
Patty, who was as competent a whip as she was a rider, was entrusted with
driving the young children around on the high road in the "sociable."
This was an open four-wheeled carriage, also known as a "whisky", with
two seats facing each other, and a box seat for the driver. At the same time
Frances, at the reins with Anne and Fanny alongside her, tried to get the
perilous whisky to Capel Curig along a rough steep road. At some narrow places the whisky party was forced to pull stones out of the gates in
order to squeeze through, and finally they met an obstacle they could not
get past. Fortunately, the walkers came up at this point and escorted the
women the last three miles to the village on foot, leaving the whisky at a
farm to be recovered later. Ben, seventeen, strode ahead to Capel Curig
to secure provisions for the six of them. The two chickens and a piece of
bacon he scrounged were enough to fuel the Smith party for the final
five-mile walk to Llanwrst, where they were to spend the night. The
women on this day walked eight miles, the men and boys twenty. In the
following days, Adams failed to make it up Pengwern with Ben and
William, though he did manage Cader Idris.

Should we protest Frances and William's unkindness in insisting that
their son Adams take walks of this kind? Today the walk to Llanwrst
would be considered a challenge for a ten-year-old, and unthinkable if
he was weak and ill-coordinated. But nineteenth-century English people, especially men, habitually walked great distances. The longevity of
all the Smiths impressed their contemporaries (even the perennially ailing Patty lived to be eighty-seven) and makes a strong case for the benefits of a youthful regimen of strenuous physical exercise.

The problems Adams had keeping up with the others on mountain
paths were indicative of a more general inadequacy. In a family of dy-

namic achievers, female as well as male, Adams fell into the role of black sheep. In school, he was already slow and indolent, to judge from a letter his mother wrote to him: "My Dear Adams[,] I did indeed very much wonder at not receiving a letter from you sooner as I think I said 'Adams will write to us once or twice a week' when we parted; but I fear that you sleep so long in the morning that the substance of your brain is quite melted, and you have no ideas to communicate to me . . . It is such a mean and low enjoyment to be passing that time in bed which might be improved to the noblest purposes. Are there not books to be had, are there not a thousand things of which you are entirely ignorant to be read about, are not the mornings fine? Have I not earnestly desired you always to walk before breakfast? I hope, Adams, I shall not have occasion to say that you are negligent of what I request you to do: you should get up at the latest at seven, and run up to the Castle every morning."[18]

If Adams had problems with his mother and was cowed by the all-round superiority of his big brother, at least he was at school, away from Frances Smith's eagle eye and sharp tongue. The Smith girls had to deal with their mother day in and day out, but fortunately all five were resourceful and energetic, to say nothing of beautiful. Anne, Fanny, and Joanna seem to have figured out fairly early how to cope with their mother, whom indeed they were to remarkably resemble when mothers themselves. The girls had a successful policy of basic compliance and minor rebellion, and decided at an early age that what their mother did not know would not hurt her.

The middle sisters were close in age, attitudes, and goals. They looked up to Patty, their marvelous older sister, but unlike Julia, the littlest daughter, they did not seek to emulate her. To judge by an 1804 letter that Anne and Fanny wrote to their sister Patty, the four older girls supported rather than competed with one another. Anne, nineteen, Fanny, seventeen, and Joanna, thirteen, had been to a ball given by the Montague Burgoynes of Mark Hall, about three miles from Parndon. Patty, who was in Brighton with friends, had demanded a full account of the ball. Fanny calls the twenty-two-year-old Patty "the bookworm" and expresses mock surprise that she should be interested in such a frivolous event. Patty, I gather, had already been recognized in the family as the nonmarrying sister, the "blue."[19]

One maternal strategy that the three middle Smith daughters learned from their mother, Frances, was that if you were having problems with a daughter, you packed her off for an extended stay away. Both Joanna and Julia had a term at one of the new schools for girls that were beginning to spring up within the Dissenter community, but more usually the girls were sent to relatives or friends like the Tolletts of Betley Hall, a family that had close relations with the Darwins, the Wedgwoods, the Milneses, and the Gaskells. The friendships between families woven by these extended visits were long-lived.

The Smith girls' married Coape aunt, Mrs. Cure, had only three children, a boy named Capel, like his father, and two girls, Caroline and Freeman. In 1807 Joanna spent some months with the Cures. Frances Smith's parenting style is again revealed in a letter she wrote to Joanna in 1807, giving her permission to stay on for a few more weeks with the Cures: "I am quite pleased with the manner in which I am told you spend your time, strictly conforming to Freeman's hours and lessons . . . if you do as she does, you will when we meet, have been in the habit for three weeks of a more ready compliance with any request that may be made to you than you are accustomed in general to practice. I cannot but mention and urge this to you, as dear Freeman has such an advantage over you in this part of her conduct, and it forms a beautiful trait in the character of a Female. Females are born to practice obedience, first to their Parents, and afterwards to their husbands, or should they *not* be called on so to exercise it, they have by the practice in early life, acquired an invaluable command over themselves."[20] Perhaps it is not just chance that we have almost no information on how Florence Nightingale interacted with her grandmother Smith!

EDUCATION FOR THE Smith children did not come only from books. In Park Street, at Parndon, and on the tours they made with their parents, the older Smith children in particular met some of the most remarkable men of the age. Patty tells a funny little story in her diary about one occasion when the family was at Park Street and Charles James Fox was meeting with William Smith and other gentlemen in the drawing room. Patty, Benjamin, and the younger children were eating a makeshift dinner in the front parlor when someone knocked on the door demanding to come in. As a joke, the children set their weight against the door.

Only when they were finally persuaded that it was the great Fox who needed to come in to wash his hands did they open up the door. They were sadly conscious of the crumbs and orange peels littering the table, as well as of the open copy of Germaine de Staël's recently published and highly touted novel *Delphine*. Madame de Staël was a controversial woman, personally as well as politically, and it is a sign of the Smith parents' exceptionally liberal philosophy of education that they allowed their daughter Patty to read her work.[21]

Some of the notable people whom the Smith children grew to know lived in Clapham. At least until the death of William's stepmother in 1804, the Smiths continued on very familiar terms with the Thorntons, the Wilberforces, and other Clapham families whose abolitionist activities had already earned them some renown. Their connections in the Dissenter community offered the Smith children even more prestigious mentors and role models. The Priestleys, the Darwins, the Wedgwoods, and the Galtons were family friends, and Patty is being daring when she says that personally she did not care for Mr. Priestley. She and all the family followed Unitarian minister and scientist Joseph Priestley's remarkable career closely and were there to listen to his last sermon and shake his hand before he departed for the United States. Erasmus Darwin, a friend of the family, was a man of great intellect, a scholar and scientist whose ideas on how there came to be different species of plants and animals anticipated Lamarckism and would have some influence on his even more remarkable and famous grandsons, Sir Francis Galton and Charles Darwin.[22]

The Smiths met other notable contemporaries on their summer tours. When in north Wales in 1792 the Smiths dropped in on Sarah Ponsonby and Anna Seward in Llangollen. These two well-bred and well-connected women, already famous in their day, led irreproachable lives once they had eloped together to the wilds of Wales, refusing all suggestions of conventional marriage. The "ladies of Llangollen" are now celebrated in the annals of lesbianism, and one wonders what Patty Smith, then age ten, made of them.[23] When in Shropshire the Smiths naturally stayed in Etruria with the Wedgwoods. The great pottery baron Josiah and his son Richard held radical political views and supported writers like William Godwin, who had run afoul of the legal system in the repressive years around 1800.[24]

When touring the Lake District, the Smiths spent several days near Wordsworth, who was then living at Dove Cottage. The poet had become a kind of walking tourist attraction but the Smiths, who knew his work, did not take to him. Patty Smith described Wordsworth as "a dirty, slouching personage, too learned to be clean, too sincere to be civil."[25] On the other hand, during this same tour of the Lake District, the Smiths were charmed by the poets Southey and Coleridge. This meeting resulted in an invitation to stay, and Julia Smith remembered the occasion when Samuel Taylor Coleridge came to Parndon. To the envy of the other girls, Coleridge gave Patty a copy of his poem "Christabel." Later, little Julia watched in fascination as Coleridge strode up and down the hall, rapt in thought, while a carriage full of guests impatiently awaited him. Here was a great poet writing a poem before her very eyes. Sadly, Coleridge's eccentric behavior and his request to be served brandy in his room, "to bathe his ankles," was too much for Frances Smith, who never invited him again.

Of all the notable members of the Abolition Society, the Smiths were closest to William Clarkson and his wife. Both were frequent and much-loved guests at Parndon. Mr. Clarkson was often closeted with Mr. Smith at Park Street and did much of his vast correspondence and journalism there. A chronic invalid who yet ran the household and business affairs, Mrs. Clarkson was a charming and cultivated lady. It was she who introduced the young Smiths to the work of Wordsworth and Coleridge, who were then part of the extreme literary avant-garde. Clarkson's main contribution to the abolitionist cause was to collect as much firsthand data as he could about conditions on the plantations and slave ships. Patty describes him often sitting long in silence at dinner and then suddenly breaking out into a story of cruelty and oppression that would reduce the company to tears.

AS AN ELDERLY WOMAN, Patty Smith was a joke in the reformist political circles she frequented as well as an embarrassment to her family. Barbara Leigh Smith Bodichon, a radical of the new stripe, was fond of entertaining friends like George Eliot with her comic impersonations of her aunt Pat. But to an astonishing degree, Patty Smith as a girl was a prototype of the young Florence Nightingale, and the story of her rapid decline into hypochondria and truculence is a tragic one. Patty in her teens impressed the often very impressive people she met with her intellect, her breadth of reading, her prowess as a horsewoman, her talent as a musician and artist, and above all her radical spirit. She was a passionate abolitionist and was also willing to applaud revolution in France or in Haiti if it meant an end to tyranny.[26] Patty reached adulthood as the campaign to abolish the slave trade was finally nearing success, and since she did not have the heavy business cares of her brother Ben, she was close to her father and to the Wilberforce group during this fascinating period. In her late teens and early twenties Patty served as her father's amanuensis and even as his hostess in London when her mother was at Parndon or on visits to friends. This was Patty Smith's heyday, and she never ceased to mourn its passing. But even at this stage in her life, Patty, like the young Florence Nightingale, was moody, difficult, and plagued by mysterious ailments.[27] By the time Patty was twenty-five the era of revolution was over and she herself had become an anachronism. Forever ill and expecting death, Patty Smith lived to be eighty-seven. It is striking, and tragic, how closely Florence would in certain aspects recapitulate her aunt's life.

Patty Smith never married. If I had to guess, I would say that Patty might have married—her father was at the zenith of his fortunes in her late teens, her mother surely introduced her to eligible young men—but could not bring herself to it. As the oldest girl in a large family, Patty had seen her mother go through a dozen pregnancies. As the family grew and her mother's interest in child care waned, Patty became surrogate mother to the younger children. Books, travel, and the friendship of unconventional women like Anna Barbauld, Amelia Opie, Mary Clarke, and the Princess Belgioioso did nothing to convince Patty that her happiness lay in marriage.

Instead, Patty developed intimate relationships with female friends, most notably, when she was in her late thirties, with Marianne Thornton, one of the Clapham Thorntons, then a teenage girl, two years younger than Patty's sister Julia. When Marianne lost her parents, she and Patty became very close, and the friendship, mainly conducted in letters, lasted all their lives. Sadly, their extensive extant correspondence was destroyed by zealous relatives after Marianne and Patty died. Where Patty was the oldest of ten, Marianne was the oldest of nine, so they had much in common. The difference between the two friends was that Marianne's adored father died young and left her comfortably set for life, while Patty's father lived to be old and lost almost everything. As her great-nephew E. M. Forster tells it in his graceful biography, Marianne Thornton was a lively, attractive woman of wit and culture, eminently suited to marriage, it seemed, who yet preferred to leave marriage and children to younger sisters.[28] Julia Smith deeply admired Marianne Thornton and wished that she had been admitted into the exclusive friendship that bound Patty and Marianne. Julia writes: "I envied MT's education under her father . . . She was about my age I admired & loved her but did not even then want to be Evangelical & Biblical I wanted to be useful & responsible to have something as she did to live for & I coveted her friendship wh she never gave me as she did Patty tho she was intensely kind & feeling."[29]

By temperament and education, Patty and Julia Smith were very different. Where Patty emerges from her letters and memoirs as cool, factual, caustic, Julia is passionate, judgmental, sensual. Patty was shaped by the Enlightenment, Julia by the Romantic movement. Patty, though she played and sang and painted as a young woman, was above all an intellectual. Julia, though she learned Greek and read the latest in German philosophy, was an artist. While Patty as an adult took to her bed and obsessed about her ailments, Julia, nicknamed the "inspired apple-dumpling" as a child, grew into a tiny, slim, attractive woman who was incapable of sitting still. Patty in her reminiscences shows us Parndon and Park Street at their apogee, while Julia paints them in decline.

Julia, like her nieces Florence and Barbara, comes alive with almost every sentence she puts on the page. Of all the Smiths, she was the real artist, and her memories are of color and pattern, as well as of feelings and images.

I loved our old Nurse dearly . . . She was a great woman for air and water, when air and water were not so much the fashion as now . . . She had a beautiful cotton gown covered with a running pattern of strawberry plants. I can see the dark and light green leaves and the red berries with the seeds in them still. I think that gown gave me my first pleasure in painting, and the decided preference I have for a running pattern over stripes, stars and spots. Her cap borders too were a perpetual feast to me, they were made of hand worked lace, every division of the pattern done in a different stitch. I think she was never cross to us, always affectionate and kind . . . Every Friday evening a wagon laden with flowers, fruit, and vegetables, eggs, chickens etc was sent to London. Every Sunday morning it returned, having traveled in the night, and when I got down to the housekeeper's room, there were letters and sometimes big parcels for me on the dresser . . . The delight of that first hour of Sunday will never be forgotten while I remember anything. My sisters and brothers . . . wrote fond letters in text hand that I could read, and there were little pictures and storybooks—The sun always shone upon the dresser at that time.[30]

On another occasion when Julia was little, she and Fred were sent over to Clapham to the house of their father's stepmother. Frances Smith would come on Mondays with the bigger girls and play with Julia and Fred, but still Julia felt the separation keenly. At Clapham Grandmama allowed Julia and Fred to play among the furze bushes on the common, but the old lady was still a disciplinarian of the old school. Once, Julia remembered, she was whipped by her grandmother for telling a story—when she had not—and after Fred came back from a walk and remarked that a lady had complimented him on his pretty curls, old Mrs. Smith immediately took out her scissors and cut them off. Sometimes at Clapham when they were naughty, Julia and Fred were punished by being put in a large cupboard.

Despite the cupboard and the unmerited whipping, Julia was deeply attached to her grandmother and was inconsolable when the old lady died in 1805. Overall, Julia was an exceptionally affectionate child. She was in awe of Patty, who gave her most of the scraps of formal education that came her way when she was little, and Fanny seems to have been her favorite sister. But Julia above all idolized her biggest and grandest brother, Ben, and craved his attention and approval. Once while he was at Cambridge Ben came to Parndon when only the little ones were there. Julia, no doubt proud of her reading skills, disturbed him by persistently reading aloud from her book while he was trying to study. Benjamin lifted Julia up bodily and put her and the book outside the room. The next evening, however, Ben, who would always be wonderful with children, made amends to his deeply aggrieved little sister. He asked the nurse to bring Julia into the dining room to keep him company after dinner—she no doubt ate her evening meal in the nursery. Ceremonially Benjamin set two candles beside Julia on the floor so she could see her book. Julia says: "I was so very fond of him, the touch of his little finger as I walked beside him was happiness, and that small estrangement was misery while it lasted."[31] As adults, Benjamin and Julia Smith would disagree on many issues—sexual morality, and the ineluctable inferiority of the female sex, most notably—but Julia's passionate devotion to Ben never faltered and was transferred to his five Leigh Smith children.

FEMINISM WAS PART of Florence Nightingale's intellectual birthright in large part because Patty and Julia Smith were her aunts. Many of the proto-feminist writers who were active in London during the last quarter of the eighteenth century—Mary Wollstonecraft, her husband William Godwin, Amelia Alderson and her husband, John Opie, Helen Maria Williams, Anna Barbauld—were personal friends of Florence's grandparents William and Frances Smith and of their eldest children, Patty and Ben.[32] Patty Smith was admired and emulated by Julia, the youngest Smith child, and Julia can rightly be called a feminist. All her life, Julia was an active part of the London intelligentsia and the political avant-garde, writing letters, raising funds, volunteering in hospitals, making nourishing soup with the great Soyer during the Irish potato famine, learning to sign so she could communicate with pupils in the new schools for the deaf, taking classes at the new Bedford College. Julia Smith was one of the older generation of women associated with the influential Langham Place group, headed by Barbara Leigh Smith and her friend Bessie Parkes, which was active between 1855 and 1865. Actually or symbolically, Julia passed the family copy of Wollstonecraft to her niece, friend, and ally Barbara, Benjamin's oldest child. Barbara's whole life echoed with Wollstonecraftian and Shelleyan themes. She was born rich but illegitimate and suffered from social prejudice all her life, yet managed to make an independent and unorthodox life, full of friendship and art and achievement. As a political lobbyist for equal legal rights

for women, contributor to an important women's periodical, and founding mother of Girton College, Barbara carried on the fight for many of
Aunt Julia's most cherished causes.[33]

Florence Nightingale and her sister, Parthenope Verney, were not
feminist like Julia or Barbara, but the ambivalence they expressed as
adults on the issues of women's rights was in part, I think, a defense
mechanism against the zeal of their female relatives. As a child and young
woman Florence was often cared for and chaperoned by her aunt Ju and
found that lady's passionate idealism tiresome. "This noon Ju & I have
had an immense talk," wrote Florence to Parthenope in the mid-1840s,
"she is positively-raving-German-mad & more excited than I ever saw
her . . . She is enough to set a whole family by the ears." In a letter to her
mother, Fanny, Florence refers to "the tempestuous Ju" and notes that
"she cannot stand under the tempest of her feelings & no more can I. I
told her truth & she was very much hurt."[34]

Young Flo was determined not to be like old Ju and older Patty, and
they loved her too much to want her to share their fate. When Flo was
in her early thirties, Aunt Patty wrote a sad little note to Fanny, begging
her younger sister to give Flo the freedom and encouragement she
craved. With the clarity of intellect and quickness of feeling that were
characteristic of the Smiths, Patty saw that Flo risked becoming like herself—an impoverished, lonely, frustrated, snubbed old Cassandra. And
in fact, in the letters written in her old age, the famous philanthropist
and lobbyist Miss Nightingale, with her yards of information, crusty
opinions, coruscating wit, and dogged idealism, reads astonishingly like
her Smith aunts thirty years earlier.

In some ways it is hard to imagine two more different women than
Mary Wollstonecraft and Florence Nightingale, yet a slim but direct and
personal thread reaches from Mary to Patty to Julia to Flo. And in the
1851 "Cassandra" fragment, which has become a part of today's feminist
canon, Florence Nightingale re-echoes Mary Wollstonecraft's demands
that women be afforded the same moral agency, the same education, the
same opportunities, the same work as men.

The link between Mary and Florence has been obscured because it
has seemed to run through Fanny, and Fanny Smith Nightingale has
come down to us as a superficial, hidebound, conventional Victorian. As
we come to consider the famously combative relationship between Flo-

rence Nightingale and her mother, we must keep in mind that many prominent Victorians chose to forget that their parents had been fiery radicals, just as a media-savvy conservative matron in the 1990s might forget that in the '60s her mother had hung out in a lesbian commune. Fanny's conservatism and conventionality were a part of the general Victorian *mentalité*, but they were also a specific reaction against her memories of living dangerously close to the cutting edge of social change and intellectual ferment during her childhood. Fanny had been fed on advanced ideas from infancy. She had seen something of revolution. For her daughters, she wanted something different.

Family traits and traditions do not die, even if they go unexpressed for a generation. The radicalism of the Smith grandparents, of the crazy aunties Patty and Julia and the reprobate uncle Ben, resurfaced in the next generation in inflected but recognizable ways. When Florence Nightingale refused to conform, she was both innovating and reverting to type.

As the Napoleonic wars finally ended in 1815, the Smiths were full of confidence in the life that lay ahead in the new century. If the abolition of slavery for which their father had fought so hard and long meant that the Smiths could not live from the sale of sugar, well, the new generation would need to learn new trades, make new investments, form new alliances, as their forefathers had done. The family was confident in its traditions and its talents. Six of the Smiths who went on to have children of their own—Benjamin, Anne, Joanna, Fanny, Sam, and Octavius—all strove, in different ways, to create their own versions of Parndon and pass on the legacy they had received from their parents.[35]

Small wonder, then, that when the shy, gawky, studious William Edward Nightingale was invited home by his school and university friends Samuel and Octavius Smith, he was enchanted by the whole family and fell deeply in love with one of the daughters, Fanny.

Chapter 3

WEN AND FANNY,
BEN AND ANNE,
SAM AND MAI

Born in 1788, Fanny was the fourth child of William and Frances Smith, and the third daughter. She was intelligent but not intellectual, religious but no zealot. She could make people laugh, and she was aware of being much admired. She had a mind of her own and meant to have her way. English novelists from Samuel Richardson and Fanny Burney to Jane Austen and Walter Scott chose spirited young women like Fanny as their heroines. Fanny knew this because she read the novels.

Fanny Smith had good looks, which, before Charlotte Brontë came along with Jane Eyre, were essential in a heroine. The charming and unpretentious portrait of the young Fanny that now hangs at Claydon House shows a natural and very English beauty—fine skin, delicate features, and casually waving auburn hair. Fanny Smith took after her tall, handsome, ruddy father.

The second eldest Smith sister, Anne, was the first to marry, and hers was a splendid match. Her husband, George Nicholson, a thoroughly congenial man drawn from the old Dissenting network, was also very rich. The fourth sister, Joanna, had always been precocious, and she became engaged in her late teens to a brilliant, up-and-coming, but poor Unitarian lawyer from Portsmouth, called plain John Carter. He, like Samuel and Octavius Smith, was a pupil at Dr. Cogan's school and went

on to Cambridge University, but compromised with his religious principles and took the exams, emerging with a first-class degree. On
Christmas Day 1816, twenty-five-year-old Joanna finally married her
John, a wedding made possible in part at least by the generosity of the
bride's eldest brother. Benjamin Smith gave John and Joanna the house
he owned at 16 Duke Street, Westminster, facing St. James Park, and all
its contents. This address was invaluable to John since in 1816 he was
elected M.P. for Portsmouth, a position virtually hereditary in his family.
In the Commons, John Carter became one of his father-in-law William
Smith's allies. At first the young Carters were hard-pressed for money but
after some ten years their fortunes changed—luckily, since Joanna was
proving as fertile as her mother. John Carter inherited a large legacy from
his bachelor cousin John Bonham and was transformed into John Bonham-Carter, the owner of ten thousand acres of land near Peterfield and
in the Isle of Wight.[1]

This left William Smith with three daughters to marry off—an unenviable position for a man with serious money problems. At thirty-
three, Patty, the eldest child, was a confirmed spinster and sinking into
depression and hypochondria. Julia, unlike Anne and Joanna, showed
little interest in beaus and babies, but she had time to change. English
women in the Dissenter community tended to marry in their twenties,
not their teens. At sixteen going on seventeen, Julia, a tiny, plump ball
of feeling and energy, was extremely marriageable.

But unexpectedly Fanny at twenty-seven was proving to be a real
problem. She was clearly not cut out to be a spinster, and she could have
had a husband if she had wanted one. But, like many attractive women,
Fanny was high-handed and particular about men. As she moved into
her late twenties she refused to get desperate. All the same, the sight of
her two sisters and their loving husbands, of the increasingly disgruntled
Patty, and of eager little Julia coming up fast behind inevitably put marital pressure on even the self-confident Fanny.

Fanny Smith had formed an attachment with the Honourable James
Sinclair, a younger son of the Earl of Caithness, and in 1816 she an-
nounced that James had given her a ring and they wished to marry. The
two apparently met in Scotland on one of William Smith's official parliamentary tours.[2] James Sinclair was an army officer, and as Jane Austen
observed in *Pride and Prejudice,* even rational young women can find

men in uniform irresistible. James was also an aristocrat, a minor, Scottish, but undisputed part of the tiny oligarchy that ruled and owned the British Isles. As the Honourable Mrs. James Sinclair, Fanny might perhaps gain an entrée into what Georgette Heyer in her Regency novels likes to call "the *ton*," a social set that was still firmly closed to a daughter of "trade." If Patty Smith longed to be a man and go into Parliament, Fanny Smith was happy to be a woman provided she could move in the best society.

Romantic Fanny may have been, ambitious (from within a traditional woman's frame of reference) she surely was, but she was also the child of pragmatism. She knew she needed an income that would allow her to live with her noble lover in something like style, and, having always lived in circles where money was plentiful, she assumed she could get enough if she pressed hard. Thus, even though she and James were well of age, they did not elope to Gretna Green. Instead Fanny worked hard on her father to find a good army post for James and make some settlement on them. James, for his part, conforming to an aristocratic male stereotype, remained passive, content to allow his beloved and their parents to work things out if they could.

To Frances Coape Smith, her daughter's desire to marry James Sinclair made no sense. James was not a Unitarian, and like many minorities then and now, Unitarians tended to marry within the faith. This choice of partner was in part an affirmation of values, but it was also a form of self-defense. Prejudice against Unitarians was almost universal. Second, Sinclair was a career army officer, and he made four hundred pounds a year, which did not even cover his expenses in the regiment. As the younger son of a peer, it was understood that his duty was to do well enough in his chosen career to bring credit to the family, handle his debts in a gentlemanly manner, and ensure his future by marrying a woman with money. Fanny, by religion, by fortune, by society, could not be what James Sinclair needed in a wife.[3]

It was thus to her father that Fanny wrote of her proposed marriage, sure that he would be sympathetic. We do not have Fanny's letters to William—at her earnest request he destroyed them—but to judge from William's response, Fanny's message was that she and James were deeply in love and sure of their feelings for each other. She assured her father that James was perfectly indifferent to questions of money and that he wished her for herself. For all her twenty-seven years, Fanny Smith was still very naive.

William wrote to his daughter at length, sadly and rationally, and with a fine sense of psychology. Far from playing the heavy father, William acknowledged, even honored, the strength of Fanny's feelings. He did not suggest that she had made a mistake or remark on the romanticism of the picture she painted. Above all, he cast no aspersions on the lover, sensing no doubt that to attack James was unlikely to win over the self-willed Fanny.

William explained as gently as possible that he had been in contact with Sinclair's family about the marriage and had also tried in vain to get James taken on as an aide-de-camp to a general.[4] The Caithnesses were irrevocably opposed to the match. Religious prejudice is hinted at in the letters, but the main reason for the Caithnesses' opposition seems to have been financial. My impression, as I tried to decipher William's barely legible scrawl, was that James Sinclair's family would not have liked a wealthy Fanny Smith but were certainly not going to accept a poor one. William told Fanny he was not in a position to keep her and her darling James, and any eventual children they might have.

Even the most intelligent and acute young women of this period had little idea of how the world worked financially, and Fanny was shocked by her father's news. She had overestimated her own powers of persuasion, her father's wealth, and his willingness to make her happy at any cost. She had wanted something very badly and was not getting it. But since it was clear that neither she nor James would be happy in a cottage, Fanny returned his ring and broke off relations. In 1818 the Honourable James Sinclair married the heiress Elizabeth Tritton. Fanny had learned something about the world, about money and marriage and women's power, something she would be anxious to pass on to her daughters. Fanny put her father's letters away and kept them to the end of her life, when they passed to her daughter Parthenope and thence into the Claydon collection. But she did not repine like Anne Elliot in *Persuasion*. In 1817 Fanny became engaged to be married to William Edward Nightingale, a man of great wealth and impeccable Unitarian lineage.

For Nightingale it was not a great match. WEN did not need wealth in a wife, but he did need sons to inherit the Nightingale estate, which constituted most of his personal fortune. Fanny was six years older than

William, closing in on thirty—old in an age when women married in their teens and, all too often, died in their twenties. Fanny had no money of her own. Her father, William Smith, had recently suffered severe business losses, and Fanny's rich brother, Ben, saw no reason to come up with a substantial wedding present, as he had for Joanna. The Smiths and the Shores, William's family, had long been friends, but if any rumor about the Sinclair affair had got about the Unitarian network, it would have done nothing for Fanny's reputation.

William's parents, William and Mary Shore, were simple and loving people of high principle who did not put their trust in mammon. All the same, they had no doubt expected their darling only son to set his sights a little higher than the third, slightly shop-soiled Smith girl. But the Shores saw how William adored Fanny, and they could not bear to see him unhappy. In a notably loving and thoughtful act, Mr. Shore, who was himself wealthy, gave his rich son's fiancée a generous wedding present, in essence a dowry, to spend as she willed.

WEN had been close to the Smith family for some years, and he surely knew that Fanny had wanted to marry James Sinclair. But what to a less truly honorable man would have been an impediment was, I think, an incentive to the quiet, introspective, intellectual William. William, like Fanny, was well read in the fiction of his period. His part would be that of the quiet, sensible, adoring man to whom the spirited heroine turns after she has had her romantic fling and with whom she will live happily ever after. Jane Austen gave two excellent versions of this in *Sense and Sensibility* and *Emma*. Later in the century Emily Brontë would reprise it with Hareton in *Wuthering Heights,* as would Thackeray with Dobbin in *Vanity Fair*. Even though he knew that he was Fanny's fall-back choice, that he was not suave and charming and debonair, William thought he had much to offer Fanny. He relied upon her to see that he not only presented the solution to her present problems but was a man whom she would always be able to rely on in the fundamental things of life. Fanny would grow to love him and make a good, if demanding, wife, William thought, and in this, as in so much else, he was quite right.

On the Smith side, Fanny's parents were overjoyed by the betrothal. On the day of her daughter's wedding Frances Smith wrote to Fanny to confer a mother's blessing. "May God in his infinite mercy," wrote Frances in her immaculate handwriting, "keep you both, may you go hand in hand happily through life, but may you never forget that there is a better . . . Your father & I have remembered you at the throne of Grace this morning." From Frances such a letter was a sign of the highest approval. But Fanny's siblings were surprisingly critical of her decision. They liked Nightingale as Sam and Octavius's friend, but with Fanny so bossy and talkative and ambitious and WEN so silent and gawky and indecisive, they felt the two would never, in the long run, suit.

Fanny and WEN's wedding on June 1, 1818, proved as full of aggravation as it was of celebration.[5] There was some problem over the wedding license, and the time of the service to be held at the bride's London home was advanced at the very last minute. William and Mary Shore, together with their teenage daughter, Mai, had come from Sheffield to London for the wedding, but they did not receive word of the change in time. They missed the ceremony and the departure of the happy couple on their honeymoon. Worse, instead of going to an inn in Herefordshire, as they had planned, WEN and Fanny decided at the last minute to go to Parndon, the Smith country home in Essex. Learning he had missed the wedding, the bridegroom's father set off on horseback to try to intercept the honeymoon couple on their journey to Herefordshire and wish them well. As Julia wrote to Fanny and WEN with her habitual directness: "Did you know that your poor old father went out on the Oxford Road & rode up and down two or three hours to see you?"

While Mr. Shore was riding fruitlessly around on the wrong road, Mary and Mai Shore arrived at Park Street to attend the wedding party given by the Smiths, which included some twenty-three guests. The Shore women were mortified to find that they had worn quite the wrong clothes. WEN had apparently told his parents and sister that no one intended to dress up for the wedding, but Sheffield and London interpreted this rather differently. Mrs. Shore was upset and Mr. Shore was indignant. As he wrote to his son on the following day: "There ought to have been some communication with the ladies in Park Street on this head—you indeed said to your mother that there would be no dressing on the occasion but this settled nothing without some information from those competent to say what that expression means."

It was Julia who rescued poor Mai from the sad embarrassment of being the worst-dressed woman in the party—apart from her mother,

who was a fashion disaster even by Yorkshire standards. Julia had also ridden over from Clapham too late to catch the ceremony or see the happy
couple on their way. In full fizz, Julia declared herself heartbroken not to
have seen her adored Fanny married, and then promptly drowned her
sorrows. She enchanted Mai with her exuberance and her promise of
sharing Italian lessons. Mai solemnly reported to Fanny in her letter of
June 2: "Poor Julia quite won my heart yesterday in her grief. She drank
one glass of wine after another in vain to raise her spirits." In her letter to
Fanny, Julia put a rather different spin on things: "Mary sweet creature
was obliged to drink 3 glasses of wine to enable me to do that & my father, whether he was drunk with joy or wine I cannot tell but his roar-
ing was quite disgusting & his kisses bestowed not only on the 3 girls but
on Mrs. Sydney too were really more than my spirits would endure."

The misunderstanding between the Smiths and the Shores was further compounded when the young Nightingales returned to London to
prepare for their journey abroad and to attend a party given in their
honor by Anne and George Nicholson, the bride's sister and brother-in-
law. The party would be held at the Nicholsons' luxurious London
home. The groom's immediate family, Mr. and Mrs. Shore and Mai, who
were still in London, were invited to the Nicholson party. However,
William wrote to his father saying that he would look forward to seeing
him and Mai but that he assumed that his mother would "not like the
bustle of meeting, etc." and would not attend.

Wounded to the quick, feeling that her son was ashamed to be seen
with her at a fashionable event, Mrs. Shore said that she would stay at
home. Shocked and mortified on her behalf, her husband and daughter
at once assured her that they would not think of going without her. Now
Mr. Shore was angry, not for himself but for his wife. He wrote in pain
and irritation to WEN explaining why he had refused the Nicholsons'
invitation and mildly chastising his son for making a casual remark that
so hurt his mother. Mr. Shore suggested that WEN and Fanny, however
busy they might be with their honeymoon preparations, should call
upon the Shores in their lodging and, in essence, make amends.

It is hard to know whom to blame for the wedding debacle. Fanny
and her mother were both such formidably organized women that it is
difficult to imagine how they could have got a wedding so wrong. It is
true that at this period it was not uncommon for people not to attend

the weddings of their children, but the Shores had made it plain they wished to see their son married and had come to town for that purpose. The Smiths must bear some of the blame for giving the Shore-Nightingale connection such a rocky start.

But the real problem, I think, lay with WEN, not with the Smiths. WEN was secretly uncomfortable at the prospect of seeing his own family and his wife's in the same room. He was in fact ashamed of his mother, whom he loved but knew to have no social graces. At the same time, he was too proud and awkward to ask Fanny for help with the problem of making his mother comfortable at the wedding. The Smith women were not malicious, and they were surely anxious to do everything in their power to make their old friends and new relatives happy.

The subtext of the Nightingale wedding drama was the cultural divide between north and south in England. From the time of Chaucer or before, the language of London and the Home Counties had become the standard English of culture and society, the language advocated by grammarians and painstakingly taught in schools as the prime means to social advancement. In other parts of the country, especially the Midlands and north, people spoke in a bewildering variety of dialects, with accents and turns of phrase that to the southern ear sounded both comic and uncouth. This was still true when I was growing up in south Wales in the 1950s and being drilled in the correct English vowel sounds.

Mrs. Shore, we may be sure, spoke broad Derbyshire and was not a woman to change her language just because she was in London. Her husband and daughter would have sounded much the same. WEN, the brilliant Edinburgh and Cambridge University student, recently returned from his sojourn in Germany and Switzerland, had probably modified his own provincial accent. That his mother, whom he now knew to be ill-dressed and coiffed, would embarrass him and Fanny in the Nicholsons' elegant drawing room was too much for him. It was easier to assume that she would not wish to go.

It would have been all too easy for the Shores to go back to the Midlands in a huff, but, remarkably, William Shore understood his son and chose to forgive the slights he and his wife had received. In the two letters he addressed to his son and new daughter-in-law, William Shore begins by expressing the warmest and most sincere pleasure in the marriage, asking God's blessings upon them as Frances Smith did, but with none of

Frances's infuriating priggishness. Shore tells Fanny how fortunate he feels his son is in his choice of partner and, rather more dubiously, mentions the great affection she has already aroused in her mother-in-law. He even manages to commend his son on his sudden decision to go to Parndon—so much better than an inn! But in the second half of the letter Shore's sadness and perplexity get the better of his tact: "I confess however I was much vexed when I first heard of the circumstance [i.e., that the couple were already married and gone] as you I have no doubt were also . . . I tell them in Park Street after this cheating your father how can you be expected to make a good husband (how do you & Fanny like the word!) to their daughter . . . Don't you think your Mother & I ought to have been at the wedding? I have heard it strongly insisted on by people who are competent judges."

I shall leave the last word on Fanny's wedding to Julia, who wrote a dazzling little parting note, full of affection, and humor, and pathos, to the sister she calls "dearest lovey-dovey." Here we get a sense of why people found the Smiths, especially perhaps the Smith girls, so wonderful: "Dear dear Fan poor John & I wander up and down like unburied ghosts asking comfort & finding none though to be sure cutting and eating & digesting the cake & hearing my mother's screams of indignation at the large pieces these are remedies against despair otherwise I should certainly hang myself Give my best fraternal love to Nightingale & tell him what I have never had the courage to tell him yet & what he cannot possibly know without, that you are the best woman in the world . . . The boys are waiting for me to go out upon the water. I do not mean to be wretched any longer."

AS AN UNDERGRADUATE William had explored some northern parts of Europe, notably spending some months in Geneva in 1816. On his honeymoon he took his bride through France into Italy, where her taste for the fine arts could be amply gratified. Like most educated men of his generation, William was soaked in the classics, and he longed to see and smell the landscape that had formed Virgil's *Eclogues* and *Georgics*. With the great French wars at last over, it was time for the British to travel south again and satisfy their passion for warm seas and brilliant sunlight, for wine and olives, for volcanoes, hot pools, colonnades, and curios.

WEN and Fanny got as far south as Naples, where they rented a house and settled down for a long stay. Italian came easily to both of them and they were quickly accepted into local expatriate society. The Nightingales found the sensuality of Naples overwhelming. The heat was tremendous, as was the street ruckus that entered the house day and night through the open windows. The exuberant architecture, the ritual and superstition of the Catholic processions constantly patrolling the streets, and the squalor and tyranny of the court of the King of Naples were all deeply foreign to these English Dissenters. Here bribery and *far nientismo* were a way of life, and just getting the customs department to release the packages sent from England took all WEN's diplomacy, linguistic talents, and ample supplies of local currency. To the Nightingales, Naples was exotic to the point of alien, and under all the brilliant color and bustling activity, disease lurked—cholera, typhoid, tetanus, malaria, run-of-the-mill diarrhea—ready to pounce indiscriminately on a Neapolitan peasant or an English milord.

Fanny wrote home to her family that WEN loved it all and would have been happy to stay there forever. She herself was full of verve, good humor, and curiosity. She gave her sisters a spirited account of the emperor and empress of Austria touring one of the great sites near Naples, finding no one willing to serve them refreshments and having their clothes almost torn off their backs by the rapacious locals.[6] But things got serious for Fanny when she gave birth to a fragile little girl whom she named Frances, after her mother and herself, and with characteristic élan Parthenope, the Greek name for Naples. In a droll, frank, chatty little piece of writing, no doubt intended for her family and entitled "Journal of My Little Life by Frances Parthenope Nightingale," Fanny ventriloquized her tiny daughter's voice and recounted her difficult first three months.[7] A terrified young mother who knew the risks she and her baby faced, separated from her family by several weeks of arduous travel, Fanny Nightingale rallied her spirits and reached out for love and comfort with this journal.[8]

Parthe was born on Monday, May 19, 1819, and the birth itself, under the attendance of a local doctor, was a horror story. The baby was small, the mother exhausted and afraid, and no one, not even Gale, Fanny's devoted nurse and maid, seemed to know what to do. "Tuesday 20. Slept & sucked as well as I could but Ma was so feverish and nervous or something or other I got about nothing, confound it, they gave me some sour acid stuff wh. I had enough to dispose of. Wedn. Slept gloriously, but was tormented beyond measure at sucking & sucking & all for nothing & gruel is but sorry stuff out of a spoon 3 times as big as one's self."

On Thursday, WEN fell ill, a not uncommon occurrence among anxious, loving young fathers, and Fanny worried about him. The baby continued to suck vigorously but got little milk, and Fanny's nipples became very sore. By the following Monday, the baby was clearly failing to thrive, but Fanny was at least able to get up and eat dinner with her husband. On Wednesday, things seemed to take a turn for the better—"I had my first belly full & the 3 doctors said we should all do well," writes Fanny, in her daughter's voice—but on Thursday night Fanny herself fell sick: "Mother caught cold she says because they didn't dress her up in flannel enough (I wish they had given her mine for I was about smothered) & all night long she tossed about & nurse rubbed & Gale rubbed & the more they rubbed, the worse she was."

At this point, the desperate little baby started throwing up blood, to general hysteria; the doctor who had attended the confinement was summoned but took his time coming, and the baby seemed likely to die. Fanny blamed the doctor: "If it had not been for his carelessness in the beginning, ignorance in the middle & brutality in the suite I should never have had to work away at my poor Ma & she would have been as good a cow as any." The next day was a confused Babel as they tried to get Fanny's milk flowing. "My poor mother tortured night & day while successive Babes, children, women nay puppies were applied to the unfortunate dairy." None of this did any good, and finally, after more than two weeks, Fanny accepted that she must bring in a wet nurse or Parthenope would die: "so I sucked away like a tiger and now I know what good living is."

The fact that Parthenope Nightingale almost died in the weeks after her birth, and that her mother saved her would profoundly shape both the character of the child and her relationship with her mother. It had been established that Parthe was frail and needed special protection. Fanny Nightingale may actually have blamed herself for waiting so long to find a good wet nurse. In 1820 and for decades to come, all across Europe, women of affluence preferred to use wet nurses, and for poor women their breast milk was a rare resource. In very affluent families, wet nurses were brought into the household as servants and often separated from their offspring. This was probably better for the child whose family was paying for the milk but not, unsurprisingly, for the wet nurse's own child. In other cases, the infants were sent to live with the wet nurse until they were weaned, often several years. During this time, their families visited them more or less often and paid the wet nurses more or less regularly for the child's upkeep. Thus for the first years of life many children of affluence lived the life of peasants, and their caretakers were free to care for them or abuse them pretty much at will.

So Fanny Nightingale was unusual in her determination to do everything she could to breast-feed her own child, following the example set by her sisters. At the time of Parthe's birth both Anne Nicholson and Joanna Carter were breast-feeding. Out of conviction, Fanny Nightingale chose to endure not only the torment of seeing Parthenope crying from hunger but the humiliation of getting other children and adults to suckle her to try and express her milk. The picture of Fanny and the puppies should be borne in mind by all who assume Fanny Nightingale was a pompous Victorian prude who cared only to keep up appearances.

Fanny's journal of Parthe's first weeks is often very amusing. Making the baby speak for herself enables Fanny to put her distress at arm's length, but at the same time she does not hide the fact that the real price for her inability to feed her own baby was paid not by herself or by Parthe but by the wet nurse's child. "Mother goes on gallantly with Joannina & the puppies," she wrote, "and sometimes takes a turn with Antonio, an ugly cross thing belonging to my nurse who does nothing but roar & disturb the whole house but she torments herself for nothing for she will never have me at her breast again." Fanny is bothered by Antonio's howls. Soon, as I gather from the journal, Antonio stops howling, grows listless, and dies. Not every woman is able to feed two infants at once, even if she wants to. When the wet nurse takes on a stranger's baby, she makes a devil's bargain, and Fanny Nightingale knows it.[9]

SOON FANNY WAS pregnant again, and the Nightingales moved to Florence in time for Fanny's next confinement. They rented the Villa Columbaia, a large, furnished villa near the Porta Romana on the edge of the city with a beautiful park and views of the Duomo and the Boboli Gardens.[10] On May 12, 1820, another daughter was born, and on July 4, in the saloon of the villa, the baby was christened by Dr. Trevor, Prebendary of Chester. Her given name was Florence.

The gap of seven weeks between birth and christening was unusual. In the Anglican faith, as in Roman Catholicism, doctrine dictated that a child be quickly baptized to wash it clean of original sin and thus clear its path to heaven should it die.[11] It seems likely that Fanny Nightingale, not the baby, was ill this time. Fanny never had another child, and two botched childbirths in thirteen months may explain her subsequent infertility. This time she did not attempt breast-feeding, and on July 1 an Italian woman called Umiliana Pistelli signed a three-year contract as nurse to Florence. Signora Pistelli was valued by her employers, and eight-year-old Florence was encouraged by her mother to correspond with her old nurse—in French, interestingly enough—and to give "Balia" news of her health and doings. When the Nightingale family returned to Florence in 1838 they visited Signora Pistelli, thin, old, and poor, and Florence met her "milk sister," Estella.[12] In later years Fanny told Florence that she had been unable to nurse, but Florence harbored still some resentment against her mother on this account.[13]

Fanny and William called their baby simply Florence, and the singularity of that name, in both senses, is important. It speaks to me of detachment and disappointment on the part of the parents. She should have been Mary Florence after WEN's mother and sister—which would have followed the pattern of Frances Parthenope—or Julia Florence after a favorite sister. As commentators on Florence Nightingale love to point out, Florence was both the name of her birthplace and a rare, old-fashioned, even outlandish name, sometimes given to boys in both England and the United States. But little Flo, as she would be known in the family, was a girl, and there was no getting around this. Indeed, however well the child was doing in the care of her Balia, the fact was that in the maternal stakes Fanny was trailing badly behind her two married sisters, each now possessed of healthy children of both sexes—and they did not have her legal problems. Florence's birth had done nothing to resolve the problem of the Nightingale entail. Fanny still had reason to quake for her sake and her daughters' every time William came down with a fever.

IF WILLIAM AND FANNY were having problems with children and nurses on their long and luxurious continental excursion, Fanny's family was having worries of a very different kind.[14] On June 2 Julia Smith reacted sympathetically to the first announcement of little Parthe's birth and Fanny's nursing problems but was forced to give her harassed sister far worse news from home. Their father's business had crashed, and he would be forced to sell Parndon and Park Street to meet his obligations. Julia and Patty were losing their home.

WEN and Fanny were aware that William Smith had been having financial problems for some time. He had been renting out Parndon and taking his family abroad, in an Englishman usually a sign that he needed to save money. In 1803 William Smith inherited sixty thousand pounds under the will of his uncle Benjamin and invested it all in a partnership in the Millbank whisky distillery on the Thames near London. When the uninsured Millbank plant burned down in 1806 Smith suffered very heavy losses. William's eldest son, Benjamin, took over the Millbank business from his father and managed to turn everything around. By 1820 the Millbank distillery was producing 373,831 gallons of spirits a year, and Benjamin Smith was a very rich man. But Ben's success did not solve his father's financial problems.

These became acute in 1813 when William Smith's partnership with his cousin Joseph Travers in the Cannon Street grocery business was dissolved amid great acrimony. As Davis summarizes the situation: "The main point of contention was Travers's disapproval of the activities of Smith's son Adams who had recently been taken into the business. After the dissolution of the old firm, Smith formed a new one with his Kemble cousins . . . By 1819 a combination of Adams's mismanagement and that, or worse, of the Kembles, had brought the firm to the verge of bankruptcy."[15] Benjamin was forced to bail his brother out of bankruptcy in 1819 and again in 1823, and Adams seems to have been a burden on his brothers and sisters until his death in 1870.

Julia's news continued to be bad: "We shall have, selling Parndon and *everything*, about £1000 a year (more or less) left." The London house, the country estate, almost all of the magnificent art collection, and even the gentleman's library had to go to meet the debt. A few months later, Julia reported to Fanny that Patty and Adams were leaving for Europe and that she feared that Adams had absolutely no idea of how to manage on five hundred pounds a year. She wrote about the house her father had rented for them at Kynsham, near Presteigne in Herefordshire on the Welsh border. Julia waxed rapturous about the beauty of the Welsh mountains but then admitted: "the house to be sure is rather awful, as the Americans say, but the view out of the window makes up for all deficiencies."

With Patty away shepherding the improvident and failed Adams around Germany, her other sisters busy with their husbands and children, her brothers Ben and Oc no doubt intent on minimizing the impact of their father's bankruptcy on their own business interests, Julia was the daughter in charge at home. She had to superintend the move and look after her mother, no easy task. Frances Smith, who had been born into affluence, could not but be deeply affected by this sudden downturn in her fortunes. Julia herself, whom no one ever accused of stupidity, must have understood that her dowry had gone with the art collection and that her life prospects had darkened a great deal. But Julia in her letters says little about herself, keeps her spirits high, and puts the best face on everything.

The only time Julia broke down was when she wrote to tell Fanny that their youngest brother, Frederic—Julia calls him Fritz—the brother nearest to Julia in the family, had determined to go out to India. Unlike Ben and Oc, Fritz had always hated business, and he seized the occasion of his father's financial difficulties to change his life. He wanted to go into the Indian army and be no more trouble or expense to his father or his oldest brother. Within a few weeks Frederic was packed, and he sailed away in a spirit of high adventure. Julia, who would probably have liked to sail away somewhere too, was heartbroken. She knew that even under the best of circumstances, it would be many years before Fritz's family saw him again, and he was all too likely to die. In fact, although Frederic Smith married and lived until 1872, he became permanently estranged from his family. He thus passed out of the family story, just as his sister had tearfully predicted.

Octavius Smith, the fourth son, was luckier than Fritz since his marriage had been arranged some time before his father's difficulties became public. His bride was Jane Cooke of Hertford, also Unitarian and the daughter of one of his father's former business partners. Octavius, thirteen years younger than brother Ben, also went into the distillery business. When Octavius and Jane (rapturously in love and sure to suit, according to Julia) were married, Mr. Cooke and Benjamin Smith gave them ten thousand pounds, an astonishingly handsome sum.[16] At the time of his father's bankruptcy in 1819, Samuel, the third brother, had left Cambridge, been called to the bar, and was earning his way, if not making much money, as a lawyer.

As for Patty and Julia, Benjamin took principal financial responsibility for them both, and they in turn were principally responsible for the care of their elderly parents, notably their mother after their father's death in 1835. One of the ironies of family life was that it was Patty and Julia, the least favored children, who had main care of their increasingly difficult mother. There is a telltale reference in one letter in the Claydon collection to Frances Smith not allowing Patty to have a fire in the drawing room and thus forcing her to entertain her friends in her own horrid little room. The lives of spinsters even in loving and affluent families were made of such small ignominies.

The four Nightingales arrived back in England in 1821. On their way home they spent some time in Paris, and here both WEN's sister, Mai, and Fanny's eldest brother, Ben, paid them a visit. Before the visit was over, Ben had swept Mai off her feet, and she had accepted his proposal of marriage, without even consulting her parents. Mr. and Mrs. Shore were furious. In an angry letter to his son, Mr. Shore described how Ben Smith had walked in and told him he intended to marry his daughter. "I shall briefly say," wrote Mr. Shore to WEN, "that the poor parent like me when Mr. Ben Smith told me I was to understand that Miss Shore had accepted him, has only left him to say (let the man be what he will) Sir you do me & my daughter honour, and I will provide the money [presumably Mai's dowry] as fast as I can."[17] In fact, however, Mr. Shore did not come up with the money fast, and he and his wife became irrevocably opposed to Benjamin Smith as a son-in-law, much to the indignation of Frances Smith, Ben's doting mother, who called the Shores "unjust and violent."[18]

Mai Shore was over twenty-one and free to marry, but she was far too sweet and scrupulous to jump into marriage against her parents' wishes. Once back at Tapton, far away from the fascinating Smiths, she began to waver. The Shores were devoted to their only daughter, and they were convinced that Mai was making a terrible mistake. They knew how to manage her and felt it was necessary on this occasion to be cruel to be kind. Faced with her parents' unaccustomed harshness, May poured out her sorrows in letters to Fanny but she did not head off to London and Ben's arms.

Mr. Shore's declining health may have had something to do with her hesitation. In September 1822, William Shore died, still unrelenting in his opposition to Ben. He blamed his son, William Nightingale, who had rushed home to see him in his last illness, for allowing the whole Benjamin Smith affair to develop. With her husband dead, Mrs. Shore became even more unsociable than before, doing her best to make her daughter's life a misery.

Mary writes in Oct. longing to get away from the sad house [i.e. Tapton] to visit the Nightingales—Oct. 6 1822 "the moment I mentioned the subject to my mother, she burst out into one of her passions, said everything that was abusive & unreasonable & then went to bed . . . my uncle Shore says that some time later in the spring is as soon as from respect to my father's memory & duty to my mother I ought to leave home . . . Mrs. Sydney [Shore] thinks so much of propriety she said remember the eyes of the world are upon you. . . . it sounds rather too ridiculous to suppose that the world can care about or notice me. What shall I do, I feel it so hard to be shut up here at the time of my life when I might most enjoy myself, without even the comfort of thinking that I do any good by it, for my Mother does not pretend to wish for me, except for the sake of propriety. This day she has breakfasted, dined & had tea in bed and here am I without a creature to speak to." Oct. 14, 1822. "My mother & I go on à l'ordinaire sometimes we are on speaking terms & sometimes not. I think her economy increases with her riches. When we are alone we dine on a table-cloth with holes so large, that Parthey could put her head through them. The cows and horses are brought to eat the grass in front of the house that it may not be wasted, & as there is no fence they gallop about the garden and where they please. The principal manias are making bonfires & cutting down trees. The labourer told me that there was one tree in the garden which bore a great quantity of apples & she ordered it to be cut down, because she said that it was so much trouble to gather them, so that now we are dependent on charity for any apples we have. "Nov. 14. 1822" Mr. Parker [Mr. Shore's partner in the bank and his executor] tells people who tell people who tell me that my mother is left immensely rich. We are not on sufficiently intimate terms to know anything of each other's concerns in any more direct way. I believe however it must be allowed for my poor Mother that she generally intends to do right & from not knowing how she torments herself at least as much as she torments everybody else."

It seems likely that Mai's engagement to Benjamin Smith lasted months at most. The Nightingales, who initially had facilitated the relationship, rapidly came to frown upon it like the Shores. Fanny seems never to have thought Ben was right for Mai, and her husband, attacked on the matter by both his father and his wife, soon came to believe they were right. It is possible that he was told things about his brother-in-law he had not known before. Margaret Verney tells us: "Meanwhile the original subject of the quarrel [i.e., Benjamin Smith] had fallen out of sight, & in March 1823, Mr. N writes to his wife 'I *more* than agree with you in all you say about Ben & Mary & shall certainly make a point of preventing their meeting as far as I am concerned' and 2 days later—'I hope you will find an opportunity of putting Mary completely upon her guard against Ben. I should wish her almost to swear that she will never listen to him for a moment—he is just as agreeable as ever, but so easily disturbed, & so completely the opposite of simplicity—good taste & what may be suited to a peaceable life that no good can come of his union with anybody, but a woman as high-spirited & determined as himself.' "

WHAT EXACTLY THE Shores had against Benjamin Smith in 1821 is not spelled out in the letters or in Margaret Verney's paraphrases. He was, of course, almost twice Mai's age, but it was far from uncommon for forty to marry twenty, and Ben was after all the eldest son of William Shore's old friend and coreligionist William Smith, and WEN's brother-in-law and friend. His behavior toward his parents in their financial trials and toward his sister Joanna had been notably generous. It is possible that Mr. Shore did not agree with the way Benjamin Smith conducted his business—the turnaround at the distillery had been achieved with conspicuous speed—but it seems far more likely that what the Shores disliked about Benjamin was his sexual morality.

The best information we have on Benjamin Smith's sexual mores can be gleaned from the relationships he is known to have contracted after 1822.[19] After his break with Mai Shore, Ben remained on friendly terms with the Nightingales and visited them at their new home in Derbyshire. On one occasion, Ben was looking around the Matlock area for a mine to buy that his brother Adams could manage, but what he found was a woman. Anne Longden was a milliner in her early twenties and presumably a beauty if she attracted the attention of a man of the world like Benjamin. The two would not have been introduced formally since Anne, though from a respectable Derbyshire family, did not move in the same social circles as the Nightingales. Her father was a corn miller and he and his family lived not far from Lea, on the estate of the Morewoods of Alfreton Hall. Ben and Anne fell in love and began an affair. When Anne became pregnant Ben did not abandon her but moved her to a rented house near Hastings, on the south coast of England. There she was known under the name of Mrs. Leigh. A daughter, named Barbara, came into the world on April 8, 1827, the first of the five children born to Anne and Benjamin, who would be known under the name of Leigh Smith.

Anne Longden's family members were far from "Victorian" in their response to her decision to go away with Benjamin Smith, and trust to his good feelings for her. Anne's mother as well as her sister Dolly Longden stayed with her, helping with the children during her life and after her death. Anne's trusted friend Hannah Walker, a Derbyshire woman with ties to the Longden family, also stayed with the children when Anne died. Barbara Leigh Smith Bodichon chose to be buried next to her aunt Dolly.

The reaction of Benjamin's family was, perhaps predictably, much harsher. William Smith was enough man of the world to understand his son's decision, if not condone it. William and Ben were extremely close, and in William's generation men like Charles James Fox and indeed the Prince Regent, later George IV, had flaunted their mistresses before the world. Mr. Smith saw no reason to break with his son over Anne Longden, especially since he was so reliant on Ben's generosity. William Nightingale, despite the old difficulties over his sister, kept Benjamin as a friend and was the member of the family to whom Ben was able to turn in the last, sad days of Anne's life. But Benjamin's mother and sisters were furious and disgusted. Patty was convinced that Anne was a conniving strumpet who had stolen the mainstay of the family, sullying his reputation and setting obstacles in his way to higher achievement. Patty claimed that Anne had had other lovers and that the man who came to visit her was not her brother but her husband or paramour. The Smiths felt that Anne's family had plotted to ensnare Benjamin and were now living off the fat of the land at his expense. "Oh, how it grieves me," wrote Frances Coape Smith to her daughter Fanny, "to think of his thraldom, for he is really as clever a man as can normally be met with, and think to what conversation he is confined."[20] Neither Frances nor any of her daughters ever agreed to meet Anne Longden or to receive her children during her lifetime. Fanny, Anne, and Joanna would maintain the taboo to the end of their lives.

With Anne Longden settled in Hastings in 1827, Benjamin bought Crowham Manor near Hastings in Sussex as well as Brown's Farm nearby. Fom there he could ride over to Anne's lodging, and a second child was born eleven months after Barbara. Despite all the vituperations of the Smith women, it seems likely that Anne was not only beautiful but a woman of sensibility whose mind grew in scope under Benjamin's influence and who loved him very much. According to biographer Pam Hirsch, in 1828, faced with the intransigence of his family and English society's growing censure of irregular sexual relationships, Benjamin took the extraordinary step of dissolving all his business partnerships and taking his common-law wife and their children to America.

The diary Benjamin wrote of this American adventure is a document both fascinating and infuriating.[21] Benjamin had been writing up such travel journals since childhood—one of the rare areas, one suspects, where he was influenced by his mother. Like Frances, Benjamin sets down events and facts, things he has seen, men he has met, towns he has visited, miles he has traveled.

The diary reveals a man with an excellent mind and a strong body deeply interested in all that he sees. While in America, Benjamin tries without much success to get in some good hunting. He fishes and plays écarté and chess, losing two games out of three to one opponent, to his great irritation. He tours jails, saltworks, hospitals, schools, colleges, monuments, botanical gardens, Native American villages, and African American churches. He attends the assizes and hears Channing preach in the Unitarian church in Boston. He has dinner with various gentlemen along the road: in Boston he refers to Ticknor, Grey, Winthrop, Sparks, and Dutton. He notices in surprise that in America it was necessary to shake hands "with men of all degrees." He describes the deep antagonism between Catholics and Protestants, who will not work together on the Erie Canal project. He is amused by news of the Pioneer, a Puritan coach service, which traveled from Albany to Niagara via Buffalo every day but Sunday and never stopped at houses of entertainment where spirits were sold. He is fascinated by Niagara Falls and devotes several pages to scientific observations on the falls as both hygrometer and thermometer.

Intermittently, however, there are hints that Benjamin Smith is not just touring America as he had once toured Scotland or the Lake District with his parents. All the travel he undertakes in his ten months in the United States has a purpose, though he never sets this down in so many words. He is looking for a property to buy, asking about farming in Canada and the United States, making contact with local men who can help him locate a good place to buy. Finally he writes: "Mr. Bose the magistrate said he could not help me in his shire. Irish emigrants stopped in their boat all Sunday near his house sympathized with me."

Perhaps it was the sympathy of those poor Irish emigrants that finally put despair into the heart of the normally determined and energetic Benjamin Smith. Certainly it was more than the mosquitoes that kept him from emigrating. One of the peculiar features of Benjamin's American travel diary is that he eschews personal pronouns, but he makes two or three cryptic references to "the babies": for example, "July 29. Babies affected with Diarrhea. Great kindness of Dr. Baldwin." What Benjamin is carefully concealing from anyone who might read the diary is that he is not alone on this exhausting and disappointing odyssey. The omitted "I" of the narrative is properly a "we," "Anne and I," but the existence and the experience of Miss Longden are allowed no place in Benjamin's account.

Yet the fact that he was accompanied by a woman not his wife, together with their two illegitimate babies, was probably at the heart of his failure to succeed in his mission. Benjamin Smith was a very wealthy man. He had sold his assets before setting sail for New York. He had the names and addresses of many notable American men and perhaps letters of recommendation from friends. And yet he could find nothing to buy, at least not on the terms he was willing to accept. Obviously Benjamin and Anne could have shipped into New York as man and wife and made a new life. Many with far slighter resources did so. But if the diary is evidence, this is not what Benjamin Smith wanted. He wanted to live a life somewhat like his English life, to be a friend to men like himself, a citizen of repute as in England. He also wanted to have Anne Longden as his common-law wife and had thought that this would be easier in America than in England. He was mistaken.

What the American journey must have been like for Anne Longden we can only imagine. Some of the time she was surely with Benjamin, always meeting new people in the steamers, canal boats, and stagecoaches and having to be introduced. When Benjamin went out hunting or to dine with local men she was left alone in the hotel or boardinghouse, enduring the stares and snubs of the other guests. When Benjamin was away on his own, on the fruitless search for a home for them, she had weeks to cope with the children in a foreign and hostile place. Probably Anne had her Derbyshire nurse Hannah Walker with her, or even her sister, but even so those months must have been a hard and humiliating experience.

When the family returned, Anne was pregnant with her third child. She was also showing signs of serious illness. Two more children were born at Brown's Farm, in 1831 and 1833, and by then it was plain that Anne was dying of consumption. Benjamin, crazy with love and grief, did everything he could to save her. To the deep chagrin of his family, he cast convention aside and openly adopted her and the children as his. He took her to luxury hotels for sea air and bathing, to fashionable spas, and finally to the Isle of Wight, the Smiths' place of origin. There she died in August of 1834, age thirty-two. Benjamin set up a stone memorial for her in which she is referred to for the first time as his wife, Anne Smith.

No one has been able to explain satisfactorily why, if Benjamin loved Anne so much, he never married her. It would surely have meant a great deal to her in her final years, and far more to their children, even if it was not possible under English law to legitimize them after the fact. Perhaps the social snobbery and family opposition Benjamin experienced after he went off with Anne reinforced his stubborn desire to lead his life as he saw fit. He was a middle-aged man of wealth and experience when he met Anne. He was also a man of great intelligence, wide culture, and radical ideas, unswayed by convention and the opinions of the world at large. I like Pam Hirsch's suggestion that Benjamin Smith's views on male-female relationships were influenced by his reading of William Godwin, a prophet of free love who cohabited with Mary Wollstonecraft until she became pregnant, and by the example of Godwin's daughter Mary and her eventual husband, Percy Bysshe Shelley. Benjamin was precisely of the generation, the intellectual caste, and the social group most likely to have been influenced by the Godwin-Shelley-Byron circle.

Or on the other hand, quite simply, Benjamin was swayed by his family and cared more about his position in the world as a rich businessman and his political ambitions than he did about Anne. When it came right down to it, he could not bring himself to marry a milliner.

Benjamin Smith proved to be an enlightened father. With the help of Dolly Longden and his own youngest sister, Julia, he gave his five Leigh Smith children a superb education, set them up for life financially, and earned their passionate love and devotion. Thus it was a profound shock to the Leigh Smiths in 1852 when their father, anticipating his own death, set about dividing up his estate and told them that a further two thousand pounds each had been set aside for Jane, Alexander, and Henry Bentley Smith. These were his illegitimate children by a certain Jane Buss. Their existence had remained a complete secret.[22]

IN 1827, ABOUT THE TIME that Ben Smith and Anne Longden began to live together, Mai Shore became after all Mai Smith, Fanny Smith Nightingale's double sister-in-law. Mai married Samuel Smith, the third of the five Smith brothers. After leaving Cambridge, Samuel went into the law and seems to have had a struggle. He was bitter over his father's failure in business. In a letter of November 17, 1823, to his sister Fanny,

Sam complained about the way William Smith had flung himself into one disastrous business venture after another, "to make him fancy himself a man of property and squander till not a penny was left for anybody." Marriage to a rich woman was Samuel's best hope of achieving something like the standard of living of Ben and Oc, of Nicholson and Nightingale. Mai Shore was not in 1827 a rich woman, but she had a dowry and excellent prospects of inheriting a large fortune when her parsimonious mother died.

Mai Shore and Sam Smith had a long and successful marriage, but the specter of Ben must have been hard for both to shake off. I have the impression Mai was marrying a family more than a man. She longed to leave the lonely life at Tapton under her increasingly eccentric mother's thumb. She was devoted to Nightingale, her only brother, and he to her, and as the dozens of letters Mai wrote to Fanny prove, she also was extremely close to and admiring of her sister-in-law. As Sam's wife, Mai would be close, geographically and socially, to the Nightingales, to Julia Smith, who was a good friend, and also to the Nicholsons and Bonham-Carters. She would be an integral part of the fascinating Smith tribe.

By marrying Sam, Mai also did her part to resolve the increasingly intractable problem of the Nightingale entail. In 1827 Fanny was thirty-eight and less and less likely to produce the desired heir. If Mai and Sam should have a son, at least WEN and Fanny could rejoice in seeing a double nephew as heir presumptive to the Nightingale fortune.

When seven-year-old Florence Nightingale, on a visit to London after a terrible bout of whooping cough, was told by her mother that Aunt Mai was to marry Uncle Sam, she wept. Flo adored Aunt Mai but did not like Sam, and the thought that he would be taking Mai away was too sad. Florence recorded all of this in her journal. She remembered, "When they got to the church she [Florence] had tried to kneel between Uncle Sam and Aunt Mai in order to keep them apart as long as possible. She also remembered that there had been a most wonderful wedding breakfast with more cakes and fruit than she had ever seen in her life, and that the festive feeling it all gave her had really been very delightful. It was curious to think about; she reflected that it had been at once the happiest and the *un*happiest day that she had ever spent in her grandmother's house at Tapton."[23]

Florence Nightingale and Samuel Smith had a long relationship and he did her many favors, but she never really changed her views on him. In 1874, at the time of her father's death and the reversion of the Nightingale property to the Samuel Smiths, she told her friend Benjamin Jowett that though Sam was intelligent and well educated, he lacked pluck and character.[24] In 1890, she discussed the old engagement between Mai and Benjamin with Margaret Verney, her stepniece-in-law, at Claydon. Margaret writes in her notes: "I said to Miss N. how happily it had eventually turned out—yes she said musingly—yet Sam was never half the man Ben was. 'Ben was such a large nature with a touch of genius in him, such a delightful companion, he used to sit with my father at Rome their feet on the empty grate talking from 2 o'clock in the afternoon till night. He was never profligate'—and yet all his domestic relations were most unhappy. His eldest son fitted out an Arctic expedition of his own—was shipwrecked and icebound thro' a winter but brought his men home safe again. Did Ben do well in the H of C [House of Commons] I asked—Very well I believe said Miss N."[25]

As we consider how Florence Nightingale turned into such a strange and powerful woman, we need to remember that one of her mother's brothers was Benjamin Smith.

Chapter 4

LEA HURST AND EMBLEY

W hen Fanny and WEN and their two baby girls returned to England in 1821, they first moved to Kynsham Court in Herefordshire.[1] This was the house Fanny's father, William Smith, had rented from Lord Oxford after his bankruptcy. Taking over Kynsham was a tactful way for WEN to help his parents-in-law financially, and he tried hard to find a suitable property near Kynsham to buy. But WEN really had his heart in his native Derbyshire, and there the family soon moved to a brand-new house he called Lea Hurst.

While still abroad, Nightingale had come to the conclusion that Lea Hall, Mad Peter Nightingale's house, was too run-down and inconvenient for a fashionable young family and was best converted into a farmhouse. What he and Fanny needed was a new, modern home, and Nightingale decided to design it himself. He probably had the site for the Derbyshire house in his mind from the start since the key to the house's beauty is the way it folds into the landscape. When he returned to Derbyshire at the time of his father's death in the fall of 1822, Nightingale had the opportunity to buy more land and get the building started. Lea Hurst's excited and proud young owner-architect designed and commissioned from Italian craftsmen some massive, heavily carved furniture for the new house. These pieces still grace Lea Hurst today.

The site that Nightingale chose for his house was in Holloway, a mile or so away from Lea Hall. Lea Hurst was about ten miles from the picturesque market town of Matlock and two and a half miles by road (less across the fields) from Cromford Bridge. This was where WEN's aunt Elizabeth Evans had her home, as did some 750 textile workers. Tapton,

Lea Hurst. Drawing by Parthenope Nightingale.

the home of WEN's parents and of his sister, Mai, on the moors on the outskirts of Sheffield, was a day's ride away. After three years abroad the Nightingales were really coming home, and one can imagine how this news pleased WEN's widowed mother and his aunt.

Lea Hurst tells us a great deal about its architect and first owner. William Edward Nightingale was already a wealthy man when he built Lea Hurst, but if he could afford the baronial, he did not choose it. Lea Hurst is a gentleman's residence, but it is also unpretentious, stern, and almost monastic in style, invisible from the road and nestling into the hill, very different from the Arkwrights' Willersley Castle, which dominates Cromford. Lea Hurst was built by local men out of the gray local stone, and, though larger, it matches the houses up the hill and over the valley. In the tradition of his rich but unworldly and antisocial Shore forefathers, WEN was seeking to suit himself, not to engage in conspicuous consumption.[2]

The glory of Lea Hurst is the view, which is both spectacular and private. The novelist Elizabeth Gaskell, struggling in 1856 to finish *North and South* for her impatient publisher, Charles Dickens, spent some weeks at Lea Hurst in early fall. With a painter's eye, Gaskell tossed off this dithyrambic description of the house: "High as Lea Hurst is, one seems on a pinnacle, with the clouds careering round one. Down below is a garden with stone terraces and flights of steps—the planes of these terraces being perfectly gorgeous with masses of hollyhocks, dahlias, nasturtiums, geraniums, etc. Then a sloping meadow losing itself in a steep wooded descent (such tints over the wood!) to the river Derwent, the rocks on the other side of which form the first distance, and are of a red colour streaked with misty purple. Beyond this, interlacing hills, forming three ranges of distance; the first, deep brown with decaying heather; the next, in some purple shadow, and the last catching some pale watery sunlight."[3]

THE NEW HOUSE was incontestably an improvement over the old Lea Hall. WEN felt at home there, but it soon became clear that Fanny would not be happy living most of the year in Derbyshire. In the early 1820s, unlike today, the Lea-Cromford area, with its lead smelting and its Arkwright mills, was sadly lacking in the picturesque, and Fanny's eye was now accustomed to Pompeii and the Boboli Gardens. But more important, Holloway and Derbyshire were cold, or so at least they seemed to Fanny.

Like all her compatriots, Fanny Nightingale had not been spoiled by the German luxury of stoves, and it would be almost 150 years before British homes were centrally heated. From the king at Windsor down to the plowman in his cot, the British in the 1820s were accustomed to dressing warmly indoors and doing calisthenics so as to withstand the dank chill. But Fanny was a woman of the English south, and the first winter in the Derbyshire dales was a bitter shock. Once the winter set in, the barely carpeted bedrooms and stone corridors of Lea Hurst, which Gaskell found endearingly homely in the early fall, were icy. When there was snow, the steep roads became impassable for days or even weeks. Holloway well knew the kind of blizzards to which Emily Brontë subjected that helpless southerner Lockwood in the opening chapters of *Wuthering Heights.* During the one winter that the Nightingale family spent together at Lea Hurst, the little girls had bronchitis and a series of coughs and chills. This was a worry, as infant mortality was high among all classes, and little Parthenope, fragile from birth, seemed especially at risk. Fanny was convinced, as she later told her girls, that Pop and Flo were failing to thrive because they missed the warmth of their Italian birthplace.

Worse than the physical cold was the isolation Fanny felt and the coldness of the local people. Fanny was used to life in London. She liked to travel and meet new people. Before her marriage, even in the country, she had been surrounded by friends and family who were ever eager to ride out, go sketching, or engage in amateur theatricals. But Derbyshire was quiet and far from the London scene, an unsettling mix of the pastoral and the industrial. It was as if a nineteenth-century New York socialite, before the advent of the railways, found herself marooned in the Black Hills of Dakota.

Holloway was in many ways more foreign to Fanny Nightingale than Naples, Florence, and Paris. In the lively expatriate communities of those cities, the Smiths had made many friends, and being a daughter of William Smith, M.P., had some cachet. But in Derbyshire few knew or cared who Fanny was.[4] As for the Lea Hurst tenants and servants, to Fanny they seemed almost like savages. In rural Essex the Smiths had warm relations with the local working classes and took their deference for granted, but in Lea things were different. If southerners tended to snub and sneer at northerners, northerners looked on southerners with surly suspicion. In time Fanny would win acceptance from the gentry, respect from the farmers, and affection from the servants in her husband's native country, but initially she felt alone.[5]

Above all, Fanny missed her sisters and brothers. The stouthearted and affectionate Julia actually seemed to like Derbyshire and could be counted on for visits, even in winter, if only to get away from her mother and Patty. Adams would spend time with anyone who would put up with him. But Anne and Joanna were so very absorbed in the care of their growing families that bringing them so far north would be difficult. The brothers and brothers-in-law had businesses and estates to run and professional duties, notably attendance at the House of Commons, all in the south. When at leisure, Nicholson, Bonham-Carter, Oc, Ben, and Sam were devoted to field sports, but the area around Lea Hurst offered poor hunting and fishing. How often could the Nightingales expect to see them?

There were still a number of Shores in the Sheffield area, and neither Fanny nor WEN would ever repudiate these connections.[6] All the same, the young couple's social position in Derbyshire was at first delicate. On one hand, being of Dissenter stock did not recommend them to

the county set. On the other hand, Fanny and WEN increasingly identified themselves as Anglicans, which did not ingratiate them to the old
Presbyterians and the new Unitarians. If the gentry turned up their noses
at "trade," the Midlands Dissenter families, even when wealthy, tended
to be xenophobic and to reprove anyone who seemed "fast." Like Fanny's
mother-in-law, they lived in the old manner, kept themselves to themselves, met mainly at church, dressed plainly, ate frugally, slept early, and
looked with disapproval at art, theater, modern literature, and politics,
all the things that were mother's milk to Fanny Smith Nightingale.

The closeness of Lea Hurst to the Shores of Tapton was no substitute to Fanny or WEN for the Smith clan. Mai Shore, a sensitive and
deeply affectionate young woman, clearly adored Fanny and did everything in her power to win her love in return. But Mrs. Shore was one of
the rare people able to resist Fanny Smith Nightingale's charm. Her
daughter's increasing involvement with Fanny and the Smiths only increased Mary Evans Shore's antagonism toward Fanny. Over the next
decades Fanny became, I think, a convenient scapegoat for her mother-
in-law's dissatisfactions. Flo, Mai, and WEN all allude in their letters to
the frustrations and stubborn disagreement that characterized relations
with the Evans sisters. Whenever they went north, Grandmother Shore
and Great-aunt Evans would greet them with a long litany of complaints.

The resentments of Mrs. Shore and her sister during Florence's
childhood probably went as follows. Fanny had stolen WEN's devotion,
even though he was not her first choice in a husband. She had made
WEN look down on his own mother, and at the Nightingales' wedding
the Smiths had done everything to make Mrs. Shore uncomfortable.
Fanny was too old for WEN, too old to give him the son he needed.
Then, to cap it all, Fanny had plotted to marry Mai to one of her brothers and thus put the Nightingale money—really, Mrs. Shore's own
money, since it was her uncle Peter Nightingale's inheritance—in the
Smith family's incapable hands. Mr. Shore had succeeded in detaching
Mai from the clutches of the unsavory Ben Smith, but the strain and distress of that affair had brought him to an untimely grave. And then, un-
believably, the intriguing Fanny had actually persuaded Sam Smith, her
last available brother, a man who could barely support himself, much less
a wife and children, to court Mai in Ben's place. And that ninny fell for it!

Interpreting silence is always a tricky business, and amid all the massive documentation left by the Nightingale family there is almost no extant correspondence between Fanny and her mother-in-law. I think, however, we get an inkling of the relationship between Mrs. Shore and Mrs. Nightingale from a little bread-and-butter letter that Florence wrote to her grandmother when she was eleven. As her daughters grew up, Fanny increasingly entrusted them with conducting parts of her huge correspondence. This was one of the many things that infuriated Florence about life at home, but she probably did not mind writing to her grandmother Shore. Thus in 1831 Florence was detailed to write a thank-you letter to her grandmother for a pair of shoes Mrs. Shore had sent to her newborn grandson, Shore Smith. This baby was Florence's cousin, the ardently desired second child of Mai and Sam Smith, and not incidentally the presumptive heir to the Nightingale fortune. At this time Mai and Sam Smith were living in smoky London and were hard-pressed for money. Shore was a delicate infant whose future seemed far from assured, and he came to Embley with his mother, wet nurse, and three-year-old sister soon after his birth.

Given all these circumstances, if all that came for baby Shore from Tapton was a pair of shoes, the Sam Smiths were very disappointed, and the Nightingales annoyed on their behalf. Mrs. Shore had, after all, inherited a very large fortune from her husband nine years earlier. Thus the fact that Fanny did not pen the note to Mrs. Shore herself is in itself significant. "Let Flo write," we can hear Fanny saying to Mai, "she gets on so well with Mother Shore and she so adores the baby. Anything we say will be wrong." But at the bottom of Florence's letter Fanny punctiliously added this chilly salutation: "Nightingale & the children join in fondest love with dear Madam your obliged & affectionate Frances Nightingale."[7]

WHEN HE ATTEMPTED to settle his family in Derbyshire in 1822, William Edward Nightingale had surely not anticipated social difficulties and family tension. But Fanny's happiness and the children's health were his first concern, and so WEN began to think again of where they might live. Another house, in another place, must be found that he and Fanny would both like. That his mother and aunt Evans would never forgive his moving away from Derbyshire was a cross that he would just have to bear.

Over more than a year WEN was away a great deal looking at different properties. He wrote to Fanny: "How would you like Leicestershire? For my part, I think that, provided I could get about 2000 acres and a house in some neighbourhood where sporting and scenery were in tolerable abundance, and the visit to Lea Hurst were annually confined to July, August, and October, then all would be well."[8]

Fortunately, Fanny did not have to settle for Leicestershire, since her obliging husband finally came upon the perfect property—Embley Park, near Romsey in the parish of Wellow, in Hampshire. Surrounded by acres of its own park, pasture, and beech forest, it was rural England as George Eliot nostalgically painted it in her fictional Hayslope.[9] From Fanny's point of view Embley could not have been better situated. The sea was only a few miles away—reportedly Southampton Water can be spotted on a clear day from the top of the house—so Fanny or her children could take healthful bathing when needed. The Isle of Wight, the ancestral home of the Smiths, was just across the water. The villages around Embley were small and picturesque, the villagers were accustomed to doffing their caps to the gentry, and there was not a mill or a mine or a speck of soot to mar the views.

There were numerous fine local families in comfortable visiting distance, most notably Lord Palmerston at Broadlands in the very next parish. The shooting was good, always an important consideration for any woman who wished for success as a hostess. Fanny's married sisters, Anne at Waverley Abbey, near Farnham, and Joanna, currently at Fair Oak, near Winchester, were within easy reach by carriage. London was close enough that, should Fanny's dear Nightingale decide to go into Parliament, he could come down on weekends when the House was in session. Embley itself, a solid brick Georgian building, was larger than Lea Hurst and had real possibilities for entertainment. "In comparison with Waverley Abbey, of course, Embley is nothing," we can imagine Fanny Nightingale happily saying to friends, "but then, the Nicholsons are so very well-to-do one simply cannot hope to compete."

If Lea Hurst was WEN's house and Florence's, corresponding on some deep level to their fantasies as well as their natures, Embley was Fanny's house and Parthe's. Late in life Parthenope Nightingale Verney painted a nostalgic picture:

Embley in Hampshire was a large picturesque gabled house, whose

handsome rooms gave ample space for its owners' wide hospitality.
Soil and climate alike favoured a luxuriant vegetation, it was em-
bowered in flowers, and the rhododendrons & azaleas which
clothed the plantations with a glow of colour in the spring & early
summer gave place to roses and lilies and a procession of bloom
lasting far into the winter. Embley was furnished with all that refined and cultivated taste could suggest, Greek and Italian marbles,
delicate watercolour drawings, draperies of rich colour, but beyond
& above all the house abounded in books. Old books in their staid
brown bindings, foreign classics in white parchment, great folios &
portfolios of choice engravings, formed a pleasant background
while the best books of the day on all conceivable subjects were
heaped on the tables & overflowed on every ledge or coign of van-
tage. It was a joke against Mr. Nightingale to the end of his life that
he could not get through a meal without covering the tablecloth
with literature . . . It was a house from which all sordid cares & pe-
cuniary anxieties were excluded & from which sympathy & help
flowed bountifully to the poorer homes around it.[10]

WITH THE PURCHASE of Embley in 1825 Fanny acquired the appropriate setting for her career as a prominent hostess to England's political
and cultural elite. In remarkably few years, she and Nightingale were receiving invitations from the Duke of Wellington and the Duke of Devonshire, receiving visits from Ada Byron Lovelace, Julia Ward Howe,
Elizabeth Gaskell, and Elizabeth Blackwell, meeting in London with
Charles Babbage, George Babington Macaulay, and Thomas Carlyle,
and rubbing shoulders abroad with Guizot, Thiers, Sismondi, Manzoni,
and Chateaubriand. By 1836, when Parthenope Nightingale was presented at court, the Nightingales and their clan were one of the nation's
leading families.

A subtle synergy of money, charm, culture, and intellect was at work
in this success. WEN's Nightingale money, which enabled him to purchase a large estate in Derbyshire and an even larger one in fashionable
Hampshire, was of course the sine qua non for social climbing. This was
a time when one-quarter of the land of England was in the hands of a
mere twelve hundred people, and when seventy-four hundred people

owned half of the country.

But though WEN himself was a man universally liked and esteemed by those who knew him, he was far too much a long, silent, detached, intellectual Shore to cozy up to the Devonshires or make the Palmerstons laugh over dinner. Fanny was the engine powering the Nightingales' rise up the social ladder. She had the makings of a social lioness and knew it, had known it back in her twenties when she tried in vain to become the Honourable Mrs. James Sinclair. A woman of competence and strong will like her mother, Fanny also had her father's good looks, social grace, and above all humor, and it was a winning combination. Fanny understood instinctively that it was essential to move away from the gritty sources of the Nightingale wealth. Once one achieved the right situation and frame, the right connections became possible, and then personal qualities could come into play. Both Fanny and WEN, in their contrasting ways, were delightful people.

Fanny exploited, first of all, the Unitarian, Quaker, Evangelical Anglican, and abolitionist networks she inherited from her parents. These connections—with the Macaulays, Trevelyans, Hallams, Wilberforces, Wedgwoods, and Darwins, with the Gaskells, Martineaus, and Davys, with the Malthuses, Arnolds, and Stanleys, with Lady Noel Byron and her daughter, Ada—were reinforced and extended rather than weakened.[11] It was this group, in large part, that provided the brilliant writers, scientists, historians, mathematicians, and artists whom Fanny would shrewdly combine with fox-hunting justices of the peace, aristocratic churchmen, and the new generation of liberal members of Parliament. In her drawing room at Embley Fanny Nightingale re-created the kind of intellectual, political, marginally aristocratic society she had known at Parndon and Park Street.

Fanny Nightingale had to work hard to leverage WEN's money and her own charm and organizational skills into social capital, and yet she had to make it all look easy. She needed to be constantly on the move, meeting people, reviving old connections, and expanding her social network, and the burden of correspondence was huge. Fanny understood that a hunting gentleman would come again to a house where the morning coffee was hot and strong and the gourmet dinner ended in a vintage claret. The wives of hunting gentlemen would also come if servants were quick and obliging and the long afternoons passed pleasantly in talk and tea with an engaging hostess. All this took a great deal of organization and management and scheduling, especially for a woman who traveled from home so often, but as time passed, Fanny trained her girls to help her. How irritating that it was the recalcitrant Florence, not Parthenope, who inherited Fanny's genius for the minutiae of household management!

Fanny Nightingale was anxious to show the world that the Smiths were not crying uncle just because their father had declared bankruptcy and their eldest brother had chosen to cohabit with a milliner. Fanny was ambitious for her husband, whom she hoped to launch on a successful political career along the lines of William Smith's, and she knew that success in politics was more a matter of whom one knew than what one knew.

In the longer term, Fanny sought to give Parthe and Flo the very best chance in life, which for her meant largely giving them the best choice of husbands. By creating a sparkling backdrop against which to stage the launching of her daughters into society, Fanny was ensuring that the Sinclairs of Caithness and similar worthies would not turn up their noses at the daughters as they once had at the mother. Fanny was also doing everything she could to insure Parthe and Flo against the provisions of the Nightingale entail. If their father were tragically to die, leaving his womenfolk much reduced in fortune, they would at least know all the very best people. It would be Fanny Nightingale's sorrow that her daughter Florence, who could so effortlessly have diversified and increased her mother's social capital, cared neither for husbands nor society.

SOCIAL MOBILITY FOR the Nightingales was literal as well as metaphorical. They were constantly on the move, even before the railway came to make travel easy. Though they owned two beautiful homes, Fanny and WEN did not usually spend many weeks on end in either one of them, and when one spouse was in residence the other very often was not. By 1825, when Florence was five and Parthe six, the four Nightingales were leading a peripatetic family life that was to last, with modifications, into the early 1850s. The months of July, August, and October were based at Lea Hurst, as WEN had anticipated, and were relatively quiet and informal, as befitted the *genius loci*. In September and again in the spring the Nightingale parents would spend some weeks in London, and when the girls came to be of marriageable age they were expected to be there too, whether Florence liked it or not. In London the Nightingales took rooms in a respectable hotel, usually the Burlington. This hotel living was rather a comedown to Fanny, but WEN could not be persuaded to take on a third home.

The rest of the year, the Nightingale family was based in Hampshire, though it was rare to find all four of them together at the same time at Embley. Sometimes the Nightingale parents traveled as a couple but more often each went his or her own way. If Fanny was in Leamington or visiting one of her bosom friends such as Louisa MacKenzie (later Lady Ashburton), WEN was perhaps in Yorkshire on estate business or London for a scholarly meeting. Parthe at the same time might be at Embley with the governess, and Flo on a prolonged visit to one of the aunts.

We know so much about the Nightingales and their many relatives because they were so often from home, wrote many letters, and kept a surprisingly large amount of the correspondence.[12] This was a family that was accustomed to having its affairs in writing, took pride in its ability to commit experience and ideas to paper, and thought, not incorrectly, that posterity would be interested in them. Florence in particular, from an astonishingly early age, seems to have been writing for an audience. Marianne Nicholson, who herself aspired to epistolary excellence, could wax satiric on cousin Flo's practice, even as a teenager, of keeping copies of her own letters and sending the best parts to several correspondents.

It is apparent from the letters and journals that there was a great restlessness in the Nightingale parents. While maintaining a front of solid respectability and mutual regard, Fanny and WEN seem to have increasingly gone their separate ways. Such a lifestyle had long been standard among the aristocratic set and was far from uncommon among people of the Nightingales' class, but there seems to have been no particular reason for the Nightingales so often to be traveling in different directions. Unlike the exceptionally busy Disraelis, Shaftesburys, or Palmerstons, for example, whose letters to one another are full of longing to be together again soon, the Nightingales did not seem unhappy when they were apart.

After her return from Europe in 1821 Fanny, so robust as a girl and young woman, became delicate, making frequent visits to the sea or to spas where WEN did not accompany her. Ill health was fashionable among affluent women in the nineteenth century, and spas like Gully's famed hydropathic center at Malvern had a mainly female clientele. Unhappy wives came to such places to escape domestic and marital cares, and it would not surprise me if Fanny Nightingale went off to Malvern or Tunbridge or Leamington when she and WEN were in dispute. For his part, WEN followed the fashion for affluent Victorian men and turned increasingly to estate management, local governance (he was high sheriff of Hampshire, for example), books, learned societies, and field sports. Nightingale spent time at his London club and also in the north dealing with his Derbyshire interests and his mother's problems. When at home, he retired as much as possible to his library, where he could stand at his specially designed desk and read in lonely peace. A sketch by Hilary Bonham-Carter showing her beloved uncle Night deeply absorbed in a book captures WEN very well.[13] But he was a man of action as well as thought, a man who loved long walks and rides, in his youth a good shot and a superb rider to hounds. As one of his tenants lovingly remembered: "A trimming smart man you may depend on't, when he used to ride wi' the red coats, he went better nor any on 'em that he did."[14]

A little undated note WEN wrote to his wife in his habitual scribble suggests both lasting affection and irritation at her tendency to nag. Fanny has evidently written to complain about her husband's management of the Embley estate, notably the cutting down of some trees: "I will venture only a word of advice in return—that you shd. in some degree shew your consent to some of my proceedings. If I cut a tree however wrongfully, if I press a work or an object not agreeable quite to your view, disturb not yourself as if I were committing a [crime?] or destroying what is essential to your existence. We both of us trouble too much in making miseries of ourselves or rather we study too little how to avoid them. So give me your assistance when I ask it & I shall fail not, but laugh at my doings instead of crying at them . . . in other words let each submit to the follies or weaknesses or error of the other & acquire if possible a positive pleasure in seeing that done in doings by which every fancy or desire or habit of one's own is tortured."[15]

AT EMBLEY OR LEA HURST, the Nightingales were almost never

alone. A constant stream of visitors came, some of them eminent, but many invited because they were good folk down on their luck who needed good food and country air. The largest single group of guests was composed of family members, coming as individuals rather than as groups and in rather complex patterns of affinity. Mrs. Shore would be invited each year, as well as—though probably not at the same time as—her sister Miss Evans. Patty Smith was at times a guest, though we hear little about her, and even less about the Smith parents, which is odd. Adams Smith could be found at one family home or another, drinking a brother's hock or tormenting a sister's children.[16] Julia Smith was constantly on the move between her siblings' homes, an invaluable help with the growing horde of little nephews and nieces. The three married Smith sisters, Anne, Fanny, and Joanna, exchanged children constantly as well as frequent letters about shopping, servants, and ailments, but they may well have spent less time together than their more mobile husbands. The married Smith brothers and their brothers-in-law enjoyed one another's company, followed the shooting or hunting seasons in one another's neighborhoods, and as time went on brought the crowd of eager nephews along. Benjamin Smith was often party to these sporting events, and he was free to stay in all his siblings' homes and welcomed the men to his own town and country homes. But he could not send his daughter Barbara to Lea Hurst in the summer or bring his eldest son, also called Benjamin, to shoot at Embley. On the subject of Ben's illegitimate children, the married sisters were implacable.

In fact, though the purchase of Embley had put virtually the whole Smith clan (with the exception of Fritz in India) in close geographical proximity, there were important divisions among them based on income and marital status, and these increased over time. The unmarried siblings, Patty, Julia, and, after his various financial and political failures, Adams, were at the bottom of the family heap and largely dependent upon the others, notably Benjamin, for support. They not infrequently went abroad, where it was cheap, but were otherwise rotating visitors, increasingly more tolerated than appreciated.

Aunt Joan and Uncle Octavius Smith, often called "the Ocs," were loving, unpretentious people and great favorites with the Nightingale girls. But they were emphatically trade, and Joan Smith did not have Fanny's social ambitions or her pizzazz. The Nicholsons were the richest and most gentrified of the families and inevitably resented for it by the others. Their Nightingale relatives compensated for the giddy magnificence of the yearly Christmas parties at Waverley Abbey by privately dismissing the Nicholsons as uncultured materialists. The Bonham-Carters, after the death of John in 1838, had the reputation in the family for being incorrigibly disorganized. Joanna Bonham-Carter inherited a very large fortune from her husband and never lacked for money, but she had no talent for the role of matriarch and was unable for many years even to settle on a permanent home for herself and her brood. All too much of the work and care of the house fell, as we shall see, on the shoulders of the eldest daughter, Hilary.

The most frequent and grateful visitors to Embley, especially in the late twenties and thirties, were Mai Smith and her children. Mai's many letters to Fanny, which Fanny lovingly kept, show that the two women were very close. Mai, I feel, took the place in Fanny's heart once held by Julia. The thing that was to threaten the relationship between Fanny and Mai, as well as that between Julia and Florence, was Mai's increasing adoration of Florence.

In the first years of their marriage Mai and Sam Smith experienced severe money problems; whether this was from Sam's mismanagement of his wife's dowry or from old Mrs. Shore's stinginess is not clear. Sam was a Cambridge man, trained as a lawyer, who specialized in mines and civil engineering. When their first child, Blanche, was small, the Samuel Smiths were dependent on his erratic earnings and rented unattractive houses in or near London. The extant letters from Mai to Fanny in the 1830s show signs of financial, social, and reproductive stress.

Sam was a cheerful, sporty, down-to-earth man, while Mai was sensitive, intellectual, intensely spiritual, and accustomed to a very quiet country life. Mai seems to be protesting a little too much about her relations to Sam in a letter she wrote to Fanny in the year before her pregnancy with Shore: "Sam & I certainly appear to suit à merveille considering we are as different as most people. He is very gay, dines out, has people at home, is in the world of a morning & is not sorry to spend a good many evenings with quiet me." Mai tells Fanny that she has found no friend among the wives of her husband's cronies and prefers to stay at home, seeing only family. Mai shyly offers Fanny the use of their rented home should she come to London but wonders if Fanny could cope with the sad offerings of her eleven-pounds-a-year cook. In another letter from about 1831, Mai tells Fanny that if Sam could actually receive the 250 pounds he has been promised for his work on two canals, she would have all she aspires to—"a lot, a garden, a house."[17]

Hanging over the heads of both Mai and Sam was the question of the Nightingale entail. It was imperative, for themselves and for WEN and Fanny, that they produce a son, and for a couple with problems, having to produce children to order is the biggest problem of all. Soon after the Smiths were married, Mai gave birth to a daughter, Blanche, but then she failed to get pregnant again. Mai worried to Fanny that little Blanche had the faults of an only child and noted how unwilling Blanche was to share with a sickly little tot whom her mother had imported to be her companion. Given that Blanche at the time was only two, this all seems very neurotic. Fortunately for the whole family, when Blanche was three a little brother arrived, to be followed soon by two more sisters, Bertha and Beatrice.

Mai enjoyed the beauty and good air of Hampshire, loved the light airy room dedicated to her use there, and appreciated the services of Fanny's superbly organized domestic staff. In exchange for this hospitality, while Fanny was away Mai took over the general management of the household, was company for her brother, WEN, when he was at home, and supervised the activities of Parthe and Flo when they were young. While pursuing those activities Mai wrote constantly to Fanny with news of her family. In a delicate sisterly balancing act, Mai bemoaned her own inadequacy—how could she produce a cup of morning coffee that WEN would condescend to drink?—deferred to Fanny's expertise, asked for her advice, and proffered her own suggestions with the greatest modesty.

Sam Smith sometimes accompanied his wife to Embley, especially when he was ill, but more often Mai went alone, with one or more children. Shore and his sisters grew to love Embley, especially perhaps after they were sent away to school, the youngest girls dispatched to Switzerland at an unusually tender age for their sex. Even after the mid-1830s, when Sam Smith was able to settle his family at Combe Hurst on the outskirts of London, he sometimes rented Embley from his brother-in-law during the summer, and his wife and children saw it as home.

Parthe clings to Father's coat-tails, while Flo trudges by his side. Sketch attributed to Julia Smith.

This love of Embley brought the Nightingales and the Sam Smiths together, but it also introduced an undercurrent of tension, especially between WEN and Sam. Their self-interests were, after all, opposed. With the birth of Shore in 1831, the Samuel Smiths consolidated their position as the legal heirs to Embley and Lea Hurst. If WEN were to die prematurely, the lavish lifestyle enjoyed by the Nightingales would be the Smiths'. Where the Smiths were now guests they would be hosts. When the Nightingales did something especially extravagant, such as enlarging and modernizing Embley and going on an eighteen-month Continental tour in 1837–39, Samuel Smith at least was surely calculating how much Nightingale had spent.

When William Edward (Shore) Nightingale died in 1874, Sam and Mai Smith moved almost immediately into Embley and made it their home for the rest of their lives. Fanny, already lapsing into senility, was forced to leave the house she had loved, taking with her only those possessions that were indisputably her private property. Fanny's two daughters, embittered to see their mother so sadly displaced, wondered whether she might take with her the beloved pictures she had inherited from her father, which had long hung in the music room. On all other issues, the Sam Smiths were affectionate and considerate to the Nightingales, but Embley was non-negotiable. It was Mai's.

Chapter 5

A Privileged
Victorian
Childhood

Observing the bustling activity and rapid growth of the
Smith clan was Florence Nightingale, who by the age of six
had a critical eye and a thirst to get as much of her experience down on paper as possible. Florence and her elder sister,
Parthenope, grew up as small fish in a shoal of grandparents, great-aunts,
second cousins, aunts and uncles by blood and marriage. They were
among the oldest of more than twenty cousins, all of whom lived busy,
structured, intensely supervised lives. Through Florence Nightingale's
letters, journals, and workbooks we get a child's-eye view of what it was
like to grow up in a big, affluent, closely knit Victorian family.

Both Fanny and WEN adored children and regretted having only
two of their own. They were determined their children should be neither spoiled nor lonely. Rather than wrapping her daughters up in a co-
coon of special attention, Fanny made sure that Parthe and Flo
experienced the ups and downs of life in a large family. As a mother, Mrs.
Nightingale had three main physical concerns: to keep her daughters
constantly busy, to promote their health in every way possible, and to
provide them with lots of companions their own age. Thus Parthe and
Flo were often left in the care of relatives, and Fanny herself always had
one or more nieces and nephews to mother when she was at home. But
whether absent or not, Mrs. Nightingale maintained full jurisdiction

Embley Park. Drawing by Parthenope Nightingale.

over her daughters, supervising their lives minutely and demanding frequent reports on their activities, both from the person in charge and from the girls themselves.

As children the Nightingale girls were almost never alone. Parthe and Flo lived in large homes that were constantly filled with visitors and servants. They usually shared a bed with each other or with a female relative or friend, and someone came each morning to dress them and do their hair. Parthe was almost eleven before her governess suggested to Mrs. Nightingale in a letter that the girls might surely now begin to attend to their own toilette in the mornings—under proper supervision, of course. They were enjoined to take frequent walks in the grounds, but whenever they left the estate they were always accompanied. Apart from Frances Gale, the children's nurse, there was always at least one adult whose special care was to keep a close eye on the girls at home. If Fanny herself was away, then an aunt, often Julia or Mai, looked after Parthe and Flo, or they were sent, usually separately, to pay a visit to one of the respectable married aunts, most often Anne Nicholson or Joanna Bonham-Carter. Children in this extended family were dispatched like parcels in the care of uncles and governesses and friends, their comings heralded, their goings planned, their lost belongings pleaded for in a constant stream of letters. To be at home with one of her parents without

guests was a rare experience that Florence Nightingale remembered with
nostalgia.

The only time the girls were alone for any length of time during the
day was when they were confined to bed after a serious illness. In her 1851
biographical sketch Florence noted that "the happiest time of my life was
during a year's illness which I had when I was six years old."[1] This illness,
a severe case of whooping cough, occurred in the winter of 1826–27, and
Florence seems to have taken months to recover from it. Flo came down
with the cough at Lea Hurst but was then moved to Embley, in a separate
carriage since special care was taken to ensure that Parthe should not catch
the disease. In the spring Florence went to London, where she was cared
for by her aunt Mai and became far too attached to her to rejoice at the
news of Mai's impending marriage to Uncle Sam. In London Florence
was able to play with her slightly younger cousin Hilary Bonham-Carter,
who also had the whooping cough. This was the beginning of Hilary's
passionate friendship for her cousin Flo.

In their childhood and teenage years Parthe and Flo were in regular
contact with twenty-five cousins—the four children of Mai and Sam
Smith, the five children of Anne and George Nicholson, the nine children of Joanna and John Bonham-Carter, and the seven children of Joan
and Octavius Smith.[2] Seven of the cousins were about their age—Jack
Bonham-Carter, the eldest of all the cousins, and his brother Bonny and
sister Hilary; Marianne, Henry, and Laura Nicholson; and Fred Smith,
eldest son of Uncle Oc.

In the background of all the complex interactions of the Smiths,
Nicholsons, Bonham-Carters, and Nightingales were the illegitimate
children of the oldest Smith, wealthy, brilliant, successful brother Ben,
acknowledged head of the Smith family. After the death of Anne Longden, their young mother, the five Leigh Smiths lived with their father in
full view of a consternated society, occupying fine establishments on the
outskirts of London and in the seaside town of Hastings. Both of the
homes of the Leigh Smiths were within easy distance of Embley, Waverley, and Fair Oak, but apparently the Leigh Smiths as children had no
contact with their cousins.[3]

Did Parthe and Flo know about Barbara, little Ben, Bella, and the
others? Did they find it odd that Uncle Ben came at times to visit at Lea
Hurst or shoot at Embley but never received anyone but Papa at his

homes? That their mother when in London never stayed with her own
mother or her sisters Patty and Julia, who lived in Uncle Ben's house at
Blandford Square? Aunt Ju could have told her Nightingale nieces about
the Leigh Smiths. But perhaps Fanny had made it clear to all, especially
to the irrepressible Julia, that in her house there would be no talk of the
Leigh Smiths.

By her teen years Florence had formed strong bonds with the two female cousins closest to her age, Marianne and Hilary, but she was also
on excellent terms with her older male cousins. Little Flo was shy, but
she had great energy and, unlike her sister Parthe, who was so often confined to the sofa, she entered easily into the play of intelligent, well-
schooled boys like these cousins. Thus Henry Nicholson came to Embley
for a long visit around 1827 and "he and Flo did everything together. He
taught her Latin and she taught him French. They made little cards with
Good and *Bad* printed upon them and hung them round each other's
necks as occasion required."[4] Perhaps this willingness to share the shame
of being bad was at the root of Henry's lifelong admiration for Flo, which
would finally lead to a disastrous proposal of marriage. Florence also got
on well with her older Carter cousins Jack and Thomas (the latter usually
known in the family as Bonny), who were not rough and bouncy.[5]

For two seasons at Fair Oak when she was about nine, Florence was
deeply involved in making a playhouse and garden under the leadership
of Jack. Flo wrote from Fair Oak to her sister at Embley on February 24,
1830: "Dear Pop, I have not put your scrap book anywhere but one day
I saw it in the drawer in the Music Room, next to the bow window, and
I think it very odd that you did not think of looking for it there!!!! We
[meaning she and the Bonham-Carter children] have banked up the
kitchen-door (of our house) and made a new one. We have made a sofa
in the kitchen, covered with heather. Our moss-beds are so wet, we cannot sleep in them. We have filled up our potato holes in the kitchen, and
made a larder." Then Florence drew up a tiny table, under the headings
"Vegetables" and "Fruits," showing the cones, acorns, and so on that she
and Jack and Hilary were using to represent peaches, potatoes, cucum-
bers, peas, et cetera in their play larder. It is fascinating to see Florence
Nightingale in this early letter already marshaling her data in tabular
form, energetically collaborating in a project with male contemporaries,
and accusing Parthe of carelessness.[6]

Sometimes when she was a little girl, Florence traveled about with her mother. In "La Vie de Florence Rossignol" she apparently gave detailed accounts of the places she went and the people she met on the journey back south from Tapton in the year of Mai's wedding. At Betley Hall in Staffordshire she was awed to learn that one of the seven daughters of the Tollett family had concealed as long as possible the terrible pain in her arm, and when told the arm must be amputated had gone alone to Chester for the operation. At Castle Downton, Agathe, the Nightingales' French maid, was confronted for the first time with a bathtub with running water and had the whole room swimming before someone came who could turn the tap off. The Nightingale sisters made frequent visits to the sea for bracing walks and cold bathing, either with their mother or Aunt Julia.

Visits to London were not always pleasant since all the Nightingale and Bonham-Carter children were taken there regularly to the dentist, which usually meant an extraction. "Has Pop had many teeth out at Mr. Dumergue's?" wrote Flo to her father in February 1829.[7] Since Grandfather and Grandmother Smith as well as Aunts Patty and Julia lived when in London with Uncle Benjamin, Parthe and Flo never stayed with them. They did, however, visit their uncle Octavius and aunt Jane Smith at Thames Bank. On a visit in the summer of 1830, Flo found Uncle Oc's house near the distillery fascinating, despite the horrid smell coming in through the window of her tiny bedroom. This was possibly the first time Florence Nightingale had slept on her own, and she found it both disturbing and exhilarating. She wrote to Parthe back at Embley: "There is a hole in the wall close to my door, which communicates with the bath-room, which is next to the room where Freddy [her eldest Smith cousin, who was exactly her age] sleeps, and he talks to me by there . . . I went up into the distillery to the very tip-top by ladders with Uncle Oc and Fred Saturday night. We walked along a great pipe."[8] Florence would sadly remember those nights talking to Fred through the hole when Fred was lost on a disastrous expedition in Australia in 1839.

ANIMALS, BIRDS, FLOWERS, the sights and smells and feel of the country were key parts of the everyday experience of the Nightingale sisters, who were brought up in two of the most beautiful parts of England.

In Derbyshire they had the hills and moors; in Hampshire they had the sea, the fields, the forests. Everywhere there were gardens filled with flowers and big enough to take walks in. When they were at the shore the Nightingale girls collected or purchased new specimens for their shell collections. Inland they grew silkworms and plants, watched caterpillars turn into butterflies, pressed flowers into albums, and enjoyed the company of creatures both tame and wild. As a child Florence had a pony at Lea Hurst for getting round the country, and as an older teenager she was able to ride to hounds with her father while Parthe was limited to staid canters on the flat. Cook tells us, "A neatly printed manuscript-book is preserved, in which [Florence] made a catalogue of her collection of flowers, describing each with analytical accuracy, and noting the particular spot at which it was picked. Her childish letters contain many references to animal companions. She made particular friends with the nuthatch. She had a pet pig, a pet donkey, a pet pony."[9]

Florence was ready to take any animal on as a pet. In a letter to her mother written when she had just turned twelve and was at Embley with her aunt Mai and her ailing grandmother Smith, Florence recounted how a maid had found a nest of newborn mice in a mattress in the blue room. "They are not an inch long with such tiny paws and a long tail, very large head, and two bits of skin over their eyes. They have no hair at all and look like little bits of raw meat, they are perfect frights. One died directly, and Aunt Mai burnt it. We wrapped them up in wadding and put them in a basket by the fire and now and then put a drop of warm milk in their mouths, which I think they swallowed. They are such queer things, always stretching out their legs. Three died in the night, so only one is left, which revived just as I was going to bury it. The other four were evidently quite dead, and I buried them in my garden by my squirrel. This one I have wrapped up and put by the fire and I have given it some milk, and it moves about, and I think it is possible it may live poor little thing! I should like to rear one, only one, so much. It would be so interesting to watch it."[10]

Florence's love of animals blended into her interest in medicine. Nineteenth-century hagiographers made much of the incident when young Florence Nightingale saved the sheepdog Cap. She and the local vicar found Cap with a broken leg on the downs near Embley, and his master the shepherd was all set to hang the dog. Florence insisted that the dog's paw could be treated, and under her care he made a full recovery, getting around handily thereafter on three legs. According to one account, before dressing the dog's paw Florence Nightingale boiled the water, something few doctors at the time thought necessary. If this is true, it is evidence of Nightingale's astonishing genius as a clinician.[11] In a book the size of a postage stamp—the oldest document in her hand, according to Cook, and, like so many others of this period, not included in the British Library collection—Florence, age about seven, carefully noted the dosage of James compound, a common medicine: "16 grains for an old woman, 11 for a young woman, and 7 for a child."

If collecting flowers, observing newborn mice, and nursing sick dogs were impromptu learning opportunities, this did not mean that formal education was in any way neglected. Lessons, in the world of little Parthe and Florence, were a serious business. Fortunately, both girls were excellent scholars, taking to reading and writing like ducks to water, and reveling in words. Thus in a letter to her sister, Flo, who was about to turn eight, excitedly described a new anagram game she had learned: "Dear Pop, Here is a new game for you. Take any word and see how many words you can make out of the letters. I took 'breath,' and I made 40 words. You need not take all the letters, you know, but as many as you please. You must not double the letter, that is, putting in two of the same kind in one word. Is it not a nice game? Here are two words for you to make 2 words out of them of the same quantity of letters, but changing the places of them. GAY ONES and GREAT HELP. The first is very easy. I have found it out, the last I have not. Your sister. [Apparently as an afterword] The best way to do those words I told you is to cut out the letters. There is a box of letters at Embley so you need not take that trouble."[12]

As they moved around the country on visits, both girls became fascinated early on by differences in local dialect. They had no doubt been alerted to this issue by their parents, who had different accents. Seven-year-old Flo told her father of visiting Mrs. Staples, an old woman living near Embley, and she attempted to reproduce exactly what Mrs. Staples said, knowing her father would find it interesting and funny: "She *be'es* very well and *he* (her leg) *be'es* very well too."[13]

Both Parthe and Flo showed a precocious talent for languages, learning to speak French from babyhood from their parents and from their mother's French maids and acquiring by their late teens virtually com-

plete mastery of the language. All the same, the few letters written by
Parthenope that survive from the early period indicate that as a child she
did not have Flo's command of French vocabulary and grammar. For little Parthe, writing in French was a school exercise, whereas Flo enthusiastically took on the challenge of writing long pieces in the new language,
completing two biographies of Agathe and Clémence, the French maids,
based on interviews with those young ladies. Then in January 1829,
when she was eight and a half, Flo undertook her own autobiography in
French, "La Vie de Florence Rossignol," which seems to have been a
document of quite considerable length and complexity. Several of Florence's letters to her parents when she was under ten were also written in
more than commendable French. Florence began to learn Latin with her
father before she was eight, and it seems most likely that Parthe began
Latin at the same time.

If Parthe was a very good student, Florence was remarkable in all but
one thing—penmanship. As a little girl she developed a rapid, spiky style
of printing, but for a girl of her generation she was unusually slow in
changing to cursive. She noted in the autobiographical sketch she wrote
in German in 1851: "I never learnt to write till I was eleven or twelve,
owing to a weakness in my hands," but this statement is misleading. The
extant letters show that from the age of eight she was alternating between
printing and cursive in letters to her mother. She reverted to printing
when she had something special she wanted to communicate or was writing to someone she was close to, like her grandmother Shore or her father. These printed letters are the fun letters to read, the ones where we
gain most insight into Florence Nightingale's remarkable mind. However, by the age of ten she had completely dropped the printing and was
writing letters for and to her mother in a notably elegant hand.

The failure to master cursive at the right age may have had some
physical cause, but there was an element of rebellion in Florence's printing, especially, as we shall see, when she came under the tutelage of a governess. Victorian children had copybooks in which hackneyed,
improving phrases, such as "Conscience is a faithful and prudent monitor" or "Humility is the foundation of preferment," were written in copperplate and had to be copied over and over again. Assigned this
laborious and boring task by Miss Christie, Florence got to the letter *T*
and then wrote, "Stupid Copybook. The use of this copy I never could

see and I do not like it, I never wish to write it and I never will if I can help it."[14]

Each day, Parthe and Flo were supposed to find some object to draw—a flower, a vase—and to practice the piano for at least half an hour. They always had some piece of needlework to do, and they were encouraged to hand-make gifts for members of the family and servants. There were also chapters of the Bible to read, poems to learn by heart, and on Sundays, if they went to church, Fanny liked her daughters to take notes on the sermon and write out a summary when they returned home. Florence, age nine, could already do this very well.[15] Reading was of course important, but for information and spiritual inspiration, not for fun. Fanny disliked "story books" and exercised tight control over what the girls were reading.

The Nightingale children made regular visits to the poor people who lived near their homes, sometimes distributing small gifts they had made or sums of money they had earned. Florence carefully reported to her parents the problems of the local folk she met, as in this letter to Fanny of October 16, 1828. "We arrived at Embley at half past three o'clock. Aunt Mai stopped at the school, and I walked on by myself to Maria Brent who was better and downstairs, working. As I was coming home, I met the two Miss Cooks. We bought two buns, three hard biscuits and two little round ones. I gave Maria Brent one of the biscuits; was that wrong? Mrs. Staples gave me a glass of her currant wine. We went to see her yesterday. Your affectionate daughter. Florence Nightingale."[16] As Fanny also insisted that her daughters account for all their expenditures, Flo ended her letter with a detailed bill of how she had spent sixpence on buns and biscuits.

In Fanny Nightingale's eyes, physical exercise was more important than lessons and second only to praying and Bible reading for her two small, skinny, delicate girls. She insisted that they take at least two good walks a day, rain or shine, and do daily calisthenic exercises inside. These were designed by a London specialist to strengthen specific parts of their bodies. In 1831, Parthe was having some problem with her arm and had been ordered to do exercises for it, which the girls called "doing arms." Miss Christie, the Nightingale governess, coldly reported to Fanny: "I knew she [Parthe] had no particular appetite for pain, but I certainly was not fully conscious of her extreme tenacity against a momentary interruption of her wonted ease which occurred whenever she attempted to move her arm."[17] When unable to go out because of truly appalling weather, the children played shuttlecock and battledore (badminton), and "valsed" (waltzed) with their governess or some other adult female. Both Parthe and Flo vastly preferred lessons, piano practice, and sketching to long walks in the cold, battledore, and "arms."

Underlying this rigid regime of exercise was Fanny's very real fear that her daughters would die young. In 1829, death came close to the Nightingales when ten-year-old Bonny Carter died after a very painful illness. According to what his aunt Mai wrote to Fanny Nightingale, Bonny had some kind of cancer or bowel constriction, which he hid "from mere decorum" from the sight of his governess as long as he could.[18]

Florence was extremely attached to her cousin Bonny. When he became ill, she planned little gifts to send him with her mother, and wrote to him with a complete list of the books she owned and which he might like to borrow from her, as well as the complete text of a very uplifting hymn. When Bonny died, Florence wrote a detailed account of his illness and death to a friend. It is the first of the many extraordinary letters that Florence Nightingale wrote telling of the death of someone she greatly loved: "Dear Miss Brydges, Do you know poor Bonny Carter, my cousin? Such a dear kind boy! He has been very ill for six or seven months, and 7 June (Sunday) between 6.00 and 7.00, he died. He was kind to everybody to the last, and very patient, he was never cross. Half an hour before he died he asked to see aunt Patty, and he was looking about the room for a sofa for her. We left Gale [the Nightingale nurse] in London to take care of him, but nothing would do; his complaint had got so much the better of medecine [sic], doctors, nursing and all, that all hope was given up. He had a great deal of pain, throughout his illness. Mama saw him once, he talked to her a great deal, and was so anxious to give her everything she liked. Gale slept by his side. One night, she got up to do something for him and he said to her, 'Come it will do very well, there's a good creature, go to bed now, go to sleep.' One day he said to his papa, when in great pain, 'I will bear it as well as I can, but if I were strong I think I should leap about the room with this pain.' "[19]

Writing down the events of Bonny's death was one way nine-year-old Florence Nightingale tried to deal with her grief. She was already a regular, absorbed reader of the Bible, where the suffering of mankind and the shortness of life were constantly emphasized. She saw that being good did not save a boy like Bonny from pain and death. She was drawn to scenes of tragedy, confiding to her diary all that she learned about Miss Tollett's amputated arm, Maria Brent's long illness, or the suicide of mad Mrs. Petty, a woman from the village. Mr. Petty had broken into his cottage to discover his youngest child dead in a pool of blood and his dying wife writing a message in her own. In the barracks hospital at Scutari, Florence Nightingale would still be trying to keep the living nightmare around her at bay by carefully noting down the facts.

TRAGIC DEATHS LIKE Bonny's are hard for anyone to bear. An intelligent and sensitive little girl like Flo was especially ill-prepared to deal with such events alone. Yet it was in the period around Bonny's death that Fanny Nightingale subjected her daughter to an especially rigorous regime. By mid-1827 Fanny Nightingale had decided that Flo was self-absorbed, unkind, and inflexible. She had been spoiled by too much attention and indulgence. Her moral character needed to be reformed.

Fanny Nightingale had read her Wordsworth but, like most early Victorians, tended to see children not as ethereal beings trailing clouds of glory but as imps of Satan, tainted with original sin. The role of a loving parent was to chide, punish, and correct. Like her mother, Frances Smith, Fanny Nightingale was a tremendous manager, of people as well as households, and she was committed to keeping her husband and children up to scratch. WEN, that affable intellectual, was a hard man to manage, and if Fanny pushed too hard he simply moved away from her, physically and psychologically. But the children were fully in Fanny's domain. Parthe was a worry because of her poor health, but with Parthe Fanny felt herself on firm ground. Parthe needed to be judiciously cosseted and encouraged, protected and pushed. Flo, on the other hand, was a problem, and when Fanny Nightingale saw a problem, she tackled it head-on.

A child, according to the Lockean educational theory the Smith sisters had absorbed, was a *tabula rasa*, and Fanny Nightingale was very clear what she wanted written on Florence's blank slate. Flo must put away her storybooks and her science projects, play better, take more exercise, and generally transform herself into the kind of sweet, obedient, happy, grateful, active little girl people liked. A girl like her sister Parthe, in fact. Fanny Nightingale knew Flo well. She saw that paradoxically Flo could be persuaded to do things if they were hard and if they were defined as a duty or an exercise in self-mastery. So Fanny felt it was right to come down harder on Flo.

Since Fanny's busy social round did not allow her to be always at home looking to her girls, someone else must be found to take Flo in hand. Julia and Mai would help but they could not do it alone. They had their own lives to lead and had already spent a good deal of time with the little Nightingales. They also gave Flo far too much affection and attention. A young, energetic, determined governess was needed to make Flo her priority, and by the summer of 1827 Fanny felt she had found the right person, Miss Sarah Christie.

The Brontë sisters have so vividly described the sad lot of governesses in the early nineteenth century that it is necessary to note that not all governesses were victims, and some were tyrants. Unlike the unhappy Brontës, Miss Sarah Christie was welcomed by her employers, the Nightingales, as a member of the family and even as a social equal. As the Nightingales saw it, Miss Christie's need to leave home to earn her own living was her misfortune, not her fault, and they did their best to make her stay with them a happy one. Thus when the Nightingale family was in London, Miss Christie was allowed to sleep at the home of relatives, coming each day to teach the children their lessons. When Miss Christie was unwell, she was cared for solicitously and given ample time to recover. When her beloved brother fell ill—he was to die very young of consumption—she was given indefinite leave to go home and care for him. We can be certain that Fanny Nightingale made quite sure that Miss Christie would not suffer from any unwanted attentions on the part of Fanny's charming but unreliable brother Benjamin when that gentleman came for his occasional visit to Embley.

In treating their daughters' governess with affection and respect, Fanny and WEN continued in the Unitarian tradition of their two families. The small but influential Unitarian community put a premium on education and, exceptionally, saw the importance of educating girls as well as boys.[20] The prevailing understanding among Unitarians was that intellectual achievement was important both in itself and as a way to spiritual enlightenment. An educated mind often led to improved economic prospects, a not unimportant consideration in an embattled minority, but mere wealth was never to be equated with virtue or worth. Among enlightened members of the Dissenting community, notably Unitarians, there was both a demand for gifted teachers and a supply of ready pupils.

Women, by the second decade of the nineteenth century, were beginning to found small schools for girls, but most girls of Florence Nightingale's generation were still educated at home by governesses.[21] For most of these young women teachers, their years as governess constituted a stage in life, perhaps a weary one, but not social derogation. For a few years they would be self-supporting and perhaps earn a small sum of money that could be invested in a family school—this was the great, unrealized dream of the Brontë sisters—but which could also serve as a dowry. Being a governess did not preclude a young woman from marrying a man of her own class, even a wealthy one, and having children of her own to bring up and educate. Poor but respectable and brilliant Fanny Byerley, the eldest in a family of eight girls and five boys, married the rich Mr. Parkes.

Sarah Christie was in her early twenties when she came to the Nightingales, the devoted daughter of a respectable, deeply religious family probably known to Florence's family through their old Norfolk friends the Taylors. We can be sure she was well qualified to teach and of impeccable moral character. She was, in Florence Nightingale's own phrase, "a just and well-intentioned woman," anxious to please her employers, show her own merit, and be a pride to her family. If she was zealous in the old Calvinist manner as well as the new evangelical one, this would not have disqualified her in the eyes of Mrs. Nightingale. What Mr. Nightingale thought of her may best be deduced from the fact that after she left the family he never employed another governess.

Standard biographical accounts of Florence Nightingale's childhood portray Miss Christie as a tragic and gifted young woman and claim that her charges adored her.[22] The first statement is correct; the second is not. Florence and Parthenope in later life both admitted that they had black memories of their time with Miss Christie.

Years later, Florence wrote: "At seven years of age we had a governess, who brought me up most severely. She was just and well intentioned, but she did not understand children, and she used to shut me up for six weeks at a time. My sister on the contrary, she spoilt."[23]

Underscoring Florence's comments is a private note Parthenope Nightingale Verney made in the 1870s or 1880s when she briefly contemplated writing a biography of her famous sister. "*Early recollections of a child a year younger.* [Florence was] Overflowing with fun + spirits + wild of every kind, a voluble little body at two. When she had the whooping cough her thirteen dolls had it too—were found with pieces of flannel round their 13 necks. Then came a very clever governess who misunderstood her completely, and turned inwards all the overflowing energy + busy child life. Two or three years altered her accordingly—and troubled her with the introversion which she long suffered from."[24]

WHY DID FLORENCE NIGHTINGALE need to be reformed? Why on earth did her own mother think this delightful little girl, so funny and energetic and curious and sensitive, needed reproof, punishment, moral stringency? We can best discover what, in the eyes of her mother and governess, was wrong with little Flo Nightingale from the sad little litany of promises the child made to her mother in January 1830. She was then five months short of her tenth birthday and the reform effort had been under way for almost two years.

> I promise to
> take run before breakfast to gate or to and from [?] ½ hour's walk
>   before dinner, long walk after, or if cold and dark long walk be-
>   fore & ½ an hour's after
> to do 20 arms before I dress, 10 minutes before breakfast & 10 af-
>   ter exercises,
> if ill done ten more
> to practise 1 hour a day if you like it as I shall not have so much to
>   do and ½-regularly
> to draw ½ an hour regularly
> not to lie in bed
> to go to bed in proper time
> to read the Bible & pray regularly before breakfast & at night
> to visit the poor people & take care of them who are sick

to take medicine when I want it
to go regularly after breakfast
on Sundays to go to Church when there is anyone to go with me,
to read, write and do the Bible
to read any book you put out for me
to read to Aunt Mai & save her trouble
to read this paper everyday
to write to you
I think I should be much better here than elsewhere. I should have
    fewer temptations.

                                      FN[25]

This document plunges us into the daily life of a girl born to wealth and privilege, but weighed down with lessons, duties, supervision, and guilt. The initials "FN" scrawled at the bottom of the paper seem to be by the child herself, but the rest is in the hurried hand of some adult. Giving up the pen and then reciting her promises aloud and having them inscribed by someone else all, I think, contributed to the complicated moral exercise Flo was undertaking. The lines toward the end of the manuscript are blotched, as if by tears. But if Florence did not pen the words we see here, they are unmistakably her own. The terse last sentences in particular, full of desolation and self-abnegation—"I think I should be better here than elsewhere. I should have fewer temptations"— could have been written at age twenty-nine or sixty-nine. It is astonishing to find Florence Nightingale so completely herself so young.

In this list of things to do to be good, there is no mention of lessons. In the schoolroom Florence shone; indeed, she was too clever for her own good. Florence's intellectual precocity, the love of fact, the dispassionate eye, the sharp wit she shows in her letters as a small girl were very much a part of the problem Fanny Nightingale had with her. The child's casual display of mastery and her fierce concentration on learning everything there was to learn were seen as self-aggrandizing. Little girls should be seen and not heard, but Flo had so much to say and write to the adults in her world that she often seemed pert and cocky. To her aunt Anne, the six-year-old Flo once wrote: "I hope you have got safe to your journey's end. I hope you saw the eclipse of the moon on the day you went. Papa says that you were blind boobies if you did not watch it for a whole hour as we did."[26] To brag and call one's aunt a booby was not commended in little girls in 1827.

Since Florence needed no incentive to get her French verbs by heart or do all her sums right, the reform emphasis was on soul and body. Bible reading and prayer are repeatedly stressed in the list of promises, as is going to church (when the adults are prepared to take her) and doing good to the poor. Even more stress is placed on physical exercise, viewed not as a pleasure but as a duty. Each day Flo will strengthen her wrists by "doing arms" for twenty minutes before dressing—a chilly business—and even ten more if Miss Christie adjudges the exercise to be "ill done." Like most Victorians, Fanny Nightingale was obsessed with the bowels, and therefore Florence will take medicine, probably a purgative, when she "wants"—that is to say, needs it—and she will try to "go" each day after breakfast, not an easy thing for a child forbidden to eat fruit.

Each day Flo will run to and from the gate, possibly some distance at a big estate like Embley. She will also take a half hour's walk before dinner and "a long walk" after dinner. Or, "if cold and dark"—one imagines the child's lip beginning to tremble here—the long walk will be done before dinner and the short one after. For the walking and running, Flo will wear the steel-lined boots that are designed to support her weak ankles. All those nostalgic about nineteenth-century child-rearing practices should keep in mind the steel boots for weak ankles, the whalebone corsets for weak backs, the iron brace for sitting up straight at table, and other amiable innovations that upper-middle-class children had to bear at this time. And these were of course the lucky ones.

Another problem with Flo being so intellectually precocious was that she cast Parthenope into the shade and then compounded the slight by being unkind and condescending to her. Florence not only kept pace with her elder sister, she passed her at every opportunity. Outside the schoolroom Florence would become so wrapped up in her own projects that she was unresponsive to the feelings of others, especially her older sister's. Parthe would lose something, her scrapbook perhaps. Flo would know quite well where it was but not tell her, and then the two sisters would squabble. These squabbles are the subject of perhaps the earliest extant document attributable to Florence Nightingale. It shows two little stick figures who are depicted in two scenes, one labeled "Anger and quarrelling" and one "Peace." In the first Pop says, "You nasty thing," and

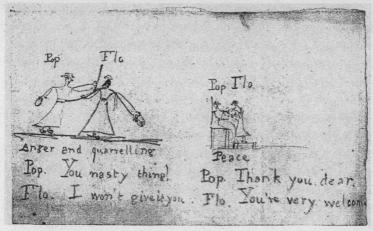

Florence Nightingale, aged about six, sketches a quarrel with her sister.

Flo says, "I won't give it you." In the second, Pop says, "Thank you dear," and Flo says, "You're very welcome."[27] Despite her constant battles with ill health, Parthe was a cheerful, affectionate, intelligent, artistic, willing little girl, fitting well into the family, easy to love. But she was simply no match for Flo, and so she was the one the grown-ups rushed to protect.

Victorian children were expected to be obedient, respectful, and affectionate, but Flo persistently had opinions of her own, asked awkward questions, and made pointed observations. Why did Mamma give nothing to the beggars when they visited Tintern Abbey? Why were the people living near Lea Hurst so poor and sick and tired? Were they, the Nightingales, not rich, and did the Bible not say that it was harder for a rich man to enter heaven than for a camel to go through the eye of a needle? Fanny Nightingale, like her mother before her, was prone to sanctimony, and she did not take kindly to criticisms from her child. Fanny came from a long and proud line of Dissenters. She sought to do good and was conscious of caring more than most people of her class for the unfortunate. It was Fanny who insisted WEN finance a school for working-class girls near their Derbyshire home, Fanny who regularly gave aid to the poor and sick, Fanny who was warmly welcomed into villagers' homes. Who was little Flo to point the moral for her mother or turn up her nose at the material advantages that her father was able to offer her?

Flo in her preteens was not just precocious and pert with adults but, in her own words, "shy to a misery and unable to like the play of other children." As an adult Florence Nightingale remembered not the academic achievements of her youth but the social miseries, the sense of being inadequate, aberrant, different. Her two most important biographers, who read more of the lost juvenilia, make this point clearly. " 'My greatest ambition,' she wrote in some private reminiscences of her early life, 'was not to be remarked. I was always in mortal fear of doing something unlike other people, and I said "If I were sure that nobody would remark me I should be quite happy." I had a morbid terror of not using my knives and forks like other people when I should come out [as a debutante]. I was afraid of speaking to children because I was sure I should not please them' " (Sir Edward Cook). "She had an obsession that she was not like other people. She was a monster. That was her secret which could at any moment be found out. Strangers must be avoided, especially children. She worked herself into an agony at the prospect of seeing a new face, and to be looked at was torture. She doubted her capacity to behave like other people, and refused to dine downstairs, convinced she would betray herself by doing something extraordinary with her knife and fork" (Cecil Woodham-Smith).[28]

Another odd thing about little Flo that upset her mother and her governess was that while refusing to play games with children her own age, Florence would become unaccountably fascinated by some older girl or young woman, follow her around, and attempt to monopolize her attention.[29] This happened with her aunt in the months before Mai's marriage to Sam Smith. In the winter of 1829–30 it happened again, only now the object of fascination was Lucy, the young nursemaid Mai had engaged to look after her small daughter, Blanche. These girlish crushes were an awkward search for love by a child all too aware that she was not a favorite with her mother and who perhaps blamed herself for her mother's frequent absences.

Of all Florence's problems, the most intractable in her own view was what she came to call her "dreaming." This was a state of absorbed reverie, when for minutes or even hours on end she would be so absorbed in some imagined adventure as to be impervious to what was happening around her. In an autobiographical fragment, she recalled: "When I was a child and was naughty, it always put an end to my dreaming for the time, I never could tell why. Was it because naughtiness was a more interesting state than the little motives which make man's peaceful civilized state, and occupied imagination for a while?"[30] In the list of promises from January 1830, Florence vows to "go to bed in proper time" and not to "lie in bed." I wonder if the prohibition on "lying in bed" was related to her habit of daydreaming. Perhaps as a small sick child Florence lay in bed and found pleasure in stimulating herself while dreaming. Today such behavior in a six- or seven-year-old would be considered normal, but the Miss Christies of the nineteenth century were especially watchful for any signs of eroticism in their charges and swift to chastise any youthful sin of the flesh.

Dreaming was one of the key aspects of Florence Nightingale's life as a young adult. She refers to the habit constantly in her diaries, especially those relating to her travels in Egypt, Greece, and Germany in 1849–50. She says almost nothing about the content of the dreams but describes them over and over again as sinful, addictive, loathsome. She says that she struggled against dreaming as the desert fathers once struggled against erotic fantasies.[31] Her inability to curb her habit of dreaming brought her close to a complete nervous breakdown in 1850. Thus it is significant that she tells us she was dreaming by the age of seven and was already convinced that she must stop it. Someone close to her, someone she trusted, must have told her dreaming was wrong. Obediently little Florence discovered that a burst of activity could keep the dreams at bay, but then, I think, she got caught in a kind of Laingian knot. She was punished in the first place for dreaming and in the second place for naughty behavior. This is a classic double bind, and it shaped Florence Nightingale's whole life, promoting an indelible sense of sinfulness and a distrust of the body.

Florence's love of solitude, her daydreaming, her reluctance to romp and play, her crushes on older girls, and her quarrels with her sister all alarmed her mother. Fanny had been the fourth child in a famously rambunctious family of ten and fondly remembered the "hurly-burly" of her old home at Parndon Hall. Throughout her life, Fanny Smith Nightingale excelled at social relations and was happiest when she found herself in the center of a large group of friends and relatives. Parthenope had the same relish for society, even when she was ill and in pain, but Flo was quite different. Fanny Nightingale saw little of herself in her second

child, and the favor shown to Flo by WEN, Aunt Mai, Grandmother
Shore, and Great-aunt Evans did not help Flo with her mother. The last
thing Fanny wanted for her daughter was that she become a Shore, a passionate, wild, shabby, antisocial creature like her paternal grandmother
and great-aunt.

Hence, I think, Fanny's willingness to entrust the care of Parthenope
and Florence to a governess and her acquiescence to what Aunt Mai
called "Miss Christie's plan" for Florence. The plan was designed to curb
her rebelliousness, correct her egotism, and make her behave like a nice,
good little girl. For some two and a half years, Parthe and Flo were under
Miss Christie's jurisdiction. They were in no way abandoned, since one
of their aunts was usually in the house, and when at home they could always rely on the love of Mrs. Gale, their old nurse. All the same, their
parents were often away from home, and their aunts Mai and Julia were
specifically requested by Fanny not to interfere. Given their dependence
on Miss Christie's goodwill and the close supervision she exercised over
them, the Nightingale girls were unable to voice directly to their parents,
grandparents, or aunts how harshly Florence was being treated by the
governess.[32]

Thus Florence's letters between 1827 and 1830 are both a detailed
and an incomplete record of what she was experiencing. The emotions
she expresses are censored and, as it were, encoded.

THUS, PERHAPS THE GREATEST burden Florence had to bear between summer 1827 and spring of 1830 was the frequent absence of
both her parents. That she also was frequently separated from her sister
no doubt exaggerated her feelings of abandonment.

During the years when Miss Christie was governess to Parthenope
and Florence, Fanny was away from home without her husband even
more than usual. Furthermore, both Fanny and WEN spent the months
before and after Christmas in Derbyshire, and they did not take their
children with them. This is odd since Fanny never liked Lea Hurst in
winter and the family pattern was to spend only the summers there.
Whether or not Fanny intended it, it was definitely a punishment for Flo
to know that her parents had gone to Lea Hurst without her.

Notes of desolation sound over and over again in Florence's letters from this period. At first she openly says how much she misses her parents, writing, "Dearest Mama, I think of you everyday," or in another letter "Ma chère Maman, Je suis bien triste sans vous aujourd'hui [Dear Mother, I am so sad without you today]." On December 18, 1827, Florence writes to her two parents in copperplate handwriting and in rather shaky French. To her father she notes, "J'ai réglé ces lignes moi-même [I ruled these lines myself]" (f. 4), the kind of self-congratulation she was being trained to avoid. Her first sentence is "Cher Papa, je voudrais que tu reviendrais aujourd'hui" [I wish you would come back today], and she carefully calculates when her father is due home. She goes on: "Je crois que tu nous a oublié tout à fait [I think you have completely forgotten us]." On March 30, 1828, Florence wrote from Embley to her grandmother Shore, giving news of a relative, Mrs. Sydney Shore. Here Flo is much more her old self, but there is a somber cast to what she recounts about finding a dead bird and giving it a burial with flowers and an inscription composed by herself and Parthe.

> *Tomtitty bird! Why art thou dead*
> *Thou who dost bear upon thy head*
> *A crown! But now thou art*
> *On thy death bed,*
> *My Tom Tit.*[33]

The solemn care taken with this bird funeral is significant since, as we have seen, Florence was thinking a lot about death at this time. On February 21, 1829, Miss Christie wrote to Fanny, who had gone to London with Parthe, who needed to have some teeth pulled. The governess apologized for "letting Flo appropriate this page, but she is so anxious to write that I could not refuse her. She has a little cold but seems well otherwise—she is very well apparently though the first evg [evening] went off very heavily in spite of a most philosophical struggle."

In the early stages of Florence's life under Miss Christie's authority, there were moments of protest or rebellion. On Sunday, November 15, 1827, in a charming and tiny new book, Florence recorded only one, desolate entry: "I, obliged to sit still by Miss Christie, till I had the spirit of obedience. Carters and Blanche [Florence's baby cousin] here, not allowed to be with them. Mama at Fair-Oaks ill. Myself unhappy, bad eyes, shade and cold."[34] In her French autobiography "La Vie de Florence Rossignol," Florence dared to write that on their first meeting she found it odd that Miss Christie should greet her as "my dear" when they had never met before. She recorded her disagreement with Miss Christie about the "stupid copybook" and admitted that she did not care at all for Miss Christie's darling brother—a very rough boy, in Florence's opinion. In an autumn letter of 1828 in French to her mother, Florence finishes a laborious line in cursive with "je n'ai pas que" and completes the sentence on the next line in the old printing "rellé avec ma soeur ni lu dans un livre [I have not quarreled with my sister or read in a book]," as if to rebel even when claiming virtue.

Gradually, however, Flo's letters show awareness that she is being punished for something and that her penance will end only when she has placated her mother by offering clear evidence of improvement. On August 14, 1829, both Flo and Parthe wrote to their mother at Cowes, Parthe in careful cursive and Flo in her funny printing. Florence notes stonily: "Miss Christie puts no more caustic to my foot, as the rag I am obliged to have has made a blister. I wear my boots now [presumably the steel boots], as they do not hurt me. We do not eat too much fruit." The letters to Fanny now consist almost entirely of lists of daily activities dutifully performed and of protestations of reform. "I think I am got something more good-natured and complying," Florence assures her mother, or again "I am going on very nicely, and, I think, am a little more yielding." Once or twice emotion breaks through. In a letter to her mother of January 20, 1830, written all in French, Flo carefully lists how she has spent her day—written a sermon, taken two long walks, drawn, and done her poetry—but finally bursts out: "Mother, must I take two walks, and so long because I was so tired today and so cold."[35] But mostly Flo is stoic. This letter, written from her aunt's home in February 1830, is fairly typical:

> Fairoaks. Dear Mama, I think I am more good-natured. I have got my duet quite perfect, called "*m'aimeras-tu?*" I play it with Hilary. I am learning another. I am making the bag Bonny gave me. Will you tell Gale, if you please, that I go on very well, except that I want night caps (having only two) and trowsers. My head was washed

Monday by Rebecca. I wear my steel boots as you told me—
Florence.

FLORENCE'S ORDEAL UNDER Sarah Christie lasted about two and a
half years, but even by the end of 1829 things were beginning to change.
The Nightingale parents, as I have noted, spent most of the winter
months in Derbyshire, but Mai Shore Smith and her baby, Blanche,
came to take charge of Embley in their absence, and Uncle Sam was there
for a time as well. With the Smiths in residence and Mai so sympathetic
toward her younger niece, there would be no opportunity for Miss
Christie to lock Florence up for six weeks at a time. In fact, at the beginning of January 1830 Miss Christie left the Nightingales to go and care
for her dying brother. She did not return until September and then for
only a few months since the following spring she was married to a German widower.

At first the Smiths' presence at Embley, especially Florence's infatu-
ation with the nursemaid Lucy, caused problems. On December 15,
1829, Florence at Embley wrote to her mother, in French and partly in
copperplate: "I am allowed to be with Blanche and Lucy but not to speak
to the latter much. I can be in the room with whomever I wish. Miss
Christie takes more interest in me . . . Miss Christie told me this afternoon that 'Lucy has not the strength to stop herself speaking to me and
that therefore I could not stay with her except to eat, dance and play.' "

Mai too wrote to Fanny that Florence was not allowed to be with
Lucy "except at meals & when holiday exercises are going on." In this
letter Mai refers specifically to "Miss Christie's plan" for Flo and notes
that Parthe is "very good & happy & appears to be much improved in
attention to other people," so apparently Parthe too was being asked to
become more "obliging." In the next letter to Fanny at Lea Hurst around
December 23, 1829, Mai wrote: "I hope Flo will profit by the present
way of going on. I will attend to all your directions," so obviously she
has not been given jurisdiction over her two Nightingale nieces. On December 25, 1829, Mai again wrote again to Fanny: "I have been very intimate with Flo these last few days & though I am afraid of trusting to
my own opinion about her & especially fearful of interfering with Miss

C[hristie], I hope she is in an improving way. I have felt much interested in her of late." The list of promises Florence made to her mother dates from early January of 1830, when Miss Christie was on the point of leaving.

On January 20, 1830, Mai Smith wrote a key letter to Fanny, who was still at Lea Hurst, reporting on the progress of the two Nightingale girls, who were now under her care. In this letter and others from this period Florence is referred to as "Bo" with the *B* written as a Greek small beta.[36]

Parthe is a fine girl I think in mind & person. How I hope she will not be spoiled by the admiration she is so sure to have. She seems to me to grow handsomer every day. I never saw a more striking improvement than her perfect truth & simplicity.

It seems to me βo gives undue importance to her doings as compared with her feelings. For instance, Parthe asked her to let her play first, because she had been told to do her music before she came to her exercises. "Oh no" said βo, it will put me quite out not to do my music now." I mean that doing her lesson at a regular time stands in her mind as more important than feeling kind & giving up herself to others. My conscience tells me I have contributed my fair share to any faults βo has so I often speculate on how they cld be put to rights. I fancy if she were mine I shd when we happened to be talking together say that I felt her lessons of no importance compared to certain other things, in which they should be an assistance but that in her case they were a contradiction because she had got into a way of thinking the lessons themselves important. I shd give her nothing to do, nor shd I let anyone else give her anything to do, I shd only make a point of her having plenty of air & exercise! I shd watch her carefully & when I saw the [?] feeling giving way I wld take up with her anything I thought likely to interest her, the less it partook of the form of a regular lesson & the more it opened & interested her feelings the better. This is the merest speculation & very likely all wrong for the more I see & think of children, the more ignorant I feel, but you will not think me an impertinente [*sic*] because I only mention what passes thro' my mind without the least confidence that I am not mistaken.

If I lived in the country & had no children I sometimes fancy I cld cut free the entanglement in βo's little mind, not from any skill of my own but from a change which I think cld be beneficial to her. You are quite at liberty to laugh at my fancies in which I have very small confidence but it occurred to me that when Carter & John are in town & the little C's left with Miss N as they are to be, it wld do βo good to be there [i.e., at Fair Oak] a little. I feel there is something fine in Flo, something deeply good which favourable circumstances wld unfold.[37]

This letter seems to me a model of tactful intercession. Mai Smith is careful not to pose as an expert in child rearing, but she points out to Fanny all that is good and remarkable with her second child. Perhaps Mai recommended sending Flo over to the Bonham-Carters because she was getting a sense of Miss Christie's severity toward Flo and saw that she needed a change.

At first Florence enjoyed being with her Bonham-Carter cousins. She was excitedly involved in the garden and playhouse project led by big cousin Jack, she loved her baby cousins, and the duets she and Hilary practiced together were but one sign of the growing closeness between the two. Flo had found a real friend. All the same, by March 28 Flo was beginning to show signs of strain. She wrote home wistfully that her aunt Joanna and older Bonham-Carter cousins had gone to stay with Uncle Oc's family at Thames Bank, leaving her with the maids and the babies, Harry and Alice. "I have been here 6 weeks and 2 days," she remarks.

By April 9, 1830, Pop had been sent over to be with Flo at Fair Oak, and by the summer Flo was cheerfully writing to various relatives of all the fun and activity of the massed family vacation at Thames Bank and on the Isle of Wight. Now ten, she has dropped her childish printing and writes an elegant cursive hand that matches her style. Florence wrote a wonderful description to her mother of a festival held for orphan children in which she had eagerly taken part. Parthe, on the other hand, according to Mai's letter, which was written across Flo's, "seemed tired of the throng & very prudently lay down on the sopha part of the time" (f. 54).

Now Florence was allowed to spend time with her mother, and she began to act as Fanny's amanuensis, crafting chatty, affectionate letters to relatives. When Fanny again went away, Flo sent her letters that proclaim a willingness to comply with whatever command her imperious mother may issue. Apparently Fanny now wants her daughter to eat less, play less, and lie down more! In a letter to her mother from Thames Bank on July 12, 1830, Flo seems almost to be parodying some pattern letter from a dutiful daughter. "The sunset was particularly beautiful. On one side the golden clouds shed such a beautiful tinge on the water, and on the other, it looked so dark and stormy, and there were 2 sweet little ends of a rainbow on each side of the sky, & 2 windmills against it, & little boats gliding up and down the river. Oh! So beautiful! And there were 2 steam boats just seen in the distance, that had passed us, with the smoke curling up. I felt so happy, mama, I thought I loved God then . . . Uncle and aunt Oc are all very kind, and so am I, I hope, to my cousins. I do not eat too much, I assure you, and I do not play too much. I lie down sometimes. I have found a very pretty book here, called The Christian's Friend, consisting of short sermons, and stories showing the shortness of life and the suddenness of death."[38]

It was now Parthe's turn to be dispatched to relatives, leaving her sister at home, and Flo wrote sanctimoniously as a postscript to one chatty letter: "Dear Pop. I think of you. Pray let us love one another more than we have done. Mama wishes it particularly, it is the will of God and it will comfort us in our trials through life."[39] The process of moral reform was complete.

CERTAIN THINGS that happen in childhood can shape the course of a life. I think that Parthenope Verney put her finger on something very important when she accused Sarah Christie of permanently warping Florence's character.

I do not wish to make facile accusations of abuse here, so let me be clear. Sarah Christie was not an ogre like something out of Dickens or Roald Dahl. She probably was, as Nightingale herself said, a "fair and well-intentioned" woman, and she was young and uncertain and far from home. When she died in childbirth only a year after her marriage, her former charges felt the tragedy of her life and wept. Florence Nightingale's parents were loving, caring, and responsive, and the Smith-Nightingale-Shore-Nicholson-Carter clan as a whole was exceptionally enlightened in its child-rearing practices.[40] Fanny Nightingale did not abandon Flo as the young Rudyard Kipling, age five, was abandoned for several years to the care of a sadistic aunt. Florence could write to her mother and so had some opportunity to express her feelings of loneliness and distress, and we can be sure that Fanny read those letters, just as she read the frequent reports sent in by Miss Christie. Aunt Mai and Aunt Julia could be counted on.

Florence Nightingale had a life of high privilege. When she was growing up, male and female children of six or even younger regularly worked twelve-hour days or more on farms and in cotton mills, clay pits, and coal mines. Boys of the Nightingales' class, again as young as six, were sent to school, where they often suffered from hunger and cold. They were beaten routinely by the masters, tortured by the older boys if they were strange, and sodomized if they were attractive. Conditions at Mr. Thwackem's educational establishment in *Nicholas Nickleby* accurately reflected reality in many English schools at this time. Francis Ashley, a younger son of the sixth Earl of Shaftesbury and scion of one of England's oldest noble families, engaged in a two-hour boxing match at Eton College, was knocked unconscious and left unattended, and died.[41] Florence's sufferings pale in comparison.

All the same, we may wonder why Fanny tended to protect Parthe and blame Florence. The reasons are, I think, not hard to find. Fanny was happy to have one daughter. She needed an aide and an echo, and Parthe fit the bill. Parthe wanted to be like her mother and her aunts Joanna and Anne and was sad when, as so often happened, she had to lie on the sofa, too ill to play games with her cousins. But Flo was more a Shore than a Smith, and even the Smith parts of her reminded Fanny less of herself than of Patty or Julia or even Benjamin. Flo should have been a boy. She did everything so well except the things that counted for a genteel young girl. Her brilliance of mind, her thirst for education, her self-absorption, her intractability would have been seen as normal in a boy. Fanny would have nurtured such traits in a son as the seeds of high achievement and worldly success.

But Flo was a girl who did everything asked of her conspicuously well and who found that nothing was ever quite enough. A girl who felt she had come into hostile terrain, sought out allies like Aunt Mai, and prepared to fight. A girl, like Mary Godwin Shelley, who had been persuaded that she was a monster.

This book is called *Nightingales,* and its theme is that Florence Nightingale was an exceptional woman born into a loving and gifted family that on many different levels enabled her to achieve great things. But this is not the message Nightingale herself wished posterity to receive. In many private notes and journal entries, above all in her huge manuscript *Suggestions for Thought,* Florence Nightingale wrote a succession of long, bitter denunciations of family life and above all of the abuse daughters suffer at the hands of their mothers. As a young adult she was implacably opposed to marriage and having children of her own. In 1857, when she fell terribly ill and seemed likely to die, Nightingale refused to let her parents and her sister into her sickroom, choosing to be cared for only by her spiritual mother, Mai Smith. For eight years, the eight years when she was at the height of her fame and influence, Florence kept the three other Nightingales out of her life, even though, as a helpless invalid, she was wholly dependent on their support. For the rest of her life, she ate alone, slept alone, rarely came out of her own rooms, and almost never saw more than one person at a time. Had she entered a convent, her renunciation of family life could hardly have been more decided.

I think Florence Nightingale's rage against her closest family members can be traced back to 1827 and the coming of Miss Christie. On the surface she recovered, was even improved. But deep down she felt betrayed and she could never forget or forgive. Complex patterns of love and hate, intimacy and separation, excellence and falling short were established before Florence was ten, and relationships between the four Nightingales were never the same again.

Chapter 6

IN FATHER'S
LIBRARY

With the departure of Miss Christie, sunshine broke through for the Nightingale sisters. The years 1831 to 1839 were the most serene and happy of Florence's life and, since she was the chief constellation in Parthenope's sky, Pop too, overall, savored her teenage years. As an adult Parthenope Nightingale Verney looked back with almost savage nostalgia on those days when she and her sister were so close.

Fanny Nightingale still thought it best for Flo and Parthe often to be in different places, but when together the sisters were able to find more common ground than they had as small children. Both were developing a love of art, music, and literature. Their friendships with the big cousins, notably Marianne Nicholson and Hilary Bonham-Carter, deepened. If Florence was the queen of the schoolroom, in drawing-room skills she lagged conspicuously behind her elder sister. Above all, Parthe and Flo worked as a team at being good daughters to their mother, no small task.

Flo's letters to Parthe from this period are affectionate, even tender, full of happy complicity. In the late fall of 1834, for example, Florence found herself stranded at Ryde, on the southern coast, helping Aunt Julia to look after the small Smith cousins, Blanche, Shore, Bertha, and Beatrice. Autumns are usually dreary months by the coast, and Fanny Nightingale had herself departed for London with WEN and Parthe in tow. Flo missed her sister, and the fact that she was suffering from both

boils and constipation did not help. She wrote to Aunt Mai, "I felt somewhat forlorn when Mama & Papa departed & my room & my bed are
too large without Parthe." In 1837 Florence is still sounding the same
note in her letter of January 17: "My Dear Pop, Disappointment & do-
lor are still my lot which even perhaps are greater when I saw them [i.e.,
Fanny and WEN] return without you than when I saw them depart
without me."[1]

Two things in particular accounted for Florence's new equanimity
and the Nightingale family's contentment—the birth in May of 1831 of
William Shore Smith, to be known in the family as Shore, and WEN's
move to take upon himself the main responsibility for his daughters'
education.

THE ARRIVAL OF baby Shore was an immense relief, not least of course
to his parents. Mai and Sam Smith had long been under pressure to produce a male child, heir presumptive to his uncle Nightingale's estate.
When Shore was born, WEN and Fanny put aside any resentment they
may have felt at their own inability to bear a male child. Little Shore became, in a very real sense, their son, and as a toddler at Embley he styled
himself, significantly, as "Martertore" (Master Shore). By temperament,
Shore and Fanny had much in common, and as boy and man Shore was
probably closer to his aunt Fanny than to his mother or his uncle Night.
The family alliance of Sam, Fanny, and Shore now balanced that of Mai,
WEN, and Florence.

If all four Nightingales took Shore to their hearts, Florence gave him
a devotion that verged on adoration. "The son of my heart," she called
him. "While he is with me all that is mine is his, my head and hands and
time."[2] Part of this devotion was a kind of friendly competition between
Florence and her two nearest and dearest female cousins, both of whom
had little brothers. Throughout Florence's adolescence, "Love to all Babies" was a common sign-off in family letters. Now, with the arrival of
Shore, Florence too had a baby, news of whose colics and tantrums and
droll sayings could be sent around the clan network. "I am very sorry to
hear your Baby is still so poorly," she wrote to Hilary on March 24, 1832,
"but our Baby is much better for he has got two teeth through."[3]

From the time when three-month-old Shore was first placed in Florence's arms by his mother, she made him her personal project, and all the family took notice.[4] The concentrated intelligence that Flo had hitherto trained on her silkworms and flower collection was now trained on this frail, precious little boy. Mai, who could not breast-feed successfully, hired a resident wet nurse, and Florence, who had recently tried in vain to keep some orphaned newborn mice alive by pipetting milk, carefully observed this woman at work. No one was more anxious for Shore to live and grow strong than Florence. All the same, she reported in a letter to her grandmother Shore that the family had decided not to tell the nurse that her husband had died, as they feared that grief and anxiety would stop her milk. Something about the process of separating some poor strange woman from her own family worried Flo.[5] Shore was almost two before he was weaned, a sign of his privilege, and a notable expense for the struggling Smiths.

In the summer of 1832 the Bonham-Carter baby boy died, and the anxiety surrounding Shore intensified. In July of that year, Mai Smith went with her four-year-old daughter, Blanche, to spend the summer at the spa at Harrogate, leaving little Shore at Lea Hurst. Mai was full of fear about this first separation from her baby, but she was once again pregnant, her third pregnancy in four years, and very run-down. Since the unborn child Mai was carrying might be another boy with better chances of survival than Shore, the family's chief priority was to keep Mai healthy. After all, sentiment aside, his mother's presence offered no guarantee for Shore's well-being. Nineteenth-century people were used to seeing small children die in their mothers' arms.

Fanny Nightingale may have accompanied Mai Smith to Harrogate. Certainly Fanny was not at Lea Hurst in July 1832, and Shore was left in the care of Fanny's old nurse, Mrs. Gale. Frances Gale, a tiny, hunchbacked woman whose title of "Mrs." was purely honorary, was legendary in the family for her devotion to her former charges, who included Fanny as well as Parthe and Flo. But Gale was not strong, and in the absence of Fanny and Mai she fell seriously ill, creating a small crisis at Lea Hurst. Twelve-year-old Florence stepped into the breach, taking over principal care of little Shore, especially at night, when he slept in her bed. When Mai Smith returned, she found the child in fine fettle.

This event marked an important stage in Florence's life. The pattern was set in the family that Florence was the one to turn to if someone was sick or in trouble. To a surprising extent the Smith-Nightingales credited Flo with keeping Shore alive. When Mai and Sam Smith's third and fourth children turned out to be more girls, Shore's importance increased, and the family's gratitude to Flo with it. Mai Smith had long had a deep interest in her younger niece, but Flo's passionate devotion to Shore forged an even stronger bond between them. It also earned Florence her mother's approbation. Who, seeing Florence with Shore, could now accuse her of egocentricity and selfishness? Here in the preadolescent girl was evidence of that tender solicitude, that willingness to sacrifice one's own comfort, which the Victorians, like many another culture, equated with true womanliness. Once Flo devoted her remarkable powers of mind and will to the service of a family member, they became valued.

But perhaps the greatest love and loyalty Florence won in the summer of 1832 was that of her nurse, Frances Gale. The Nightingales and their kin composed Gale's world, and if anything had happened to "Master Shore" while Gale was in charge, Gale never would have forgiven herself. If Frances Gale had adored her little mistress Florence before, she now saw in her an ally and a friend, and the feeling was reciprocated. Throughout her life Florence Nightingale would find it easier to establish close relationships with women like Gale than with women her own age, class, and nationality.

Flo would often find herself in the next years charged with the care and education of Shore and his sisters, as Mai Smith followed the example of her sister-in-law Fanny and frequently left her children in the care of relatives. At Embley or Lea Hurst the Smith children were officially in the charge of their aunt Fanny, but since she was often away and always busy with guests, it was in fact their cousin Florence who supervised their activities. Parthe was a friendly presence but Florence, stronger, more energetic, more committed, more amusing, was like a second mother to the growing Smiths. Throughout her life Florence Nightingale had a magical effect on children.

We get a good sense of what Florence's cousinly duties included from a set of letters she wrote to her sister in January and February of 1837. Florence was at Embley with Shore and Bertha when a flu epidemic broke out, laying low most of the servants and many other local people. WEN and Fanny returned to Embley, leaving Parthe in safety at Waverley, but then themselves fell ill, leaving Florence and a cook to cope with more than a dozen sick people. Shore unexpectedly resisted the flu, but little Bertha, called Puff by her family, was very ill. Florence not only worked all day as nurse and housekeeper but kept a close eye on Shore. She reported to Parthe: "Shore is expelling the nine lives out of my body one by one yet he & I are great friends, but I grow thin under his discipline." In another affectionate and chummy letter to Parthe Florence comments on her nights with Shore, "whose extraordinary snortings, groanings & grumblings à la walrus mingle agreeably with my dreams."[6]

An evolutionary biologist might point out that Florence's care of her cousins was adaptive. Like many other young female primates, she was assisting an older woman with child care and thus rehearsing the skills of motherhood and promoting the common gene line.[7] But though Florence loved and often looked after all four of her Sam Smith cousins, her special devotion was to the male, Shore. This devotion was a result not of evolutionary instincts but of legal, social, and psychological pressure.

Florence saw clearly that she and Blanche and Parthe mattered little in comparison to Shore. She immediately picked up on the fact that when Blanche was a tiny baby her mother had referred to her as "the thing."[8] Florence knew that because she was not a boy she could not inherit her father's estate and thus secure the comfort of her mother and fragile sister. But she could do everything in her power to ensure that her cousin Shore survived and that he became the kind of man the family valued. As she said in a letter to Hannah Nicholson in the mid-1840s, with the exaggerated rhetoric of self-abasement that was typical of her: "And my boy [i.e., Shore] has such a pure heart & affectionate soul. As for me, I have said to corruption, Thou art my brother & sister. But he might be all that I could have been."[9] When she contemplated her cousin's future as he entered his teens, what Florence feared above all was that he would become "ill or a sporting man." Sadly for her, this is more or less exactly what happened.

IN LATER YEARS Florence also gave her male cousins Shore Smith and William Nicholson special cramming to prepare them for careers in the law and the military. For a woman to have such competence in fields exclusively reserved for men was rare. But Florence and her sister as teenagers were lucky enough to receive an education not only commensurate with their intelligence but comparable to that given to privileged young men in elite schools. As she recalled: "When I was ten my mother would have no more governesses and my father took us himself in hand. He taught me Latin and Greek and mathematics and whatever he knew himself. I had the most enormous desire of acquiring—for seven years of my life, I thought of little else but the cultivation of my intellect. And even now when I think what a human intellect may become by industry, ambition comes before me like Circe with her cup to tempt me."[10]

For a girl of Florence's generation, even one born into a wealthy family, to learn Greek, Latin, and mathematics was extremely rare. For her to be taught by her father was almost unheard of. Florence knew this as well as anyone since her aunt Julia Smith was vocal on the subject of the neglected and unreported state of female education in Great Britain. Early-nineteenth-century English society in fact waged a fierce rearguard action against education for women. It would take the efforts of women like Julia Smith, her close friends Harriet Martineau and Anna Jameson, and younger women like Barbara Leigh Smith Bodichon, Emily Davies, Frances Beale, and Dorothea Buss to begin to level the educational playing field for girls.

Science was progressing at giant leaps at this period, but all too often scientists and medical doctors in particular provided new weapons in the old misogynist campaign. Did girls have the abilities to learn as boys did? Most Victorians thought not. By training a girl's intellect did you make her unmarriageable? Many people thought so, and respectable medical men went so far as to argue that education weakened a girl's body, fed her hysterical impulses, and impaired her reproductive capacity. Even if some rare girls had the ability to learn like their brothers, might they not lose more than they gained? Education was meant to train a person to think, to give him a solid basis of fact, and to prepare him for professional life. But what respectable professional opportunities for women were there around 1830 except as teachers to the next generation of girls? What would a woman gain from thinking for herself or having a great many facts at her disposal? What man would care for her if she did? Even the royal princess Alexandrina Victoria, heiress to the throne of Great Britain, born in 1819, received a notably undemanding education. She was a willing, capable, energetic, but ill-informed and untrained teenager

Florence Nightingale at thirty, photographed in
Berlin on her way back from Egypt.

William Smith, Florence's maternal grandfather, as a boy with his doting father, Samuel.

William Smith, the radical Member of Parliament who campaigned for the abolition of slavery, the widening of the franchise, and the extension of civil rights to religious minorities.

Fanny Smith Nightingale with baby Parthenope, whose natal mountain, Vesuvius, appears in the background.

Fanny with Parthenope and Florence as very young children.

Parthenope and Florence Nightingale in 1839, Florence's debutante year.
Florence is in the pink dress.

Barbara Leigh Smith Bodichon,
painter and women's rights activist.
She was first cousin to the Nightingale
sisters but never allowed to meet
them as a child.

Elizabeth Cleghorn Gaskell. The
novelist was present at the birth of the
legend of Florence Nightingale.

Mary Clarke Mohl, the renowned
salonnière. Her great charm lay in the
absence of it.

Ada Byron, Lady Lovelace, the
mathematician. 'I deem her fair, yes
very fair! Though some there are who
pass her by,' wrote Ada of Florence.

Richard Monckton Milnes, later Baron Houghton. Florence was tempted to accept his reiterated marriage proposal, since it seemed an easy escape out of her difficulties.

Anthony Ashley Cooper, seventh Earl of Shaftesbury, known to history as the Great Reformer, friend to factory workers and young chimney sweeps.

Queen Victoria and Prince Albert re-enact their wedding vows for the camera. The Nightingales, like many Britons, saw the royal marriage as a romantic ideal.

The Barrack Hospital at Scutari, a village across the Bosphorus
from Constantinople.

Balaclava harbour, the British army's communications centre,
during the winter of 1854–55.

Patients lining the wards and corridors at the Barrack Hospital during the first winter.

Florence Nightingale's sketch of the living quarters afforded to her party of nurses on their arrival at Scutari in late November 1854.

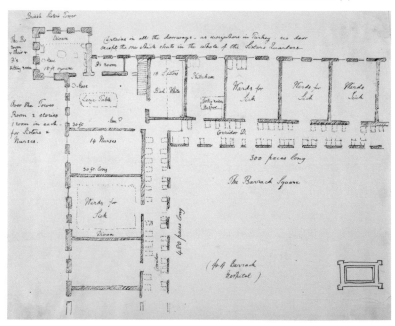

when she succeeded her uncle William in 1837. One of the tasks that awaited Albert of Saxe-Coburg-Gotha was to educate his queen wife.

A gifted man like James Mill might devote himself to the education of his precociously brilliant little son John Stuart Mill, but had the Mills' child been born Joanna instead of John, she probably would have seen little of her father. Some girls of extraordinary ability like the Brontë sisters, Elizabeth Barrett, Mary Ann Evans (George Eliot), and Christina Rossetti were suffered by their authoritarian fathers to acquire the learning freely offered to their brothers. They learned piecemeal, largely on their own, often with pain and sacrifice, and their short, sad, and difficult lives gave little cheer to the promoters of female education.

Why did WEN teach his daughters? The first reason was ideological. William Edward Nightingale was one of the rare men of his time who had been taught to believe that women too should be educated. This was part of his Unitarian heritage. The second was that he had time on his hands. A thinking man of ample independent means with no taste for libertinism could chase only so many foxes and eat so many rich dinners. The third was that WEN felt intellectually isolated within the big family circle and yet lonely and amateurish when he left it for the world of London clubs and learned societies. A busy social life full of county dinners, family shooting parties, and visiting children did not satisfy him, as it did Fanny, and the increasingly evangelical tone of her new friends did not suit him. WEN's brothers-in-law George Nicholson and Sam Smith, though excellent fellows, did not share WEN's taste for metaphysics and political theory. Talking to Patty was impossible, Julia and Mai, in different ways, had both become too radical. Benjamin Smith and John Bonham-Carter were men of ideas but increasingly busy with their constituencies, their business and philanthropy interests, and their large, growing families. Benjamin was an important friend, but since he was barred from bringing his children with him on visits, WEN saw relatively little of Ben. So WEN was looking for stimulating company, and in eleven-year-old Flo he spotted a soul mate and a prospective ally.

Under the care of Miss Christie, WEN saw his lively, pert, accomplished, infinitely curious little Florence turning into a gloomy, sanctimonious puppet, mouthing the sentimental pieties of Evangelical tracts and second-rank poets like Felicia Hemans. For a Unitarian Brahmin like WEN, this was cause for alarm. Something deep and intense and pained in Florence called out to her father, and he heard it. Thus WEN took the unusual step of trespassing upon his wife's sphere and taking an active role in his daughters' lives.

AT FIRST, faced with Miss Christie's announcement that she was leaving to be married, the idea was to send Flo away to school.[11] In the last months before Miss Christie left the family Parthe and Flo were taken by their governess to visit two girls' schools with excellent reputations. They first went for a day or so to the school of the Miss Byerleys. Florence came away with some precious seedlings in pots, which she tended with characteristic zeal, but that was all that came of that visit.[12] Miss Emily Taylor, a brilliant and cultured woman and a close friend of Julia Smith's, also had a small school in Norfolk that she financed through her poetry and other publications. In the early winter of 1831 Miss Christie and Parthe and Flo spent several weeks at Miss Taylor's home. Although she knew Sarah Christie, Miss Taylor seems initially to have taken the children's part against their governess. She wrote tactfully to Fanny, saying she wished she had been able to talk to Florence without Miss Christie being present, and she seems to have doubted the wisdom of the course Christie was taking with her charges. In a peevish letter to Fanny, Miss Christie complained that while they were with the Taylors Parthe was willfully disinclined to do her painful arm exercises. Even worse, Flo had rebelled against the work set for her by her governess and felt free to abscond to the kitchen, where she sat cheerfully knitting and chatting with Miss Taylor's aunt.

But if Miss Taylor gave Florence support against Miss Christie, she resolutely refused to take her as a student in her school. She continued to refuse for several years, though she agreed to carry on a correspondence with both Nightingale girls. At first Miss Taylor opined that Flo would gain too much ascendancy over the other students in her school and that this would not be in her interests. Subsequently she wrote to Fanny Nightingale that she was "not very easy" in corresponding with Flo. "I find so much disposition in her to detach herself from her sister in everything," Emily Taylor wrote, "and almost to turn her own faults to account as entitling her to a more confidential and separate mode of communication." Miss Taylor went on: "I do not find I *can* conscientiously indulge her in this—because I am quite sure that she already both knows her failings and their best remedy—and that speculation, in words, on the difference between her and Parthe are very bad indeed for her . . . In her last to me she is left with her aunt Julia 'to break me of some of my peculiarities'—and adds, 'Parthe & I are so different, that we require quite different treatment, so that while it is good for her to go, it is good for me to stay.' "[13]

In another letter, written this time to WEN in 1834 or 1835, Emily Taylor said that in her view what Flo herself dubbed "peculiarities" might get ironed out if the girl were in a class of contemporaries who were not her cousins. Taylor noted Florence's excessive habit of introspection and suggested that, despite Fanny's distrust of "story books," the novels of Walter Scott would help the girl. "I do not like Flo's *concentrated imagination,*" Taylor wrote, "and think it may be a real injury upon herself & here & there one chosen object."[14] One can see from these comments why WEN was anxious to see his daughter in this perceptive woman's care, but the fact remained that Miss Taylor refused the challenge of educating Florence Nightingale. The ball was back in WEN's court.

The Nightingale girls were not taught exclusively by their father since he and they were frequently separated and away from home. When staying with Mrs. Bonham-Carter and Mrs. Nicholson, Parthe and Flo took lessons with their cousins' governesses, most notably Sarah Sophia Hennell, a woman of remarkable talent and scholarship who was the Bonham-Carter governess for some five years.[15] Aunts Julia and Mai were often in charge of their Nightingale nieces and supervised their lessons. Julia was a fierce autodidact, taking on sign language, so that she could communicate with the deaf, as well as Greek and German so that she could read obscure books by modern German philosophers and taste for herself the glories of the ancient world. She was also a fine artist, who encouraged her nieces Parthenope and Hilary to explore their talent. In the period 1831–37 Julia Smith became more and more of an influence on the teenage Florence, not just for what she knew but for her active involvement in political reform and philanthropy.[16] Mai Smith, married and with a growing family, had less time to study and campaign than Julia, but she too encouraged her Nightingale nieces to learn and excel.

But for all the brilliance and dedication of Sarah Hennell, Julia Smith, and Mai Smith, they were women sunk in the mire of nineteenth-century misogyny. It was far more empowering for a scholarly father to teach his daughters, take an interest in them, read their work, and accept them into his library. The Nightingale sisters were lucky enough to receive an enlightened version of the standard school curriculum of their day at the hands of a loving, engaged teacher-father. Though Parthenope and Florence devoted fewer hours in the day to their studies than boys in school did, they had more opportunities for independent thought, creative projects, and wide reading than most boys their age. Better, they did not have to endure the flogging, toadying, and buggery that so perverted the educational process at elite schools like Eton and Harrow.

Their father's lessons were an extraordinary gift that both Nightingale girls remembered with pride and appreciation. Thus in a letter to her sister from Rome in 1847, Florence wrote: "I assure you I feel more and more every day my gratitude to that father, who taught me all I ever knew, who gave me all the ideas I ever had, who taught me interest in nations as though they were personal existences, and showed me how to look upon all churches as but parts of the one great scheme, all opinions, political and religious, as but accidental developments of the one Parental Sap which comes up oats in one case and oranges in another. I do so feel, and gratefully acknowledge, the advantage of it now."[17] For his part, William Edward Nightingale enjoyed for the rest of his life an intimacy and an intellectual community with his daughters that few men of his day could claim.

WILLIAM EDWARD NIGHTINGALE had an excellent mind and had received a superb education, at a Dissenting academy as a boy, then at Edinburgh University and finally at Cambridge. After coming down from the university, Nightingale retained a lively interest in the arts, the humanities, and the sciences. He traveled in Europe, meeting some of the best minds of the day. He was one of the founding members of the British Association for the Advancement of Science, including the statistical section, established by Charles Babbage in 1833. Unlike the more ancient Royal Society, the British Association addressed the emerging social sciences, and it allowed women to contribute papers and take part in its proceedings. As Parthenope Verney told her daughter-in-law Margaret Verney, WEN had a passion for books and was rich enough to afford a scholar's library. In affluent nineteenth-century homes, the library was the male sanctum par excellence, but like his father-in-law William Smith before him, Mr. Nightingale shared his books with his daughters. The Nightingale library contained not only the great classics in several languages but modern poetry, fiction, and scientific monographs as well as philosophy from Plato and Aristotle to Hobbes and Locke. WEN subscribed to some of the best contemporary reviews which not only published new fiction but reported the latest findings in the sciences, economics, and public policy.

WEN developed lesson plans and exercises for his daughter-pupils and he expected them to work hard, but he was not all rote and routine like Miss Christie. His essential pedagogy was to offer to teach his daughters what he knew and then wait to see how they responded. If they made progress, he became more engaged; if they failed to show interest or commitment, so did he. Since both girls proved to be worthy pupils, full of intelligence and application, a positive synergy grew up around the lessons. Fanny as well as WEN could feel pride in the schoolroom prowess of her teenage daughters. The risk that, led on by their brilliant, idealistic father, Parthe and Flo might turn into "blues" like their spinster aunts Patty and Julia was a problem Fanny was confident she could solve when the time came.

Modern-language study was the single most important segment of the Nightingale girls' education, the area where Parthenope most easily kept pace with her sister. When they began to work under the supervision of their father, Parthenope and Florence already had an excellent grounding in French, both oral and written, and had begun Latin. WEN built on this and added Italian. Parthe and Flo may also have begun German when they were teenagers, though here, I believe, their teacher was their aunt Julia, not their father.[18] Translation was at the heart of language learning at this time, and both Nightingale girls took to it like ducks to water. As adults both would be highly proficient translators. In January of 1837, Flo at Embley wrote to Parthe at Waverley Abbey: "Papa desires me to say that you are to go on where you left off in Dante, & that he will be anxious to see the translation you will produce of Canto 1 revised and corrected by Miss J."

Globes were a standard part of the Victorian young lady's education, but WEN had the knack of making geography entrancing. As Florence remarked as she was sailing through the Greek Islands in 1850, "The finest scenery one ever sees in all one's life is what one sees as a child in a map. I have never seen any scenes like what I used to see in Papa's little old torn Latin map book on that dirty Greek page."[19] The sisters also applied themselves seriously to history, ancient and modern, and to basic science. WEN was enthusiastically involved in the development of what would now be called social science and this was an interest he passed on to both of his daughters. In arithmetic and geometry Parthe and Florence had probably received the basics from Miss Christie, and Florence at least continued to work on mathematics with her father, though his taste for it was less than her own. As we shall see, Florence's desire in her early twenties to do serious work in mathematics was to prove one of the *casus belli* between her and her mother.

One gets a particularly sharp sense of what Florence learned as a teenager from a tiny notebook, about two inches by three and a half, that she acquired in August 1836, when she was just sixteen. This "Compendium of Useful Facts," written in a minute hand, is fascinating, not only for what it tells us about the mind of this particular Victorian girl but for what it tells us about the state of knowledge, especially scientific knowledge, at this time.[20] Some letters of the alphabet—notably *N* to *Q*—get short shrift, and Florence is most diligent in her entry under letter *A*, whose pages start thematically with a list of famous beginnings and go on to "Aeronautics," "Animal Strength," and "Atmosphere." Page 1 reads:

	B.C.
Creation	4007
Deluge	2351
Greek Olympiad	776
Rome built	752
Death of Alexander	323
First of Julius Caesar	44
Christ born	A.D.
Hegira	622

Aeronautics

First balloon ascended	1783
To 4 and ½ miles	1804

Proportion of oxygen & nitrogen & magnetic
influence *same* in every part of atmosphere

Animal Strength

Human strength depends on climate

English	71.4
French	69.2
Van Diemen's Land [Australia]	51.8
New Holland	50.6

Atmosphere, properties of

Fluidity, elasticity, gravity, expansibility

nitrogen	79
Oxygen	21

Under "Atmosphere," Florence goes on to list the mean temperatures in cities all over the world. Under *B* we find all the main bridges in the world, with number of arches, date of erection, and length in feet. Under *C* we have a chronology of inventions, beginning with the first recorded observation of the eclipse of the moon (Babylon) and ending with "the telegraph (France) 1794." *E* gives us "Echo" and "Elasticity," *G* the seven wise men of Greece, *H* "heat," *I* "Iceberg," *J* "Jupiter," *L* "Lever," "Light," and "Lead." Under *M* Florence offered a careful comparative table of ancient and modern monetary units, calculated in pounds sterling, as well as a list of the world's highest mountains, with the heights of St. Peter's in Rome, the Pyramids, and the first balloon ascent thrown in for good measure. *M* also includes a list not only of the Muses but the Furies and the Graces. *R* has a careful discussion of refraction, a list of the world's great rivers with length and volume of water, and a table showing the average rainfall in Great Britain each year from 1790 to 1821. Under *S* Florence discusses satellites, sects, and sound, under *T* telescopes, under *V* volcanoes, and under *W* winds. The back cover of the tiny book contains a list of the kings of both England and France with dates of their ascension and number of years in power.

Perhaps the most important thing William Edward Nightingale offered to teach his daughters was ancient Greek. His Greek was excellent, and he was a passionate lover of Plato. Florence Nightingale once remarked that her sister, Parthenope, had shown a greater initial aptitude for Greek, but it was in Greek, more than geography or history or Italian, that Florence showed her true intellectual mettle, leaving her sister in the dust. Greek is much harder than French or even Latin, and Florence had not only a natural flair for language but perseverance and concentration. By the age of sixteen, she had read a good deal of Homer and the *Phaedo*, the *Crito,* and the *Apology* by Plato in the original, and she continued to work on Greek well into her twenties. Florence Nightingale's command of Greek literature was still good enough in the 1870s for Benjamin Jowett to ask her comments on the introduction to the translations of the dialogues of Plato that would make his fame.

Greek had enormous symbolic value in nineteenth-century English culture, functioning in many ways as the seal of professional ability and as the distinguishing mark for high caste. Furthermore, in the key matter of religion, Plato was almost as influential on Florence Nightingale's development as the Bible. Plato's conception of the sensual world as a mere representation of the spiritual reality confirmed her deepest religious instincts. In the *Republic* Plato envisaged an ideal society ruled by philosopher-kings and philosopher-queens, a heady concept for an intellectual, ambitious girl. In a sense, Nightingale saw her whole life as a striving to move out of Plato's dark cave of materiality with its reversed, flickering shadows, up into the light where divine truth is experienced without mediation.

Florence Nightingale's superb Greek, her familiarity with not only Plato but her father's favorite Scottish philosopher, Dugald Stewart, and her command of multiple facts about the world set her apart from her female contemporaries, even from the other women reformers in the family. Thanks to her intellectual training as well as her intellect, Nightingale was accepted as both colleague and adversary by men in real-world affairs. Encouraged by her father to excel, trained to compete handily with men in their own game, Florence Nightingale had neither love nor fear of the old-boys' network that increasingly ruled Britain and its empire. Her intimate knowledge of Greek literature, with its celebration of refined male bonding, gave Florence Nightingale a key to the developing public school culture of Victorian England that few women possessed. When, during the Crimean War and after, the chance to wield power came her way, she regarded the Victorian establishment rather as an anthropologist would—respectful but not cowed, more inclined to judge and chide than to admire.

Rightly or wrongly, Nightingale was more confident in her intellectual ability than almost any other woman in England of her generation. This helps to explain both her achievements and the hostility she aroused. Glory and anomaly, Florence Nightingale's intellectual self-confidence was a gift given her by her father.

EDUCATION BROUGHT Florence and her father together, but it also at times roused the old tensions with her sister. The letters from the teenage years indicate a happy and healthy rivalry between the sisters. In January 1837, when Embley was faced with floods as well as a flu epidemic, Florence not only directed the household, nursed the sick in the house and the village, and supervised two small children but also got up before dawn to study. She reported to Parthe: "It is incredible what some people's industry will perform e.g. the piles of manuscripts which have arisen like mushrooms under my pen during this last month, while I have been nurse, governess, assistant curate & doctor in the absence of Mr. G., at all events I have killed no patients though I have cured few. But the lives of British Worthies, the histories, the analyses which I have achieved, enough to smother Papa when he returns. I feel rather awed & subdued by your boasted achievements ma chère soeur & hope you will communicate them gently & by degrees to me on yr return & do not stifle me at once. I wish to put the best leg foremost & boast of my own doings too as much as possible." Florence continued in the same jocular vein in her next letter to Parthe of February 19, which she opens: "Dear exemplary Pop, Daily & hourly are the praises bestowed on your epistolary merit in this house devoted to Calomel & Castor Oil."[21]

But there was a limit to how far Parthenope Nightingale could compete. In pursuit of knowledge Florence was remorseless. She was brilliant, she was focused, she was competitive, and she identified learning, correctly, as an avenue to power.

For Parthenope, to be second in a class of two must at times have been a nightmare. Where many biographers of Florence accuse Parthe of envy and jealousy of a more talented sibling, I am surprised that she was not more resentful. To judge from the extant documents, Parthe was willing, even eager, to grant her little sister preeminence in the classroom. What upset her was not Florence's brilliance and her achievements but the exclusive intimacy growing up between her sister and her father. On my reading of the documentation from this period, Parthe did not quickly weary of the demands her father made and retreat to her mother in the drawing room. She pleaded and struggled to stay in the library with Flo. In 1834 she wrote a letter of protest to her father, accusing him of neglect and favoritism, to which he replied with quizzical affection: "My dear Pop—not one word . . . among my waking dreams I sometimes fancy that you and I have not made half as much of each other's society as we might have done . . . I have more subjects than one in hand, or in mind, which are likely enough to lend themselves to our future intercourse. In the meantime I feel that you're satiating (*perhaps* usefully) with many matters which suit your infantine and merry days of 15—or is it 16?—and thro' a nervousness of interfering with them, I curtail my letter to a simple expression of my rejoicing at your merriments and your happiness."[22]

At times, it seems, WEN complained to Flo that Parthe was not working hard or doing her best, and that he was tired of trying to teach her. When Flo conveyed these sentiments to her sister, Parthe was distraught. This was the kind of spat that the Nightingales would indulge in throughout their long lives, as much a measure of their love as of their hostility to each other. Parthe wrote to her father in London in 1835: "Flo in bed coughing, told me all . . . so exonerate her pray . . . I really did not know I was laying the ban on my own happiness by such heedlessness of other people's feelings. I am properly punished for it, if you knew how very bitterly I feel your messages through her and your acknowledgment in your own letter, that you have ceased to care enough for my society, to be sorry I behave so ill."[23]

Overall, I think it is a mistake to emphasize the differences and the quarrels between the two Nightingale sisters when they were teenagers.[24] In fact, only if we realize how close the two sisters were before 1840, how much they relied upon each other, can we understand Parthenope's extravagant grief and bitter resentment when her sister later tried to leave home. The key to the difficult relations between the Nightingale sisters is to be found, I think, not in Parthe's envy but in her chronic ill health, which aroused Fanny's protectiveness, and eventually cast the newly altruistic and always efficient Flo into the role of her sister's caretaker.

WEN and Fanny had been worrying about Parthenope's health since her birth, but their fears were revived and strengthened in February 1836, when she fell ill with a high fever and a terrible cough that shook her thin body and raised the ugly specter of galloping consumption.[25] Mr. Nightingale was away from home when his daughter fell ill and was himself in pain after a fall from a horse. In her daily letters reporting on Parthe's condition, Fanny begged her husband not to come home since he could be of no help and the ever-valiant Julia had come to assist her. There is not a single mention of Florence in Fanny's dozen or so letters to WEN. Flo was presumably away somewhere on one of those incessant visits to the cousins, and Fanny had no time to think about her.

Fanny panicked over Parthe's condition, convinced that her daughter was going to die. She undertook to nurse Parthe herself, with the help of Gale, who, as usual, proved a treasure. Refusing to call in a London specialist, Fanny put her whole faith in the local doctor, Mr. J. M. Biddone. He was a hardworking man who visited his patient regularly and even spent several nights by her bedside. He was also, however, a devotee of the "heroic" school of medicine, and he convinced Fanny that Parthe would recover only if subjected to the full battery of leeches, bleedings, and blisters. For the modern reader, it is heartrending to read Fanny's descriptions of Parthe meekly suffering. "Saturday morning. I was disappointed when Biddone felt her pulse to find that it had risen to 112. He left us and the cough came in again . . . and I was just going to put on Leeches when she fell asleep for three hours, and a most refreshing sleep it was, & enabled her to bear the Leeches which were put on immediately upon her waking. Biddone came again to stay the night. I got up at 3 to examine her, as it depended upon her state whether or not another blister should be applied. I sat beside her a delightful half hour watching." This was the kind of advanced medical treatment that speeded the death of many patients. Mr. Biddone kept remarking on the strength of Parthenope's constitution, and in this at least he was right, since she survived his ministrations.

This illness confirmed all Fanny's fears for Parthe and increased her sense that she alone stood between her daughter and death. "Your letter was a great comfort to me," wrote Fanny to WEN. "You take this trial dearest as I imputed you would. I too have *generally* felt quite resigned to the event whatever it might be. At one moment I was strongly impressed with the idea that she would go. It appeared to me as if the Closed and thick darkness which separates us from heaven opened to receive her & did not close again—& I was impressed I cannot tell you how much with the train of glory which she seemed to leave behind her as a link between Heaven & her sorrowing Mother. But she will be spared to us, & we may hope that her excellent constitution will overcome the series of disease which are so often left behind—at least so Biddone says."

Parthe would live and indeed recover enough within the year to realize her mother's hopes by being presented at court. In a letter to her sister, Fanny wrote that she planned to put Parthe "in white satin covered with *tulle illusion* and ornamented with little pink hyacinths" and herself in either "mouse coloured satin with pink ribands or green watered silk with black lace." All the same, the noble Dr. Biddone's strictures about future health problems did not go unheeded by mother or daughter. From now on, in her own mind as well as others', Parthe was identified as a chronic invalid who expected to be cosseted. All of this would dramatically inflect the course of her own life and the life of her sister.

One year after Parthe entered the land of disease as patient, Florence confirmed her vocation as nurse. An outbreak of influenza raged at Embley and in the village of Wellow. Fanny, WEN, Bertha Smith, Gale, and fifteen servants fell sick, and for a time Florence and a cook were the only people available to care for the others in the house.[26] Flo wore herself thin, but in her letters to her sister, who was of course kept carefully away from the scene of infection, she sounds almost jubilant. On January 12, 1837, Florence writes to "my dear Pop" with a report of how she has been in charge of the household, has gone to bed at eight, got up at dawn, and been thoroughly busy and useful. She notes, "Gale has been most maternally careful of me & has been my playfellow besides." Flo told her sister that she had been studying hard, getting up at six or even five in the morning to work on her studies before the small children awoke.

While the influenza raged, evenings at Embley were unusually quiet and therefore much to Florence's taste: "Mama & I have been doomed to solitude & anxiety in February but we sing a duet of our own composition every evening to the tune of Nod, nod, nodding & Mama actually went to bed last night *before 10 o'clock*." More seriously, Flo also reported that one of the village children had been dreadfully burned. "Mama saw it today. It made some impression on our delinquents [i.e., the little Smith cousins] who eat cheese set for traps etc. etc. & then ask if it's poison."

It was on February 7, 1837, soon after the flu epidemic and the floods at Embley had stretched Florence Nightingale to the limit, that God spoke to her and called her to His service.

This we know not from the jaunty, chatty, comical letters she wrote at the time but from a private note that was written in 1867.[27] Even here, Nightingale, whose pen habitually flew over the page, makes no narrative, gives no details. That she heard her voices under the cedars of Lebanon in the park at Embley is an unconfirmed tradition.

There is no evidence that Nightingale told anyone about her experience at the time. In whom would she have confided—her skeptical, philosophical father, her fashionable, evangelical mother, her no-nonsense, new-German-criticism aunt Ju, her adoring but conventional sister? Perhaps Aunt Mai would understand, but even she might confide the story to someone else and then in no time the whole clan would be abuzz with the news that poor cousin Flo was hearing voices like some vulgar Mediterranean peasant.

Nightingale's mysticism is especially interesting since in 1837, when she claims first to have heard God's voice, she had next to no knowledge of the mystic tradition. The two major religious cultures that shaped Nightingale—enlightenment Unitarianism and latitudinarian Anglicanism—were both almost peculiarly alien to mysticism. This makes Florence Nightingale's experience all the rarer and more surprising, as she herself realized. Where Joan of Arc or Teresa of Avila were brought up in a culture profoundly inflected by a belief in visions and voices, any epiphanies Nightingale knew as a child would have been those in the Bible—the infant Samuel answering "Here am I, Lord," the Virgin Mary declaring herself the handmaid of the Lord to the angel. It was only in her late forties that Nightingale undertook a long, learned, and devout study of Catholic mystics like Angela of Foligno and John of the Cross.

She did so because she wished better to understand herself and also because she wanted to explain the great tradition of Christian mysticism to an ignorant and indifferent English public.

From 1836 onward, by her own account, Florence Nightingale was torn between her mystic conviction that God had personally chosen her and her inability to decide how to perform the service He demanded of her. Did God's service forbid or enjoin her to accept the traditional roles of wife and mother or, failing these, as daughter and sister?

DOING EUROPE
IN STYLE

I n 1834, William Edward Nightingale decided to seek election as Member of Parliament for Andover. The long years of Tory ascendancy were waning, so the moment seemed propitious for a man of WEN's strongly liberal views to come forward. The two Nightingale sisters were at Ryde on one of their chilly autumn seaside sojourns when they received a letter informing them of their father's candidacy. Parthenope went wild with joy. She knew just how much this electoral venture would appeal to her mother, especially as their father said that if elected he would buy a house in town, something Fanny had always wanted. While Florence too longed for her father to succeed, she was not tempted by life in London and feared losing her close relationship with him.[1]

As it turned out, Parthe's exuberance and Flo's dismay were both as short-lived as their father's political ambitions. Fired with enthusiasm for a broader-based electorate and an end to corruption at the polls, candidate Nightingale refused on principle to lay out the sums traditionally associated with elections in England. For their part, the electors of Andover, now slightly greater in number, were in no mood to give up the traditional perks of the voter, which they knew Mr. Nightingale could well afford. They declined to elect him.

The election of 1835 was the last that William Smith, Fanny's father, lived to see, and one wonders what the old abolitionist campaigner made of Nightingale's fine conscience. Smith had never hesitated to spend what it took to get elected, even if the money came out of his eldest son's pockets. But WEN was fired by ideas, not by ambition, and he had nothing in him of the tactician or the wheeler-dealer. Declaring he would never again submit to the indignity of a political campaign, he went back to his old pastimes.

For Fanny Nightingale, the defeat at Andover was a bitter pill to swallow. Parliament and politics were in her blood. London, when the Commons was sitting, was for her the only place to be. Had she been in charge of the Andover campaign, her husband would have won. Fanny had now to give up her dreams of becoming an influential London hostess, close to the political action, like her mother before the turn of the century. But never one to repine, Fanny bided her time, kept her social calendar full and her gowns fashionable while spinning a fine web to catch interesting and influential acquaintances. One day soon, Fanny trusted, Parthe and Flo would show their mettle, marry Members of Parliament or even lords, and carry on their mother's version of the great Smith political tradition.

IN THE SUMMER of 1837, when most of the Smiths were breathlessly following the family's electoral fortunes, the Nightingales were preparing to go abroad for a grand tour that would keep them from home for many months. Fanny's idea was to delay Florence's debut until their return and give both girls a patina of European sophistication. A Continental tour offered a combination of culture and exercise, self-improvement and entertainment, lonely reverie and high society that was synonymous with the Smith way of life. And it would be economical. For English people who lived and entertained on the scale of the Nightingales, European travel, even on the luxury level WEN envisaged, was cheaper than staying at home. While the Nightingales were away, Lea Hurst could be shut up or rented to friends. The house at Embley, which had begun to seem small and shabby now that the Nightingales were moving in such high circles, was to be extensively remodeled to accommodate more visitors and grander dinner parties on the family's return.

Parthenope and Florence were wild about the travel plans. For years the two sisters had been practicing their French, Italian, and German, memorizing historical facts, poring over old maps, and acquiring statistics about mountains, rivers, average rainfall, and currency exchange.

To accommodate his family party, WEN commissioned the building of a capacious vehicle, jam-packed with customized comforts and conveniences.[2] To his wife's distress, he refused to take his valet with him, but he did agree to hire a courier to assist in finding horses and accommodation. Fanny took along Thérèse, the latest in her succession of French maids, and also, rather against her better judgment, Mrs. Gale, her old nurse. Gale had seen enough of France and Italy to know that she did not like them. She had little use for any person not born within the British Isles, loathed foreign food, and found carriage travel a sad trial. At home, keeping an eye on the renovation work at Embley or maintaining a skeleton staff at Lea Hurst, Gale could have been both useful and comfortable. But the idea of being parted from her family for so many months was more than she could bear. She needed to feel needed by her darlings, and her distress at the prospective separation was so acute that Fanny included her in the party. Jolted, revolted, unmoved by chasm or cathedral, Gale could at least look forward to her return, when she would regale the other servants with tales of her second Grand Tour.

On September 8, 1837, the Nightingale party set out from Embley for nearby Southampton to take sail for Le Havre at night. Prone to seasickness and undaunted by the light drizzle falling over the English Channel, Florence prowled the decks. She listened avidly as a seaman told her about his experiences on the terrible night when the vessel *Amphitrite* went down off the coast of Boulogne. It was a prison ship, transporting 103 women convicts with 12 children to New South Wales, Australia. When the ship went aground on the sands, the captain refused to allow the women and children to be put aboard boats and taken to shore, for fear of blame if they should escape. All the prisoners were lost, within sight of land, and all the crew except three.[3] This was one of the first of many poignant anecdotes that Florence noted in her new travel diary.

Throughout her twenties, Florence Nightingale strongly resisted any attempt to make a writer of her, but her travel diaries, and some of her letters written from abroad, deserve inclusion in the canon of nineteenth-century English writing. Nightingale had a gift for landscape painting, lively anecdote, incisive analysis, and witty commentary. Unsatisfied with mere words, Florence did the odd sketch—she was a capable artist—and also kept statistics. She charted in columns the times the family set out and stopped for the day, the places they began and ended in, and the exact distance covered. Florence used her diary to keep her obsessive dreaming at bay over the long stretches of road when the weather was too bad for her to take her turn on top of the coach next to her father.

Fanny too kept a diary, and so did Parthe. In her journal Parthenope did more drawing than writing, and her finest work as an artist was done during this tour. Parthe's gift, I would say, was for landscapes and cityscapes, not portraits, and some of her first letters from abroad in 1837–38 have ink drawings of remarkable power.

Quite apart from the journals, during the eighteen months they were abroad, all four Nightingales were indefatigable letter writers. Patty and Julia Smith probably received more letters from the travelers than other members of the family. Between them, they had an address book that was a virtual who's who of intellectuals, reformers, and revolutionaries in France, Germany, Italy, and Switzerland, and they opened it wide for the Nightingales' service. Since Patty and Julia's connections contributed so much to the success of their tour, the Nightingales were careful to send back news.

The letters from the three Nightingale ladies were a joint enterprise. We find, for example, Fanny adding a postscript for her sister Joanna on a letter that Parthe wrote to Hilary. Obviously Fanny had the opportunity to read and comment on what her daughters had written, and even though a letter might be written from one cousin to another, it needed to pass muster with aunts and grandmothers too. When a letter from the Nightingales arrived, the titular recipient was expected to copy it out, or at least the best bits, and send it off to other family members and friends, rather as we might forward an interesting e-mail message today. This was the informal but highly efficient system that twenty years hence would carry news of Florence's doings in the Crimea to people all over the country.

The understanding among family members was that their letters should ultimately be returned to the Nightingales to complete the memorial of their journey. The Nightingale ladies' letters are chatty, comic, and well paced, and appear to be dashed off on the spur of the moment. This informal style had a long literary pedigree, however, and Fanny, Parthe, and Flo were consciously inspired by the famous letters of Madame de Sévigné and Madame de Genlis. In their letters to Marianne in particular, we can feel Florence and Parthenope striving for effect, expressing a sophistication that did not yet come naturally. Together with the personal diaries, these letters from abroad constituted a record of enlightened tourism that would duly go into the family archives alongside Frances Smith's diaries of Wales and Scotland in the 1780s or Benjamin Smith's carefully self-censored account of his travels in the United States in 1829–30. In 1849, Parthenope Nightingale would insist on issuing her sister's letters from Egypt in a private edition.

What we do not find much of in the letters to the cousins and aunties is confidences. Precisely because they are a shared project that aspires to the status of literature, the letters from Europe tell us little about the Nightingale women's intimate thoughts—how badly Florence was assailed by her dreaming, for example, or what impression Parthe was making on the young men she met at parties.

AFTER ARRIVING AT LE HAVRE, the Nightingales traveled through France, visiting Chartres, Blois, Tours, Nantes, Bordeaux, and Biarritz. They entertained some thought of going over the Pyrenees into Spain, and the family records offer a spirited account of the four traveling on horseback over slippery and precipitous mountain tracks in driving snow.[4] On this occasion even Parthe showed her share of Grandmother Smith's resilience, and was prepared to tackle very rough country, riding sidesaddle. But the Pyrenean region was desperately poor and racked by dynastic strife. Old women covered with flies sat in the street, children ran naked, old soldiers begged for food, and misery engendered passivity and cruelty. Repelled as much by the social conditions as by the bad food, dirty lodgings, and cold weather, the Nightingales came out of the mountains and back to the Mediterranean coast. In a tourist orgy of medieval fortress towns and Roman ruins, they visited Carcassonne, Nîmes, Avignon, and Toulon before settling down in Nice for Christmas and New Year.

Nice at that time was more Italian than French, a free port under the thumb of the kingdom of Piedmont. Here the Nightingale parents had spent some weeks of their honeymoon, and the family was rapturously received by the expatriate community. The girls had a thoroughly good time, though, as young sophisticates, they felt obliged to tell their cousins at home that the musical offerings were thin and the dancing partners distressingly consumptive. Parthe felt positively robust in comparison.

On January 7, the Nightingales moved from Nice toward Genoa, an ancient Mediterranean port then part of the kingdom of Piedmont. Florence was at first inconsolable at leaving so many new friends in Nice. She dutifully inscribed in her diary her impressions of the glorious views along the Mediterranean coast but insisted she could take no pleasure in them. Here Florence sounds refreshingly like a modern, sulky teenager. But she then fell deeply in love with "Genova la Superba," though her romance with the past did not prevent her from seeing the problems of the day. In her diary she noted the brand-new fort built to maintain order in the town and wondered how it could be true that of thirty thousand Genoese citizens, eight thousand were priests and eight thousand soldiers. A true disciple of her aunt Julia Smith, Florence made a point of visiting a Genoese institute for the deaf, noting the intelligence of the children, their sad eyes, and the cold, dirty rooms they lived in.

It was in Genoa that Florence first attended a performance of Donizetti's *Lucrezia Borgia* and turned overnight into an operamaniac. It appears that Florence and Parthenope were not taken to the opera as children, though their mother and maternal aunts certainly had been. But now in Italy Fanny happily gave her daughters the chance to see some of the greatest singers perform work by the greatest of modern composers. Here was a living tradition that bound three generations of women in the family together, since Fanny's maternal aunt Maria Coape was in her era an enthusiastic early admirer, and exponent, of the vocal music of Handel.

By the time the Nightingales arrived in Italy, works by Italian composers dominated the opera houses throughout Europe. Castration had long ceased to be an acceptable way in Europe to produce soprano voices for the professional stage (though not for the Vatican choir), and since the time of Mozart a class of female superstars had arisen, the divas— Giuditta Pasta, Isabella Colbran, Giulia Grisi, Adelaide Kemble, and perhaps the greatest of all, the sisters María García Malibran and Pauline García Viardot.[5]

A new opera in 1830 had more in common with the opening of *Oklahoma!*, *Tommy*, or *Evita* than with a Philip Glass premiere at the Metropolitan Opera house today. Top composers like Rossini, Donizetti, and Bellini were looking to create hits and make money as well as please the cognoscenti, and they had an international mass audience in mind.

The appeal of opera was not restricted to the small number of people who could attend live performances. This was a time when middle-class children practiced piano religiously every day, and the caliber of amateur musicianship was high. Sheet-music versions of operas and oratorios circulated widely, and arias and lieder were performed in parlors and drawing rooms all over Europe and North America. In 1836 when the Spanish diva María Malibran died in England of septicemia at the age of twenty-eight, fifty thousand people in Manchester followed her funeral cortege. Opera gave a tiny group of talented women power.

Florence took opera appreciation, like everything else, to new levels. In her notebook she listed the works she had seen in what theater, noted which roles were sung by which singers, and made detailed comments on the performances. She collected libretti and scores, committed whole operas to memory, and dedicated herself to singing lessons with her new Italian teachers with fresh zeal. My guess is that one of the dreams that played out in her imagination was of herself as a diva. Such dreams were of course absurd for a woman of her background.[6] In the first decades of the nineteenth century actresses and singers lived outside respectable society since even talented young women were obliged to rely on rich male protectors or to submit to the Victorian version of the casting couch.[7]

But Florence Nightingale's obsession with opera as a teenager, however short-lived, gives us a crucial clue to her nature. The opera stage was that rare place where a woman could use her talent to carve out a life for herself and be famous. Opera was the genre of passion and pleasure and torment, over and over again enacting the agon between attraction and repulsion, Eros and Thanatos. In an opera the female voice soared, triumphant even in death.

All too soon, Florence Nightingale was recalled in horror and self-rebuke from the world of the senses that opera represented. Once her birthplace Italy was left behind, swiftly Nightingale reminded herself that passion and pleasure were temptations and music a sin. In her brief 1851 autobiographical sketch she has this to say: "I had also the strongest taste for music. But God was merciful to me and took away my voice by constant sore throat. Otherwise I think, if I could have sung, I should have wished for no other satisfaction. Music excited my imagination and my passionate nature so much that I recognize this as a real blessing."[8]

IN MID-FEBRUARY OF 1838, WEN and Fanny felt the need to move on from Genoa. Their younger daughter was again extravagantly unhappy—opera, after all, had given her excellent lessons in picturesque despair—and sat grumbling in the carriage as the family traveled toward Pisa and then on to Florence. The Nightingales planned to spend the spring in Florence, and they found a magnificent set of rooms close to the Ponte Vecchio. Their suite included a salon fifty feet long, a superb dining room looking out onto the river Arno, and frescos on the bedroom walls with mythological themes that deliciously scandalized Gale.

Italian masters were as cheap as Italian lodgings, and in Florence Parthe and Flo settled down to work seriously at their accomplishments, taking lessons in music, drawing, and Italian. The family gave every church, palace, and *pinacoteca* its due, attended the opera three times a week, received tickets to all the most exclusive official events—including the viewing of the grand ducal camels—and hosted some successful soirées of their own. The weak ankles and steel boots of her childhood, the sad waltzing with Miss Christie when it was too wet to walk out—all this was forgotten, and Florence was now an accomplished and tireless dancer. Fanny was gratified to see how much her younger daughter was admired.

In Italy, Florence Nightingale became infected with the revolutionary virus that had already, in the eyes of the world, addled the wits of her aunts Patty and Julia. She became an enthusiastic supporter of the Risorgimento movement, which sought to rid Italy of foreign hegemony in the north, papal corruption in the center, and royal decadence in the south. The city of Florence languished under the heel of the Austrian tyrant, to use the language of the day, and foreigners of advanced political views like the Nightingales had to tread carefully. Even some of the histories they were reading—parts of Sismondi's mammoth *History of the Italian Republics* and Guerazzi's *Siege of Florence*—were officially banned by the Tuscan authorities.

The Nightingale family's interest in the cause of Italian unity and independence was, somewhat paradoxically, sharpened when in the summer of 1838 they moved to Switzerland. They took up residence in Geneva and found that the Swiss city was home to many illustrious Italian exiles. Members of wealthy families had been forced to leave their estates in Italy behind and now lived in poverty. In her diary Florence ardently recorded the histories of men and women she and her family were introduced to. Confalonieri had been chained up in solitary confinement for fifteen years and learned of the death of his wife only on his release. He still walked with a limp. Ricciardi, a Neapolitan aristocrat, had been locked up in a madhouse in an attempt to break his mind and health. For the first time, Florence Nightingale was meeting people who suffered for their political views, and the contrast with the idle indifference of high English society impressed her forcibly.

Geneva, the city of Calvin and stern stronghold of the Protestant faith, was as full of serious scholarship and high idealism as Florence was full of Renaissance art, romantic music, and aristocratic revelry. WEN and Florence in particular felt at home in Geneva. WEN had made a prolonged stay in Geneva before his marriage and had friends there, but his most important acquaintance in the city was a Swiss of Italian origin whom he had met in England, Jean-Charles-Léonard de Sismondi. This gentleman was an ugly, gnomelike man, but the liveliness of his spirits, the generosity of his temperament, and the brilliance of his intellect overcame the deficiencies in his physique.

Sismondi was known throughout Europe as a political economist, and his *New Principles of Political Economy* (1819) had attempted to move beyond Adam Smith and David Ricardo. Sismondi was anxious to consider how a nation's wealth might best be spent once acquired, a question that could not have interested Florence Nightingale more. "All [Sismondi's] political economy seems to be founded on the overflowing kindness of his heart," wrote Florence in her diary in 1838. "He gives to old beggars on principle, to young from habit. At Pescia he had 300 beggars at his door on one morning. He feeds the mice in his room while he is writing his histories."[9] After publishing the sixteenth and last volume of his history of the Italian republics in 1819, Sismondi engaged to write an even more vast history of the French people. By the time of his death in 1842 he had completed twenty-nine volumes. Sismondi was a mine of information on almost any topic, and in Florence Nightingale he found the ideal listener.

One other Italian exile in Geneva made an impression on Florence—the poetess and journalist Madame Ferucci, a character worthy of both de Staël and Dickens. Equipped with a decorative, idle aristocrat of a husband and a holy terror of a daughter, this lady was forced to support the family herself by giving Italian lessons to "*grandi asinoni*" (big fat donkeys) of Swiss. Florence was fascinated by La Ferucci's operatic temperament and her creative talents, so strangely at odds with her material circumstances. Imagine Germaine de Staël's superb heroine Corinne, rescued from death and tragedy but now dressed in a dirty wrapper and living in squalor on the fourth floor of a third-rate boardinghouse. What especially amazed Florence was Signora Ferucci's incompetence as a housekeeper. She was quite unable to keep a clean house, order a good dinner, or discipline her child, and saw no reason to learn. Life was too precious for such trivia, and guests came to her house for her, not the food. Florence, already a pattern of organization and efficiency at eighteen, found casa Ferucci infuriating yet instructive.

A political crisis drove the Nightingales out of Switzerland and into France. By the late fall of 1838 the Nightingales were established in a magnificent apartment on the Place Vendôme in Paris, eye to eye with the emperor Napoleon on his column. It was in Paris, on this the final leg of their grand tour, that the Nightingales made the most important friend of the whole trip, Miss Mary Clarke. Clarkey, as the Nightingales came to call her, was one of the most fascinating women of her generation, and like so many others, a friend of Aunt Patty. For over forty years, the home of Miss Mary Clarke, later Madame Mohl, was the meeting place of choice for brilliant and influential people from all over the world.[10]

In 1838 when the Nightingales arrived in Paris, Mary Clarke was forty-five, though she hated to admit it even to herself. She had recently moved with her invalid mother into a large apartment on the third and fourth floors of the Clermont-Tonnerre mansion at 120 rue du Bac, the same building inhabited, not incidentally, by Monsieur and Madame de Chateaubriand.[11] Mary Clarke would not have offended Patty Smith for the world. All the same, the prospect of the Nightingale family filled her with gloom. Mr. Nightingale, a civilized man from all accounts, might

be able to hold his own with Guizot, Hugo, Mérimée, Ampère, and the
rest, but the ladies, she felt sure, would never do. Though born to a Scottish mother and Irish father, Mary Clarke had lived almost all her life in
France, and found England a cultural backwater and English gentlewomen a strain. As she saw it, English ladies were obsessed with sexual
shibboleths and accustomed to being both physically cosseted and intellectually snubbed by their menfolk.[12] The mothers talked all the time,
and the daughters rarely opened their mouths. The first duty of a successful *salonnière,* Mary Clarke knew, was to keep meritorious but boring
people at bay.

Thus Clarkey's first invitation was for the Nightingale ladies to attend a party she gave for children every Saturday night between eight and
eleven. In such a gathering the visitors' presumed conversational lacunae
would not gape too wide. As Parthenope Verney was later to recall in an
affectionate tribute, she and her mother and sister were rather bemused
when they arrived at the Clarkes' apartment for the first time to find a
group of small children and elderly gentlemen playing a vigorous game
of blindman's buff in the double drawing room. By the fire, two gentlemen, who turned out to be the famous Oriental languages scholar Julius
Mohl and the equally famous expert in comparative European literature
Claude Fauriel, were preoccupied with getting the teakettle boiling.
Deep in the game was a tiny, disheveled whirlwind of a woman whom
the Nightingales correctly assumed to be the celebrated Miss Clarke. Fortunately, Florence proved a standout at blindman's buff, and the Nightingale ladies passed the children's party test with flying colors.

That season of 1838–39 the Nightingales were Miss Clarke's special
pets, almost as dear as her Persian cats. She took them everywhere and
introduced them to everyone who was anyone. They were even taken, as
a supreme favor, to the home of the legendary Madame Juliette Récamier
at l'Abbaye-aux-Bois and heard Chateaubriand declaim from his
Mémoires d'outre-tombe. Today, at the beginning of the twenty-first century, literati are so rarely hot tickets that it is difficult to find a suitably
momentous equivalent to this event. It was also probably in Madame
Récamier's rooms that the Nightingales heard a private dramatic reading
given by the seventeen-year-old actress Rachel. A small, skinny girl,
daughter to impoverished Jewish itinerants, Rachel that summer had
made her sensational debut at the Comédie-Française in Pierre

Corneille's *Horace*. Between 1838 and her death from consumption in 1858, she managed to revolutionize the performance of classical tragedy much as Giuditta Pasta had done for opera a few years earlier.[13]

MISS CLARKE LIVED with her invalid mother, a lady who had been told by her doctors years before that she must never again risk her health by stepping out of doors. Mrs. Clarke followed this advice and lived to see ninety-two. Mrs. Clarke in turn had lived for much of her life with her mother, Mrs. Hall, a lady born into the Edinburgh intelligentsia, related to the minor Scottish nobility, and possessed, it appears, of an income that enabled her to eke out an independent life abroad. Mrs. Clarke had two daughters, and when in 1801 she and Mr. Charles Clarke decided to separate, the parting was amicable. Eleanor, the elder daughter, went to live with her father in England, while Mary, a young tomboy of eight or nine, stayed with her mother and grandmother in France. The division between the English/male and French/female sides of the Clarke family was perpetuated when at twenty-two Eleanor Clarke married Frewen Turner, M.P., a neighbor in his fifties who had fallen madly in love with her. Mr. Frewen Turner was a man of substance, the owner of Cold Overton in Leicestershire, one of the most perfect Tudor houses in England, and other property, and a pattern of the Tory, Evangelical squire. Until her sister's death, Mary Clarke went each year to spend a month or two at Cold Overton. She loved the place, she told Hilary Bonham-Carter in a letter, because "the total absence of incident leaves me more leisure for my dreamy life than I have anywhere else."[14] Dreaming was one of the things that brought Clarkey and Florence together.

   The lovely Eleanor Clarke Turner was quiet and dignified. Her little sister, Mary, was quite the opposite. Her grandmother Mrs. Hall used to say of her as a girl, "Mary, you are as impudent as a highway man's horse." She attributed the successes of her adult life to the fact that her mother never snubbed her as a child. Mary Clarke liked to recall how, as a young woman, she had been so consumed by a desire to meet the great Madame de Staël that she had bluffed her way into the lady's presence, pretending to apply for the position of governess. Passionately fond of animals and an early crusader for animal rights, Mary Clarke once waded waist-high into a pond to hold up the head of a drowning sheep and then made sure that the dog that had worried the sheep went unpunished. As an elderly woman she on one occasion threw herself down on the ground in hysterics in front of a carriage when the coachman started brutally flogging his horses. Miss Clarke "had never a breath of posing or of 'edifying' in her presentation of herself," Florence Nightingale wrote. "She was always undressed—naked in full view. A little clothing would have been decent."[15]

The Hall-Clarke trio successfully negotiated life in France during the Revolution, and they moved to Paris after Mr. Clarke's death in 1813. Money was tight, but already writers, politicians, artists, and scientists were finding that it was pleasant to spend an evening in the apartment of the charming and disarming Scottish ladies. Being a Presbyterian in Paris made Mary Clarke somewhat exotic, and her wit and frankness endeared her to everyone. "Her great charm lay in the absence of it," wrote her friend Jean-Jacques Ampère. "I never knew a woman so devoid of charm in the ordinary sense of the word and yet so fascinating. She was hardly a woman at all."[16]

However, the key to Miss Clarke's success as a cultural hostess, or *salonnière,* was the friendship that developed between her and Juliette Récamier, one of the most fascinating and notorious women of her generation. Born Jeanne Françoise Julie Adélaïde Bernard, Madame Récamier (1777–1849), like that earlier great beauty the Marquise de Pompadour (née Poisson), was a daughter of the rising French commercial and administrative class. The fortunes of families like the Bernards and Poissons depended heavily on the favor of the royal family and the nobility, and beautiful, witty, obliging married women were often the key to securing that favor.

In the years before and after the Terror Madame Récamier had one of the most brilliant salons in Paris, but when she first met Mary Clarke in about 1820 she was a widow in reduced circumstances. She occupied several suites of rooms in a former convent on the outskirts of Paris called l'Abbaye-aux-Bois and continued to welcome an illustrious group of politicians, writers, and savants to her salon.

As Mary Clarke Mohl would later describe it in her 1862 book on French culture, the lady leading the salon did little of the talking herself, though at times personal opinions had the habit of coming out. "One's opinions are the most troublesome, noisy, snarling dogs I know," she once wrote to Hilary Bonham-Carter. "It is like having a pack of hounds in a handsome bedroom when one is visiting, and striving to keep them down, shutting doors and windows that they may not be heard, and now and then an awful 'bow-wow' bursts out!"[17] The *salonnière*'s job was first of all to be charming, to create a space where people were comfortable, to get the conversational ball rolling, and to make sure no one was humiliated. Men were the stars in the salon since men ran the world and necessarily had the most to say about it. But men were not allowed to be bores. Anyone admitted to the salon was expected to say something interesting, but no one grandstanded.

After the death of Mrs. Hall and a disastrous lawsuit, the Clarke ladies had severe financial difficulties and Madame Récamier offered to sublet to them at very modest rates a large suite of rooms she had on the first floor of the convent. The Clarkes moved in 1831 and stayed at l'Abbaye-Aux-Bois until 1838, when they moved in next to the Chateaubriands. Throughout this period, Miss Clarke and her mother received friends every evening, and Mary gradually took over from Madame Récamier as the reigning *salonnière*. In the Clarke salon French was the common language, but since so many of the guests were foreign and many were redoubtable linguists, English, Italian, German, Russian, Polish, and more exotic tongues could be heard. In the early days Benjamin Constant and Germaine de Staël, the Marquis de Lafayette and Alexis de Tocqueville could be seen. Later Victor Hugo and Prosper Mérimée came by from time to time, as well as Anthony Trollope and his famous mother, Frances Trollope, Elizabeth Gaskell, Ivan Turgenev and William Thackeray.

Apart from Madame Récamier, Mary Clarke had a number of other women friends who came regularly. One of these was Louise Swanton, a young French writer whose serene beauty, often compared to that of a Raphael Madonna, caused a sensation. Mary Clarke was "especially captivated" by Louise Swanton, who was forced to choose between Mary and another friend, Adélaïde de Montgolfier. "Deformed of person, but of a most amiable, affectionate disposition," writes Simpson, "Adelaide clung with ardent affection to her beautiful friend [Miss Swanton], sharing her literary labours, and leaving no room for any other close friendship."[18] Later, when Mademoiselle Swanton became Madame Belloc and Mary Clarke became Madame Mohl, she and Louise papered over their differences.

Here we have an example of passionate friendship among women and of how openly and unself-consciously it was discussed in the Victorian era. In fact, the intimate group clustered around Mary Clarke had a pattern of famously intense yet oddly unrequited and thus chaste love. Everyone knew that young Ampère, the rising comparatist and son of the famous scientist, worshipped the ground on which Madame Récamier walked, though she was almost old enough to be his mother and cared only for Chateaubriand. Ampère lived for many years in happy bachelor squalor with Orientalist Julius von Mohl, who silently adored Miss Clarke.

Miss Clarke nursed a passion for Claude Fauriel, an extraordinarily handsome man, another comparatist, this time specializing in modern Greek poetry and medieval Provençal and Italian literature.[19] Mary and Fauriel exchanged letters of great physical passion at first. She was clearly aroused by his embraces and anxious to become his wife.[20] He was an accustomed seducer and was far from unattracted by her. But, even though by the standards of her fanatically religious English family Mary Clarke put her reputation in danger, she seems never to have yielded to him, and he accused her of being a "stick." In certain ways, Mary Clarke was still much more British than French, and what she wanted was marriage.

Mary Clarke's most assiduous suitor, after the politician Thiers gave up hope, was Julius Mohl, a man some twelve years her junior. But Mohl's passion for Miss Clarke did not prevent him from enjoying the company of Fauriel each evening. When Fauriel died in 1844, not only Miss Clarke but also Mohl was inconsolable. Mohl wrote to Manzoni that he was "crazy with grief," that he had loved Fauriel "more than all the world besides," and was "suffering from his death more than anyone else."[21]

One of the secrets of the success of Miss Clarke's salon was that beneath the surface of urbane debate, learned speculation, and witty gossip lay a certain rich ambiguity, a sexual tension created by a combination of passion, sensibility, intelligence, and celibacy. Mary Clarke called it "amitié amoureuse." The Anglo-French microcosm of loving friendship she created played itself out against the notorious Paris world of child prostitutes, cabaret, and absinthe bars we know from Balzac and Baudelaire, Toulouse-Lautrec and Degas.

One literary lion Mary Clarke did not invite to her salon at the Rue du Bac was Amandine Aurore Dupin, Baroness Dudevant. This lady had left her husband and two small children behind in the provinces in the early 1830s and established herself as a journalist and novelist in Paris. Under the pen name of George Sand, she had by 1839 published a series of scandalous bestsellers whose heroines (Indiana, Lelia, Mauprat, Valentine), flamboyant, cross-dressing, promiscuous, frigid, women-loving artists, made an indelible impression on women everywhere.[22] Mary Clarke did not meet George Sand in society, but she knew a great deal about her. She knew that George Sand had taken for a time to wearing a boy's long coat and iron-heeled boots so that she could walk the boulevards alone, swift, comfortable, unmolested. She knew Sand was the mistress of several men, including the poet Alfred de Musset and the composer Frédéric Chopin, and that she was the intimate friend of the novelist Marie d'Agoult.

Mary Clarke read Sand's novels avidly and recommended them to her new friends the Nightingales. In the great Smith tradition of cultural radicalism, Fanny raised no objections to her daughters reading the work of this notorious woman. Thus in the fall of 1839 we find Florence Nightingale mentioning in a letter to her sister, Parthenope, that she is reading Sand's newly published work *Gabriel* and is anxious to discuss it with her when they are next together. *Gabriel* is the story of an aristocratic girl who is brought up as a boy so that she can inherit a dukedom that, under French Salic law, was restricted to male heirs. This fictional premise was sure to intrigue the Nightingale sisters, who themselves were barred from inheriting their father's estate. Gabriel loves the independence of her male life but she falls passionately in love with her cousin and is willing to sacrifice everything, her fortune, her title, her reputation, if only he will tell her unequivocally that he loves her. As so often in George Sand, the heroine is passionate, brilliant, athletic, decisive, single-minded, and loyal, while the male she loves is charming, fickle, and unreliable.

Sadly for us, Florence was too prudent to commit to paper what she thought of Gabriel and of George Sand, but one can see how Sand's fiction would have nourished her dreams. Sand's decision to break with family ties, rely on her own wits, and earn her own living was an inspiration. How marvelous to stride around London without a male servant or relative, or to travel without a fidgety old Miss Johnson!

FROM THE TIME of their meeting in 1838, Mary Clarke was a key person in the lives of the Nightingales and all four carried on a lively correspondence with her and later with her husband, Julius Mohl.[23] For WEN, Clarkey was an ideal woman, civilized but not chic, frank but kind, intelligent yet unpretentious, original but not radical. At the rue du Bac WEN encountered the kind of men who interested him, men willing to make a point and argue back, men who could satisfy his curiosity about what, really, was going on in the world. In later years, asked once why he had not gone to Paris as planned, WEN replied simply that Madame Mohl was ill. Paris without her made no sense. For Fanny and Parthenope, Mary Clarke Mohl was a wise, loving, amusing friend, someone they took counsel from, someone they looked forward to seeing at Embley or Lea Hurst for several weeks almost every year. Fanny and Parthe both aspired to practice the ancient female art of the salon that their friend had perfected.

For Florence, Clarkey represented a phenomenon too complex easily to assimilate, and she developed for Clarkey one of the passions for which she was famous in the family. Florence had no wish to live as Miss Clarke lived, but she saw that Clarkey was managing spinsterhood better than Patty or even Julia. The loving, supportive, yet chaste triangle between Fauriel, Mohl, and Miss Clarke was a model of male-female relationships that both Florence and her cousin Hilary Bonham-Carter were drawn to. Florence and Clarkey had much in common. They were both intelligent, acerbic, and energetic, impatient with artifice and convention. They shared a love of literature, art, music, and animals, as well as a disdain for dressing up and fancy hairstyles. Each had a remarkable way with words, in several languages. They both rebelled against women's traditional roles and had a love-hate relationship with their mothers. Clarkey once wrote to her would-be lover Fauriel that she felt like a galley slave shackled to her mother, that she wished she could be a man, "live in the public eye, and work for the public good, and have a busy life, instead of sitting by the fireside imagining."[24] These were things Florence herself could have written and which she and Clarkey surely discussed when tête à tête.

Yet there were also important differences between the two women. Religious faith did not play a great part in Miss Clarke's life, and she had no desire to enter a convent or give up the world of the flesh. Living in France, the most openly libertine country in the world, Clarkey knew things Florence had no wish to know. Clarkey had felt the stirrings of passion even if she had not yielded to it. Florence had yet to experience such things. Above all, Clarkey dreamed of influence, Florence dreamed of power.

Chapter 8

COMING OUT

T he remodeling of Embley Park was far from complete when the four Nightingales returned to England in April of 1839. On the exterior of the house, fuddy-duddy Georgian had given way to nouveau Tudoresque—no half-timbering, let me hasten to add—but the new rooms were unfinished and the rest uninhabitable. Fanny frothed at the unreliability of builders, but fortunately the family had expected to spend the months of May and June in town for the London season—Florence's first. In between the morning visits, afternoon musicales, and evening parties, Fanny found time for shopping. She had long been weighing different color schemes for the new Embley. In the magnificent drawing room, could fawn walls with gold moldings be reconciled with a sky-blue ceiling, the superb yellowish green carpet specially commissioned by the Nightingales from the Axminster company, and the sofas covered in crimson damask?[1] Fanny decided that they could. And while she toured the capital's emporia, WEN had fun of his own. The transformation of Embley was a project that appealed to him, and he was not unhappy to be on site to superintend its final stages, even if Fanny did keep nagging about the ivy.

Meanwhile, Florence found herself whirling about in the eddies of a London debutante season. Whether she liked it or not, once she had made her courtesy to the Queen, Florence was entered in the marital stakes, and her mother and father were determined to give their talented but balky young filly the best possible run. Together with the Nicholsons, whose eldest daughter, Marianne, was also making her debut that season, the Nightingales took over a whole floor of the Carlton Hotel on

Regent Street, noisy but in the heart of London. Armed as they were with the latest news from Europe on almost any subject—Paris fashions, Italian revolutionaries, Chinese science, Provençal love lyrics, Lobachevski's post-Euclidean geometry, Rossini's unaccountable retirement from opera—the Nightingales were gloriously in demand.

One thing Fanny accomplished soon after landing was to commission William White to do a painting of her two daughters. Sadly, White was not in the same class as Zoffany and Opie, who did portraits of earlier generations in the family. Florence on her high-backed chair seems to be in a living room, but Parthe is posed near a stone balustrade against either an inside wall sadly in need of repair or an ill-rendered sky. Yet by its very awkwardness this picture shows us how Fanny liked to see her daughters.

The two young ladies in the picture are more maidenly than alluring, their figures small, slender, and flat-chested. Both Nightingale sisters had ball gowns from Paris, but for their portrait they wear day dresses, high-necked, high-waisted, long-sleeved, lace-collared, almost Puritan in style, and identical except that Parthe's dress is gold and Flo's is reddish pink. The main fashion feature of the dresses is the sleeves, low on the shoulder, elaborately puffed to the elbows, and then tight over the forearms.[2] Both girls are bareheaded, their smooth dark brown hair decorously parted in the middle and coiled high at the back of their heads, exposing the ears and neck. Parthenope looks out of the picture full face, her slim hands holding a book toward her sister. Florence is sitting, her eyes cast down, one narrow foot extended from the folds of her dress. She is wearing black half mittens and a striped apron and is intent upon a piece of elaborate embroidery.[3]

The two sisters could easily be taken for identical twins. Not only do they wear the same dress and put up their hair in the same way, but their bodies and faces are almost interchangeable. Parthe has perhaps the rounder face, but like her sister she has a rosebud mouth, small neat nose, smooth long neck, and dainty hands. This doppelgänger effect is not entirely the painter's whimsy. Parthenope and Florence Nightingale in youth did look a good deal alike. All the same, the White painting is deceptive since we know that Florence was bigger than her sister and widely viewed as more attractive. Physical differences that were to play an important part in the lives of both women are denied in this portrait.

The Nightingale family papers are reticent on the subject of Parthenope's looks, in part because they did not write about appearance in general, in part because they loved her and sought to spare her feelings. Parthe, I think it safe to assume, was plain, and sadly conscious of it. From the little information we have, Parthenope Nightingale was a small, brown-haired woman who had not inherited her mother's elegant figure and glowing complexion. Persistent ill health kept her thin, undeveloped, and sickly-looking. Though she had the consumptive's cough, she did not have the ethereal, seductive delicacy of such young women as Ellen Tucker Emerson, Virginia Clemm Poe, and Lizzy Siddal Rossetti. Miss Nightingale was not the kind of girl who looked to advantage in a low-cut evening dress or who was likely to find a husband in a crowded ballroom. When seated next to a healthy, blooming girl like her cousin Marianne Nicholson, Parthe faded into the wainscoting. I have found no reference in the family papers to Parthe ever having a beau or falling in love until the elderly widower Harry Verney came on the scene in 1857.

Miss Florence Nightingale did not particularly resemble her beautiful mother either. Moreover, where Parthenope from early childhood had been outgoing, sociable, and anxious to please, Florence was farouche, taking refuge from visitors whenever she could. But Flo had outgrown her youthful ill health. She was strong enough now to ride to hounds with her father and, if permitted, to lope the hilly miles through the fields to her great-aunt's house at Cromford. Florence's face was plump and round, her complexion good. She had beautifully white, even teeth and a charming smile, and when she was young her hair—such an important feature for women of this period, as so many Pre-Raphaelite paintings show—was thick and red-gold.[4] If she took trouble with her dress, Flo could more than pass muster in ballroom or drawing room, and one of Parthenope's roles as a loving sister was to badger Flo to wear the right frock or the right bonnet. For all her shyness, Flo, when she chose, could more than hold her own with the Marianne Nicholsons of the world. Flo attracted notice without, apparently, wanting it, and when she emerged from her shell and talked, she held men and women in the palm of her hand.

A poem Ada Byron Lovelace wrote about Florence records the effect she had on people. Ada was six years Florence's senior, but the two moved in much the same circles as girls since their mothers were friends. In 1847, Florence and her father were invited to spend a few days at the home of the Lovelaces, and according to Cecil Woodham-Smith, Ada had a "passion" for Florence.[5] Ada Lovelace, not incidentally the daughter of the poet Byron, handed round a set of verses in which she celebrated her friend's superior qualities and challenged the world to give Florence the admiration she merited:

> I saw her pass, and paused to think!
> She moves as one on whom to gaze
> With calm and holy thoughts, that link
> The soul to God in prayer and praise.
> She walks as if on heaven's brink,
> Unscathed thro' life's entangled maze.
>
> I heard her soft and silver voice
> Take part in songs of harmony,
> Well framed to gladden and rejoice;
> Whilst her ethereal melody
> Still kept my soul in wav'ring choice
> Twixt smiles and tears of ecstasy.
>
> I deem her fair,—yes, very fair!
> Yet some there are who pass her by,
> Unmoved by all the graces there.
> Her face doth raise no burning sigh,
> Nor hath her slender form the glare
> Which strikes and rivets every eye.
>
> Her grave, but large and lucid eye
> Unites a boundless depth of feeling
> With Truth's own bright transparency,
> Her singleness of heart revealing;
> But still her spirit's history
> From light and curious gaze concealing.[6]

This is a fascinating tribute from one brilliant and troubled young mid-Victorian woman to another.

To return to the watercolor portrait, I see the directive hand of Fanny Nightingale here. I think she had decided that this late teenage portrait should stress the likeness, not the difference, between her two girls. Parthe, the elder but smaller girl, would be made the dominant figure, placed with a book in her hand to connote the intellectual life. Florence would be shown in apron and mittens, her eyes cast down, attentive to her handwork, a model of female serenity and domesticity. In the portrait at least, Flo, that brilliant and dedicated scholar, that cool yet fiery presence, would play Martha to her sister's Mary. It was all highly ironic, as Flo's debutante season soon proved.

AS A SHY, awkward child Florence had dreaded the prospect of coming out, and in later years she still felt her "courage fall into her shoes" as she walked into a fashionable drawing room.[7] But when it turned out that she was not a young woman who picked up the wrong gold fork at dinner parties or tripped over her train as she backed away from the Queen, Florence was understandably relieved. People in London seemed to like her just as they had in Genoa or Paris, and despite all her resolutions, Florence yielded once again to the temptation of shining in society.[8]

Fanny Nightingale and her sister Anne Nicholson had long planned to have their daughters Flo and Marianne presented at the same time, and the success of the plan exceeded everyone's expectation. A passion for opera, especially, brought the two cousins together during their debutante months and set them apart from other girls. Florence explained this to her new friend in Paris, Mary Clarke: "As Marianne Nicholson is as music-mad as I am, we are revelling in music all day long. Schulz, who is a splendid player, and Crivelli, her singing master, give us lessons, and the unfortunate piano has been strummed out of tune in a week, not even having its natural rest at night, as there are other masters as well." As the two girls played and sang together, the newly permissive mamas beamed to have so much maidenly beauty and energy on display, and the fathers delighted in seeing their favorite daughters admired, even if the bill for singing masters and hotel pianos was rather steep.

Florence had always felt Marianne's magnetism. When they were very young, the two had shared a private language until Flo's guilt at having secrets from her mama compelled her to give it up.[9] Florence was both fascinated and worried by Marianne's ebullience, her talent for holding center stage and getting what she wanted. Marianne, age eight or nine, could use things like a supply of embroidery silks to reward her favorites and make the others jealous. When little Flo was given some silks of her own, she was tempted to follow Marianne's example, and then felt noble for resisting.[10] As she grew into adulthood Marianne Nicholson was an intoxicating presence, charming her father, dominating her mother, the darling of the large, deeply self-absorbed Nicholson clan.[11] Beautiful, confident, conventional, she was a nineteenth-century alpha girl, the cousin whom all the others in the family vied to be friends with and longed to be like.[12]

How delicious it was for Florence to now find marvelous Marianne accepting her as equal and bosom friend. Suddenly they were sharing the spotlight, playing off each other's strengths and contriving a capital performance. Both girls had the right frocks, the right manners, the right invitations. Both were witty and entertaining, and if Marianne was more handsome and outgoing, Florence's fervent mind impressed people. So Florence made a success of her debutante season, and when Flo condescended to shine, everyone around her was able to relax and enjoy life.

THE YEAR WHEN Florence was presented at court was especially exciting for the upper ten thousand who ruled England. Le tout Londres was aflutter when Prince Albert of Saxe-Coburg-Gotha returned to En-gland for a second, even more carefully orchestrated visit to his cousin the Queen of England. Victoria had come to the throne two years earlier, and Florence Nightingale accurately described her to Clarkey as "vibrating between popularity and unpopularity."[13] The young Queen was charting an erratic path through her royal duties. As a second Virgin Queen, Victoria was problematic, and to her advisors, especially her maternal uncle Leopold of Saxe-Coburg-Saalfeld, newly King of the Belgians, finding Victoria the right husband was imperative. But Victoria was reveling in her new independence and in no hurry to marry.

Victoria's distaste for marriage melted away once she took a second look at her cousin Albert. The Saxe-Coburg men were famous for their beauty, as any visitor to Buckingham Palace today can verify from the portraits that line the walls there. In the years since Victoria had last seen him, Albert had been transformed from a gawky, pedantic adolescent to a tall, elegant, accomplished man. *Coups de foudre* happen in life as well as novels, and within days Victoria, as protocol demanded, proposed marriage. Albert, a dutiful son to his ambitious ducal house, stoically accepted her proposal, and the wedding day was set.

The news of Victoria's marriage riveted the nation. It was all so very romantic, especially for young girls like Parthenope Nightingale. Parthe was exactly the same age as the Queen, and a royal wedding, with its combination of simple vows, plain gold rings, princely pomp, and high fashion, could not have been more interesting to her. Thus it was a little sad for Parthe to find herself in the country in February and having to rely on Flo in London to send her all the latest details about Victoria and her prince—of how, for example, the young queen had cast protocol to the winds and thrown herself into the arms of her betrothed when he arrived at the palace for the wedding.[14]

The Nightingales, as it turned out, were exhilaratingly well placed to get the latest in court gossip. William Smith, Fanny's father, it may be remembered, had been a member of the King of Clubs with Prime Minister Melbourne when he was still the Honourable William Lamb, and the Nightingales, Smiths, Bonham-Carters, and Nicholsons were part of the resurgent Whig party network. WEN and Fanny counted many Members of Parliament and royal equerries among their friends. James Clarke, whom Victoria had chosen for her personal physician, was one of WEN's friends.

After 1842, when the Tories under Mr. Peel were back in office, the Nightingale family continued to be well informed about the royal household, notably through their new friends the Bunsens and the Palmerstons. Lord Palmerston had been foreign minister under the Whigs, and Lady Palmerston knew everyone who was anyone. Christian Bunsen, the Prussian minister in London, and his English wife, Frances, were part of the intimate circle that formed protectively around the new German Prince Consort. Both couples were on dining-out terms with the Nightingales and took an immense interest in Miss Florence Nightingale. Thus around 1845 Flo was able to gossip knowledgeably to her cousin Hilary and others not only about the Palmerstons, whom she had been staying with, but about the Queen.

This letter, which has Florence chatting amusingly to the fabulously rich and influential Lady Ashburton, gives a good sense of just how Florence Nightingale could shine in society when she had a mind to.

[Lady Ashburton] is an American and we swore eternal friendship upon Boston; I having, you know, much curious information to give *her* upon that city and its inhabitants.[15] She had a raspberry tart of diamonds upon her forehead worth seeing. Then Mesmerism, and when we parted, we had got up so high in *Vestiges* that I could not get down again and was obliged to go off as an angel. The Ashburtons were the only people asked to meet the Queen at Strathsfieldsaye (of her society). It was the most entire crash ever heard of, and the not asking the Palmerstons considered almost a personal insult; but they say the old Duke [i.e., Wellington] now cares for nothing but flattery, and asks nobody but masters of hounds. He almost ill-treated the Speaker. After dinner they all stood at their ease about the drawing-room, and behaved like so many soldiers on parade. The Queen did her best to enliven the gloom, but was at last overpowered by numbers, gagged, and her hands tied. The only amusement was seeing Albert taught to miss at billiards.[16]

For young English ladies like Parthenope and Florence, to have a female monarch of their own age was exciting. They followed Victoria's life closely and were anxious for her to succeed in what they knew to be an exacting life. In some obscure way, this small, dumpy, rather ditsy young woman signified new opportunities for women. Victoria was to be an adoring wife and the reluctant mother to a horde of children, but she also had a demanding job and a multifaceted public role to play. This made her especially interesting to ambitious young women like Florence Nightingale. As the royal marriage ripened over the years, as fears for German influence on English politics waned, Albert, whose intelligence and integrity matched his good looks, became Victoria's chief advisor, principal private secretary, and emissary. Their marriage was a partnership, symbolized by the entwined *V*'s and *A*'s that decorated their homes. All the same, no one was in any doubt about who was monarch and who consort. The international power of Great Britain and its growing empire demanded a reversal of sexual hierarchy, and Victoria made it seem normal.

A loving, fruitful partnership between husband and wife may have been new to the British monarchy, but to families of Dissenting tradition like the Nightingales it was familiar. Of course, Prince Albert had to have irreproachably blue bloodlines to win the hand of a queen, but culturally he was a middle-class meritocrat. For ambitious mothers like Fanny Nightingale, Albert of Saxe-Coburg-Gotha represented a new "beau idéal" that put the Lord Byrons and Viscount Chateaubriands of the Romantic era in the shade. What Fanny wanted for her daughters was a scaled-down version of the Prince Consort, a handsome, intelligent, educated, chaste young man, as suitable in the eyes of the world as he was lovable in the eyes of his intended. One day, Fanny was sure, Florence would look into the eyes of some young man and her resistance to marriage would melt away as Victoria's had done.

Florence too, from what she tells us in the 1851 "Cassandra" fragment, dreamed throughout her twenties of finding a "phantom companion of her fancy." This person would be a soul mate to whom she could pour out all her thoughts and aspirations, someone who would work selflessly with her to do great things, rather as Albert did with Victoria.[17] But Florence never found her Albert. Perhaps when she met him he had, like Sidney Herbert, just married someone else. Or else the fantasy companion might have looked like Clarkey, or Cousin Hilary Bonham-Carter, or taken the unique and unacceptable shape of a new and more occasional friend, Elizabeth Blackwell. That lonely, penurious, one-eyed Anglo-American woman had somehow, against all the odds, managed to qualify as a doctor. Once, in 1851, Florence took her new friend Elizabeth Blackwell down to Embley on a weekend visit. According to O'Malley, "Florence told Elizabeth during that weekend that if she might work with her she should want no other husband."[18] But Elizabeth went back to America.

IF MARIANNE NICHOLSON had been asked who would be the "ideal companion" for Flo, she would at once have replied, "My own brother, Henry." Marianne and Henry were close, and Marianne knew that her brother had loved Flo since he was a boy of six and he and Flo had hung placards saying "Good" and "Bad" around each other's necks. Mrs. Nightingale and Mrs. Nicholson also saw that Henry Nicholson was very fond of Flo, and they were not displeased. That Henry and Flo were first cousins was not considered to be a problem.

The advantages of a connection between the Nightingales and the Nicholsons were too obvious to need comment. The families had always been close. Henry was a pleasant, hardworking young man, and if he had little of his elder sister's verve or Florence's brilliance, he would make an admirable husband and father like his father. As the eldest son of a very wealthy man, Henry stood to inherit a fortune. To imagine Florence—many years in the future, of course—succeeding her aunt Anne Smith Nicholson as mistress of Waverley Abbey was thrilling to the whole family, except, unfortunately, Florence.

Not that anything should be rushed, of course. Among Unitarians it was traditional to marry late, and in the eyes of their doting parents, Henry and Florence were still too young to name a day. Henry must get his degree in mathematics at Cambridge, and girls like Florence deserved a few years of carefree enjoyment before settling down to motherhood. All the same, it was expedient that Henry and Florence should be given the opportunity to get to know each other better. For example, Fanny decided that Henry would be invited to stay as long as he liked at Lea Hurst in the summer of 1839. Florence was always more reliably pleasant in Derbyshire, and Henry would tempt her to spend less time nursing sick babies or holding the hand of some old woman on her deathbed. Flo and Henry were both so interested in mathematics. They would put their heads together over some silly book of equations, in a sort of latter-day version of Dante's Paolo and Francesca, and hit it off splendidly.[19] Later, perhaps, Florence could be invited by her aunt and uncle to accompany the Nicholsons on some tour—to the Lake District, for example. Florence was such a reader, she would have them all up on their Wordsworth and Coleridge in no time, and write wonderful letters for the family archives. And at Christmas, of course, the families were always together for several weeks. It was all a delightful prospect for Fanny and WEN, though WEN did worry more than most over the dangers of inbreeding.

And how did Parthenope view the new closeness with the Nicholsons? If Flo during their girlhood had become especially close to Aunt Mai Smith and her family, Parthe had been given ample opportunities by her indulgent mother to develop her relationship with the Nicholsons. Parthe adored sitting in the lap of luxury at Waverley, and since she and Marianne were the eldest of the female cousins they were surely meant to be best friends.[20] Parthe was of course very fond of Hilary Bonham-Carter, the other female cousin in her age group, but Parthe was happy to let Flo have Hilary if she could have Marianne.

But now Parthe saw Marianne and Flo deliberately brought together by their mamas, playing and singing together all day long and conspiring to have a successful debut season. She saw Henry dangling after Flo, and Fanny planning to bring them together. If Parthe as a girl had a dream, it was of being mistress of a place like Waverley and marrying a man like Henry Nicholson. Yet, now in her twentieth year, the realization of such dreams receding, Florence, with all her much-repeated protestations of reluctance, was outrunning her elder sister in the marital stakes just as she had in Latin and Greek.

Parthe's response to the situation might have been predicted: she fell ill. During the strenuous year and a half that the Nightingale family had spent touring the Continent, Parthe had been equal to anything. But as the 1839 London season wound down, Parthe seemed again in danger. While Florence spent the summer at Lea Hurst, entertaining Henry Nicholson, Hilary Bonham-Carter, and the marvelous Mary Clarke among other visitors, Parthe took the cure at Harrogate spa with her newly widowed aunt Joanna Bonham-Carter. Over the next few years, to judge from the family correspondence, Parthe, who loved company and the London life, was frequently dispatched by her mother to visit friends in the provinces. Flo, meanwhile, who had always wanted to be left alone at home, was pressed to make the social rounds in London and to be available to visitors at home. It was all, as I remarked earlier, very ironic.

WHILE FLORENCE, Parthe, and Marianne bobbed about in a sea of pleasure during the London season, their cousin Hilary was at Miss Rachel Martineau's Unitarian boarding school in Liverpool. There she improved her mind, took healthful walks, attended closely to the sermons of the Reverend James Martineau, and heard about the power of invalidism as explained by the celebrated but sadly deaf authoress, Miss Harriet Martineau.[21] Hilary's dresses were gray, and her moods were black. She had often longed to have time for herself, but now she missed her mother and the little brothers and sisters at home. Above all she missed her father, who in February of 1838 had died after a long battle with kidney disease.[22] Hilary's main comfort was her correspondence with Flo.[23]

When John Bonham-Carter died, the whole family was devastated, and Hilary, the eldest daughter, had her hands full. Joanna Bonham-Carter was prostrate with grief and anxiety, the five little ones, Alfred, Henry, Alice, Hugh, and Elinor, needed extra comfort and care, and Fanny Bonham-Carter, though only one year younger than Hilary, was considered too delicate to be of help. Yet of all the children, Hilary was perhaps the one who felt most grief and loss over John Bonham-Carter's death. She had grown close to her father during his final illness, when he was forced to withdraw from active public life and when her elder brother was up at Cambridge. Hilary and her father delighted in each other's company just as Flo and WEN did.[24]

Hilary Bonham-Carter, like her cousin Florence, was an intensely serious young girl, but Hilary was soft and vulnerable where Flo was spiky and assertive. Hilary knew her Bible and Prayer Book, had been fed a rich diet of devotional works like the *Imitation of Christ,* and had heard many sermons. She identified herself passionately as a Christian and sought to cleanse her mind and body of imperfection and to make prayer an integral part of her daily routine. For some months when she was sixteen or seventeen, Hilary Bonham-Carter kept a journal to monitor her spiritual life and give herself instructions and reprimands.[25] Entries like the following make for painful reading as we see this innocent and well-meaning young girl paralyzed by a sense of sinfulness:

Wednesday [April 24]
Got up. Came here. Babe. Mama read. We are to copy Jesus Christ but as we cannot make such great sacrifices we should be the more ready to *give* up our will in everything at all times. Breakfast. Came up. Wrote J [Journal]—now remember this morning's reading. Let it have an effect . . .

   Dinner—painted little scene for Harry etc—took Harry & Alice out, got wild hyacinths—came in supper, played with Fan & Alf [two more young siblings] etc—went up, *read little.* Oh dear I am always doing wrong I did not pray—I *read*—Oh Father canst Thou pardon me, I am very sinful. Alas yes, I never am good you should give your spirit a meal in the day, Oh Father support me. I will try Oh Yes to please Thee I do wish to be happy. I am weak. I must make efforts—went up—undressed—bed.

In her late teens Hilary, like many girls of her generation and caste, found herself in a Mary and Martha dilemma. She was not only torn between her duties to her family and her spiritual aspirations but confused by her society's assumption that, for women, there was no difference between the two. The great religious thinkers have known that spiritual exercises require silence, aloneness, and concentration, yet these were luxuries for an upper-middle-class girl like Hilary Bonham-Carter. In the big house at Ditcham there were daily prayers and Bible reading, but these were communal activities, serving mainly to discipline unruly children and proselytize pagan servants.[26] Hilary could go to church on Sundays only if her mother felt up to ordering the carriage or well enough to cope with the children and their governess. Hilary was almost never alone, and if she had a moment to herself and left the living room to go upstairs to pray, she often found someone in the bedroom—a maid dusting, perhaps, or the sister she shared her bed with. So she would take up a book, become absorbed in reading, and then chastise herself for failure of purpose and guilty pleasure.

Hilary Bonham-Carter's greatest temptation was not, in fact, reading, but drawing and painting. Like Florence, Hilary was already convinced she would never marry, and her secret dream was of living independently and being an artist. In a letter to her cousin Florence, Hilary reported a discussion she had had with her drawing master, William Mulready. He had thrown up his hands in disgust when she remarked that women could never be expected to draw well, and declared that if that was her real opinion, she should stop taking lessons at once. Application was as important as talent in the making of an artist, and the problem with women was that they could not or would not take the time to practice. What happened, Mulready explained, was that, if one hundred men and one hundred women were theoretically to set out at the same time to train as artists, ninety of the women would be held back from the rigorous demands of art by the needs of their family and friends.

Thus one hundred male artists came to compete with only ten female artists, and unsurprisingly the men were more productive. "Where a man is," wrote Hilary, "his business is the law and a woman must adapt herself and hers to circumstances."[27]

Hilary was also encouraged to pursue her work as an artist and seek independence by her beloved aunt Julia Smith. After John Bonham-Carter's death, Julia spent more time with the family, and the love and trust between her and Hilary increased. But Mr. Mulready's advice and Julia's encouragement were difficult to heed. As Hilary was coming of age the very idea of a woman professional artist seemed to English society to be inappropriate to the point of obscenity. There was no way for women to enroll in art school. The respectable gentlemen who were hired by wealthy families to teach art to their daughters necessarily confined their instruction to watercolor landscapes and portraits in charcoal since the smell and mess of painting in oils was unthinkable in a drawing room or bedroom. Studies from the male and female nude were considered out of the question for young ladies, and any form of apprenticeship was impossible given the notorious immorality of studios.

But as Hilary Bonham-Carter entered her twenties women like Rosa Bonheur in Paris and Harriet Hosmer in Rome were beginning to make a dent in the all-male world of art, and to a woman of Smith heritage, social obstacles were there to be conquered.[28] Money was not a problem for the Bonham-Carters, and had John lived a few years longer, the fate of his eldest daughter might well have been different. More fatal for Hilary's ambitions than social shibboleths were the familial responsibilities that came to her after her father's death and her religious imperative to meet those needs before her own.

From the day John died, it was clear to all in the family that Joanna Smith Bonham-Carter was not equipped to handle a household and eight children alone and that young Jack Bonham-Carter was no chip off the old block, ready to step into his father's shoes. The task of keeping the Bonham-Carter family together, of educating the younger children and providing their mother with support and companionship, would fall mainly on Hilary's shoulders. Whereas Florence Nightingale was under tremendous pressure from her parents to marry, Hilary's declarations that she was not interested in marriage fell on grateful ears. Unlike her sister

Fanny, Joanna Bonham-Carter had daughters as well as sons to spare. It suited Joanna to imagine Hilary a spinster, as useful as her sister Julia, though with none of Julia's intransigence and unconventionality. Gentle, sweet, religious Hilary was an easy victim for a weak, conventional, self-absorbed mother and a horde of thoughtless siblings.

But Hilary in 1839 was still young, and so she still had hope. She knew she could count on cousin Flo to help her do the right thing. Flo knew so much and had ambition and drive enough for the two of them. Flo had said that in the summer when they were together at Lea Hurst again she would introduce Hilary to her marvelous new friend from Paris, Mary Clarke, herself an amateur artist, who knew all kinds of ateliers where Hilary could study.

Marianne Nicholson and Hilary Bonham-Carter personified two sides to Florence Nightingale's nature, two kinds of aspiration. On the one hand, there was energy, ambition, humor, and social success; on the other, meekness, gravity, self-sacrifice, and submission to the divine will. Florence was torn between them.

IN SEPTEMBER OF 1839, after a summer of visits and living at Lea Hurst, Fanny, WEN, and Florence came back south. For the first time the family traveled by rail, a not unadventurous move, as accidents were still common. On this maiden journey, the Nightingales were given all the latest court gossip by Sir Frederick Stovin, one of the queen's equerries. They arrived at Embley House determined to camp out at the lodge and bully the builders into finishing up. Perhaps to shield her elder daughter from cold and inconvenience, Fanny decided that Parthe should remain in Harrogate with her aunt Joanna Bonham-Carter and then move to the Nicholsons' at Waverley.

The weather was appalling that fall, with floods spreading over the Romsey-Southampton area. When at last the three Nightingales struggled up to the main house at Embley one evening in a sturdy cart capable of handling the mud, they were wet through and hungry. For some hours the three huddled in the kitchen, waiting for the servants at the lodge to finish their tea and to bring over lights, food, and bedding. The butler, who was the first to arrive, was shocked to see his master and mistress sitting in the dark in the servants' quarters. But in fact the three Nightingales quite enjoyed bivouacking in their own home those first few days back, especially as they soon had family guests.

Fanny's brothers Octavius Smith and Sam Smith together with their nephew Henry Nicholson arrived unannounced at Embley to do some shooting. Only a lingering illness prevented Benjamin Smith from coming too. The three male visitors were forced to take cold baths, sleep on straw, and dry out their sodden clothing piece by piece over the fire after a day's sport, but when they rode off home they were in high spirits, promising to return to Embley soon. For her part, Florence was happy to be sleeping in the old nursery, as her new bedroom was still uninhabitable. She found it amusing to do her piano practice "with the little minute glass" before her, surrounded by washstands and piles of musty carpets.[29]

Knowing that Parthenope was desperate to see the house, Florence wrote several long letters, giving a comic account of the first days' discomfort and describing the new rooms in detail. To make her sister laugh, Flo affected what I would call her Marianne Nicholson style, introducing some comic German syntax at one point and gleefully narrating how furious Fanny had been to find that some hideous pink rosettes had unaccountably appeared in the new drawing room.

When Parthenope Nightingale was at last allowed to return to Embley she was enraptured. As she wrote to Hilary Bonham-Carter in June of 1840, Embley in the rhododendron season was as close she could imagine to "Eden, or *il paradiso terrestre* as depicted in the 25th Canto, stanza forty something." She went on to describe herself sitting in the sun, "Florence reading and talking so my immortal profited too," with "nightingales all around, blue sky above (*such* long shadows sleeping on the lawn), and June smells about me."[30] But all too often, Florence's presence was a cloud on Parthenope's sun-filled sky. Where Parthe saw the nightingales and smelled the roses, Florence saw the men, women, and children sweating all day in the sun of the fields near Embley, begging on the streets outside the Carlton Hotel, and emerging late at night from the mills near Lea Hurst. The conventional woman's life of her caste could not satisfy Florence. Over the next twelve years, the Nightingale family vessel would come close to breaking up on the rocks of Florence's anger and frustration.

Chapter 9

PROBLEMS WITH
THE NICHOLSONS

Over Christmas and New Year of 1840, Mr. and Mrs.
Nightingale celebrated their new, improved Embley with
a large family party that included all eight Nicholsons and
a number of Bonham-Carters. Fanny and WEN in the next decade
would not only enjoy many such jolly family parties but also ride a wave
of social success. Yet, as their younger daughter was all too ready to point
out, the Nightingales' life of pleasure, prosperity, and ease was deeply at
odds with the growing misery experienced by large segments of the
British population. Great Britain was entering a decade of trade reverses,
manufacturing slowdowns, and cuts in investment, and the retrogressive
Corn Laws, which favored the interests of big Tory landowners, kept the
price of bread high. The men, women, and children who labored in the
mines, factories, mills, and claypits suffered horribly, and thousands died,
especially in the Midlands, England's industrial heartland. As unem-
ployment and famine grew, anti-government sentiment rose, and
middle-class people became afraid to walk the streets at night. This was
one reason why Fanny Nightingale would not allow her daughters to
travel or go out onto London streets alone. The Chartist movement,
which organized largely peaceful demonstrations and collected more
than a million signatures demanding wider representation in government and economic reform, was ruthlessly put down.[1]

Members of the middle classes also suffered losses at this time, including some of the Nightingales' nearest relatives. Old Mr. Shore,

WEN's father, had left his considerable fortune in his family's bank, Parker and Shore. WEN had pulled most of his money out and tried to persuade his mother and aunt to do the same, but his words fell on ears that were figuratively as well as literally deaf to anything new. When Parker and Shore went bankrupt in 1842, almost everything the old ladies owned was lost, as well as Mai Shore Smith's inheritance. For Sam and Mai, whose financial situation had always been precarious, it was a setback that mirrored all too bitterly the failure of Sam's father's business in 1814.[2]

Without fuss, Mrs. Shore and Miss Evans set about making economies, dismissing most of their servants and allowing their rambling old houses to crumble around their heads. When WEN expressed concern about the burglaries she had suffered, his mother cheerfully assured him that the thieves never came upstairs to disturb her. The lives of both Mrs. Shore at Tapton and Miss Evans at Cromford were woven into the fabric of their industrial communities; though poor and lonely, they were not abandoned by their neighbors. In some way these two deeply Christian souls rejoiced to bear a small measure of the common misery. One economy neither sister seems to have contemplated was to move in together and pool expenses. Passionately devoted to each other, they could not, it seems, bear to occupy the same house for more than a visit. In February 1843, WEN wrote from his mother's house in Tapton to Fanny: "This house is bitter, the passages freezing, the smells & draught from the offices intolerable, but [my mother] heeds it not . . . She & I are in most perfect harmony. I propose something to her, she says don't say another word: I smile and we chatter on another subject."[3]

William Edward Nightingale made sure his mother and aunt did not die in penury, and he lent money to Sam and Mai to tide them over. In fact, though Fanny writes sometimes about needing to return home and economize for a few months, the Hungry Forties, as historians have named this period, seem to have had little negative impact on the fortunes of the Nightingales. Socially they were soaring, as their circle of acquaintance grew ever more numerous and more illustrious.

When the great Egyptologist and biblical scholar Christian Bunsen was appointed Prussian minister to London he and his wealthy English wife, Frances Waddington Bunsen, soon came to know the Nightingales. Florence Nightingale had the knack of getting close to a great man without alienating his female relatives, and Frances Bunsen liked and approved of Miss Florence Nightingale and was happy to take her up socially. Frances saw Florence as an excellent influence on her own small daughters, a fact that Fanny Nightingale may have found somewhat ironic. The Bunsens were important because they were close to the new Prince Consort, Albert of Saxe-Coburg-Gotha, and thus to the Queen herself. It was extremely gratifying to WEN and Fanny that people whose personal distinction equaled their social prominence made such a fuss of Florence.

For all their eminence, the Bunsens (who had not yet become baron and baroness) were from the Nightingales' own social caste, but, as Florence laughingly remarked to Clarkey in 1839, Fanny and WEN were now set to welcome "a duke and some countesses" as well.

One of the dukes for whom Fanny Nightingale was at pains to have especially nice wallpaper in Embley's best bedroom, just in case, was William Hartington Cavendish, sixth Duke of Devonshire. He was a shy, charming, generous man of liberal views whose childhood had been scarred by an illness in infancy that left him deaf, the perverse conduct of his parents and their friends, and the tragically short life of his beautiful and brilliant mother, Georgiana.[4] Hart, as his mother and siblings called him, never married, and the closest relationship in his life was with his friend Sir Joseph Paxton, a man of humble origin and great ability who became one of Britain's leading horticulturalists and architects.[5]

The Cavendishes were, and indeed still are, about as grand as one can be, south of royalty, and in the nineteenth century they were also fabulously rich. The sixth Duke of Devonshire owned huge tracts of land that happily included not only rich coal seams in Derbyshire but large sections of central London. The Cavendishes were the kind of people who saw the Saxe-Coburgs (and Queen Victoria was as much a Saxe-Coburg as Alfred) as impecunious, jumped-up German nobodies, and looked down on Buckingham Palace, the royal family's main London home, as a modern, middle-class maisonette. Buck House was simply not in the same class as Chatsworth or the Churchills' main place, Blenheim.

A social chasm divided William Edward Nightingale from William Hartington Cavendish, but somehow the two built a frail but viable bridge across. It would be an exaggeration to say that they were friends, but they were more than just Derbyshire neighbors. Both were intelligent, principled, and urbane, well up on things like architecture and geology and Italian literature. Both maintained a core of silence and distance in extremely busy social lives. Nightingale was certainly happy to find himself and his family rising in society, but he was no toady and Devonshire was too grand to care about the class of anyone born lower than himself. And so when they had occasion to meet, at some semi-official dinner in the country or over port at a London club, there was a sense of conviviality between Nightingale and the Duke.

Thus the Duke was charmed to run into the Nightingales in Geneva in 1838 when he and Paxton were taking their long European tour. He obligingly recommended his Derbyshire neighbors to his sister Lady Granville, the wife of the English ambassador in Paris, securing the young Nightingale ladies access to some of the most fashionable soirées.[6] Such attention was already gratifying, but in August 1842 the four Nightingales were invited to a three-day house party at Chatsworth. People almost as grand as the Cavendishes, such as that witty, much-traveled novelist the Honourable Emily Eden, took pleasure in describing Devonshire house parties as a great bore. No one, certainly, went there for creature comforts. But however drafty the bedrooms and congealed the breakfast kippers, a middle-class family like the Nightingales had to be a little awed to find themselves sleeping at Chatsworth.

Fanny Nightingale wasted little time in sharing her experiences at the ducal pile with her Paris friend Mary Clarke. "During the three days we were there we had every variety of amusement," wrote Mrs. Nightingale. "One day, a stately progress to Hardwick [Hardwick Hall, the ancestral Tudor mansion of the Devonshires] in a coach and six and two carriages and a cloud of outriders; a cook and fourgon having preceded us to prepare luncheon."[7]

To share a ballroom with the Duke of Sussex was an immense social coup, but the capstone of Fanny Nightingale's social success was the dinners en famille that the Nightingales in Hampshire shared with the Palmerstons. If Devonshire was rich and high, Lord and Lady Palmerston were powerful, both independently and as a couple, and in the mid-nineteenth century political power was beginning to trump blood, land, and money in the social game. "The great world was still very exclusive in the early 1840s," Benjamin Disraeli would later recall, and it was much rarer for a family like the Nightingales to be invited to dine or have tea at a relatively small country home like Broadlands than to receive an invitation to a huge place like Chatsworth.[8]

As with the Duke of Devonshire, Mr. Nightingale first got to know Lord Palmerston because they lived in the same part of the country— Broadlands, Palmerston's Hampshire estate, was next to Embley—and because they had political interests in common.[9] Nightingale had always been a Whig, and though Palmerston began life as a Tory he jumped to the Whig side in 1830 when offered the position of Foreign Secretary under Lord Grey. Having lost his Cambridge University seat as a result of this apostasy, Palmerston decided to seek election for his local constituency of Romsey. There his candidacy was seconded by his neighbor William Edward Nightingale, who worked hard to secure Palmerston's election. As Palmerston rose to be the leader of the Whig party, the Nightingales were among his most devoted supporters. Hence their star rose with his.

The intimacy between the two families began in 1840, after Lord Palmerston's marriage, when he and his wife began to entertain on a large scale. While the Whigs were out of office between 1842 and 1846, the former Foreign Secretary and his wife were often in Hampshire and saw a good deal of their neighbors. Lord Palmerston was a man of prodigious strength, tireless in the saddle or on foot, dedicated to sport of all kinds. Yet after washing off the mud and blood from a long day in the field, he liked nothing better than an informal dinner with agreeable friends. His neighbors the Nightingales turned out to fill the bill remarkably well. Nightingale was a fine shot and a man of thoroughly sound views. Mrs. Nightingale was excellent company, witty, not at all prudish considering her Unitarian background, and a damn fine woman. Miss Nightingale was pleasant, and Miss Florence was remarkable. She could be relied upon to handle that rather difficult young man, Lord Ashley, the estranged heir to the Earl of Shaftesbury. After a long courtship, Lord Ashley had managed to persuade Lady Palmerston's delightful elder daughter, Minny Cowper, to be his wife, and the Ashleys were often at Broadlands.

Coming into the orbit of the Palmerstons was a major step in the social rise of the whole Nightingale family, but Florence was the one who benefited from it most. Lord and Lady Palmerston and Lord Ashley—

or Lord Shaftesbury, as he is better known to history—are among the most fascinating personalities of the mid-Victorian era, and among the most influential. Palmerston and Shaftesbury between them personified contrasting but crucial aspects of Victorian Britain—its hegemonic power and ruthless pragmatism on one hand, its religious zeal and tireless pursuit of social equity on the other. Between them they offered Florence Nightingale a high-level course in political reform, and she proved to be an especially apt pupil. Over the next ten years, Florence Nightingale came to know virtually all the liberal political establishment. These relationships were to be of incalculable value to her in the 1850s.

Lord Palmerston began life as a poverty-stricken Irish peer. A man of great brilliance, ambition, and energy, it took him thirty years to make his way up to the Foreign Ministry, but once there he became known as a tireless, unrelenting, even unscrupulous advocate for British interests. By ambassadors and foreign rulers Palmerston was loathed. In his own ministry he was detested as a harsh taskmaster, and he often upset his cabinet colleagues. But by the British people Palmerston was idolized as the voice of the nation. Palmerston was Foreign Secretary at exactly the time when Great Britain was becoming the greatest power in the world. From 1855 until his death in 1865 he was, with one brief interval, Prime Minister.[10]

Lady Palmerston, born Emily Lamb, subsequently Lady Cowper, was the only daughter of the ambitious and promiscuous first Lady Melbourne and thus the sister (or more probably half sister) of the Lord Melbourne who was Victoria's first and favorite Prime Minister. Lady Palmerston and her three brothers were reared in the nursery of Georgiana, Duchess of Devonshire, and after her marriage she became a key member of the notoriously fast, high-rolling set of the Prince Regent, later George IV. Lady Cowper lived all her life at the heart of English social and political power, and it was as much through her connections and advice as through his own redoubtable talents that her second husband, Lord Palmerston, finally, in his mid-fifties, became Prime Minister.

Lord Shaftesbury, known to history as the Great Reformer, was the husband of Minny Cowper, Lady Palmerston's elder daughter.[11] Where Palmerston was a man of the Enlightenment, cool, rational, cynical, pragmatic, promiscuous, a deist if not an atheist, Shaftesbury was moody, emotional, idealistic, chaste, weighed down by a sense of sin, and driven by Christian zeal. In matters of personal finance, both Palmerston and Shaftesbury as young men accepted uncritically the aristocrat's freedom to live on credit. But when Palmerston had money, he used at least some of it to improve conditions on his estates and give his tenants, especially in impoverished Ireland, the infrastructure of roads and drains that allowed economic progress. Shaftesbury would give the last shilling in his pockets to a beggar, but the tenants on his estates were among the most miserable and neglected in England, as his political opponents did not fail to point out. To support his wife and growing family Shaftesbury relied largely on the generosity of friends and relatives, notably his mother-in-law and Lord Palmerston.

In their sexual mores Palmerston and Shaftesbury could not have been more different. In February of 1840, on the eve of the royal wedding and two months *after* his marriage to Lady Cowper, Lord Palmerston created a scandal at Windsor Castle by trying to rape one of Victoria's ladies-in-waiting in her bedroom at night. Victoria and Albert never forgave him. By contrast, Shaftesbury probably had sexual relations with only one woman in his life, his wife. Shaftesbury adored Minny, and she him, and they were faithful to each other. Yet Lady Shaftesbury, like so many respectable Victorian women, paid a bitter price for abjuring the sexual expertise of her mother and maternal grandmother, each of whom managed to have a good deal of sex and few children. Lady Shaftesbury spent most of her married life pregnant.

Palmerston cared for power and attacked the old political oligarchy only when it frustrated his personal ambition. Lady Palmerston, one of the most delightful as well as most beautiful women of her generation, had no interests or sympathies outside her family and her caste. But Shaftesbury, abandoned and abused from birth by his aristocratic parents (his mother was a Churchill), burned with sympathy for the poor and tormented, and devoted his life to improving their lot. The only love Shaftesbury knew as a child was from his nurse, before he was sent away to school at age seven, and from her he derived the evangelical faith that would inspire his life and power his work. For decades Shaftesbury worked to enact his Ten Hour Day Bill, but he was simultaneously involved in virtually every major reform effort of mid-Victorian England. One of Shaftesbury's most selfless campaigns was to make it illegal for small children to be used as chimney sweeps. Poor boys were sold as in-

fants to master sweeps, who forced them up hot, narrow, smoke-filled
chimneys and even lit fires under their feet to prevent them coming
down until the soot had been dislodged.[12] Even the liberal middle classes,
who liked clean chimneys and clear flues, preferred not to see the chimney sweep boys. Shaftesbury was savior to many half-starved mites, covered with scrapes and burns, their lungs seared by smoke and soot.
England's Great Reformer had looked on the face of more misery, perhaps, than any other man of his class in England.

Not only did Florence meet the Palmerstons and Lord Ashley over
dinner at Embley and Broadlands, but on one occasion at least she was
invited to stay for the weekend and meet both of Lady Palmerston's
daughters. Florence Nightingale was both astonished and gratified to
find that she fitted in at the Palmerstons', that they were nice to her, and
that she liked them enormously. "I must tell you," wrote Florence to
Parthenope, "how devoted the lord & lady seem to one another—it is
quite a worship. His care for her & her watchful attention to him. I shd
get quite fond of him, if he were not Ld Palmerston—they do seem
people of such feeling."[13]

Old Palmerston was far too busy a man to discourse to young ladies
on political theory. However, he and his wife had perhaps the most intimate and acute knowledge of the English political system to be found at
that time, and for such a rapt observer as Florence Nightingale they informed without needing to lecture. As for Lord Shaftesbury, in him Florence Nightingale found the very pattern of the life she herself wished to
lead. Though a Tory and an aristocrat, Shaftesbury was far closer in ideas
and ideals to the educated, reform-minded liberal middle class to which
the Nightingales and their clan belonged. Over the next decade, Florence
Nightingale would follow Lord Shaftesbury as closely as her mother
would allow. Most important, the large circle of reformers that clustered
about Shaftesbury would learn to turn to Miss Florence Nightingale as
the expert when it came to hospital management and international public health.

In the relationship between Palmerston and Shaftesbury, Florence
Nightingale saw a model for political action. The Shaftesbury way of
solving social ills, based on the Wilberforce anti-slavery campaign, was
mediated not just by individual acts of philanthropy but by parliamentary legislation and civil service implementation. Yet, somewhat para-

doxically, such national reform movements were often set in motion and facilitated by individual relationships. For all his religious zeal and social idealism, Shaftesbury knew just how important it was to his reform efforts that he was son-in-law to a man of power who could block or second the reforms he sought to put into law. Though cynical and conservative by nature, Palmerston was amenable to evidence. Once Palmerston, a man justly proud of his strength and energy, was persuaded to walk in an hour the same distances as a mill worker, to imitate the manipulations at a loom, and to imagine the multiplication of this labor by fourteen or more hours a day, six days a week, fifty weeks a year. Convinced by this demonstration that the normal workload in a mill was inhumanly heavy for a man, much less a child, Palmerston agreed that something needed to be done to enact the Ten Hour Day Bill so dear to Shaftesbury's heart.

Social reform had been part of the family tradition for three generations in the Smith family. Florence Nightingale understood without being told in so many words that the relationship of a Pitt to a Wilberforce, of a Palmerston to a Shaftesbury, on a lesser level of a William Wilberforce to a William Smith, was often the fuel that kept the legislative and executive machine in motion. But this fruitful interplay between single individuals and large-scale movements worked almost exclusively between men, since only men could be politicians or administrators. Even a woman as knowledgeable and engaged as Lady Palmerston exerted political influence only indirectly.

By the early 1840s, power was already a key concept for Florence Nightingale. She saw that, for all their many excellencies, the women she knew had no desire for power. It did not occur to them to want it. But she did want it and this made her different. In the eyes of the world it made her aberrant. Could any circumstances be imagined, Florence wondered, in which a woman of high social status—herself, for example—might use her personal network of friendship and alliance to effect larger social goals, an improvement in national health care, for example?

IN THE NEW YEAR of 1840, Florence Nightingale went to stay with her aunt Mai at Combe Hurst. Over Christmas the two of them had concocted a program of serious study, and at Combe they began getting up to read in the chilly pre-dawn. Florence was still passionately set on "acquiring," that is, on gaining more skills and more knowledge of the world. Her recent contact with Henry Nicholson had served to remind Florence how much she would have liked to go up to Cambridge like her father and uncles and male cousins. How pleasant it would have been to have three years to think and read as much as one wanted, in the company of one's peers.[14] Fanny had no sympathy with Flo's passion for "acquisition." If anything, Flo had already acquired too much. Problems between mother and daughter crystallized over the issue of Florence's earnest desire to continue with mathematics. Only through the tactful intervention of her aunt Mai and her uncle Octavius was Florence able to have a precious few sessions with a tutor.

Fanny Nightingale's refusal to let Florence have math lessons has often been cited as an example of how her conventional views on what women could do blocked her younger daughter's career. But though Victorian society as a whole massively subscribed to the presumption that women had no business doing taxing intellectual subjects like math, this was not true of either WEN or Fanny Nightingale. They were both personally acquainted with the most famous English woman mathematician of their time, Mary Somerville, and Mrs. Nightingale was a good friend of Annabella, Lady Noel Byron, and her daughter, Ada.[15] Annabella Milbanke had been famously labeled "the princess of parallelograms" by Lord Byron before their marriage, and the Byrons' daughter, Ada, was known for her mathematical brilliance.

But tutors, especially in mathematics and science, were almost always male, and allowing rich, unmarried girls to spend hours alone studying with smart, ambitious, and impoverished tutors was, as any reader of Rousseau knew, a recipe for disaster. Just as Fanny had been keen to see Flo and Henry working together at Lea Hurst, by the same token she was reluctant to bring in a mathematics tutor.[16]

Florence's few precious weeks of math tuition at her uncle Oc's home were possible because a small crisis had broken out among the members of the Smith family based in London. Aunt Jane Smith, Oc's wife, already the mother of six children, was near the end of another pregnancy when the news came that Frederick, her eldest son, only nineteen, who had gone out to Australia as part of Captain Grey's expedition, had been abandoned to die of hunger and thirst. In family emergencies Julia Smith had typically been the one called on, but she had her hands completely full with her mother, Frances Coape Smith, who was dying.[17] So Octavius Smith turned for help to his niece Florence, to whom he and his wife had always felt close. Jane Smith's serene fortitude (assisted, it seems, by massive doses of opiates prescribed by her doctors) brought her through the crisis of grief and loss. She was delivered of a healthy child, Edith, and some credit for this happy outcome was clearly due to her niece. Thus Flo was stung into protest when her mother wrote demanding to know why she remained in London instead of coming home as promised. "My Dearest Mum," she wrote, "How thankful you should be that your daughter for the first time in her life is doing some little good in her generation; do not grudge it her. Aunt Jane was not well enough to go out today. I really think Flora [one of the younger Smith cousins] has improved a little and I trust I feel it a blessing, as I ought, that a creature so nearly spiritualized as Aunt Jane is should cling to such as me as all now in her distress."[18]

IN THE SUMMER of 1840, Florence embarked on a tour of the Lake District with the Nicholsons. The weather was exceptionally wet, and Florence was bored, not so much by the scenery as by the company. She wrote to Parthenope, saying how much she missed her. Parthe was so very good at admiring things, and Flo was aware of not admiring things enough for the Nicholsons. In October, Flo was still with the Nicholsons, now at home at Waverley Abbey, and enjoying the fox hunting but not much else. She wrote to her sister: "I want to see you very much you spoil me for all other society & you know when I have you I don't want anyone else . . . Write speedily my dear—it is very odd how undecided I sh'd be without you."[19]

In mid-December of 1840 all four Nightingales repaired to Waverley Abbey for a long visit. Aunt Anne Nicholson, ably seconded by her eldest daughter, Marianne, outdid herself that year, finding beds for more than eighty people on one night and arranging a whirl of social activities that culminated in a public ball. A prime interest for the large group of houseguests was the dramatic entertainment that Marianne and Henry wished to stage. After much discussion *The Merchant of Venice* was decided upon as the main play, with Henry taking the starring role of Shylock.

Parthenope was prevailed upon to be "scene-painter, milliner, and cap-and-fur maker."[20] Florence was stage manager, and everyone agreed that the performance would never have come off without her remarkable talent for organization. One of Flo's jobs was to drill the actors in their lines. The play was pronounced a huge success by the audience. Marianne, who had taken the small role of Nerissa, did it to perfection, and at the ensuing ball, which continued until five o'clock in the morning, she was the undoubted star.

I can't help finding it significant that the dazzling Marianne did not take the part of Portia in *The Merchant of Venice,* which seems tailor-made for her. Marianne and Henry had concerted, I would bet, that on this occasion Henry as Shylock would be the unquestioned star, watched in admiration offstage by stage manager and prompter Flo.

BY THE TIME December 1842 rolled around, the situation between Florence and her cousin Henry Nicholson was still unresolved. Once again the Nightingales intended to spend Christmas and New Year's with the Nicholsons, and the two families would be even more intimate than usual since the Bonham-Carters and the Octavius Smiths were all on the Continent.

At Waverley, Florence got word that her Scottish friend Hope Richardson Reeve was dying, having just given birth to her first child. Hope's sister Helen Richardson, racked with grief, appealed to Florence to come to her brother-in-law Henry Reeve's house in London and help her cope.[21] Florence begged leave to go, but Fanny refused. The Richardson sisters were not especially close friends, and tragedies like theirs were far from uncommon. Fanny was not pleased to see Flo forever running off to look after sick people. Florence was outraged. Usually in her letters to her mother she is a model of filial affection, but in the note she wrote from Waverley on this occasion her tone is bitterly sarcastic: "If I can persuade Helen to put off her sister's death till next year, as I have sanguine hopes of doing when I get to town, you will certainly see me on Saturday. She can have no possible objection at least to put off her mourning for her until another year."[22]

Florence then took a leaf out of her sister's playbook and promptly fell ill, too ill to take part in most of the Waverley Christmas festivities.[23] One can imagine how pleased Fanny Nightingale and her sister Anne Nicholson must have been by this turn of events. When she did come down to the drawing room, Florence was especially nice to William Nicholson, Henry's younger brother. He had recently returned home with his regiment from Australia and had fascinating stories to tell of that land.[24]

Florence also became deeply attached to Miss Hannah Richardson, her uncle George Nicholson's maiden sister, and this too probably rubbed her mother the wrong way. Guests at Waverley over the busy Christmas season were expected to double up, and for some nights Florence shared a bed with Miss Hannah Nicholson as well as spending a good deal of the day in the room set aside for Miss Nicholson's use. Thus the two women had the opportunity to talk at length, often of religion, a matter of passionate concern to both. Hannah Nicholson was deeply sympathetic to Florence in her illness, mothering her and receiving in return a subsequent outpouring of affection and gratitude that probably surprised her. "You let me love you & that is all I want," wrote Florence in an early letter, which she ends "believe me when I say, I am yours, ever yours, Florence."[25] In another letter, written after a subsequent visit to Waverley, Florence wrote: "I saw so very little of you at Waverley, that I often wished to be ill again, in order to be allowed to come in quietly to your place of rest."[26]

Hannah and Florence exchanged letters and devotional works for some five years, and Florence's letters to Hannah have been subjected to a great deal of analysis. For the older woman, a spiritually uplifting correspondence with the admired Miss Nightingale must have been gratifying. What pious gentlewoman, unmarried and of a certain age, unaccustomed to adoration from her relatives and friends, would not like to be told: "Your whole life seems to be love, and you always find words in your heart which, without the pretension of enlightening, yet are like a clearing up to me. You always seem to rest on the heart of the divine Teacher, and to participate in His mysteries"? All the same, it was not Hannah who kept Florence's letters, but Florence who kept drafts of what she had written.[27] In fact, though much that we know of Florence Nightingale in the mid-1840s derives from the "Dear Aunt Hannah" letters, Florence was never as close to Hannah as she was to Hilary or Clarkey or as she would become to Selina Bracebridge. Their time of intimacy was extremely short, only a few days. When Florence returned to Waverley for visits, Hannah Nicholson was usually not there, and she never accepted Fanny Nightingale's invitations to come for a visit to Embley.

Florence's drafts do give us precious information about her thinking and emotions. For example, Florence told Hannah that she preferred London to the country, where her family received a constant stream of visitors: "A country house is the real place of dissipation—sometimes I think that everybody is hard upon me, that to be forever expected to be looking merry & saying something lively, is more than can be expected mornings, noon & night, of anyone."[28] In her letter of September 24, 1846, Florence lamented the fact she has been forced to leave Lea Hurst, where she had begun to feel useful to the local people: "I feel my sympathies all with Ignorance and Poverty—the things which interest me interest them—we are alike in expecting little from life, much from God . . . My imagination is so filled with the misery of this world, that the only thing in which labour brings any return seems to me helping or sympathizing with *these*—& all that poets sing of the glories of the world appear to me untrue—all the people I see are eaten up with care or poverty or disease . . . Life is no holiday game, nor is it a clever book, nor is it a school of instruction, nor a valley of tears—but it is a hard fight, a struggle, a wrestling with the Principle of Evil, hand to hand, foot to foot, & every inch of the way must be disputed."[29]

At times Florence Nightingale seems to open her soul. "Pray write to me, dear Aunt Hannah—the struggle is too hard . . . it is a long while before we shall sleep side by side" (f. 1). "There is no pure thought in me" (f. 13). "All that I do is poisoned by the fear that I am not doing it in simplicity & godly sincerity" (f. 33). But many of the major portions of the letters devoted to religion can be found verbatim in letters Florence was writing at the same time to Hilary Bonham-Carter. Even when she was most sincere and most troubled, there is a performance element in Florence Nightingale's letters, and of course she could more or less count on Miss Nicholson sharing some or all of her letters with members of the Nicholson family circle.

If I had to evaluate the influence of Hannah Nicholson on Florence Nightingale, I would say she was exactly the wrong kind of friend coming at exactly the wrong moment. Hannah apparently preached to her young friend a doctrine of Christian submission and asceticism, watered down by bourgeois affluence and inflected by high Victorian notions of female passivity and passionlessness. The Christian woman must suffer, renounce, bow her head, yield her will, give up the intellect, and await divine Providence. For Florence, such a message brought torment and frustration. Florence's inability to rebel against Fanny's bossiness and Parthe's dependency can be related directly to the message of Christian self-abnegation preached by people like Hannah Nicholson.

AFTER THE CHRISTMAS 1842 standoff at Waverley, Fanny relented and allowed Florence to go to London and stay with Helen Richardson. Marianne Nicholson was planning to stay in town also, and the cousins may have been able to travel up to town together—with a chaperone, of course. Florence spent all of February helping Helen to care for her grieving brother-in-law and do what she could for the baby, who was living with a wet nurse. Fanny seems now to have accepted Florence's absence with good grace, but Parthe became angry. She insisted that Florence had already "honourably acquitted" her responsibilities to Helen and should now come home to Embley. Flo wrote to Fanny: "Parthe's letters are my misery, & if you cannot stop her I suppose I must come home on Monday, tho' I shall have to smother my face under a pillowcase when I tell Helen & I cannot think it necessary as you say you are quite happy to have me here."[30]

In letters to her mother Florence sent messages designed to placate Parthe with humor and the kind of news she knew her sister was interested in: "If Parthe cd. see me in my new straw bonnet I sh'd not wonder at her wanting to have me. It cost 16/- [shillings] & Marianne gave me some beautiful flowers for the cap & you can have no idea of how I look." To Parthe herself Florence wrote in a different idiom: "My dear I cry unto you, do this thing for me for no one else can do it—you will have me all your life, for I shall never die and never marry." Between February and March 1843, Florence wrote some twenty notes and letters to her mother and sister, and it seems that they wrote almost as many to her. Obviously, more than Helen Richardson's sad situation was involved here. It was becoming clear that Flo was trying to break away from home and that she preferred looking after an orphaned baby to dining out. The other three Nightingales found this trend both dismaying and incomprehensible.

Over the Christmas season of 1843–44, Florence Nightingale again went to Waverley, and again fell ill. When her parents and sister left, Florence was too ill to be moved from Waverley even though she found staying in her aunt Nicholson's home increasingly stressful and longed to be at home.

In my opinion, Waverley made Florence Nightingale ill because it was increasingly plain to her that she could no longer deflect the attentions of Henry Nicholson. He had now come down from Cambridge and was reluctantly pursuing a career in the law. Though Florence had always seen Henry as a trusted and admired friend, she did not want to marry him, and she foresaw all too clearly the family furor that would ensue if she refused him. Hints, absences, and illnesses did nothing to curb Henry's ardor, and at some point in late 1843 or 1844 Henry formally proposed and was decisively rejected.

Henry was shattered. Mr. and Mrs. Nicholson were very angry and made no secret of their feelings. They felt that Florence had encouraged Henry and cruelly kept him dangling after her for years. Relations between the Nightingales and the Nicholsons would never be quite the same again. As for Marianne, she had surely assumed that one day her cousin and intimate friend Flo would metamorphose into a sister-in-law and make Henry happy. Now, seeing her beloved brother Henry in such despair, Marianne passionately turned on Florence as a kind of traitor.

What Marianne Nicholson said and did to Florence Nightingale we do not know since their correspondence was destroyed, probably soon after their friendship ended. In the summer of 1845, however, Florence did write about her feelings about Marianne to her other cousin Hilary Bonham-Carter in raw, melodramatic, spontaneous letters.

Those things pass away which make our happiness or misery in this world, it is their substituting in our souls distrust and despair for faith, hope and love—the making us *méchant* and solitary, the killing our souls which is the harm. She [presumably Marianne] has broken my faith in immortality . . . I was not a worthy friend for her. I was not true either to her or to myself in our friendship. I was afraid of her: that is the truth . . . I have walked up and down all these long summer evenings in the garden and could find no words but 'My God, my God, why hast thou forsaken me?' How anyone can find *ennui* in life I cannot think—as it hurries along in what seems to me its wild, headlong course, it is as much as I can do to run with it . . . I have no idea why we suffer so from such insufficient causes . . . only this that there are strange punishments here for those who have made life consist of one idea and that idea not God. Oh dearest, pray for me . . . I can perform my duties as well at home without it, indeed I am more use to my father and mother than I was five years ago—but for truth, truth, truth and a manifestation of God . . . If anyone would know, what are the miseries of indulging the diseased cravings of the heart, or how weary, flat, stale and unprofitable seem all the uses of the world after it . . . And last night, dear child, as I stood looking out on that solemn procession of stars, and a few hours after on the loveliest sunrise that ever slept on the grass, I said to myself that the earth wandered through these suns, themselves changing and burning out, and all would die and pass away, yet that on this wandering earth my love to her could never change, no unkindness could affect it and that it was, without any effort of mine, a love of which I could say "for ever."[31]

There was cruelty in Florence's confiding her passion and her despair to Hilary. She knew that Hilary felt for her the kind of passion she felt for Marianne. Hilary's love for Flo would indeed prove in sober truth, not heated rhetoric, to be forever. A year or so later, cooler and less bitter, Florence made a scattershot attempt at writing a character analysis of Marianne. To explain the extraordinary effect Marianne had on people, Florence finds the remarkable image of a geyser suddenly welling up:

"Since I have convinced myself that she acts always from impulse and never from premeditation, many things have become clear to me and I delight to think (for my sake, not hers) that one's judgments of her have become less severe, and therefore more just. I loved but one person with passion, and that was her—*à ne rien pardonner le pur Amour éclate*. I really think every-

thing should be excused in a person where the geyser of vehement excited sensation overflows all maxim and theory for the
moment under its boiling current. Since I saw her, when Papa
told her that V. was coming, lay hold of him and shake him with
delight, I felt, while I was internally screaming with laughter (I
should think no one ever shook my sacred Papa's person before,
kith or stranger), that everything could be explained by such a
nature, where the present is so strong and vivid that all the past
and the distant future seem to it like cold abstractions, lifeless
forms. Few will ever judge her candidly. Some who know her
very well are too hard upon her for that ever to be possible. To
others to whom that brilliant face is almost as the face of an angel, one has a sorrow in unveiling things they have not the idea
of. Her own nearest, again, have that sort of reverence for her
which one must feel for someone so richly gifted, and yet who
knows so little of her aim in life or what her gifts are for but
amusing herself and other people."[32]

Florence is trying to be fair here and to put her own intense emotions at rest, but even as she grapples with the question of what it was
about Marianne that made her so fascinating, Nightingale is again overwhelmed with emotion. Searching for words, she has recourse to French,
notably in the phrase she underlines, "*à ne rien pardonner le pur Amour
éclate*" (from forgiving nothing, pure Love bursts forth). What I think
Nightingale means is that a measure of the absoluteness of love is one's
inability to forgive if the loved person proves not to be perfect.

FLORENCE NIGHTINGALE's relationship in her late teens with her
cousin Marianne has attracted a good deal of attention. The dearth of
documentary evidence has fed rather than extinguished a forest fire of
sexual innuendo lit, I think, by a spark from Cecil Woodham-Smith who
picked up on a phrase quoted by O'Malley and gave it new prominence.
"[Florence Nightingale] had been seized by a 'passion' for her cousin,
Marianne Nicholson. 'I never loved but one person with passion in my
life and that was she,' she wrote in 1846."[33] When I first read this, it

struck me very forcibly. Could it be, I thought, that Cecil Woodham-Smith, pillar of the genteel school of English historiography, was insinuating—as delicately as possible in the late 1940s when homosexuality was still a taboo subject—that Florence Nightingale had lesbian proclivities? This was a biographical bombshell. Even (or especially) Lytton Strachey, in his scathing attack on Nightingale, had not suggested that this eminent Victorian lady was gay.

The assertion by her most popular biographer that Florence Nightingale had "passions" for women may have helped to bring her to the devoted attention of American academics in the 1970s who were interested in gender issues. These included two first-class scholars, Martha Vicinus and Mary Poovey, whose work caused a much-deserved revival of Nightingale studies in the United States. But the lesbian innuendo also stoked the fires of men like F. B. Smith who found Nightingale power-hungry and overrated. Reportedly, both sophisticated English columnists and lecturers in schools of nursing anxious to raise a snigger have liked to toss off the "fact" that Florence Nightingale was gay.[34]

Since the lesbian accusation is important, let me be very clear and explicit. Florence Nightingale was not a lesbian. History, as opposed to imaginative literature, is based on evidence, and no one has produced any evidence that Florence Nightingale ever engaged in sexual relations with women. This I assume to be the standard working definition of a lesbian. Given the immense volume of documentation we have about Nightingale's life, this lack of evidence must be given full weight. No one during her life reported or suspected anything that can be construed as sexual acts with men or women. From everything we know about Florence Nightingale, if ever there was a woman conspicuously chaste, resolutely celibate, and absolutely virginal, it was she.

It is true that Florence Nightingale was a lifelong spinster, but anyone inclined to argue that her refusal to marry is evidence of her homosexual tendencies must be prepared to entertain the possibility that Oscar Wilde, with his wife and two sons, was actually straight. It is true that, because of her exceptionally wide reading of literature from Plato to George Sand, Florence Nightingale was probably more aware of the possibility of sexual relations between women than most women of her period. It is also true that until her return from the Crimea in 1856, she often shared a bed with a girl or woman. "My experience of women is al-most as large as Europe," she wrote to Mary Clarke Mohl in 1861. "And it is intimate too, I have lived and slept in the same bed with English Countesses and Prussian Bauerinnen. No Roman Catholic Supérieure has ever had charge of women of the different creeds that I have. No woman has excited 'passions' among women more than I have."[35] But the fact that Nightingale could make this remark so casually, in a letter harshly critical of women, indicates that there were no lesbian skeletons to hide in the Nightingale closet. Indeed, if sleeping beside a person of the same sex were prima facie evidence of homosexuality, then virtually 100 percent of British men and women before the twentieth century were gay.

As a child and young woman Florence Nightingale was not free to know her body or to explore her physical needs. Even by the standards of her day and her class, she enjoyed remarkably little private space, whether at home or away. When Florence traveled, it was always with a personal maid appointed by her mother, who usually slept in her room, and she was invariably chaperoned by her parents, aunts, uncles, or re-spectable married couples. Yes, Nightingale did have beloved female friends, but once they were past puberty, they were rarely alone in a room together. Once into their teens, the Nightingale girls and their female cousins may have slept with aunts or older female friends, but not with each other.[36]

That being said, passionate friendship between members of the same sex was a key part of the experience of many great nineteenth-century British men and women, and it is no more impertinent or irrelevant to discuss it in Nightingale's case than in anyone else's. It is counterproduc-tive to shirk documentary evidence of Nightingale's feelings for men and women or, worse, censor that evidence. Surely in twenty-first-century Western culture it is possible to honor celibacy, accept homosexuality in both men and women, and refrain, in general, from censuring what in-dividuals do in the privacy of their own homes. We can admire a woman who never had a love affair and never married. We can examine without prejudice the achievements of a woman who freely admitted to herself and to others that she once passionately loved her cousin and that, in the course of a long life, other women were precious to her.

Precisely because Nightingale was an Eminent Victorian and because one of the great defining myths of the Victorian era was that women had no erotic feelings, we need to grasp the nettle of Florence Nightingale's sexuality. We need to see that her urgent insistence on lifelong celibacy was fully compatible with passionate friendships for men and women. Without indulging in reductive sexological labeling, we need to think about why a woman who so prized passion in herself and others did not marry, had no affairs, aroused no sexual jealousies, in fact is never on record as having committed an improper act—and yet prayed obsessively for "purity." Why did she write to a woman she hardly knew, "As for me, I have said to corruption, Thou art my brother and sister"?

Chapter 10

MRS. NIGHTINGALE
SAYS NO

I n 1845, Florence Nightingale secretly made plans to train as a nurse in a public hospital and then perhaps start a Protestant sisterhood dedicated to the care of the indigent sick. To prepare herself, Florence used every spare minute to read everything she could about hospitals, nursing, and the social conditions of the poor. In the late 1830s the Poor Laws Commission, under the direction of Edwin Chadwick, had begun an exhaustive inspection of every aspect of public health, especially in the new industrial communities and the slums of the great cities. The Commission's reports, notably *The Sanitary Conditions of the Labouring Classes* of 1842, sold thousands of copies and caused a sensation. In his position as assistant Registrar General, William Farr had begun collecting data on what we would now call mortality and morbidity, issuing his own annual reports, and founding the whole discipline of medical statistics. In his *Philosophy of Public Health* (1837–39) the Unitarian T. Southwood Smith had begun to educate the public in the need for clean water and good drainage. Charles Dickens was giving Britain's poor the unforgettable faces of Oliver Twist, Smike, and Joe the crossing sweeper.

Florence Nightingale, like Lord Palmerston and Lord Shaftesbury, had become convinced that improved public health measures were the royal road to making Britain a healthier nation, and she was already becoming known in her social group for her panoramic expertise in what we would now call health care provision. But Nightingale was increas-

ingly desperate to stop reading and do something to relieve human suffering. She was ashamed to spend her days in the mixture of idle pleasure and earnest discourse that was characteristic of her set. She had had
years of playing duets, listening to brilliant young Tom Macaulay discourse on national policy over dinner, and waltzing into the small hours,
and now she was tired of it all.

By the age of twenty-five, Florence Nightingale was clear that what
she wanted to do with her life was to care for the sick in public institutions—municipal hospitals, orphanages, fever hospitals, lying-in wards,
prison infirmaries, madhouses. She also was aware that there were immense obstacles to her doing this. In Britain in 1845, middle- and
upper-class families cared for their sick at home, with the help of privately hired doctors and nurses, and so hospitals were almost by definition places of last resort for the indigent. From the official reports she
eagerly read and from the personal testimony of medical friends Florence
knew that hospitals were crowded, filthy, meagerly funded, and badly
run. All too often the staff consisted of brutal doctors, drunken orderlies, and women down on their luck. Middle-class women were neither
common nor welcome in such places.

Florence Nightingale had all the makings of a great clinician. Yet she
did not aspire to be a doctor, and to the end of her life she rather disap-
proved of women who sought to be doctors and not nurses. The reasons
for this were partly societal, partly intellectual, partly religious. In the
middle decades of the nineteenth century only a handful of women succeeded in getting formal medical training. The mere idea of a lady doctor
was considered aberrant by Victorian society at large, and to the end of
the century the medical profession remained monumentally committed
to keeping women out. None of Florence Nightingale's education was
in biological science, and in her youth medical science was not in the
vanguard. With its reliance on bloodletting, purges, emetics, blisters,
opiates, and medications based on heavy metals and alcohol, medicine
still owed more to Galen than to Lister. The great advances in treatment,
notably anesthesia and antiseptic practices, were just coming over the
horizon, so even surgery was skilled butchery on living human bodies.
Many patients were treated but few were cured, and some died from the
treatment. As a result, most early Victorian doctors were still humble
bonesetters and apothecaries, men who came to the servants' entrance,

not the front door. But, above all, Nightingale's idea of nursing was based on an ethic of public service. She believed that middle-class women entering the workforce for the first time could be of more use to the community as nurses than as doctors.

The more sick people she attended, the more dissatisfied, even ashamed Nightingale was about the Lady Bountiful role of mopping a sick person's brow and praying for his or her soul. Nightingale lived at the heart of Britain's intellectual community, and she was in touch with the progress being made in science, economics, and statistics. Her spirituality was matched by her intelligence, her powers of observation, and her obsession with recording and tabulating facts. She became convinced that with enough knowledge and enough intelligent care, it was possible not only to ease pain but to make people healthy again.

The year 1845 gave Nightingale the chance to put some of her nursing ideas into practice. She did everything she could for Mrs. Hogg, the steward's wife at Embley, blind and dying in terrible pain, yet still obsessed by the indecorousness of being nursed by a woman of the upper classes. "It is horrible," Florence wrote to her mother, "to see habit strong in death & half painful & half ridiculous to hear a dying woman say . . . when I lifted her up, 'That is Miss Florence. Do not let her lift *her*. *She* is too heavy.' One w'd. have tho't death w'd have levelled all ranks."[1] No sooner had Florence reverently observed Mrs. Hogg's last days than Grandmother Shore had some kind of stroke and seemed close to death. Florence was allowed by her parents to spend some weeks in the ruinous old house at Tapton, and she nursed the old lady back into a semblance of health. Then Florence went to Lea Hurst, where her old nurse Frances Gale was suffering from what was probably congestive heart failure.

When Gale died, sitting up straight in her chair, Florence was with her, holding her hand. Afterward she sat in the room alone for some hours in case Gale's spirit might "still be lingering there among her tablecloths and may want us." Florence loved Gale very much; they had been friends as well as mistress and nurse. Convinced that death was just a transition to another state of being, Florence imagined Gale "now going to animate the body of a moral Napoleon or a Mère Angélique."[2] But she knew that this was her perception, not Gale's. If Gale found her way into heaven, it would be not because of her Christian beliefs or religious

observances but because she had led a life of selfless, loving service and
had suffered much. "You know," Florence wrote to Hilary, "she never
had the habit of a walk with God and perhaps she may require human
sympathies now to give her the impulse of resurrection."

With a strange eagerness, Florence watched people die, expecting to
see in them some word or expression that conveyed an awareness that
they were "communing in dreams with other invisible spirits, on the eve
of becoming like them."[3] But what she observed in the cases of both Mrs.
Hogg and Mrs. Gale was quite different. In her last weeks, Gale thought
more of her duties as housekeeper than of her immortal soul. She talked
of "being sadly off my teas and breakfasties lately," expressed great satisfaction in imagining how much the next person to occupy her bed would
appreciate the new pillowcases, and planned her own funeral. Gale's last
words were addressed not to the angels but to her fellow servants: "Don't
wake Burton. Hannah, go to your work." "How death always comes at
last as if nobody had ever heard of it before!" wrote Florence. "Two hours
before [Gale's] death her voice was as strong as ever, and she Hollowed
[*sic*] out to me to 'mind how I went down them stairs.' And now nothing
in her room to remind one of life excepting the tick of her watch, and
that stopped just before I came away . . . She will have 'a *great* funeral,'
white smocks carrying her across the common, 'not over the stiles,' she
said. There are a half a hundred of her friends to be invited, and we shall
all go together, and with *her*. How *unheimlich* it is coming out of the
room where there is only her and God and me, to come back into the
cold and false life of prejudices and hypocrisy and conventionalisms."[4]

Florence told no one in her family of her plans to nurse, not even her
cousin Hilary, whom she had grown very close to since the break with
Marianne Nicholson, but she did confide in two sets of family friends—
the Bunsens and the Howes—and received some mild encouragement.
To Christian Bunsen, she poured out her longing to try and "lift the load
of suffering from the helpless and miserable," and he told her about the
philanthropic work being undertaken by women in his own country. It
was from Bunsen that Florence Nightingale first heard of the religious
institution at Kaiserswerth near Frankfurt that trained lay deaconesses
to serve the indigent poor. Bunsen encouraged Nightingale to go to
Kaiserswerth to visit and learn.[5]

Samuel Gridley Howe and his new bride, Julia Ward Howe, came to

England on their honeymoon. The Howes were part of the old Unitarian-abolitionist network, and they accepted an invitation to stay a few days at Embley. This was one of Fanny Nightingale's social coups, as Samuel Gridley Howe was a celebrity. He had fought for six years in the war of Greek independence and then gone to Poland when a nationalist insurrection broke out there. Back in the United States Howe became the director of the Perkins School for the Blind, and he was famous all over the world for his work with a brilliant little girl who had lost both sight and hearing, Laura Bridgman.

Mrs. Howe, who was only one year older than Florence, noticed how absorbed she was by Dr. Howe's stories about the Perkins School. Florence requested a private interview with Samuel Howe and asked him if "it would be unsuitable and unbecoming for a young Englishwoman to devote herself to works of charity in hospitals and elsewhere as Catholic sisters do? Do you think it would be a dreadful thing?" Mr. Howe replied: "My dear Miss Florence, it would be unusual, and in England whatever is unusual is apt to be thought unsuitable; but I say to you, go forward if you have a vocation for that way of life; act up to your inspiration."[6] Had Mr. or Mrs. Nightingale known at the time what advice these worthy gentlemen were giving their daughter, they would have been indignant.

Florence also wrote to Hilary begging her to get from Mrs. Jameson, via Aunt Ju, the name and address of a German lady she had heard about, "who, not being a Catholic, could not take upon herself the vows of a Sister of Charity, but who obtained permission from the physician of the hospital of her town to attend the sick there, and perform all the duties which the Soeurs do in Dublin and the Hôtel Dieu, and who had been there fifteen years when Mrs. Jameson knew her. I do not want to know her name if it is a secret, but only if she has extended it further into anything like a Protestant sisterhood, if she had any plans of that sort that would embrace women of an educated class, and not, as in England, merely women who would be servants if they were not nurses. How she disposed of the difficulties of surgeons making love to her, and of living with women of indifferent character, who generally make the nurses of hospitals, as it appears she was quite a young woman when she began. These are difficulties which vows remove and one sees nothing else can."[7]

Aunt Julia and Anna Jameson were probably happy to send the information Florence requested, but her other friends and relatives in England were wary of encouraging her to pursue her dreams of hospital nursing. They knew that her parents and her sister did not share Florence's nursing vision, that in fact it horrified them. Taking soup, clean shirts, and words of comfort to local cottagers was every Christian's duty. To teach in a village school was right. To devote one's pocket money to Christian missions in the jungles of Africa or the slums of Manchester was admirable. But as Fanny and Parthe and WEN saw it, to desire to spend one's days in a hospital was mental sickness, not Christian charity. How could one imagine fine, fastidious, cultured Florence cleaning up human waste, stripping the rags and vermin off diseased bodies, and holding howling patients down during amputations?

Thus at Christmas of 1845, when Florence submitted a plan whereby she would work as a nurse for several months at the Salisbury Infirmary under the supervision of its chief physician, Dr. Fowler, a close family friend, quarrels broke out at Embley between Florence and her mother and sister, and WEN stalked off to his London club. Florence told her cousin Hilary that her mother was terrified "not of the physically revolting parts of a hospital but things about the surgeons and nurses which you may guess." Many years later, Florence remembered that Fanny had accused her of an illicit liaison with some "low vulgar surgeon." "My mother was so afraid I should hear indecencies. I heard far more indecencies from her evangelical friends with whom I had to play hostess in the nursery."[8] The Nightingales were also convinced that Florence's health would never stand the strain.

Florence was in despair over the failure of her plan. She had dared to try to realize a dream, and she had failed. As she says in her diary: "Ach ich fühl es wohl, ein Scheiden kaum so schwer von wahren Freuden als von einem schönem Traum [Oh how strongly I feel that it hurts less to lose actual joy than a beautiful dream]." She wrote to Hilary on December 11: "Well, my dearest . . . I dug after my poor little plan in silence, even from you. It was to go to be a nurse at Salisbury Hospital for these few months to learn the 'prax' . . . And then I had such a fine plan . . . of taking a small house in West Wellow.—Well, I do not much like talking about it, but I thought something like a Protestant Sisterhood, without vows, for women of educated feelings, might be established.[9] But there have been difficulties about my very first step, which terrified Mama . . . nothing will be

done this year at all events, and I do not believe, ever; and no advantage
that I can see comes of my living on, excepting that one becomes less and
less of a young lady every year. You will laugh, dear, at the whole plan, I
daresay; but no one but the mother of it knows how precious an infant idea
becomes; nor how the soul dies, between the destruction of one and the
taking up of another. I shall never do anything and am worse than dust
and nothing . . . Oh for some strong thing to sweep this loathsome life into
the past."[10]

Not allowing Florence to work at Salisbury Infirmary under the devoted eye of Dr. Fowler was one of the biggest mistakes Fanny and WEN
ever made. By claiming to know better, impugning her motives, and generally treating her like a silly child, they twisted their daughter's character
without softening her will. What Florence needed was not hysteria and
lectures but a taste of reality. A few months of full-time squalid drudgery
would have shown her that "prax" was not the best use of her talents and
that the average doctor and nurse had only so much to teach her.[11] Fears
for her virtue seem ludicrous. On the other hand, if Flo had come upon
some young doctor with a brilliant mind, a shining soul, and a shabby
coat, if they had fallen in love, would this have been so very bad? Flo
would have had her dream companion, and there might have been a
grandchild at Embley, botanizing with Grandma or reading Greek with
Grandpa in the library.

OVER THE NEXT FIVE YEARS, Florence Nightingale's life, to the
superficial eye, was one of privilege and pleasure. She was a superbly educated lover of literature who received all the latest books and articles—in
three modern languages and two ancient. Whether it was the newest
novel by Dickens or the poetry of the mysterious Acton, Currer, and El-
lis Bell, or Farr's mortality and morbidity reports for the year, Florence
Nightingale got hold of a copy and read it. A lover of music in the era
before recording, she was in the rare position of being able to compare
the great sopranos of the recent past with the new Swedish singing sensation and conclude that Miss Jenny Lind "really requires a new language
to define her."[12]

Nightingale's cultural resources were not limited to the arts. Fascinated by mathematics, economics, and science, from her teenage years

she regularly attended meetings of the British Association. As a girl Florence Nightingale stepped up to assist the great Michael Faraday in one of his legendary demonstrations of electromagnetism, duly recording what she had learned in her microscopic book of useful data. Such was the Nightingale family's commitment to botany that Florence's mother could write a personal note to their friend Sir W. J. Hooker, the great botanist of Kew Gardens, begging him to identify a fern that she had found, which proved to be extremely rare.[13] Mesmerism was an enthusiasm that gripped Florence Nightingale, like so many of her contemporaries, and she was keen to practice her skills on people and animals. In Oxford, in the rooms of Christ Church undergraduate Frank Buckland, Florence was ready to mesmerize a bear cub that was threatening to bite her, until Richard Monckton Milnes stepped in gallantly and put the animal to sleep.[14]

And at a time when few women ventured beyond the boundaries of their native village, Florence Nightingale traveled constantly and travel gave her a vital window on the world. Even as she lamented her family's peripatetic ways, pleaded to be left quietly alone in one place to do her work, and chafed at having to always travel "tacked on to someone's apron strings," Nightingale got detailed knowledge of three very different parts of England—the industrial Midlands, the agricultural South, and the metropolis. This firsthand experience of the world would be crucial in the days ahead.

Furthermore, when Florence was away at a safe distance, in a place where Fanny could not nag, Parthe moan, or WEN pontificate, she felt nothing but love and merriment and complicity with her "dear people." In fact, the letters Florence Nightingale wrote at this time offer crucial insight into different sides of her character. They help us to understand why family and friends adored Florence so much, why she was so important to each of the other three Nightingales, why they just could not let her go her way.

With her sister Parthe, Flo shared gossip about their extensive acquaintance, an intellectual comradeship born of those long shared hours in the schoolroom, and an enjoyment of the complex comedy of their parents' interactions. After an exhausting journey with both her parents, during which WEN insisted that they had no time to stop for rest and food, Florence wrote: "Of course you know it was an affair of the first importance to accomplish the journey in the least possible space of time, which brooked *no* delay, as the fates of thousands depended on our reaching the Romsey Lodge at ten minutes past five o'clock London time (consequently six minutes past Southampton time). I poured into [her young cousin Alf, who met them at the station] as much news as I could in 7-tenths of a minute, a fatal delay at the inn, occasioned by the post-boy's requiring spiritual support, but providentially made up by the increased velocity consequent on such support being administered . . . At Winchester Mama rushed wildly into a shop, crying 'Buns, buns' & holding out certain coins of great value in one hand, & fell prostrate across the counter into the shop boy's arms, in her search after food, while I endeavoured, by a preternatural solemnity, to maintain our dignity with two princely men in the shop, & turning my head without an inch of my body, said to the shop-boy, Tardy of purpose, give *me* the buns."[15]

The talent for comic writing emerged again in several letters Florence wrote in the late fall of 1848 from Great Malvern in Worcestershire where she and her mother went to take the cure. Men like Charles Darwin and Lord Aberdeen, sometime Prime Minister, found regular comfort at Dr. James Gully's hydropathic clinic, but the doctor was most successful with women patients.[16] Fanny Nightingale duly fell under the doctor's spell, and Florence wrote to Parthe: "Mama was so taken with him [Gully] that I was obliged to tell him that I had a father living."[17]

In letters to her mother, Florence is cheerfully chatty and informative. She wrote of visits from friends, interviews with the local schoolteacher, the cost of rented pianos, servants who might do, keeping the overpowering Aunt Julia away at all costs from poor little lame cousin Beatrice, the hairpiece Cousin Hilary had embarrassingly left behind and which Flo relied on Fanny not to brandish at the breakfast table. Thus Florence described to her mother her first visit to the home of the new vicar, the Reverend Empson, and his wife: "We were philosophical, rhapsodical, & a most eloquent trio on the physiology of blue carpets & bad characters (in Willow Woods) & swore eternal friendship over their muddy drinking water."[18] The letters show that, as far as religious feeling went, or relations with the tenants and villagers, or art and music appreciation, Fanny and Flo were astonishingly in tune. Peeping through the text, we can see that when it came to ordering a good dinner, telling a funny story, or keeping the gentlemen entertained and the ladies topped up with tea, Fanny and Flo were a mother-daughter duo that carried all before them.

WEN remarked in a letter that his daughter Florence was "not like other folk of a truth, and I shall be her humble servant in many matters."[19] In letters to her father, Florence shows off her erudition, spreads her philosophical wings, and argues her political case, but she is also astonishingly frank about her frustrations. She tells him quite bluntly that she is desperate to escape the bitterness and pain of women like her aunt Patty and his aunt Evans, who had never been allowed to put their talents to good use. "Why cannot a woman follow abstractions like a man? Has she less imagination, less intellect, less self-devotion, less religion than a man? I think not. Yet she has never produced one single great work of art, or science or literature. She has never, with the exception perhaps of Deborah, the Virgin and the Mère Angélique [of Port-Royal] been deemed a fitting vessel for the Spirit of God . . . And why? . . . Is it not because *the habit* of never interesting herself much in any conversation, printed or spoken, which is not personal . . . renders her powerless to rise to any abstract good or general view. It cuts her wings, it palsies her muscles, and shortens her breath for higher things and for a clearer, but sharper, atmosphere, in which she has no lungs to live. She has fed on sugar plums, her appetite is palled for bread."[20]

Florence joked about her father groaning to receive yet another of her "pamphlets," but she knew that in fact nothing gave him such pleasure as a free flow of lyrical-philosophical prose like the following. "I have given up riding and all sports of the field, even my gun [Florence wrote to WEN from Lea Hurst], and subsided into an excellent plain cook and housekeeper. Walking down the road to poor Poyser's, I found an immense field spider finishing his morning's work, walking round and round drawing the thread out of his tail with his right hind leg, and (as cleverly as any Manchester machine, working under the highest degree of excitement) hooking the thread on to each radius with his left hind leg, as he passed them. His morning's work done, he began to catch flies, and meanwhile ants were dragging away large moths and all scales of animals were at the work of destruction. And I, moving grandly on my pivot, stood watching the consumption and wondering whether there were superior intelligences, whom we are equally unconscious of, who in the same grand way are observing on us killing each other to the tune of slow music, and are thinking why we cannot eat each other fair like savages at that rate."[21]

CULTURAL PURSUITS and social junketing did not take up all of Miss Florence Nightingale's time in her late twenties. By a careful use of time, she was able to devote a not inconsiderable number of hours in the day to nursing village folk like "poor Poyser," Elijah Humby, and Mary Flint, as well as to the study of international public health policy at night. In London, she spent 2–4 p.m. three afternoons a week looking after patients at the Verral Institute for Diseases and Distortions of the Spine.[22]

Teaching was an area of public service where women were more tolerated than in medicine. While continuing to tutor younger cousins like Shore Smith and William Bonham-Carter at home, Florence became actively involved in the charity schools for poor children that many members of her parents' wealthy social group supported. This was a time in Great Britain when there was no national system of even elementary education for all citizens and when a high percentage of the population, especially the female population, was illiterate. The Nightingale family was practically and philosophically committed to educating all citizens, and in this, as in so many other social issues, they were much in advance of general public opinion.

Fanny Smith Nightingale's family had long been involved in founding and financing schools for the poor, and she took an active interest in the village schools both at Lea Hurst and at Embley. Uncle Ben Smith and then his daughter Barbara were both at different times at the financial helm of a small experimental school in London. But Aunt Ju was the Smith family education maven, constantly visiting schools at home and abroad and collecting information on international trends in education. Julia Smith was soon to become an enthusiastic member of the group, led by fellow Unitarian Elizabeth Reid, that offered higher education courses to women at Bedford College, London.

Florence Nightingale moved into teaching as a way of obeying her call from God even though she never felt she had a "genius" for education. She remarked once that she would have preferred to teach the bad than the young, which perhaps means that she would have liked to work with the inmates of prisons and reformatories, as her male friends Lord Shaftesbury, Sidney Herbert, and Richard Monckton Milnes did. I think Nightingale was haunted by the knowledge that teaching was all too often the pet activity of a class of ignorant, proselytizing, condescending, busybody middle-class women somewhat on the lines of Dickens's Mrs. Pardiggle in *Bleak House.* Such women, as she once fiercely argued in a letter to her father, were more concerned to save their own souls by working with the poor than to impart useful information and skills, and yet was she so very different? In this, as in so many things, Nightingale was much too hard on herself. She was a superb teacher, and her pedagogical uncertainties were certainly not caused by any sense of intellectual inadequacy. What she lamented in teaching, as in nursing, was her lack of training.

Nightingale did some work in one of the Ragged Schools that Lord Shaftesbury, Charles Dickens, Angela Burdett-Coutts, and others were organizing for the poorest of the poor in London. Teaching in a Ragged School was not for the dainty or the faint of heart.[23] But Florence loved her school and on one occasion smuggled some of her dirty, vermin-ridden pupils up into her bedroom for treats and high jinks. Unsurprisingly, Mrs. Nightingale was less than thrilled. She refused to allow her daughter to go out in London without a male escort, and so Florence's involvement in the Ragged Schools project was limited.

In the country, Florence was freer to move about independently, and through her twenties she became increasingly involved in the schools for the girls and young women who lived in the villages near Lea Hurst and Embley. Florence seized on the fact that these village schools for girls served a key social purpose. Many women who worked in the factories, on the farms, and at home thirsted for the information, entertainment, and stimulus books provided. Numeracy too was essential in an increasingly commercial and consumerist world where women were well advised to think about things like prices, wages, debt, and inheritance. And so Florence planned the program of studies and taught the older or more intelligent girls, who then passed on what they had learned to the others. This modest two-tier educational system made the most of her own talents and time as the chief organizer while at the same time promoting confidence and independence in her students.

Nightingale once made a detailed set of notes on what she planned for her pupils. Here we can see her mind at work. She had always been fascinated by physical geography, and so she had her students work with maps and think about the course of distant rivers and glaciers, and the way the globe showed the continents fitting together. History, she decided, was best started locally, with the girls reconstructing the stories of their own families and villages, and then moving back in time. She had the students discuss politics and the power of the Queen and the Parliament as it related to themselves. Nightingale also promoted hygiene and good work habits by insisting that her pupils arrive punctually, keep their hands clean and their slates neat, and pay their weekly penny for tuition on time.

The girls and women who were taught by Florence Nightingale responded with enthusiasm. Even after a twelve-hour day in the mill or the dairy they came to school, and they somehow managed to fit in their homework. Nightingale's own charisma and commitment were the keys to this success. She not only gave instruction, she made the girls laugh with her jokes and her mimicry. "She's different from most other rich people," I imagine her students saying to one another as they clattered home in the dark over the cobbles in their clogs. "She doesn't assume that you're stupid just because you're poor and female."

But when Florence really put her heart into teaching, when she ran back home from the village, out of breath, hair untidy, skirt muddied, late for dinner, she was greeted with angry recriminations by the other Nightingales. Once again she had crossed the invisible line that divided part-time do-goodery from full-time social work. "When I was 30," Florence wrote some years later, resentment still hot within her, "I had an Adult Evening school for factory-girls which was, on the whole, the most satisfactory thing I ever did. My sister went into hysterics because I attended this. And my mother requested me to abstain for 6 months & to give up that time entirely to her."[24]

FLORENCE DREAMED obsessively of leaving home, being her own mistress, and working philanthropic wonders, but while her dreams got a sympathetic hearing from relatives like Mai and Hilary and friends like Mary Clarke and Selina Bracebridge, they got a frosty reception at home. Her mother tasked her for ingratitude. Her sister clung to her like a limpet. Her father played the skeptic and disputed the mere idea that one person could make a difference in the hard world outside the gates of Embley Park. And whereas Uncle Ben Smith gave his daughters an ample independent income as they turned twenty-one, Mr. Nightingale kept his purse strings drawn tight.[25] None of the people who claimed to love Flo best would help make her dreams come true. In fact, they accused her of vanity and grandiosity.

It wasn't that Florence's family was cruel or neglectful—it was their utter predictability and lack of vision she could not bear. They were all three so boring, so satisfied with their lives, doing exactly the same this year as last, the petty pace creeping on from day to day just as Shakespeare had remarked. Her father read interminably from the newspapers, force-feeding her like a goose. If only the man had something worthwhile to do! Her mother and sister dashed about to parties or lay about complaining how tired they were. In the splendid salon at Embley, Florence would sit, night after night, doing fancy needlework while the men twaddled and the women twittered, until the clock at last struck ten and she could escape to her own room and her own work.

If her family had disowned her, like so many daughters in popular fiction, or thrown her to the Victorian equivalent of lions at the Coliseum, her road to heaven would have been easier. But instead the other three Nightingales persisted in loving Florence, prizing her, putting up with her, suffering under her dissatisfaction, and missing her atrociously when she went away. The burden of their love and need was insupportable, as was their inability to understand why she could not be happy with them.

Like the Buddha, like St. Francis, like St. Teresa of Avila, Florence Nightingale considered the wealthy society into which she was born to be trivial and degraded. The pleasure it offered was in her eyes a snare and a delusion. What Florence wanted to do, what gave her joy and stopped the dreaming, was to take care of sick people, rub their backs, apply poultices, administer potions. On July 16, 1846, she wrote in her journal: "Rubbed Mrs. Spence for the second time. Very sorry not to stay with Grandmama. I am such a creeping worm that if I have anything of the kind to do, I can do without marriage, or intellect, or social intercourse, or any of the things people sigh after . . . My mind is absorbed with the idea of the sufferings of man, it besets me behind and before. A very one-sided view, but I can hardly see anything else and all the poets sing of the glories of this world seems to me untrue. All the people I see are eaten up with care or poverty or disease. When I go into a cottage I long to stop there all day, to wash the children, relieve the mother, stay by the sick one."[26]

Nightingale never forgave her parents and sister for not accepting her vision of life while she was still young. In diaries, on scraps of paper, she gave vent to her feelings of anguish, boredom, and frustration. These papers she carefully retained throughout her long life, even copying some of them out again on fresh notepaper. It was important, she was sure, for future generations to know just what she had suffered, just why she had, for so long, failed to do God's will.[27]

So vivid, so passionate, so extensive is Nightingale's indictment of her life before 1853 that most biographers have taken her line, galloping to reach the end of that perplexingly lengthy period when their soon-to-be heroine Florence failed to respond to the personal call from God she had received in her seventeenth year. For myself, I feel obliged to observe that the years 1846–53, as they were lived rather than remembered, were the most diverse in Florence Nightingale's life, filled with interest and activity, information and emotion, experience and analysis, all of which would be crucial in the long decades of reclusion and lonely labor ahead.

Chapter 11

FLORENCE
NIGHTINGALE
IS TEMPTED

There were moments in Nightingale's ongoing self-analysis when she came to the painful realization that it was not just the demands of family that limited the scope of her activity, but her own internal turmoil and its deleterious effects on her health. She could have done more to address the problems of the poor and afflicted in her immediate vicinity if she had not spent so much time dreaming and scheming, chastising herself for the dreams and schemes, and then falling ill. We could label this the Aunt Patty Smith syndrome. A woman's frustration leads to hypochondria and on to marginalization, ridicule, weakness and so down in a vicious spiral.

When she was at home—which, as Parthenope liked to observe mordantly, was less and less often—Florence Nightingale alternated between frenzied activity and apathy. One month she would rise before dawn to write the hated courtesy letters, inventory the household linen, china, and cutlery ("Can reasonable people *want* all this?" Flo demanded indignantly of Clarkey), make fifty-six pots of jam, slog through the *Phaedo* in Greek, translate German scholarly articles for her father, read Disraeli's latest hit, *Coningsby,* aloud to her mother, regale visitors with gossip and quips and classical quotations, and generally be the perfect daughter, without neglecting her patients and students.[1] The next month, exhausted by so much self-imposed labor, she would collapse, take to her bed, wrap the whole household in the pall of her misery, and then be carried off for a visit by adoring, sympathetic friends.

But if Florence found life with Papa and Mama so unsatisfactory, why did she not marry and set up her own home? Whereas Parthe and thousands of other middle-class young women at that time seemed doomed to spinsterhood because of a dearth of young men, Flo never lacked for admirers.[2] Even during one chilly stay with her mother at Malvern she attracted the attentions of George Dawson, an earnest young lecturer on "Xtianity & Democracy."

By 1847, Florence Nightingale was a good deal longer in the tooth than the average English bride, but women in her set often married at thirty or even forty. "I wish for grey hairs," Flo wrote to Hilary. "They are of the greatest possible convenience & if they could be had before other infirmities would be of as much value as brevet rank."[3] No one in Florence's generation of the family was rushing into matrimony. Marianne Nicholson was older than Flo and she was not married, nor was her brother Henry—still pining after Flo—nor Hilary Bonham-Carter, nor, of course, Parthe. Aunt Julia at forty was actually rumored to be marrying a certain German widower. In a letter to her sister, probably in 1848, Florence wrote tartly: "I was glad to hear of Mary F's marriage, though I thought she was married to Sarah. How often an attack of Terror of Old Maidenhood comes over a woman about forty. If she can weather it, the mad dog goes off, and she does very well. Otherwise, I think that it is a very common age for people who have been Sisters of Charity all their lives to take fright and become wives."[4]

There were obliging friends like Fanny Allen in Mrs. Nightingale's social group, ready to opine that, considering the signal happinesses and comforts of their parental home, Parthe and Flo were only rational to avoid matrimony. This was the brave fiction that Parthe and Fanny maintained, and yet everyone knew that it was Parthenope Nightingale's pinched face and sickly body that made her the perennial bridesmaid, never the bride. Everyone knew that Mr. and Mrs. Nightingale wanted nothing better than to order the cake and rice for their daughter Florence's wedding to the eligible Mr. This or Lord That.

But to remain celibate was Florence's firm intention. She believed that this was God's expressed will for her, and she aspired to live a righteous life patterned after the Catholic saints. A mystic with a deep and abiding sense of the numinous, she once explained in a letter to Mary Clarke that everyday life for her resembled a two-story house in a quattrocento painting. On the ground floor leading onto the street, men and women go about their business, while God, a shadowy old gentleman separated from his neighbors only by a flight of stairs and a curtain, benignly watches all the bustle from his first floor apartment. Or else, Nightingale goes on, human life is a dark landscape where all is indistinct, alien, hidden, until the moon comes out to etch in silver the beauty of the transcendental landscape.[5] According to Nightingale's idiosyncratic, Plato-inflected theology, if she could only achieve a saintly life *hic et nunc*, in the next stage of life that attended her after death she would rise onto a higher plane of spirituality.

Celibacy has deep roots in Christian culture.[6] From the early days, Church Fathers like Paul, Augustine, and Jerome preached that holiness and celibacy were narrowly linked—if you were a man. The swiftest and surest way to God was asceticism, and while starving the body of food, warmth, and comfort was salutary in general, such severe practices were especially enjoined as they helped men to repress sexual desire and avoid erotic pleasure.

For women, the official Church mandate was quite different. Celibacy, one might say, was too good for them. A woman was enjoined to be chaste beyond reproach before marriage, take the husband of her father's choice, be a modest and compliant sexual partner to her husband alone, and produce as many children, preferably sons, as she could. Any sexual fault, for maiden or wife, was harshly punished on earth, and the divine forgiveness hereafter was not assured. Only Mary Magdalen and a handful of other women were allowed by Christian hagiographic tradition to accede to sainthood as reformed sinners who had enjoyed a youth of sexual pleasure.

St. Paul and St. Augustine did agree that there was a tiny minority of women who might remain virgins and live the ascetic life, either as solitary eremites or as members of religious communities. Some few women, they acknowledged, received a personal and specific message from God that the Church was prepared to endorse and that authorized them to dedicate themselves to asceticism. Joan of Arc, Maid of Orleans, was burned at the stake in part because the religious authorities of her day refused to believe that her message came from God, not the devil.

Though she prudently refrained from talking much about her call from God, Florence Nightingale was convinced that she had indeed received a special message.

This spiritual imperative was reinforced by Nightingale's jaundiced view of Victorian married life and of Victorian men's contempt for women. For example, Florence had a beloved and admired friend, Caroline Archer Clive, an acclaimed poet and novelist who published under the pseudonym V. Mrs. Archer Clive was an unusually happy wife and mother, but she was lame, and many even in the enlightened social group the Clives frequented felt that the Reverend Clive was a poor dog to have taken such damaged goods for his wife. Florence was outraged by the men who dared to pity V's husband: "I admire her husband for disproving the general proposition that *we* are to be treated as furniture or a piece of clothes for the man's vanity while *they* are to be as ugly as they please & no one is to wonder at anybody's marrying *them*. I was in ten thousand rages with Mr. Hamilton Grey having the impudence to worry to *me* 'how any man could marry V.' He who himself is much lamer than she, and has married Pots and Pans, you know, the famous Etrurian Lion."[7]

Nightingale saw that English spinsters like her aunts Patty and Ju were all too often poor, dependent, and despised, but she felt that marriage was jumping out of the frying pan into the fire. She remained unconvinced that her financial and social situation would improve if she married. Married women lost all legal standing and claim to their inheritances and earnings and were dependent on their husbands' goodwill and good humor. It was true that a handful of married women in the Nightingales' social network were permitted by their husbands to work for the causes closest to their hearts, and Fanny surely reminded her daughter of this fact. One such woman was Elizabeth Fry, the Quaker woman who had become well known for her work on prison reform. In America the Nightingales knew about the American abolitionists Angelina Grimké Weld, Elizabeth Cady Stanton, and Harriet Beecher Stowe. But as Florence could have heard from friends like Julia Ward Howe, even these exceptionally strong, energetic, talented, and privileged women found their work in the public sphere slowed by domestic cares.

And for Florence physical motherhood held no special charms, though she loved children and got on exceptionally well with them. Children, she once remarked to Cousin Hilary, saw one for what one was and didn't talk twaddle about one's advanced research or beautiful epistolary talents. But Flo had seen friends and relatives like her other aunts, Joanna and Joan and Ann, reduced to weakness, immobility, and irritability by years of childbearing and breast-feeding. A woman's fertility was a giant wild card in the game of life. On the one hand, there was the risk of bearing a succession of children one must in conscience bring up, and quite possibly dying in the attempt. On the other hand, one might, like Florence's own mother, Fanny, be unable to bear the desired child, the male heir, and suffer in other ways.

And just as, generally speaking, monastic women throughout history have had far less difficulty than their male counterparts in quelling sexual desire, so Florence Nightingale was not, it would seem, at the mercy of raging hormones.[8] If she was tempted, she did not fall. Unlike other brilliant women contemporaries, Florence Nightingale did not fall madly in love with a man. The dreams that beset her were not of romance but of ministry, shared preferably but not necessarily by a beloved, ideal companion. What she sought passionately was not physical intimacy but spiritual communion and active collaboration. This, at least, is what her extant papers tell us.

IN THE LATE SUMMER of 1847 Florence received some amazing news from her aunt Julia. Their great friend in Paris, Miss Mary Clarke, now in her early fifties, had married Julius Mohl. Florence learned of the marriage within weeks of its occurrence, and two months later she sent two letters of congratulation to the new Madame Mohl.[9] This delay of two months seems to me significant, since all the Nightingales were punctilious in their correspondence. Florence knew very well that Clarkey would be looking for a letter from her and depended on her, the most empathetic of friends, to triumphantly proclaim that marrying Julius was the right thing. Julius too was one of Florence's favorite people in the world, and she certainly wished both of them nothing but happiness.

My sense is that she was unable to write because the Mohl marriage shocked her into silence, and when at last she wrote she could not control her emotions or say everything in one letter. Her October 17 let-

ter was full of the wit and pathos and philosophy people expected from
the younger Miss Nightingale, but it also betrayed the writer's conster-
nation and disarray. "In single life the stage of the Present & Outward
World is so filled with phantoms . . . of Vague Remorse, Fears, dwelling
on the threshold of every thing we undertake alone. Dissatisfaction with
what is, & Restless Yearnings for what is not, Cravings after a world of
wonders . . . The stage of actual life gets so filled with these that we are
almost pushed off the boards & are conscious of only just holding on to
the foot lights by our chins." Surely Florence is talking about herself here.

And Florence wrote another letter, dated October 13 (i.e., four days
earlier).[10] In this letter, Florence narrates at length a dream she has had,
an allegorical retelling of Clarkey's life, in which she describes Miss
Clarke high up on a promontory overlooking the Mediterranean and
about to leap into the sea. This scene reproduces the legend of the poet
Sappho, who allegedly gave up the love of women on meeting Phaon,
and when that young man spurned her, she jumped to her death from a
cliff at Leucadia. In the dream, Life offers Mary Clarke first a wreath of
rosebuds signifying "the first love, the love of fancy," but the Genius will
not allow her to take this. Then Life offers "a pale scentless flower—and
its beauty was only the ideal existing in one's own mind . . . Its name is
the Besoin d'aimer [Need to love]." This too is declined. Next, Life offers
a crown of gorgeously colored and perfumed hothouse pomegranates
representing the Love of Passion. But the Guardian genius would not let
her take it. And when I looked I saw the petals of the beautiful exotic
falling off with their own weight." Next in the dream Mary Clarke, as
her summer comes to an end, is offered "a wreath of Oak from under the
open heaven & among the everlasting hills. Take it said the Guardian
Genius, it is the strong love of the Soul, the love given in the full force
of the inquiring and discriminating spirits."

Mary Clarke must make the great leap into the sea, where a small
boat awaits her, sailed by a trusty captain: "And the Guardian Angel said
to her: A vigorous intellect, uncommon powers, instead of affording an
easier descent, only raises you upon a higher eminence & gives you a
wider view of dangers & possibilities . . . For as has often been said, we
must all take Sappho's leap, one way or another, before we attain to her
repose & though some take it to death & some to marriage & some
again to a new life even in this world."

IN THE MIDDLE of October 1847 Florence Nightingale was in a dreadful state, thin, hollow-eyed, lying apathetically in bed but unable to sleep, trembling on the brink of a nervous breakdown, in the terrible grip of her dreams. Help came in the shape of another beloved female friend, Selina Bracebridge. Florence and other intimate friends liked to call her Sigma, since Selina was such a Hellenophile, and they often referred to her in writing by the Greek symbol Σ.

Selina and her husband, Charles, were embarking on a trip that would take them to Rome for the winter months. The Bracebridges were far from elderly, but they enjoyed poor health, and Florence, the couple explained to Fanny and WEN, would be of immense service in helping them survive the rigors of the journey. Of course, Mr. Nightingale would be responsible for paying all his daughter's expenses, but nonetheless, the opportunity to go abroad with such experienced, respectable, and agreeable married friends was a huge piece of good luck. Almost in a daze, Florence watched her mother and sister do her shopping and packing for the trip. WEN, for his part, drew up a detailed plan of what Florence must see when in Rome. So great was the family sense of Florence's privilege in going to Rome and Parthe's sacrifice in staying home that the Nightingale parents allowed the sisters a few days to themselves just before Florence set out.[11]

While Selina Bracebridge suffered terribly from neuralgic headaches throughout the long and arduous journey to Rome, Florence metamorphosed into a figure of unflagging energy and ebullient spirits. On the strength of two cups of black coffee, she was chipper even during the thirty-five-hour coach journey from Paris to Châlons, during which the passengers were allowed to alight only twice for a brief stop. Florence had already seen many Italian cities but not Rome, and her excitement was immense at the end of the eight-hour drive from Civita Vecchia when she got her first sight of the dome of St. Peter's by starlight. The magic was only beginning. "Oh how happy I was! I never enjoyed any time in my life as much as my time in Rome," Florence Nightingale later remembered.[12]

There seems to have been a general awareness in the Nightingale set that Rome was to be the occasion for a gifted, if unpublished, lady writer

to strut her stuff. Florence was ready to meet the challenge, and her letters from Rome caused a sensation in the family. Fanny wrote to Parthe:
"I am anxiously looking for Florence's letters . . . Is she not in the third
heaven, dear soul, how pleasant it is to think of her—instead of being up
to her neck in mud at West Wellow." And later: "We can never rejoice
sufficiently when we read these letters. Another this morning which having read four times, twice to Papa, twice to the Maids, & once to the
Empsons [vicar at East Wellow] (only selections). I have no doubt writing this journal will be invaluable to her in after life or I should fear she
was overdoing herself in order to take us along with her."[13]

As a young woman who had long had a thirst for "acquisition," Florence delighted in Rome with its wealth of art and architecture. The
Bracebridges were in touch with leading classical scholars and archeol-
ogists in the city, and so Florence not only read all the best books but
was escorted around the sites by experts. She could hardly bear to see
the Coliseum for memory of the Christians who were tortured there.
On the other hand, she loved the newly opened catacombs and remarked quite unself-consciously that among the souvenirs she picked
up on-site was a bone fragment of a martyr and the knee bone of a child
"whose skeleton I saw quite entire." With enlightened European tourists
like Florence Nightingale collecting bone fragments in Rome and
Richard Monckton Milnes using his personal chisel to remove ancient
inscriptions at Luxor, one wonders that there is anything at the great
ancient sites for us to see today. Florence's reaction to the Church of St.
John's fuor le Mura was similarly idiosyncratic. She found the place
"painfully disagreeable—like Almacks—from the galley slaves working
in the atrio." Who but Florence Nightingale, I wonder, would compare
the workplace of galley slaves to Almacks—the rooms where London's
most exclusive parties were held?[14] This former debutante's scars obviously were cut deep.

Very different was her first ecstatic visit to the Sistine Chapel. Florence lay down on the stone floor and simply gazed up in silence for
some hours. In a special letter to Parthe that must have taken the best
part of a day to compose, Florence does not so much offer criticism as
reveal deeply emotional reactions to works of art. When she gazed at the
Sibyl of Delphi, she projected onto Michelangelo's fresco her own sense
of divine mission. "There is a security of inspiration about [Michelan-

gelo's portrayal of the prophet] Isaiah, he is listening and he is speaking 'that which we *hear*, we say unto to you.' There is an anxiety, an effort to hear, even, about the Delphian [Sybil], she is not quite sure, there is an uncertainty, a wistfulness in her eyes—she expects to be rewarded rather in another stage than this for her struggle . . . there is no uncertainty in her feeling of being *called* . . . but she fears her earthly ears are 'heavy' and gross, and corrupt the meaning of the heavenly words."[15] This is less an interpretation of Michelangelo's painting than a cry from Florence Nightingale's own heart.[16]

She also looked attentively at a very different piece—the portrait of Beatrice Cenci by Guido Reni in the Palazzo Barberini. This famous picture was supposedly painted just before Beatrice was beheaded on the charge of having conspired to assassinate her father. He had killed one of Beatrice's brothers, raped her, and threatened the lives of her mother and other brother, but none of this could excuse patricide. "I have seen the Cenci," wrote Florence to Parthenope. "You cannot imagine how it makes one's heart swell. I could not live in a room with that picture . . . you go away with an iron hand grasping your heart that such a sorrow should be on earth."[17] Florence knows that Parthe will understand about Beatrice Cenci. When they were not together the two sisters had so much in common.

IF ROME IN 1847 was peculiarly capable of satisfying Florence Nightingale's intellectual appetite, history, art, and architecture were not at the core of her delight. She was in a rare state of contentment because she was with the Bracebridges, friends who not only adored her but gave her an intelligent combination of structured support and freedom of movement.

Charles Holte Bracebridge of Atherstone Hall was a man of large independent means and a certain eccentricity of conduct. He affected wide-brimmed hats and flowing capes à la Garibaldi. Bracebridge claimed descent from Lady Godiva, spoke several languages fluently, had traveled a good deal in both Europe and the Near East, and raised Arab thoroughbreds on his estate near Coventry. Intellectually Bracebridge came several notches below Florence's father, but when it came to making his way about Europe, Charles was efficient, and he and his wife, a friend of Mary Clarke who had lived for some years in Paris, had interesting contacts everywhere.[18]

Charles was a man of radical views. It happened that he and his wife and Florence Nightingale came to France and Italy at the very time when a great wave of revolutionary fervor began to wash over the Continent. Specifically, they were in the city of Rome in the first months of the papacy of Pius IX. The advent to the throne of St. Peter of this apparently mild, charming, and liberal cleric was mistakenly heralded as the forerunner of massive reforms in the corrupt Vatican states and an end to the fragmentation and foreign domination of Italy. Florence and the Bracebridges had several opportunities to see the new Pope and even talk to him in his private study, and they were wildly impressed with him. Over and again the Roman populace took to the streets en masse for peaceful demonstrations, and Charles Bracebridge was more than happy to get out and witness these events firsthand and to take his young friend Flo along.

Florence Nightingale was fond of Mr. Bracebridge and grateful for his bluff, uncomplicated help. She relished sitting down with him and working out the budget for travel, converting all the scudi and bajocchi into pounds, shillings, and pence, and advising her father on the exact exchange rate she had got for his banker's orders. But it was without any doubt Mrs. Bracebridge who made Rome such an uncomplicatedly magic place for this extremely complicated young woman. In many ways, Selina was a new, improved version of Aunt Mai and cousin Hilary. She had no children, and was delightfully anxious to dedicate herself to friends. She showered Florence with the combination of motherly concern, sisterly support, and admiring friendship that the younger woman craved. For his part Charles was only too pleased when his wife brought some surrogate daughters into their lives. He soon became as mad about Flo as his wife, especially as she proved so adept at applying leeches when he had one of his headaches.

Of her deep love for Selina Bracebridge, Florence wrote in her diary: "I wonder whether she [Selina] knows what a difference she has made in my life. The very fact of there being a person with whom one's thoughts are not pronounced fit only for a dream not worth disputing, who does not look upon one as a fanciful spoiled child who ought to take life as it is and enjoy it—that mere fact changes the whole aspect of things to one . . . As long as one believes that one's inmost self—i.e. the ideas which make one's life, are hollow, there is no support from within or without . . . God himself is at a distance. But given one heart of fellow feeling and the scene changes."[19] Florence wrote ecstatically to Hilary: "Many a plan which disappointment has thinned off into a phantom in my mind, takes form and shape and fair reality when touched with her Ithuriel's spear."[20] For Hilary, such paeans of praise must have been bittersweet. Florence had written to Hilary in 1846 that they must henceforth see less of each other since she felt friends were like the apples strewn at the feet of Atalanta to slow her down in the race.[21]

Florence's admiration for the Bracebridges was a little over the top. Charles and Selina were younger and less fashionable than the Nightingales, but essentially they ran with the same people and did the same things as the Embley crowd. But somehow, for Florence at this stage, everything the Bracebridges did was perfect. Unlike her French maid Mariette, who found their Roman lodgings "fort commun" [very commonplace], Florence liked the modest rooms the Bracebridges took, slightly off the fashionable map for English expatriates. Her mother, she knew, would never have been seen dead in the place. Florence liked the simple breakfasts of bread and fruit and ricotta that she was able to pick up in the local shops herself.

Selina and Charles's poor health kept them late in bed in the mornings and eager to avoid evening parties, and this suited Florence since she was able to move around Rome under her own steam. At one point in her letters she gave a bravura description of the Roman fountains at dusk, and this elicited a rapid and horrified response from Embley. Surely, Mrs. Nightingale wrote, the Bracebridges were not allowing Florence to be out in the city at nightfall alone? Florence wrote back lightly, reassuringly, that, of course, she was always accompanied by Mr. Bracebridge's manservant Giuseppe when she went out, if that gentleman himself was not able to escort her. Perhaps!

One afternoon, Mr. Bracebridge felt too unwell for sight-seeing, so Selina and Flo deposited him at the library and then sallied forth alone to pay a return visit to their beloved Sistine Chapel. At about 2 p.m. they emerged into the sunshine of the piazza outside the Vatican, then went into a *caffè* for black coffee and bread, which cost each of them five bajocchi—a penny farthing, Flo happily specifies for the folks at home. Back on the street, Sigma and Flo purchased a pocket handkerchief full of hot chestnuts for two bajocchi each, and walked along munching. "We spent an exquisite half hour mooning or rather sunning about, the whole Campagna & city lying at our feet, the sea on one side like a golden laver [water basin] below the declining sun, the windings of the Tiber & the hills of Lucretius on the other, with Frascati, Tivoli, Tusculum (places in whose very names is magic) on their cypressy sides. For in that clear atmosphere, you could see the very cypresses of Maecenas' villa at Tivoli—with long stripes of violet & pomegranate coloured lights sweeping over the plane like waves." As evening fell, the two women walked to the basilica of St. Peter and once again prevailed upon the "custode" to let them in, even though the church was officially closed for the day and there were no other visitors. Then they ran home in the growing dusk.[22]

How many of us have enjoyed golden days like this one, savoring the beauties of an ancient place, blessed with sunshine and good local food, in the company of a friend? But for Selina and Florence this afternoon was especially precious and its pleasures rare because they were so simple. Who could blame Parthe for feeling discontented and envious when she received letters like this?

WHEREAS THEY DID not care to go out into society very often, the Bracebridges knew many interesting people. Most important, Florence in Rome became intimately acquainted with Selina's other surrogate daughter, Elizabeth A' Court Herbert and her husband, Sidney.

Of the new Mrs. Herbert's beauty and charm Florence gave her family a rapturous account, and she also narrated with comic verve the exhaustive investigation of ecclesiastical architecture she and Mrs. Herbert engaged in, to the surprise, amusement, and weariness of their companions. Florence gives the impression that she and Liz have become chums, and this was more or less the case. But of Mr. Herbert Florence says very little, a silence in the midst of so many words that is significant. It was left to Selina Bracebridge, in one of her letters to Parthe, to indicate how well Flo and Sidney were hitting it off. "Did you hear of [Flo's] dissipation that day? Going out to dinner with the Herberts & then on to an evening party at the Stanleys? Mr. Herbert put off an engagement to dine with the Duke of Newcastle that he might dine with Flo at home—& *very* agreeable he was as usual—Let me whisper in your ear that Flo wore her new velvet gown made in Paris by Mme Roget her hair *very nicely* done & looked so well dressed that you would have been charmed to see her."[23]

Parthe would surely have liked to hear more from Flo about Sidney Herbert since he was a man who struck most people, male and female, dumb with admiration. Sidney Herbert was the second, and deeply preferred, son of the Earl of Pembroke by his second marriage. Sidney's mother, Countess Catherine Woronzov, was a lady of the Russian aristocracy who had

Sidney Herbert.

come to England when her father was Russian ambassador to the court of King James. A delicate boy of extraordinary beauty, intelligence, and charm, Sidney was the darling of his parents, became the rage at his prep school, and then one of the most fêted men at Oxford. By the age of twenty-one he was already being touted as a future Prime Minister of England. Modest and sweet-natured, Sidney seemed unspoiled by all the attention, and there was a strange but charming sense of melancholy about him. If he had a fault, it was a certain lack of energy.

Sidney's father died while he was still a young man, and though his half brother now became Earl of Pembroke, Sidney inherited a large fortune from his godfather and probably one from his mother also. Sidney's brother, the new earl, continued to live in Italy with his mistress, and so Sidney was able to rent the huge and beautiful family estate of Wilton, where he had grown up.[24] For a time in his twenties, when he was already a Tory junior minister, Sidney Herbert sowed some wild oats in the company of Lady Caroline Norton, who was separated from her husband and who was the onetime mistress of Lord Melbourne.[25] Then family duty reclaimed Mr. Herbert and he married his adoring and beautiful young cousin Miss Elizabeth A' Court.

The marriage of Elizabeth and Sidney was happy, and the couple produced seven children. Mrs. Herbert adored her husband and gave him the single-minded devotion that religion has often seen as the heart of female piety. But she was not as intelligent and amusing as Lady Caroline, and she knew it. Beneath the surface perfection of the Herberts' marriage, boredom lurked on his side and jealousy on hers. After Sidney's death, Liz would confide in Florence: "It is strange but I think his whole family believe *he did not love me*."[26]

Both Herberts courted and fêted their new friend Florence Nightingale. She and Sidney could talk for hours, they had so much in common, yet Liz did not see Flo as a rival. Cecil Woodham-Smith refers to the "strange and fatal intimacy" that sprang up between Sidney Herbert and Florence Nightingale in that Roman winter, and I think there was an attraction between them that went beyond mere friendship. Sidney was so soulful and earnest, so deeply religious, as well as so beautiful, that he seems exactly the man to realize Fanny's dream scenario and sweep Flo off her feet. Sadly, the two met when Sidney was married, and for them adulterous dalliance was out of the question. But that winter Florence Nightingale and Sidney and Liz Herbert built the foundation of a friendship that would have important consequences in the years ahead.

THE HERBERTS WERE TORIES where the Nightingales were Whigs, and they were high church while the Nightingales were broad church, with Unitarian undertones. One of the reasons the Herberts came to Rome was that Liz Herbert was anxious to have an audience with His Holiness the Pope.[27] The 1840s were a time when the Anglo-Catholic revival called the Oxford Movement was sending cracks through the ecclesiastical establishment. English people like the Herberts came to the city not so much to haunt the ateliers and excavate the temples but to visit monasteries and convents, go on retreats, and talk earnestly with Catholic divines. Soon three of the nation's most prominent Anglican churchmen—Wiseman, Newman, and Manning—would "go over to Rome" and become cardinals in the English Catholic Church.

Florence talked in her letters of attending Catholic services and of climbing the Scala Santa at St. John in Lateran on her knees, a conspicuous act of Catholic piety.[28] Even though Fanny and WEN were gratified to know their daughter was now so intimate with the son of the Earl of Pembroke and his wife, they were uneasy about the religious influences she was feeling. And in fact Florence was feeling the pull of the Catholic faith far more than she told her family. In all the hundreds of bravura pages that Florence wrote home, she makes no mention of her burgeoning friendship with Madre Santa Colomba of the convent of Santa Trinità dei Monti. As so often in her epistolary relationship with her family, Florence uses a plethora of detailed description and racy narration to conceal the fact that something very important is not being told. The story of Florence's relationship with Madre Santa Colomba was reserved for notes in her private diary that unfortunately seem no longer to be extant.

At a church service on February 6, Florence noticed a delightful little girl of about five, one of the many poverty-stricken urchins that swarmed around the city. Unable to forget this child, Florence found out that she was called Felicetta Sensi and that she lived with a so-called aunt, a woman whom Florence instinctively mistrusted. She determined to see if there was any way that the child could be given an education and kept off the streets, and after making inquiries she found herself summoned to a meeting with Madre Santa Colomba, who ran the local orphanage. Florence Nightingale entered the convent with some trepidation. She was sure that the *madre* was going to tell her in no uncertain terms that Protestant English women had no business interfering in the lives of small Catholic children. But in fact the *madre* was warm and welcoming, and over meetings during the next days it was agreed that the *madre* would take Felicetta into her convent school for a sum Florence would be able to squeeze out of her dress allowance. Florence faithfully paid this money over the next years and received news of Felicetta as she grew up.

But Madre Santa Colomba and Florence Nightingale soon took to discussing more than the child. Florence visited the orphanage school several times and took careful notes on the calm, sweet, and effective way the nuns dealt with pupils who had known little soap and less saintliness in their young lives. She would try to incorporate some of this in her village schools at home. Toward the end of her stay in Rome, Florence was permitted to make a retreat at the convent. She and the Bracebridges must have come to an agreement that this would be a secret from the Nightingales at home.

Madre Santa Colomba was a warm, plump, jolly, rather plebeian

Frenchwoman who did not get on well with her more refined sisters in the convent. Like Florence, she was extremely quick at practical things, and one of her trials was to watch her pupils slowly and inexpertly doing simple tasks she could have finished in a moment. She made no secret of the fact that she had taken an immense liking to the young English lady. More than anything she wanted to convert Florence to Catholicism. "I have made my self-examination many times before Him, since I knew you, to see whether the love I feel for you is from nature (for I do feel birth pangs for you)," Florence remembered the *madre* saying. "I don't think it is only that, because what I long for is not to go on seeing you, but to know that you are God's."

The Italian nun chided Florence for being so dissatisfied with her life at home. Help the people close to you and take satisfaction in that, Madre Santa Columba advised; "it is not good separating yourself from people to try and do the will of God." For perhaps the first time, Florence confided in the Roman nun that she had heard the voice of God. She recalled that at the end of her retreat, she and her *madre* had this dialogue:

C. Did not God speak to you during this retreat? Did he not ask you anything?

F. He asked me to surrender my will.

C: And to whom?

F: To all that is upon the earth.

C: He calls you to a very high degree of perfection. Take care. If you resist, you will be very guilty.

Florence made a vow to her "mother" that she would strive to crush self-will and do *only* the will of God. In the end, the advice of Madre Santa Columba was much the same as that of Hannah Nicholson, and proved equally impossible for Florence to follow.[29]

IN ROME IN JANUARY 1848, Florence Nightingale wrote: "This is the most entire and unbroken freedom from dreaming that I ever had." The combined charm of Rome, Selina Bracebridge, Sidney Herbert, and

Madre Santa Colomba had worked a miracle on her, and she longed to see her family and rejoice with them in her new happiness and resolve. When she arrived home in the late spring, the auspices at first seemed good. Parthe and Flo were both bridesmaids at the elaborate wedding of their two cousins Jack Bonham-Carter and Laura Nicholson. Florence spent a good deal of time with the Bracebridges in Coventry and the Herberts at Wilton. Herbert was a good friend of Lord Shaftesbury, and at Wilton Florence met many influential people who were involved in the administration of hospitals and poorhouses.

In September 1848, Parthenope was very ill, and her doctors advised that she take the cure at Carlsbad, near Frankfurt. It was now becoming obvious that Parthe fell ill when Flo was not at home. Julius and Mary Mohl were planning to be in Germany at the same time, and Julius of-fered to introduce WEN to the learned society of his native city. The nursing institute of Kaiserswerth that Florence had long ached to visit was also near Frankfurt, and, unbeknownst to Fanny and Parthe, WEN agreed to let Florence make the side trip to the Anstalt. But 1848 was the year of great revolutions, there was social unrest in Frankfurt, and WEN decided at the last minute that it was not an opportune time to visit the Continent. They would all three accompany Parthe to Malvern instead. Once again, Florence's plans to get nursing training were scotched. Worse, Richard Monckton Milnes had tired of an eight-year courtship and demanded a final answer from Miss Nightingale. The answer was no, and the gap between Florence's ambitions and her family's ambitions for her gaped wider than ever.

In Nightingale biography Monckton Milnes has played a significant role. He was the man Florence Nightingale loved but sacrificed to her vocation. Clearly, biography has a stake in Florence Nightingale re-maining single, since if she had yielded to the temptation of Monckton Milnes, she would never have gone to the Crimea, and her picturesque name and striking myth would have been lost to the world. But at the same time, part of the luster of that name depends on the public know-ing that Miss Nightingale had been sorely tempted at least once and had only with great pain given up the joys of love and marriage. By contrast, James Pope-Hennessy in his biography of Milnes devotes only a few pages to Florence Nightingale and scornfully rejects the notion that he was ever in love with her.

Florence was tempted to marry Milnes. She says so explicitly in the autobiographical sketch she prepared for the Kaiserswerth Institute in 1851: "There came a marriage for me which fulfilled all my mother's ambition: intellect, position, connections, everything, not that she ever tried to influence me. I myself was tempted."[30] But Richard Monckton Milnes was not, or not just, the Great Victorian worthy we learn about in standard books on Florence Nightingale. To understand the strangeness and pathos of their relationship, we need to look at the man more carefully.

On his father's side, Richard Monckton Milnes came from an old Yorkshire cloth-manufacturing and brick kiln family of Dissenter tradition. Robert Pemberton Milnes, Richard's father, was a tall, handsome, eccentric, foxhunting man, a true-blue Tory who earned the nickname of "Single Speech Milnes" after he unexpectedly refused the cabinet position of Chancellor of the Exchequer and retired from Parliament. Robert Milnes's wife, née Henrietta Monckton, was a daughter of Lord Galway, a privy councilor to George III, if a notoriously alcoholic one. Mrs. Milnes was a lovely woman whose talent for music and love of art were attributed by her contemporaries to Portuguese-Jewish and Antiguan-Creole strains in her maternal bloodline.[31] Such tastes did not endear her to her West Riding neighbors, and Mrs. Milnes always pined after the London life that her husband had so arbitrarily abandoned. Richard and Harriette, the two children of Robert and Henrietta, both took after their mother's side of the family in looks and tastes, and both identified with her aristocratic Anglo-Irish relations. But if the Monckton Milneses were more aristocratic than the Nightingales, they were also poorer. Robert's only brother, Rodes (that is to say, Richard Monckton Milnes's paternal uncle), a charming rake, gambled away the fortune of his elder brother, his mother, and his seven sisters. As a result, Robert Pemberton Milnes teetered on the edge of bankruptcy for almost thirty years, and the family's two estates, Fryston and Ferrybridge, had to be rented out.

Richard Monckton Milnes was extremely delicate as a child and was educated at Thorne Hall, the isolated Yorkshire property his father rented. Perhaps the Milneses could not come up with the fees for Eton or Harrow. Until his late teens, Robert lived largely in the company of Mrs. Milnes and his younger sister, and the three were exceptionally close. Biographer James Pope-Hennessy states flatly that Richard Monckton

Milnes "doted on his sister with an exclusive affection he never gave to another woman."[32] A voracious reader with a jackdaw mind, Richard showed some promise as a student when he went up to Trinity College, Cambridge. His real talent, however, was for making the right friends, and at Cambridge he came into his own, managing to get himself elected to that now legendary group, the Apostles. Milnes's fellow Apostles included Alfred Tennyson, Arthur Hallam, and A. W. Kinglake, who, not incidentally for our purpose in this book, was to be the author of a multi-volume history of the Crimean War. This whole Cambridge set came to bask in the golden glow cast by *In Memoriam,* Tennyson's masterpiece, a long elegy to Hallam, who died suddenly at twenty-two.

At Trinity Milnes and his friends spent as much of their time together as possible during term, visited one another's homes, and took trips abroad during the long vacs. In letters and poems, they airily declared their love for one another, very much as undergraduate Bosie did for Oscar Wilde at Oxford University sixty years later. In fact, in these 1830 Apostles, who had all been fed a steady diet of Greek and Latin literature as boys, we can see the prototypes of those curiously Victorian platonic lovers whom playwright Tom Stoppard portrays in *The Invention of Love.* Milnes made a bid for Hallam, but the gloriously handsome and talented Arthur could not be divided from his bosom friend Alfred Tennyson. Milnes fell back principally on the friendship of an Irishman, Stafford Augustus O'Brien, whom Pope-Hennessy describes as "irresistibly charming." When O'Brien went down from the university, Monckton Milnes could gossip to him unself-consciously that "Garden & Monteith have not cooled at all," "Cavendish's brother is a charming creature & so well fitted for Montjoy," and "Sir Jacob and I are inseparable, he is one of the dearest creatures I have ever seen. You would, I am sure, approve of our friendship, it is so unlike the routine of Cambridge arm-in-arm."[33] Pope-Hennessy says that "the qualities which made Milnes loved and a little distrusted by his Cambridge friends—the *engoûments* and the kaleidoscopic opinions, the vulnerability and the anxiety to be fascinated by whatever was new—merely became stronger . . . as he grew older."[34] Pope-Hennessey is telegraphing as clearly as possible in 1949 that Richard Monckton Milnes's homosexuality made him stand out even in an all-male culture where passionate friendships were the norm.

Milnes's nerves were not up to the strain of taking his final exams. He left Cambridge early, without a degree, and, more important for such a poor man, with no obvious way to make a living. He first spent some time studying German philosophy at the University of Bonn and was delighted by the unrestrained emotionalism he observed in his new German acquaintance. He wrote to a friend that "I think Goethe would have fallen in love with me and I am not sure Platen did not."[35] According to Pope-Hennessy, Platen was a young German dramatist and an "avowed homosexual" whom Milnes met again in Rome. After Bonn, Milnes spent the next several years roaming about Europe, living with his family when he could not scrounge the money to travel from his father. The impoverished Milneses were still obliged by their English debts to lead a peripatetic European life, but it actually seemed to suit them well.

In 1832 Monckton Milnes wangled 150 pounds out of his father to embark on a lengthy tour of Greece and Turkey with some rather distinguished old Cambridge friends. Richard soon tired of ruins and digs, but in Athens he became passionately committed to returning to Greece the Parthenon marbles purloined by Lord Elgin. He also got from Byron's close friend George Finlay an insider's account of the private life and sexual proclivities of the great poet. Byron had also been a Trinity man. In Turkey, Milnes was invited to a pasha's dinner party at which the guests were entertained by Greek dancing boys dressed as women. In a letter to his mother, Richard noted that the dance became increasingly "lascivious and violent." Pope-Hennessy summarizes: "The dance ended with the Turkish guests getting thoroughly involved with the Greek dancing boys. Milnes who had had too much to eat said he dropped off to sleep." As a fellow biographer, I can only admire the delicacy of the expression "thoroughly involved," and the positioning of the word "said."[36]

After publishing a volume of poetry based on his travels, Richard Monckton Milnes would have chosen the life of poet and aesthete had his father been willing to finance it. Instead he went into politics as soon as the family could scrape together the money for election expenses at Pontefract. Richard's father was determined he should become at least a junior minister, but Richard's intricate speeches in the Commons went unappreciated, and politics fundamentally bored him. In order to get ahead Richard needed the help of powerful friends, and he made it his business to know everybody who was anybody, male or female, English or foreign, in politics, art, literature, high society, or the demi monde.

Thus William Ewart Gladstone, the most coming politician of his generation, was a friend of Milnes from the time they clashed in an 1829 debate at the Oxford Union over the relative merits of the poets Byron and Shelley.[37] Thomas Carlyle, a notoriously difficult man, had a soft spot for Milnes, who was also the rare man permitted to turn up unannounced at the Isle of Wight lair to which the reclusive Tennyson retired when Poet Laureate. Lord and Lady Palmerston invited Milnes to Broadlands house parties because he could be relied on to entertain. Women like Lady Blessington and Lady Caroline Norton, whom scandal had thrust beyond the pale of society, found in Milnes a loyal friend, but he was also a frequent guest at the exclusive parties of the fabulously rich and respectable Lady Harriet Baring. In Paris, Milnes inevitably spent his time with George Sand, Lamartine, Montalembert, Guizot, Thiers, Tocqueville, and the like. Mary Clarke was happy to welcome him to her salon. Tocqueville noted in his diary that he had never seen Milnes when he was not crazy (engoué) about someone or something.

In London the eccentric, deaf, and stridently ex-Unitarian journalist Harriet Martineau affectionately harangued Milnes in person and in letters. Elizabeth Gaskell liked him so much she actually showed him the confidential letters she received from her painfully shy protégée Charlotte Brontë—an atrocious betrayal of confidence on Gaskell's part, as Jenny Uglow has pointed out. Years later, when the Americans Nathaniel Hawthorne and Henry Adams came to London and found the initial going rough, they had a friend in Milnes, who actually read and liked American writers from Emerson and Thoreau to Walt Whitman. Both Hawthorne and James left subtle and gracious pen portraits of the older Milnes in their memoirs of the period. Henry Adams called Milnes "the good nature of London; the Gargantuan type of its refinement and coarseness, the most universal figure of Mayfair."[38]

Benjamin Disraeli despised Milnes and left a cutting fictional picture of him as Mr. Vavasour in his novel *Tancred*. Yet even Disraeli was not above sardonically surveying the gnawed chop bones at one of Milnes's breakfasts and noting in his daybook that his fellow guests that day had included Milnes's father, his Cambridge pal Kinglake, Lady Blessington's "dear friend" the so-called Count d'Orsay, William

Cobden, Prince Louis Napoleon (later Napoleon III), and Suleiman Pasha. Such a wild mix of guests was more the rule than the exception for Milnes and one of the reasons people accepted his invitations. As Carlyle once quipped, if Jesus Christ had risen from the dead and turned up in London, within the day Richard Monckton Milnes would have secured his presence at breakfast in the rooms over the tailor's shop at 26 Pall Mall.

By the mid-1840s, the Milness's family fortunes took a decided turn for the better. Mrs. Milnes got a legacy that allowed her and her husband and daughter to return to England. Old Mrs. Milnes, Richard's grandmother, died at last, leaving Fryston and the remains of the family fortune to her older son, Robert Pemberton Milnes, who also managed to make a packet by speculating on railway stocks. In 1838 Harriette Milnes, who proved, remarkably, to be as irresistible in Pontefract and Crewe as in Rome and Venice, snagged her cousin Lord Galway and became châtelaine of Serlby. Richard's own life was a nonstop whirl of parties and country house visits and improbably successful breakfasts. Nonetheless, his mood was increasingly somber.

Richard had always detested his cousin and brother-in-law Lord Galway, and his relations with his darling sister were affected. In 1847 his mother died—killed off, it seemed, not just by the cholera in Bath but by the move back to Fryston. The windows at the Milneses' ancestral pile were now blackened with soot from the surrounding industry, its pastures polluted, its river a running sewer. Milnes's political prospects got worse by the year. Even though in 1846 Milnes moved from the Tory to the Liberal side of the House, Palmerston proved as inexplicably reluctant to give him an undersecretaryship for foreign affairs as old Robert Peel had been. Meanwhile, his Oxbridge contemporaries were rising to the top of the tree. Gladstone was the Liberals' new golden boy, and after Peel's sudden death Disraeli became the leader of the Tories in the Commons. Both men were to become great Prime Ministers. Given Milnes's excellent connections, a peerage and consequent accession to the House of Lords was a reasonable prospect, but it would have to be offered first to his notoriously unpredictable father, who showed no sign of dying.[39]

As littérateur, Milnes had little more success than in politics. Friends were prepared to admire his several slim volumes of verse, but in comparison with Tennyson, Browning, and Rossetti, or even Browning's wife, Elizabeth, or Dante Gabriel's little sister, Christina, Milnes was obviously third-rank. With the help of young Coventry Patmore, he was finishing his pioneering book on the life and work of John Keats, but given Keats's low social class and notoriously radical ideas, that labor of love was unlikely to bring Milnes much glory anytime soon.

Milnes, a small, ruddy man who had never been handsome, was getting fat and gouty from all those breakfasts and dinners. In 1849 he would turn forty, and the loss of youth was a personal nightmare as well as one of the main themes of his poetry. Milnes's bachelor existence in London, his tours of the Continent with male companions, and his collection of louche acquaintances like Russian merchant Charles Brown (who gave him the Keats documents), wild-man explorer Mansfield Parkyns, and notorious libertine Count Potocki were beginning to raise eyebrows. What Milnes needed, it was clear, was a wife, and in his late thirties he apparently courted a number of ladies, all of them "high-minded, religious, intelligent, and cultivated."[40] But increasingly Milnes fixed his choice on the younger daughter of his old friends the Nightingales. He and Florence knew the same people and met each other socially all the time, in London and in the country.

Florence liked Richard very much. He bought books by the yard and had read absolutely everything, ancient and modern, in at least five foreign languages, taking copious notes, just as Florence did. Milnes had strong philanthropic urges, though his purse was too slight to permit him to do much, and he had refreshingly radical views on subjects like industrial reform, Polish independence, and Irish liberty. Florence applauded his speeches in the Commons against the death penalty, as well as the efforts he made from Ireland, where he had many friends, to organize relief for victims of the potato famine in 1846. When she saw Richard kneel down and talk to a ragged boy as if they had been friends all their lives, Florence's heart melted. With Richard, Florence felt she could talk about anything and he would never be shocked. As Florence acknowledged rather confusedly, marriage to Milnes would have been "such an easy way out of my difficulties." As his wife, she would be able to "do pretty much what I liked."[41]

So Florence Nightingale was tempted, but she did not fall. In June 1848 at Embley, Richard Monckton Milnes proposed again, and was again refused. Both parties knew that this time the courtship was at an end. Florence says that "an accident" prevented the marriage and then quickly adds, "I will believe that it was God who saved me from casting myself down from the temple." She has to "will" this belief, even for the pious authorities at the Kaiserswerth Anstalt.[42] In her diary Florence wrote passionately of her misery and regret over losing Richard: "I have an intellectual nature which requires satisfaction, and that would find it in him. I have a passional nature which requires satisfaction, and that would find it in him. I have a moral, an active nature which requires satisfaction, and that would not find it in his life. I can hardly find satisfaction for any of my natures. Sometimes I think that I will satisfy my passional nature at all events, because that will at least secure me from the evil of dreaming. But would it? I could be satisfied to spend a life with him combining our different powers in some great object. I could not satisfy this nature by spending a life with him in making society and arranging domestic things . . . To be nailed to a continuation and exaggeration of my present life, without hope of another, would be intolerable to me. Voluntarily to put it out of my power ever to be able to seize the chance of forming for myself a true and rich life would seem to me like suicide."[43] In a separate note, as Woodham-Smith narrates it, she "wrote again with a pencil that trembled, hesitated and dug itself into the paper. 'I do not understand it . . . I am ashamed to understand it . . . I know that if I were to see him again . . . the very thought of doing so quite overcomes me. I know that since I refused him not one day has passed without my thinking of him, that life is desolate without his sympathy.' "[44]

Florence was still in this state of mind vis-à-vis Monckton Milnes in March 1851 when she chanced to meet him at a London party given by Lady Palmerston. He came across, made some light remark about the noise in the room being like a cotton mill—an apt comment for the children of two old Yorkshire textile fortunes, I may say—and then moved on. She wrote in a private note: "Last night I saw him again for the second time. He would hardly speak . . . I was miserable . . . I wanted to find him longing to talk to me, willing to give me another opportunity, to keep open another decision; or perhaps I only wanted his sympathy . . . He was not ready for it. He did not show indifference but avoidance. No familiar friendship. No confidence such as I felt towards him."[45]

Monckton Milnes was surely anxious to avoid any intimate conversation with Miss Florence Nightingale at Lady Palmerston's since he was within weeks of announcing his engagement to the Honourable Miss Annabel Crewe. Miss Crewe's family was part of the Yorkshire gentry, and the Nightingales would have known of her through friends like the Tolletts. Annabel was thirty-seven when Richard Monckton Milnes proposed, six years older than Florence Nightingale and much less affluent. A sweet-natured, attractive woman, she had lived most of her life in the depths of the northern countryside. Her older brother and sister were very eccentric, and both were single. Given Annabel's options in 1851, she was quite right to grab the proposal from Richard Monckton Milnes with both hands.

The Milnes marriage was very successful. Annabel Milnes was a tactful hostess and gracious if unexciting conversationalist at the fashionable dinner parties at her London home. On those rare occasions when she accompanied her husband abroad on one of his frequent trips, she was an enthusiastic traveler who retired to bed conveniently early. From the beginning Annabel was an overwhelming favorite with her husband's father, now increasingly sick, lonely, and difficult. Robert Pemberton wrote to his daughter-in-law every day and expected a reply. Best of all, the fashionably fragile Mrs. Milnes presented her husband with three children. The first two were daughters, named Amicia and Florence. And then, to cap her astonishing reproductive success, Annabel Milnes presented Richard with a healthy son, named Robert Offley Ashburton Milnes. Annabel's crazy bachelor brother, Hungerford, Lord Crewe, who had never liked Richard, accepted the new baby as his heir. Annabel's rich sister, Henriett (sic) Crewe, who also had snubbed Richard, was placated and left her fortune to lucky little Robert. Predictably, Robert Pemberton Milnes was ecstatic over the birth of his grandson, and soon graciously died, allowing his son to inherit the family estate at last. In 1863 Palmerston finally came through with a peerage for his old friend Milnes, and the new Baron Houghton happily moved up to the Lords.

AFTER HE HAD MARRIED, inherited his family estate of Fryston, become a peer of the realm, and acceded triumphantly to the status of paterfamilias, Richard Monckton Milnes led a successful double life that would have made Oscar Wilde green with envy. The truth about Monckton Milnes was delicately hinted at in early biographical accounts, but it was not until the mid-twentieth century that Georges Lafourcade, the French biographer of Algernon Swinburne, revealed that Fryston not only housed an almost unrivaled collection of hard-core pornography and sadomasochistic memorabilia but also was the site of Sadeian revels.[46] Lafourcade referred to Fryston as "the inn of strange encounters" and paints it vaguely as a damp Yorkshire version of Minski's castle in *The 120 Days of Sodom*. In *The Romantic Agony*, Mario Praz described Monckton Milnes as a man of "Mephistophelian malice," a "sinister Virgil, guiding Swinburne through the Inferno of his library, crouching at Fryston like a spider to catch some unwary young fly."[47]

Perhaps moved to protest by these slurs, the descendants of Richard Monckton Milnes authorized James Pope-Hennessy to write a two-volume biography in 1949 and opened the family archives to him. Pope-Hennessy was writing when homosexual activity between consenting male adults was still punished by imprisonment or chemical castration in Britain, yet allusively but unmistakably he made Milnes's sexual orientation clear and in fact heralded him as a remarkable gay success story. He portrayed Milnes as sentimental, melodramatic, entertaining, and gossipy, given to hugs of delight and tears of dismay, almost a parody of the gay man. Given the prejudice such men have traditionally aroused in male heterosexuals, it becomes easy to understand why gruff, laconic, conservative old Robert Peel would not give Milnes a ministry, why the oft-despised dandy Benjamin Disraeli publicly mocked him, why Palmerston would not send him on a diplomatic mission.

Pope-Hennessy documents in detail that Milnes was already interested in sadomasochism in the 1830s and 1840s, when he was courting Florence Nightingale: "[Milnes's] wish to abolish the death penalty did not prevent him from indulging his bizarre taste for hangmen's autographs, and his later zeal for boys' reformatories went hand in hand with an interest in flogging and a collector's attitude to books on school punishment."[48]

Monckton Milnes's collecting of erotica accelerated in the late fifties when he and his wife became affluent, and he inherited Fryston, which he jovially nicknamed "Aphrodisiopolis." In 1869, Swinburne wrote excitedly to Dante Gabriel Rossetti, "[Milnes] is *the* Sadique collector of

European fame. His erotic collection of books, engravings, etc. is unrivalled upon earth, unequalled I should imagine in heaven . . . There is every edition of every work of our dear and honoured Marquis."[49] In fact, Milnes had not only the complete published work of Sade but unique pieces written in Sade's own hand. The gems of the Fryston collection were bought in Paris and smuggled into England by friends or concealed in the diplomatic pouches. Milnes's agent in the Paris sales was a notorious individual called Frederick Hankey. This man's sadistic tastes were, by his own account, so extreme that the brothels of Paris would not accommodate him, and he was obliged from time to time to return to London.[50]

Pope-Hennessy concludes that "to prudish and illiberal persons [Richard Monckton Milnes's] name has become a bogey, to the prurient a decoy," and his biography makes it clear that Milnes was no Sade.[51] Yes, he took pleasure in collecting the works of Sade; yes, he passed them on to his young friend Swinburne; yes, he discussed them with his other great friend and celebrated sensualist, Sir Richard Burton. With consenting male friends he may well have acted out his fantasies. But for all this, as Pope-Hennessey documents, Richard Monckton Milnes was a nice man, just as Flo and Parthe said he was in the memorial letters they wrote to his family. He was a loving, reliable, attentive son to both of his parents, and a fond brother. He was a good husband and father. He was a true and loyal friend to many men and women. He was a discerning critic and champion for such great poets as John Keats and Walt Whitman. As a public citizen, he consistently took unpopular stands, defended the rights of the disenfranchised, and sought relief for the suffering of the poor.

But still, and yet . . . to imagine this man the husband of Florence Nightingale is grotesque. Richard Monckton Milnes, who spent his old age collecting the most extreme pornography the world had seen before the invention of film and the Internet, was quite extraordinarily not the ideal companion of Florence's philanthropic dreams. She was not the woman to give him children, write daily to his father, preside at his official dinners, retire early to bed when his friends came to stay, and keep out of the library.

Florence was not a prude, but nothing she had read would have prepared her for opening a copy of Nerciat, much less Sade, and since the women in her family had always had the use of their father's or husband's library, she would have found them. When Florence in a Roman art gallery came face-to-face with Raphael's semi-naked "La Fornarina," she turned away in disgust and tried to erase the unclean image from her mind. What would she have made of the eighteenth-century etchings in Richard's special collection, or of the extraordinary piece of erotic sculpture that decorated his study? Obsessed by the impurity of her own mind, how could Florence begin to understand, much less accept, the fantasies that occupied Richard's?

Annabel Crewe Milnes loved her husband, was polite to Swinburne and Burton, and looked the other way. But if Florence Nightingale had married Monckton Milnes, one cannot imagine her being so blind, so besotted, or so compliant. My guess is that Florence would have reacted with horror and flight to evidence of her husband's hidden tastes and habits. The resulting public uproar would have put Effie Ruskin and her 1853 nonconsummation suit against husband John quite into the shade, and both Florence's and Richard's lives would have been ruined forever.

Chapter 12

DE PROFUNDIS
CLAMAVI DOMINE

Florence's decision to dismiss Monckton Milnes hardly took the other Nightingales by surprise. However, when Milnes went off in search of a Miss Crewe, tears flowed and tempers snapped in the family circle with monotonous regularity. Embley Park began to gain a reputation for domestic Sturm und Drang as well as roses and rhododendrons, and the Nightingales' tightly knit kinship group was dividing into a pro-Flo faction, led by Mai, Ju, and Hilary, and an anti-Flo faction, led by the Nicholsons.

WEN hated the scenes more than anyone, and he decided to accept the offer made by Charles and Selina Bracebridge that Florence should accompany them to Egypt and Greece. The Bracebridges planned to make their way through Italy to Alexandria in the late fall of 1849, lease a boat in Cairo to take them up the Nile and back, spend the early spring in Athens, where they owned a house, and return at a leisurely pace through Germany in the summer.[1]

The plan to send Florence out of England for yet another long period of independent travel was not an easy or uncontroversial one. Even for an affluent father, WEN was showing uncommon generosity toward his younger daughter. Aunt Patty, who in previous years had been rather pro-Flo, now gave it as her decided opinion that Florence was being pampered. For once Fanny agreed with her eldest sister. Why indeed should Flo be given special treats when she already enjoyed so much privilege at home and showed so little gratitude for it? The weekends with the Bunsens or at Broadlands with the Palmerstons had now become weeks or almost months at Wilton with the Herberts or the Bracebridges at Atherstone, to say nothing of Aunt Mai at Combe. When Fanny was expecting a flood of guests at Embley, she had to positively command Flo to come home to do her share. Sending Flo to Egypt was like a reward for making life thoroughly disagreeable for her family—and it was so unfair to Parthe! Why did Flo receive all the really nice invitations while Parthe got to pack Flo's trunks, stay home, and wait for Flo's latest epistolary masterpieces from abroad?

Grandmother Shore and Great-aunt Evans were upset to hear their adored Flo was going abroad again—not because she did not deserve a treat but because the journey was dangerous. Europe, according to the newspapers, was nothing but nasty revolutions and horrid reprisals, and as for Egypt, it was like setting foot on a nest of vipers. And those Bracebridges were hardly the best people to ensure Florence's safety. In Egypt Charles Bracebridge was talking of trying to get past the cataracts and up into Nubia as far as Abu Simbel. How many white women had been that far? Did WEN not comprehend that he might never see his daughter again?

In fact WEN's decision to let Flo go was a calculated risk. WEN knew that Egypt was poor and disease-ridden. It was only in the last fifty years—since the invasion of Napoleon's army and Admiral Lord Nelson's heroic victory at Aboukir Bay—that anyone really had gone to Egypt. After that, of course, a good many scholars from all over Europe had explored and brought back some wonderful antiquities. The ruler, Mehemet Ali, had been effective in making tourism safe for Europeans, though one heard that his methods were rather heavy-handed—whole villages being massacred just because one white man's baggage was stolen, and that sort of thing. But Egypt was still dangerous. Even if you frequented the best hotels and stuck to the established tourist route (picnic at the Pyramids, sketching opportunity at the Sphinx, luxury tour of Luxor and Thebes, back to Cairo for a few tombs and a banquet à la Turque), you were sure to get ill. There were people one knew who had died in Egypt! And in Alexandria and Cairo, it was so difficult and disagreeable for European women to go about. Even if they covered every inch of skin, wore a veiled bonnet, and had several male escorts, they could hardly go out into the streets without attracting a hostile mob.

But WEN held his ground on letting Florence go to Egypt. He determined to make it up to Parthe by sending her and Fanny to Europe as soon as travel was safe again.[2] They would take the waters at some elegant spa, relax in pleasant company, show off their languages, tour the galleries, and have carte blanche in the shops. Fanny, who had refused point-blank to allow her daughter to encounter the horrors of the Salisbury Infirmary, agreed in the end to allow Flo to go to Egypt.

Florence was very aware that she was getting many more treats and rewards than her sister, and she sincerely regretted that this was so. Pleasure was not her goal in life. She had no talent for it. But Florence's asceticism did not extend to refusing the Bracebridges' invitation. She knew quite well that Egypt was her parents' last-ditch effort to get her interested in something more suitable than hospitals—hieroglyphics, Hebrew, travel writing, a bachelor Orientalist, who knew exactly?—and was sure that she was going to hold her course. But the prospect of Egypt appealed to her even more than Rome had, both as a Christian and as a classical scholar. Homer, Pythagoras, Plato, Aristotle, and Herodotus had all drunk deep from Egyptian culture and history. Hermetic religions such as gnosticism, to which Nightingale had been introduced by her friends Bunsen and Mohl, had grown up in the mid-East. Christian monasticism, of which Florence was an increasingly devoted student, had begun with Pachobius in the deserts of Egypt. She expected the journey would be a spiritual as well as a cultural feast.

Florence Nightingale had gone to Rome hurriedly, in a kind of daze, but for Egypt she made careful preparations. Thus she set out with a princessly abundance of linen and underclothes, virtually all of which she gave away en route as presents, rewards, and bribes. Florence presumably took some fashionable dresses, but she and Sigma distinguished themselves in Egypt by wearing the ugliest, most practical, and least constricting garments possible. Brown Holland (unbleached linen) was their preferred fabric, and in the privacy of their Nile boat they took off their stays and wore wrappers—a kind of loose dressing gown.

The most important, and innovatory, thing Florence took with her was a levinge, a strange hybrid of sleeping sack and mosquito net, which was quite an adventure to get into at night but did keep off the mosquitoes, as advertised. Other vermin would prove harder to escape. Nightingale was soon telling her family that anyone who arrived in Egypt thinking they wouldn't get fleas was deluded, and mentioning casually how she needed to get up from time to time to kill bugs. Like the locals, she became resigned to the blackflies clustering on her head and face. The Nile boat crew, who adored her, gave Florence a special gift of two chameleons, and one of the many delights of these pets was that they ate flies. The boat had lots of rats, and the Bracebridge party imported several cats, one of which proved to be a good ratter, as well as a huge turkey that terrified not just the rats but the crew too. Florence was bitter when Selina decided that the turkey must be sacrificed for one of their rare dinner parties. Florence did save the chameleons, carefully carrying them ashore.

The thing that Florence took to Egypt that she could best have done without was a personal maid. This person she refers to as Trout; whether it was Miss Trout or Mrs. Trout, she never tells us, but Trout was clearly *de trop*. While Florence's letters home brim with affectionate and admiring references to individual members of the Arab crew and to Paolo, the Maltese guide who supervised the party, Florence has only one single reference to Trout. She describes "T" sitting crocheting a pattern for a polka (a short, fitted jacket), with her back resolutely turned to the temples. In her personal diary Florence is a bit more open, mentioning several terrible rows she had with Trout and the relief she felt when Trout was ill, in need of nursing, and presumably less contentious. What Florence quarreled with Trout about, she never says, but we can assume that this woman had no wish at all to be chaperoning a willful, ungrateful, and unfashionable mistress around Europe and Egypt. Nine months of intense heat by day and bitter cold by night, of seasickness and flea bites, of rats and lice and terrifying foreigners, must have been a nightmare for Trout. And her inescapable presence, full of resentment and criticism, surely tarnished the pleasure of her three European traveling companions, especially during the three months on the Nile.

The boat had three cabins: a day cabin, a sleeping cabin for Charles and Selina, and a smaller one for Florence. The crew lived unsheltered on the foredeck. Trout presumably shared the cabin with Florence, but Florence never refers to her presence in the letters. She comments on her shared living space only once, indirectly. When she got back to a hotel in Cairo, Florence wrote in her diary: "Enjoyed the luxury of having a room to myself for the first time—what use shall I make of it?"[3] In

Rome, Florence had been able to get away from her French maid, Mariette, but in Egypt there was no way she could get away for more than a few hours of the occasional day from Trout.[4]

In the Balkans and in Egypt, Western women were essentially precluded from conducting business, so there was to be no question on this expedition of Florence managing her own money and doing odd bits of food shopping, as she had in Rome. Mr. Bracebridge took charge of all the finances as well as negotiations with local officials. Florence's roles would be those of companion, nurse, interpreter, and scribe. This third role she took seriously indeed. When it came to ancient Greek, New Testament Greek, and early monastic cultures, Florence was the party's acknowledged expert, and she had also learned some Hebrew so that she could attack the Old Testament in the original. Before and during her Egyptian journey, she applied herself seriously to learning hieroglyphics, and her incidental comments in the letters indicate that, to the admiration of her companions, she made considerable headway in reading inscriptions. Florence was encouraged to tackle Near Eastern languages by two close Prussian friends who happened to be among the greatest Orientalists of the period—Julius Mohl and Christian Bunsen. Before leaving on her trip, Florence spent some days with Ambassador Bunsen, getting a concentrated private tutorial on ancient Egyptian history, architecture, and writings.

The Bracebridge party took a huge trunk of books with them, including *Eastern Life Past and Present* by their friend Harriet Martineau. This redoubtable journalist had visited Egypt with friends in 1847, and her reflections on the ancient Semitic roots of many Christian beliefs and on the condition of Islamic women impressed Florence. Selina and Flo also took along a novel hot off the presses in England—*Shirley.* This story of an independent Yorkshire heiress and of Caroline, her struggling friend, said many of the things Flo and Sigma wanted said about contemporary English women's lives. They knew from Lizzy Gaskell and Richard Milnes that *Shirley*'s author was a woman called Charlotte Brontë, who, like themselves, came from the English Midlands.[5]

Florence Nightingale was also committed to writing as fine an account as possible of the party's expedition. Between her arrival in Alexandria in the middle of November and her departure back across the Mediterranean in mid-March, Florence Nightingale wrote some thirty-nine letters to her family at home, all or parts of which were then circulated about the kinship network. In my view they constitute one of the masterpieces of Victorian travel writing. It took time and energy to write so much, especially as candles were a precious commodity and in the day Florence spent hours every day reading aloud to her companions. On several occasions Nightingale mentions that she and her letter paper are being covered with new layers of sand as the khamsin (sandstorm) raged about the boat.

The letters were a labor of love, but the act of writing filled Nightingale with anxiety. Was she reaching out for the world's praise even as she vowed to become "the handmaid of the Lord . . . not the handmaid of correspondence"?[6] When, on her return, Florence found her sister insisting on putting her letters into print, Florence refused to cooperate, though she did not forbid the project. Parthenope Nightingale sometimes understood Flo better than Flo liked, and she knew that on some level her sister was really writing for posterity. In fact, if these letters had disappeared, an important part of Florence Nightingale would have been lost to us.

WHEN THE BRACEBRIDGE party arrived in Cairo, small steamboats were already beginning to ply their way up and down the Nile. The large party of the Marquis of Northampton and his daughter the artist Lady Marian Alford was on the Nile at the same time as the Bracebridges, and they traveled in a steam-powered launch. But Charles Bracebridge and his Maltese dragoman Paolo decided to hire a dahabieh (as Nightingale spells it), a traditional vessel powered by sail and raw manpower. The hired crew rowed when there was no wind, and walked along the shore towing the boat when it was not possible to put out the oars. The dahabieh Charles found was the largest and most luxurious on the river—the private vessel of a local pasha—and, at thirty pounds per month, it was considered extremely expensive.

Every boat carrying passengers on the Nile was obliged to register with the authorities and fly a personal flag of identification. These flags gave European tourists plenty of opportunity to see who else was on the river and decide whether or not they wanted to meet them socially. Thanks to the flags, the Bracebridges were able to avoid the Northampton party for the most part, as Fanny was no doubt dismayed to learn. Florence was allowed to christen the boat, and she chose the name *Parthenope*. She herself sewed the flag, "blue bunting with swallow tails, a Latin cross upon it, and ΠΑΡΘΕΝΟΠΗ in white tape . . . it has taken all my tape and a vast amount of stitches, but it will be the finest pennant on the river, and my petticoats will joyfully acknowledge the tribute to sisterly affection,—for sisterly affection in tape in Lower Egypt, let me observe, is worth having."[7] Here Flo sounds the old note of affectionate camaraderie, and the flag decorated with sisterly petticoat tape remained one of Parthe's prized possessions.

The *Parthenope* gave its passengers an unusual amount of room and privacy, and Florence ever after insisted that the only way to really see the Nile was on a dahabieh. Whether the crew would have agreed on the day they pulled the heavy boat along in the 110-degree heat, we may wonder. It also chanced that the Bracebridge party met quite remarkably bad weather during their months on the river. It rained torrentially for about ten days on the way up, reducing the crew to shivering wrecks, and on the way down, lack of wind and then days of blinding sandstorms several times made it impossible to advance. A steamboat would probably have been more practical, but steamboats could not yet get farther upriver than Aswan because of the sequence of fierce rapids, known as the cataracts. In fact, the *Parthenope* was so big that it seemed likely that she too would have to stop below the first cataract. But after much parleying and deliberation, the chief of the tribal group who specialized in getting vessels through the rapids agreed to try. What Trout thought about the whole thing we can imagine.

Nightingale's descriptions of the hair-raising rides through the cataracts are two of the great moments in her book. An astonishingly large group of men from the local village was hired not only to steer and row the boat, but to dive into the foaming water and push the boat off the rocks with their legs and backs when necessary. At another point on the way upriver, the boat got becalmed on one shore, and its passengers watched enviously as a smaller vessel, carrying local people, passed quickly by on the other side. However, when the next cataract had been negotiated, the Bracebridge party saw the empty, shattered wreck of the same boat floating by. All of the passengers were, it seemed, killed. On the way back downriver, Selina Bracebridge elected to walk around at least sections of the cataracts, but Florence sat on the top of the cabin, drenched to the skin from the huge waves that passed all over the boat, but determined not to miss a moment.

Charles Bracebridge's decision to get upriver into Nubia proved to be inspired. Florence had days at the temple of Abu Simbel with not another tourist in sight. Watching the rising sun light up each in turn of the great stone faces of the temple, placing her own crucifix in the tomb of Osiris in Philae, and sitting for hours writing and thinking in the Ramesseum at Thebes were for Florence the highlights of this extraordinary journey, and they occurred on the way upriver. But Charles's plan was to make the most of the wind on the way upriver and to explore the most celebrated sites in depth only on the slow way back. Thus Florence was almost at the end of her river experience when she spent her weeks at Karnak and Luxor. By the time she came to Gizeh, the Great Pyramids, and the tombs of the sultans near Cairo, she was positively jaded. It was at Thebes on the way back, that, according to her personal diary, Florence began the slow descent into depression and panic that was to last until the following spring. My guess is that the constant sandstorms, the fleas, the mosquitoes, and Trout had a lot to do with this.

Enforced dependency also ate away at Nightingale's spirits. In the Arab heartland of Upper Egypt it was quite impossible for Europeans to walk out alone, and as the Bracebridge party traveled around on land, they had a posse of aggressive Arab guides to protect them. Even so, she and Selina were, as Nightingale remarked, treated by men in the street like unclean dogs. When Florence early on walked unsuspectingly into a mosque, her guides had to drive the outraged worshippers back with swords. This incident filled her with remorse, as she came to value mosques as places where men of all classes could go to pray, to think, to listen, and to chat. If only women could have done so too, she thought, the mosque would have been a perfect place of worship, far preferable to a fashionable church in London.

Florence seems to have fallen head over heels in love with Cairo as soon as she arrived. From the terrace of one of the city's mosques, she says, she had "the finest view in the world," and in her opinion Gothic architecture could not hold a candle to the intricate yet chaste Arabic style. The Cairene streets were a maze of houses with overarching roofs, and suddenly at the end of an alley there would be a perfect archway, pierced by a single point of light from above. But even as she gloried in these treasures of artistry and craftsmanship, Florence found the crowds, the chatter of the tourists, the shouting of the Arabs, and the feeling of ostracism by reason of her sex increasingly hard to bear. Still, there was to be no shirking of the cultural mandate, and only the increasingly satirical tone of her letters home suggested that all was not well with her.

After all the wonders she had seen upriver, Florence Nightingale took an immediate dislike to the Pyramids, which she dismissed as monotonous testaments to tyranny. "You remain from first to last insensible of its great size," she remarks of the Great Pyramid of Gizeh, "which, as it is its only quality, is unfortunate."[8] However, to go up the Great Pyramid was for the European visitor *de rigueur*, and so one morning, hoping to avoid other tourists, Florence and the Bracebridges set off for Gizeh in the midst of a minor khamsin (sandstorm), guarded by their loyal boat crew. As always, they rode not in a carriage but on donkeys, whose breakneck pace and apparent disregard for obstacles Florence described hilariously in her earliest letters. As soon as they arrived at the Great Pyramid they began the ascent, which involved being physically hauled up each course by the local guides. "As to the difficulty," wrote Florence airily, "people exaggerate it tremendously;—there is none, the Arabs are so strong, so quick, and I will say so gentlemanly; they drag you in step, giving the signal, so that you are not pulled up piecemeal."

Charles and Selina perhaps found all this hauling up and down more tiring than Florence, and they declined to enter the maze of passageways inside the pyramid, which was accessed by a tunnel near the bottom. They made no objection to allowing Florence to go in alone, however, and she was aware of how different everything would have been had her mother been in charge of the party. Florence devoted several pages to her dark venture inside the pharaoh's tomb. "Here, clad in brown Holland and flannel . . . having taken off your shoes, you are dragged by two Arabs (before you had three) down one granite drain, up another limestone one, hoisted up a place . . . and at last find yourself in a lofty groove . . . You look up to what seems an immeasurable height, for your light does not approach the roof . . . After you have crawled, ramped, and scrambled for two hours in black granite sheaths, without an inscription, without a picture of any kind, but the Arabs fighting for the candle, 'the mind,' I assure you, 'is satisfied.' As to the difficulty, here again, there is none: people talk of the heat, the Theban tombs are much hotter; of suffocation, I did not even feel the thirst, which in Egypt is no joke; of the slipperiness, it is impossible to fall with those Arabs. The only danger you cannot possibly avoid is that of catching an awful cold in your bones."

Florence was pulled out of the last few feet of the passage by Abool Ali, one of her beloved crewmen, "with the usual Hel-e-hel with which they haul up the yard or pole the boat off a sandbank." Getting to her feet, dirty, shoeless, disheveled, in a dress that looked pretty much like a shift, she found she was the object of close attention from a party of fifty fat Turkish harem women, sitting about the entrance to the tunnel, drinking coffee, "all looking like feather beds in their huge 'habarahs,' veiled up to the eyes, and three grave Turks, their happy possessors."[9] Selina, convulsed with laugher, clapped a shawl around Florence's shoulders and a bonnet on her head.

Selina and Florence had a brief firsthand experience of wearing a habarah on one of their first days in Alexandria. Their new friend the English consul reluctantly agreed to take them to visit a mosque on the condition that they wear full Egyptian costume, remain wholly silent, and keep their hands hidden. Florence describes getting dressed in "an immense blue silk sheet . . . then a white stripe of muslin which comes over your nose like a horse's nose-bag, and is fastened by a stiff passe-menterie band, which passes between your eyes and over and behind your head like a halter; then a white veil; and lastly, the black silk balloon, which is pinned on the top of your head, has two loops at the two ends, through which you put you two wrists in order to keep the whole thing together. You only breathe through your eyes; half an hour more and a brain-fever would have been the result."[10]

On the long ferry journeys between Alexandria and Cairo, where the women sat all night "nine to the square yard" beset with "Circassian, Chinese, and Coptic fleas," Florence had her best opportunity to meet women of many different nations and classes.[11] There was a Greek bride with two aged crones to chaperone her, traveling out to her husband in Cairo. The bride, who had been married at eleven, was fat and ugly but dressed in silk, velvet, and fur and covered with pearls and diamonds. Sigma could follow some of the conversation of the Greek women and was amused to hear them speculating as to what she and Florence could possibly be doing in Cairo. In their culture, a woman of thirty was old, and to be thirty and unmarried was almost incredible. Florence concluded: "I would not have missed that night for the world; it was the most amusing time I ever passed, and the most picturesque."

On the day of their departure, Florence and Selina paid a visit to Engeli Hanum, wife to Said Pacha, the man who would soon rule Egypt. Engeli Hanum was a woman of extraordinary beauty who had been born a Circassian slave, was adopted as a child by the wife of the ruler Mehemet Ali, won his love, was married to his son, and now lived in her royal husband's harem in Alexandria. "Oh, the ennui of that magnificent palace," wrote Florence, "it will stand in my memory as a circle in hell! Not one thing was there lying about, to be done or to be looked at . . . [Engeli Hanum] was dressed in a green pelisse, lined with fur, over yellow trousers and train, and was sitting in an immense marble hall, with no article of furniture but the divan . . . Coffee came of course, and pipes covered with diamonds; and the Circassians, the most graceful, and the most sensual-looking creatures I ever saw, stood in a semicircle, or knelt round us. The very windows into the garden were wood-worked, so that you could not see out. The cold, the melancholy of that place! I felt inclined to cry."[12]

THE JOURNEY FROM Alexandria to Athens in the winter of 1850 was unusually difficult, as the British fleet was patrolling the Mediterranean in force in protest of the Don Pacifico affair, and Lord Palmerston had decreed the naval blockade of Piraeus, the port of Athens. The Bracebridge party was obliged to zigzag to and fro across the Mediterranean, and Florence was laid low by seasickness. One of the first things she did on arrival was to run over to a Turkish bathhouse to wash off the stale misery of the journey. The Bracebridges' house in Athens was on Eucharis Street, and the terrace of Florence's library-bedroom looked right up at the Acropolis. Yet finding herself at last in the city of Plato and Aeschylus failed to energize Miss Nightingale. Instead of boning up on the latest archeological finds, she spent a good deal of time with John Henry Hill and his wife, Frances.

The Reverend Hill was a former American businessman who had come to Athens as an Episcopal missionary, and Mrs. Hill and her

American associate Mary Baldwin ran a non-denominational school for girls that had won favor with the Athenian people. One of the teachers was an extraordinary wizened gnome of a woman, Elizabeth Kontaxiki, who had spent her childhood on the run with her family, hiding from the Turkish army. The hardships of Kontaxiki's life deeply moved Florence. She also talked at length with Mrs. Hill and Miss Baldwin about their vocation to do missionary work, just as she had done with Madre Santa Colomba in Rome. The message from all three women was remarkably the same. "We moved no finger in the matter," Mrs. Hill told her. "We had neither act nor part in it—the way was opened for us to come here. If I had been told before I came where I was going to, the life I was going to lead here, the responsibility, I should have said 'It was impossible,' for I am unfit for it. Before I came here I had nothing at all to do—& I used to wish for something. I *did,* but when I thought of a missionary life, I did not know whether I could do it, you know. Then we came here, and I did. I did the duty each day presented me & I left it to Providence to open the way I should follow."[13]

Florence Nightingale's depression deepened. All the women she met who were actively engaged in successful philanthropic work emphasized that God had brought them into a situation where certain work opportunities arose, and they had simply obeyed. But Florence Nightingale, however much she tried, was full of will and ambition and plans, and she never doubted her capacity to realize those plans, if only given the chance. As events in the Crimea and after would prove, Florence was right to be confident in her own abilities, right to be looking hard for opportunities to put them to use. But the idea of willed philanthropy for a woman went against the Victorian *mentalité,* and when Nightingale caught herself planning and aspiring, she was overwhelmed with remorse. On the day before Whitsunday she wrote, "I have read over all my history, a history of miserable woe, mistake and blinding vanity, of seeking great things for myself."[14] As a very little child Nightingale had thought of herself as a monster, and this perception was now confirmed as she entered her thirties. God had perversely given her great abilities, enabled her to get education and training, spoken to her, asked for her service, and then refused to show the way.

As Florence became more and more apathetic and distressed, she continued to write long and charming letters home.[15] All the same, the people at home sensed that something was wrong, and to ward off anxiety Florence confessed that she had indeed caught some kind of low fever in Athens that kept her in bed. She assured her dear people that Sigma had taken her to an English doctor, who had bled her from the foot, and that she was now much better. What she did not tell them was that she was in the grip of dreaming, and that on many days she could not find the energy even to get out of bed and look up to the Acropolis.

Two years earlier Florence had elatedly recorded in her diary that she had been free of dreaming while in Rome, but this triumph was short-lived. On the journey down the Nile she was horrified to find herself again lost in inner reverie while the greatest temples of antiquity stood all around begging for her attention. At Ptah's temple cave at Jerf Hossayn, for example, she wrote in her private journal, "Oh heavenly fire, purify me—free me from this slavery." By the time she arrived in Athens, Florence was more than ever before in the grip of what she called the "murderer of thought." She began to doubt her sanity. "Friday I sate before breakfast & thought of my despair—this day twelve months, June 7, 1849 I made that desperate effort, that Crucifixion of the sin, in faith that it would cure me. Oh what is Crucifixion—would I not joyfully submit to Crucifixion, Father, to be rid of this? But this long moral death, this failure at all attempts at cure. I am in just the same state as I was last June 7. I think I have never been so bad as this last week. When Plato's plane tree, when riding in the Academy, when living intercourse with these dear Hills could not recall my attention to actual things. And I thought, when I was 30 I should be cured. 8 months since the last incentive to sin, & not a day has passed without my committing it."[16]

Nightingale's agony of mind is all too clear, but its reasons are not. Exactly what sin did she try to crucify once and for all on June 7, 1849? Is it related in some way to her refusal of the marriage proposal from Richard Monckton Milnes? What was the "last incentive to sin" that occurred on October 7, that is, just before her departure for Egypt? What sin could possibly be worthy of "crucifixion"? Only one thing is clear: the agonizing cycle of sin, repentance, and renewed sin has something to do with what Nightingale calls "dreaming."

In her diaries and private notes, some of which have come down to us, Nightingale referred constantly to her habit of dreaming and dates it back to early childhood.[17] She says that she suffered not from night dreams or nightmares but from what she calls variously dreams, visions, and fancies. These could take hold of her mind for long periods of time in almost any place—at a dinner party, while walking out, while visiting a friend or touring a famous site. In her diary, she obsessively records the measures she has undertaken to stop dreaming, and their persistent failure. She says that when she is nursing the poor or similarly doing what she regards as God's work, she is untroubled by dreams. One of the main reasons why she cannot forgive her family for blocking her way to full-time employment as a nurse is that they have left her prey to her dreams. Nightingale's diary refers to dreaming in the most negative possible terms. It is "sin," "slavery," "the enemy," "the long moral death," an addiction more loathsome than the use of opium, et cetera.

But in all the hundreds of extant pages she devoted to private self-analysis, Florence Nightingale does not tell us what she dreamed about. The dreams themselves are, it seems, so terrible, so loathsome, she cannot commit them to paper.

"Dreaming" is thus, by Nightingale's own account, a key feature of her mental landscape, yet everything we know about her "dreaming" is both agonizingly sincere and logically nonsensical. Even if we agree that it is not healthy for a young woman to be so often lost in reverie that she is unresponsive to the world around her, the revulsion, the self-chastisement, the despair Nightingale feels after she has dreamed seem quite disproportionate to the offense.

There is one place where Nightingale appears to offer an account of the content of her dreams, and this is in the fragment of *Suggestions for Thought* that she calls "Cassandra." This, I believe, was first drafted when she was in Athens in 1850,[18] and "Cassandra" is clearly autobiographical even though Nightingale never uses the pronoun "I."[19] In fact, "Cassandra" reads much less like a fiction than like a dream narrative. It proceeds by fits and starts, it has no logical development, and it is full of emotion, especially anger. Nightingale begins by talking of the temptation "one" feels to escape the bitterness of life by committing suicide. She then asserts that men cannot bear women to be unhappy: "To God alone may women complain, without insulting him." Mothers teach their daughters to be meek and submissive, since " 'women have no passions,' " but, Nightingale states, this is lies and hypocrisy. She then apostrophizes "Suffering, sad, female 'humanity' " and alludes to the fate of

Chinese women whose feet have been bound. Hereupon she devotes two passionate pages to the habit of dreaming, which, she alleges, is epidemic among respectable, unmarried women of the leisured classes in Britain. "If the young girls of the 'higher classes' . . . were to speak, and say what are their thoughts employed upon, their *thoughts* which alone are free, what would they say?"[20]

I, for one, am dying to know, and since this is I believe a unique passage in Nightingale's massive oeuvre, I will quote the next page in full:

That, with the phantom companion of their fancy, they talk (not love, they are too innocent, too pure, too full of genius and imagination for that) but they talk, in fancy, of that which interests them most; for they seek a companion for their every thought, the companion they find not in reality they seek in fancy, or, if not that, if not absorbed in endless conversations, they see themselves engaged with him in stirring events, circumstances which call out the interest wanting to them. Yes, fathers, mothers, you who see your daughter proudly rejecting all semblance of flirtation, primly engaged in the duties of the breakfast table, you little think how her fancy compensates itself by endless interviews and sympathies (sympathies either for ideas or events) with the fancy's companion of the hour! And you say, "She is not susceptible. Women have no passion." Mothers, who cradle yourselves in visions about the domestic hearth, how many of your sons and daughters are *there,* do you think, while sitting round under your complacent maternal eye. Were you there yourself during your own (now forgotten) girlhood?

What are the thoughts of these young girls while one is singing Schubert, another is reading the review, and a third is busy embroidering? Is not one fancying herself the nurse of some new friend in sickness; another engaging in romantic dangers with him, such as call out the character and afford more food for sympathy than the monotonous events of domestic society; another undergoing unheard-of trials under the observation of some one whom she has chosen as the companion of her dreams? another having a loving and loved companion in the life she is living, which many do not want to change.

And is not all this most natural, inevitable? Are they, who are too much ashamed of it to confess it even to themselves, to be blamed for that which cannot be otherwise, the causes of which stare one in the face, *if one's eyes were not closed?* Many struggle against this as a "snare." No Trappist ascetic watches or fasts more in the body than these do in the soul. They understand the discipline of the Thebaïd—the life long agonies to which these strong Mohicans subjected themselves. How cordially they could do the same, in order to escape the worse torture of wandering in "vain imaginations." But the laws of God for moral well-being are not thus to be obeyed. We fast mentally, scourge ourselves morally, use the intellectual hair-shirt, in order to subdue that perpetual daydreaming, which is so dangerous! We resolve "this day month I will be free from it"; twice a day with prayer and written record of the times we have indulged in it, we endeavour to combat it. Never, with the slightest success.

This is a *locus classicus* in nineteenth-century English feminism, and it is very, very strange. Dreams are nothing if not vivid, exciting, and unexpected, Nightingale was an accomplished storyteller, yet here her prose becomes vague, disjointed, limp. Florence Nightingale, in passionate rage, claims that mothers (perhaps like her own) would react in horror if they knew that their prim daughters were absorbed in imagined endless conversations with ideal companions. Can she be serious? The dream adventures Nightingale adumbrates here would be too tame for the most anodyne woman novelist of her time. There is not even the quivering touch of a hand, the arm clasped about a slender waist, the little head laid tenderly on a manly bosom, the chaste kiss under the stars, and other stock-in-trade love tokens of Victorian romance. And yet then Nightingale goes on to imply that to give oneself up to such preternaturally chaste dreams as she has described is a sin comparable to that of St. Jerome in his cave. What is going on here?

Unlike earlier scholars, I find it impossible to believe that the dreams Nightingale calls a sin, an addiction, the enemy, and so on were in fact the ones she sketches here. The discrepancy between the imaginative sins Nightingale is prepared to confess, her sense of defilement, and the punishment she calls down upon herself is too great. Something crucial is missing in this account, and I would hazard the guess that what Nightingale calls the passional side of her nature is being transferred from the dream to the imagined punishment. She invokes the desert fathers whipping and starving their uncontrollably lustful bodies into submission because she too could not control her desire. I think it is probable that when Florence Nightingale became absorbed in one of the imagined philanthropic adventures with an ideal companion she describes, she became physically aroused and experienced an erotic pleasure that filled her with the guilt and shame she records so obsessively.

The Christian religion taught Florence Nightingale to be pure and chaste. Victorian ideology taught her that virtuous women had no passion and experienced no sexual pleasure. Doctors taught her that masturbation led infallibly to mental and physical degeneracy. Educationalists taught her that parents, governesses, and teachers must do their utmost to prevent children from masturbating, even if it meant tying their hands, interrupting their sleep, and strapping on brutal mechanical devices. The mind of a Victorian girl with a passional nature was more tightly laced than her body. I would bet that Miss Christie, the Nightingale governess, tried hard to break little Flo of her habit of "dreaming," just as she was under instructions to stop her mooning around after young women like her cousin's nursemaid. We know that from the age of seven on, Florence Nightingale tried to spend as little time as possible in bed, that acts of active naughtiness delivered her from her dreaming, and that she loved to get so tired that she slept as soon as she lay down.

We shall never know what happened in Nightingale's dreams. The passion that in "Cassandra" Nightingale insistently claims for herself and other women but never, never renders in a physical image, the sympathy she cries out for and claims never, never to find in reality, speak to me of a deep, dark pit in Nightingale's mental landscape that was constantly threatening to open up and swallow her. And in Athens in the spring of 1850, the pit gaped wide.

But—and it is a very, very important but—it was also during the times when she was afflicted by dreams that Florence Nightingale heard the voice of God. Into the black pit of despair and apathy came shafts of intense light. Out of the eternal silence of infinite space came a voice.[21]

This is what Nightingale reports unequivocally in the entries to her 1850 travel diary, both in Egypt and in Greece, and this is where her experience links up with that of mystics throughout the centuries.[22] Here is an abridged version of the February and March diary:

> [February 16] Karnak. And where was I? All the while that I was on the Propyleion & half the afternoon dreaming. Karnak itself cannot save me now it has no voice for me.

> [February 22] Luxor before breakfast. Long morning by myself at old Kourna. Sat on steps of Portico moving with the shadow of the sun & and looking at that (to me) priceless view. God spoke to me again.

> [February 28] God called me with my Madre's words.

> [March 7] Gale all night & all day. Lying under Gebel Heredu. God called me in the morn[in]g & asked me "Would I do good for Him alone without the reputation."

> [March 9] During half an hour I had by myself in the cabin . . . settled the question with God.

> [March 10] Everyday during the ¼ of hours I had to myself after dinner & breakfast in my own cabin, read some of my Madre's words. Can you give up the reputation of suffering much & saying little, they cried to me.[23]

TWO THINGS PULLED Florence Nightingale back from the pit. The first was Athena, her owl. One day when Florence was walking about the Acropolis she saw some boys tormenting a tiny owl that had fallen from the nest. She bought the bird from the children and managed to rear it. At first, in order to get the wild creature into a cage, Nightingale mesmerized her owl, but soon the new pet, who full-grown was some seven inches high, took to spending much of the day asleep in her pocket.[24] Florence christened her owl Athena, after the owl goddess of the owl's native city. The goddess, she noted in her diary in May 1850, united wit and intelligence. These were qualities Florence herself had in abundance and to which she often gave scant value. Thus Athena, owl and goddess, a little warm ball of fuzz that pecked her and an ancient inspiration, were balm to Nightingale's wounded psyche. As we shall see, Athena will feature in Florence Nightingale's waking dreams for years to come.

And second, Selina Bracebridge watched and worried over Florence. Sigma could see that her young friend was going though some kind of crisis, that Egypt was not succeeding as Rome had. At some point the Bracebridges decided that on the way back through Germany they would allow Florence to make a visit

Florence Nightingale with her owl, Athena. Drawing by Parthenope Nightingale.

to the Kaiserswerth Anstalt. This was a risk of a different kind from the cataracts into Nubia. Fanny Nightingale would be certain to see the Bracebridges' taking Florence to Kaiserswerth as a betrayal of trust.

The Bracebridge party traveled home slowly, via the island of Corfu, Trieste, Prague, Dresden, and Berlin, and Florence's mental condition fluctuated. As she prepared to leave Athens she wrote: "After a sleepless night, physically & morally broken down, a slave. Glad to leave Athens. I had no wish on earth but to sleep, an unbroken sleep in my little bed at Lea Hurst. There it seemed to me as if forgetfulness opened her mother's arms to me. There I wished to be, but only to sleep." On the voyage back across the Mediterranean from Greece to Italy, things were no better. "I had no wish to be on deck. I let all the glorious sunrises, the gorgeous sunsets, the lovely moonlights pass by.[25] I had no wish, no energy, I longed for sleep. My enemy is too strong for me—everything has been tried."[26]

On the boat to Italy, Nightingale was free of dreaming and able to sleep. She notes "gradual respite from animals delightful," which, given that Florence never saw a critter she didn't like, may mean that this particular ship was not infested with vermin. In Prague, Florence again lay in bed in despair—"past redemption, a slave that could not be set free"— but in Dresden, she felt up to visiting the art gallery and gave a beautiful description of Raphael's "Ecce Homo" she knew would please the ladies at home. In Berlin at first things were worse than ever, and the prospect of Kaiserswerth made her more miserable not less. "A miserable week in Berlin—I did not think it worth while to get up in the morning. What could I do but offend God? I never prayed. All plans, all wishes seemed extinguished, and now, on the brink of achieving my greatest wish [i.e. going to Kaiserswerth], with Σ [Selina] positively planning for me, I seemed to be unfit, unmanned for it—it seemed not to be the calling for me."[27]

But then things started going well again. In Germany she had all sorts of useful contacts, and the Bracebridges seem to have allowed her to travel around on her own in a private carriage—alone, that is to say, with Trout. In Berlin she visited the Bethanien, a deaconess hospital, as well as the institute for the deaf and dumb. She took a side trip to Hamburg to visit Amalie Sieveking, a deeply religious woman who had helped found a school for poor girls, worked in hospitals during the cholera epidemic of 1831, and then founded her own hospital for destitute children. All these visits and contacts helped Florence to better define what she herself hoped to achieve. Also in Hamburg, unexpectedly, Florence met up with Richard Monckton Milnes, who, she says, "was himself again." On behalf of her father, Florence made careful inquiries about treatment for failing eyesight with a famous German eye doctor. Hearing her account of WEN's symptoms, the doctor agreed that something might possibly be done surgically.

Finally, at the end of July, Florence found herself driving up to the Kaiserswerth Anstalt, where she was kindly received by the founders and organizers of the hospital, Pastor Fliedner and his second wife, Caroline. "My hope was answered. I was admitted within the Diakonissen Anstalt. Went to the inn to dismiss Trout & get my things. My first night in my own little room within the Anstalt. I felt queer, but the courage which falls into my shoes in a London drawing room rises on an occasion like this. I felt so sure it was God's work." The next morning, for the first time in her life, she did her own hair.[28]

Florence Nightingale stayed at Kaiserswerth only two weeks, as an honored visitor. She was taken around the various wards, was introduced to the deaconesses and observed their life, but she did not have much chance to work with patients or students. The Fliedners saw the arrival of the well-connected Miss Nightingale as quite literally a godsend, and they convinced her to write a pamphlet in English describing the work at the Anstalt and recommending that her countrywomen begin something similar in England. Florence set to work on this pamphlet at once, and she was deeply grateful to the Bracebridges for delaying their return to England until she had finished it. Charles edited the manuscript and sent it off to a publisher in London.

Gales kept the Bracebridge party from crossing the English Channel for a few days, and when they finally took the ferry, the way was stormy. But now mere bad weather could not curb Florence's feeling of euphoria. She spent the first night at the Burlington Hotel, where she and her family always stayed in London, then said farewell to the Bracebridges and set off for home. "Up at 5. Saw Σ off. Off myself by 8.30 from Euston Sq. Amber Gate at 2 & home by 3—Surprised my dear people sitting in the drawing room & not thinking of me, with the owl in my pocket." Then Fanny found out that Florence had been at Kaiserswerth, and once again the fat was in the fire.

Chapter 13

BREAKING FREE

WEN, Parthe, and Fanny had all longed for Flo's return. Without her, each of them felt incomplete, but the elation caused by her unheralded arrival was soon over. No one was pleased to know that the last months of Flo's adventure had been devoted to investigating philanthropic institutions. Even harder to bear were Florence's professions of fervent admiration for the various Catholic sisters she had fallen in with during her travels. She admitted that in Alexandria she spent so much time at the convent of the sisters of St. Vincent de Paul she was "like a tame cat there . . . and went in without ringing."[1] If the idea of Florence as an English Mrs. Hill was unappealing, Florence as Sister Mary This or Mother Teresa of That was positively abhorrent to the whole Nightingale clan. Parthe threw the bracelets Florence had brought her back from Egypt in her face. Remembering this some ten years later, Florence wrote in a private note, "The scene that followed was so violent that I fainted/first felt the symptoms of that disease which is now bringing me to my grave."[2]

The news that Mr. Bracebridge had taken upon himself to send Florence's pro-Kaiserswerth pamphlet off for publication caused another furor, as the Bracebridges had probably anticipated. The whole notion of celibate Protestant sisterhoods smacked of popery to Fanny's Evangelical-Anglican friends. Of course the pamphlet was to be anonymous, but people would be sure to put two and two together, point the finger of blame at Flo, and wonder how dear Mrs. Nightingale could have countenanced such a thing. Indeed, in July 1852, Fanny received a rather disingenuous letter from her eldest sister, Patty: "People seem to understand that Flo wrote the little Kaiserswerth pamphlet—I have never thought so—neither have I any belief that it would succeed in England, neither as regards lay nuns, nor as superceding workhouses."[3] As if Fanny had ever cared about wretched Kaiserswerth!

Thus the fall of 1850 found all four Nightingales sunk in rage and depression. WEN was as miserable at home as Flo, and her lengthy absences abroad over the last two years had been hard to bear. He and Fanny had less and less to say to each other, and Fanny and Parthe together formed a pressure group that WEN was weary of resisting.[4] He had advised Florence to send her letters to him to the Athenaeum, since Fanny insisted that all letters be made public property.[5] While he clearly saw the love-hate relationship that was destroying the health and happiness of both his daughters, WEN felt powerless to address it, and it irked him to find himself a fugitive from his own home, especially as his health was poor. WEN was suffering from increasingly severe eye problems, and it seemed all too likely that he would lose his sight, a terrible prospect for a man who spent so much time with his nose in a book. When WEN was ill, Fanny and Parthe got frantically anxious, and this only grated on his nerves more.

Florence's attitude toward money and success also stuck in WEN's craw. With little fuss he had steered the family ship through the hungry forties, no small achievement in an age rife with Ponzi schemes, speculative bubbles, and their attendant bankruptcies. He did not seek praise for succeeding where so many louder men of business failed, but he was aware that in Florence's eyes he was an amiable failure. Flo would have liked him to work a seventy-hour week running a manufactory or to go into Parliament and campaign for labor reforms with Lord Shaftesbury. Moreover, Florence preached poverty while taking affluence for granted.

While WEN fretted largely in silence, Fanny Nightingale gave voice to enough anger for the two of them. Her temper was not improved by an awareness that there were relatives and friends, her sister-in-law Mai Smith chief among them, who blamed her for WEN's unhappiness and Florence's frustration. In her younger daughter Fanny saw a force of will more than equal to her own, and an energy that seemed set on destroying the social capital the family had labored to build up. Flo had unexpectedly developed the social skills Fanny prized, and without seeming to care she attracted the interest of the most desirable people. Yet of late it was hardly possible to keep Flo in the drawing room when there was company at Embley, and sometimes over the dinner table she might just as well have been sleepwalking. As a domestic manager, Flo could run rings around poor Parthe when she chose, but nowadays, choose she did not. And then there was her treatment of poor Mr. Monckton Milnes— leading him on all those years and then deciding he was not good enough for her. Of course, Florence had the right to remain single if she wished, and Fanny needed no convincing that no marriage was better than a bad marriage. But how dare Flo dismiss her father as a parasite and her mother as a parvenue? And then there was the entail, forever sitting at Fanny's shoulder like a succubus. At any moment Mr. Nightingale could fall victim to the cholera or stumble blindly into a culvert, and then the Sam Smiths would inherit almost everything. Overnight, Fanny and Parthe could find themselves living in a cottage the size of the Embley butler's pantry, or so Fanny's nightmares went.

Florence Nightingale knew how much her mother worried about her father, fretted about Parthe's health, and blamed her for not helping. Using the kind of sociological analysis encouraged by the British Association meetings she liked to attend, Florence saw Fanny as an upper-middle-class English mother caught in a generational trap. In one passage of *Suggestions for Thought,* Florence, who was an excellent mimic, ventriloquized her mother's voice to convey the deep differences in mother-daughter relations that had developed since the time of her autocratic grandmother Frances Coape Smith: "Many a mother of this day would speak . . . thus:—'My mother did not think of what her daughter thought; her daughter had no business to think, *she* thought in her stead. *I* allow my daughter to think, but I expect she shall always think like me. This is the least she can do, in common gratitude, in return for all that I have done for her. I don't desire her to obey—no such tyranny can exist in the nineteenth century; but she is always to act as I should do . . . I am excessively indulgent, that is, I take immense pains (*my* mother took no pains of the sort) to make her happy, in my way; to please her, according to my taste . . . and she is not grateful."[6]

The disagreements between mother and daughter, though marked, were not so great as to provide no hope for rapprochement.[7] If Florence got her intellect and taste for metaphysical speculation from her father, it was from Fanny that she got her ego, her "genius for order," her plans to conquer the world. Florence not only loved her mother, she respected her and longed for her sympathy and support. For her part Fanny was, to quote Mai Smith, "wrapt up in" Florence and wanted only her happiness.[8] Fanny had always given her intellectual freedom, as well as offering her a good deal of pleasure. The problem was that Florence wanted more autonomy and less pleasure. Both mother and daughter were armed with a blueprint for the future, and each was convinced that hers was right.

If Fanny and Parthe formed an alliance, it was because their interests dovetailed, not because their characters were alike. Fanny was strong and Parthe weak. Parthe was her mother's faithful ally, constant companion, and obedient echo; in return she got Fanny's unconditional protection and support, and she needed it. If all four Nightingales had problems, the one who seemed likely to founder on the rocks of her own frustration was Parthe. Now in her thirty-first year, Parthenope Nightingale was a confirmed invalid. If I may attempt a risky *ex post facto* diagnosis, a satisfactory explanation for Parthenope Nightingale's physical symptoms would be that a childhood attack of rheumatic fever, a common and untreatable disease in the nineteenth century, had left her with permanent cardiac and neurological impairments. Furthermore, the arthritis that would make Parthenope Nightingale Verney a cripple by her early fifties was already affecting her in her thirties. Yet organic factors do not account for Parthenope Nightingale's deteriorating condition, since in later years she endured pain with remarkable fortitude and continued to write and research when she was incapable of holding a pen. In 1850 Parthenope was in a state of rising hysteria about the future that all the Harley Street specialists could do nothing to stem, and this manifested itself chiefly in a growing obsession with her sister.

When she returned from Egypt, Florence wrote what Victorians called a "character" of Parthe.[9] It was customary to begin with a "leading feature" or "startling projection" that offered the key to the subject's personality, but Florence confessed that she was unable to find such a thing for Parthenope. Her sister was a happy, guileless child of nature, a creature of instinct and impulse, "like the Bird of Paradise, who floats over this world without touching it, or sullying its bright feathers with it, rather than the nightingale, which makes its nest in it and sings." Florence admiringly acknowledged Parthe's artistic talents, her imagination, and her gift for language. She praised Parthe's grace, her selfless devotion to the people she loved, her absolute discretion, her natural gift for accommodating herself to the world. "She hated the sight of sorrow—it did not even interest her. To admire was her passion and jealousy she could not understand."[10]

Even as she strove to be fair to her subject, Florence's pen was tipped with acid. Florence remarked that her sister was "the true type of woman" since she had "not the smallest ambition. The love of distinction or of power would not make her raise her hand to grasp them, if they were within her reach." This seems on the surface to be praise, but then Florence spoils the compliment by going on: "She would be called remarkably frank, but she had nothing more to tell to her sister than to her fortnight's acquaintance . . . She liked everybody and cared for scarcely any . . . A friend to all, she interested herself particularly in none."

With her sister, Florence swung between hot and cold. As children she and Parthe fought, but as a teenager Flo treated Parthe like a special chum. But after the family returned from their European travels, Florence grew bored with her sister and irritated by her assumption of intimacy. Parthenope, in contrast, was consistently warm with people outside the family, carefully maintaining friendships through the years, but the adamantine core of her emotional life was always her love and devotion for her parents and her sister. For Florence to write that Parthe was not "particularly interested" in anyone was cruel. As everyone knew, Parthe was passionately interested in "her own Flo, her idolatrized, wondrous Flo."[11]

Florence misread Parthenope's resolute cheerfulness. The "leading feature" or "startling projection" that Florence sought in vain for this character sketch was, I think, Parthenope's ill health and lack of physical beauty. Illness was one subject, Florence admits in another note on Parthe, that her sister absolutely refused to discuss. Flo says that Parthe would be perfectly happy if she only had her health—a very large if. She writes: "Such pure *existence,* without question, without introspection, without consciousness I never saw in anyone. It does not matter what she is as to beauty for the question never seems to have entered her own mind."[12] Can we really believe this to be true? Far from being an exotic bird of paradise, Parthe was at best a sparrow.

My impression is that Parthenope's combination of hysterical outbursts when Florence went away and irritating chirpiness when she was at home formed a double smokescreen under which a growing desperation lurked. Parthe's determined wish to see only the sunny side of life—so diametrically opposite to Florence's emphasis on the world as a vale of tears—may have begun as a predisposition, but it became a strategy. If Parthe at thirty-one, in competition with the other three strong personalities in the family, was playing some combination of affectionate child, feckless woman, and cheerful invalid, this was perhaps the best casting she could obtain from a grudging Providence at this point in her life.[13]

Parthe had her own dreams, which Florence was too absorbed to see or too contemptuous to acknowledge. Parthe remained pathetically attached to her sister not just because Flo had exceptional charisma but also because no husband and children came to take precedence in Parthe's affections. As a girl Parthe had seemed destined to become a successful Victorian upper-middle-class wife and mother. Parthe expected the things in life most women expect, the things Flo disdained—husband, house, children. If in her early twenties Parthe had been healthy enough to find these, life not only for herself but for her parents and for her sister might have been much simpler. Imagine Parthe married young and we can imagine Fanny happily preoccupied with Parthe's household and Parthe's confinements and Parthe's children. We can imagine Flo off the leash, living in a little London house her father rented for her, beavering away in hospitals and schools, chairing lots of committees, and romping on weekends with her adoring nieces and nephews. We can imagine WEN, less henpecked, less anxious about the future, spending chummy nights in London with his younger daughter and taking the train with her down to Parthe's place for the weekend.

But Parthenope was ill, and illness made her plain and undesirable. For fourteen years, Parthe played the part of the Victorian debutante as well as she knew how. She did the devoted daughter, the selfless sister, loving cousin, loyal friend, and cheerful companion. None of it worked. There was no proposal of marriage, no establishment of her own, not even a star-crossed love affair. By the age of twenty-five, Parthe had already resigned herself to forever playing second fiddle to virtuoso Flo, but then she had to confront the fact that Flo had no interest in music and refused to pick up her instrument. Flo, so glum, so moody and ungrateful and hypercritical, so different, could have had all the things Parthe wanted. To Parthe, this was heartbreaking and incomprehensible, and it made her more ill and more unbalanced, and her hysteria threatened to split the family.

AND SO WHEN FLORENCE finally came home from Germany in late August, her mother told her in no uncertain terms to put her philanthropic plans back in her trunk and devote herself entirely to her sister. Flo's job, for six months, was to make her sister well and happy and thus relieve the load on her mother. After all the money that had been lavished upon Flo in the last two years, this was the least she could do.

Unsurprisingly, the next months were unhappy for all. On the good days, when she was not lying in bed longing to die and thus accede to the next "stage" to come after death, when she might happily find herself an orphan without siblings, Florence wrote notes to herself urging pragmatism in dealing with Parthe. At times, Florence saw Parthe's rising distress.[14] But most of the time she angrily refused to take on the role of her sister's keeper and bitterly resented Parthe's attempts to be hers. "Why didst [Thou] make me what I am?" she wrote. "I have never known a happy time except at Rome and that fortnight at Kaiserswerth. It is not the unhappiness I mind, it is not indeed, but people can't be unhappy without making those about them so. Oh, if we could but have been alike, either I like her [Parthe] or she like me."[15]

At Whitsunday in 1851 Florence was still "vibrating between irritation & indignation at the state of suffering I am in—& remorse & agony at the absence of enjoyment I promote in them—I wish for nothing but death in order to relieve them & relieve myself." But after this characteristic explosion of hyberbolic despair, she concludes: "This cannot be true. This is childish."[16] She was right—it was childish, especially since in fact her situation was changing and she was slowly but surely shaking off what she saw as the chains of family life.

The six months of exclusive attention to Parthe that Fanny had demanded of Florence lasted three months at the outside, and a good deal of that time was spent planning her definitive escape from Embley. Nightingale corresponded on social and medical policy with people all over Europe and wrote a long, wandering, and astonishingly bitter indictment of family life in her new manuscript, *Suggestions for Thought*.

It is hard to keep track of Florence Nightingale's activities between fall 1850 and her move to Harley Street in the summer of 1853 because she traveled around so much, met and corresponded with so many people, and engaged in so many productive and interesting projects. These appear insignificant only when compared with those that engaged her after 1854.[17]

To pick out just a few plums from the rich mix, this was the period when Nightingale was introduced to both George Eliot and Elizabeth Barrett Browning, when she was absorbed in her friendship with the Anglo-American doctor Elizabeth Blackwell, when she corresponded with the newly ordained Roman Catholic priest Henry Manning, when she kept up close relationships to Sidney Herbert and Lord Shaftesbury, when she taught in Ragged Schools and village schools, when she volunteered in hospitals, when she got involved in the struggle to save poor women from prostitution.[18] It was also the time when she did a good deal of field research on the opinions and beliefs of England's educated artisans and got to know a number of socialists of the Owenite persuasion.[19]

Florence's incursions into Chartist and Owenite territory were to do research for her projected book *Suggestions for Thought to the Searchers After Truth Among the Artisans of England*. This was intended as a rebuttal to Robert Owen's assertion that religion was an unnecessary or even harmful influence on the lives of the poor, and Florence's friends Lord Shaftesbury, Charles Kingsley, and F. C. Maurice, to say nothing of her aunt Mai, encouraged her to write it. The shocking finding of the 1851 national census that five and a quarter million Britons did not attend Sunday worship crystallized the conviction of many earnest Christians in the Nightingales' reformist circle that the English industrial workers and city dwellers had been abandoned by the churches.[20] Nightingale hoped her book would lead the atheist artisans of England back to the Christian religion, but it was never published in her lifetime and had no influence on public opinion. In the end the artisans of England had far more influence on Florence Nightingale than she on them. The socially egalitarian nursing policies she was to adopt in the Crimean War hospitals, the extraordinary rapport that developed between her and the non-officer class of soldier-patients, can be explained in part by the people she met, the sermons and lectures she heard, and the books and pamphlets she read in the early 1850s.

IN OCTOBER OR EARLY November of 1850, Florence was relieved of Parthe duty by two successive calls for help that even Fanny saw as priorities—to go first to Cromford Bridge and help her aunt Mai look after Great-aunt Evans, and then to Waverley Abbey to give what comfort and support she could to her aunt Anne and uncle George and her Nicholson cousins. Fanny and Parthe were annoyed when Aunt Mai wrote asking that Flo might be allowed to accompany her to Cromford. Why on earth couldn't Mai take her own eldest daughter, Blanche, with her? However, everyone in the family knew that for Mrs. Shore and Miss Evans the sun rose and set with Florence and that no one else could possibly be the comfort to them that she was.

Mai and Flo went up north to look after the old ladies in a spirit of decided affection, but their assignment was not an easy one. Both the Cromford Bridge and the Tapton houses were now cold, damp, smelly, tumbledown places. The owners were in equally poor shape and gave a good deal of trouble, in part because they were so intent on offering their guests vast quantities of food and drink, in part because they were constantly quarreling. Since their lonely childhood, the lives of the two sisters had been passionately intertwined, but their love and concern for each other found no harmonious expression. Mrs. Shore, the elder sister, tyrannized the younger and made Miss Evans's life a misery, all with the best intentions. Seeing the tortured relationship between these two old sisters, one wonders what conclusions Florence Nightingale reached about her own relationship with Parthe.

Miss Evans was to live until the end of 1852, and Mai and Flo seem to have spent some weeks with her and her sister each year after 1849. These visits were happy occasions for all three generations, to judge from a letter Mai Smith wrote to Fanny in 1852, a few months before Miss Evans's death: "I am constantly feeling how much happiness Flo's visit has given to our dear old lady [i.e., Great-aunt Evans] . . . We always have pleasant walks in this dear and interesting country. Florence lets me tell all my tales of my dear old people, who have been so good, so loving, so wrapped up in their affections yet so

curiously have wrung one another's & their own hearts . . . The owl is
our constant & sociable companion, sometimes on the hearth like a [?]
sometimes perched on my aunt's armchair or on her lap seized by a
longing for her tangled cotton, just now in Flo's hands being beaten for
a frequent & dangerous offence, the jumping within the fender . . . We
went to a school where my mother & I at 6 or 7 used to go. I fancied
the sturdy little girl pegging up the clattered way & looking round the
room I then stood in."

While Florence was in the Midlands with her aunt Mai, word came
that tragedy had struck the Nicholsons, the family of her aunt Anne and
uncle George. Henry Nicholson, the family's eldest son, had been killed
in an inexplicable carriage accident in Spain. He was the second of Florence's adult male cousins to die in an accident abroad, and the whole
clan was deeply upset.[21] Parthe, who had long been a regular guest at Waverley, was with her aunt and uncle when the blow struck, but swiftly returned to Embley. WEN hurried down to his brother-in-law Nicholson's
house to do what he could, but he found that his visit went almost un-
noticed. The Nicholsons were extravagantly upset and besieged by visitors. To WEN they seemed more distracted than grieving, but when
WEN was asked if Florence might come to Waverley he of course agreed.
Since her teenage years, Florence's combination of psychological acuity,
spiritual comfort, and practical assistance made her invaluable. All the
same, it was odd for Florence to be summoned by the Nicholsons. Years
before, she had rejected Henry's proposal of marriage, causing a split in
the family that had at best been papered over.

In the written comments she sent home, Florence, like her father,
was inclined to be censorious about her Nicholson relatives, especially
Marianne, whose wild and bitter grief over Henry's death she found almost unseemly. In one of the many apologetic notes to Fanny and Parthe
explaining why she had yet to return to Embley, Florence wrote on December 3: "I am going tomorrow to Henry's chambers [i.e., his London
legal offices] with Marianne which I think it quite worthwhile to have
staid for, as I doubt whether she would ever have the courage to have
done it alone, which I think a great pity, converting God's comforts into
terror. But her path is a hard one, & I think must give Henry great
pain."[22] How like Florence to have a clear conviction of what Henry was
feeling in the next "stage" after death!

As FLORENCE DREW farther away from her mother and sister, she grew closer to Mai Smith. When they went up north, Mai and Flo had weeks in each other's company and felt marvelously free. They shared a dank bed, strode across the wuthering moors, and exchanged complicitous smiles when yet another slice of seed cake was pressed upon them. They could talk for hours, with no one to interrupt or comment. Even as Flo found it unbearable to be in the same house for long with her mother and sister, so she loved to be tête-à-tête with Mai. In her aunt, Flo found an admiration, almost a worship that was very sweet. Mai was willing not only to sacrifice herself but to subordinate the interests of her own family to her remarkable niece. Her husband, the jovial, snide, outgoing, yet insecure Sam Smith, appears to have accepted this, and the three daughters, Blanche, Bertha, and Beatrice, were obliged to do so too, though it cannot have been easy to have their mother so dote on their cousin. The three B's, as they were known in the family, were all growing into intelligent, accomplished, socially responsible young women, but their lights dimmed when set next to Florence's.

Part of Mai's absorption in Flo was based on Flo's absorption in Shore, Mai and Sam Smith's only son. From the time of his birth, a heavy weight of expectations was laid on Shore, heir presumptive to his uncle's Nightingale estates, not only by his parents but by the Nightingales. Florence was eleven years older than Shore, and in her teens and twenties she projected her own ambitions onto the boy. She envisioned Shore in the future as a great political reformer and philanthropist and hoped that, as the cherished companion and tutor of his youth, she would play the role of *éminence grise* in his adult life.

When Shore entered his teens, he went as a boarder to Mr. W. King's school at Brighton, in the company of his angelic little cousin Hugh Bonham-Carter. At school Shore became rowdier and coarser, that is to say much like other boys his age, and he was probably happy to get away from all his doting and difficult female relatives, if only as far as Brighton. Unfortunately, his mother and all four of his Nightingale relatives were appalled by the changes school wrought in him.

Florence was especially troubled by Shore's emergence into male adolescence. "How is it," she wrote to her cousin Hilary Bonham-Carter in 1844, after Shore and Hugh had come for a visit to the Nightingales, "that the intercourse between boys seems always to bring out all the evil and none of the good . . . From the moment he came, Shore was méconnaissable [unrecognizable], I did not know what was become of him, everything was forgot, everything neglected, even his prayers. Oh is it possible that the happier we are, the less we wish to think of Him, the giver? Everything was altered, even his voice, for his voice to Hugh was like a bulldog's and his manner to him so coarse and untender. And, curious! since Hughie has been here, Shore has used a word which I never heard him use before, and which Hughie does not use. My dear, there was nothing left of him!"[23] How interesting it would be to know what this terrible word was that young Shore had picked up at school. But Florence did not easily give up her mission to make a great man of Shore. She redoubled her efforts to keep the boy's affection, to enter his world, and maintain her influence over him. When Shore was away, Florence wrote him long, engaging letters, full of jokes and anecdotes and news of the animals Shore loved, especially Flo's dog Teazer.[24] When Shore fell ill, he came to Embley, and he and Flo renewed their old camaraderie.

Shore did not make much academic progress at Mr. King's school, and he was brought home. Mai wrote to Fanny that since there was no good school available to Shore, she planned to find a private tutor for him when he was fifteen who would prepare him for the university. Meanwhile, could Flo take him on again? "My delight would be to ask her to take carte blanche," wrote Mai to Fanny, "to teach him Mathematics, Algebra, Trigonometry, Astronomy, German or what she would, wishing however to let no stitch drop of his classics."[25] We can assume from this heavy academic program that the family expected Shore to go up to Trinity College, Cambridge, which still required classics from all students. At Trinity, Shore would be following in the footsteps of his father, his uncles Nightingale, Octavius Smith, and Benjamin Smith, and his cousins Henry Nicholson and John Bonham-Carter. After coming down from Cambridge, he might then make a career in the law with a view to politics and the Houses of Parliament. In Shore's mid-teens Florence was already entertaining dreams of learning enough law to get her cousin through his legal studies.[26]

One of the tutors Mai and Sam Smith found for Shore was Arthur Hugh Clough, an eminent man in his late twenties from a distinguished

Liverpool family who had fallen on hard times. As a scholar in classics at Balliol College, Oxford, Clough succeeded well enough to become a fellow of Oriel. He was also a poet who won the friendship of peers like Dante Gabriel Rossetti, Matthew Arnold, and Francis Palgrave.[27] Clough seemed set for life as an Oxford don, but then the old Dissenter strain in his makeup came to the fore, and he suffered a crisis of faith. In 1848, Clough decided he could not take holy orders and was forced therefore to resign his college fellowship. From this time Arthur Hugh Clough was a poor man. After leaving Oxford, he traveled around Europe, observing the sack of Rome by French forces in 1849. He also went to Massachusetts at the invitation of Ralph Waldo Emerson and found himself at home among the Transcendentalists.

By the time he started coming to Sam Smith's house to tutor Shore, Clough was quite a romantic character. Blanche Smith, Sam's eldest daughter, promptly fell in love with him, and he with her. Tutors, as I have noted, often spelled trouble for upper-middle-class parents. For all his remarkable talents, Clough was not the Smiths' idea of a son-in-law. He had no money and neither did Blanche, and Mai and Sam Smith, who had struggled for years against financial adversity, had few illusions about the joys of love in a cottage. Though Sam was now making a decent living as a lawyer for large engineering projects, he was in no position to support his eldest daughter and her impractical poet. Shore had still to be educated, and there were two younger girls to consider, one of them severely lame and perhaps therefore unmarriageable.

The stalemate was broken by Florence Nightingale. She and Arthur Hugh Clough became friends at her uncle and aunt's home after her return from Egypt. Florence and Arthur were close in age, and they had a thousand things to discuss, from modern theology to classical literature and Italian politics. According to Cecil Woodham-Smith, Clough became another of Florence's "enthusiastic admirers," and if this is so, one wonders how Blanche felt about it.[28] Florence, who so often dreamed of an ideal companion, was sure that Blanche had found just such a person in Clough. She drew up complex budgets showing just how much income the couple would need, with projected increases in expenditure with the birth of the statistically likely children.[29] Blanche and Arthur were finally married in June 1854, shortly before Florence left for the Crimea. In later years, Florence Nightingale was to construct complicated emotional triangles with Arthur and Blanche, as well as with Sidney and Elizabeth Herbert, and, later, with Marianne Nicholson Galton and her husband, Douglas Galton.

If the marriage of Blanche and Arthur was a problem that Florence could solve, the issue of Shore's future was not so easy. In the fall of 1851 Florence wrote to her father: "Shore is going on Monday to Mr. Simpson's, an Engineering Manufactory near Thames Bk. His father pays down £100 for a year—but this binds Shore to nothing. He is to sleep at Thames Bank [i.e., at the distillery home of his uncle Octavius Smith]. Aunt Mai begged me to tell you."[30] The dreams of Trinity College, of the Inns of Temple, and the Houses of Parliament faded. The family would have to get used to the fact that Shore Smith was, in William Gilbert's phrase, "a commonplace young man, a matter of fact young man, a steady and solidly jolly bank holiday everyday young man."[31]

If anyone was disappointed in Shore, it was Florence. But since love should go only to God, she needed to swallow her disappointment and submit. She wrote in 1851: "Among the many stones I ate, one piece of bread God always granted me; a nephew of my mother's, whom I almost brought up, and who was the apple of my eye. He was a sickly child. When he went to school I prepared him. In the holidays I taught him. When he later went to college, I was his instructress. He never had any particular affection for me, otherwise I should have made him my idol, but God kept my affection for him pure. I was ambitious for him and he did not succeed in the way in which I wished. So much the better; God has other views for him."[32] One more chamber in Nightingale's strange, cold, passionate heart was put under lock and key.

WILLIAM EDWARD NIGHTINGALE had seen with approval how Florence had nursed his aunt and comforted the family of his Nicholson brother-in-law. As he battled with blindness he felt the benefit of Florence's loving, intelligent care himself. WEN was becoming the leader of the pro-Flo faction in the family, and so in the summer of 1851, Florence was allowed to return to Kaiserswerth and to spend three months there. The trip to Germany came about because doctors recommended to Parthenope that she try various German spas to see if they would help her regain her health. While Parthe and Fanny took the waters and toured some German cities, Florence could train at the Kaiserswerth Institute. WEN himself would remain at Lea Hurst.

The Kaiserswerth plan seems to have been withheld from Parthe for as long as possible. When she understood that her visit to Carlsbad to regain her health was to be the occasion for Florence to go to Kaiserswerth, she became recalcitrant. Parthe wanted above all to prevent her sister from leaving home, and she saw Kaiserswerth, quite correctly, as the thin end of the wedge that would separate the two of them for good. Parthe managed to persuade her mother to cut their German stay from six months to three and stipulated that no one should know that Florence was not spending the time with her. Keeping Florence's stay at Kaiserswerth a secret was of course ridiculous, as Florence remarked to her mother. All the friends who really counted—Mai and Sam Smith, the Mohls, the Herberts, the Bracebridges, the Bunsens, and so on—were thoroughly in favor of her going. The Bracebridges and the Herberts actually planned to pay her a visit at Kaiserswerth.

If it had been in any way her decision, Parthe would have stayed in England, but for once all the other three were united against her. In the end she had to go. Her feelings of loss and betrayal came out into the open at Carlsbad on the night before Flo was to leave them to travel to Kaiserswerth. Parthenope attacked her sister with a pyrotechnic of reproach, and Flo, who did not blanch to see legs sawn off and cataracts removed without anesthesia, fainted dead away.[33] The theatricality of such displays, on both sides, was probably not lost on their mother, but it was just as well that WEN, who abhorred scenes, had elected to stay at home.

The summer proved very hot, and Fanny and Parthe trailed around Germany, staying at the very best hotels, going to the finest galleries, shopping at the finest emporia, and being thoroughly out of sorts. They were, rather surprisingly, accompanied by the owl Athena, to whom Parthe was now deeply attached. Florence sent careful instructions about how to give Athena sand baths, and issued warnings that she must not be allowed to drink ink. But all this epistolary solicitude did nothing to make Parthe feel less aggrieved.

Meanwhile, at the Kaiserswerth Anstalt, Florence plunged joyfully into the dour, ur-Protestantism of her English Dissenter ancestors. She slept in a little room in the orphan asylum, rose at five o'clock, ate four rapid, meager meals a day of black bread, vegetable broth, and rye tea, and had not even enough spare time to send out her clothing to be washed. She saw almost nothing of the Fliedners, who ran the institute, had no good word to say of a visiting Prussian princess, took pleasure in the superb choral singing of the staff, accompanied the children on nature walks to the river, and spent as much time as she could in the infirmary. "The world here fills my life with interest and strengthens me body and mind," she wrote to her mother on July 16.[34] "The weather is intensely hot, too hot I am afraid for you," she wrote smugly to Parthe on August 4. "I like it and am perfectly well, body and mind (though I am afraid you would much rather hear that I was not)."[35]

The institute at Kaiserswerth with its ninety-odd deaconesses in residence was divided into several small sections that included an orphanage, a penitentiary for fallen young women, and two separate infirmaries for male and female patients. Theodor Fliedner, who had founded the Anstalt, was a pastor, not a doctor, and the training he gave the deaconesses was more spiritual exhortation than medical internship. Even in the infirmary, the main concern was for the soul of the patient, not the body, though Florence noted that the wards smelled much cleaner and fresher than those in English public hospitals. Florence Nightingale was exceptional in the careful way she observed the patients, both male and female, and in the intelligent way she handled them. She assisted at an amputation and later watched the patient succumb to infection and die, as most amputation cases did, taking detailed notes that would prove all too relevant to the cases she was to meet in the Scutari hospitals a few years later. As Pastor Fliedner told Sidney Herbert, Miss Nightingale was the most talented and expert nursing intern the institute had ever had.

It is unlikely that Florence Nightingale learned anything important about hospital management and patient care at Kaiserswerth.[36] For so many years she had dreamed of apprenticing herself to some experienced nurse or doctor at the Anstalt, and when she finally found herself there, there was little she could learn and much she could teach. But if the months at Kaiserswerth did not "qualify" Nightingale in the way she had expected, they did give her the first, delicious taste of living independently of family and friends. They also helped her to formulate more precisely what she wanted to do. Her goal now was to have charge of a public medical facility, the bigger and busier the better.

While Fanny and Parthe were abroad alone and relatively unsupported, Florence lobbied them vigorously. She wrote a series of well-crafted letters astutely working on their Christian ideals, their affection for her, and their progressivism. The most notable letter is the one she wrote to Fanny on August 31: "I should be happy here as the day is long and wish that I could hope to have your smile, your blessing, your sympathy upon it, without which I cannot be quite happy. My beloved people, I cannot bear to grieve you. Life, and everything in it that charms you, you would sacrifice for me. But, unknown to you is my thirst; unseen by you are waters which would save me . . . Have other paths *right for others* been untried by *me?* But, my beloved people . . . little do you know how long that voice has spoken . . . how I have turned this way and that, trying if there were other path for me than the one which might look like estrangement from hope and parents, so loving, so loved . . . When I was six years old, with Miss Johnson, this had been my first thought, for the last seven years, my first and last."[37]

In other things she was writing at about this time, Florence breathed less affection and conciliation and more anger and resentment. On December 7, some six weeks after her return from Germany, Florence was still working out ways to win her mother over. She hastily sketched out a kind of dialogue with Fanny: "Why my dear, you don't think that with my 'talents' & my 'European reputation' & my 'beautiful letters' and all that, I'm going to stay dangling about my mother's drawing room all my life—I shall go & look out for work, to be sure—you must look upon me as your son, your vagabond son, without his money. I shan't cost you near so much as a son would have done. I haven't cost you much yet—except my visits to Egypt & Rome. Remember I should have cost you a great deal more if I had married or been a son."[38]

Anger really erupted in the manuscript of *Suggestions for Thought.*[39] Here Nightingale allowed herself to develop a long, rambling, and astonishingly vitriolic critique of Victorian upper-middle-class family life. Family life is nothing but internecine strife and mutual exploitation, she asserts. Parents rarely speak to one another, siblings have nothing in common, and the weak prey on the strong. Sons are lucky since parents are anxious to get them out of the home. Girls use marriage to escape the stifling atmosphere chez Papa but then reproduce it for lack of education and understanding. Unhappiest are the unmarried women, whose slavery ends only when both parents die. Nightingale insists that parents should in fairness allow each child to go his or her own way and that each child had a right to a share in the family resources in lieu of maintenance, dowry, or inheritance. All the heroines of fiction, Nightingale remarks, have lost at least one parent, and usually both.[40]

FANNY'S OBDURACY to the idea of Florence leaving home and leading an independent life was not merely selfish or stupid. She believed it was in the ultimate interest of both her children for her to resist Flo's plans. Fanny now accepted her daughter's dedication to philanthropic work, but she could not see why this required Flo to remain single. The right husband who could offer both financial and moral support was exactly what Florence would need to succeed. On this point, Mai Smith, Mary Clarke, and Selina Bracebridge were probably much of Fanny's mind. Since Fanny clung, not unreasonably, to the idea that Flo might still marry, she temporized. Perhaps when Florence turned thirty-five she would be allowed to leave home with her mother's blessing. But the main reason why Fanny dug her heels in was for Parthe's sake. If Flo left home, Parthe would sink even farther into misery and illness.

In the fall of 1851, Florence Nightingale came down with the measles, but by early December she was writing to her father in high spirits that they should both take at least three weeks at the Malvern spa and then repair to Birmingham for a British Association conference on managing juvenile delinquency. In January 1852, she went with her father to Dr. Johnson's establishment at Umberslade Lodge in Wiltshire. WEN had finally made up his mind to risk letting a surgeon operate on his eyes, and though the operation was successful, the recovery was long and full of anxiety. Florence's task was to keep her mother and Parthe, frantic with anxiety, at bay. She read to WEN, accompanied him on long walks at night, and generally kept him amused while his eyes healed. Father and daughter talked endlessly, and the old alliance was revived and strengthened.

Meanwhile, Florence's dalliance with the Roman Catholic Church continued, and the possibility that she might convert was a kind of sword of Damocles held over her mother's head. In June of 1852 she wrote to her proselytizing friend Father (soon to be Cardinal) Henry Manning: "You think it would be a sacrifice to me to join the Catholic Church, a temptation to remain where I am. If you knew what a home the Catholic

Church would be to me!"[41] In fact, there was little real danger of Florence becoming a Sister of Charity. When in the summer of 1852 Florence, properly chaperoned by old, blind Dr. Fowler of the Salisbury Infirmary and his wife, went over to Ireland, her visit was not a success. The hospitals, run by Catholic nuns, that Nightingale had planned to visit were closed, and the charity institutions she did see disgusted her.

Whereas it was true that she had little respect for the Church of England, Nightingale was too well versed in the latest Biblical criticism, religious history, and comparative mythology to be awed by Catholicism's patristic tradition. She had little use for ritual or priestly castes, she found God as readily in a mosque as in a church, and she was a product of the Protestant reformation in her recourse to the Bible as a source of guidance. Her indifference to theological niceties, her strong religious activism, and her emphasis on individual judgment all harked back to her Unitarian roots. Above all, Nightingale understood the politics of religion in England well, and she felt no urge to provide Henry Manning or any other gentleman ecclesiastic with a trophy convert.

As Florence spent more and more time away from home with friends and relatives, Parthe's health plummeted. Alarmed, her parents put her under the care of Sir James Clark, a good friend of WEN's and one of Queen Victoria's personal physicians. Clark diagnosed "rheumatic headaches" and declared the patient to be "nervous, fanciful, and unstable." Clark was convinced that it was essential to separate Parthenope from her family and her usual way of life, and so he suggested that she come and stay with him and his family in Scotland. Clark lived for much of the year in a grace-and-favor residence at Birk Hall, a small property next to the Queen's estate at Balmoral Castle. Here Parthenope was sent in the late summer of 1852.

Sir James Clark believed that Parthenope Nightingale suffered from hysteria, an illness reaching epidemic levels at this time among upper-middle-class women all over Europe and North America. Even though fashionable doctors like Clark preferred to refer to the complaint—and how those women complained!—as neurasthenia, not hysteria (i.e., womb sickness), they attributed it to abnormalities of the reproductive organs, just as their ancient Greek forebears had. Widows, childless wives, and spinsters were predisposed to hysteria/neurasthenia, and in the past, congress with the male, followed preferably by pregnancy and motherhood, was held to be the sovereign remedy.

Advanced Western medical opinion gave out that modern women were becoming neurasthenic largely because they were spoiled. Life in industrialized society gave women too much leisure, too much attention, too much time to fret, too many novels to read, too many dreams to rot their minds. For their own good, these patients must be treated with severity, as if they were naughty children. To coddle, to sympathize, was to convince the neurasthenic of the advantages of the invalid life and impede her recovery. A neurasthenic who was thin and hyperactive should be confined to bed, deprived of stimuli and amusements, and fed a good deal of fat.[42] Someone like Parthenope Nightingale, who was spoiled to death by her mother and spent her days on the sofa, must be required to take vigorous exercise, separated from her family, and supervised by some kindly but firm stranger. In those unfortunate cases where neurasthenia became hysteria proper, modern surgical interventions—clitoridectomy, ovarectomy—could be necessary, especially if the patient was poor.[43]

In Scotland, far from her family and friends and subjected to "observation," Parthenope Nightingale broke down completely. Sir James Clark reported "delusions," "chronic delirium," and "extreme irritability." Fanny Nightingale, who was in constant communication with Parthe by letter, was frantic with anxiety and insisted that Florence should cut short her Irish trip and hasten up to Ballater in Scotland to collect her distraught sister. In this emergency, Florence was allowed to travel from Ireland to Scotland on her own—that is to say, with her maid, Mariette.

As soon as her sister arrived, Parthe reverted to normal, as Florence immediately reported to her mother on September 17. In this and subsequent letters, Florence adopted a rather supercilious form of "we" to designate her sister: "This is to announce that we have made our first walk this beautiful day and we come downstairs now at 10 o'clock; we sleep well and eat well and I see no reason why we should not set out homewards, except that the *time* [the onset of Parthe's menstrual period] is the *end* of next week again, and Sir James is not quite certain whether we had better go before or after it." Florence also had some interesting royal gossip to convey. "Yesterday, as we were out, we came upon the royal party in a scompiglio [a state of confusion]. The Queen came out into the middle of the road by herself and said, My niece has had an accident. Luckily Sir James was with us and he went to her directly. It was

the young Princess Hohenlohe who had been thrown from her horse and
we have not seen Sir James since."[44]

Florence, always a cool head in a crisis, no doubt made a favorable
impression on the royal party, and she certainly became a huge favorite
with the Clarks, whose small children soon fell under her spell. When
Florence left Ballater, the youngest Clark cried. In the convivial atmosphere that Florence conjured up as if by magic, Parthe became increasingly cheerful and ceased to complain of weakness and paralysis. Seeing
Parthe come downstairs and even take walks, Sir James Clark was further convinced that the sickness was in her mind, not her body. Florence
wrote to Fanny: "Sir James says, if she [Parthe] could but think herself
well she would be so, or rather if she could but think of something else."

The visit to Birk Hall turned out to be extremely important. In Sir
James Clark, her sister's chief physician, Florence now had a most valuable ally. Clark had told the Nightingale parents that Parthenope's health
depended on her being separated from her sister, and they had accepted
his advice and sent her up to Scotland. But by producing a particularly
threatening set of symptoms, Parthe had successfully manipulated her
mother, brought her sister hurrying back from the snares of Catholic Ireland, and made Clark look foolish. She had shown that she could be well
only if Florence was with her, looking after her. Sir James Clark was at
the top of his profession, and he did not care to be outsmarted by patients like Nightingale's elder daughter. Clark made a point of instructing
Florence that Parthenope would never think herself well as long as she
and Flo lived in the same house. He also convinced William Edward
Nightingale that this was so. As Florence wrote in a private note some
ten years later, "A very successful and justly successful physician once seriously told a sister who was being Devoured that she must leave home in
order that the Devourer might recover health and balance which had
been lost in the process of devouring. This person was myself." In another note, Florence Nightingale wrote that Sir James Clark had taught
her "a terrible lesson which tore open my eyes as nothing less could have
done. My life has been decided thereby."[45]

IN THE LATE FALL OF 1852, Parthenope Nightingale's mood was
dark. All her life she had loved and admired and needed her sister, Flo-

rence, and now she was instructed that that love was excessive, devouring, the product of a diseased mind. Her impulse had always been to put Flo first, and now she was accused of sacrificing her sister's interests to her own weakness. For once the power of positive thinking failed Parthe, and she felt a bitter need to tell her side of the story.

So Parthenope Nightingale developed her own "character" of Florence. "Truth is a good thing," wrote Parthe to Madame Mohl,

> and the history of the last year (the others much like it) is one month with the Fowlers in Ireland, three months with aunt Mai in London, three more with her at Harrogate [a spa] and Cromford Bridge [i.e., attending to the dying great-aunt Evans], three more with her at the water cure and Grandmama's. Now Aunt Mai is the person she [Florence] loves best in the world, and whose metaphysical mind suits her best, so that I hope she has passed a very pleasant year, but meantime those eternal poor have been left to the mercies of Mama and me, both very unwell, and whose talkey-talkey broth and pudding she holds in very great contempt. Now, dear Clarkey, you are a very clever man and wise . . . and what you say is very true, I believe she has little or none of what is called charity or philanthropy, she is ambitious—very, and would like very well to regenerate the world with a grand *coup de main* [course of action] or some fine institution, which is a very different thing. Here she has a circle of admirers who cry up everything she does or says as gospel, and I think it will do her much good to be with you who, though you love and admire her, do not believe in the wisdom of all she says, *because* SHE says it. I wish she could be brought to see that it is the intellectual part that interests her, not the manual. She has no *esprit de conduite* [gift for management] in the practical sense. When she nursed me [presumably on the trip back from Scotland], everything which intellect and kind intention could do was done, but she was a shocking nurse. Mariette was ten times better. Whereas her influence upon people's minds and her curiosity about getting into the varieties of mind is insatiable. After she has got inside, they generally cease to have any interest for her.[46]

Chapter 14

MANAGING
HARLEY STREET

I n December of 1852, Great-aunt Evans died. On hearing the
news, Florence went at once to Cromford Bridge to arrange the
funeral and then on to Tapton to try to give comfort to her
grandmother. Cromford Bridge House lay empty and was inherited by
WEN and Mai—or, more precisely, by Mai's husband, Sam Smith.
Convinced that Florence could no longer be prevented from undertaking full-time work in some kind of medical facility, Fanny and
Parthe hatched the plan that Great-aunt Evans's house should be converted with family funds into a nursing home under Florence's supervision. If not the house at Cromford, then perhaps Forest Lodge near
Embley could be put to use—or then again Mr. Nightingale could at
last buy a house in London to serve as a base for Florence to do her
work there.

But Florence turned every one of her mother's options down. From
Tapton she escaped to the Smiths at Combe Hurst and persuaded her
aunt Mai to write to Fanny on her behalf. Though the offer was most
kind, Mai wrote, a house in London was far more apt to appeal to Parthe
than to Flo, and Flo was the one whose needs must be considered.

As far as Cromford Bridge House went, Florence took it upon herself
to turn that idea down. She explained to her mother in a letter in January
of 1853 that someone as inexperienced as herself would surely fail in the
effort to start a nursing institution from scratch.[1] What Florence really
meant to say, I think, was that the Cromford scheme was completely im-

practicable. The village was in a remote, heavily industrialized, and thus unfashionable part of the country, and people would be reluctant to come there. The house was virtually a wreck, and just to make it habitable would be expensive.

On the same day she wrote in this practical and businesslike way to her practical and businesslike mother, Florence wrote a most affectionate and conciliatory note to her sister: "Oh my dearest Pop, I wish I could tell you how I love you and thank you for your kind thoughts as received in your letter today. If you did but know how genial it is to me, when my dear people give me a hope of their blessing and that they would speed me on my way, as the kind thought of Cromford seems to say they are ready to do. I will write to Mama about Paris and Cromford. My Pop, whether one or the other, my heart will be with thee. Now, if these seem mere words, because bodily I shall be leaving you, have patience with me my dearest, I hope that you and I shall live to prove a true love to each other."[2]

As Florence herself was beginning to realize by the beginning of 1853, the long years since her mama had vetoed her proposal to do the "prax" at Salisbury Infirmary had been not a waste of her powers but a period of hard, rigorous training. After visiting hospitals all over Europe, she had discovered that there was no one to teach her to nurse. She had to learn it for herself and prepare to teach it to others. Florence's inspections and research confirmed that female nurses came from the humblest classes of society and were employed mainly to watch patients and keep them clean. Most were drunken, callous, and, willingly or not, accustomed to providing sexual services for the doctors, dressers, and patients. There was little to be learned from them since the technical nursing in hospitals—dressing wounds, giving physic, attending to surgical patients—was done by male dressers. The doctors and boards of trustees who ran medical facilities in Great Britain had no intention of giving nurses more responsibilities because they held them in such low esteem. To work alongside such women might be an act of piety worthy of a medieval saint, but was it useful?

It was true that Catholic nursing sisters were better trained, had an ancient tradition of selfless service, and were viewed as sex-neutral. But after long and careful study of the Roman Catholic religion, Florence Nightingale could not find it in her conscience to convert just in order to become a Sister of Mercy. From a medical standpoint, Kaiserswerth had been a disappointment. The smaller Protestant nursing institutions recently founded in England had attracted few adherents and were regarded by English society at large with a killing mixture of derision and hostility. Florence Nightingale had come around to her aunt Patty's view that if England was ever to allow women to perform all nursing functions, those women would have to be trained lay professionals, modeled on the emerging profession of women educators, not on nuns.

Florence Nightingale was now confident in her abilities and clear in her goals. She was a first-class practical nurse who could provide a model for others as well as teach them. And men of importance—Lord Palmerston, Lord Shaftesbury, and Sidney Herbert, to name only the most prominent—knew this too, believed in her, consulted with and confided in her.

Nightingale's revised nursing plan was to take charge of a hospital or infirmary and there train an elite corps of women supervisors who would gradually revolutionize patient care in the whole of the public hospital system. This was an ambitious goal, but she thought she could pull it off, and her large circle of reform-minded, sanitarian friends strongly encouraged her to pursue it. Their help would be crucial since Nightingale, like all the other women in Victorian society, had no qualifications. Nightingale's friends, male and female, held the appointments to charitable institutions in the palms of their hands and could bend the rules if they chose. And it was not irrelevant that Florence's own family was wealthy and well connected. Most Victorian institutions to serve the health needs of the poor were privately financed, and when it comes to fund-raising, it always helps to be on intimate terms with the people who have money.[3]

FLORENCE NIGHTINGALE'S newfound confidence is expressed in the summary of the events of 1852 she wrote on December 31. For years she had penned a New Year's Eve jeremiad of frustration and despair, but this entry was almost chipper. "I am so glad this year is over, nevertheless it has not been wasted I trust . . . I have re-modelled my whole religious belief . . . All my admirers are married . . . and I stand with all the world before me . . . It has been a baptism of fire this year."[4]

In February, Florence was finally able to escape to Paris. Hilary Bon-ham-Carter was awaiting her there, at the home of Mary and Julius Mohl. Florence assured Hilary in a November letter that travel to France was perfectly safe, but her mother was not of the same opinion, and so time was lost finding some lady to accompany Florence across the Chan-nel. She arrived at the rue du Bac looking thin and stressed, but once in-stalled chez Mohl, Florence made a fast recovery. Parthenope was not the only member of the family who used illness as a strategy and a form of self-expression. For a woman who only a month ago had been, according to her aunt, far too ill to sustain a London conversation, Florence Nightingale in Paris was a whirl of activity. Julius Mohl secured permis-sion for his English friend to visit all the city's public medical facilities, and Nightingale was as assiduous in attending operations and touring wards as she had once been in visiting museums and churches. Her plea-sure in her visits was greatly enhanced by the fact that she was able to get around the city on her own and tasted the joys of omnibuses for the first time. Nightingale collected "reports, returns, statistics, pamphlets," and she was already putting together the statistical analyses of medical facil-ities and preparing the questionnaires that were to form the basis of her work after her return from the Crimean War.[5]

In between the visiting and the note taking, Florence Nightingale participated happily in the busy social life of the Mohl household. She went to parties, to the opera, even to balls. She sparkled at dinners and agreed without difficulty to have several gowns made up for her by a fashionable modiste. Anna Mohl, Julius's niece, was fascinated by Flo-rence and wrote that she was "on the point of falling in love" with her. Hilary Bonham-Carter, busy with her art classes in the day, basked in the sunshine of her favorite cousin's happiness.

After this initial visit, Florence planned to take up residence for sev-eral months at an institution run by the Sisters of Charity of St. Vincent de Paul. But just as she was due to move to the convent, news came from home that Grandmother Shore, who had lost the will to live after the death of her sister, was taking no nourishment and seemed certain to die soon. Florence at once packed her bags and set off on the journey to Der-byshire, escorted across the Channel this time by the elderly and dis-gruntled English governess of Madame de la Rochefoucauld.

Stopping in London for one night, she stayed at the home of Mai and Sam Smith in Victoria Square, which her youngest Smith cousin, Beatrice, opened up for her. Here Florence received urgent messages from her friends Lady Canning and Mrs. Herbert intimating that the ladies' committee of an Institution for Ill Gentlewomen wished to offer her the position of superintendent. Florence hurried round for a brief meeting with Liz Herbert to discuss the position, but she declined to dally in London or at Atherstone with Selina Bracebridge, who was all agog with news of the Canning offer. Afraid her grandmother might be dead before she got to her, Florence took the train to Sheffield the next morning, arriving at the house at Tapton on Monday, March 14, to the immense relief of her aunt Mai.

Florence loved Mrs. Shore and her sister Miss Evans, less critically and conditionally than anyone else in her family. "There are many (to me) more painful contemplations than her [Mrs. Shore] in her decline," Florence wrote to her mother from Tapton in 1852. "She seems to me a giant among pygmies. There is nothing mean, nothing worldly, nothing humbuggy or hypocritical about her. I shall never be ashamed of her. Her affections are colossal, her ways are impetuous, straightforward, simple. When she and Aunt Evans are gone, I shall feel there are two great Ichthyosauri gone extinct."[6]

Florence's love for her grandmother in turn had a strong impact upon both her father and her aunt Mai, whose relationship with their mother had often been fraught. As Nightingale recalled toward the end of her life: "My 'Aunt Mai' as we used to call her was the very first in afterlife to say to me how unfair she was to her mother . . . My father and [his?] sister were, as you perhaps know, singularly subject to the 'caprice des yeux.' If St Paul had been ungraceful, he would have found no favour in their sight. But he and I have often talked in afterlife of a certain greatness there was about his mother. My dear sister never really knew her."[7]

Mrs. Shore seemed barely alive when Florence arrived, and it took a while for her to rouse enough to recognize her granddaughter. Mrs. Shore was in pain from bedsores, she struggled horribly for breath, and her mouth and throat were infected by thrush; she spoke mainly of her longing for death, but her body refused to give up life easily. Terribly restless, she was constantly in and out of bed. Her terrible breathing and her occasional cries of pain filled the house.

Deathbeds were a place of authority for Victorian women, and Florence wrote to her father on March 19 advising him not to come north, as his mother would not recognize him and to see her would only distress him unnecessarily. But WEN left home before this letter arrived, and, regretting her attempt to keep her father away, Florence wrote telling her mother to destroy it. WEN came into his mother's room once; she recognized him and expressed joy that he had come. The next day he went out on business and then left Derbyshire, as there was nowhere in the house for him to sleep. Florence and Mai shared the only decent spare room.

On March 21, Florence wrote home to her mother: "What with frequent vomiting, having been now since Friday night without even one drop of water passing her lips, and with an exertion of voice which would kill a healthy person, that she is still alive is miraculous. Aunt Evans's nineteen hours' talking were nothing to this. Still her mind is clear, she recognizes us and what she says is full of love and trust. I think she bears it like a hero." Finally, on March 25, Good Friday, Mary Evans Shore passed away, "so calmly," wrote Florence, "that though I had hold of her, I could not mark the last moment." Florence noted with amazement that the terrible bedsores, which had been spreading rapidly, had actually responded to the silver nitrate she had been painting on and were almost healed. Florence kept vigil over the body, and in the morning she wrote to let her parents know that the end had come at last. "Love to all. I hope the sun shines on you, dear Papa. The full moon shone on the waste of snow last night, as the face grew beautiful in the light of death and young in the hope of life. I almost wish that you could have seen her as she is NOW. There is no trace of suffering or decay. She might be fifty . . . I never before admired the noble cast of her features; it is a face which might have done anything." Florence scattered fresh flowers all around her grandmother's body and filled the coffin with them.

WEN, along with Mai's youngest daughter, Beatrice, but not Fanny or Parthe, came north for the funeral on March 30. WEN was deeply grateful for all Florence had done for his mother. "Great had been the occasion for her usefulness, great the comfort she had administered—her hands in hers till the last of her moments on earth. Judge of the sensation of Love in the mind of the dying sufferer."[8] On the day of the burial, the sun shone but the wind blew up a gale. The bier was torn as the bearers carried the coffin over the moors to the little local church, and on the last steep climb they almost dropped their load. The small group of family mourners following behind was pushed hither and thither by the wind, and Beatrice with her lame leg could barely be dragged along. On the way back in the carriage, there was a period of brilliant sunshine, then a sharp shower of rain. "The whole thing was so characteristic of her," Florence wrote to her mother, "the *vehement* storms, the bright daylight, without a moment's pause or interval, forgetting all the past and clearing up without a shadow of a cloud upon her brow. Now she is gone, the house deserted and all is over, soon to go into the hands of strangers, and I shall not ever see the Ribes [currant bushes] blossom. Somebody else will mark the tender green of the larch against the dark yew tree, as we did, with her, last spring."

FLORENCE'S NEGOTIATIONS with the lady trustees of the Institution for Ill Gentlewomen proved long and arduous. The institution was a private clinic for sick governesses, financed largely through charitable gifts, and governed by two committees of prominent citizens: the gentlemen who took care of finance, and the ladies who took care of management. The establishment had run into serious difficulties under its previous superintendent, and the decision had been made to move it from Chandos Square to 1 Upper Harley Street. Someone efficient was needed to oversee the move and then provide firm leadership. Florence Nightingale made it quite clear that she would agree to take the position only if she had authority to run things as she saw fit. She insisted that she must be able to observe the surgical operations performed at the facility and be present when the doctors interviewed the patients so that she could be sure that medical instructions were scrupulously carried out. She agreed to live on the premises, to accept no salary, and to bring with her, at her own expense, a respectable lady housekeeper who would serve as her chaperone as well as doing work in the house.

Given those terms, it is surprising to note that several members of the ladies' committee were opposed to appointing Miss Nightingale. Her willingness to leave home seemed to these women unnatural, her interest in matters surgical and medical most indecorous. Miss Nightingale looked too young for the post, and her recent incursions into the territory of Catholic nursing orders abroad rang warning bells in the ears of the more evangelically inclined. These hostile ladies were known among Florence's allies as "respectable asses" (Mary Clarke Mohl) and "old cats" (Liz Herbert). Fortunately, the pro-Flo faction on the committee was energetic and powerful. Mrs. Herbert came onto the ladies' committee specifically to ensure her friend Florence's appointment.

Miss Nightingale was to accept no remuneration and employ a housekeeper "at her own expense." To Florence Nightingale, these last were sweet words indeed, for finally William Edward Nightingale, with the consent of his brother-in-law Sam Smith, contracted to give his daughter Florence five hundred pounds a year, payable quarterly, for her personal use. With this income she would at last be able to live independently. So violent was the emotion aroused by this decision in the breasts of Fanny and Parthe that WEN decamped for several days to the Athenaeum. There he contemplated whether it would be possible to send Parthe into the country somewhere. "*Memorandum of April 20*. I have this day reached the conclusion that Parthe can no more control or modify the intensity of her interest in Flo's doings than she can change her physical form, and that her life will be sacrificed to the activity of her thoughts, unless she removes from the scene immediately—the only question being where to go."[9]

The negotiations with the ladies' committee might have dragged on longer if Cousin Marianne Nicholson, Flo's old passion and enemy, had not decided to put her oar in. Marianne was now married to the army sanitary architect Captain Douglas Galton, and she was acquainted with one of the members of the ladies' committee for the Institution of Ill Gentlewomen. Asked by this lady how Florence's family viewed her wish to become superintendent at Harley Street, Marianne Galton told the truth—that Fanny and Parthenope Nightingale were bitterly opposed to it. The committee lady, deeply gratified to find all her suspicions confirmed, rushed back to tell her colleagues, and a letter was written informing Miss Florence Nightingale that since she did not have her parents' consent, the offer to her had been withdrawn. Marianne, for her part, spread to the extended clan the exciting misinformation that Cousin Flo had in fact never been approached with an offer to fill the post. She had first volunteered, then actually pressed her services on a deeply reluctant committee, just as if she was herself some vulgar, indigent governess desperate for a post.

Florence took this piece of cousinly malice in her stride, and WEN wrote a letter to the committee officially declaring that he gave his daughter his permission to accept the post at Harley Street. However, Marianne's interference proved a blessing in disguise, since it infuriated Fanny and Parthe. They felt fully in their rights to oppose Flo, but they were certainly not going to put up with Marianne Nicholson Galton doing the same. If Florence, unaccountably, wanted this ridiculous position at Harley Street with those pathetic, moth-eaten governesses, then she must certainly have it. Thus, in high dudgeon, Parthenope Nightingale wrote to Miss Hannah Nicholson, Marianne's aunt, to give her own account of the matter: "In the winter when the Committee were sending their proposals to Flo at Paris, one of them came to Marianne to enquire about F & her family. Marianne replied that F was doing it without, indeed against the consent of her family, & a great many other particulars which were wholly incorrect. I do not of course mean that we have chosen or desired such a course for her but that we are honestly & lovingly anxious that she should do what she thinks right & as she likes. Marianne had never at any time heard any one of us mention that subject *in any manner.* You may conceive the mischief which such a report occasioned, the difficulties it has put in F's way, the trouble it gave us in going about disabusing the Committee, the strange reports it gave rise to in London when we were not there to tell our *own* story, indeed it was weeks before we heard of it, all that painful time when F was nursing her Grandmama. I quite acquit Marianne of unkindness, but her love of talk is such, of being 'au courant,' of knowing more than other people, that the mischief done (not only in this case) is very painful."[10]

Unsurprisingly, letters like this caused a commensurate swell of protest from the Nicholson camp. Marianne had recently lost her first child, and her younger brother Lothian Nicholson rushed to defend her. It was left to Florence to smooth troubled waters and assure everyone concerned that she knew very well the whole matter was a misunderstanding. From this point on, Florence could count among her devoted allies both her cousin Lothian Nicholson of the Royal Engineers (later General Sir Lothian Nicholson) and her cousin-in-law Captain Douglas Galton (later Sir Douglas Galton).

HAVING SUCCESSFULLY negotiated the terms of her position as superintendent, Florence returned in secret to Paris and entered the Convent of the Sisters of Charity, as she had long planned. Mary Clarke Mohl was paying her usual summer visit to England at this time, so Florence could not stay with her. At the convent, Nightingale spent a busy two weeks, making copious notes not only on the patients she saw but on the life of the nuns and on the different rules of the different Catholic nursing orders.[11] But then her visit was again cut short by illness. In Paris, eighteen months years earlier, while engaged in exploring Catholic hospitals, she had contracted measles, and now, to the frank disbelief of her French doctors, she came down with a measleslike rash again.[12] Fate, or God, seemed determined to prevent Florence from carrying out her French convent plans.

For some days Florence remained in her squalid little cell at the convent, alone, feverish, and far from pampered. Apprised of her plight, Julius Mohl transported Florence to recover in the back drawing room of the apartment on the rue du Bac and insisted on coming into her room and chatting from time to time. It was excessively improper for an unmarried lady to be lying in bed recuperating in the home of a gentleman whose wife was abroad. What Florence's mother and sister thought of the whole affair we can only imagine, but WEN wrote to thank Julius for all the fatherly care he had lavished on Flo.[13]

By mid-July Florence was back in London supervising the move to Harley Street.[14] With the assistance of Aunt Mai, she had found a small apartment to rent in Pall Mall, and she elected to stay there until she was able to move into the Harley Street facility. Even her great ally Clarkey Mohl thought that it would have been kind if she had spent her last weeks with her family, but Florence could not be budged on this point. Her decision to leave home was the result of years of careful consideration and fruitless negotiations with her sister. It was now a fait accompli.

To be superintendent of the Institute for Sick Gentlewomen was hardly an important post, but it was a difficult, complex, and irksome one. Florence was in her element. She had begun to assume control by stipulating a number of renovations to the property. A dumbwaiter must be installed to carry supplies and meals to the different floors, as well as an up-to-date system of bells that would allow the nurses to know at once which patient was in need of assistance. Such newfangled amenities were quite outside the competence of the lady managers, and when Nightingale returned from abroad she was obliged to oversee the work herself. The patients moved in before the workmen were out. As Nightingale remarked in an August 20 letter to Madame Mohl: "From Committees, Charity and Schism, from the Church of England, from philanthropy, and all deceits of the Devil, Good Lord deliver us."[15]

In fact, before she could set about making the house comfortable for its inmates, Nightingale had to settle a religious issue. Told that the committee would refuse to accept any patients who were Catholics, Florence issued her first ultimatum. She would resign on the spot unless not only Catholics but women of all religions were accepted, and their ministers allowed into the house to give them the consolation of religion. "So now it is settled, and *in print,* that we are to take in all denominations whatever, and allow them to be visited by their respective priests and Muftis, provided that *I* will receive (in any case *whatsoever* that is *not* of the Church of England) the obnoxious animal at the door, take him upstairs myself, remain while he was conferring with his patient, make myself *responsible* that he does not speak to, or look at, *anyone else,* and bring him downstairs again in a noose, and out into the street. And to this I have agreed! And this is in print!"[16]

Having got the building itself into some kind of shape, Nightingale discovered that the furniture and equipment from the previous establishment were completely inadequate. Towels, counterpanes, and tablecloths were all tattered and in need of mending. The chair covers were so filthy it was impossible to discover their original color. Most of the bedlinen was rat-eaten. The windows were bare. Many of the nearly new mattresses as well as the blankets and pillows, Nightingale reported, "were spoiled, *even to rotting,* by large stains, owing to having been used (in certain cases) without the proper Mackintosh. Vermin ran about tame in all directions."

So Nightingale first got the house scrupulously clean, then had the old carpets pieced out and relaid on floors and stairs—"not a square inch remains unused," she triumphantly reported—and curtains and blinds put up at the windows. Her personal housekeeper, Mrs. Clarke, and two helpers made from scratch dozens of pillowcases, towels, tablecloths, dish cloths, dusters, pincushions, and pincushion covers (whatever a cover for a pincushion might be). A large amount of darning and mending was also done. Old curtains were converted into chair covers, or at least chair cover linings and blind linings. Nothing was wasted except women's time and women's eyesight in this age before the invention of sewing machines.

Nightingale persuaded the local grocer and butcher to give her advantageous bulk prices on meat, vegetables, and dry goods. Hitherto, all the jam needed for the house—and it seems a great deal of jam was consumed—had been purchased ready-made from the local grocer's shop. This was clearly scandalous, and under Miss Nightingale's direction the household set about making its own jam at a fraction of the cost, as well as baking its own biscuits. Several members of the nursing and domestic staff were dismissed for inefficiency, and new ones engaged. "I have changed one housemaid," reported Nightingale on May 15, "on account of her love of dirt and inexperience, & one nurse, on account of her love of Opium & intimidation." With measures of this kind, all described and listed in minute detail in the superintendent's reports, Nightingale managed to cut the cost per inmate per day from one shilling and ten pence to one shilling and a halfpenny.

The patient population was never larger than twenty-seven, composed of governesses who were either ill or had fallen on hard times and taken to their beds. Most of the women had been more or less abandoned by their families. All paid something toward their living and medical expenses. All had come to the institution on the recommendation of one of the members of the governing committees. Some of the women patients were desperately ill, and the institution provided a hospice for them in their last weeks or months. Some women had physical ailments, such as severe skin complaints, that responded well to treatment. These women went back to their families or found new positions as governesses.

Nightingale was untiring in the personal attention she gave to the sick women, who soon came to adore her just as the villagers at West Wellow and Lea had in earlier years.[17] For example, at night she was known to come around and rub cold feet until they were warm. Some of the inmates liked this so much they stood barefoot on cold stone before Miss Nightingale made her rounds. Nightingale saved the lives of several inmates. On one occasion, the flue on a new gas oven had been improperly installed, and Nightingale caught it in her arms before it could fall on one of her patients. When the pharmacist delivered a bottle of ether mislabeled as "Spirits of Nitrate" she caught the mistake before any of the patients had taken a dose. One woman had a cancerous breast removed, and Nightingale herself did the post-operative nursing so successfully that the woman recovered and was able to work again.

As superintendent, Nightingale provided top professional care by nurses and doctors, cheerful and efficient service by the staff, good food, and a comfortable living space. However, a fairly large proportion of the patients admitted to the institute were what Nightingale calls hysterics, and she became rapidly convinced that what they needed was not medical care but encouragement and practical support, in the shape of small sums of money and letters of recommendation. While generously providing these out of her own pocket, she nonetheless advised her governors to be more careful in screening the women who requested admission. "A Hospital is good for the seriously ill alone," wrote Nightingale in her February report, "otherwise it becomes a lodging house where the nervous become more nervous, the foolish more foolish, the idle & selfish more selfish & idle. For two of the elements essential to a Hospital are *want of occupation & directing the attention to bodily health*. There is not a trick in the whole legerdemain of Hysteria which has not been played in this house . . . Conclusion—that, if the Medical certificate be not strictly enforced, this will become, not a Hospital for the Sick, but a Hospital for incompatible tempers & for hysterical fancies."[18]

As for her relations with the medical gentlemen employed to treat the governesses, and with the ladies and gentlemen of the committees, Nightingale wrote to her father in December of 1853, describing her methods of dealing with both groups. "When I entered into service here, I determined that, happen what would, I *never* would intrigue among the Committee. Now I perceive I do all my business by intrigue . . . Last General Committee I executed a series of Resolutions on five subjects, and presented them as coming from the Medical Men . . . all these I proposed and carried in Committee, without telling them that they came from *me* and not from the Medical men; and then, and not till then, I showed them to the Medical Men, without telling *them* that they were already passed *in committee*. It was a bold stroke, but success is said to turn an insurrection into a revolution. The Medical men have had two meetings upon them, and approved them all *nem. con.* [i.e. with no one opposed], and thought they were their own. And I came off with flying colours, no one suspecting my intrigue."[19]

WITHIN A FEW MONTHS, Florence Nightingale had the Institution for Ill Gentlewomen neatly fitted out and running like clockwork. Doctors doted upon her; patients looked upon her as their savior. Even the members of the ladies' committee who had been most opposed to her appointment now sang her praises, largely because she had been so successful in cutting expenses. Florence was able to take time for herself and accepted evening invitations from her intimate friends Lady Canning, Lady Palmerston, and Mrs. Herbert. She also spent time at her private flat, where she retired especially on Sunday mornings to conceal the fact that she was not attending church. Her disaffection with the Church of England was evidently very deep.

After six months at Harley Street, Nightingale was ready to move on to some more challenging medical facility.[20] The young surgeon Mr. Bowman was anxious for her to come over to Kings College Hospital and see if she could repeat her miracle of reorganization there. Sidney Herbert asked her to collect as much information as she could on nursing conditions in the different London hospitals. Nightingale discovered that hard data of any kind were difficult to come up with, as people refused to talk for the record for fear of being replaced. When asked by a French doctor she had met in Paris to recommend two reliable nurses to serve in colonial hospitals, she replied regretfully that such persons were not to be found. On February 22, 1854, she wrote to her father: "I am sorry to say that the information I have had concerning the morals and manners of Grays Inn Hospital is so bad (among the bad this is the worst) that I should not feel inclined to assist it, if it were I. Of the Westminster, which I have always considered one of the best, though the poorest, I had a head nurse with me last night (a very admirable woman) and she told me that, in the course of her long life's experience with the *Westminster* Hospital she had never known a nurse who was not drunken, and that there was *immoral* conduct practiced within the very walls of the ward, of which she gave me some awful instances. So much for our moral boards [boards of trustees and governors]. That this impinges on the *principle* of hospitals I cannot think. Without hospitals, where would be our surgical science? If you do away with hospitals you must, of course, do away with lunatic asylums, union houses and all the rest of the machinery of overpopulated civilization."[21]

Thus, when cholera broke out in London in the area of Broad Street, just off Oxford Street, Florence Nightingale volunteered her services in admitting and nursing patients. At the Middlesex Hospital, unlike 1 Upper Harley Street, no one was pretending to be ill. So great was the influx of cholera cases that many of the medical staff walked off the job in fear for their lives, and the regular patients had to be sent elsewhere. At one point the cholera-related mortality rate was 10 percent, and the disease struck down members of all classes. Some patients turned into hideous dark, dry husks of humanity and died within hours of getting the first symptom of the disease. Some patients suffered terribly for many hours but survived. In 1854, the cause of cholera was unknown. Few effective measures had been taken to prevent its transmission even though it was several years since Dr. John Snow had established the link between cholera and polluted water by temporarily disconnecting the Broad Street pump. No one in the medical establishment, from the most famous physician to the local herbalist, had any idea how to treat the disease.[22]

Florence Nightingale was convinced that she was immune to cholera. She told Elizabeth Gaskell that cholera was "*not* infectious i.e. does not pass from one person to another."[23] This was an accurate observation since cholera in fact is transmitted not by person-to-person contact but by the ingestion of water contaminated with *Vibrio cholerae*. Nightingale's minute attention to personal and domestic cleanliness served her well at the Middlesex Hospital, as later at Scutari. At the end of August she was up with patients a whole day and a night, watching two of her fellow nurses die of the disease. Prostitutes who plied their trade along Oxford Street were hardest hit by the cholera. Nightingale spent much of her time undressing these women, "and awfully filthy they were," by Elizabeth Gaskell's account, "& putting on turpentine *stupes* &c herself as many as she could manage—never had a touch even of diarrhea." One night, Nightingale was up alone with one of the porters since the other nurse had gone to bed in exhaustion. A half-tipsy woman came in who insisted "for all I am so dirty I am draped in silks and satins sometimes, real French silks and satins." This woman was a nurse, earning five guineas a week, and she survived.[24]

FANNY AND PARTHENOPE Nightingale had been opposed to Florence's removal to Harley Street. The initial filth and the enduring seediness of the house and its inmates grated upon their sensibilities.[25] But once Florence started tackling the problems at the Institution for Ill Gentlewomen, her mother and sister rallied to her side. It was, after all, a matter of pride in the Nightingale family that anything attempted by one of its members should be done superbly. When Parthe condescended to cross the threshold of 1 Upper Harley Street, her heart went out to the women there, and she began volunteering for little jobs. The change in relations between the three Nightingale women can be felt in this funny little note Florence wrote on October 20, begging her mother to send her an old pair of comfortable boots: "Oh my boots! My boots! Dearer to me than the best French-polished, my brother boots. Where are ye, my boots. I never shall see your pretty faces more. My dear I *must* have them boots . . . More flowers, more game, more grapes." Fanny Nightingale would be sending more flowers, more game, more grapes, more everything to her younger daughter's protégées, both individual and institutional, for the rest of her life.

As for WEN and Flo, during the Harley Street year they were allies and comrades as of old, and happy about it. It was to WEN, who had just undergone eye surgery himself, that Florence gave the sad account of a cataract operation that Mr. Bowman, one of the great Harley Street specialists, had performed on an old woman in the institution that left her blind, mad, and suicidal. Florence continued to explore in letters to her father the religious and philosophical issues raised by the practice of philanthropy that they two had long debated. She and WEN had both read Strauss's *Life of Jesus,* a key text for many Victorian Christians struggling to keep their faith, and Florence wrote to WEN: "I remember you were struck with Strauss's comment on the tendency of some 'to soar in the skies,' instead of 'mending' what is at hand. Man, says he, will never improve as he might, till he ceases to believe in a future state. But I believe there is, within & without human nature, a revelation of eternal existence, eternal progress for human nature. At the same time I believe that to do that part of this world's work which harmonizes accords with the idiosyncracy of each of us, is *the* means by which we may *at once* render this world the habitation of the Divine spirit in Man, & prepare for other such work in other of the worlds which surround us—The kingdom of Heaven is within *us*."[26]

IN SEPTEMBER OF 1854, Florence Nightingale left London, where the cholera epidemic was dying down, and went up to Derbyshire to have a holiday at Lea Hurst. She was exhausted and needed time to think and plan for her next move. One of the Nightingales' guests at Lea Hurst was Mrs. Elizabeth Gaskell, the wife of a Manchester Unitarian minister and an increasingly popular and controversial novelist. The Gaskells were not friends of the Nightingales, and they were much less grand. However, Nightingales and Gaskells were all part of the old Unitarian network, and they had a great many friends in common both in London and in the Midlands. Not only was Mrs. Gaskell welcome to be at Lea Hurst while the family was there, but she was invited to stay on for as long as she liked after they had gone back south.

Elizabeth Gaskell was a friendly and charming woman, and though she was somewhat awed by the Nightingales' erudition, she got on very well with all four. She was a tremendous gossip, the heart of a lively group of friends and relatives, and despite her deadline and the terrible wrath of Mr. Dickens hanging over her head, she could not resist writing a number of long letters describing the Nightingales and their home. The beauty of Lea Hurst and its surroundings thrilled Gaskell. The size of the house rather awed her, especially when she became the only guest in residence, but at the same time she noticed with surprise how simple, even monastic were the rooms habitually used by both the Nightingale sisters on the top floor. It was these low, bare rooms, with their glorious view, that she herself occupied once the family had left.

Gaskell was fascinated by the Nightingales, especially Florence, and she wrote a long description for the delectation of her friend Catherine Winkworth, who she knew would pass it on. "[Florence] is tall; very slight & willowy in figure; thick, shortish rich brown hair very delicate pretty complexion . . . grey eyes which are generally pensive and drooping, but when they choose can be the merriest eyes I ever saw; and perfect teeth making her smile the sweetest I ever saw. Put a long piece of soft net . . . round this beautiful shaped head, so as to form a soft white framework for the full oval of her face. . . . and dress her up in black glacé silk up to the long round white throat—and a black shawl on—& you may get *near* an idea of her perfect grace & lovely appearance. She is like a saint."[27]

Observing the prodigious effect Florence was having on their novelist guest, Mrs. Nightingale regaled Mrs. Gaskell with stories about Florence's youth—her loving care for poor villagers when she was a teenager, her superb Greek and Latin, her many proposals of marriage, her ability to speak to Catholic monks in Latin, her extraordinary travels in Italy, Greece, and Egypt. Fanny gave a rapturous picture of Florence's devotion to philanthropy—her visit to Kaiserswerth, her current position of responsibility at Harley Street, where she was, Gaskell underlines in awe, *"present at every operation."* Elizabeth Gaskell commented of Florence: "She has a great deal of fun and is carried along by that I think. She mimics most capitally the way of talking of the poor governesses in the Establishment, with their delight at having a manservant and at having *Lady* Canning and *Lady* Monteagle to do this or that for them . . . She must be a creature of another race so high & mighty & angelic, doing things by impulse—or some divine inspiration & not by effort & struggle of will. But she sounds almost too holy to be talked about as a mere wonder. Miss Nightingale [i.e., Parthenope] says—with tears in her eyes that they are ducks & have hatched a wild swan."[28]

Here we have the firsthand account of a woman giving birth to one of those "passions" Florence Nightingale inspired in both men and women. Elizabeth Gaskell was already comparing her exciting new acquaintance to St. Elizabeth of Hungary before Florence had done anything more noteworthy than superintend the lives of a couple of dozen impoverished spinsters. Furthermore, Mrs. Gaskell's instant eyewitness testimony proves that the Nightingale family legend about Florence was being constructed by her mother and sister before she took ship for Istanbul. Parthenope had already come up with the famous comparison of Florence to the ugly duckling of Andersen's fairy tale.

On October 27, Elizabeth Gaskell felt impelled to confide more juicy tidbits to another bosom friend, Emily Shaen. Parthe had stayed behind at Lea Hurst for a few days after the other three had gone south, and she had lots of stories. As a child Florence had eighteen sick dolls all in a row in bed. Mr. Nightingale (such a brilliant man!) had tutored both his girls himself. Florence was so influenced by Catholic legends. This last comment is of interest, given Florence's claim to have heard the voice of God when she was sixteen, rather like Joan of Arc. As Gaskell came under the influence of Parthe, and Florence's charisma receded into memory, her view of the younger Nightingale sister changed subtly. Cracks began to appear in the saintly figure. Parthe, Gaskell told Emily, "is plain, clever, and *apparently* nothing out of the common way as to character, but she *is* for all that. She is devoted—her sense of existence is lost in Florence's. I never saw such adoring love. To set F. at liberty to do her great work, Parthe had annihilated herself, her own tastes, her own wishes in order to take up the little duties of home, to parents, to poor, to society, to servants—all the small things that fritter away time and life, *all* these Parthe does, for fear if anything was neglected people might blame F. as well as from feeling these duties imperative as if they were grand things." Parthe told Elizabeth Gaskell—in the deepest confidence of course, knowing that she would pass these things on only to her closest acquaintance—that Florence had the greatest "natural intense love of God" of anyone she had ever known but that Florence did not care at all for individuals, only for the whole race of God's creatures. For example, a poor woman in the village was passionately grateful to Florence for nursing and comforting her little son while he was dying. But now the same woman had lost her husband too, and longed for Florence to comfort her, but Parthe had the greatest difficulty in getting her sister to walk over and pay even a short visit. Flo said that she was too busy with her hospital plans to spend time in the village.

Elizabeth Gaskell now remembered some odd things that had occurred when Florence was with them. She remembered how Florence no longer read books and was unwilling to answer any of the questions about Egyptian myths that her sister, who was preparing a private edition of Flo's letters from Egypt, had asked her. Florence "used to sit with her head bent a little forwards, one hand lying in repose over the other on her knees in that steady way which means that people are not seeing the real actual before them." Here is an eyewitness description of Florence Nightingale in the act of dreaming.

One day, Elizabeth Gaskell had a "grand quarrel" with Florence when the latter advocated putting all children, rich and poor alike, in communal crèches. Gaskell felt guilty whenever she noticed herself putting her own needs as a busy writer before those of her children, her friends, her husband, and his parishioners, and so she was deeply shocked by Florence Nightingale's refusal to admit that family had the highest claims on a woman's time. Gaskell wrote to the pregnant Emily: "She has no friend—and wants none. She stands perfectly alone, half-way between God and His Creatures."[29] When Florence abruptly informed her family that she would be leaving for London the next day, Mrs. Gaskell was impressed by their ready acquiescence. "Considering how decidedly this step of hers was against their judgment as well as against their wishes, it was very beautiful to see how silently and diligently they all tried 'to speed the parting guest.' "

Was Parthenope deluding herself and others when she claimed to spend her time doing all the little, caring, unimportant things her sister was too busy and grand to be bothered with? Can we blame Florence for wanting to get away from this fluttery, ingratiating, incompetent, interfering, needy busybody of a sister? Through the eyes of that born observer and storyteller Elizabeth Gaskell, we see both sisters in action and understand both of their points of view.

ELIZABETH GASKELL stayed on at Lea Hurst, working on her latest novel in glorious isolation, but missing the hurly-burly of normal life. It was to Parthe that she reported a terrible tragedy that had occurred—Athena the owl had been found dead. "Last night about five, in came Mrs. Watson [the Lea Hurst housekeeper] almost in tears. 'Oh dear! Mrs. Gaskell, whatever shall we do?' (She had it in her hands.) 'It was quite well at dinner, and hopping about my room; and just now I found it on it's [sic] back quite stiff and cold.' I took it in my hands. I fancied I could just feel a fluttering, and I held it in my warm hands near the fire. But it was but a fancy." So, by Elizabeth Gaskell's testimony, Athena the owl died of natural causes, was mourned by all the household at Lea Hurst, and was affectionately sent to be stuffed. But Florence Nightingale could never forgive the fact that while she was undertaking her preparations to go out to save the dying soldiers in the hospital at Scutari, her sister, who claimed to adore her, had let Athena die.[30] Couldn't Parthe get even the simplest things right?

Within days of the Nightingale family's departure from Lea Hurst, Elizabeth Gaskell received from Parthenope herself the thrilling news that Florence had been asked by the government to lead an official party of women nurses out to the army hospital at Scutari in Turkey. Like all the Nightingale acquaintances, Elizabeth Gaskell was swept up in the enthusiasm of the moment, and memories of Florence's imperfections were banished. This was the biggest story in England—bigger than poor Effie Ruskin's divorce suit or sad little Charlotte Brontë's wedding—and she had a good lead on it. "My *dear* Miss Nightingale," she wrote breathlessly to Parthe on October 30, "I do so want to hear about you all. I know I have no right from recent acquaintance to expect to hear at such a time as this; so I don't come as a claimant, but only as beggar; but sometime,—in some odd leisure ¼ of an hour would you mind writing a little about what I am so greedy to know. I pick up all the scraps I can out of the newspapers; but I think they only whet my hunger; and they tell me nothing, of course, about you and Mr. and Mrs. Nightingale, and I do so want to know about you all! The more I think about it the more it seems that all these steps in her life seem to have been 'leading her on' to this last great work . . . Don't think I should have written to you, solely to worry you for a letter when you have so much to do & to think of— (dear Miss Nightingale if it had not been for your careful performance of the quiet home duties she would not have been at liberty for what she is now free to do—) but I wanted to return you the formal thanks I render, not the less truly than formally, for my happy happy 'pause of life' at Lea Hurst."[31]

And so Florence Nightingale entered upon the great adventure that would stretch her to the breaking point, and Parthenope and the rest of the Nightingale clan took on the enthralling task of making sure that the whole world knew about it.

Chapter 15

BRITAIN GOES TO WAR

In late March of 1854, while Florence Nightingale was warming the feet of governesses at 1 Upper Harley Street, Great Britain and France declared war on Russia, in support of their sometime ally Turkey.[1] There was no pressing reason for war.[2] True, Russia had dared to try and assume control of the Christian shrines in Palestine, but it backed down under concerted pressure from the other great powers. True, the Tsar had sent a small force into the Danubian principalities of Moldavia and Wallachia (today's Romania) but he withdrew as soon as his imperial brother Austria to the north protested. The government of Sultan Abd-el-Mejid (known in diplomatic parlance as the Porte)[3] declared war on its hostile neighbor Russia in 1853 paradoxically because it knew it would take a beating and counted on Britain and France to come to its aid. By Turkish calculations, the allies between them would eke out some kind of victory, and the Russian noose about Turkey's neck would loosen for a few more years. Sure enough, the Russians had then inflicted a minor naval defeat on the Turks at Sinope.

Small things like the engagement at Sinope had happened before without raising much interest in London and Paris. The Turkish empire had been dying for decades, and governments had refused to panic. Everyone who mattered had been happy to play the princely game of diplomacy. Ministers had amused themselves sending secret coded communications to ambassadors that their foreign counterparts routinely read. Special envoys armed with illustrious names and capacious baggage trains spurred off to distant lands.[4] Diplomats convened in chic resorts for powwows. Treaties were signed, secret clauses were duly leaked. Europe's small professional armies had been squeezed for money and allowed to drink and whore themselves to death in the long peace.

But by 1854 Napoleon III, France's brand-new emperor, was eager to oblige Turkey and have a proper war. The erstwhile Louis Bonaparte's imperial crown still wobbled, and he fancied going head-to-head with some of the other emperors. An alliance with England against Russia would offer a good opportunity to wipe that sneer off the Tsar's face and cozy up to Queen Victoria.[5] The French army was lean and mean following its campaigns in Algeria, and a triumph in Turkey would brighten the French nation's *gloire,* tarnished at Waterloo. Above all, the world would learn that the martial valor of the Buonapartes had not died out on St. Helena with the current emperor's illustrious uncle.

While its Turkish and French allies thundered defiance and geared up the war machine, the British government, a new coalition of Tories and Whigs, dithered, drifted, and (to use Foreign Secretary Lord Clarendon's own word) shilly-shallied. Lord Aberdeen, the new Prime Minister, and a majority of the members of the cabinet saw absolutely no reason why the Eastern Question, as it was known, could not be solved by diplomacy. All the facts, all the experts, both on the state of the international negotiations under way and on the British nation's preparedness for war, supported their position. Aberdeen's personal experience of war as a young man had made him a confirmed pacifist.

Aberdeen and Clarendon's opposition to war with Russia was stoked by personal animosity to their cabinet colleague Lord Palmerston, the former foreign secretary now sulking at the Home Office. Palmerston had been breathing fire against the Tsar for years. In speeches in the Commons, articles in his pet daily newspaper the *Morning Post,* and conversations over port with friends like Nightingale and Monckton Milnes, Palmerston warned his compatriots that the tsarist eagle was spreading its wings and looking to sink its talons into Turkey's moribund body. Russia and England, as Palmerston saw it, were covertly involved in a Great Game to determine control of the vast wild tracts between the Caucasus and the Himalayas. If Russia were allowed to find its strength, England's power from Europe to India would be in danger. Blustering, bellicose old "Pam" was extremely unpopular with ministries abroad, with his cabinet colleagues, and with Queen Victoria and Prince Albert, but with the general public Palmerston enjoyed a status not unlike that of Winston Churchill in the twentieth century. He seemed to be the voice and the conscience of the nation.

Britain in 1853 was governed by a group of able, dedicated men, all with their own agendas, and fighting, in the most gentlemanly way, for turf. No one was in charge. No one in London had a firm grip on foreign affairs, and so the French and the Turks could set the pace. But more important for the British government than what the Turks did or the French said was the force of public opinion at home. Inexorably the government's intelligent, informed, and principled resistance to war was countered by public opinion. Across the political spectrum the English were in favor of war with Russia.[6]

The liberal middle classes, increasingly a power in the nation, as well as the still inchoate but emergent educated working class, had all somehow become convinced that Turkey—a corrupt, anti-Christian autocracy that ruled its vast territories with a toxic mixture of inefficiency and sadism—was a small, pitiable victim that must be protected at all costs against the big bully Russia. A war against Russia was a blow for freedom, claimed the liberal press, for an independent Hungary, for an independent Italy, for an independent Rumania. War with Turkey against Russia amounted to a crusade.

English Tories cared no more for Turkey than for Russia—they couldn't even stand the French. But they too had been persuaded that national values were at stake in the Black Sea. Britain stood as guarantor for the Turkish navy, and so when that navy was routed at Sinope ("massacred," said the popular press), the Tories considered that a gauntlet had been thrown down to British power. In France, the spirit of Napoleon's *grande armée* lived on, and that nation was hearing the bugle call to new victories. By contrast, the great Duke of Wellington, who had just been laid in the ground, seemed to have left no heirs. Was the Englishman today no more than a shopkeeper?

Politics apart, the Tory aristocracy and squirearchy were bored with peace. War was a sport that interested the aristocratic male if only because it was so much like hunting. The sons of dukes and earls who spent most days jumping fences after foxes or shooting widgeon were, it would seem, divinely appointed to lead a nation's forces into battle. Unfortunately, from the point of view of this privileged set, since Waterloo

Europe had seen no more than the odd skirmish. Two generations of blue-blooded generals and lieutenant colonels in England had kicked their heels, drilling their troops on the parade ground, designing expensive new uniforms, and raising the cash to pay for their next promotion. The British navy in the same period had gone from strength to strength, but great men did not go into the navy, a low-class, mongrel operation ever since Drake. Horatio Nelson had certainly had his victories, but was he really a gentleman? Of course, for the militarily minded there was plenty of action in places like India, but no one who was anyone wanted to be out there. Indian society was notoriously low, and proper standards of military discipline and turnout were hard to maintain. When the temperature oozed up to 100 degrees Fahrenheit in the shade, even a duke sitting his steed on the parade ground was not at his best in full dress uniform.

At the beginning *The Times* was also against the war, and *The Times* was a political power in its own right in England. *The Times's* circulation of forty thousand almost equaled that of all its daily newspaper competitors put together, and its editors and reporters, led by the brilliant Irishman John Thadeus Delane, had unrivaled access to the corridors of power. Foreign governments believed that *The Times* was the mouthpiece of British government, while English ministers knew that *The Times* belonged to no party. As Lord Clarendon wrote, "It is a well known fact that *The Times* forms or guides or reflects—no matter which—the public opinion of England."[7] *The Times* had a most exalted view of journalism. "The responsibility of journalists is in proportion to the liberty they enjoy," wrote foreign affairs lead writer and old Etonian barrister Henry Reeve. "No moral responsibility can be graver . . . Those on whom the great part of political action devolves are necessarily governed by other rules."[8] But in the end, even *The Times* was dependent on its subscribers. After trying for months to persuade its readership that intervention on behalf of Turkey was against British interests, *The Times* gave up and halfheartedly backed the declaration of war.[9]

British society was possessed by the sentiment that the long years of peace since Waterloo in 1815 had left the nation soft and effeminate, "enervated by a long peace, by easy habits of intercourse, by peace societies, and false economies," as one leading journalist put it.[10] Yes, England was rich and powerful as never before, but had it lost its soul? The

Reverend Charles Kingsley, the Christian socialist and popular novelist, was convinced that war would "sweep away the dyspeptic unbelief, the insincere bigotry, the effeminate frivolity which paralyses our poetry as much as it does our action."[11] And so in early 1854, jingoism ran high, and Englishmen in pub and club talked of clipping the pinions of the Russian eagle, teaching the Tsar a lesson he wouldn't forget, hitting Johnny Rooskie where it hurt, et cetera, et cetera.

ONE REASON WHY the British government had been reluctant to go to war was because ministers knew what the public did not: the British army was a mess. Even Palmerston, who loved to tweak the tail of France with his dispatches or play diplomatic chicken with Russia, actually had no desire to mobilize the nation and undertake a full-scale European war. The British army was large but spread thin over the world in Britain's distant colonies. Above all, the command structure of the British army was fatally divided and inefficient.

Ever since the reestablishment of the monarchy at the end of the English Civil War, officers in the English army had been drawn almost exclusively from the landed gentry and the aristocracy. Commissions had to be purchased, and promotions depended on money and connections, not ability. Men of small means could buy their way into the army and work their way up a few rungs of the ladder by meritorious service—in the colonies. There ability, efficiency, and success, mattered. But if those colonial officers came home and tried to move to the top, they met insuperable obstacles.

Yet if the officer class was riddled by inequities and riven by grievances, it was united in its feelings of contempt for the ranks. Yes, they were all, officers and men, soldiers; yes, they were all British and thus superior to any other nation's citizens; but there the common ground ended. Officers, even poor officers, ate better food, lived in better accommodations, and enjoyed the services of men from the ranks to forage for food, cook and clear up, look after their clothes, bring along their baggage, and attend to their horses. If an officer chose to bring his wife along, as Captain Henry Duberly of the Eighth Hussars did in the Crimean War, then she must have the same services.[12] When an officer was taken prisoner, he was given special treatment. When he died, he was buried in an individual, marked site, while the men from the ranks were put into a communal grave. The Duke of Wellington had described the ranks that defeated Napoleon's army in the Peninsular War and at Waterloo as "the scum of the earth enlisted for drink," and forty years later few officers felt inclined to challenge this view.[13] Officers were gentlemen, the men were brutes.

As a result of the system of buying promotions, the British officer class in 1854 at the highest level was both inexperienced and old. The oldest had not seen a battle since Wellington's day; the younger ones—like the cavalry commanders, Lord Lucan, fifty-four, and Lord Cardigan, fifty-seven—had seen little or no combat. When the British government needed to choose a commander in chief to lead its expeditionary force to Turkey, it had the choice of four senior generals, but since three were over seventy, the youngster, Lord Raglan, at sixty-five, was the inevitable choice. Raglan had served with great gallantry as a staff officer during the Peninsular War and at Waterloo, where he suffered his right arm to be amputated above the elbow without uttering a murmur. Intimate friend and disciple of the Duke of Wellington, Raglan had served for forty years as Wellington's top aide and latterly as the master-general of ordnance. He was an aristocrat of the old school, a man of sweet nature and few words, courteous to a fault, and of imperturbable calm. He had never had independent military command at any level. He was used to standing in the shadow of a great man. He was the best Britain had got.

To compound the problems arising from the age, inexperience, physical debility, and limited capacity of the officer class, the army's affairs in London were divided up among a bewildering set of different ministries, all underfunded and pathologically resistant to reform. Each administrative entity had its own bureaucracy and its own regulations, and since the government starved them all for funds, each was determined above all to protect its territory and admit no interference. Whereas the French army had a trained, experienced, well-organized command structure, no one involved in the British army knew how to put a large body of men into the field some thousands of miles away from home and maintain them there.

Once war had been declared, the poor pacifist cabinet worried in private about the nation's readiness to fight, but they kept the army's dirty linen out of the public view. When troops of the British expeditionary force marched through the streets of London before taking ship for Turkey, thousands of citizens came out to cheer and admire. As a result of the recent Limited Service Act, the ranks of the army included a good number of volunteers, and the proportion of old lags, drunkards, and ya-hoos was notably smaller than in the days of the great Duke of Welling-ton.[14] Many wives and sisters of modest but respectable families watched with pride and dread as their young menfolk marched off to war. Only a handful of these men came back.

In their bright red wool jackets and archaic leather stocks keeping chins high, the infantrymen with the new Minié rifles looked magnifi-cent, but of course they could not bear comparison with those sons of privilege, the cavalry. The Eleventh Hussars of the Light Brigade of Cav-alry under Lord Cardigan, Prince Albert's own regiment and the *crème de la crème* of Britain's military might, caused a sensation wherever they appeared. "They wore overalls [close-fitting trousers] of cherry colour, jackets of royal blue edged with gold, furred pelisses, short coats, worn as capes, glittering with bullion braid and gold lace, high fur hats adorned with brilliant plumes."[15] Here, surely, was the personification of British strength and wealth, ready to charge.

THE BRITISH ARMY, numbering some thirty thousand men, that was dispatched to the Black Sea had the might of the world's foremost in-dustrial power behind it, and it was transported on the largest and swiftest fleet the world had ever seen. The journey from Southampton to Constantinople had been cut from two months under sail to two weeks with the latest steamships. Britain's factories and mills churned out the products needed for war—the new bored rifles, ammunition, woolen clothing, blankets, tinned goods, tents, prefabricated huts, and cannon large and small. On paper, the British soldier who found himself travel-ing out to Turkey in the late spring of 1854 was better equipped and pro-visioned than any fighting man in history. The smart money in London was ready to bet that the campaign in the Black Sea would be over by the summer.

The English troops made their way to the Black Sea via Malta and finally congregated in and around Constantinople by late spring. The

French troops, happy to demonstrate the superiority of their transport and supply units, were already settled in the Turkish capital, and the English were obliged to settle for Scutari, across the Bosphorus. The losses from disease soon gave cause for concern, and it was decided to move the armies across the Black Sea to the little coastal town of Varna. To the people of the region, but apparently not to the French and English high command, Varna was known as a pesthole. William Howard Russell, special correspondent for *The Times,* who had done his homework, was able to remind his readers that in the 1828–29 Russo-Turkish campaign the victorious Russian army had lost eighty thousand men to "plague, pestilence, and famine" near Varna.[16] Traveling gentlewoman Fanny Duberly, who found herself under a tent at Varna, noticed that the troops about her were camped on irregular mounds, which proved to be the shallow graves of the Russian troops. As the summer progressed dysentery, typhus, "Varna fever," and especially cholera began cutting a swath through the French and British armies.

Nothing about cholera was understood in the British army medical corps at Varna. Now we know that *Vibrio cholerae,* the bacterium that causes cholera, is endemic in warm brackish water, and it is adapted to living on the shells of crustaceans. In most histories of the Crimean War, the French are credited with bringing the cholera with them from North Africa, but cholera does not survive well on ships. A simpler explanation would be that both French and British soldiers caught cholera directly at Varna, where they swam in the warm waters of the Black Sea, fished, and ate their catch. Once one or two men came down with the disease, water supplies quickly became contaminated with human feces, and cholera then spread rapidly.[17] In the Varna area some seventy thousand men were concentrated at the height of summer, and no efforts were made to deal systematically with human waste. No latrines were dug, and when a camp became too smelly and revolting, the army unit simply moved on and fouled the next place.

In the best hospital in London, England's greatest doctors could do little for cholera patients but watch them recover or die. At the General Hospital at Varna, "exhausted orderlies watched the writhing, sweating bodies of the sick with a kind of dazed indifference, while the lice and fleas and rats, 'great big fellows' that made you shudder, crawled over the mouldering floors . . . It was generally believed that no man came out of that packed hospital alive, and men did what they could to conceal their sickness for fear of being sent there."[18] As the troops deserted Varna, which had fast been converted to a running sewer, they carried disease with them to neighboring villages. The thick wool scarlet uniforms and leather stocks the men had worn with pride in a British spring were a burden in the Turkish summer. Men screamed in agony on the grassy, flower-scented meadows, and others lay dead beneath fruit trees bowed down with peaches and apricots.[19] Though the English officers staged horse races and the French bands played rousing tunes, the mood was sinister.

When the Tsar capitulated to pressure and moved his troops out of the Danubian principalities, thereby removing the apparent *casus belli*, England, France, and Turkey were taken by surprise. Diplomacy would easily have secured the four points the allies claimed to care about, and yet it seemed impossible to back down with nary a shot fired. So much taxpayers' money had been spent, so much martial fervor roused. After more weeks of ministerial dithering, during which the army death rate continued to soar, the decision in London and Paris was made that an attack should be launched forthwith on the Russian naval stronghold of Sevastopol, on the Crimean Peninsula. The armies had been keen to fight, so let them have a battle—or was it a siege?

For the third time in six months, the army had to pack up and take ship. Britain had men, horses, and ships, it had goods to pack into the holds, and it had money to buy anything it needed *in situ*. What it lacked was the means to transport the goods overland and officials able to do the army's business efficiently. Merchants, *cantinières,* sutlers, thieves, and whores of all nations flooded into Varna from countries all around the Black Sea and the Mediterranean, but mules and oxen were hard to come by. The British were in a losing competition with their allies. The French were experienced foragers who managed to get everywhere first. The Turks could actually talk to the local people in their own language, which gave them a very unfair advantage in English eyes.

Despite the hundreds of merchant vessels and ships of the line sent from the mother country, plus the craft procured locally, the British army found they could not take everything with them when they finally disembarked from Varna. The Duke of Cambridge, the Queen's cousin, alone had come to the Crimea with enough baggage for seventeen carts. Several thousand horses were abandoned in a depot, where they subsequently starved to death. Several hundred army women (each army unit had an official quota of women) almost met the same fate but won a reprieve and were transported with the army. Most of the Army Medical Corps' equipment—stretchers, operating tables, medical supplies—was left behind. The French had brought in with them ten field hospitals as well as many ambulances, but the British had not. General Sir George Brown, one of the most senior officers, thought ambulances were for sissies. On the transport ships, every man was packed tight as a sardine, and dozens of cholera-stricken corpses were being thrown overboard before the huge flotilla set out for the northern shore of the Black Sea. After some parleying and a lengthy stand-to, the fleet moved along the shore nearer to Sevastopol. Many of the men spent seventeen days on the transport vessels, and they had brought the cholera with them.[20]

Neither the elderly Raglan nor Saint-Arnaud the French commander in chief could make hard decisions. They had no good maps, no local intelligence they were prepared to trust, no idea of how many men the Russians had at Sevastopol or how the city was fortified.[21] It was easy enough for the men at the Horse Guards in London to say capture Sevastopol, but how? One military expert sent out from home hotly pressed for a fast, all-out attack on the Russian stronghold. Another was equally determined to conduct a siege. Some things were clear: the whole of Russia lay behind Sevastopol, and it was impossible to cut the city off totally on the landward sides. The capital of the region, Simferopol, a center for the Russian army, was only miles away, and troops, supplies, and serfs to construct and repair the earthworks protecting the city could all be brought in from the hinterland. In contrast, the expeditionary armies, numerically inferior to their Russian counterparts, could be reinforced and supplied from the sea.

But, ill-informed, jostling courteously for supremacy, divided on strategy and tactics, sick at heart, and ailing in body, Raglan and Saint-Arnaud had no choice but to embark for the Crimean Peninsula. Like the humblest infantryman, theirs was not to reason why. Unlike the humblest infantryman, they were not up to the job that had been given them.

IN BRITAIN, the bellicose spirit of the spring had died down. Steamships and the electric telegraph, which in 1848 had been extended as far as Belgrade, now made it possible for news from the front to arrive within days.[22] Each morning over breakfast Englishmen learned from their daily papers how the war was going and how their army fared. Government couriers were often slower than reporters using the telegraph, and there were occasions when British government ministers received the first news of events before Sevastopol from the newspaper.

The most detailed and most brilliant reports were sent by William Howard Russell, the special correspondent of *The Times.* Editor John Thadeus Delane gave Russell astonishing freedom to call things as he saw them, and since *The Times* had never been keen on war, the newspaper was not inclined to protect official reputations. Thanks to Russell, the epidemic at Varna and the dithering about what to attack and where to land were front-page news. Lord Raglan protested in private to the government that Russia could learn all it needed on troop dispositions and military targets from the pages of *The Times,* and questions about Russell's patriotism were raised in the Commons. Delane and Russell shrugged off the criticisms. The arrival of the war correspondent had changed the nature of military expeditions, and they knew it. In her memoir of the Crimean War, the innkeeper and "doctress" Mary Seacole notes that in the summer of 1845 "nothing of consequence was done in the front for weeks, possibly because Mr. Russell was taking a holiday & could not return until August."[23]

Thanks to Russell and his journalistic colleagues, the British public knew that the leather stocks were stifling the men. They knew that hundreds or even thousands had died of cholera from all ranks, though of course only the names of the most prominent officers appeared in the *Times* columns. They knew that the French officers, especially in the areas of supplies and medical services, seemed well prepared, while their British counterparts flailed about in disorder. When at last fighting broke out, they followed the action day by day with rapt attention and in unparalleled detail.

In late August of 1854, British, French, and Turkish troops, by now down to some fifty thousand despite reinforcements, were put ashore on the thirsty beaches of Calamita Bay on the northern shore of the Black Sea. A small party of the irregular Russian cavalrymen known as Cossacks watched with interest as the foreign troops milled about. Their elegant officer took notes, hardly bothering to keep out of rifle range. Despite everything published in the *Times* of London, the Russian commander in chief, Prince Menchikov, had refused to believe that the allies could actually be so foolish as to attack so great a stronghold so late in the season. Among the first on shore, General Sir George Brown and Quartermaster-General Richard Airey began reconnaissance with a handful of aides. Watched in suspense from the ships at sea, Airey's party almost rode into the arms of the Russian soldiers. This mixture of incompetence and disregard for personal safety was to be the hallmark of the British high command.

The infantrymen were instructed to leave not only their tents and heavy artillery but their packs, containing spare clothing and mess kits, on the transport ships. They marched from the stony beachhead toward Sevastopol in blistering heat with only three days' ration of salt pork and dry biscuit and a canteen of water, shedding their packs, their greatcoats, and their brass-studded helmets as they marched. There was no potable water until the army got to the steep, winding banks of the River Belbec, and there Lord Lucan, in command of cavalry, strictly forbade his troops to allow their horses to stop and drink.[24] And on September 21, when the army reached the river Alma, perched on the rocky heights dominating the river were the Russians, confident of victory in the place they had selected for battle. On the heights, ladies who had driven out from Sevastopol with picnic hampers raised their champagne glasses and prepared to enjoy the greatest show on earth—a battle, with a cast of almost one hundred thousand.

The Russians expected to defeat the French and British and drive them immediately into the sea, but the British and French infantrymen fought like men possessed. Better trained and better armed than their Russian counterparts, these were soldiers of a new kind: volunteers, not mercenaries or pressed men, inspired with patriotic zeal, and conscious that their actions would become a matter of public record. They had come to fight, and they won. News of this astonishing victory of September 21, captured in William Howard Russell's marvelous reports, thrilled the British nation.

But, after the battle, Lord Raglan, terrified to lose his cavalry that guarded the left flank of the whole allied army, refused to allow the cavalry to ride to pursue and harry the enemy in retreat. The main Russian army under Menchikov was allowed to retreat in good order to Simferapol.[25] Saint-Arnaud, worn-out, refused to allow his men to make the frontal attack on the north side of Sevastopol that Raglan suggested. Ever polite and deferent, Raglan did not press the point. The citizens of Sevastopol, defended by a mere eleven thousand marines, waited in dread for the anticipated attack. When—by a miracle, the Russians believed—that attack did not come, they set to, men, women, and children, under the inspired direction of the engineer Todleben, to raise a massive ring of earthworks all around the city. Russian pride demanded that Sevastopol resist to the end, whatever the sacrifice in men and money.

The British army marched inland around Sevastopol, in full view of its startled defenders, and was happy to find that no one bothered to shoot. Lord Raglan, who was at the head of the whole army, made the rash decision to establish the British connection with its fleet at Balaclava. This was a picturesque little fishing village sandwiched in below high red cliffs at the head of a narrow, deep, protected harbor. The French settled in the capacious ports of Kamiesch and Kazatch, closer to the city of Sevastopol and their front lines, and protected once again on one flank by the sea and the navy and on the other by the British. By contrast, Raglan's headquarters on the plain below the city was some seven miles to the harbor, and another three miles to the trenches. His right flank was completely unprotected from the Russian cavalry.[26]

The severe disadvantages of Balaclava harbor soon became apparent. Every biscuit, every bullet, every gun, every coat, every cannon would have to be landed at the tiny dock, unloaded on the tiny foreshore, and carried up the narrow, unmade cliff path and then another ten miles or so to the encampments. The War Office in London had decided that all the severely wounded and the gravely sick would be transported across the Black Sea to Scutari, where the Turkish government had given the British army a large hospital and an even larger barracks to convert into a hospital. All the casualties would need to be carried down the cliffs from the siege positions, loaded onto little boats, and hoisted onto the ships for the increasingly storm-tossed journey to Constantinople.

A forced retreat under fire to the port of Balaclava was Lord Raglan's nightmare, and the Russians knew it. With larger forces and from superior positions, the Tsar's army launched an attack to push the foreigners into the sea. Once again, unaccountably, the Russians were repulsed, lost their appetite for slaughter, and withdrew to their strongholds. This engagement, fought principally on October 25, was known to the world as the Battle of Balaclava.

This was the occasion when the famous "thin red streak tipped with a line of steel," of the Scots Greys, the Irish Enniskillens, and the Royal Dragoons, outnumbered three to one, charged and drove back an attack by a force of Russian Cossacks. This was the occasion that the Light Brigade under Lord Cardigan, misdirected by ambiguous instructions from Lord Raglan, was sent by its commander, Lord Lucan, to make a suicidal charge on the main Russian battery, with a loss of some 300 men and 381 horses. On November 5 another engagement was fought on the same terrain, near the deserted village of Inkerman. By this time the allied armies were exhausted, but again the Russians did not press their attack. The Russian winter, which had defeated the French under Napoleon I, was closing in.

On November 14, a terrible gale with torrential rains stripped away every tent, leaving all the men on the plains crouching sodden in open fields, the trenches streaming with icy water. In the harbor of Balaclava, all was destruction and chaos. The magnificent new English steamships *Prince* and *Resolute*, bearing winter clothing, food, and guns from home, went to the bottom, as did several other supply vessels. By the end of November, Balaclava had become a pesthole far worse than Varna. Fanny Duberley described it in this bravura piece of scene painting: "If anybody should ever wish to erect a 'Model Balaklava' in England, I will tell him the ingredients necessary. Take a village of ruined houses and hovels in the extremest state of all imaginable dirt; allow the rain to pour into and outside them, until the whole place is a swamp of filth ancle-deep [*sic*]; catch about, on an average, 1000 sick Turks with the plague, and cram them into the houses indiscriminately; kill about 100 a-day and bury them so as to be scarcely covered with earth, leaving them to rot at leisure—taking care to keep up the supply. On to one part of the beach drive all the exhausted *bât* [pack] ponies, dying bullocks, and worn-out camels, and leave them to die of starvation. They will generally do so in about three days, when they will begin to rot, and smell accordingly. Col-

*Sick and wounded British soldiers are carried down to the
transport ships in Balaclava harbor.*

lect together from the water of the harbour all the offal of the animals
slaughtered for the use of the occupants of above 100 ships, to say nothing of the inhabitants of the town,—which, together with the occasional
floating human body, whole or in parts, and the driftwood of the wrecks,
pretty well covers the water,—and stew them all up together in a narrow
harbour, and you will have a tolerable imitation of the real essence of Balaklava."[27]

As snow began to fall, despair chilled the hearts and minds of the
British army, from Lord Raglan down to the twelve-year-old bugle boy.
William Howard Russell wrote: "We have defeated the enemy indeed
but have not advanced one step nearer towards the citadel of Sevastopol.
We have abashed, humiliated, and utterly routed an enemy strong in
numbers, in fanaticism, and in dogged resolute courage . . . but we have
suffered a fearful loss, and we are not in a position to part with one man.
England must give us men. She must be prodigal of her sons as she is of
her money and of her ships."[28]

The French, who had a better hold on their press, sent reinforcements. More Turkish troops were brought up, and Piedmontese men
came, anxious to look like the army of a sovereign Italian nation in the
Crimea. But though British men cheered the "the most brilliant val-

our . . . the excess of courage" that Russell celebrated, they were no longer thronging to volunteer for the army. The manifest inadequacies of the British army's fighting machine had become common knowledge even as officials in London scrambled desperately to remedy them. Not just journalists but private citizens, male and female, had come out to the Crimea to see a magnificent demonstration of British power, and the reports they sent back shocked the nation. Criticisms centered on the failure of the Commissariat and transport authorities, the disorder and filth of the harbor of Balaclava, and above all the care of the wounded— on the battleground, in the field hospitals, in transport down to the ships, on the sea voyage to the hospitals in Scutari.

For months, William Howard Russell had reported how cholera killed dozens of men in a day, how dysentery weakened all the army.[29] This was terrible but, given the state of medical knowledge, perhaps beyond the power of human intervention. But on October 9, following the Battle of Balaclava, Russell was angry to see the terrible sufferings of the wounded, and he pointed the finger of blame at the government and at the army commanders both in London and in the field.

The alarm and indignation in Britain greatly increased when the October 11 report came from Russell's *Times* colleague Thomas Chenery in Constantinople, whither the wounded and sick were being transported.

It is with feelings of surprise and anger that the public will learn that no sufficient preparations have been made for the proper care of the wounded. Not only are there not sufficient surgeons—that, it might be urged, was unavoidable; not only are there no dressers and nurses—that might be a defect of the system for which no one is to blame; but what will be said when it is known that there is not even linen to make bandages for the wounded? The greatest commiseration prevails for the sufferings of the unhappy inmates of Scutari, and every family is giving sheets and old garments to supply their wants. But why could not this clearly foreseen want have been supplied? Can it be said that the Battle of the Alma has been an event to take the world by surprise? Has not the expedition to the Crimea been the talk of the last four months? And when the Turks gave up to our use the vast barracks to form a hospital and depot, was it not on the ground that the loss of troops was sure to be considerable when engaged in so dangerous an enterprise? And yet, after the troops have been six months in the country, there is no preparation for the commonest surgical operations! Not only are men kept, in some cases, for a week without the hand of a medical man coming near their wounds; not only are they left to expire in agony, unheeded and shaken off, though catching desperately at the surgeon whenever he makes his round through the fetid ship; but now, when they are placed in the spacious building, where we are led to believe that everything was ready which could ease their pain or facilitate their recovery, it is found that the commonest appliances of a work-house sick-ward are wanting, and that the men must die through the medical staff of the British army having forgotten that old rags are necessary for the dressing of wounds.[30]

On October 13, Chenery's wrath rose higher. Well aware that this comparison was guaranteed to make his fellow Englishmen's blood boil, Chenery wrote in The Times: "Here [i.e., in the area of medical care] the French are greatly our superiors. Their arrangements are extremely good, their surgeons more numerous, and they have also the help of the sisters of Charity who have accompanied the expedition in incredible numbers. These devoted women are excellent nurses."[31]

BACK FROM HER family holiday in Derbyshire, Florence Nightingale read the reports in The Times with rapt attention. Her father was a friend and supporter of Lord Palmerston, whose pro war views were well known, and the whole Nightingale family was deeply involved in the "Eastern Question." As her subsequent letters would show, Florence Nightingale was a firm "Palmerstonian," convinced that it was crucial to defeat Russia, not just for Great Britain but for democracy.[32]

Florence Nightingale conferred with her friends in London. She wrote on October 14 to her dear friend Liz Herbert, then at Brighton with her husband, Sidney, Minister at War in the Aberdeen government, explaining that she was planning to leave for Constantinople on October 21 at the head of a small band of nurses. The nurses would be paid out of private funds—Lady Maria Forester had already offered to pay two hundred pounds for the expenses of three nurses—but obviously the cooperation of the army medical officers, both in London and in the East, would be essential. Florence begged her friend Selina Bracebridge and her uncle Sam Smith to intercede with her parents and get permission for her to go to Turkey.

Also on October 14, Nightingale, who was not one to let grass grow under her feet, secured an interview with Dr. Andrew Smith, the head of the Army Medical Board. He was, unsurprisingly, livid about the reports in *The Times*. Smith did not forbid Miss Nightingale to go out to Turkey as long as her party was very small, went "quietly and privately," and made no efforts to "take possession of the Hospital." But Smith was of the opinion that Sevastopol would surely fall before the Nightingale party reached Constantinople. In that case, the sick and wounded might be moved from Scutari, and "you cannot follow the army about like Sisters of Charity."[33] Obviously any woman who moved with the men and whose dress did not absolutely proclaim her religious vows of chastity and obedience risked falling into the disgraced category of camp follower, one small step up from whore. None of the nuances in Smith's response was lost on Nightingale.

Sidney Herbert in Brighton had perhaps been even more unpleasantly surprised by Chenery's reports in *The Times* than Dr. Smith. As Minister at War, his job was to oversee the financing of the war, and issues of supplies and commissariat, though directly the responsibility of his senior colleague at the Treasury, came within his purview. Clearly, if things in the Crimea turned sour, the current government would fall, and Aberdeen and his cabinet members would exit under a cloud. For Herbert personally the situation was even more delicate. Sidney Herbert's mother, Countess Woronzov, was Russian. One of his first cousins was a senior officer currently serving in the Russian army in the Crimea. The Woronzov Road, the only made road that led from the plain below Sevastopol to the cliffs above Balaclava—the British army's main supply route, the road that had tragically, inexplicably been allowed to pass into Russian control after the heroic Battle of Balaclava—was named after Sidney Herbert's maternal relatives. Sidney Herbert needed not only to solve the purveying and supplying problems that were leaving the hospital at Scutari short of bandages when literally tons of lint had been sent off from England, but also to persuade the British public that he cared just as deeply about the plight of the men as any other patriotic Englishman.

So on October 14, Sidney Herbert, in his official capacity as Minister at War and with the approval of Lords Aberdeen and Newcastle, wrote a letter to Miss Florence Nightingale that crossed with her own, begging her to lead a group of nurses out to Turkey to minister to the troops. The Aberdeen cabinet had considered the idea of sending women out as nurses "at a very early stage" in the planning for the war but dismissed it as impracticable, since no suitable nurses could be found.[34] Only when Herbert told his colleagues about Miss Nightingale and her unique qualifications for the job of superintendent was the idea revived.

Herbert's letter was an appeal, first to Florence herself and then to her family, who would have to give their consent. "There is but one woman in England that I know of who would be capable of organizing & superintending such a scheme," Herbert wrote. "The selection of the rank & file of nurses will be very difficult . . . The difficulty of finding women equal to a task after all full of horror, & requiring besides knowledge and good will, great energy, & great courage, will be great. The task of ruling them & introducing system among them, great; & not the least, will be the difficulty of making the whole work smoothly with the medical & military authorities out there. This it is, which makes it so important, that the experiment should be carried out by one with administrative capacity & experience. A number of sentimental, enthusiastic ladies, turned loose into the Hospital at Scutari would probably after a few days be mises à la porte [shown the door], by those whose business they would interrupt, & whose authority they would dispute."[35]

Florence Nightingale gave this letter her most careful attention. She understood that her job was to keep tight control over her nurses, work as smoothly as possible with the doctors and army officials, interrupt no man in the conduct of his appointed business, and dispute no official's authority.

On October 20, in concert with Miss Nightingale who wished to have things as clear as possible, and in writing, Sidney Herbert wrote out a set of instructions, copies of which were sent out to Lord Raglan, to the English ambassador to Turkey, Lord Stratford de Redcliffe, and to Dr. Duncan Menzies, principal medical officer at Scutari, but not, in a significant omission, to Dr. John Hall, chief medical officer in the East and Menzies's superior. Nightingale was given the "Office of Superintendent of the female nursing establishment in the English General Military Hospitals in Turkey." These last two words would turn out to be critical since they seemed to say that Nightingale would have no authority in the Crimea itself. Nightingale was told to report on arrival, as any officer would, to the principal medical officer at Scutari, Dr. Menzies. Nightingale or her own delegates would have total discretion over the choice of the nurses under her authority, and would arrange for their duties in consultation with the medical officers. Each nurse would have a certificate to present, and no woman without a certificate would be permitted to attend the patients. Nightingale was authorized to dismiss or discharge any nurse as she saw fit. Nurses given an official discharge would have their passage paid back to England. The nurses would be accommodated and fed at the army's expense, their travel expenses defrayed with money supplied to Nightingale on departure, and a wage paid where necessary. Herbert enjoined the nurses to pay strict attention to all military regulations and avoid all forms of insubordination. In conclusion, Herbert told Miss Nightingale that he relied upon her to ensure that none of the nurses used their position at the hospital "to tamper with or disturb the religious opinions of the patients of any denomination whatever," using "severe measures" if necessary.

To this letter of accreditation Sidney Herbert added a letter to the *Morning Chronicle* (of which he was part owner), published on October 24, that summarized its essential points. Herbert again asserted that Miss Florence Nightingale alone had the qualities needed to undertake the position of superintendent of female nursing. As Goldie notes, "He stated clearly and categorically that no further nurses were to be sent out except on the specific requisition of Miss Nightingale."[36]

Florence Nightingale had four full days to prepare for the journey and plan for the task ahead. Her housekeeper at Harley Street, Mrs. Clarke, volunteered to accompany her, as did her good friends Charles and Selina. The Bracebridges had ever been ready for an adventure, and it is not clear that Florence Nightingale could have gone had they not agreed to escort her. Only two years earlier, Fanny Nightingale had refused to allow Florence even to cross the English Channel without an older female chaperone. Fanny and Parthe, now ensconced in a rented house at 4 Cavendish Square, packed Flo's trunks for an expedition far more dangerous and difficult than a journey up the Nile. Their house also served as a depot for the extraordinary flood of clothing and supplies that people of all ranks began sending for the troops. The Nightingales engaged in an orgy of correspondence with family members and friends desperate to hear exactly what Flo was intending to do. "I am well nigh writ out," wrote Parthe to Madame Mohl on November 6. "170 letters to answer in the last fortnight . . . Old linen is abating, I am happy to say; even knitted socks are slacker; but nurses, rabble and respectable, ladies and *very* much the reverse, continue to rain."[37]

While her sister wrote letters and counted socks and Charles Bracebridge raced all about London in a new hackney cab at the extraordinary speed of ten miles an hour, Florence herself remained calm, quiet, and controlled. Everyone who saw her was in awe. Her only sign of emotion was when Parthe put the tiny, embalmed body of Athena into her hand. "Poor little beastie," she said, "it was odd how much I loved you." In between her negotiations with government officials, her discussions with Henry Reeve at *The Times* (which was sending out an agent to disburse a large fund), her receipt of seven thousand pounds in private contributions to disburse at her own discretion, and the winding up of her affairs at Harley Street, Nightingale yet found the time to prepare the lessons she had promised to the Sunday school at Embley. Parthenope Nightingale was now convinced that God had brought Florence to this mission. "I must say the way in which all things have tended to and fitted her for this is so very remarkable one cannot but believe she was intended for it. None of her previous life has been wasted, her experience all tells."[38]

The press, not just in England but all over the world, was now extremely interested in the woman to whom the government had given such unprecedented authority and responsibility. "Who is 'Mrs.' Nightingale?" queried the *Examiner* of October 28, and then went on to tell its readers the happy news that Miss Nightingale was a "young, graceful, feminine, rich, and popular" lady who delighted in the "palpable and heart-felt attractions of home." The article concluded: "There is a heroism in dashing up the heights of the Alma in defiance of death . . . but there is a quiet forecasting heroism and largeness of heart in this lady's resolute accumulation of the powers of consolation, and her devoted application of them, which rank as high and are at least as pure . . . There is not one of England's proudest and purest daughters who at this moment stands on so high a pinnacle as Florence Nightingale."

This paean was circulated internationally, and the myth of Florence

Nightingale was born. Unsurprisingly there were many, not only in the army, who regarded with indignation the comparison of the heroism of the troops at the Alma with that of Miss Nightingale going over to Scutari to "render the holiest of women's charities to the sick, the dying, and the convalescent." It was not Nightingale's fault if she was so extravagantly praised before she had so much as taken ship for Scutari. The British press had touted this war that was turning into a national disaster. It needed a hero.

FINDING WOMEN to go out with the remarkable Miss Nightingale proved even more difficult than anticipated.[39] The task was taken on by a committee of noble philanthropic ladies including Liz Herbert, Selina Bracebridge, Mary Stanley, Lady Canning, and Lady Cranworth, and they had a tough time of it. In the end they managed to recruit thirty-eight women: fourteen "secular" nurses drawn from the public hospitals, six sisters from St. John's House, eight more from Miss Sellon's Anglican sisterhood, five Roman Catholic nuns from the Norwood orphanage, and five more nuns from the Sisters of Mercy at Bermondsey. The fact that a quarter of Miss Nightingale's party were Roman Catholic nuns came as a shock to many in England. Even though the nurse to go out to Scutari was idealized as the English counterpart of the French Sister of Mercy, even though many men in the ranks of the British army were Roman Catholic, the idea of Catholics having access to wounded soldiers was repugnant.

In fact, the first five women from England (though all of them were actually born in Ireland) to volunteer to go out to Scutari to nurse the troops were from the small house of the Sisters of Mercy in the London suburb of Bermondsey. The Bermondsey convent had been founded by a most remarkable Irishwoman, Catherine McAuley. Dedicated explicitly to serving the needs of the poor, it was located in a poverty-stricken area of London, the kind of area where Mrs. Nightingale would have been loath to see her daughter go, even with a male servant. The Bermondsey sisters were a small, savagely overworked band, too busy to notice much when the country declared war. However, as soon as they became aware that things were going badly with the troops, they determined to send out a party. The Mother Superior, Mary Clare Moore, insisted on going herself, though her health was not robust. The Bermondsey sisters packed their tiny bags and crossed to France while Miss Nightingale was still settling her affairs at Harley Street and negotiating with the War Ministry.[40]

There were also in England three small Protestant sisterhoods devoted to the service of the poor and sick. After some arm-twisting by the Herberts, both the sisters of St. John's House and the Sellonite sisters agreed to send some of their members and to accept Miss Nightingale as their direct superior. The Evangelical sisterhood of the "Protestant Institution," to the contrary, horrified by the idea of associating not only with the Tractarians but with actual Papists, refused to send any nurses out to Scutari with Miss Nightingale. This meant that the powerful Evangelical faction in the Church of England regarded the Nightingale mission *ab initio* as a creature of the Catholic Counter-Reformation in England. As the Evangelicals saw it, Sidney Herbert's injunction that no nurse under Miss Nightingale's superintendency would seek to use her position as a nurse to influence the religious views of the troops was whistling in the wind. The Bermondsey sisters, the Sellonites, and the St. John's House sisters were going out to spread their faith, and nothing could persuade the Evangelicals to believe anything different. And in fact, as Florence Nightingale knew very well, given the slight medical expertise of the sisters as a group, it would be impossible to tell at any one moment where Christian charity ended and religious proselytizing began.

Finding nurses posed other problems. The honorable lady interviewers threw up their hands in horror at the kind of woman who walked through the front door of Mrs. Herbert's elegant London town house at 49 Belgrave Square, asking for a job. These women nursed for a living, and they were willing to go out to the pestiferous wards at Scutari because the government offered to pay a good wage and cover all expenses.[41] The nurses were suspected by the ladies, not unfairly, of seeing the expedition to Scutari as a great lark, a chance to see something of the world, to drink and eat on the government's tab, and find a nice soldier husband, perhaps even an officer. If in the case of the sisters the authorities feared religious proselytism, in the nurses they anticipated disgraceful behavior—drink, opium, promiscuity. As Madame Mohl wrote jokingly after meeting the Nightingale party in Paris, the nurses "were of no particular religion, unless the worship of Bacchus should be revived."[42]

Hence Mrs. Herbert, Miss Stanley, and their associates carefully eliminated women who were too young or too attractive—or too drunk. They emphasized that all the women who nursed would be required to wear a gray woolen uniform cut to no woman's actual figure, designed to wear well and look ugly. The uniform cap was hideous. As one nurse, Mrs. Lawfield, was to remark to Florence Nightingale: "I came out Ma'am, prepared to submit to everything—to be put upon in every way—but there are some things, Ma'am, one can't submit to—There is caps, Ma'am, that suits one face, and some that suits another's, and if I'd known, Ma'am, about the caps, great as was my desire to come out to nurse at Scutari, I wouldn't have come Ma'am."[43] In fact, Mrs. Lawfield was to become one of the most effective nurses at Scutari.

FLORENCE NIGHTINGALE was seen off at the harbor by her cousin Blanche's husband, Arthur Hugh Clough. In her pocket was a little black case containing three letters, one from her mother, one from her friend the Catholic priest Henry Manning, and one from Richard Monckton Milnes. "So you are going to the East," Milnes wrote, "you can undertake that, when you could not undertake me." This self-absorbed missive shows rather clearly why Nightingale had refused Milnes, but she kept all three letters in their case until she died, so they obviously meant a lot to her.

Florence was accompanied not only by the Bracebridges and Mrs. Clarke but by her uncle Sam Smith, who planned to go as far as Marseilles. His job was to observe everything his already legendary niece did and send news back home. *The Times* reported that at Boulogne the so-called "fish-women," many of whom who had menfolk in the French army in the Crimea, carried the Nightingale party's bags and refused payment. Relations within the party were less cordial. In the railway carriages the Anglican sisters refused to sit with the nurses. In Paris they refused to eat with them and expected the nurses to do the washing and mending for the whole party. Nightingale ate with the nurses and did

Boulogne fisherwomen carrying the luggage of Miss Nightingale and her nurses.

everything possible to get them comfortable and make them feel appreciated. "We never had so much care of our comforts before," one nurse told Sam Smith. "It is not people's way with us."[44]

In Marseilles, the party waited a few days while Nightingale used some of the private funds she had been supplied with to buy goods—tinned foods, clothing, bedlinen, portable cooking stoves, and so forth. Despite Sidney Herbert's earnest assurances that everything a wounded soldier and his doctor could possibly want was in plentiful supply at Scutari and that she would get full cooperation from the commissariat, Nightingale made her own decisions. "In her bedroom, but NOT," explained Uncle Sam, "at bedtime she received a motley crowd of merchants, shopkeepers, dealers, officials from the French government and the British Consulate, army officers, *The Times* correspondent and a Queen's Messenger 'with the same serenity as in a drawing room.' She was looking handsomer than ever, he noted, and the impression she created was extraordinary."[45] The party was joined at Marseilles by the nurse Mrs. Wilson, who had arrived drunk at London Bridge Station and missed the boat but had then traveled first class to catch up. Nightingale wrote home to her family that Wilson had "proclaimed her intention publicly that *she* did not come for the paltry 10/- a week, but to nurse noblemen, and intended to desert the first opportunity. She has made acquaintance with all the surgeons & is a regular bad one."[46]

The women then boarded the steamer *Vectis,* a vessel that rolled horribly in heavy seas and was notorious for shipping water into the cabins belowdecks.[47] The sisters and nurses were allotted tiny berths, but those who were not immediately prostrated with seasickness preferred to stay on deck as much as possible, however cold and wet they became. One sister lay on the cabin floor for much of the voyage, soaked in seawater and vomit, in a kind of coma. She never recovered from the voyage out and was soon shipped back home. When the *Vectis* lost its engines for a time and seemed likely to break up, the women were sure their hour had come. But then the engines started up again, the weather improved, and the crew carried some of the women onto the stern deck to get air and some food. Florence, a perennially bad sailor, spent most of the voyage helpless in her berth, but she at least had a cabin with some air and the resilient Selina Bracebridge, who was never seasick, to look after her.

As the ship approached the Dardanelles, Florence Nightingale too got up on deck in time to see the fabled plains of Troy. When the boat anchored off Seraglio Point near Constantinople, she managed to write her family the kind of brilliant, descriptive, funny letter they had long been accustomed to. The weather was bad, heavy rain fell. "The Golden Horn looked like a bad Daguerreotype washed out," she wrote, "& Sta Sophia was drowned in tears."[48] When Lord Napier, one of the secretaries at the British Embassy, came aboard the *Vectis* to greet Miss Nightingale, he found her lying pale and exhausted on a sofa.[49] Soon the two were talking animatedly of the situation, and Florence Nightingale had made her first important ally, and a lifelong friend. Napier brought news of the great victory at Balaclava, of the tragic charge of the Light Cavalry, and of the four hundred sick men already on their way to Scutari to join the thousands already there.

As the nursing party gazed across at the enormous yellow bulk of the Barrack Hospital, one woman said: "Oh, Miss Nightingale, when we land don't let there be any red tape delays, let us get straight to nursing the poor fellows." Florence Nightingale's reply gave an indication of what the nurses could expect in the days ahead. "The strongest will be wanted at the wash tub."[50]

Chapter 16

STEEPED UP TO
OUR NECKS IN BLOOD

There was no question of Florence Nightingale and her party taking time to recover from the rigors of the sea voyage with a little sightseeing in Constantinople or a stay at the elegant seaside resort at Therapia, where British ambassador Lord Stratford de Redcliffe had his villa. From on board the *Vectis*, the members of the Nightingale party embarked in the graceful little open boats called caiques and were rowed across the choppy waters of the Bosphorus toward the General and Barrack Hospitals, the two big army base hospitals at Scutari. As they were helped out onto a small, rotting landing place, the nurses noticed the bloated body of a horse floating just offshore, under assault from a pack of skinny dogs. High above the dock was the Barrack Hospital, some quarter of a mile up a causeway that soon turned into a narrow dirt track. About another half mile farther on was the General Hospital. Around the two hospitals a host of tents and wooden stalls had sprung up to serve the new population of foreign soldiers. As in the great city across the water, fleas, flies, mosquitoes, rats, and lice abounded in the area, and a man could "get drunk for sixpence and syphilis for a shilling."[1]

The view from Scutari across the Bosphorus to Constantinople and out to the Black Sea was one of the wonders of the world, but the village itself was a huddle of wooden huts and in 1854 it had no bazaar. Finding a house there to rent was a problem for the whole English colony, and all supplies had to be purchased in Constantinople. When weather was bad, landing at the dock below the hospitals was impossible, so goods had to be ferried across to the little port of Scutari a mile and a quarter away, transported along a bad road, and finally carried uphill. "English people look upon Scutari as a place with inns & hackney-coaches & houses to let furnished," wrote Florence Nightingale to Sidney Herbert on December 10. "It required yesterday (to land 25 casks of sugar) four oxen & three men for six hours—plus two passes & two requisitions, Mr. Bracebridge's two interferences, & one apology from a Quarter Master for stealing the Araba."[2] No wonder Lord Raglan had determined to move the British army from Scutari to Varna four months earlier, and the French authorities soon decided they must buy up every possible building in Constantinople to house their own sick and wounded.[3]

The General Hospital was a large, multistory building, meant to accommodate about six hundred patients. It had served as a military hospital under the Turkish authorities, was more or less intact structurally, contained some rudimentary hospital fittings, and even had a garden. Unfortunately, before the British army exchanged a single shot with the Russians, hundreds of its soldiers were struck down with acute bowel diseases and fevers, and by late October all the wards at the General Hospital were filled with officers. Ordinary soldiers lined one side of the corridors, lying on hard, thin palliasses as there were no more beds.

To serve a patient population running with diarrhea, there were very few latrines and an estimated twenty chamber pots. The latrines were of the stand-up-and-let-fly type and emptied into subterranean drains, which no one had yet cared to look into. The smell from the drains wafted back into the wards, and the men plugged up the latrines with anything they could find, so raw sewage often trickled across the floors. When Sidney Godolphin Osborne toured the General Hospital on November 15, many windows had been boarded up against the cold, and the stench was almost unbearable. Augustus Stafford, M.P., who was there about the same time, claimed that he had got dysentery simply by looking into one of the hospital cupboards. Sarah Anne Terrot, a Sellonite sister and experienced nurse who worked for some months at the General Hospital, thought it was worse than any workhouse or infirmary she had seen in England. Nonetheless, the General Hospital had certain amenities and so Dr. Menzies, the principal medical officer at Scutari, had his quarters there, and the medical care was a little better supervised.

The Barrack Hospital was by common agreement a far rougher place than the General. As its name implies, the building was originally the Selimiye Kislasi Barracks of the Turkish army. It was empty and almost derelict when the Porte made it available to Lord Aberdeen's government, initially as a barracks when the British army arrived in late spring and then as a hospital. The building was immense, a hollow square built around a central courtyard that had once been a parade ground but was now a vast mud pit encumbered with refuse. Each side of the building was about one and a third miles long, and at each corner there was a tower. Inside, the building took the form of a wide continuous corridor, with rooms opening off it that had become wards. The corridor windows faced into the courtyard, and there were staircases only at the corners. The building nestled into a hill, so that some sides had more floors than others. One whole side of the square had been ravaged by fire. It took experience to find one's way from one floor and one side to another, and sometimes it was necessary to walk three complete sides of the building to find a stairwell. Providing medical care in such a building was a nightmare under the best of circumstances.

Underneath the main floors of the Barrack Hospital, just above the drains, was a warren of dark and fetid spaces, occupied by some two hundred "camp followers"—the wives, mistresses, and growing contingent of children who were attached to the British soldiers in Turkey. Sarah Anne Terrot tells of one time early in her days at Scutari when a chaplain persuaded her to go down into the cellars where a young woman, filthy, starving, lying on a heap of rags crawling with vermin, was dying of tuberculosis while drunken women and ash-faced children looked on. Terrot had seen the slums of London and Plymouth, but this was worse. It is to the everlasting credit of Charles and Selina Bracebridge, ably assisted by Lady Alicia Blackwood, that in the course of the fall and winter they were able to channel some of the aid coming into Turkey from Britain toward this sad and savagely neglected group.[4] Within a month or so, given a little help, the soldiers' wives, or at least those still strong and sober enough to work, did their bit for the war effort as washerwomen, seamstresses, and scullery maids—once Florence Nightingale had begun to organize the washing of the army's linen and serve digestible food to its sick.

On their arrival at Scutari, the Nightingale party, which numbered

forty-one women and two men (Bracebridge and a courier), was taken
to the Barrack Hospital. They were allotted seven rooms on three floors
in the northwest tower, located to the left of the hospital's principal entrance. Three junior medical officers and their servants normally occupied a suite of this size, and, in accordance with military hierarchy, the
hospital commandant, currently Major Sillery, had an equivalent
amount of room all to himself.[5]

On one level of the women's quarters there was a large room, twenty
feet square, which was at once designated the storeroom. In the months
ahead this room became the dynamic center of the whole hospital, ruled
over by Selina Bracebridge and the Reverend Mother Mary Clare Moore.
A little farther down the corridor was a room Nightingale converted into
a kitchen using the portable stoves she had purchased in Marseilles. Here
Mrs. Clarke, Nightingale's housekeeper, was in charge. Clarke was an energetic, resourceful woman of little education, devoted to Miss Nightingale. She loved to remind the men, as she ladled out the soup or
arrowroot laced with port wine, just how fortunate they were that
Madam had come to help them. Within days of Nightingale's arrival this
makeshift kitchen was turning out quantities of soup, cereal, beef tea,
and other special invalid foods, little of which had been available before
and which were greeted by the sick with ravenous enthusiasm.

On each side of the storeroom were two smaller rooms, perhaps
eighteen feet by twenty, one occupied by fourteen nurses, the other by
sixteen Roman Catholic nuns. Opening out of the storeroom was the
tower room that became Nightingale's office and the administrative center for the group. Another party of nurses and a party of sisters were
stacked in the tower rooms on the two floors above. From one of these
rooms, the neglected corpse of a Russian general had been hurriedly removed just prior to the Nightingale group's arrival. The dead man's
white hairs lay on the floor until at last a broom could be found to
sweep them up.

Florence moved her things into the office room, setting up a cot behind a curtain. Except for the months of her convalescence, this tower
room was Florence Nightingale's whenever she was at Scutari. "Occasionally the roof is torn off our quarters," she wrote on November 14 to
Dr. William Bowman of Kings College Hospital, "or the windows blown
in—and we are flooded and under water for the night."[6] When it rained

on the sisters on the top floor, the water poured through onto Florence Nightingale below, and thence down to some medical officers, who complained that she was trying to drown them.

For middle-class women, such quarters were appallingly squalid, and even the nurses, who had lived in crowded hospitals, were shocked by the lack of space and privacy they would have to endure. It was a relief when, within weeks, almost a quarter of the original number had returned to England, for various reasons.[7] Yet for all their disadvantages, the three tower rooms in particular were desirable accommodations by Scutari standards. They had tall windows along one side, they faced out to the sea and the sublime view, they were high enough to get fresh air, and the voracious hordes of flies that tormented the men in the wards and the long corridors could be kept at bay. Though at first they suffered from cold and ate off the floor, the women who occupied these rooms remained relatively healthy.

When the women arrived, there were no chairs or tables—Sarah Anne Terrot was told that the whole of the Barrack Hospital did not contain even an operating table—and no beds. The sisters and nurses put what they had in the way of pillows and covers on the flea-ridden divan, about a foot high, that ran along one side of the rooms. In Nightingale's inspired phrase, vermin ran tame everywhere, and everything was filthy.

The Nightingale party had been assured in London that the army would feed as well as house them, but it was hard to get anything out of the miserably equipped and undermanned central kitchen. The women were glad that Miss Nightingale had thought to bring some provisions with her from France and had both private funds to spend in the markets of the city and a male friend to go to the markets. Any kind of container was at a premium in the Barrack Hospital, and each of the women had a copper basin that she used for drinking, eating, and washing and which she cleaned out with paper. For some weeks, the party also relied for their ministrations on a small green pail that was passed religiously from one woman to another to carry whatever the patients needed—water, soup, cereal. When the pail disappeared for a time, the nurses shed tears of frustration.[8] It is not hard to see how disease might spread in such conditions.

Water was more of a problem than food. Each floor of the hospital had a single fountain where orderlies queued up all day long to catch the

trickle of water in their precious pails and basins. The women were allocated one pint of water a day for all uses, and it had a nasty cloudy, yellow
cast that made even tea barely palatable. Beer, wine, and spirits were a
standard part of the diet of most British men and women of this period,
and port wine was considered a sovereign remedy by doctors and patients
alike. Unsurprisingly, inebriation was a chronic problem among doctors,
officers, orderlies, and patients, and many of the nurses who accompanied Nightingale, including Mrs. Clarke, fell victim to alcoholism and
had to be sent home. However, at Scutari it was sane to drink wine or
beer rather than water, and as time went on, Florence Nightingale found
it easier to forgive the drunkenness of her nurses than the idleness of her
ladies or the proselytizing zeal of her sisters.

    More distressing to the sisters and nurses than the tight, dirty quar-
ters and bad food was the hostility of the army medical personnel. The
women were astonished to discover that the doctors and orderlies were
extremely reluctant to have them on the wards.[9] On her arrival Nightingale engaged in negotiations with the medical officers, and Dr. McGrigor
volunteered to allow one or two selected nurses to go into the so-called
"cholera wards." Sarah Anne Terrot was one of these, and she found that
her work consisted mainly in making a man a little more comfortable
before he died. Even more distressing for Terrot was the fact that she was
obliged to ignore the lines of men desperately begging for help in those
sections of hospitals where the MOs had absolutely forbidden any nurse
to so much as touch one of his cases.[10]

    While a few women tasted the terrors of the wards, the rest were
forced to remain in their cramped quarters, setting up a kitchen, mending old linen, sorting through the supplies that had been bought at Marseilles. The women had not come all the way out to Turkey to do
darning, and they bitterly blamed Florence Nightingale for not putting
up a fight. Couldn't Miss Nightingale hear the patient groans of men dying without so much as a cup of water? Was she made of stone?

    Unsurprisingly, the nurses and sisters did not understand how the
British army worked. Florence Nightingale might politely present her
credentials and mention Sidney Herbert and the Duke of Newcastle. Dr.
Menzies could listen politely, accept the letters, chat, and go his way.[11]
The instructions Herbert had given Nightingale stated explicitly that she
and the nurses were to serve as the doctors saw fit and must above all give

no hindrance to the medical personnel. If the doctors refused to have nurses on the ward, that was their prerogative. Prerogatives, not patients, were what counted. Like most officers in the British army at that time, a staff surgeon could be fairly sure of keeping his job, drawing his pay, and creeping up the promotional ladder if—and it was a big if—he could manage not to offend his senior officer by an excess of zeal. Any surgeon who showed more energy, ability or humanity than his fellows could expect to receive a thunderbolt from on high.[12]

Morale among the doctors at Scutari was extremely low. The General and the Barrack Hospitals were deeply unpopular places. Officers and men wanted either to return to the front or else to be sent home. Army doctors, normally called surgeons, were much more interested in surgical cases than medical ones, and the amputations and wound repairs done on the battlefield were often brilliantly executed. Surgery was, pun apart, the cutting edge of medicine in the mid-nineteenth century, which is one reason why Florence Nightingale, that keen student of all things medical, observed every surgical operation she could.[13] Unfortunately, surgery performed at the base hospitals had far lower survival rates than that conducted in the field. At Scutari almost all the amputees died from diseases such as gangrene that they developed while on the wards, and this further lowered morale among the surgeons, with predictable results in patient care. Worst of all, only perhaps one in ten of the cases that came into the base hospitals was surgical; the rest were medical and therefore, in the experience of the army doctors, untreatable. Just by going into a fever ward, a doctor risked his life—and to what end?

After a long, hard day sawing off men's limbs, watching them die, and walking through corridors where mortality from fever and dysentery was at epidemic levels, the doctors gathered in their quarters, ate the tinned grouse, dumplings, and pudding heated up for them by the orderlies, drank their claret, smoked their pipes, and agreed that war had ever been thus.[14] This too would pass. If lucky, they themselves would manage to stay healthy and exploit the accelerated promotion schedule prevailing in wartime. The really distressing part of the business was the scandalous way the whole Army Medical Board was being scrutinized by interfering civilians, analyzed in the press, and blamed by the public for doing its duty according to the rules.

It was in fact the first time in the history of military engagements that army surgeons had come under attack for providing inadequate care to their soldier patients. The doctors' response to the criticism was not to undertake reforms and try to do better but to close ranks and cultivate denial.

And when Dr. Menzies and his staff learned from the pages of *The Times* how Miss Nightingale and her nurses had been fêted as heroes on their progress through France, they did not roll out the red carpet and breathe sighs of relief that help was on its way. They already had Traveling Gentlemen like the Rev. the Hon. Sidney Godolphin Osborne and Augustus Stafford, M.P., poking their noses in everywhere. They had journalists like Thomas Chenery of *The Times* filing hysterically condemnatory reports every other day. Now a band of lady do-gooders, anxious to smooth a pillow, mop a fevered brow, and murmur soft words of comfort, had arrived in a hospital where many a man died on the floor before an MO so much as looked at him, was sewn into his blood-soaked blanket if he still had one, and was hurried down to the communal burial pit.[15] Not, of course, that any of this was to be mentioned in an official report. Nurses on the wards, even if they helped the patients and obeyed the doctors' orders, would be sure to observe and report. They were nothing better than spies. As for Miss Nightingale, she was Espionage personified.[16] So Dr. Menzies and his staff hoped Miss Nightingale and her nurses, discouraged by the cold welcome they received and the dismal quarters assigned them, would just give up and go away.

Florence Nightingale remained calm, kept her own counsel, enforced iron discipline, and seemed if anything to take the doctors' side when the complaints of her nurses began to rain down on her head like water from the roof. Yet how easy it would have been for her to beat a dignified retreat before any of her party had succumbed to the fetid air and cloudy water of the hospital and she had their deaths on her conscience. How easy it would have been to act the woman, to weep, and expostulate, and explain. But since childhood Nightingale had wanted to take care of the sick. Now, throughout the miles of wards and corridors of the Barrack Hospital, men lay dying. As she wrote to Dr. Bowman on November 14: "In the midst of this appalling horror (we are steeped up to our necks in blood)—there is good . . . As I went my night rounds among the newly wounded that first night, there was not one murmur, not one groan, the strictest discipline, the most absolute silence

& quiet prevailed, only the step of the sentry, and I heard one man say, I was dreaming of my friends at home, & another said And I was thinking of them. These poor fellows bear pain & mutilation with unshrinking heroism, and die or are cut up without a complaint. Not so the Officers, but we have nothing to do with the Officers."[17] Florence Nightingale had never had a child of the body, but now the fifty thousand men in the British expeditionary army, here and at the front, became her children of the spirit. This is how she would refer to them for the rest of her life. The men were in terrible need. She would not leave them. She would "identify her fate with that of the heroic dead."[18]

On perhaps the fifth day, the impasse between the doctors and the nurses was broken. Suddenly, more and more casualties poured in from Balaclava, and in consonance with the Panglossian system of asserting that nothing was wrong, the military officers at the hospitals had made nothing ready to receive them. With death and agony on one side and inefficiency and inertia on the other, even the façade of order at the base hospitals broke down. "The wounded are now lying up to our very door, and we are landing 540 men from the [transport ship] 'Andes,' " Florence Nightingale reported to Dr. Bowman on November 14.[19] Terrified, run off their feet, the doctors reached out for help. As he watched the suffering of the sick men lying neglected on the ground, Augustus Stafford, M.P., suddenly found a canteen of water thrust into his hand by one of the medical attendants. Even a Traveling Gentleman spy could help out. Sidney Osborne and his son worked day and night with the dying men, saying prayers, writing last letters to families at home.

Miss Nightingale and those nurses who had experience with wounds appeared with basins of water and clean rags. Bathing and clean clothing would have to wait until Florence Nightingale had managed to introduce baths, hot water, and soap at Scutari. On the days when the sick were being disembarked, Nightingale spent eight or more hours on her knees, soaking off the bloody, dirt-sodden bandages from wounds that had been dressed ten days or more earlier on the field of battle. Meanwhile she set her less experienced and hardy nursing companions to sewing up big bags and stuffing them with straw so that the men need not lie on the cold, filthy, rat-ridden stone floors. Hot soup was served from the nurses' own kitchen. Quiet, calm, authoritative, Nightingale personified order, raised morale, and inspired the orderlies and medical staff to do their best, if only out of shame. Denial at Scutari was ceasing to be an option.

When involved in what we would now call first aid and triage, Nightingale turned first to the men who needed her help most, regardless of rank. This policy, which she observed as nurse and superintendent of nursing throughout her time in the East, went against tradition and entrenched opinion, and it immediately caught the attention of all observers. Officers in the army, gentlemen in civilian society, were accustomed to getting precedence in everything. Nightingale explained her policy vis-à-vis officers most clearly in a note to her aunt Mai of November 16, 1855: "I have never declined to nurse an officer. I have uniformly declined to send them Nurses—to take away a woman from nursing 100 men to sit or lie the 24 hours in an Officer's room, as *they* wished. But *in* the Hospitals, Barrack and General, wherever we were sent for, whether to Military, Medical or Ecclesiastical Officers, Mrs. Roberts & I have always gone. I have farther found (i.e. provided) everything that was necessary. And few have died without me or Mrs. Roberts—& few have recovered without acknowledging us. But I have always nursed an Officer like a Private—that is, visiting him at regular times. If he did not choose to be nursed that way, he was not nursed at all."[20]

In his stirring encomium to Miss Nightingale, Sidney Osborne felt obliged to defend her to his readers on this issue: "I heard a good deal of observation made on the spot, and also since I came home, with regard to the fact that Miss Nightingale and the 'sisters' did not pay the same attention to the wards of the wounded and sick officers, which was given to those of the soldiers; I believe as a rule, Miss Nightingale did consider her own and the services of her 'corps' confined by previous understanding to the soldiers only, though I have known her on special request from a medical officer, cheerfully order small matters of extra diet for a wounded officer."[21] But, observing with astonishment that this well-bred woman did not place the interests of her own class first, the ordinary English soldier began his long love affair with Florence Nightingale.

FLORENCE NIGHTINGALE'S HEART went out to the sick men in the Barrack Hospital, but as her hands were busy cleaning wounds, her mind was scrambling to understand just what had brought them to this hideous condition. Yes, some men showed the terrible effects of cannon and rifle and saber, but the battlefield wounded accounted for only a small proportion of the cases, and these were the most hopeful. The wounded (as opposed to the sick) who came to Scutari were mainly taken into the General Hospital, the doctors showed some interest in them, and their chances of survival were relatively good. As observers were astonished to report, though the wounded were often horribly disfigured and subjected to terrible pain when limbs were amputated or wounds were probed, their morale remained high. They felt like men and heroes, enjoyed recounting their battle exploits, and remained extremely interested in the news of the war, reading the newspaper out loud to one another, to the astonishment of TGs like Osborne, who assumed all the men were illiterate. Most important, the wounded found the energy to look out for one another. Before the arrival of the women, almost all of the nursing in the General Hospital was done by the wounded men themselves. Sarah Anne Terrot, one of the sisters who came out with Nightingale, noted in her diary how one older soldier with a serious thigh wound lovingly fed a young lad who had lost one whole arm and the hand off the other. This boy died on the transport ship home, probably because he had lost the active protection of his comrades in arms.[22]

However, the men sick with disease outnumbered the wounded by ten to one or more, and this population got larger and sicker as the winter progressed. These men sank into an apathy that appalled all observers. Racked with fever, lying in their own filth, their life energies draining away, they were viewed with horror, not compassion. They were spreaders of pestilence, burdens to be borne by the strong. Abandoned, they abandoned hope and died in horrendous numbers. "One poor dying fellow, called Nichols, seemed to be neglected by the orderlies because he was dying," wrote Sarah Anne Terrot in her diary. "He was very dirty, covered with wounds, and devoured by lice. I pointed this out to the orderlies, whose only excuse was—'It's not worth while to clean him; he's not long for this world.' I washed his face and hands, cut away his hair, and tried to make him a little less uncomfortable, and he was so grateful, he would scarcely let me leave him. His eyes were inflamed, and I gave him a little soft cambric rag for them, as he injured them by rubbing them with his dirty hands; in fact, by conveying bad matter from his wounds to his eyes and his face, they had got into a fearfully painful state. His flannel shirt was dark, and seemed moving with lice; it stuck to his bed-sores; he needed a woman's constant care, but I was unable to return to him."[23]

To the great distress of her family and friends, who rightly feared for her life, Florence Nightingale spent many hours a day during that first terrible winter doing individual nursing, and she chose to work predominantly in the fever and dysentery wards, with the most serious cases. Most of the men she nursed died, often within hours of arrival, and as she gazed into those dead faces she struggled to understand why death came so swiftly to young men who had been so full of life and strength when they left England six months earlier. She was sure that army life in time of war, not war *per se*, had killed these men, and one of the things she could do to honor their memory was to work out exactly how that happened and find ways to stop it happening in the future.

THE PROBLEM, as she saw it, lay in the army's failure to protect its men against disease, and to promote their recovery once they fell sick. The failure was in the system, and so, in Nightingale's view, could be prevented if men only found the will and allocated the resources to do so. Efficiency and order were not more expensive than chaos and ineptitude. In her belief in the perfectibility of human institutions like the British army, Florence Nightingale was very much the Great Victorian.

The central issue facing the Army Medical Board in the hospitals at Scutari and the Crimea was an epidemic of several infectious diseases, which no one in 1854 understood. It would be years before Koch and Pasteur came up with the germ theory, decades before their discoveries revolutionized the public health field by introducing good drainage and clean water, many more decades before cure became possible through –antibiotics. For her time Florence Nightingale had done a great deal of serious reading in what might now be called epidemiology, and she had an unusually informed understanding of what was happening at Scutari. For example, she immediately condemned the standard use in the hospitals of a single sponge to wash one man after another, and instructed her nurses to use separate clean rags.[24]

Through her research, Nightingale was familiar with the work of doctors like John Snow and public health specialists like Edwin Chadwick. They had established a causal link between disease and contamination, most notably between cholera and contaminated water, though they were far from identifying the agents. Having worked on a cholera ward, Nightingale knew just how ineffective medical treatment was, and had reached the conclusion that prevention was the best way to approach disease. In other words, at a time when the study of public health or sanitarianism was an avant-garde, hotly contested, deeply unpopular subject in Britain, she was a convinced sanitarian. As she saw it, a healthy man who breathed bad air, drank impure water, and was unable to keep his body clean tended to fall ill. If that man was surrounded by thousands of others living in the same conditions, his illness was easily passed on to them.

On the whole, the officers of the British army were not sanitarians. Army historians had established that in time of war more soldiers died of disease than of wounds and extrapolated that modern armies, which tended to be larger and to be in the field longer, lost more men to disease. However, officers considered such losses to be natural and unavoidable. They preferred where possible to live at a distance from the men in isolated farms and villages, but this pattern of living reflected their habits of privilege not their sanitary theories. Lord Cardigan, who found a charming rustic site and a clean private spring for himself at Varna, and then at Balaclava lived aboard his private yacht, was, in this respect, exemplary of his class. But even though a growing body of evidence indicated that digging adequate latrines, protecting the water supplies from contamination, and keeping the camps as clean as possible cut the army's death rate, few officers had any interest in organizing sanitary brigades. Hence the army was hit increasingly hard by cholera, dysentery, and the debilitating catchall malady known as "Varna fever" and then "Crimean fever." By the end of November 1855, "out of a nominal army of 37,232 men, there were 9,003 sick."[25]

If the British army was too ignorant and careless to take reasonable measures to protect its men against disease, it was culpably negligent in its provision of medical care. At the dock at Balaclava, the wounded and sick had to be loaded into small boats and unloaded into large ships, a difficult business even when the weather was calm. Officers were given cabins while the rest of the men were crammed into every space above-

and below-decks. Frances Duberly watched this happening day after day
with a kind of resigned horror.

> The dignified indifference of the medical officer, who stood with
> his hands in his pockets, gossiping in the hospital doorway,—the
> rough and indecent way in which the poor howling wretches were
> hauled along the quay, and bundled, some with one, and others
> with both legs amputated, into the bottom of a boat, without a
> symptom of a stretcher or a bed, was truly an edifying exemplifica-
> tion of the golden rule, 'Do to others as you would be done by.' On
> board the steam-ship 'Avon,' I hear the sights and sounds are too
> dreadful to imagine. An officer, who was sick on board, tells me the
> wounded men were laid on the deck with nothing but a blanket be-
> tween them and the boards . . . He said the groans and moans of
> those poor creatures, on the first night he spent on board, were
> heart-rending; but the next night the noise had considerably de-
> creased—death had been more merciful to their pain than man.[26]

Almost a quarter of the men loaded onto the ships in the Crimea
that first winter were dead before they reached Constantinople. When
finally unloaded from the ship onto one of the docks at Scutari, the sick
men either hobbled up the hill to the hospital or waited to be carried up
by a small and reluctant group of porters. Once in the hospital, sadly, the
men's trials were far from over.

A good friend of Sidney Herbert, Sidney Godolphin Osborne was a
doctor, an Anglican minister, and a writer for *The Times*. Osborne and
his son arrived in Constantinople within days of the Nightingale party
and one day after John Cameron Macdonald. He was the almoner appointed by *The Times* to disburse the large sum that the newspaper had
solicited from private donors to make good the shortages at the hospitals reported by Chenery and others. Macdonald and Osborne acted as a
team. Osborne (subsequently Lord Osborne) was well connected, and
on arrival he and his son and Macdonald were taken on a tour of the
General Hospital by Dr. Menzies himself. Osborne had worked in public hospitals at home and abroad and he volunteered to work with the
medical officers at Scutari, but Menzies refused his offer, insisting no
help from civilians was needed. When Macdonald asked Menzies for a

list of the most urgently needed supplies so that he could purchase them with money from the *Times* fund, Menzies replied emphatically that "they had everything—nothing was wanted."[27] When the British ambassador Lord Stratford de Redcliffe, under specific instructions from London to purchase anything needed in the hospitals, again asked Menzies to list things he wanted, the reply came in writing that "we are satisfactorily supplied, and more expected daily from England and Varna."[28]

Osborne did not take long to discover that Menzies was lying. Unable to serve in his medical capacity, he went over to the Barrack Hospital and volunteered to act as chaplain. He then found his way to the sisters' quarters and made himself known to Florence Nightingale, who had been there for two days. In this early alliance of Nightingale, Osborne, and Macdonald we see the model of that small but dedicated civilian force that for the ten years after the war would work under Nightingale's leadership to reform the War Office and improve health care in the British army.

As a chaplain, Osborne had full access to the wards and all too many opportunities to exercise his spiritual calling since the men were dying like flies. What Osborne saw appalled him. "These vast hospitals were absolutely without the commonest provision for the exigencies they had to meet . . . there was in and about the whole sphere of action an utter want of that accord among the Authorities in each Department, which alone could secure any really vigorous effort to meet the demands, which the carrying on of war was sure to make upon them. It is quite true, that as ship after ship brought down their respective cargoes of wounded and sick, the Medical and other Officers with Miss Nightingale and her corps of nurses, did work from morning till night, and through the night, in trying to meet the pressure upon their scanty resources; but the whole thing was a mere matter of excited, almost phrenzied energy, wholly inadequate to what was really required."[29]

THIS WAS THE SITUATION that Florence Nightingale found at the Barrack and General Hospitals, and within weeks of her arrival she had made a difference. This was the immediate and unanimous report of disinterested observers who were in the wards before and after her arrival. Augustus Stafford, who was constantly in the hospitals in November and

December, saw this change and talked about it in his memorable speech in the House of Commons on January 29. Sidney Osborne wrote an encomium to Florence Nightingale that made an immense impression: "I do not think it is possible to measure the real difficulties of the work Miss Nightingale has done . . . Each day had its peculiar trial to one who had taken such a load of responsibility, in an untried field, and with a staff of her own sex, all new to it. Hers was a post requiring the courage of a Cardigan, the tact and diplomacy of a Palmerston, the endurance of a Howard, the cheerful philanthropy of a Mrs. Fry or a Miss Neave; Miss Nightingale yet fills that post, and in my opinion is the one individual, who in this whole unhappy war, has shown more than any other, what real energy guided by good sense can do."[30]

Above all, the men in the ranks saw the difference. Robert Robinson came to the Barrack Hospital as a casualty and had an excellent opportunity to compare the situation before and after Nightingale. A Protestant from the North of Ireland, Robinson enlisted with the Sixty-eighth Light Infantry at the age of fifteen, one of the many Irishmen who saw the army as a desirable option following the potato famine of 1847–48. When Robinson disembarked with the rest of the troops at Calamita Bay on the Crimean Peninsula in late August, he was so seriously ill that he was immediately shipped back to Scutari. In the account he wrote of this time in 1860, Robinson notes stoically that he was one of thirteen hundred sick men stacked on board a transport ship designed to carry four hundred that arrived in Constantinople on September 22, a few weeks before the arrival of the Nightingale party. Robinson recovered, and though he was too small and weak to be a stretcher-bearer, he was at hand to watch the debarkation at Scutari from the *Golden Fleece* of four hundred more soldiers, wounded in the Battle of the Alma. "It was a frightful sight to see some of the cases which came ashore that day," wrote Robinson, "& still more frightful to see them lying on stretchers in the passages of the Hospital & the men who were carrying them standing beside the stretchers, sometimes for two hours, waiting for orders where to take the men." From November, Robinson observed, "everything underwent a change for the better. The sick were not kept waiting in the passages but went at once to bed, were washed & had clean linen & were attended as well as in England." This reversal of fortune was due, Robinson specifies, to the efforts of Miss Nightingale and her assistants.[31]

Robert Robinson was Nightingale's man through and through. Noticed as a bright, able boy by Charles Bracebridge, Robinson was taken on as Nightingale's messenger and rarely left her side throughout the next twenty months. He escorted her at night when she crossed the three-quarters of a mile of muddy track between the two hospitals. When she walked the wards at night, he trimmed her lamp for her. When she went to the Crimea, he went with her. When she fell ill at Balaclava, he walked by the stretcher carrying her up to the Castle Hospital, wishing he could bear part of the load or at least hold the sunshade over her head as the colored gentleman Mr. Taylor did. After the war, Nightingale took Robinson into her home for some time and helped him make his way in civilian society. Robinson was not an objective witness, but he probably saw more of Nightingale at work than anyone, and the extent of his devotion to her is in itself a testimony to the surprising connections she was able to make with working-class soldiers.

AS THAT SUPREME ANOMALY, a female very junior officer in a war zone, Florence Nightingale had very little power, but official powerlessness could in some ways count as an asset. As an aging spinster of means, she did not have a career to make or a family to feed, and intellectually she could run rings around any aide-de-camp or embassy man in Turkey.

She would do everything she could, even if it did not stem the tide of disease. She would testify truthfully to what she had seen, keep accurate records and statistics, and make recommendations for improvements based on a shared admission of failure. This attitude of moral superiority and spiritual enlightenment won her the fervent support of some and the undying enmity of others.

Florence Nightingale understood that men did not die at the base hospitals primarily because they received no medical care. Her years of research into international hospital management and medical statistics had taught her that in an epidemic, a European hospital served not to cure or treat but to warehouse the sick, to isolate them from the general population, and to dispose of the dead. Experience in fever hospitals had shown her that the medical profession was largely powerless to prevent, cure, and or treat infectious disease. The reasons for this are obvious to us today. A medical practice that still relied *grosso modo* on bleeding,

blistering, and purging, together with a pharmacopoeia based on opiates, heavy metals, arsenic, and alcohol, would tax the strength of even
the healthy and could prove fatal for the sick. It was not known as
"heroic medicine" for nothing.

Unlike her nurses, Nightingale sympathized with the plight of the
medical officer, but she was convinced that nursing could solve problems
that doctoring could not. She had seen enough sick patients to believe
that the best-case scenario for a person who fell ill was to be isolated from
other sources of contagion, to be spared the rigors of "heroic medicine,"
and to be given constant, intelligent, responsive care. For a wide variety
of illnesses and medical conditions, good nursing at home was more
likely to produce results than even first-class doctoring in the greatest
hospital in the world. In her postwar classic *Notes on Nursing*, which
mainly deals with how ordinary women can keep their loved ones
healthy and out of the hospital, Nightingale would lay out these principles for the general public. But since hospitals were unavoidable for the
indigent and friendless, for the imprisoned and the mad, and for soldiers
in war and peace, the question became how hospital care could be
brought up to the standards of home care. Part of the answer was to bring
women, with their long tradition of caregiving, into public facilities. Today we can see that, in the absence of modern medications, Nightingale's
system of good sanitation on the societal level and good nursing on the
individual level would work in many cases because it would give the patient's immune system its best chance of fighting off disease.

Thus Nightingale arrived at the heterodox view that the men at Scutari suffering from contagious diseases were little worse off than the patients at the major London teaching hospitals at the time, or indeed the
private patients of Harley Street doctors. What the soldiers lacked was
good sanitation, good nursing, and a decent chance to get better. Need I
say that such views, which Nightingale was to argue for the next four
decades of her life, were not apt to ingratiate her with members of the
medical profession?

Finally, Nightingale brought to Scutari a taste for organization and a
talent for getting practical things done fast. From afar, Turkey had
seemed Florence Nightingale's God-given opportunity to get her foot in
the hospital door, and demonstrate and document her theory of nursing. Close up, Scutari proved to be lacking in the most basic elements

needed for good nursing care. And so it became clear to Nightingale that before any nursing could begin, she and her helpers must take on the basic domestic functions that the army was signally failing to address. Within days of arrival Nightingale had embarked on a vigorous campaign to wash the men, feed them regular, digestible, nutritious food, and give them clean clothes, clean sheets and blankets, and reasonably comfortable beds. These were the first, admittedly timid steps toward bringing sanitary principles to the hospitals, but they were steps men might not take. Because they were related to the traditional female roles in society, they might also arouse less opposition.

To clean a patient's wounds you need at the minimum a basin, a washcloth, a towel, and soap. To clean a ward you need at the minimum a broom, a bucket, a scrubbing brush, a floor cloth, and soap. These were to be found in the poorest workhouse in England but not at the hospital at Scutari in November 1854. At Florence Nightingale's instigation, all of these items, together with a hundred other humdrum, essential things, were scrounged up in the markets at Constantinople by Mr. Macdonald and Mr. Bracebridge, using the private funds Nightingale herself had brought from England and the money from the *Times* fund.

Next was the question of laundry. When the soldiers from the ranks arrived at Scutari, they usually had nothing but the shirts on their backs, heaving with lice, and a blanket that had served to cover them through all the horrors of the last six months. To keep the men in clean linen and bedding, the hospital needed a supply of spare shirts, sheets, and blankets. Changing a shirt or sheet was not useful unless there was an efficient laundry to wash them. In her first letter to Sidney Herbert on November 25, Nightingale launched without preamble into an itemization of the problems she saw: "(1) It appears that, in these Hospitals, the Purveyor considers washing both of linen & of the men a minor 'detail'—& during three weeks we have been here, though our remonstrances have been treated with perfect civility, yet no washing has been performed for the men either of body-linen or of bed-linen except by ourselves & a few wives of the Wounded."[32] One of her first acts was to set up large boilers that would destroy the lice, and find women to do the washing who would not steal the sheets.

The provision of food at the base hospitals was so inefficient as to be laughable if the corridors had not been filled with half-starved men.

Whereas most officers had discretionary funds, servants to procure and prepare food, and regular parcels from home, the men from the ranks were dependent on service by the orderlies and on food from the central kitchens. The orderlies lined up at the purveyor's office for several hours twice a day to procure the basic supplies, mainly whole sides of beef, and lamb which they butchered in the crowded corridors and took to the kitchens to be cooked. All the meat, as the orderlies brought it in, was thrown into thirteen vast cauldrons that were removed from the heat and emptied each evening, though never washed out. To distinguish the meat allocated to his service, an orderly tied it in a kind of rough parcel and labeled it with pieces of fabric or metal. All the food got to the men cold; some of it was uncooked, and some of it consisted entirely of bone and gristle. Since most of the orderlies were young and very hungry, they made little attempt to feed men unable to feed themselves. Sarah Anne Terrot saw one orderly eat the rations of eight men.

Florence Nightingale inspected the kitchens and managed to make progress by installing new cooks and encouraging the orderlies to be more prompt. However, when she suggested that the meat might be boned before it was distributed, she was told that that was impossible since it would require a new regulation. Seeing how the men who could eat kept tight hold on a precious plate or mug and tore their food apart for want of cutlery, she set about providing everyone with cup, plate, knife, fork, and spoon. All these items had already been issued to the men, but were then abandoned in the knapsacks the men were ordered to leave on the transport ships at the beginning of the campaign.[33] Under army regulations, any item issued was the man's individual responsibility, sick or not, and he had to replace it at his own expense if lost. It was over regulations like these that Florence Nightingale was close to coming to blows with the purveyor's office.

Leaving the central kitchen problem for the time, Nightingale concentrated most of her human and financial resources on preparing and supplying extra diet items in her own kitchen, especially soups, beef tea, jellies made from fruit and meat, thin cereal, and various concoctions based on wine. The healing properties of wine were universally lauded by the medical authorities of the day, and in this respect Florence Nightingale was of her time.[34]

Feeding sick, undernourished men at no extra cost to the army might seem an unexceptional innovation, but Nightingale soon discovered that the operation of an extra diet kitchen was a highly controversial and politicized act at Scutari. The most important single thing the medical officers did for the rank and file patients was to determine each day which of three diets each man should receive on the following day, if he was still alive and able to eat it. The full diet consisted of one pound of meat, one pound of potatoes, one pound of bread, two pints of tea, and half a pint of porter. Half diet was half of this. Light or spoon diet consisted of one pound of bread and two pints of tea plus, at the surgeon's discretion, two or three from a list of extras that comprised chicken, mutton chops, arrowroot, sago, rice, and lemons for lemonade.[35] The fact that surgeons were often too busy or too lazy to fill out the daily diet rolls accurately and that men often went hungry was irrelevant. Drawing up the diet rolls was the doctors' prerogative. On the other hand, the doctors had no power over the commissariat and the purveyor, and if these gentlemen refused to provide the items the doctors requested, that was their prerogative.

It was obviously a matter of supreme importance to the patients who should receive extra diet items, and since the items on the extra list were notoriously unavailable from the purveyor, anyone who could supply them became a person of great popularity and even power in the wards. Thus the nurses' ability to provide extra diet meals was viewed with dark suspicion. Florence Nightingale tried to skirt this particular minefield, which endangered her whole policy of rapprochement with the medical officers, by decreeing that no food item should be supplied to a patient that a doctor had not requisitioned in due form and that the purveyor had not declared in due form to be unavailable. The fact that on many occasions she knew the doctors failed to make the requisition out of carelessness or malice, knew positively that the item requested in fact sat in the purveyor's storeroom, was not to the point. Through her personal efforts and the private and governmental funds she commanded, essential needs would be met in part, if tardily.[36]

By December it was clear to the medical officers and the orderlies that if they wanted anything on their service, from morphine to lint to stump pillows, they could get it from Miss Nightingale without flouting any regulations. Her quarters became the hub of the whole hospital system. Frances Margaret Taylor, who came out with the Stanley party in December, described them in her memoir as the Tower of Babel. "In the middle of the day everything and everybody seemed to be there; boxes, parcels, bundles of sheets, shirts, and old linen and flannels, tubs of butter, sugar, bread, kettles, saucepans, heaps of books, and of all kinds of rubbish; then the people, ladies, nuns, nurses, orderlies, Turks, Greeks, French and Italian servants, officers and others waiting to see Miss Nightingale; all passing to and fro, all intent upon their own business, and all speaking in their own tongues."[37]

The mystery of the disappearing supplies was one that sorely plagued the officials of the army and the Treasury back in London. Tons of lint, hundreds of beds and basins and brooms, thousands of shirts and socks and comforters had been sent out from England. Menzies, eyeing the official cargo dockets provided by the Commissariat and Purveyor, insisted that nothing was lacking, and Lord Stratford took his word for it. Chenery and Osborne and Stafford and Nightingale insisted that everything was lacking. Where did all that stuff go? In her letters to Sidney Herbert, Minister at War responsible for purveying the army as well as her personal friend and ally, Nightingale endeavored to clear up the mystery.

Things sometimes went down in ships when they sank, as in the famous case of the *Prince,* but more commonly things were stolen. They disappeared into the Turkish customs offices, to furnish the homes of officials or reappear in the markets of Constantinople, where Nightingale's representatives Bracebridge and Macdonald, as well as purveyors to the French army, could buy them again. Theft, by local people or the eternally scavenging French allies, whether at Constantinople, Scutari, or Balaclava, accounted for a high percentage of losses. Goods sent to the East were often unlabeled or mislabeled and so never delivered. They were usually packed in the wrong order, so that morphine or bandages for Scutari was placed under ammunition, taken to Balaclava, and never seen again.[38] When items did find their way into the storerooms of Mr. Wreford, the paralytically ineffective Peninsular War veteran in charge of purveying at Scutari, they sat for weeks, waiting for the paperwork to be completed. A board must needs be convened to officially determine that goods had arrived and whither they should go, and convening a board was no small matter. Since all the customs sheds were insecure,

Nightingale recommended that the government should establish an off-shore hulk staffed by reliable, active clerks sent out specially from England, in which all the goods brought out would be placed, checked, reorganized, and rapidly distributed. She also made detailed recommendations as to how the wards should be stocked and the medical attendants made responsible for keeping track of them.[39]

Nightingale's letters to Sidney Herbert were devoted in no small part to lists of things lacking. Thus a final postscript in her long letter of December 15 reads: "I must again refer to the deficiency of knives and forks here, the men tear their food like animals. The Medical Officers request me to state that boxes of Sheffield cutlery, say 1000 knives & forks 1000 spoons should be sent out immediately—as there are none in store. I will meanwhile do what I can in Constantinople to stop the gap."[40] On December 21 she wrote acerbically: "Dear Mr. Herbert, The brain is wanting at home in the combination of the authorities between the purchasing & shipping & sending off & landing, not only here. The 'Army & Navy' [a ship] is just reported with nothing but Hospital Clothing & Bedding on board not an utensil of any kind. The head or the will is wanting in the Admiral here. Twelve days ago, in obedience to requisition from Balaklava, stores of Arrow-root, Sago etc. were shipped on board the 'Medway' for Balaklava where everything is deficient, with the promise that the 'Medway' would sail the next day. The 'Medway' is still here & her hold is filled with things *above* the Medical Stores. The hospital at Balaklava is still in want. This morning I foraged in the Purveyor's store—a cruise I make almost daily, as the only way of getting things. No mops,—no plates, no wooden trays (the Engineer is having these made)—no slippers, no shoe brushes, no blacking, no knives & forks, no spoons, no scissors (for cutting men's hair which is literally alive, & for the Hospital Serjeants)—no basins, no towelling—no Chloride of Lime."[41]

Through the offices of *The Times,* which loved to assert that its funds were supplying the army, the shortages at Scutari and at Balaclava were headline news in Britain, and the name Florence Nightingale was voiced abroad as a symbol of sanity and efficiency. In late December, Queen Victoria wrote a personal message of concern for the men, which she begged Miss Nightingale to make known. The Queen also asked what she could send as extra comforts—perhaps the men would appreciate some eau de cologne since the smells at the hospitals were said to be so unpleasant?

This question of extra comforts for the men was one that people of all classes in Great Britain were anxiously asking, and for the whole of her time in the East Nightingale took on the extra and onerous duties of almoner of the free gifts. She was responsible for receiving, acknowledging, storing, and distributing parcels of miscellaneous items in every shape and size. If only they would save the postage and just send her money, she privately complained to Herbert. And yet, contradictorily, when the Palmerston government recommended selling off the contents of the parcels, she protested vehemently. All over England, she pointed out, from the Queen down to the village seamstress, people were worrying about the men and expressing their love and concern in little parcels. The value of the parcels was not monetary. When a man got a pair of mittens or a few ounces of tobacco he knew that someone had thought about him. If the public was to learn that its parcels were being sold off by the army for pennies, the news could bring the government down. As Queen Victoria, who regarded the army as a primary concern of her own and who ordered that Nightingale's letters be sent to her, once remarked: "We are very much struck by her . . . wonderful, clear, and comprehensive head. I wish we had her at the War Office!"[42]

In one of two long letters written on Christmas Day 1854, Nightingale wrote to Herbert: "The things we want are (1) Socks 1000 prs. I get them also by the 100 from Const[antinopl]e.) (2) Flannel 10,000 yds or Flannel shirts, as you prefer. (3) Slippers 2000 prs. Warm shoes I would suggest for the troops. But that is not my affair as Deputy Inspector of Hospitals. (4) Drawers & Mitts the Doctors suggest—you will judge. (5) Soap ad libitum—the soap here is bad. (6) Knives & forks & spoons. 3000 more beside what we asked for. (7) Cocoa Nut Matting with the long pile such as is used for mats to clean feet in Workhouses is most necessary here, where our *Sick* corridors become by feet of Orderlies like muddy roads. (8) Air cushions 100—fifty round with a hole in middle— for bedsores. But the Queen ought to give something which the man will feel as a daily extra comfort which he would not have had without her. Would some woolen material do cut up into comforters for the neck when the man begins to get out of bed? . . . Or a brush & comb for each man? Or a Razor for each man? As to the Eau de Cologne, a little gin & water would do better."[43] Who but Florence Nightingale could have permitted herself this last remark about the gin, in a letter the Queen was likely to read?

In this Christmas Day letter Nightingale gives herself an official title—deputy inspector of hospitals. In fact this title was never hers, though she exercised the functions the actual inspectors, like Menzies and Hall, shirked. In her letters to Herbert, Nightingale allowed her anger and frustration to show, and her dismissal of powerful men like Admiral Boxer and her tone of irritated admonishment to Herbert himself are startling. Historian Trevor Royle calls her a "bossy-boots."[44] But in person, on the wards, Nightingale remained calm, cordial, and polite whatever the provocation, and was famous among her nurses for never raising her voice. This combination of strategies was extremely effective, and Nightingale's capacity as a leader awed her friends and put the fear of God into her enemies.

Nightingale's willingness to cut through red tape and take boldly entrepreneurial measures became especially obvious in December. Facing the imminent arrival of hundreds of even more debilitated men in a hospital crammed to overflowing, Nightingale planned, organized, and in the end paid out of her own pocket for a team of two hundred Turkish carpenters to refloor and refit the side of the Barrack Hospital that had been destroyed by fire. When news of this executive *coup de main* reached Balaclava, Colonel Anthony Sterling thought it the most extraordinary piece of female effrontery he had ever heard of. Nightingale's power had become in his view "fabulous." Lady Stratford, who had failed to get the carpentry work done, was deeply affronted by Nightingale's preemptive move, as was her lord, the ambassador.

But when the men whom Sarah Anne Terrot describes as "miserable skeletons devoured by lice" arrived at Scutari, now suffering from severe frostbite as well as the usual wounds, bedsores, fever, and dysentery, they were all bathed, issued clean linen, put in clean beds, and fed good food by gentle nurses.[45] A high percentage of these men still died since, for all Nightingale's efforts, the Barrack Hospital was crawling with infection. But what was the alternative? Leave the men on the transport ships until death had cleared a space for them on the wards and then let them in turn die in their rags?

PURVEYING TO THE ARMY until the new Palmerston government could get its act together was a virtuoso display of administration, entrepreneurship, and negotiation. That a woman could do such things evoked wonder in the minds even of Nightingale's enemies, but in fact this was probably the easiest part of her work in Turkey. She happened to be very good at this kind of job. Where once she had carpets laid and jam made at Harley Street, now she got a mile of floor laid and fed extra diets to hundreds. Writing long reports to government ministers, making careful recommendations in the matter of training orderlies or lading ships, was a profound satisfaction to her, even if it had to be done in the small hours of the morning after a long day. She knew she was laying out a detailed road map of how the purveying problems could be solved not just in the hospitals but at Balaclava. There the besieging British army was being decimated by hunger, cold, and disease even as they watched the Russians reinforce the fortifications around Sevastopol. In the months ahead, when the government commissioners arrived with powers to act, Nightingale had the satisfaction of seeing many of her recommendations put into force.

But it was as a nurse, sitting by the bedside of a sick man, the personification of feminine compassion and maternal solicitude, that the British public liked to imagine Florence Nightingale, and that image, though partial, was not false. For at least half of her twenty-one months in Turkey and the Crimea, Nightingale spent as many hours a day as she could on individual patient care. On the days when hundreds of new patients were disembarked from the transport ships, she was the nurse who worked the longest hours and was one of the most effective. During the first, terrible winter, she took on the neediest cases in the most neglected areas, and when one of the other women fell ill, she took on those patients with her own. Nightingale was famous among the medical staff for appearing when least expected and most needed. At Christmas, when cholera had broken out in the Barrack Hospital, Sarah Anne Terrot observed two doctors quarreling over a dying man, while Florence Nightingale, without saying a word, ran to fetch a hot-water bottle and then rubbed the man's feet until he could feel no more. As Osborne tells us in his book: "Her nerve is wonderful; I have been with her at very severe operations; she was more than equal to the trial. She has an utter disregard of contagion; I have known her spend hours over men dying of cholera or fever. The more awful in every sense any particular case, especially if it was that of a dying man, her slight form would be seen bending over him, administering to his ease in every way in her power, and seldom quitting his side till death released him."[46]

Little of what the nurses, Florence Nightingale included, did at Scutari was nursing in our modern sense, and Nightingale's duties as a nurse shaded into her work as an administrator and purveyor. It would seem that the first wards in the General Hospital she personally was allowed access to were those dedicated to the wounded. These were, by common consent, the wards where the surgeons spent most of their time and where the men most often recovered. All the same, when Nightingale saw the surgeons cutting off men's limbs in full view of their comrades, she felt that the soldiers were being unnecessarily traumatized. She managed to find some screens and arranged for them to be put around the beds of men undergoing amputation. One of the most appreciated and least romantic things she did was to get the buckets of human waste in the wards emptied regularly. Orderlies, unsurprisingly, had little appetite for this job, and so she would stand by the vats until the men were shamed into carrying them out.[47] The image of Florence Nightingale standing patiently next those large, open, portable privies was not one that appeared in the pages of *The Times,* but it is the kind of thing the men remembered.

Another, indirect way in which Florence Nightingale improved patient care in the wards was in her effect on the orderlies. These were usually young soldiers detailed by their regiments, much against their will, to serve in the hospitals. The orderlies were under the command of their regimental officers, who, understandably, entered the hospitals as little as possible, and the staff surgeons had no authority over them. If an orderly kicked a man because he groaned too loudly, ate the men's rations, stole from the dead and incapacitated, slept soundly all night when supposed to be on duty, and played leapfrog over the men in the corridors for a bit of fun, there wasn't much a doctor could do. According to regulation, nurses could influence the conduct of orderlies only by example, or by taking on the tasks the men found most unpleasant. Florence Nightingale was the personification of domestic order, the mother, mistress, and teacher whom the young men respected. When she appeared on a ward, things might get done properly.

Florence Nightingale was an outstanding nurse. She was ready to dress the most appalling wounds or stuff lint into a spurting artery until a surgeon appeared. She was undeterred by the terrible physical deformities of the wounded. Nightingale was possibly the only nurse routinely authorized by the doctors to give the drugs that had been prescribed. She was also unusually good at treating bedsores, having had a good deal of experience with this problem with her elderly relatives and neighbors. She liked to do massage, a comforting therapeutic technique she had learned at such fashionable spas as Harrogate and Malvern and which was not in the repertoire of the army surgeons and orderlies. Nightingale would also bring water, beef tea, and jelly; she would wash parts of the man's body in an attempt to make him more comfortable; she would change a shirt or a sheet, wipe away sweat, and supply that comfortable old staple of British home life, a hot-water bottle.

But much of what she did was psychological, and here none of her nurses could come close to her. Nightingale was funny, an expert mimic, full of weird information, interested in everything, and she had always found it easy to get on with men. With her cultivated voice, graceful demeanor, and modest but elegant dress she was obviously a lady, and to be nursed by a real lady was, for these intensely class-conscious British men, a kind of tonic in itself. The men could see that Miss Nightingale liked them, even admired them, and they liked her and admired her in return.

Nightingale talked to the men, listened to them, and, especially for the dying, wrote letters. These hundreds of letters written to loved ones in England on behalf of sick or illiterate men were sometimes accompanied by little parcels containing the man's personal effects. She also wrote letters on her own account, telling the families at home of a man's illness and the circumstances of his death. Nightingale ensured that these letters were mailed, and paid the postage out of her own pocket. Sometimes, when she knew circumstances in a soldier's home were especially hard, she included a few banknotes. How wonderful it was that she finally had five hundred pounds a year of her own money to spend as she liked![48]

For Nightingale, nursing was a practical imperative and a spiritual exercise, providing a nexus of body and soul that gave her the deepest satisfaction. It was, in her own words, "the great serenifier."[49] The physical reality of the men kept her grounded, banished all her doubts, and eased her anxieties. When she was weary of arguing with the purveyor, writing letters to ministers, listening to the complaints of a nurse, or coping with the ego of a doctor, she found strength at the bedside. Florence Nightingale did not believe that God wanted or intended men to suffer, and she was fiercely convinced that the job of a nurse was to relieve the physical suffering of others, not to save her own soul by tending the sick. At the same time, she had a bedrock certainty that death was only a transition to another level of existence. Therefore, tending the dying did not hold the horror for her that it holds for most of us.

As an administrator, as a substitute purveyor, as a superintendent of nursing, Florence Nightingale helped to save many lives and ease many others. I would put that number in the thousands. As a nurse, she personally saved a few lives, perhaps dozens. But by her own account and that of others, she closed the eyes of hundreds of men, since she chose to devote herself to the most desperately ill patients. Nightingale knew that the final, ineluctable role of the medical attendant is to give solace to the dying and that this too must be done well. To nurse was also to hold a hand, to look with love, to be there for the dying. And since at the Scutari hospitals, with their large, crowded wards and echoing corridors, no act could be private or unobserved, the men saw the way she had with their living and dying companions, and they were grateful. A handful came forward fifty-five years later to carry Florence Nightingale's coffin.

Late at night, when all the nurses and doctors had gone to bed, when the orderlies on duty were usually sound asleep, Florence Nightingale walked the four miles of beds, a small Turkish lamp in her hand, stopping to talk or meet some simple request. "One night, a soldier of seventeen years old, sobbing with pain and crying for his mother in England as he had cried to her when he was a little boy, felt someone bend over him and heard a gentle voice say: 'Let me kiss you for your mother.' "[50] But mostly the men lay quiet and watched.

Florence Nightingale began to walk the wards at night within days of her arrival at Scutari. What began as an exploratory tour of inspection turned into a routine and then into a ritual. It symbolized the covenant between her and the men, and they understood its meaning very well.

In perhaps the most famous single passage in the Nightingale legend, one man wrote home: "What a comfort it was to see her pass even. She would speak to one, and nod and smile to as many more; but she could not do it all you know. We lay there by hundreds; but we could kiss her shadow as it fell and lay our heads on the pillow again content."[51]

The British soldier's feelings of thanks and reverence of Florence Nightingale are perhaps best expressed in two stanzas from a popular ballad that was circulated during the Crimean War:

> On a dark lonely night on Crimea's dread shores
> There'd been bloodshed and strife on the morning before;
> The dead and the dying lay bleeding around,
> Some crying for help—there was none to be found
> Now God in His mercy He pitied their cries,
> And the soldiers so cheerful in the morning do rise.
> Refrain
> So, forward my lads, may your hearts never fail
> You are cheered by the presence of a sweet Nightingale.
>
> Her heart it means good for no bounty she'll take,
> She'd lay down her life for the poor soldier's sake;
> She prays for the dying, she gives peace to the brave,
> She feels that a soldier has a soul to be saved.
> The wounded they love her as it has been seen,
> She's the soldier's preserver, they call her their Queen.
> Refrain
> May heaven give her strength and her heart never fail.
> One of Heaven's best gifts is Miss Nightingale.

Chapter 17

WOMAN TROUBLE

The greatest frustrations Nightingale met in her Crimea venture came in her dealings with other nurses, and her Achilles' heel was her failure as superintendent of nursing to build a cohesive, effective, contented female team.[1] Of the original thirty-eight women who accompanied Nightingale out to Turkey, some dozen returned to England within weeks or even days of arrival. Of the Norwood nuns Nightingale wrote, more in sorrow than anger: "Excellent, gentle, self-devoted women, fit more for Heaven than for a Hospital, they flit about like angels without hands among the patients, and soothe their souls, while they leave their bodies dirty and neglected. They never complain, they are eager for self-mortification. But I came not to mortify the nurses, but to nurse the wounded."[2] So the Norwood nurses too did not stay long.

Nightingale had trouble with women in the Crimea in part because her relationships with women in general were often tortuous. Since infancy, she had had a love-hate relationship with her mother and her sister, and this formed a template for all her intimate relationships with women. Overall, Nightingale despised women of her own class. When she did find a friend, Nightingale tended to laud her to the skies, but when the friend failed in some way to be what Nightingale expected or to satisfy her needs, the relationship turned cold. Each of the five great female friends of Florence Nightingale's life—her aunt Mai Smith, her aunt Julia Smith, her cousin Hilary Bonham-Carter, Mary Clarke Mohl, and Selina Bracebridge—were all for many years adored and considered

Florence Nightingale, "the Bird," supervises the work of an "angel" nurse.

indispensable, only, in the end, to be unaccountably, unforgivably set at a distance.

Forced intimacy with strangers placed Nightingale under stress. At Scutari the women were obliged to live very much on top of one another, and this was very difficult for her to endure since she had an almost obsessive need to be alone. At the same time, she had never in her life been without the company of family or close friends, and being among strangers was also unnerving. Both the need for solitude and the need for sympathy, by which she meant total, empathetic support, were at the core of Florence Nightingale's being. As a child she never went to school. As an adult she opted out of social events as far as she was allowed, and her experience with group living and teamwork was limited. Accustomed to thinking and acting in isolation, Nightingale was far too passionate, too opinionated, too focused, and at the same time too erratic to be comfortable in a large group of strange women.[3]

Above all, Nightingale failed as superintendent of nursing because as soon as she arrived at the Barrack Hospital, her priorities changed in fundamental ways that her female companions for the most part neither understood nor accepted. For a decade or more, establishing nursing as an honorable profession for women and proving herself as a professional leader had been of consuming importance to Nightingale, but now, at Scutari, nursing, in and of itself, faded into the background. In the short term, Nightingale saw that her job in Turkey was to alleviate the suffering of the men. To do this she wanted only women who would directly and quickly help her. Anyone else was expendable. In the middle term, she was determined to address, if not solve, the purveying problems of the army, which she saw would pose a terrible threat to the men camped on the plains above Balaclava as winter drew on.[4] In the long term she aimed to try to prevent the kind of suffering that had occurred—not only at Scutari but on the Crimean Peninsula—from happening in the future.[5] Reform of the army health care system, not nursing, was the cause that absorbed Nightingale, and her relationships with other nurses now hinged on their capacity to help or hinder.

Once she realized how much damage the ill will of the other women could do to her work on every level, Nightingale worked extremely hard on restoring good relationships and building trust, but certain resentments only grew with time.

BUT IF NIGHTINGALE refused to be charming and needed to learn by bitter experience how to lead women—she proved to have a natural talent for leading men—the nurses she had to deal with were difficult. As she herself explained in a letter to Benjamin Hawes in April 1855: "Forty women, living closely packed in narrow quarters under new discipline & in a barrack—women too whose tempers & habits are unknown—present *great obstacles to management.*"[6]

The women who took the risk of going out to nurse in the Crimea and at Scutari were, like Nightingale herself, of strong character. In general, women in Victorian England had little experience of working in business or administration and tended to identify themselves as individuals or family members, not as colleagues or co-workers. With the exception of the Catholic nuns and possibly the Anglican sisters, discipline, collegiality, and team spirit were not qualities society asked of its women. Even in the domestic hierarchy, women were far more inclined to take orders from men than from women. A cook in a large household would defer to the butler but would often have the upper hand with her "mistress." Thus in the hospitals a woman would, however disapprovingly, obey the orders of a doctor but would be reluctant to "take a hint," in Nightingale's phrase, from another woman, especially if that woman was of lower class.

In fact to call the women who came under Nightingale's superintendency "nurses" implies a common identity that she ardently wished them to adopt but which the women themselves fiercely denied. The women who went out East to nurse fell into three main categories—ladies, sisters, and nurses. The categories were distinct to all observers and identified on the wards by dress. Ladies—who in this respect included Nightingale—wore a plain, serviceable version of normal middle-class dress. The Roman Catholic nuns wore the highly distinctive habit of their order, even if the trains, flowing sleeves, and headdresses were hardly functional in the Barrack Hospital.[7] Some of the Anglican sisters, like Sarah Anne Terrot and Elizabeth Wheeler, were ladies, and all sisters aspired to be ladies, but they cared more about religion and the competition with the nuns than class, and so they too usually wore the uniform of their order. Nurses, much to their chagrin, wore the uniform designed for them by Mrs. Herbert's interview team, who themselves were, of course, not just ladies but Ladies. This uniform was intended to be unattractive; it served the key purpose of distinguishing the nurses from the "camp followers."

Florence Nightingale aroused resentment and resistance in the other women for three main reasons. First, she had no interest in marriage and was convinced that a key barrier to the employment of educated middle-class women in public hospitals was the promiscuity that had hitherto marked relationships between female nurses and medical personnel. Second, she was deeply contemptuous of women of her own privileged class and, while hardly an egalitarian, was good at forming relationships with sensible, efficient, hardworking women regardless of class. Third, she had an ecumenical religious philosophy radically at odds with that of most of her contemporaries.

Nightingale's goal as superintendent was to ensure that when they went on the wards, all the women obeyed orders and worked hard, even if the tasks were unpleasant and menial. This is what Nightingale herself did. She also expected the other women to respect her authority, and she demanded discipline. This system, as she herself referred to it, tended to rub the other women the wrong way. If all the women did the same things on the wards, and were seen to do so, the class barriers between them would be blurred, which the ladies hated. If nurses could not take a drink when they needed one and were forbidden to have a bit of a laugh with the orderlies, the job was nothing but a grind. If the women had to be constantly busy and spend their time looking after the men's physical needs, what time and energy would the sisters have for their spiritual mission? And why should any woman obey another woman who wasn't her mother, her Mother Superior, or the mistress who paid her wages?

At the Barrack Hospital at Scutari, Nightingale was determined to prevent the other women from forming sexual relationships with doctors, staff soldiers, or convalescents. Victorian England found the picture of a single, unrelated woman tending to the physical needs of a virile young soldier to be erotic. Furthermore, in 1854, a woman who married almost inevitably dropped out of the workplace or was dismissed, so when a nurse married she ceased to be a nurse, which for a superintendent of nursing was provoking. However, it would be idle to assert that what could be called Nightingale's anti-fraternization policy was based solely on logic and tactics. There were personal forces behind it too. From her teenage years, Nightingale had found in nursing a way to sublimate sensual feelings that she had been taught were sinful. Having espoused nursing as her divine vocation, Nightingale was unsurprisingly intolerant of women who saw it as a means to find a husband or, worse, a lover. She was especially hostile if the amorous women were middle-class like herself. Of course, Florence Nightingale's attempt to stop men and women from falling in love in the Crimean hospitals was doomed. The puritanical regime she imposed upon the nurses under her authority is, I think, one of the main reasons why so many people, male and female, held her in such antipathy during the twentieth century. Young women believed it was their right to consort with whom they chose and identified marriage to a doctor as a way to find happiness and move up in society. Hence they deeply resented Florence Nightingale's attempt to equate nursing with chastity. Today, as increasingly strenuous efforts are under way to keep love and sex out of the workplace, it could be argued that Florence Nightingale was ahead of her time.

Social class was an ongoing, absorbing concern for most of the women at Scutari. The ladies and the Anglican sisters may have nursed, but they emphatically did not wish to be called "nurses," since "nurses" were common and were paid for their work. In truth, there was no mistaking a nurse for a lady. Nurses had seen the seamy side of life, were inclined to take a drop too many, and enjoyed giving people a piece of their minds. In other words, they were the kind of persons middle-class women employed as cooks and maids but did not take tea with. The ladies and sisters also tended to look down on the nuns for being Roman Catholic and Irish. English Catholics, though reviled as religious traitors, were indisputably high-class, but Irish society was divided, more or less, between upper-class Protestants and lower-class Catholics. Thus the Anglican sisters felt it necessary to ignore the nuns and "cut" the nurses who were living and working alongside them.[8]

Florence Nightingale would have none of this. At Scutari, she often expressed her appreciation for the work the nurses did, and she was tolerant of their failings. Certainly she kept a close eye on them. Certainly she sent home any nurse whose taste for drink or men interfered with the performance of her duties. Certainly she got cross when nurses who had proved their worth found husbands in the wards and gave in their resignations.[9] But on the whole Miss Nightingale was warm and human toward her nurses. In report after report she said that the nurses consistently did the best job. She also understood their financial problems and did her best to make life easier for them. One of the many support functions Fanny and Parthe Nightingale performed for Florence during the war was to make sure the dependent relatives of the Scutari nurses were all right, and to find good positions for the nurses themselves when they returned home. In return for her consideration and praise, the nurses tended to like Miss Nightingale.[10] She was the kind of fair, appreciative, supportive lady employer they were all looking for, and they knew how to handle her.

Nightingale's willingness to cross the class barrier in her female friendships was demonstrated most clearly in the close relationship she developed in Turkey and the Crimea with Elizabeth Roberts. Mrs. Roberts (all the nurses were given the title of "Mrs." even when they were not married) was Nightingale's age or older, and a pioneer of nursing for women. She had for a number of years worked with surgical cases at Kings College Hospital and proved to be unusually good at the job. At some point, however, the doctors at Kings decided that only male dressers would be employed in such work, and Roberts was put back to doing the menial domestic work of the typical nurse. Eliza Roberts thus had special reasons for volunteering to go out to Scutari. Watching Mrs. Roberts dressing the wounds of men in the General Hospital at Scutari, senior medical officer Dr. Cruickshanks commended her. None of the dressers or assistant surgeons was nearly as skillful, he said. But all the same, Cruickshanks refused to allow Roberts to do such work on his service, at least when he was watching. "It is not a question of efficiency, nor of the comfort of the patient," Cruickshanks remarked, "but of the Regulations of the Service."[11]

Nightingale admired Roberts's expertise and envied her experience. Here at last was a woman she could learn from, a tireless worker and a reliable colleague. When it came to bedside nursing, Roberts became Nightingale's right-hand woman, and their working relationship developed into friendship. In the famous painting by Jerry Barrett, "Florence Nightingale Receiving the Wounded at Scutari," Elizabeth Roberts, wearing the Scutari nurses' sash, is shown kneeling to give a cup of water to a soldier on a stretcher, directly beneath the figure of Florence Nightingale.[12] Roberts joined the Bracebridges and the boy Robert Robinson in Nightingale's inner circle and accompanied her wherever she went. But Nightingale's closeness to Roberts was not likely to conciliate her with the middle-class sisters. And indeed, when Mai Smith came to replace Selina Bracebridge at Scutari, Smith's letters to the Smith-Nightingale family at home reveal an undercurrent of dissatisfaction and even jealousy in her references to Mrs. Roberts.

Of the groups of women who originally accompanied her from England, Nightingale was closest to the five Roman Catholic nuns from the Bermondsey convent in England who came out with their own superior, the Reverend Mother Mary Clare Moore. She was intelligent, active, well educated, and a member of a religious house that had known a number of remarkable women leaders. When Moore showed herself willing to become, in effect, Nightingale's chief lieutenant, when she accepted Nightingale's conditions, especially in regard to proselytizing, the other nuns buckled down and did any job that was assigned to them. Uncomplaining, cheerful, hardworking, reliable, sober, disciplined, selfless, and loved by the men, Catholic and Protestant alike, they personified the nursing virtues and in Nightingale's eyes served as both an example and a rebuke to the other women.[13]

If Florence Nightingale was warm and forgiving toward the nurses and rapturously appreciative of the nuns, she was usually stiff and judgmental toward the Anglican sisters. A number of sisters believed they had come out to Scutari to figure as angels of mercy, not to work as chambermaids, but Florence Nightingale construed their conduct as laziness and indifference. She found it hard even to be polite to them. The sisters were surprised and upset by this turn of events. At the outset they surely felt that they and Miss Nightingale shared the same vision and would have the closest relationship. Like the sisters, Florence Nightingale was an Anglican; indeed, had she not been a member of the Church of England, she would not have been sent out as superintendent of nursing by the British government.

It was in the area of religion, however, that Nightingale and the Anglican sisters really fell out. Though proselytizing had been explicitly forbidden in the instructions Sidney Herbert had given to the nurses, in fact conversion, especially of the Roman Catholic soldiers, was number one on the High Anglican sisters' agenda. Their essential concern was with the men's souls, not their bodies, and they saw nursing as a way to pave their own personal way to heaven. They assumed Miss Nightingale would feel as they did.

The idea that an Anglican sister might take the opportunity given her as a nurse to make a last-minute conversion of a Roman Catholic soldier, or a Roman Catholic nun of a Protestant soldier, made Nightingale angry. Deeds, not dogma, were what mattered to her. She believed in God with all her heart; she had been born an Anglican Protestant in an Anglican Protestant culture and intended to stay that way because she believed that denomination did not matter.

To the Anglican sisters, the idea that denomination did not count and that they were not missionaries was bewildering, even heretical. When they saw Miss Nightingale commend the work of the Bermondsey nuns, when they saw her closeness to the Reverend Mother Moore, they inevitably concluded that secretly she was of the papist persuasion, and they spread the word through their communities.[14] The religious affiliation of the women nurses in the war zone, especially of their leader Miss Nightingale, became a matter of national debate. Nightingale wrote to Sidney Herbert in January: "I never look at *The Times,* but they tell me there is religious war about poor me there & that Mrs. Herbert has generously defended me—I do not know what I have done to be so dragged before the Public. But I am so glad that my God is not the God of the High Church or of the Low—that he is not a Romanist or an Anglican—or an Unitarian. I don't believe He is even a Russian—tho' His events go strangely against us."[15]

Nightingale's great champion, the Reverend Sidney Godolphin Osborne, was obliged to defend her: "That she has been equally kind and attentive to men of every creed; that she would smooth the pillow and give water to a dying fellow creature who might own no creed, I have no doubt, all honour to her that she does feel that hers is the Samaritan's, not the Pharisee's work. If there is blame in looking for a Roman Catholic priest to attend a dying Romanist, let me share it with her—I did it again and again. Those who walked that field of suffering, had too many pressing calls on every energy which could be enlisted to save pain to the body, to stop to question the faith of the sufferers. It was not the least frightful of the many features of that awful scene, that the demand for active physical help, did sadly interfere with the aid which would have been cheerfully given in higher matters. We all did what we could in both; but this was a hospital, Miss Nightingale and her staff were nurses, cooks, purveyors; they were not, they could not be, but in a very minor degree—missionaries."[16] Here was the gospel according to St. Florence.

EVERYTHING GOT FAR WORSE in December when Nightingale's former personal friend Mary Stanley arrived with a large and disparate group of ladies, Roman Catholic nuns, and nurses. When Florence Nightingale first got wind of the departure of this party, she tried in vain to stop them. Herbert, who had given the party his permission, received the brunt of her bitter complaint. She accused Herbert of reneging on the written agreement between them that more nurses would be sent *only* if she asked for them in writing. This she had certainly not done. "You have sacrificed the cause, so near to my heart. You have sacrificed me, a matter of small importance now. You have sacrificed your own written word to a popular cry . . . You must feel I ought to resign, where conditions are imposed upon me which render the object for which I am employed unattainable—& I only remain at my post till I have provided in some measure for these poor wanderers. You will have to consider where the 22 are to be employed—at Malta, Therapia or elsewhere—or whether they are to return to England—& you will appoint a Superintendent in my place, till which time I will continue to discharge its duties as well as I can. Believe me, Dear Mr. Herbert, ever yours very truly . . ." Having got that off her chest, she went on to write a lengthy postscript, repeating that she had never asked for more nurses, that the proportion of Roman Catholics in the Stanley party would enrage almost everybody, and asking for a thousand knives, spoons, and forks, immediately![17]

To say Florence Nightingale was overwrought is clearly an understatement, and the two letters she wrote to Herbert about the Stanley party have become exhibit A in the case against her. Poor, diligent, overworked, Minister at War Herbert, with his bad kidneys! Here he was doing his job and the Duke of Newcastle's, assailed by press and public, trying his best to sort out the mess in the Crimea and salvage the reputation of the government he served with. What had he done but send out reinforcements to a woman who claimed to be fighting a desperate battle against terrible odds? Surely Charles Bracebridge in a letter had spoken for the superintendent of nursing in opining that more nurses would take some of the strain off poor Florence's shoulders. Mr. and Mrs. Nightingale had been so upset to hear that Flo was doing so much actual nursing—eight hours a day on her knees, General Bentinck had reported—and begged to know why she had so little help. Herbert had merely tried to do the best for everyone. Lytton Strachey was only the first in a line of male critics who have felt that Sidney Herbert was a saint to put up with a harpy like Florence Nightingale!

The brouhaha over the Stanley party was not Florence Nightingale's finest hour, and Sidney Herbert and his wife, Elizabeth, showed great forbearance in their response.[18] As Elizabeth Herbert wrote to her dear friend Selina Bracebridge just after Christmas: "My own Σ, what *is* come to her [Florence Nightingale]? In the same way she takes copies of her letters to us, it seems. Are we then become her enemies? People of whom she is suspicious and afraid? We have not so dealt by her. We have not a single letter that we have written to her, and Sidney naturally feels as hurt as I do. The whole matter is painful and unaccountable to the last degree. But perhaps it is wholesome for us to be reminded that she is *still a mortal,* which we were beginning to doubt."[19]

On the other hand, Mrs. Herbert was wrong even to suspect that Miss Nightingale protested so vigorously because she saw Miss Stanley as a rival. Mary Stanley was exactly the kind of woman—privileged, idle, self-absorbed, disorganized, untrained, undisciplined, demanding—that Florence Nightingale had been trying to get away from all her life. She saw her as a nuisance, a troublemaker, and a burden and events proved her to be absolutely right. But Florence Nightingale's private rhetoric was usually more intemperate than her public actions, and when the Stanley party arrived she decided (reluctantly) to do all she could for its members.

Miss Stanley and Miss Nightingale had known each other for some years and seemed to have a great deal in common. They had met in Rome, under the auspices of the Herberts and the Bracebridges, at the time in Florence's life when she was talking of conversion with her beloved Madre Santa Colomba. The Stanleys were an upper-middle-class family with strong roots in the Anglican episcopacy and the Oxbridge intelligentsia. However, Miss Stanley was increasingly under the influence of that ecclesiastical spellbinder and recent convert to Catholicism, Henry Manning. If Miss Stanley converted to Roman Catholicism, it would be a coup for the emergent Catholic party in Britain and a large feather in Manning's cap. And perhaps she could secure what Manning himself had not—the conversion of their friend, Florence Nightingale, now famous the world over.

In many ways Stanley's health care services résumé, if I might call it that, was more extensive than Nightingale's. Mary Stanley had been deeply involved in the preparations for the departure of the Nightingale party for Turkey and was one of the ladies who interviewed the nurses and designed their uniform. There can be no doubt that she knew quite precisely that Sidney Herbert had contracted with Florence Nightingale that no more nurses should be sent out to Turkey unless she specifically requested them. Nonetheless, Miss Stanley and her friends, enchanted with their interviewing role, continued to entertain applications from women desirous of going out East to nurse. Within weeks of the Nightingale party's embarkation, a second, larger, and even more disparate group of women had been identified as nurses for the Crimea, and Miss Stanley had been prevailed upon to lead them. She had persuaded herself that her dear friend Flo would greet her with open arms, accept her as colleague, and, not incidentally, share her glory. As O'Malley notes with great perspicacity: "Next to Manning, the friend who gave [Mary Stanley] the most emotion was Florence Nightingale, who inspired in her the passion which is not incompatible with sub-conscious envy."[20]

Miss Stanley's party was larger than Miss Nightingale's, but it included no Anglican sisters. The twenty-odd nurses had by common consent even less hospital nursing experience than the first group and were perhaps even more inclined to follow the worship of Bacchus. The ladies saw their mission as a spiritual one, imagined themselves hovering about the bedsides of attractive young officers, and intended to work strictly in a supervisory capacity, though their supervisory capacities were at best unproven. The nurses and the ladies had been told by Miss Stanley that she and Miss Nightingale had worked together in hospitals but had never been friends, since Miss Nightingale was generally lacking in religious feeling and had distinctly Romish tendencies, which Miss Stanley said she could not condone.[21] If the fifteen Irish nuns heard this casuistical remark, they no doubt smiled.

In fact, before she left Turkey in April 1855, Mary Stanley had secretly become a Roman Catholic. I say secretly, in the sense that she had made no announcement of her act to her family in England. The news of her conversion was known to virtually the whole English colony at Scutari except Lord and Lady Stratford, whom Miss Stanley could not afford to alienate.

The Aberdeen government gave the Stanley party fifteen hundred pounds to meet their expenses, but when the group arrived in Constantinople in early December all that money had been spent, and serious disputes had already broken out between the different factions. The first thing Miss Stanley did on arrival was to present her compliments to Dr. Cumming, the new chief medical officer in the base hospitals. In the eyes of all parties, this established *ab initio* that Miss Stanley saw herself as an equal to Florence Nightingale and not a subordinate.

The Stanley party was escorted by two young upper-middle-class gentlemen, Mr. Jocelyne Percy and Dr. John Meyer. Mr. Percy and Dr. Meyer came to see Miss Nightingale and were dismayed by their reception. Miss Nightingale was icily calm, Mrs. Bracebridge was upset, and Mr. Bracebridge was raging mad. It was Charles Bracebridge's letter to

Sidney Herbert that had apparently precipitated the arrival of the Stanley party, and Bracebridge felt he had been misunderstood and indeed betrayed by his friends at home. Miss Nightingale told the visiting gentlemen in person what she had already told Herbert in her letters: there was no room in the hospitals, the doctors were refusing to accept any more nurses, and there were no houses to rent in Scutari. When Meyer and Percy revealed that their party was now without financial resources and that Cumming had declined to pay their expenses in Turkey, Miss Nightingale said that she too had received no instructions from the government about the Stanley party. She was not free to use government funds without authorization, but she would agree to lend ninety pounds out of her private purse.

On December 21, Miss Stanley finally herself made her way to the Barrack Hospital, sure that everything could be speedily resolved if only she and dear Flo were together again. As she reported in a chatty letter to Liz Herbert, she was charmed to see for herself Miss Nightingale's quarters, as these had already achieved almost legendary status from reports in *The Times*. People hurried in and out asking Florence questions about a hundred matters of business, while she herself continued to write a letter to Mr. Herbert since it was mail day. Flo was in splendid health, Mary reported, dressed in black merino trimmed with black velvet, clean linen collar and cuffs, apron, and white cap under a black silk handkerchief. This was not the kind of detail that Florence herself was imparting in her letters to Mr. Herbert.[22]

Both Miss Nightingale and Mrs. Bracebridge were civil to Miss Stanley and offered her coffee, but they were not helpful, and Miss Stanley returned to her ship in the harbor. She was very tired of being cooped up on board with a set of squabbling women. When it became clear that no accommodations for the forty-eight members of the Stanley party were forthcoming in the base hospitals, and when the physical realities of those places impinged in the shape of a fierce attack of fleas, Miss Stanley was rowed over to Therapia to take tea, counsel, and consolation with Lord and Lady Stratford.[23] The ambassador and his wife proved gratifyingly sympathetic. Room was found for Miss Stanley and her companions at the Palace or Seraglio convalescent hospital at Therapia. Lady Stratford was all too ready to agree that Miss Nightingale had grown far too big for her boots, had lost the last shreds of gentility and womanly charm, was such a bore, and so forth. On the subject of money the ambassador was less forthcoming.

In the end, Florence Nightingale gritted her teeth and negotiated. The most accommodating and useful of the women who had come with Mary Stanley could replace some of those now living in the Barrack Hospital who wished to go home or had proved unsuitable. If Mother Bridgeman would agree to divide up her nuns and put them under Miss Nightingale's superintendency, some of them too could find a place at the big base hospitals. When Mother Bridgeman absolutely refused, Miss Stanley proposed her own plan. Ten of the Irish nurses should work in the base hospitals as assistants to the Roman Catholic chaplains, and ten of the ladies would do the same for the Anglican chaplains. Miss Nightingale told Miss Stanley that only Dr. Cumming could approve such a plan, and he categorically refused. Then in January, when the number of men coming in from Balaclava rose even higher, a new hospital was opened up at Koulali.[24] On January 29, Miss Stanley and the bulk of her party moved from Therapia to Koulali. Dr. Meyer's connections in England secured him the position of head of the new civilian hospital at Smyrna.[25] Mr. Percy returned to England. Florence Nightingale wrote to Sidney Herbert on December 31: "Mr. Percy has sneaked home like a commander who has set so many Robinson Crusoes on a desert island and said 'Now you will shift very well for yourselves.' "[26]

Nightingale officially renounced all authority over the Koulali hospital, which was lavishly supplied and furnished at the behest of Lady Stratford, who at one time presented the War Office with an unitemized and unsupported bill for eighty-five hundred pounds. Expenditure per patient was some four shillings a day at Koulali as opposed to one shilling at the other base hospitals.[27] Miss Stanley ran the nursing at the hospital according to her own system, and it was disaster for all concerned. Miss Stanley did not manage to set up extra diet kitchens or laundries, and she exercised no discipline over the other women. The army kept shipping men in from Balaclava who kept dying, and conditions on the wards were so horrid that after two days Miss Stanley could not bear to go near them. Asking for money from the government was an odious business, and the ninety pounds from Florence in December, followed by another draft for four hundred more did not go far. As for keeping accounts, who had a head for it? The nurses spent their time drinking and flirting with the orderlies or else acting as ladies' maids. The ladies wafted around aimlessly, "pottering and messing about with little cookeries of individual beef teas," as Nightingale cuttingly put it in a letter to Sidney Herbert. None of them paid Miss Stanley any mind. When Dr. Cumming came to inspect the hospital at Koulali he was most rude, wrote a dreadful report, and refused Miss Stanley's request to bring out more ladies from England to help her. At least dear Lady Stratford was sending her over food from the embassy, since army rations of stringy meat and sour bread had proved quite inedible.

The drama of Miss Stanley's rebellion against her own faith also proved short-lived. The Reverend Mother Bridgeman, who was really not someone a lady would usually associate with, proved more intransigent and demanding by the day. Everyone at Scutari and Constantinople disliked Mary Stanley and told dreadful stories about her conversion. Miss Stanley's family at home were ready to complain when Miss Nightingale refused to give her government funds, but they too were not sending their errant daughter much hard cash. Finally Mr. Sabin, the senior chaplain at the Barrack Hospital and a great friend of Flo's, summoned by Lady Stratford to hear of Miss Stanley's many woes and worries, took it upon himself to tell Lady Stratford that Miss Stanley was secretly become a Catholic. Once the Stratfords turned against her, Miss Stanley's position in Turkey became quite impossible, so, after much tedious discussion, she appointed one of the other ladies in her place, packed her bags, and took ship.[28]

Mary Stanley returned to England in early April, a bitter and vengeful woman. Nothing had worked out as she had planned, and it was all Florence's fault. Florence, who had once been such a chum, had turned cruel and cold. She refused to let Mary into that charmed inner circle at the Barrack Hospital with Selina and Charles and that unaccountable person, Mrs. Roberts. Attack was always the better part of defense, so Mary Stanley in London at once began to intrigue against Florence Nightingale. She presented herself in the guise of one who loved and was wronged by a woman she had thought a friend. To maintain all her religious and social options, she kept the fact of her conversion a secret.[29] When Florence, during her convalescence in the summer of 1855, was obliged to send her employee Miss Salisbury back to England in disgrace, Miss Stanley took that lady's part. Yet all the while, Mary Stanley wrote to Florence repeatedly, vowing eternal friendship. Such a course of action was not just mean and dishonest, it was stupid. Everything Miss Stanley did in England was reported quickly to Miss Nightingale in Turkey.

In October 1855, Mary Stanley wrote to Florence Nightingale, affecting a tone of equality and common interests, seeming even to patronize her friend.

> I wish you had come back in the summer. It would have enabled you to go back to work with added experience. I feel myself how much I have learnt since I returned which would have greatly helped me had I gone back to the East. Through Lady Coltman I heard you were now turning your attention from the bodily to the moral diseases. I greatly rejoice to hear this. You know how earnestly I desired to combine the two, and grieved when you told me that your War Office instructions only recognized you as a nurse and the morale was not your province. So far I have written to you in your official capacity. Now I go back to my own Florence of past days who I will not believe is lost in the Florence of the public. Would that I could have you up in my rooms as of old and talk over the wondrous chapter of life that has passed over us in this year. Dearest Florence, if I have given you pain by any words or deeds of mine, I heartily ask your forgiveness . . . In lonely hours I feel all you have been to me, I miss the words of sympathy that used to cheer me . . . My conflict continues. I have not moral courage enough to brave my family's pain over the step [i.e., conversion to Catholicism] I would take at once were I free. If you hear the deed is done, contradict it. Would it was. I am half crazed by the difficulty of being honest on the one side and paining those I love on the other . . . God bless you, my dearest friend, and give me one line to say you still love me.

On the envelope of this letter Florence Nightingale wrote: "Does she know that she lies? Does she know that I know that she lies? Does she know that I know that she knows that she lies? Is she 'mad, bad, or silly?' " Her reply to the letter was as follows: "December 19th [1855] I have no Mary Stanley and to her whom I once thought my Mary Stanley

I have nothing to write. She has injured my work. She has damped my courage to pursue it by the grievous blow of finding want of faith in her whom I so loved and trusted."[30]

But Mary Stanley would not give up. She continued to write to Florence Nightingale, nine immense letters. Finally, in January 1856, Florence found the words to put an end to it. "I have nothing further to say. And for explanation I refer you to yourself. I have nothing to forgive. There has been no 'difference' between us, except a slight one as to the distribution of articles, and the manner of doing so to the patients. The pain you have given me has not been by differing nor by anything for which forgiveness can be asked, but by not being yourself, or at least what I thought yourself. You say truly I have loved you. No one will ever love you better. Florence Nightingale."[31]

Chapter 18

SPRING AT LAST

As winter in the Crimean Peninsula wore on, greatcoats, boots, woolly drawers, knitted socks, sweaters, mitts, and the now famous "Balaclava helmets" began arriving at the port for the men. Each officer was to receive in addition a fur cloak, a pea jacket, and a fur cap.[1] Getting the new winter clothes from the congested and polluted Balaclava harbor up to the camps was still very difficult, however. The famous Russian mud made the steep road almost impassable, and horses and oxen were so few and so weak that they could not get up their own forage. "Let an araba [a local cart] once stick or break a wheel or an axle, and the Zouaves [French infantrymen] sniff it out just as vultures detect carrion," wrote William Howard Russell, war correspondent to *The Times*. Russell commented on the horrible profusion of dead horses all along the road between port and camp. Some of the carcasses had been torn apart by wild dogs, while others had been skinned and even sliced up for meat by the French scavengers, a barbaric thing in the eyes of the horse-loving Irishman Russell.[2]

In January, an international team of laborers of the newly constituted Land Service Corps arrived at Balaclava and began the brutally hard job of building not just a road but a railway line that would carry the heavy ammunition and weaponry to the front. In the meantime the army was still living on mud under canvas and suffering severely from malnutrition, frostbite, and the deficiency diseases Nightingale called "scorbutus." The flood of men going down to the port to be transported to the hospitals at Scutari swelled. Russell, though he looked hard for news of improvement to encourage people at home, could not resist describing one grisly scene he had witnessed:

> Before Sevastopol. Jan. 23. There was a white frost last night. . . . A large number of sick and, I fear, dying men, were sent into Balaclava today on French mule litters and a few of our bât [packsaddle] horses. They formed one of the most ghastly processions that ever poet imagined. Many of these men were all but dead, with closed eyes, open mouths, and ghastly, attenuated breath, visible in the frosty air, alone showing they were still alive. One figure was a horror—a corpse, stone dead, strapped upright in its seat, its legs hanging stiffly down, the eyes staring wide open, the teeth set on the protruding tongue, the head and body nodding with frightful mockery of life at each stride of the mule over the broken road. No doubt the man had died on his way down to the harbour. As the apparition passed, the only remarks the soldiers made were such as this,—'There's one poor fellow out of pain any way!' Another man I saw with the raw flesh and skin hanging from his fingers, the naked bones of which protruded into the cold air, undressed and uncovered. This was a case of frost-bite, I presume. Possibly the hand had been dressed, but the bandages had dropped off.[3]

Florence Nightingale and her nurses were waiting to receive these men in the newly clean beds with the laundered sheets, but these skeletons heaving with lice defied her best efforts, and she came close to despair. "Yesterday and the day before, the frost-bitten men, landed from the 'Golden Fleece' exceeded in misery anything we have seen—they were *all stretcher* cases, and the mortality is frightful, thirty in the last twenty-four hours in this hospital alone. One day last week it was forty, and the number of burials from the Scutari hospitals seventy-two. We bury every twenty-four hours."[4] As she herself would demonstrate after the war in the famous coxcomb diagram that plotted mortality in the army in the East between April 1854 and March 1856 against mortality in Manchester, the unhealthiest of all British cities, "in January 1855 the Annual rate of Mortality per 1000 was 1174; a higher rate than that which prevailed during the month (September) when the Mortality was highest in the year of the Great Plague, 1665."[5]

The number of amputations at the General Hospital picked up sharply as men lost their limbs not to cannonballs but to frostbite. It was all so tragically unnecessary, and in a letter to Sidney Herbert of February 5, 1855, Florence Nightingale pointed the finger of blame. "The hospitals of Scutari are only the result of the want of transport in the Crimean, as consequence follows cause. Had there been any body to draw the novel inference that after autumn comes winter,—that roads would be wanted to bring the provisions etc. from Balaclava to the camp, the sick from the camp to Balaclava—that forage is necessary to keep horses alive as well as men, & that where the forage is, there should the horses be also, Scutari would never have existed on the gigantic scale of calamity it does now."[6]

But the tide was turning. Spring was coming to the Crimea, and wildflowers in profusion were springing up all around the carcasses of men and horses on the plains above Balaclava. On February 19, Florence Nightingale reported to Sidney Herbert: "The last few days have made a marked improvement in the health of the patients—whereas in the first days of February we buried 506 from the Hospitals at Scutari alone, on the ninth day 72—during the last twenty-four hours we have lost only ten (out of twenty-one hundred in this [i.e., the Barrack] Hospital)— only thirty (out of the whole of the Hospitals of the Bosphorus). It is not much more than ½ per cent."[7]

The religious feuds in the various hospitals continued to rage.[8] Sweet, mild, devoted Sister Sarah Anne Terrot created a furor when she claimed she had observed one of the nuns rebaptizing a Protestant soldier on the point of death. This was exactly the scenario that Florence Nightingale had feared from the outset. The doctors were livid, and ever more hostile to the employment of female nurses in army hospitals. Nightingale had the greatest difficulty in calming everyone down.

In her letters to Herbert, which were now real letters rather than official reports since he was no longer a member of the cabinet, Nightingale spoke her mind more and more freely: "A great deal has been said of our [i.e., her own] 'self-sacrifice,' 'heroism,' so forth. The real humiliation, the real hardship of this place, dear Mr. Herbert, is that we have to do with men who are neither gentlemen, nor men of education, nor even men of business, nor men of feeling, whose only object is to keep themselves out of blame, who will neither make use of others, nor will be made use of."[9]

But the very extravagance of her grumbling in letters to a sympathetic friend shows that Nightingale was in fact emerging from the valley of the shadow and looking to the future with renewed hope and zest. On February 22, out of the blue, she floated a radical new scheme—to set up a medical school in an abandoned kiosk on the esplanade above the Barrack Hospital. She would pay out of her own pocket to prepare the building for occupancy, and then doctors would come out from England, armed with their own scientific instruments, and both teach and do research. With a scientific zeal that would have frozen the hearts of her sister or Miss Stanley, Nightingale saw in Scutari "the finest opportunity for advancing the cause of medicine & erecting it into a science." She meant, presumably, that there was an ample supply of patients with all kinds of interesting problems, to say nothing of dead bodies. Nightingale was also anxious for the army medical officers to begin keeping proper medical statistics. The French army medical corps already did this routinely. "There is here no operating room," she wrote to Sidney Herbert, "no dissecting room, post mortem examinations are seldom made . . . (the ablest Staff Surgeon here told me that he considered that he had killed hundreds of men owing to the absence of these) no statistics are kept as to between what ages most deaths occur, as to modes of treatment, appearance of the body after death etc. etc. etc. & all the innumerable & more important points which contribute to making Therapeutics a means of saving life & not, as it is here, a formal duty." In other words, Florence Nightingale wanted the army to use the current calamity to make real progress in treatment of diseases and wounds.[10]

ON MARCH 5, Florence Nightingale wrote to her family: "Dear people, I saw Athena last night. She came to see me. I was walking home late from the Genl. Hospl. Round the cliff, my favourite way, & looking, I really believe for the first time, at the view—the sea glassy calm & of the purest sapphire blue—the sky one dark deep blue—one solitary bright star rising above Constantinople—our whole fleet standing with sails idly spread to catch the breeze which was none—including a large fleet of Sardinians carrying up Sardinian troops—the domes & minarets of Constantinople sharply standing out against the bright gold of the sunset, the transparent opal of the distant hills (a colour one never sees but in the East) which stretch below Olympus always snowy & on the other side the Sea of Marmora when Athena came along the cliff quite to my feet, rose upon her tiptoes, bowed several times, made her long melancholy cry, & fled away—like the shade of Ajax—I assure you my tears followed her."[11]

Athena's ghost was the herald of better times. In the first week of March, Florence Nightingale was heartened by the arrival in Constantinople of powerful new allies, in the shape of two royal commissions. There was a commission on the provision of supplies in the Crimea, headed by Sir John McNeill and Col. Alexander Tulloch.[12] There was also a sanitary commission, led by Dr. John Sutherland, Dr. Hector Gavin, and Mr. Robert Rawlinson, a civil engineer. The two commissions represented the most radical attempt so far by the new Prime Minister, Lord Palmerston, to bring the government's will to bear on the Crimean war zone. The McNeill-Tulloch commission grew out of the parliamentary inquiry into the state of the army before Sevastopol, known usually as the Roebuck committee. The sanitary commission was the brainchild of Palmerston and his son-in-law Lord Shaftesbury, both convinced sanitarians who had received digests of Nightingale's reports and letters to Sidney Herbert.[13]

Lord Shaftesbury's most important contribution in the matter of appointing the sanitary commission was to ensure that it had teeth. Shaftesbury persuaded his father-in-law, Palmerston, to give broad executive powers not only to McNeill's commission on supplies but also to Sutherland's sanitary commission. Lord Shaftesbury drafted the sanitary commission's instructions in his own hand, and the commissioners' authority exceeded that of the army officers, both medical and regimental, in the war zone. If Sutherland decided to get the drains at the Barrack Hospital cleaned out, he had the power to go over the head of the army commandant, Lord Paulet, and order the engineers to do the job. If Sutherland decided the wards were overcrowded, he could go over the head of Dr. Cumming and get half the beds moved out. To give civilians such power over army matters was unheard of, and Palmerston found it necessary to keep part of his instructions to the Sanitary Commission secret from officials in London and in Turkey, and even from Queen Victoria.

The new commissioners who arrived in Turkey in early March thus possessed powers that Florence Nightingale had only dreamed of. For months, she had longed for men with ideas, energy, and ability who were prepared to risk their careers to save lives, and in Sutherland, McNeill, Rawlinson, and Tulloch she found them at last. Thus the commissioners had a joyful meeting of minds with Florence Nightingale, became her firm allies, and followed a concerted strategy for the rest of the war. After the war, several of these men became key members of the "kitchen cabinet" she gathered around her to strategize and lobby for health care reform in ever larger areas of British society.

Historians have unanimously acclaimed the work done by the McNeill and Sutherland commissions. In her written testimony before the 1857 royal commission, Florence Nightingale credited them with saving the army in the Crimea, a pardonable hyperbole. However, Rawlinson, Tulloch, and especially Sutherland had to pay a big price for their idealism, their hard work, and their success in curbing mortality from disease when the army itself had failed to do so. One of the blots on the record of the British army high command and the army medical service is that they sought to protect themselves by blackening the names of all the commissioners, including that of the veteran diplomat McNeill, and blocking the professional advancement of both Sutherland and Tulloch.[14]

PALMERSTON CHOSE a remarkable team of men to go out to Turkey. Sir John McNeill was a brilliant, witty, urbane Highland Scot of tremendous charm. Trained as a doctor, McNeill had a distinguished career as a diplomat, serving as minister plenipotentiary in Persia for many years. After returning from the East McNeill served as Poor Law commissioner in Scotland and was credited with limiting the dire effects of the failure of the potato harvest in that country. Florence Nightingale thought the world of McNeill, and they would remain friends and allies until his death.

Alexander Tulloch was a little younger than McNeill, a career army officer who had spent years in India. Tulloch was an enthusiast and an idealist. Like many people of his generation in England and the United States, he had strong feelings about nutrition, and was convinced that good health was correlated with good bread. One of the first things that Tulloch did on landing in the Crimean Peninsula was to set up a bread oven, get some flour and yeast, and demonstrate exactly how to produce a good loaf.[15] Tulloch's other great interest, one that obviously endeared him to Florence Nightingale, was medical statistics. When the statistical section of Tulloch's report was suppressed by the minister of war, Lord Panmure, because it was considered too damning, Tulloch published it as part of his 1857 book, *The Crimean Commission and the Chelsea Board.*

John Sutherland was a young man in comparison with McNeill and Tulloch, a medical doctor but one who fervently espoused Edwin Chadwick's doctrine of sanitation. He too was a Scot, but not a charming diplomat like Sir John. O'Malley says he was "hot-tempered, strong-headed, tenacious," qualities that had long been needed at Scutari. He was also erudite, eccentric, and, to judge by his letters, very funny. Dr. John Sutherland became Nightingale's medical advisor while he was in Turkey, and for the rest of his life he was to be her most devoted, if not her most appreciated, ally and assistant.

McNeill and Tulloch spent little time in Constantinople. Their business lay at Balaclava and on the plains around Sevastopol, but they had time to talk at length with Florence Nightingale. McNeill and Tulloch were extremely able men, they had been given unusual authority, and they were highly motivated to succeed. For these very reasons, they recognized expertise when they saw it, welcomed information, and were willing to strategize with someone more familiar with the issues than themselves. And they were not afraid to take advice from a woman.

In the Crimea, the effect of the commission's recommendations was rapidly felt. McNeill's charm and intelligence oiled the wheels of reform, and since money had suddenly become a matter of no object to the British government, the harbor at Balaclava was cleaned up and its shipping and docking reorganized with amazing rapidity. The streets of Balaclava were cleared up, the carcasses of dead animals were burned and buried, and something, one hopes, was finally done about the tragic condition of the Turkish soldiers and citizens, supposedly Britain's allies. Such quantities of supplies of every kind now flowed to the British army camps on the plains that the depredations of the rats and the French became quite tolerable. Cannonballs and rifle shots still continued to take their toll as the siege of Balaclava continued, and cholera raised its ugly head as soon as the weather turned hot again. But in the allied armies around Balaclava, there was now time and energy to stage horse races, attend concerts by the magnificent military band of the Piedmontese contingent, plan picnics at picturesque local sites like St. George's monastery, and arrange for Mother Seacole of the English Hotel at Kadikoi to cater elaborate dinners for officers. Army life in the sweet interludes between battles was once again seductive.[16]

Meanwhile, the Sanitary Commission had divided into two groups, with Sutherland remaining at Scutari and Hector Gavin going to the Crimea, where his brother was in active service. Tragically, Hector Gavin killed himself accidentally when taking hold of his brother's pistol. The engineer Robert Rawlinson was struck on the head by a cannonball on the plains above Balaclava and was obliged to return to England. Given these events and the determined resistance to reform of John Hall, the chief medical officer in the East, sanitary reforms in the Crimea received a setback. Nonetheless, the combined efforts of the McNeill commission and the Sanitary Commission brought results.

The remaining director of the Sanitary Commission, John Sutherland, brought all his energy and stubborn determination to bear on the General and Barrack Hospitals. There the sanitary way had already been paved by Florence Nightingale. Sutherland brought with him from England a team of gentlemen who rejoiced in the title of "inspectors of nuisances" and specialized in drains and privies. One inspector proudly reported that he had with his own hands cleaned out the privy of the commandant, Lord Paulet, and laid down the correct charcoal filter. The inspectors descended into the bowels of the hospitals and discovered the huge sewer festering underneath the buildings. They set about clearing the refuse and dead animals, created a clear air passage, and re-engineered the flow of sewage into the sea so that the stench from the drain did not back up into the privies and thence into the wards. All the walls in the hospitals were whitewashed, a broad passage was cleared through the corridors, the reflooring of the wards and corridors that Nightingale had begun was completed, and the windows were repaired and opened up. For the first time clean sea air circulated throughout the hospitals, though the patients were also carefully protected from drafts. Fleas, rats, and lice continued to be a problem, but they were a problem everywhere in Turkey, and one that many Englishmen dealt with in their daily lives.

By May 1855, the base hospitals at Scutari had metamorphosed into model institutions that French and other foreign visitors toured with admiration and envy. There were now specialized army hospitals at the former sultan's palace, at Koulali, and at Smyrna, so the wards and corridors at the Barrack and General Hospitals were no longer crammed to overflowing with sick men. At Renkioi a new, revolutionary hospital was started, designed as a series of separate pavilions by the famous British engineer Isambard Kingdom Brunel. This establishment opened in October and was closed in February and served only 1,321 patients. However, Florence Nightingale, among others, inspected it with enormous interest and became convinced that a cluster of small pavilions, not one enormous building, was the best way to serve patients and avoid the transmission of disease.

IN THE SPRING OF 1855 Nightingale and Sutherland at Scutari found another unexpected but not unimportant ally. This was the Frenchman Alexis Soyer, a chef of international renown, best known for his work in England at the Reform Club. Soyer was a fascinating man who fancied himself as a writer almost as much as a cook, and in 1857 he published a book about his experiences during the Crimean War called *Soyer's Culinary Campaign*. On February 4, Soyer read in *The Times* of the continuing poor condition of the English soldiers, and he impulsively wrote to the newspaper declaring his readiness to go out and teach the men how to prepare simple nutritious food. Soyer had already done some work along these lines during the Irish potato famine, when he instructed philanthropic English ladies in how to make good, cheap soup. One of those ladies was Florence Nightingale's irrepressible aunt Julia Smith.

Over the next weeks Soyer engaged in a whirlwind of visits, gaining interviews with Mr. and Mrs. Herbert, with Lord Panmure and his deputy Sir Benjamin Hawes, with Lord Shaftesbury, the Duke and Duchess of Sutherland, Isambard Kingdom Brunel, and others. He was strongly advised to stay at home, since the risk of dying from contagious disease was so high, but he persisted, and managed to design and get a prototype built of a camp oven, which he planned to introduce to the average soldier bivouacking on the plains above Balaclava. Soyer's greatest difficulty was in persuading someone to go with him as his secretary, but this was solved on the very day of his departure when he met "T.G."

in the street. T.G. agreed to pack up and be ready to leave in two hours, and twenty friends of T.G.'s turned up at the station to wish him and Soyer bon voyage. It all reads very much like a real-life version of Jules Verne's *Around the World in Eighty Days*—but some three decades *avant la lettre*.

"T.G."—or Mr. Taylor, as the Robert Robinson memoir once refers to him—is one of the many surprising elements in the Crimean story, for T.G. was a "coloured gentleman." For a time in Soyer's memoir, T.G. figures rather prominently, and we get a glimpse of what it was like to be a "coloured gentleman" traveling in Europe in 1855. Sleeping the first night in a coastal inn, Soyer thinks he has lost his pocketbook, so he sends T.G. back on the train to retrieve it. No sooner has T.G. left than Soyer finds the pocketbook behind his bedstead and sends word via the railway company for his secretary to return at once. However, the railway passengers and officials jump to the conclusion that T.G. has stolen Soyer's pocketbook, and he has to be extricated from the hands of the law. Once T.G. and Soyer are reunited, there seems no difficulty in their traveling together in the same compartment, sharing a hotel room, or eating together in very expensive restaurants.

Unfortunately, once he arrives in Turkey, T.G. fades from the picture, though other accounts specify that when Soyer accompanied Florence Nightingale on her first expedition to the Crimea, he had his "coloured" secretary with him. Oddly, when Soyer describes how Florence Nightingale, stricken down with fever, was taken from on board the *Robert Lowe* and carried up to the Castle Hospital, he places neither himself nor T.G. on the scene. In his unpublished memoir the young Irish messenger boy Robert Robinson noted specifically that Soyer's secretary went with Nightingale and protected her from the fierce sun with a parasol.[17] It would be so interesting to know why T.G. decided at a moment's notice to go to the East with Alexis Soyer, what had made them friends, and what happened to him thereafter.

On his way to Constantinople, Soyer got the recipe for bouillabaisse in a top restaurant in Marseilles, visited the birthplace of Napoleon at Ajaccio (a gentleman's kitchen, he notes in relief), and at the Parthenon cooked on his new camp oven a "petit déjeuner à la fourchette" for his shipboard friends. All these adventures he communicated to the British public in a letter to the *Illustrated London News* telegraphed in from

Athens. Finally, however, Soyer reached Constantinople, and as he steamed through the Bosphorus he was chastened to observe the immense size of the Barrack Hospital at Scutari and to calculate the thousands of soldiers expecting culinary miracles from him.

If we were to believe his own account, Alexis Soyer found the officials he met in Turkey uniformly charming, helpful, and accommodating. Soyer seems determined to offend no gentleman who might later be a restaurant client. From other accounts it emerges that Soyer was given the brush-off by army and embassy officials who saw him as a comic character, not a culinary savior. The idea that a French gourmet chef could have a worthwhile effect on camp and hospital cookery appeared ludicrous. Of course, it was also possible that, if M. Soyer were to take a look at the kitchens in the Scutari hospitals, the honor of a great nutritionist would prevail over the prudence of a professional restaurateur and Soyer would write another damaging exposé of life for the men at Scutari for the British press. Fortunately for Alexis Soyer, Florence Nightingale was thoroughly receptive to his ideas and respectful of his expertise, and once he threw in his lot with her he began to make progress.

Nightingale had long been anxious to radically change the preparation of rations for the men in the hospitals, and in Soyer she found the perfect tool to get what she wanted. Soyer toured the kitchens at the Barrack Hospital and was appalled both at the filthy state of the great cauldrons the men's meat and tea were prepared in and by the fact that once the meat was boiled, the nutritious cooking liquid was thrown away. Alexis Soyer had his own book of easy recipes for inexperienced cooks, and he could both demonstrate and teach how to make basic ingredients taste better. Like Nightingale, Soyer was to remain in the East, shuttling between Constantinople and Balaclava, until the summer of 1856. Though his recipes did not always find favor with the British soldier, Soyer's culinary genius, unflagging energy, and cheerful acceptance of risk and hardship made him a good companion for Nightingale as well as a valuable ally.

When Florence Nightingale set off for the Crimea in May 1855, Soyer and T.G. accompanied her, but shortly before that departure Soyer was summoned to the Barrack Hospital for a dinner with Nightingale's great ally among the MOs, Dr. MacGrigor. After the dinner, Soyer made his way out from the doctor's quarters. The next section from his book, which probably first appeared in one of the London periodicals, shows how Florence Nightingale's legend was being constructed:

> On arriving at the second door, which opened upon one of the grand avenues of sick and wounded, we retired in a silent and mournful procession—except the groans of the sufferers, nothing was heard but the friction of our boots upon the stone floor, already worn into a kind of groove between the rows of beds upon which lay the sick and wounded, caused by the constant passing and repassing of the doctors, Sisters of Mercy, orderlies, and other officials in attendance upon the patients.
>
> As we turned the angle of the long corridor to the right, we perceived, at a great distance, a faint light flying from bed to bed, like a will o'-the-wisp flickering in a meadow on a summer's eve, which at last rested upon one spot . . .
>
> But alas! as we approached, we perceived our mistake. A group in the shape of a *silhouette* unfolded its outline in light shade. As we came nearer and nearer the picture burst upon us. A dying soldier was half reclining upon his bed. Life, you could observe, was fast bidding him adieu; Death, that implacable deity, was anxiously waiting for his soul to convey it to its eternal destination.
>
> But stop! near him was a guardian angel, sitting at the foot of his bed, and most devotedly engaged in pencilling down his last wishes to be dispatched to his homely friends and relations. A watch and a few more trinkets were consigned to the care of the writer; a lighted lamp was held by another person, and threw a painful yellowish *coloris* over that mournful picture, which a Rembrandt alone could have traced, but which everybody, as long as the world lasts, would have understood, felt, and admired. It was then near two o'clock in the morning.[18]

THE SWIFT AND PRECIPITOUS decline in mortality at the Barrack and General Hospitals at Scutari that occurred in the spring of 1855 has been endlessly analyzed. In the nineteenth century too much credit for that drop was probably given to Florence Nightingale in person. In the twentieth century she was certainly given too little.

"The Lady with the Lamp."

We know in great detail what Florence Nightingale did in her first four months, and her actions prove conclusively that, for a person of her generation, Florence Nightingale both had an expert understanding of disease and possessed the financial resources to allow her to take various measures. To recapitulate, Florence Nightingale was the first person to institute a rational system for receiving and housing the patients as they arrived. Appalled by the filthy, blood-and-waste-soaked condition the men arrived in, she made it a priority that the men and their linen should be washed and kept clean. She bought huge quantities of shirts and sheets so that the linen could be changed. She campaigned untiringly, and against great resistance, to set up a laundry where the hospital linen would all be boiled to destroy the lice. She spent hours with her most skillful nurses washing wounds and changing dressings. She instructed her nurses to take a clean piece of rag for each patient, not use the same sponge for all the men, as had been the practice for medical officers and orderlies before. She bought mops, buckets, scrubbing brushes, and soap, and induced orderlies to clean the wards. She began to get the walls whitewashed and the flooring replaced so that it could be scrubbed to keep the vermin at bay. She instituted an efficient extra diet kitchen to provide the sickest men with thin cereal, chicken and beef broths, savory jellies, and lemonade. With the help of Alexis Soyer, she did what she could to improve the patients' regular diet by directing that the cooking vessels should be cleaned out regularly, that all the meat should be cooked through and distributed quickly, and that as many vegetables should be used as could be procured. The care and attention she personally gave to the patients, symbolized by her nightly patrol through the wards, raised the general morale. By her constant vigilance and intelligent participation in all aspects of medical care, she put the orderlies and doctors on their mettle and challenged the "force of inertia" that had prevailed in all the army hospitals.

We now know that typhus is spread by body lice, that fleas and rats and flies are key vectors of disease. We know that good nutrition is especially important to the sick and that dysentery, diarrhea, and fever can often be caused by improperly prepared food. We know that a wound that is not properly cleaned and debrided of necrotic tissue every day will develop gangrene. We know that vitamin C is essential to the formation of scar tissue. We know that morale has an important bearing on the human immune system. The measures Nightingale was permitted to take were not enough to stop the epidemic disaster overwhelming Scutari, but they were all essential and life-promoting. She was not exaggerating when she wrote to the Herberts on July 11, 1855: "Now, I will say what I would not, except under this pressure, & what I would not, if you were in office have said—what I will never say to anyone else. We pulled this Hospital through for 4 months & without us, it would have come to a stand-still."[19]

When the Sanitary Commission arrived, the mortality rate had been falling for three weeks, and this progress has to be attributed to the changes instituted by Florence Nightingale. Thereafter, the progress was rapid. As Nightingale told Sidney Herbert unequivocally, Scutari was only a symptom of the army's malady, not a cause, and once things began to improve at Balaclava, things improved at Scutari. Once the men on the plains below Sevastopol began to get better food and the weather became warmer, their strength increased, they became more resistant to disease, the numbers arriving at Scutari went down, the wards became less crowded, and the medical personnel were under less pressure. At this point, the measures taken by the Sanitary Commission, notably in providing good ventilation in the wards and further combating the vermin, tipped the balance completely, and the men started to get rapidly better. The one key thing that neither Nightingale nor Sutherland and his inspectors of nuisances managed to achieve was to provide the hospital patients and staff with clean water. The Scutari water supply was contaminated with human waste, and as soon as the warm weather came in, the *Vibrio cholerae* began to grow and cholera once more broke out at Scutari. The energetic and innovative young doctor Alexander MacGrigor died of cholera in the fall of 1855.

But Nightingale was not just a trained expert working twenty-hour days in the infectious-disease trenches. She had personal relationships that made her a unique catalyst for change. From the moment of her arrival, Nightingale had the ear of the British government. Her reports and private letters to Sidney Herbert and other influential men in London shaped the responses to the war of the men who held the reins of power. The success of the 1855 commissions depended in no small part on the fact that Florence Nightingale had accurately reported on the issues and suggested detailed solutions before the commission members had left England. She was, in the end, a powerful combination of government spy and agent provocateur.

Nightingale's personal influence with key members of the British government was magnified a hundredfold by the legendary identity created around her as the Lady with the Lamp. Everything she did was reported and embellished by the British press and taken up by a British public ravenous for heroes. As success on the battlefield proved more and more elusive, the ordinary unnamed British soldier became the nation's hero. He had triumphed against the odds at the Alma, he had been needlessly sacrificed in the Charge of the Light Brigade, he had been allowed to die like a dog—until the Lady of Scutari came along to treasure and care for him. Florence Nightingale became an incarnation of the values of the British people. She personified courage, selflessness, determination, industry, initiative, tenderness, compassion. By a unique combination of events, Florence Nightingale had attained a unique power.

Chapter 19

IN THE CRIMEA

Florence Nightingale spent her thirty-fifth birthday on
board the *Robert Lowe*—nicknamed by the passengers the
Robert Slow—as the vessel labored across the Black Sea to
Balaclava. The principal members of her party were Charles Bracebridge,
Eliza Roberts, Alexis Soyer, his secretary T.G., and the boy Robert Robinson. Also on board were some 420 convalescent soldiers from the Scutari hospitals, "returning to their Regiments to be shot at again," as
Nightingale tartly put it in a letter to her family. The sea voyage was mer-
cifully calm, and perhaps because Soyer was with them, the ship's menu
was far from unappealing. The passengers were treated to roast beef
washed down with "quantities of exquisite pale sherry, good old port,
with a fine crust, properly decanted . . . with the inseparable and justly
famed Stilton cheese and fresh plain salad." In his capacity as reporter,
Soyer offered a description of his celebrated companion.

She is rather high of stature, fair in complexion, and slim in person; her hair is brown and is worn quite plain; her physiognomy is
most pleasing; her eyes, of a bluish tint, speak volumes, and are always sparkling with intelligence; her mouth is small and well-
formed . . . when wit or pleasantry prevails, the heroine is lost in
the happy good-natured smile which pervades her face, and you
recognize only the charming woman. Her dress is usually of a gray-
ish or black tint; she wears a simple white cap, and often a rough
apron . . . In conversation no member of the fair sex can be more
amiable and gentle than Miss Nightingale. Removed from her ar-

duous and cavalier-like duties, which require the nerve of a Hercules . . . she is Rachel on the stage in both tragedy and comedy.[1]

Once their boat had moved slowly through the narrow entry into the crowded harbor of Balaclava and anchored, the party was greeted by a raft of officials. These included Sir John McNeill, Colonel Tulloch and Dr. John Sutherland, all government commissioners who were firm allies of Miss Nightingale. Lord Raglan, the commander in chief of the British army, who had engaged in a long and harmonious correspondence with Nightingale ever since her arrival in Turkey, sent a message of welcome. One man notable by his absence was John Hall, the chief medical officer in the East.

Nightingale's official task was to inspect the contingent of eight nurses, fifteen nuns, and three ladies from the Stanley party who were working in and around Balaclava. So that she could make her rounds, one of the officers lent Florence Nightingale a fine chestnut horse; forsaking her nursing dress for an attractive riding habit, she cut a dashing figure. Selina Bracebridge, Parthenope Nightingale, and Lady Anne Blunt between them would later produce a drawing of Florence Nightingale gazing over at Sevastopol in which she appears a small, dainty figure on a powerful horse, bareheaded, her skirts extravagantly long. Since none of the lady artists was present at the event, this is a work of the romantic imagination, but it helped to satisfy the public's thirst for images of the heroine of Scutari.

Florence Nightingale had once enjoyed riding to hounds, and on a fine May day, with a good horse under her, she was in an exuberant mood and rode much closer to the lines of siege than her escort thought wise. As she rode over the sharp little hills between cliffs and sea that had proved such difficult terrain for soldiers, Florence Nightingale was overwhelmed to see Sevastopol "like a fairy palace, so gorgeous in the sun."[2] "It was a wonderful sight looking down upon Sevastopol," she told Parthe, "the shell whizzing right and left. I send you a Minié bullet I picked up on the ground which was ploughed with shot & shell—& some little flowers. For this is the most flowery place you can imagine— a beautiful little Tormentilla which I don't know, yellow Jessamine and every kind of low flowering shrub." One of the men who rode with her, a sergeant of the Ninety-seventh, picked her a little nosegay. "I once saved Serjt.———'s life by finding him at 12 o'clock at night lying—wounds undressed—in our Hospl. with a bullet in his eye & a fractured skull," wrote Nightingale to her family. "And I pulled a stray Surgeon out of bed to take the bullet out. But you must not tell this story. For I gave evidence against the missing Surgeon—& have never been forgiven."[3]

The sight that affected Nightingale most was that of the men mustering at dawn to march off for trench duty. "From those trenches 30 will never return. Yet they volunteer, press forward for the trenches. When I consider what the work has been this winter, what the hardships, I am surprised—not that the army has suffered so much but—that there is any army left at all, not that we have had so many through our hands at Scutari, but that we have not had all as Sir John McNeill says. Fancy working 5 nights out of 7 in the trenches, fancy being 36 hours in them at a stretch—as they were, all December, lying down or half lying down—often 48 hours without food but *raw* salt pork sprinkled with sugar—& their rum & biscuits—nothing hot—because the *exhausted* soldier *could not* collect his own fuel, as he was expected, to cook his own ration. And fancy, thro' all this, the army preserving their courage & patience."[4] No praise pleased Florence Nightingale as much as the rousing cheer the men of the Thirty-ninth Regiment raised when they identified the lady who had ridden over to visit them.

The letter to Parthenope describing the ride up toward Sevastopol breaks off abruptly. Within a few days of her arrival at Balaclava, Florence Nightingale fell seriously ill from what was diagnosed at the time as Crimean fever.[5] She was carried from her ship's berth to the Castle Hospital, where her nursing ally Jane Shaw Stewart was superintendent, and was then put in isolation in a small hut. There her friend Eliza Roberts nursed her, refusing to allow anyone else, even Charles Bracebridge, to come in. Several times a day, the boy Robert Robinson climbed the hill for news that could be brought down to Balaclava and then reported to the waiting world. For days Nightingale was delirious, and all the time she kept filling page after page with letters to imaginary officials about imaginary disasters. "One day, a Persian Adventurer came and stood by her bedside and told her that Mr. Bracebridge had drawn on her for 300,000 pounds." And so Florence Nightingale must needs write at once to Sir John McNeill, who was obviously the man to handle Persian

NIGHTINGALES

adventurers, and Sir John kept the letter, and returned it to her after her recovery as a memento.[6]

One day, Lord Raglan rode up to the hut, dressed as usual as an English country gentleman and with no escort. Eliza Roberts had no idea who this strange man was, and refused to let him in, fearing he would tire her patient. But Nightingale recognized his voice, and the two had a long talk. At one point, Raglan asked Florence Nightingale if her father "liked her coming out." She replied with pride, or so she told her family in her letter of November 14: "My father is not as other men are, he thinks that daughters should serve their country as well as sons—he brought me up to think so—he has no sons—& therefore he has sacrificed me to the country—& told me to come home with my shield or upon it. He does not think, (as I once heard a father & a very good & clever father say,) 'The girls are all I could wish—very happy, very attentive to me, & very amusing.' He thinks that God sent women, as well as men, into the world to be something more than 'happy', 'attentive' & 'amusing.' "[7]

On June 25 Lord Raglan died, some said of cholera, others said of overwork and a broken heart. Writing on July 5 to her family, Nightingale delivered an unsentimental obituary to the dead commander that most of the army would have echoed. "It was impossible not to love him for his kind & gentle courtesy. I did. But I shd. think his death an equal gain to him & us—to himself, because a good man has been taken from the evil to come—to us, because few perhaps could have done worse for us than he has done . . . Peace be with him & his hecatomb of twenty thousand men."[8]

After several weeks, Nightingale's fever dropped and the doctors declared her out of danger. Her friends decided that she must return to Constantinople, and she was carried down to the port and placed on the *Jura,* a steamer that had just been used to transport horses. For a woman in poor health who had always suffered from seasickness and who was almost fanatically committed to fresh air and cleanliness, the ship was signally ill chosen. When it transpired that the *Jura* was scheduled to sail to England without making a stop at Scutari, Nightingale's friends, especially the hot-tempered Charles Bracebridge, smelled a conspiracy. Someone, most probably John Hall, had thought to find an easy way to get rid of the superintendent of nursing. As luck would have it, Alexis

Soyer prevailed on his aristocratic patron Lord Ward to lend the Nightingale party his steam yacht, *London*.[9] On the eve of the boat's departure, Selina Bracebridge, crazy with anxiety, arrived at Balaclava. As Nightingale wrote to her family on June 18, "I think seeing her [Sigma] did me more good than all their [her doctors'] blisters."[10]

The sea voyage back to Scutari, in the luxury of the private yacht, lasted only thirty-six hours, but then the captain lost his way and drifted back forty miles, so two more days were spent at sea. Florence Nightingale was once again very ill. When she was carried ashore at Scutari, people were shocked to see how white and thin she was, her shorn head covered by a white handkerchief. Two relays of guardsmen bore the stretcher, while twelve other volunteers carried her luggage. A large group of men followed behind the stretcher in silence.

Nightingale was a long time recovering. In mid-June she jokingly reported to her family that she was "suffering from a compound fracture of the intellect," but in fact her mind was back at work long before her body was ready. Her friends were convinced that if she remained in her tower room at the Barrack Hospital, she would die, so she spent a short time in Therapia, at the Naval Hospital, accompanied as always by Eliza Roberts. Then, since Florence was aching to be back at Scutari, the senior chaplain, Mr. Sabin, who was returning to England on leave, rented his villa to her. The house was far from perfect. It had no kitchen and all the food had to be brought in from the hospital, but it was large and airy, it had a garden, and it was only fifteen minutes' walk from the Barrack Hospital.

Gifts and visitors of all sorts flooded into the villa, but, as always, pets and babies cheered Nightingale up best. The men at Scutari found her another little owl. Sidney Herbert sent her a small terrier that would not only love her but catch rats. Mrs. Brownlow, a sergeant's wife who was working as a washerwoman, left her baby in a kind of playpen in the living room of the Sabin villa next to Miss Nightingale's bed. Parthenope from home sent a little book called "The Life and Death of Athena, an Owlet from the Parthenon," which she had written and illustrated especially for her sister. Florence laughed and cried to read it, and reported to Lea Hurst that the terrier howled in jealousy.[11] A plate from this book, showing Florence with Athena perched on a small pillar, was massproduced and popped up in shops all over England. Novelist Elizabeth

Gaskell saw one in Manchester, as she wrote to tell the artist, noting at the same time: "Babies ad libitum are being christened Florence here; poor little factory babies, whose grimy stunted parents brighten up at the name . . . these poor unromantic fellows are made, somehow, of the same stuff as *her* heroes of the East, who turned their faces to the wall and cried at her illness."[12]

The Nightingale family was desperately anxious for Florence to return home. Her father, who was not known to be demonstrative in his affections, wrote telling her how much he loved and valued her, and begging her to consider her own health. In reply Florence wrote: "When I left England for Scutari, little expecting ever to see my dear father again, I left for him words true then & true now—that I loved him as I never loved any but him."[13]

A large part of the Nightingales' anxiety was caused by the fact that the Bracebridges were intending to leave Turkey at the end of July. Florence Nightingale recognized just how much her friends had contributed to her work, and she dreaded losing them. All the same, she was anxious to see them go for her own sake as well as their own. Selina and Charles had assumed responsibilities for which they had had no previous training. Neither one was an accountant, and Nightingale knew that the complexity as well as the sheer amount of the work they had to do increasingly overwhelmed them. She worked under intense scrutiny from the press and from hostile army officials, and any suggestion of financial impropriety could be fatal.

Furthermore, Charles Bracebridge's paternalism was increasingly irksome. He felt that his friends the Nightingales had entrusted him with their daughter—as indeed they had—but Florence had been chafing under parental control for too long to relish a surrogate father. When Nightingale was attacked Charles rushed to her defense, not always to good effect. His letter to Sidney Herbert had provoked the Stanley debacle, and the recent time in the Crimea, when Florence had been so close to death, only exacerbated Bracebridge's paranoia. He had become deeply unpopular with army men and therefore less useful. As Nightingale confided to her aunt Mai in October: "I find much less difficulty in getting on here [at Balaclava] without him [Bracebridge] than with him."[14]

But if Florence was not unhappy to be left to manage her own affairs alone, her family was convinced that she needed more support than the Reverend Mother Mary Clare Moore and Eliza Roberts could give. Nightingale's position as an unmarried woman dealing almost exclusively with men was a difficult one, especially as the eyes of the press were trained on her. As she told her sister after the war: "Officers spoke of me in their messes I have no doubt from what I did hear, as of liking to come down and live there [presumably Balaclava] because of the officers, etc."[15] Any number of people, both in Turkey and in Britain, would have been happy to see Nightingale discredited. In fact, the summer of 1855 demonstrated the difficulties of Nightingale's situation, as she crossed paths with two other single British women much her own age who had gone out to Turkey alone in hopes of changing their lives—Martha Clough and Charlotte Salisbury.

Miss Martha Clough arrived in Turkey in December 1854 with Miss Stanley's party.[16] She made a great mystery to her companions of the fact that she had been engaged to a brave and noble gentleman in a Highland regiment who had died in the fall of 1854. She came east, she said, to visit the grave of her lost love and lavish upon his fellow officers the affection and care she could no longer give him. The dead gentleman she had loved and lost turned out to be Colonel Lauderdale Maule, the brother and heir presumptive of Lord Panmure, who had died of cholera at Varna. Whether Maule and Clough were actually engaged to be married is far from certain, but she carried about a portrait of Maule that Panmure had given her. When in January 1855 Lord Panmure took over from Sidney Herbert at the War Office, no one in the East needed it spelled out that Miss Clough must be given kid-glove treatment.

Miss Nightingale's system at the Barrack Hospital, which specifically precluded the nursing of officers, was not at all to Martha Clough's taste, and she quickly chose to leave Scutari for the Crimea. The Seventy-ninth Highland Regiment under Brigadier General Sir Colin Campbell was stationed on the heights above Balaclava, and in her letters Martha Clough gushed how tall, handsome, considerate, and gentlemanly she found the officers—so like her dead love! In a matter of weeks, Martha Clough quite suddenly left the hospital in the port of Balaclava and settled down at Campbell's encampment on the heights, purportedly to manage the regimental hospital. For an unmarried, middle-class woman to act like a camp follower was considered extraordinary behavior, especially since Miss Clough had no known income. Miss Langston told Miss Nightingale, off the record of course, that Miss Clough had stolen the hospital's money when she left. In any case, Miss Clough hired a soldier and his wife as her servants and moved in with them; when that arrangement did not suit, she was given a small hut of her own and allowed to draw army rations. Rumors flew around in the Crimean and at Scutari that Miss Clough was often the worse for drink. For a few months, Colin Campbell and the other officers of the Seventy-ninth Highlanders treated Martha Clough like a strange pet, and in general the army afforded her, in Nightingale's phrase, "not only toleration but sanction."[17] But in the late summer Clough fell seriously ill and she became an impossible burden on a regiment that was, after all, fighting a war. Jane Shaw Stewart took Clough into the Castle Hospital and nursed her personally night and day, but it was obvious she needed to go home. Sadly, Martha Clough did not survive the sea voyage.[18]

In her letters and reports Nightingale calls Clough variously "that queer fellow," "drunken isolated Miss Clough," and a "mad freak" who brought dishonor on the title of nurse and represented the worst in upper-middle-class English women. People who knew Martha Clough at Scutari and Balaclava saw her not as a tragic heroine but as a deluded victim. Since Clough had consistently flouted her authority and moved as far away from her as she could go, Nightingale clearly bore no responsibility for her miserable death. Nonetheless, Florence Nightingale took charge of Miss Clough's body when it arrived at Scutari, attended her funeral, erected a cross over her grave, wrote the news of her death to friends in Britain, and paid for Clough's belongings and papers to be sent back. Nightingale and General Campbell out of their own pockets paid the wages of the soldier of the Forty-second Highlanders and his wife whom Clough had engaged as her servants. It is hard to see how Nightingale could have done more.

While Florence Nightingale was obliged to take charge of the remains of sad, mad Martha Clough, she was also coping with mean, bad Charlotte Salisbury, who bore a strong resemblance to the Becky Sharp and Lady Audley of Victorian fiction.[19] A vivacious Irishwoman with the gift of the gab and charm to spare, Salisbury served the family of the British Consul at Patras as a governess for eleven years and then moved on to Turkey, determined, it seems, to make as much money and as

The Mission of Mercy: Florence Nightingale Receiving the Sick and Wounded at Scutari (detail), by Jerry Barrett, a painting completed in the year after the war, from existing images. As an engraving, the work was popular with the nation but not with Nightingale. It features Nightingale's key civilian allies (Selena and Charles Bracebridge, Mother Mary Clare Moore, Eliza Roberts, Robert Robinson, and Alexis Soyer) but also several military men (notably Lord William Paulet and Dr William Cruikshanks) whom she despised.

Florence Nightingale with Charles Bracebridge on Cathcart's Hill, looking
toward Sevastopol, May 1855. Parthenope Nightingale and Lady Anne Blunt
produced this popular image from a sketch by Selena Bracebridge,
who was not an eyewitness.

Florence Nightingale in the mule carriage she was occasionally able to use
to get from one hospital to another on the plains above Balaclava in 1856.

The inadequacy of British medical provisions was already apparent after the army's first great victory at the Alma in September, 1854.

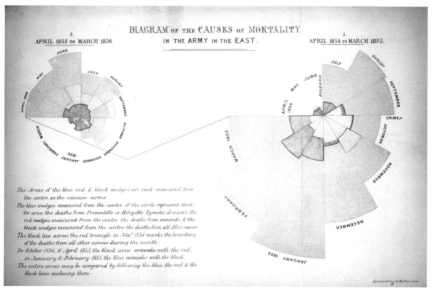

The famous 'coxcomb' diagram Florence Nightingale devised in 1857 for her government report that launched a radical reform in the housing and medical treatment of soldiers.

One of a series of photographs taken of Florence Nightingale, probably (to judge by the length of her hair) in 1857. These pictures were widely distributed as *cartes de visite*.

Arthur Hugh Clough, poet, cousin-in-law, secretary and deeply mourned ally.

Mai Shore Smith, Florence Nightingale's double aunt and most devoted comrade and protector.

Hilary Bonham Carter. A self-portrait by the cousin who worshipped Florence Nightingale but was unable to please her.

William Edward
Nightingale with his
daughter Parthenope at
Embley, *circa* 1870.

Fanny Smith
Nightingale in her
declining years, with
Parthenope, Lady
Verney.

Sir Harry and Lady Verney entertain a group of nurses at Claydon House.
Florence Nightingale stands apart from the others at the open window.

Florence Nightingale and Sir Harry Verney in the garden at Claydon,
circa 1880.

Florence Nightingale in her bedroom at South Street, *circa* 1887.

much trouble as she could. Salisbury arrived at Scutari while Nightingale was still in the Crimea and was immediately hired to help Selina Bracebridge. While worming her way into that lady's favor, Salisbury at once began writing home to friends about Mrs. Bracebridge's mishandling of the Free Gifts. Salisbury did not take long to discover that the most important grievance the sisters, ladies, and nurses all held against Florence Nightingale as superintendent was that she did not allow them free access to the supplies. Salisbury reported to her friends in London that Nightingale's obsession with army regulations meant that precious supplies moldered on the shelves. Meanwhile, good-hearted nurses were punished for freely giving to the men food, wine, and clothing that they needed and which had been sent to the East specifically for their use. Salisbury also complained that Miss Nightingale refused to allow officers to hire nurses as their private attendants, thus, in Miss Salisbury's view, sacrificing the health of gallant men and spoiling the chances of needy women.

When Florence Nightingale arrived back at Scutari in late June, weak and frustrated after her long illness, she too fell under Charlotte Salisbury's spell. She welcomed her as a new ally, sought her company, and trusted her completely. Nightingale asked Miss Salisbury to act as her housekeeper, moved her into the private villa at Scutari, and gave her the keys to the house. On top of the eighteen shillings a week paid by the army, Salisbury received an extra seventy pounds a year out of Nightingale's own pocket. Nightingale also agreed to find work for a Maltese couple for whose honesty and industry Miss Salisbury stood guarantor. After Selina Bracebridge's departure, Salisbury took over complete management of the Free Gifts, an invitation to larceny she was happy to accept.

Charlotte Salisbury had a weakness for drink, and she rapidly got careless. When large quantities of goods, including a great deal of wine, went missing, Florence Nightingale asked Salisbury about them, only to be told that the nurses were to blame, especially poor Mrs. Wreford. On her deathbed, Mrs. Wreford accused Miss Salisbury of unkindness and dishonesty, but Florence Nightingale, who was nursing Wreford, assumed her patient was merely delirious. Finally the nurses and the soldiers' wives who shared the villa could stand it no more and told Nightingale of the strange behavior of her new employee—large bags and parcels constantly moving in and out of the house, mostly at night.

They advised Nightingale to look in the rooms of both Salisbury and the Maltese couple in her employ. These were found to be stuffed with purloined merchandise.

When General Storks, the new commandant at Scutari, was informed of the matter, he made a thorough investigation and discovered that Salisbury and her associates had been stealing and selling government stores as well. Confronted with the evidence, Salisbury groveled hysterically on the floor and begged for forgiveness in a scene straight out of Victorian melodrama. Anxious to avoid scandal at all costs, Nightingale decided, against Storks's advice, to send Salisbury home in disgrace, but not to prosecute her. Distraught, Florence begged Charlotte to explain why she had so deceived her, and actually offered her the money to emigrate to Australia, where she had relatives.

Dismissed on September 27, Charlotte Salisbury left Turkey on October 1. In her haste, she left behind her desk, and the letters in it made it clear that she had been an agent provocateur as well as a thief. Allowing her Gothic imagination full rein, Salisbury had gone so far as to suggest that there was something improper about the personal care Florence Nightingale had given to the decaying corpse of Martha Clough. Once in London, Salisbury found allies in high places, notably the disgruntled Mary Stanley. She insisted that she had been unjustly persecuted. Benjamin Hawes, Lord Panmure's Permanent Under-secretary at the War Office and a leader of the anti-reform faction in the government, seized upon Miss Salisbury's accusations. A four-man commission of inquiry was set up. Salisbury's testimony was completely discredited, but the whole sordid affair exhausted and discouraged Florence Nightingale.

In an effort to assess the situation at Scutari and if possible persuade Florence to return home, her uncle Sam Smith and his son, Shore, arrived in Turkey in early August. They stayed only for a few weeks. A letter Florence wrote to Shore in January 1856 indicates that there was some feeling in the family that Shore had let Florence down by not staying with her. Florence took the time to assure her young cousin that she harbored no resentment and understood that he had his work, as she had hers. Written at a time of great stress, Nightingale's letter was magnanimous, but in comparison with the letters she addressed to Shore when he was a boy, her tone is chilly. Flo had loved Shore very much and had done so much for him that she must have found it hard to see him come and go so quickly. To have a young man of practical abilities and proven loyalty by her side would have been a comfort.[20]

But perhaps because Shore Smith could not see his way to devoting the next months or years to his cousin Florence, the family agreed, with extreme reluctance on Sam Smith's part, that Mai Smith, Shore's mother, should have her earnest wish and go out to Scutari in place of Selina Bracebridge.[21] Mai Shore Smith's journey out to Turkey and the ten months she spent at Scutari were the great adventure of her life. And she turned out to be exactly the person Florence Nightingale needed because she understood Florence so well and was accustomed to both supporting her and deferring to her.

For Mai, as for Selina Bracebridge, the Crimean War was a defining moment. They were well aware that Scutari was their opportunity as well as Flo's, that by braving the fleas and rats and fetid water of Turkish army hospitals they were demonstrating, not just to their own families but to society at large, what women could do. As Lord Stanley said at the public meeting in November 1855 that launched the Nightingale Fund: "Mark, what, by breaking through customs and prejudices, Miss Nightingale has effected for her sex. She has opened to them a new profession, a new field of usefulness . . . A claim for more extended freedom of action, based on proved public usefulness in the highest sense of the world, with the whole nation to look on and bear witness, is one which must be listened to, and cannot easily be refuted."[22]

WHEN MAI SMITH arrived at Scutari in the middle of September, she burst into tears to find her niece so thin and run-down. During the heat of the Turkish summer, Florence Nightingale had cropped her hair short again, so that she could wash it once or twice a day, and the small childish curls that escaped from her cap contrasted with her worn face. After two months of enforced inactivity, Nightingale was once again back in her tower, confronting official indifference and apathy on all sides. She was surely a very difficult woman to deal with on a hot summer day, and rarely showed the feminine charm that Alexis Soyer had described so eloquently. As she wrote to the Bracebridges, "If I could have condescended to make these men in love with me, it wd. have been better. But that I could not do."[23]

Nightingale was convinced that although the army was now swimming in public and private money, the "system" remained not merely unaltered but unconvinced of the need to alter. Even if Sevastopol was to fall, she saw plenty of problems ahead. In the August heat, Nightingale was already writing to Lord Panmure and friends in England about the need to procure fur-lined mittens for the soldiers during the coming winter. She also imagined waterproof coats made of gutta-percha, and a waist-high, one-size-fits-all waterproof trench outfit that sounds rather like our modern fisherman's waders.[24] There was a new purveyor at Scutari, Mr. Robertson, who seemed better than Wreford, but Nightingale still found it necessary to go out and buy "lemons, vinegar, lime-juice."[25] Vitamin C is now known to be essential for the formation of scar tissue and the healing of wounds, so Nightingale did well to keep buying lemons for the patients. Shirts and sheets were now supplied in abundance, but in September, in a letter to Lady Canning, Nightingale begged for needles, thread, and buttons "by the million."[26]

Florence Nightingale's biggest concern during the dog days of summer was to keep the soldiers occupied and sober. In a carefully drafted passage that she included in letters to several people, Nightingale wrote: "I have never been able to join in the popular cry about the recklessness, sensuality, and helplessness of the soldiers. On the contrary I should say (and no woman perhaps has seen more of the manufacturing and agricultural classes of England than I have—before I came here) that I have never seen so teachable and helpful a class as the Army generally. Give them opportunity promptly and securely to send money home & they will use it. Give them a School & a Lecture and they will come to it. Give them a book & a game & a Magic Lanthorn & they will lay off drinking. Give them suffering and they will bear it. Give them work and they will do it. I had rather have to do with the Army generally than with any other class I have ever attempted to serve . . . If Officers would but think thus of their men, how much might not be done for them."[27]

And so Florence Nightingale arranged to provide the soldiers with books, magazines, candles, and a pleasant reading room where they could smoke and drink coffee. She set up schools for the men in different regiments as well as for the soldiers' children. She found models, footballs, cards, and board games, not just for Scutari but for the men in the Crimea. She arranged play readings and lectures. She offered to send money home quickly and reliably for officers and men. Fortunately, the new commandant at Scutari, General (later Sir Henry) Storks, a new and important ally, cooperated enthusiastically with Nightingale's plans. Nightingale wrote to the Bracebridges: "By dint of Pincoffs, & men, and the incessant exertion of money, the Coffee-House was opened yesterday. I advanced others 150 pounds—& sent them hams, butter, brandy, tea-urn, tent, prints, a band, newspapers, etc. for the opening day when everything was gratis."[28]

The small army of middle-class reformer volunteers in England, led by Florence's sister, Parthenope, was mobilized to acquire recreational, educational, and decorative materials of every kind. In November 1855, Parthenope wrote to her old friend and frequent confidant, Ellen Tollett: "I don't know whether Mrs. Milnes told you how hard we worked to send off boxes for F.'s education of the army! Let me tell you, Ma'am, to instruct 50,000 men is no joke. Seriously tho', my love, it is small things any one can do amid such a mass, which made one the more anxious to enable her to do what she could, and we have sent a dose of 1000 copybooks, writing materials in proportion. Diagrams, Maps, books illustrated and other. *Macbeth* (6) to read 6 at a time, and the music in the interludes, which Mr. Best . . . recommended as having been successful in his village. Chess, Footballs, other games, a magic Lanthorn for Dissolving views, a Stereoscope (very fine!), plays for acting, music, &c. &c. Finally I thought a little art would be advisable, and had a number of prints stretched and varnished which are to be my subscription towards the improvement of the British Army."[29] Queen Victoria volunteered a print showing "the Duke of Wellington presenting May flowers to the little Prince Arthur, his godson." The print was a huge success with the men.

Lord Panmure was more annoyed than impressed by the news that Miss Nightingale was sending home money for the men. He felt she was once more poking her nose into army affairs where she had no business.

It was slightly crazy of Florence Nightingale to get into the remittance business. The sums involved were small, and the labor involved was great. After January 1856, Nightingale's uncle Sam Smith took on the job of arranging for the monies to be deposited and the relatives informed, but all the same Nightingale herself spent hours every week handling the money, and there were constant problems. A soldier would demand to know what had happened to the pound he swore he had given Miss Nightingale and that his old woman in England never received. Almost certainly the pound had been spent on drink and the man had forgotten, but in the meantime Florence Nightingale needed to come up with the pound. In the end, about two hundred pounds a week, seventy thousand pounds in all, found their way to England from men in the ranks through Florence Nightingale's good offices, not a great sum. But the remittance scheme, like so many others that Florence Nightingale launched at Scutari, was more important for its symbolism than its practical usefulness. She wanted to demonstrate that many soldiers cared about their families and wanted to look after them.

WHILE NIGHTINGALE battled the heat and the flies of a Scutari summer, she continued to have trouble with the remaining members of the Stanley party. Most of these women had gone over to the hospital at Koulali that had opened up in January, and mortality there quickly climbed as high as at the Barrack Hospital. In the end, the army medical corps decided to exercise stringent controls over the rations and extra diets at Koulali, which was costing the government unheard-of amounts of money. Since most of the nursing there consisted in doling out treats to favored patients, several of the ladies decided that they might as well go home.[30] The Reverend Mother Bridgeman, on the other hand, who had been instructed by the Catholic hierarchy in Britain to stay on in Turkey at all costs, began to negotiate with Dr. John Hall about moving her group of fifteen nuns en masse to Balaclava. When Florence Nightingale finally got word that the Irish nuns were moving out to the Crimea, she at once decided that she would go with them and use the occasion to assert her authority as superintendent of nursing in the base hospitals across the Black Sea. Her sudden illness had prevented her from doing this in May, and since her enforced return to Scutari in June the medical situation across the Black Sea had deteriorated.

Florence Nightingale was convinced that good nursing would be needed in the Crimea through the winter, even though in September, after suffering horrendous losses in men and money, the Russians decided to abandon the shattered city of Sevastopol and withdraw a few miles into the Crimean Peninsula. But if the siege was over, the war was not, and the British soldier—who by this time was typically an Irish teenager—was still at risk from cannonballs, Cossack attacks, cholera, alcoholism, and the oncoming winter. Hall had instituted the policy of opening more base hospitals in the Crimea and sending what he called convalescents directly back to England, bypassing Scutari. Nightingale had had a look at some of these so-called convalescents, and their condition was horrendous.[31] She strongly suspected that, though supplies were now abundant, the sanitary conditions in the Crimean hospitals were comparable to those at Scutari a year earlier.[32]

On October 9, Florence Nightingale set out for the Crimea for the second time, this time aboard the *Ottowa*. She was accompanied by Eliza Roberts and Robert Robinson. The crossing of the Black Sea was made in only forty-eight hours, but the harbor authorities refused to allow the vessel into the port. After three days, Florence Nightingale determined to get to land at any cost, but the small steamer sent out to collect her crashed against the *Ottowa* in the heavy swell and promptly held off. "The little steamer being a failure," wrote Robert Robinson, "a boat was immediately lowered & brought round to the stern of the vessel, & then with great risk to herself & a very heavy swell on the water, she allowed herself to be lowered into the boat. The task was accomplished with safety, Miss Nightingale being held suspended by the arms over the side of the vessel, until the next wave elevated the boat to such a height that she could be dropped into it. Mrs. Roberts was lowered in like manner, & I stayed on board until the vessel should get into harbour, two days later."[33]

Florence Nightingale spent two months in the Crimea and had a very wearisome time of it. Mother Bridgeman and her nuns hardly spoke to her, Miss Weare was both elusive and rebellious, and Elizabeth Davis, who, under Miss Weare, had enjoyed free range of all the food and wine at the Balaclava General Hospital, was outraged that Miss Nightingale should presume to enter her kitchen on a tour of inspection. The new commander in chief of the army, General Simpson, was an ally of Hall. But the commander of the new Land Transport Corps, charged with building the road and railway between the port and the camp, was desperate to have some nurses, since his men, many of them Slavs, were grossly neglected by army officials, who looked down upon them as mere navvies. The commander sent over for Nightingale and her nurses two precarious two-wheeled vehicles similar to jaunting carts. Predictably, at one turn, the wheel of one cart carrying Florence Nightingale, Jane Shaw Stewart, Robert Robinson, and two nurses hit a rock and turned over. Robinson, who had been riding on the shaft, hopped off quite nimbly. Nightingale landed on the top end of the cart and jumped off, but the two nurses were underneath and were badly bruised and shaken. For two weeks they were unable to work, and Florence Nightingale looked after them and did their work. When the nurses felt better, Nightingale took them on an expedition to see the ruined city of Sevastopol, whence they returned laden with trophies and very happy. If at Scutari Florence Nightingale's work was essentially that of an administrator and lobbyist, in the Crimea she was once again deeply immersed in bedside nursing and in the close supervision of the other nurses' work.

The animosity of Dr. John Hall to Nightingale and her nurses was now out in the open. "Dr. Hall is dead against me," wrote Florence to Aunt Mai. "He descends to every meanness to make my position more difficult."[34] Hall and other army officials had been newly provoked by an article in *The Times* of October 16 describing a lecture given in Coventry by Charles Bracebridge in which he not only indicted the Purveying Department under Mr. Wreford but accused the army medical corps of using outdated treatments. By Bracebridge's account, Florence Nightingale, with the help of money from *The Times,* had within a few days revolutionized the situation at Scutari and saved countless lives. Florence Nightingale was very upset by what Bracebridge had said. Her dear old friend, attempting to support and defend her, had in fact done her incalculable harm.

In her official communications with Hall, Florence Nightingale was suave and diplomatic; in her everyday dealings with doctors and army officials, she was calm, soft-spoken, and undemanding. But in letters home, Florence's anger and frustration, fueled by the rheumatism, sciatica, and boils from which she was suffering, erupted. On November 17 she wrote to Liz Herbert from the Castle Hospital at Balaclava: "In April I undertook this Hospital—& from that time to this we have cooked *all* the Extra Diets for 500–600 Patients & the *whole* Diets for the wounded Officers by ourselves in a shed—& until I came up this time . . . I could not get an Extra Diet Kitchen built promised me in May, till I came to do it myself, viz. in October. During the whole of this time, every egg, every bit of butter, jelly, all of Eau de Cologne which the sick Officers have had have been provided out of Mrs. Shaw Stewart's or my private pockets. On Nov. 4, I opened my Extra Diet Kitchen—but, for 24 hours, I would not bake the Officers' toast in this kitchen, because it disconcerted the Extra Diets for 550 patients. In those 24 hours, the Officers made a complaint to Head Quarters of our 'ill-treatment' in re. Toast. And Dr. Hall, with the PMO of Balaclava, came down in their wrath, & reprimanded the—Cook's Orderly . . . Dr. Hall then published to his inferior Officers that the ladies at the Castle Hospital meant to throw off all subordination to the Medical Officers—& that this was the reason he had brought the Nuns to the General Hospital, Balaclava . . . These things are nothing excepting in as much as they thwart the work.[35]

WITHIN WEEKS of the Balaclava battle of the officers' toast, news came from England that Nightingale's work was receiving the most extraordinary accolades. To express her personal appreciation for all Miss Nightingale had done for the troops, Queen Victoria sent her a brooch that Prince Albert himself had designed. The brooch, which is remarkably ugly, features a St. George's cross with the letters *VR* and the royal cipher superimposed, and there are three little diamond stars on the top. Around the cross are the inscriptions "Blessed Are the Merciful" and "Crimea." On the back of the medal is written: "To Miss Florence Nightingale, as a mark of esteem and gratitude for her devotion towards the Queen's brave soldiers—from Victoria R. 1855."

And on November 29, at Willis's Rooms on St. James's Street in London, a public meeting was held to launch the Nightingale Fund. Conceived as a special kind of testimonial to Florence Nightingale, the fund's organizers had decided that any money contributed should be given to the foundation of a Kaiserswerth-like institution in England for the training of nurses. More people flocked to the meeting than the rooms could accommodate. The Duke of Cambridge, the Queen's cousin, who had decided within a few months that Crimean campaigning was not after all quite his thing, chaired the meeting. Various worthy gentlemen—Sidney Herbert, of course, who was leading the appeal for funds, the Duke of Argyll, Sir John Pakington, Lord Lansdowne, Richard Monckton Milnes—all made speeches that were rapturously received.

The three Nightingales did not attend the meeting—the ladies felt that they would be too overcome with emotion, and Mr. Nightingale was afraid that he would be called upon to make a speech. However, their friends rushed around immediately to tell them exactly what had happened, and the Nightingales quickly put pen to paper to tell Florence everything. "This 29th of November," wrote Fanny Nightingale to her daughter at Scutari. "The most interesting day in thy mother's life. It is very late my child, but I cannot go to bed without telling you that your meeting has been a glorious one. I believe that you will be more indifferent than any of us to your fame, but be glad that we feel this is a proud day for us; for the like has never happened before, but will, I trust, from your example, gladden the hearts of many future mothers."[36]

Florence Nightingale had had word from the Herberts of the effort to launch a fund in her name and had responded with little enthusiasm. There was cholera again at Scutari and several of her friends had died, and the open recalcitrance of Hall and his allies was wearing her down. Nightingale feared that everything she had striven to achieve was still at risk, that the Dr. Halls would win in the end. What she might do with her life after the war had no reality for her, and heading up a kind of college of nursing was no longer her cherished dream. After all the experiences she had had with the management of nurses in army hospitals, she now saw only the difficulties and pitfalls, and she was also cynical about public opinion and the power of the press. And so Florence Nightingale parried all the urgent requests for plans for the nursing school that her friends sent her. Her only decision was to defer decisions and ask for a board of trustees to be set up who would take good care of the money.

Nightingale's friends had sought to please her by offering her what she had long desired, only to find that she had changed. As usual, she was unfathomable. At least Nightingale seemed moved by her parents' emotion after the November meeting. "If my name," she wrote to WEN and Fanny in response to their rapturous letters, "and my having done what I could for God and mankind has given you pleasure, that is real pleasure. My reputation has not been a boon in my work; but if you have been pleased that is enough. I shall love my name now, and shall feel that it is the greatest return that you can find satisfaction in hearing your child named,—and in feeling that her work draws sympathies together—some return for what you have done for me."[37] Such expressions of filial piety seem positively Roman, and they told at best half the story.

The person who gave Florence Nightingale the soundest advice on the subject of the Nightingale Fund was Charles Bracebridge. He had been allowed to say only a few words at the very end of the London meeting, and he resented the fact that so many aristocratic gentlemen had been allowed to wax eloquent on a subject they knew only at third hand. But if Charles Bracebridge was cynical about the sponsors, he was not cynical about the fund itself, to which eventually some forty-five thousand pounds would be subscribed. He urged Florence Nightingale not to throw away the opportunities represented by the fund simply because she was tired and discouraged. Florence was prepared to listen to Charles Bracebridge because his letter showed that he at least understood what her mission was about. "After all, what a joke," wrote Bracebridge, "that of 'My Lords and Gentlemen' and His Royal Highness none dared to tell what you did! Stood in gap when officers deserted; loved the soldier when his officers left him; cured him when his doctors left him to die; found out his wants, forced them to be acknowledged and then supplied them. These *élite* of a free country neither said it nor let me say it."[38]

WHILE FLORENCE was at Balaclava, Mai Smith took over many of her supervisory tasks, settled endless disputes, kept an eye on the distribution of those wretched Free Gifts, and carried on a good proportion of her niece's less important correspondence. To the frank surprise of her own family, Mai was making a great success of Scutari. She lived in Florence's villa alongside three nurses and Miss Ann Morton, a zealous Evangelical, fierce worker, and amateur artist who left some interesting little sketches of the Barrack Hospital and of the villa. Also living in one room at the villa was Robert Robinson; Vickery, an army orderly who served as a bodyguard for Mrs. Smith and Miss Morton; and two younger lads, a one-legged sailor called William and a Russian boy called Peter, both of whom Nightingale had taken under her wing. Mai Smith got on splendidly with everyone and became a second mother to the boys.[39]

In December, Florence returned from the Crimea, and Mai Smith was able to feed the home network's insatiable appetite for news about the heroine of Scutari. She explained that she and Florence were almost never alone, rarely had time to speak, and were sometimes in each other's company for only a few minutes in the day. Nightingale at Scutari no longer did much individual nursing and spent only an hour touring the wards—the best hour in her day, she said. The rest of the time, clad in ladylike black, she received a stream of visitors and wrote interminable reports and letters. Much of the time she and Aunt Mai communicated via notes. Mai and Flo would each sit at her own desk, back to back, writing, in complete silence. The room was cold, as the stove that had been sent from England smoked, and charcoal burners gave Florence a headache. Though once she had been terribly sensitive to cold, Nightingale seemed now wholly impervious to it. From time to time Mrs. Roberts, whose constant chatter Mai found annoying, would come in asking Miss Nightingale if she was ready for her tea or her dinner. Nightingale ate at her desk, absentmindedly taking the odd sip or the odd bit of toast. "The wind roars, the rain patters; I don't think Flo is conscious of the bluster," wrote Mai Smith. "I never saw a mind so continuously concentrated on her work. Is it a mind that belonged to some other planet, though, in accordance with God's love, falling like a meteor on this? For it does not seem adapted to the human frame, though it has forced that frame to obedience."[40]

In a January letter, Mai again wrote with reverence of her niece's capacity for work: "She is extremely quick and clear too, as you know, in her work. This I suppose has increased upon her, and she can turn from one thing and one person to another, when in the midst of business, in a most extraordinary manner. She has attained a most wonderful calm and presence of mind. She is, I think, often deeply impressed, and depressed, though she does not show it outwardly, but no irritation of temper, no hurry or confusion of manner, ever appears for a moment."[41] As Mai Smith noted to the folk at Embley: "Nothing can be so different as your atmosphere and ours. You hear of her at the pinnacle of human admiration; here opposition and dislikes are an atmosphere, and she is too busy contending with these to realize the other."[42]

At Christmas Mai Smith persuaded Florence to accept the invitation from Lady Stratford to attend the embassy party. Dressed in a high-necked, long-sleeved black dress, her cropped hair showing under a white lawn handkerchief, the Queen's brooch her only ornament, Florence Nightingale cut a curiously nunlike figure at the brilliant gathering. Lady Stratford made much of her, but the next day Nightingale learned that the ambassadress had warmly defended Miss Salisbury to Dr. Blackwood. From that time on Florence Nightingale could not be prevailed upon to attend embassy functions. "Why seek to convince her," she remarked of Lady Stratford, "she does not really exist enough to hold a conviction. She only exists to build up something she thinks is a very important Lady Stratford and to put down whatever interferes with it."[43]

In February 1856, Florence Nightingale managed to find a wonderful gold dress as a present for her mother. It was a heavily embroidered garment, upon which a chapter from the Koran—"God be with you, God protect you, May you live long in happiness—altho' you are in joy, remember the words of the Prophet"—was worked several times. Florence told Fanny that the dress was "the life's work of a poor Turkish widow," and that the woman had offered it to her directly, as she herself never had the opportunity to go to the bazaar in Constantinople. "They call me the sultana of the Bosphorus," she remarked jokingly, "& if I am, I think I have a right to insist upon the mother of the Sultana wearing a very fine gown."[44]

IN THE SPRING OF 1856, the peace treaty was signed. The Crimean War was over, but the diplomatic and bureaucratic war between those for and against reform of the army bureaucracy was only heating up, much to the despair of Lord Panmure at the War Office. He was congenitally disinclined to ministerial work of any kind, and his energetic deputy Benjamin Hawes was determined to maintain the status quo at all costs. Hawes was in constant communication with John Hall at Balaclava and with the new purveyor there, David Fitzgerald. He was an Irishman strongly in the camp of Mother Bridgeman and Father Ronan who took every possible opportunity to attack Florence Nightingale and her nurses in his reports and make their daily lives miserable.[45] Fortunately, Nightingale found a new and influential ally in Colonel John Lefroy, Panmure's special envoy in the East. Lefroy persuaded Panmure to issue a general order specifically giving Nightingale, as superintendent of nursing, jurisdiction in all the hospitals in the Crimea as well as at

Scutari. When Hall wrote to protest, Panmure, thoroughly fed up, issued a sharp rebuke telling Hall to do what he was told.

Even as the War Office was moving to resolve the dispute in Nightingale's favor, it was carefully placating the still powerful and active members of the anti-reform party. Sir John McNeill and Colonel Tulloch had written up their commission's findings in a judicious, carefully framed report, strong on statistics and detailed reporting, that pro-reform advocates like Sidney Herbert thought was masterly. But the report raised howls of protest from the army, and Panmure agreed to suppress the most damning sections, notably Tulloch's statistical tables on mortality. These were in sharp contrast to the figures put out by the Army Medical Department. Worse, Panmure caved in to the army's cry for a special board of inquiry that would allow the regimental and medical officers accused by McNeill and Tulloch of neglecting the care of the men to defend themselves. This inquiry, known generally as the Chelsea Board, was a blatant exercise in whitewashing, and poor Alexander Tulloch, who was subjected to extremely hostile questioning, suffered a nervous breakdown. He resigned his commission and was denied the knighthood that McNeill had requested for him.[46] In February, the latest honors list finally was published, and the world learned that John Hall had been awarded a KCB—"Knight of the Crimean Burying Grounds," as Nightingale bitterly put it. The medical officers who had remained loyal to Hall had been promoted, while those who had protested at the way the patients were being treated or who had cooperated in the reforms recommended by Nightingale and the McNeill and Sutherland commissions had been held back. Andrew Smith and Benjamin Hawes, chiefs of the anti-reform party in London, were also given knighthoods. Lords Lucan and Cardigan, the men largely responsible for the disastrous Charge of the Light Brigade, were exonerated of all blame by the Chelsea Board and received honors suited to their exalted station.

Hearing this news, Florence Nightingale let loose an apocalyptic fury in letters to her uncle Sam and to Colonel Lefroy in the first week in March: "From this time forth can a K.C.B. ship or a promotion from Horse Guards or War Dept. ever be anything but a title of disgrace? If you have friends among those men, so have I. But I would have given up my own father in such a cause. England has never realized the eight thousand graves at Scutari, and more in the Crimea. But I, who saw the

men come down through all that long, long, dreadful winter (four thousand sick we received in seventeen days—Dec. 17/54–Jan. 3/55—& of
these we buried more than the half) without other covering than a dirty
blanket & a pair of old Regimental trowsers [sic], when we knew that
the Stores were teeming with warm clothing—living skeletons, devoured with vermin, ulcerated, hopeless, speechless, dying like the
Greeks, as they wrapped their heads in their blankets & never spoke a
word, 70–80 we lost per diem on the Bosphorus alone up to Feb. 13/55
on which day we buried 85 in one grave without a Register—in that
month there were 1000 more burials than deaths registered. Can we
hear of the promotion of the men who caused this colossal calamity, we
who saw it, without thinking, will the next thing be the 'Decline and
Fall of the' British 'Empire.' "[47]

All the same, Nightingale was fiercely determined not to let Hawes,
Hill, and Fitzgerald win. Once again she took ship for the Crimea, and
immediately on her debarkation at Balaclava she went over to the General Hospital. After requesting a personal interview with Mother Bridgeman, Nightingale exerted all her charm and tact and begged Bridgeman
and her nuns to stay on. Bridgeman refused and gave notice she and her
party would leave as soon as they could get packed.[48]

The day the Bridgeman party departed, Florence Nightingale arrived
at the General Hospital at Balaclava. Night was falling, and the weather
was still wintry. She asked for the keys to the nurses' storerooms and
kitchens and to the huts where the Irish nuns had been quartered, and
when told that they were not available she said that she would sit outside
and wait until they were brought. To Fitzgerald's disgust, she prevailed
upon one of the junior MOs to give her access to some of the rooms in
the hospital, and she and her nurses took over the service. Perhaps, in
this and other dealings with Hall, Nightingale was high-handed, but she
was surely under great provocation.[49]

Florence Nightingale reported, both informally in letters of the
spring of 1856 and in the official written report she presented to the
Royal Commission in 1857, that she found the General Hospital at Balaclava in a state of indescribable filth and the patients horribly neglected.
"Your pig sty is cleaner than our Quarters or than the wards of the Hospital, as left by Mother Bridgeman," wrote Florence Nightingale on April
17 to her uncle Sam. "The patients were grimed with dirt, infested with

vermin, with bedsores like Lazarus, (Mrs. Bridgeman, I suppose, thought it holy.)" Nightingale and her nurses spent "two days hard whitewashing & cleaning—after three days washing & dressing the Patients, one of whom takes Mrs. Roberts six hours daily—being one mass of bed sores."[50] Sir John Hall came to inspect the hospital, declared that he wished it returned to precisely the admirable condition in which it had been hitherto, and instructed that none of the MOs should henceforward interfere in any way with the provisions of Purveyor Fitzgerald. However, Hall and Fitzgerald had essentially lost the medical battle. With the war over and all the troops returning home, they determined to keep their powder dry and their resentments hot for the bureaucratic battles they could see coming.

In fact, in the 1857 inquiry on medical care during the Crimean War, Hall and Bridgeman vigorously denied Florence Nightingale's assertions about the condition of patients in the General Hospital under their administration. The horrible fate of one poor man called McDonald became a minor *cause célèbre*. This was the patient whose bedsores Mrs. Richards spent six hours a day dressing. In her testimony for the Report of the Royal Commission on the Sanitary State of the Army, the Reverend Mother Bridgeman wrote that indeed McDonald was a tragic case, a man who had entered the hospital with severe frostbite and had suffered amputations. His bedsores became so extensive and his pain so great that the kindhearted Irish nurses could not bear to torture him by changing his bedlinen. The orderlies, who alone had permission from the MOs to change wound dressings, had also rightly refrained from doing so, out of compassion. Bridgeman admitted that indeed McDonald's sheets had probably not been changed in the two weeks prior to her departure, but insisted that he had been assisted in relieving himself. Mrs. Roberts's attempt to clean this man's wounds, in Bridgeman's view, was barbaric, a heaping of agony upon pain, since the poor creature was obviously going to die very soon.[51]

The feud between Nightingale and Bridgeman has been intently scrutinized. In my view, the importance of the religious issues that set Bridgeman and Nightingale in opposing camps cannot be overestimated. Frances Bridgeman and her fifteen nuns were good-hearted, well-meaning women—Nightingale always acknowledged this—but all the available testimony shows that they were not good nurses.

Mother Bridgeman's conception of her nuns' mission in the East was diametrically opposed to that of Florence Nightingale, and she therefore felt it her solemn religious duty to deny Nightingale's authority, escape her jurisdiction, and thwart her wherever possible. But if Mother Bridgeman's party had accepted Miss Nightingale's system, kept the wards as clean as possible, boiled the sheets and the shirts to kill the lice, and given the men chicken soup and lemonade as well as selfless, prayerful attention, their patients would have been the better for it.

BRIDGEMAN'S DEPARTURE stoked the ire of Hall and Fitzgerald, and Florence Nightingale knew they would take revenge on her for the other women's intransigence. Anticipating problems, Nightingale had brought with her to Balaclava all the nonperishable goods her nurses would need over the next months, "leaving the Queen to provide only meat, bread, porter, fuel & candle," as she put it in a letter to her uncle. These were the basic items the Bridgeman party, Miss Weare, Mrs. Davis, and Miss Clough had all drawn as their army rations, and Nightingale and her party were certainly entitled to them too. Nightingale was now an advanced student of the imposing volume *Regulations for the Management of Army Hospitals, at home, & abroad, & for the rendering of Hospital Accounts; with an Appendix of Forms.* Even as she was cleaning up the filth at the General Hospital and getting her nurses properly settled in other hospitals, she filled in requisition after requisition for food and fuel, complied with every regulation, waited on Fitzgerald's good pleasure for hours without obtaining an interview, and was generally treated more like a "tramp"—the word is hers—than an international heroine.

The weather in the Crimea in March and April was snowy, and the roads between Nightingale's set of huts at the Castle Hospital up on the heights of Balaclava and the General Hospital and administrative headquarters at the port of Balaclava were still difficult. The mule cart that Nightingale had been given for her use in October was useless in such conditions, and she was forced to ride and at times to lead her horse when the way got especially dark and treacherous. Often she was on horseback all day, the loyal Robert Robinson by her side, with only a little brandy and water to maintain her courage. As she joked to friends, the Crimea was driving even her to drink. Regimental officers, especially the officers at the Land Transport Corps, who had seen what Nightingale and her nurses did for their sick men, were now warmly on the women's side. They offered to give Nightingale meat and bread and fuel from their own supplies, but she refused. From the beginning of her great venture, she had engaged to submit to army authority and obey army rules to the best of her ability. She would not give Hall and Fitzgerald any ammunition by taking anything from the army that the army did not choose to give her as of right. She would smile at Fitzgerald's impertinent underlings. She would ask politely to see him, kick her heels in his anteroom, and finally take a quiet exit when his door remained closed. She would not act like a prima donna or a darling of the press.

But in the midst of this standoff with the Purveyor's department, Florence Nightingale received a letter Sidney Herbert had written more than a month earlier, begging her to control her emotions and curb her tongue when dealing with men like Fitzgerald if she wished to get the Panmures of the world on her side. Herbert remarked that ministers of the Crown like himself were accustomed to living in whole beds of thorns, while she had received merely a prick. Nightingale was in no mood to be condescended to. On April 3 she fired back a vintage piece of the old Nightingale emotional rhetoric.

> We have now been ten days without rations. Lord Cardigan was surprised to find his horses die at the end of a fortnight because they were without rations & said that they 'chose' to die, the obstinate brutes! The Inspector General [Hall] & Purveyor [Fitzgerald] wish to see whether women can live as long as horses without rations. I thank God—my charges have felt neither cold nor hunger, & are in efficient working order—having cooked & administered in both Hospitals the whole of the Extras for 260 bad cases ever since the day of our arrival. I have, however, felt both. I do not mean to make a martyr of myself; within sight of the graves of the Crimean Army of last winter (too soon forgotten in England) it would be difficult to do so. I am glad to have had the experience. For cold & hunger wonderfully sharpen the wits . . . You say this is but one bud of the bed of roses upon which Secretaries of State are wont to lie. I have seen enough of Govt. to know what that bed must be. But, till Secretaries of State have known what it is to have

the reputations of their wives & daughters slandered, for party purposes, till you have known what it is to be uncertain for many days where you should get food or warmth for those beautiful children who are standing round your table, & to feel that grinding anxiety for the responsibility of the lives and healths of those under your charge, & to doubt whether you are not sacrificing them, in your turn, to considerations for the good of the work, I deny that you can cull one bud from my bed of roses, or feel its fragrance afar off.[52]

Nightingale was always prone to exaggeration and melodrama. Ten days of sleeping in a cold hut, eating canned food, riding about in the snow for many hours of the day and night, and meeting bureaucratic rebuffs is hardly a martyrdom. But all the same, Nightingale's situation and her reactions mark a stage in the history of women's slow, contested entry into the public sphere. Florence Nightingale was not a mother trying to feed her children, though this was an image she liked to use. She was a junior woman officer in a war zone, responsible for the health and safety of her women subordinates, and this was unprecedented.[53] Nightingale upset the Fitzgeralds and Halls of the world in part because she dared to enter their territory and challenge their competency. She, Eliza Roberts, Jane Shaw Stewart, and Sister Mary Gonzaga were showing men how to do their job.

Having got all her complaints off her chest to her dear friend Herbert, Florence Nightingale soldiered on. The rations and the fine spring weather probably came at about the same time to raise her spirits and stiffen her resolve. In her last months, Florence Nightingale was once again deeply involved in individual bedside nursing. In April, Sister Mary Martha, one of the Bermondsey nuns who had only recently arrived in the East, fell ill with fever, and Florence Nightingale, fearing she had brought this woman from England to her death, undertook to nurse her. She wrote a humorous letter to her sister Parthe:

Would you like to see me hunting rats like a terrier dog? Me!
Scene in a Crimean hut.
Time midnight
Dramatis Personae—

Sick Nun in fever perfectly deaf
Me the only other occupant of the hut
Except
Rat sitting on rafter over sick nun's head
& rats scrambling about.
Enter me, with a lantern in one hand & a broom-stick in the
    other . . . me, commonly called "Pope" by the Nuns, makes ye
    furious Balaclava charge, i.e. the light cavalry come on & I am
    the Russian gun.
Light cavalry ensconces itself among my beloved boots & squeak—
    Desperate Papal aggression.
Broom-stick descends—enemy dead—"Pope" executes savage war
    dance in triumph, to the unspeakable terror of nun & of him-
    self
Slain cast out of hut unburied.[54]

The rats were even more of a threat at Balaclava than they were at
Scutari, and one day a nurse who had plumped down on her bed in exhaustion shot up quickly to find that she had squashed a whole nest of
newborn rats. When a non-commissioned officer presented the nursing
ladies with a little yellow cat, they were ecstatic.[55]

FLORENCE NIGHTINGALE remained in the Crimea until the last of
the soldiers had been sent home. She personally intervened with General Stokes and General Wyndham to secure a paid passage home for the
women and children who were attached to men in the ranks and who
had been employed in various ways but were now viewed as a nuisance.[56]
She paid a final visit to the plains of Inkerman and Balaclava and picked
a little bunch of flowers from soil nourished by the bodies of thousands
of men, most of them buried in unmarked graves and now forgotten.
When all the hospitals in the Crimea had been closed, she returned to
Scutari to repeat the process. By the end of her tour of duty, Florence
Nightingale had become the most conscientious and supportive superintendent, worrying over her nurses like an old sheepdog with her prized
ewe lambs. Her subordinates adored her. Before the nurses left the
Crimea—and this group of nurses, nuns, sisters, and ladies were now all

happy to bear the title of nurse—Nightingale arranged a series of picnics for them in the famous sites in and around Sevastopol, and they were surprised and delighted with the savory little meals she sent with them. When Lady Cranworth, at Nightingale's suggestion, sent over some caps like the ones she herself wore, with a lovely little sprig pattern in the muslin, the nurses were charmed. With scrupulous care, Nightingale completed the business of writing reports on each woman who had served, paying their wages, arranging their transport home, and finding them good positions if they needed them.

The British government was anxious to send a man-of-war to bring Miss Nightingale home. Entire regiments, complete with military bands, were gearing up to greet her on her return, and the press planned to be out in force. "Triumphal arches, addresses from mayors and corporations, and a carriage drawn by her neighbours were at once suggested."[57] Florence Nightingale refused the man-of-war and dreaded the welcoming committees, bands, and reporters. All too aware by now that things she wrote in private letters often became international news, she was elusive in her communications with her family about exactly when she planned to leave Turkey and what ship she would take. She sent ahead of her the one-legged sailor boy William and the little Russian boy Peter as well as a cat and Roosh, a huge and rare Russian dog that had been found as a starving pup on the heights above Balaclava and given to her as a present by the men.

On about July 27, Florence Nightingale, her aunt Mai, and Eliza Roberts traveled back to England on the steamer *Danube*. They came via Athens, Messina, and Marseilles and spent one night in a modest hotel in Paris. Mai and Florence traveled under the names of Mrs. Smith and Miss Smith and arrived in London at night, quite undetected. Early the next morning, August 7, the nuns at the Bermondsey Convent were astonished to find Miss Nightingale at their door. She had come to give thanks with them in their chapel. Nightingale then took the train up north, arrived at her little local station at Whatstandwell, confided her luggage to the stationmaster, and walked across the fields to Lea Hurst. The Nightingales' housekeeper, chancing to look out of a window, saw her entering through the back gate. And in this way, in her thirty-seventh year, Florence Nightingale moved decisively off the stage and into the wings of Victorian history.

Chapter 20

LIVING TO FIGHT
THEIR CAUSE

I n Turkey and in the Crimea, Florence Nightingale's work constantly made the front page. For twenty-one months she was the
most famous woman in Europe, perhaps in the world. Everything she did was scrutinized, publicized, denigrated or, more often, applauded. It is as the Lady with the Lamp, the heroine of Scutari, that she
remains imprinted on the world's memory even today, almost one hundred and fifty years later.

But Nightingale's really important work, in her own eyes and in the
eyes of those contemporaries who knew her, was done behind the scenes
after her return from Turkey. It went on for decades, proceeding slowly
and painfully. It had nothing of romance, of myth, of sensation. The
enigma of Florence Nightingale's life centers in this seemingly overnight
transformation from a high bright flame to a steady, cooling, smolder-
ing heat.

Nightingale's first instinct on her return was to take a hospital position far away from London, in a mission, for example, like her friends
Frances Hill in Athens or Paulina Irby in Bosnia. But the reputation, the
fame which she both cursed and counted on, made a modest retreat of
this kind impossible. The world demanded that she stay, and since the
world's demands were expressed in terms of service and sacrifice, she was
unable to resist. She had tasted power, she had tested her abilities, she
had seen her authority grow. She wanted to do more of what she had
done in the Crimea. But she also feared to lose her soul. Was it possible

The three homeless boys Florence Nightingale brought back with her from the war zone, together with the Russian dog given to her as a pup by the soldiers. Sketch by Parthenope Nightingale.

for a woman living in the England of Victoria to do as St. Catherine of Siena or St. Teresa of Avila had done—live the disciplined, ascetic life of the religious recluse while consulting with kings and having a hand in public policy?

When she first returned from Turkey, the faces of the men she had seen die at Scutari and Balaclava haunted Florence Nightingale. She could not sleep and could not bear the sight of food; she paced the floor at night wringing her hands or spent hours sitting looking fixedly out of the window. She refused to see anyone and barely glanced at the flood of adulatory letters and gifts that poured in from well-wishers. When the Duke of Devonshire arrived at Lea Hurst to present Florence with a silver owl, Fanny and Parthe were obliged to try to explain to the deaf old man that Florence was simply too unwell to come downstairs. And then, at the end of August, a unique opportunity arose for Nightingale to use her influence on behalf of the army. The Queen and Prince Albert, who had been deeply impressed by Miss Nightingale's work in the Crimea, invited her to come to Balmoral and tell them personally what she had seen and learned during the recent war. They wished, they made it known, to find out what they could do for her.

McNeill, Tulloch, Stafford, Lefroy, Sutherland, and Rawlinson were dazzled by the possibilities raised by this invitation. These were all brilliant, dedicated, able men with more ideas than power who were anxious to reform the organization of the British army's support services from top to bottom, and they were convinced that Florence Nightingale was the person to get the ball rolling. In that quiet, witty, ladylike, rapier way of hers, she could persuade the Queen that the troops to which both she and Victoria were so devoted needed and deserved reforms. As for Prince Albert, Florence Nightingale was exactly the kind of intelligent, informed, capable, yet religious person with whom he felt most comfortable. Her Majesty, once brought into the reformers' camp, would know how to put pressure on Lord Panmure. He was an amiable gentleman, but lazy and far more interested in grouse shooting than in the War Office.

The plan was that Florence Nightingale would ask the Queen to give her a royal commission to look into the state of the army. The commission would be the reforming party's opportunity to expose to the world the polluted, immoral, treacherous life that the army forced upon its soldiers, in peace and in war. Amazingly, the plan worked. The Balmoral visit, or visits, proved a huge success. As John Sutherland wrote to Nightingale in high glee on receiving the miraculous news that there was indeed to be a royal commission on the state of the army and that, thanks to her influence, he was actually to be a commissioner: "I am led to believe that there must be a foundation of truth under the old myth abut the Amazon women somewhere in the East of Scutari. All I can say is that if you had been queen of that respectable body in old days, Alexander the Great would have had rather a bad chance."[1]

Nightingale in fact needed little persuasion and even less coaching to lead the army reform party. This, she was sure, was the ultimate service that divine Providence had put before her. The task at hand was not to take vengeance on men like Hall and Cardigan and Wreford. It was to try to prevent the same thing happening again next time. As Nightingale wrote in December 1856: "We can do no more for those who have suffered and died in their country's service; they need our help no longer; their spirits are with God who gave them. It remains to us to strive that their sufferings many not have been endured in vain—to endeavour so to learn from experience as to lessen such sufferings in future by forethought and wise management."[2]

For some fourteen years Florence Nightingale and her kitchen cabinet of dedicated men forced a raft of reforms through a benevolent but inert government and a resolutely hostile military bureaucracy. Sidney Herbert, by his high pedigree, great wealth, and extraordinary personal connections and diplomatic skills, made the reform campaign palatable to the aristocrats in political power and glamorous to the public. However, except for Herbert, the reformers were men of Nightingale's own upper middle class, men determined to create a society where ability, not birth, was what counted.[3] Nightingale was the chief strategist, chief statistician, chief correspondent, chief worker—the one essential person upon whom the whole male team of experts relied.

Her greatest achievements were the two royal commissions that reported in 1858 and 1863. The first commission in particular was essentially her work from beginning to end. Before he finally, reluctantly, acceded to appointing the commission, Lord Panmure asked Florence Nightingale for a full report on the Crimean War. In six months of frantic work, Nightingale produced a report of 830 octavo pages, to which she subsequently added another 184 pages when official army responses began flowing in. Modestly entitled *Notes Affecting the Health, Efficiency, and Hospital Administration of the British Army,* this report presented a formidable raft of hard information, statistical tables, and tart analysis, larded with firsthand testimony, personal observations, and a unique sensibility. The royal commission's ultimate report is largely based upon it. *Notes* was probably the best thing that Florence Nightingale ever wrote, and it is almost unknown. Nightingale had a small number of copies privately printed and sent to chosen friends, but since 1857 few people have read it.

Having successfully persuaded the Queen and bullied Lord Panmure into agreeing to a commission, Nightingale handpicked the commissioners and proceeded both by inspections and correspondence to gather even more information, this time about the army in peacetime. She wrote much of the testimony to be given before the commission and planned most of the interviews. She even directed how best to cross-examine key witnesses like Sir John Hall, that old "Knight of the

Crimean Burying Grounds" and now the top prospect to succeed his old
friend Sir Andrew Smith at the head of the Army Medical Board. Sidney
Herbert, who chaired the royal commission, applied to Nightingale almost hourly for facts, analysis, drafts of speeches. The final report was
largely written by her, mostly with her own pen. The one thing she did
not do was put her signature to any document or give her evidence before the royal commission in person. There was never, even from her
most adoring supporters, the suggestion that she might serve as a commissioner. Even an Amazon was still a woman.

The great conclusions reached by the Nightingale team and duly
written up in the commission's report were the following. First, mortality among the troops during the Crimean War had risen by the beginning of 1855 to hitherto unprecedented heights and then plummeted
even more rapidly in the spring once basic sanitary measures were enacted and basic support services were reliably supplied. As Nightingale
pointed out with devastating accuracy, the British army had in the
Crimea conducted a huge experiment on sanitation, using real human
lives, and the results were incontrovertible. Clean water, fresh food, good
latrines, and suitable clothing and housing saved lives. Second, saving
lives by taking precautionary sanitary measures was cost-effective for an
army at war since there were more healthy soldiers to do the fighting.
Third, and this was the real thunderbolt, new data that Nightingale and
her team collected especially for the commission revealed that in peacetime the mortality rate for men in the army aged between twenty and
thirty-five was almost double that of civilians. Wherever a barracks was
situated, be it in tony Kensington or seedy Chatham, two of the soldiers
confined to that barracks died each year for every person, regardless of
age and sex, living in the surrounding community. The *peacetime* mortality rate among army recruits in the mid-nineteenth century exceeded
that recorded at the height of the Great Plague of 1665.

Nightingale and her group now made sure that their commission's
findings and recommendations hit the front page. The British people
howled for reforms, and the government and the civil service were
obliged to give ground. Over the next few years, the training, professional advancement, and institutional organization of the British Army
Medical Department were restructured. An army medical school was set
up as well as an army statistics department, just as Nightingale had

recommended in her letters to Sidney Herbert in 1855. The construction and maintenance of army barracks and stations at home and abroad were redesigned. Following the introduction of these reforms, mortality in the army based in England fell sharply. And then the Nightingale team, encouraged by their success, went on to tackle the problem of the army in India with a new royal commission.

India, which then comprised the whole of the Indian subcontinent, was Britain's largest and most important colony. Florence Nightingale was never able to realize her dream to go out to India, but through correspondence she became an expert on Indian land tenure and irrigation, its patterns of disease and famine, its caste system, its attitudes toward women, its village life. "How People May Live and Not Die In India" became not only the title of one of her few signed publications but the absorbing interest in her life for ten or more years. On the days before the mails went out to India, the Prime Minister might call, the Queen of Prussia might ask for a few minutes, but no one got in to see Florence Nightingale. Her own sister, who lived a few houses away, did not even try.

Nightingale's influence over public affairs was greatest between 1858 and 1872, a period when her friends in the Whig-Liberal party were in power. During this time she wrote one minor classic under her own name—the famous *Notes on Nursing* that earned her money she could find good uses for, and is still in print today. Nightingale wrote speeches for cabinet ministers to deliver in Parliament and tried not to wish she could be in Parliament and speak for herself. She endlessly drafted and redrafted regulations for various public bodies. She leaked information to key journalists, like Harriet Martineau, to keep the public informed and clamoring for reform. She labored over the construction of forms to be used in the collection of medical data and charmingly twisted the arms of powerful medical men like Sir James Paget to use her forms in major hospitals like St. Bartholemew's. Many of these forms were still in use in the twentieth century.

Nightingale was of the firm opinion that reform could be effective only when the facts in the matter were known. Action must rest on solid information. One of Nightingale's most ambitious research projects was to send out what we would now call questionnaires to all the military stations in India. She was for the first time attempting to establish objectively and in detail what effect the British Raj was having not only upon the occupying forces but upon the civilian populations. Nightingale herself received all the answers to the questionnaires and, with the help of John Sutherland, William Farr, and Arthur Hugh Clough, collated, analyzed, and wrote up the data. The whole enterprise was creative, innovative, influential, and exhausting. Florence Nightingale's name continued to be revered in India through the twentieth century.

As a young woman Nightingale had studied statistics and corresponded with the great Quetelet. Now, with the help of her new friend William Farr, the great British pioneer in medical statistics, she developed the famous "coxcombs," colored diagrams that conveyed complex information at a glance. She also became fascinated by planning and engineering blueprints. She pored over the designs of existing hospitals and drew up plans for new ones in Lisbon, Rangoon, and many English towns. She engaged in an international correspondence whose full extent is only now becoming apparent.

Nightingale loved facts and absorbed details. She knew how far it was possible to travel on a winter day in Canada by sled, how to make a good kit for a canvas bed to be assembled in a war zone, the number of inches there should be between hospital beds, the recipe for a tasty, cheap, nourishing soup. But through the facts she always saw lives. "No one can feel for the Army as I do," Nightingale remarked to a friend in 1857, and emotion charged everything she wrote. She developed a rhetoric of outrage that would reach people's hearts and puncture bureaucratic complacency. Sometimes the rhetoric consisted in extreme brevity, as in this section from her report to the first royal commission on the army: "Question: To what do you mainly ascribe the mortality of the hospitals [during the Crimean campaign]? Answer: To sanitary defects." Sometimes she would make a staggeringly large pronouncement: "Let us now ask, how it was that our noble army all but perished in the East? And we shall at the same time learn how it has happened that so many hundreds of millions of the human race have by pestilence perished before our time . . . The three things which all but destroyed the army in the Crimea were ignorance, incapacity, and useless rules; and the same thing will happen again, unless future regulations are framed more intelligently and administered by better informed and more capable officers."[4]

Sometimes she invests a piece of data with dramatic intensity. "With our present amount of sanitary knowledge, it is as criminal to have a mortality of 17, 19, and 20 per 1000 in the Line, Artillery, and Guards in England, when that of Civil life is only 11 per 1000, as it would be to take 1100 men per annum out upon Salisbury Plain and shoot them." Sometimes, she begins tamely, only to strike at the end like a scorpion: "If there be an exception, that is, if there be a single station in India with a good system of drainage, water supply and cleansing for itself and its bazaars, with properly planned and constructed barracks, provided with what is necessary for occupation and health—a station where the men are not encouraged to drink, and where they are provided with rational means for employing their time—to such a station these remarks do not apply. But I have not found it."

When civil war broke out in the United States in 1861, officials of the federal government turned to Florence Nightingale for advice on military hospitals. When war broke out between France and Prussia in 1870, Florence Nightingale was deeply involved with the efforts of the newly formed Red Cross organization to bring good medical care to the wounded of both nations. The Queen of Prussia, Queen Victoria's eldest daughter, corresponded and even managed to secure an interview with Nightingale in order to discuss nursing and hospital services. Successive viceroys of India, before sailing out to take up their posts, conferred with Miss Nightingale, who appeared to know more about India than anyone else.

When in the early 1870s Nightingale's personal influence with the highest echelon of government ceased, she turned her prodigious energy and her vast network of allies back to the problems of British civilian hospitals, lying-in wards, and workhouses. For the first time she interested herself directly in the work of the Nightingale Fund and in the training of nurses. One of her key goals was to train women nurses who, working both in hospitals and in the community at large, would, she believed, transform the provision of health care on every level and save an untold number of lives. The "Nightingale Nurse" became established as a model of trained, disciplined, dedicated professionalism.[5]

Throughout her sixties and seventies, Florence Nightingale was in touch with idealists, reformers, and iconoclasts from all over the world. She maintained a loving correspondence with George Gordon, the tragic hero of the siege of Khartoum. Giuseppe Garibaldi, the exiled hero of the Risorgimento, visited Nightingale at her home and saddened her by his airy impracticality. Benjamin Jowett, the controversial master of Balliol College, Oxford, became her dear friend and spiritual counselor and asked for her comments on his new edition of the works of Plato. John Stuart Mill begged her in vain to come out of the shadows and lend her name to his campaign to extend the suffrage to women. Nightingale did, however, wholeheartedly back the campaign to repeal the misogynist Contagious Disease Acts.[6] As a private individual, Nightingale made countless donations and subscriptions to individual charities, though she rarely allowed her name to be used as a fund-raising tactic.[7] For many years, for example, she was a loyal correspondent and financial supporter of Paulina Irby, who ran a mission for the poor in Bosnia.

After 1857, Florence Nightingale worked in obscurity, promoting the advancement of others, rarely allowing her name to come before the public, refusing all honors. By the 1870s, most people in Britain probably assumed she was dead. When in 1909 she was given the Order of Merit, Britain's highest civilian decoration, which had never before been given to a woman, she was completely blind and largely unaware of what was happening around her.

Her executors were under instructions that, after her death, her body was to be given for dissection. There was to be no state funeral, Nightingale stipulated, no burial in Westminster Abbey with the famous dead. In partial obedience to her wishes, after her death her body was brought to the little churchyard of East Wellow and buried next to her parents. The simple, four-sided monument to the four Nightingales reads on one side simply: "F.N. Born May 1820. Died 13 August 1910."

FROM EARLIEST CHILDHOOD Nightingale had been a person who made an impression on anyone who met her. Her voice, her manner, and her conversation were striking, and though far from beautiful, she remained in people's memories. She had charisma, and everyone felt it, from the soldier with one leg lying on a straw bed in the Barrack Hospital at Scutari to Queen Victoria at Balmoral. After 1857, Nightingale gave up the weapon of presence, exerting her influence mainly at a distance. For the last fifty-two years of her life, she lived the life of a recluse. People all over the world knew her handwriting, felt the force of her personality leap off the page, but never set eyes upon her in person. Harriet Martineau, for example, who worked with Nightingale on many campaigns and was a family friend, could never wangle an invitation to South Street. Prime Minister Gladstone, the Grand Duchess of Baden, and Lord Stanley, viceroy of India, alone and without acolytes, might be admitted to the Nightingale sanctum. But even they might be disappointed to learn, when the appointed day arrived, that Miss Nightingale was after all too unwell, or perhaps too busy, to receive them.

Florence Nightingale believed that she was compelled to lead this extraordinary life because she was ill, at times so ill that doctors feared for her life. For at least a decade after her collapse in the fall of 1857, she was convinced that she was dying. The acute attacks were followed by months of exhaustion and depression when Nightingale could not get out of bed even to walk to the window. During these years, only a carefully selected handful of people were allowed near her, most of them her professional colleagues. Even with John Sutherland, her chief lieutenant, even with Arthur Clough, her secretary, even with collaborators working downstairs from her in her own house, Nightingale preferred to communicate in writing. During this period Nightingale adopted a way of life that she would retain with some modifications until her death. She rarely left her house, always ate alone in her room, and saw people exclusively by appointment, and then only one at a time. There were years when her parents and her sister were specifically barred from seeing her, and old friends like Clarkey Mohl could not get past the door.

Florence Nightingale's period of greatest activity and achievement (1857–72) was exactly the period when she was bedridden, in an agony of pain, exhausted, depressed, and apparently on the edge of death. To her, this was not paradoxical but logical. God had called on her to serve and had made it clear in her mid-thirties that her service was to take the form of public health reform. Since it was working, not living, that counted, then all the time and energy she had must be devoted to work. Social life, friendships, and leisure activities like music or riding took up time and so must be ruthlessly sacrificed. If dedicating herself to work meant that she grew weak and ill and died, that was a sacrifice to offer to the Lord. In the next stage of existence, after death, she was sure, she would be closer to God and things would go better for her.

It is all too easy to understand how Florence Nightingale first fell ill. The twenty-one months of the Crimean War, added to the hard work of the previous year at Harley Street, left her exhausted. While abroad, she had regularly worked eighteen hours or more a day in difficult and distressing situations. She had been exposed to all kinds of pathogens and suffered one major illness. She had been under enormous, unrelieved stress. A deeply private person, a lover of solitude, she had been living in a room constantly thronged with people who demanded to speak to her. She had dressed, washed, slept, and performed all the most intimate bodily functions behind a curtain.[8] Constantly frustrated, angered, and desolated, she had remained outwardly serene and kept her voice low and sweet. It was all an excellent recipe for a nervous breakdown.

Once the great army reform campaign began in the fall of 1856, Nightingale spent hours in concentrated work, reading, writing, talking to her group, traveling all over the country. At the end of a day she would fall onto a couch in virtual catatonia. Constantly urged by family, friends, allies, and medical advisors to rest, eat, get away from work, take a break, Nightingale worked all the harder and lashed out bitterly against anyone who tried to stop her. And then she fell ill, a combination of nervous breakdown and, very probably, an acute attack of the severe brucellosis that would eat away at her body for the next fifteen or more years.

In this crisis, Nightingale became a volcano of conflicting emotions. The brunt was borne by her sister and her mother, but John Sutherland, who had been her physician and was never afraid to speak his mind, got his share of her tongue. He wrote begging her to eat meat, stop working, and stay away from London. Florence was sure that Sutherland had been egged on by Parthe, and she was furious.

> Now in what one respect could I have done other than I have done?" she wrote to Sutherland. "Or what exertion have I made that I could have left unmade? . . . Had I lived anywhere but handy would Mr. Herbert have used me? . . . Had I 'lost' the Report [i.e., the long report on the Crimean War demanded by the War Office], what would the health I would have saved have 'profited' me? Or what would ten years of life have advantaged me, exchanged for the ten weeks this summer?"[9]

Florence Nightingale and her doctors were sure she was dying, but she did not die, not in 1857 and not in 1861, when, as she told her father, she surely meant to die. Nightingale began her life of invalidism and reclusion on the assumption that God meant for her to die young— before she was forty. Instead Nightingale was to live for fifty years in elegant, cosseted solitude and watch as other people died. It was a fundamental miscalculation, and during the long years when both the work and the pain of illness seemed unrelenting, she raged against her fate, in letters and in private notes.

Her entries and marginal notes written on her 1877 desk diary offer poignant evidence of her state of mind.[10] As we saw in an earlier chapter, when she was a teenager, Florence Nightingale tried to put all the facts she had learned in one tiny book she could keep in her reticule. By the time she was fifty-seven, the publishing world had caught up with her, and it was possible to buy a *Gentleman's Pocket Companion,* which was a kind of mini-encyclopedia. For each day of the year, the diary supplied the day in the Anglican calendar (Epiphany, Whitsunday, Circumcision), the phase of the moon, the times of the rise and set of the sun, the dates when Parliament and the central courts were in session, and the births and deaths of famous people, ancient and modern. Every empty space in Florence Nightingale's copy of the *Gentleman's Companion* of 1877 is filled with her tiny handwriting. Here she notes her day's appointments and records what she has paid in taxes and rates and what she has laid out for coal, water, and gas as well as for her servants' wages, washing, and groceries. She tells us what she was reading, among much else, Harriet Martineau's *Autobiography,* Anthony Trollope's *Phineas Redux,* Thackeray's *Pendennis,* Thomas Hughes's *Tom Brown's Schooldays,* and George Eliot's *Daniel Deronda.* She notes on June 8: "Sorted & burned papers."

With sorrow, regret, guilt, and anger, she remembers family members who once meant so much and were now gone, either dead, or forever out of her life. The entry of February 7 ("End of 3 years slavery after my father's death") shows that Nightingale still resented the time she was forced to devote to her senile mother's care. From the entry of Saturday, April 6 ("O Mai, Mai, Mai, how art thou fallen?") it appears that she still views Aunt Mai's departure from her life as live-in companion in 1860 as treachery. But on October 31–November 1, guilt is uppermost in her thoughts of the dead Charles Bracebridge ("Mr. Bracebridge deserted by me"). The accompanying notation referring to her uncle Sam ("Kiss of reconciliation to Uncle S.") is ambiguous, though it seems probable that she never physically gave Sam such a kiss. She notes the anniversary of stages in her spiritual journey: "Forty years since first called Feb.7/37" and, more mysteriously, "March 16 Friday. Two years ago, my great repentance." She empathizes with the fate of animals hunted for sport: "Feb. 26. Picture of hare run down by 2 greyhounds & man galloping behind: all for the pleasure of the greyhounds & the man & not one to sympathize with the hare. That fate is thine."

Almost incongruously, a practical compendium of gentlemanly knowledge becomes for Florence Nightingale a repository for obsessive soul-searching, doubt, guilt, despair. On Saturday, April 7 she writes:

> 6am Because you have prostituted my gifts, show cause why you
>   should not be condemned
> I have no cause to shew
> Apr. 7 40 yrs

On the inside cover in tiny handwriting, we find a particularly poignant spiritual meditation that shows that in her fifty-seventh year, Florence Nightingale continued to be ravaged by repentance and self-reproach. Twenty years after the war, she is still wrestling with her Crimean experiences and poring over her own motivations—had she worked for God, for love of her fellow men, for Sidney Herbert, out of personal ambition and thirst for fame? Was her sin above all the sin of discontent and doubt and confusion, of being unable to feel God's love and trust Him?

> Oct. 29–30
> It isn't as if God was not here. Why do I moil and toil in their sights
> as if there were no others. I'm ready to [sic] whatever he wishes me.
> An old woman, nearly sixty years of age, who will not want anything earthly for long.
>   [Quote from Young's Night Thoughts] "Will God forsake & not
> return?

NIGHT "Down to the grave I sink alone
And have I then his love forgot?
Who gave His son unto the grave
Thy soul from endless woes to save.
And has he done all this for me *in love?*
& all this for SH [presumably Sidney Herbert] in love?
NIGHT: "And thy rebellious worm is still
the young man with the riches
would have done a great work like
the Crimea: but would not give up all
My work: an idol, A Moloch to me . . .
up the hill of difficulty—& down the valley
of Humiliation alone
And yet I am not alone for the Father is with me
And were all those five years 1856–1861
(for which so much was sacrificed) for nought?"

This is as close to stream-of-consciousness as one can get, and as I pored over the tiny crowded pages, I felt that to enter on someone's soul in this way was an unpardonable intrusion. Here was a document of extraordinary fascination that either Miss Nightingale or her executors should have destroyed, as they destroyed others.

FLORENCE NIGHTINGALE's invalidism is an issue that has exercised generations of biographers, historians, and critics. Was she really ill, and if so, what illness did she have that could account for so many symptoms and ninety years of life? Was she a hysteric, inventing symptoms, caught in the web of her unconscious, and then made really ill by dint of manifesting illness and receiving treatment that confirmed the diagnosis? Was she a malingerer, using illness to have her way and take revenge on her family? Was she a tragic victim, obliged to take on the life of an invalid because her family would give her no peace, would not allow her to do her work and achieve her destiny? All of these positions have been argued cogently and passionately.

In 1974 George Pickering, a distinguished professor of medicine, wrote an influential book in which he cited Florence Nightingale as an example of "creative malady." According to this post hoc diagnosis, Florence Nightingale had a strong healthy body but a tortured mind that expressed itself in physical symptoms. Pickering was sympathetic to Nightingale, but he gave it as his opinion that her illness was psychosomatic, born in the childhood stresses of her relation with her mother and her sister, and developed unconsciously to allow her to do the work to which she was committed. In 1983, the Australian historian Frank Smith went farther, arguing that Nightingale was not a neurasthenic but a conscious malingerer. Smith saw her as a cold, power-hungry woman who manipulated those around her by pretending to be in pain and close to death.

In 1995, D. A. B. Young revolutionized the whole field of what could be called Nightingale diagnostics by identifying a specific, well-documented disease that would account for the symptoms Nightingale reported over the years, and the strange course of her life.[11] This disease was severe chronic brucellosis, often called Malta fever, which begins when someone drinks the infected milk of goats or sheep. Within some ten days of ingestion, the bacterial agent causes acute illness and symptoms that correspond closely to those reported by Florence Nightingale when she fell ill with "Crimean fever" at Balaclava in May 1855. Then the bacterium may become an intracellular parasite, occasioning subsequent acute attacks, when the patient suffers agonizing pain in the joints and in the back, delirium, neurological damage, and severe depression. Recovery is slow, with frequent relapses; the patient is unable to eat or sleep and suffers a severe change in personality. An inability to move is common, because of the severe pain, and temporary paralysis is not rare. Brucellosis was not clinically described until 1861, its causal agent was not isolated until 1887, and effective treatment became possible only with the discovery of antibiotics.

One well-documented case bears a striking resemblance to Florence Nightingale's. Dr Alice Evans (1881–1975), a woman bacteriologist, was terribly ill for six years. Though she had been working with brucellosis, Evans's doctors could find nothing obvious wrong with her and dismissed her illness as neurasthenia. Finally, however, it became possible to culture brucellosis, and the bacterium was found in her blood. Evans still had recurrent acute and painful episodes of brucellosis for a further seventeen years, but she lived on into her ninety-fourth year. It was only through the experience of this woman scientist that the diagnosis of chronic severe brucellosis became possible.

Florence Nightingale's symptoms and the course of her illness correspond to a few documented cases of the virulent strains of brucellosis. In Turkey and the Crimea, she had every opportunity to contract the disease. Brucellosis is one of the diseases against which Nightingale's abstemious habits and strict attention to cleanliness would not have protected her. Refusing to drink the contaminated water of the Barrack Hospital, unwilling to drink only beer, wine, and spirits like most of the doctors and nurses, she probably felt she was safe drinking goat's milk. To me, the diagnosis of brucellosis is compelling. It explains so much that is enigmatic about Nightingale's life.

All the same, we will never know for certain that Florence Nightingale actually had chronic brucellosis, and the question remains: how would a remarkably intelligent and strong-willed person like Nightingale cope with a chronic, undiagnosed, untreatable disease? How would it affect her sense of self, her patterns of interaction, and her work habits? How would she relate what she was feeling in her body to her ideas, her ambitions, and her religious beliefs? As Dr. Monica Baly, the noted historian of nursing and one of the major experts on Nightingale, remarked, whatever might have been the physical cause, the psychosomatic element in Nightingale's condition cannot be ruled out. "There is a strong case," wrote Dr. Baly, "for suggesting that once she became bedridden Miss Nightingale manipulated her illness and those around to get her work done . . . Anyone who has spent long periods with her letters will conclude that she was inclined to dramatise everything, including her illness . . . The conclusion must be that, like so much Victorian illness, Miss Nightingale's illness was multifaceted, and compounded by the advice and treatment of the day."[12]

This remark makes excellent sense. From the very outset Nightingale's doctors gave her conflicting advice—eat more meat, take walks and drives, or, on the contrary, lie down, keep still, and eat no solid foods. In 1861, when her back pain was so excruciating that for forty-eight hours she tried to remain perfectly still, the subcutaneous injections of morphine which the Harley Street experts employed to ease her pain did her no lasting good and risked turning her into a functioning addict like her contemporary Elizabeth Barrett Browning. Fear of such terrible pain, together with morphine, can easily persuade a woman that she cannot get out of bed. Anyone who has lain on a couch for six years finds it hard to get up and start walking again.

But Florence Nightingale's retreat into her bedroom cannot be wholly explained by illness. Many sick people, forced to live much of their lives in bed, thrive on company and do everything they can to get about as soon as they feel a little better. Parthenope Nightingale Verney was precisely one of these. She suffered from what was probably rheumatoid arthritis that reduced her hands to claws by the time she was fifty. In her last years she was racked with cancer, and she died when she was only seventy-one. Parthe in her last three decades, as her sister testified many times, was constantly in an agony of pain, but she still researched, wrote, and published a series of books and articles. She traveled, paid visits, entertained, got about as much as she could, and loved to have visitors. That was her way to get past the pain, and in this, as in many other respects, she was different from her younger sister.

The unique conjunction of her illness, her conviction of a special divine mission, and her love of solitude turned Florence Nightingale into a recluse. As a small child she had found illness seductive. She enjoyed being in bed, even as she was told that it was sinful not to get up betimes. As she remembered it, her happiest time as a child was at age six, when she spent most of a year ill in bed being lovingly nursed by her aunts Julia and Mai and regarded tenderly by her mother. On some level, the life of a cosseted, protected invalid suited Florence.

Furthermore, Florence Nightingale had since childhood been instructed by her religion to fear the body. As an adolescent she became absorbed in the philosophy of Plato, who advised her to look beyond materiality. As a young woman Nightingale came under the influence of several outstanding Catholic nuns in Italy and Egypt and was so tempted by the monastic life that she contemplated converting to Roman Catholicism. Obsessed with the question of what God wanted from her, cerebral rather than sensual, Florence was prepared by her late thirties to sacrifice the body to the spirit. After thirty-six years of great activity and constant stimulation, after the stress and trauma of Scutari, after seeing so many people die in the prime of life, she presumed that she had no time to waste. And so she created a strange version of the monastic life. People would hear from her. Occasionally one person would be allowed to come and see her, as a visitor comes to the grille of the parlor of an enclosed order of nuns.

Thus the long battle Florence had fought over her duties to her family, her rights in society, and her needs for fulfillment ended in stalemate. She would play no more waltzes, paint no more oils, pour no more tea, attend no more dinners, make no more small talk. She would be by herself, free to fill her day with the activities she chose. No one would tell her what to do, no one would get on her nerves. Her illness guaranteed that.

The price of this stalemate was high for all the Nightingales. WEN, Fanny, and Parthe all loved Flo, relied on her, and delighted in her company, but they now saw little of her. For years, WEN and Fanny to all intents and purposes lost one of their daughters and Parthe lost her only sister. All three suffered from Florence's contumely, bitterness, and rejection.

For Florence the price was far higher. She found herself—"*nel mezzo del camin di sua vita,*" as her beloved Dante put it—constricted to the narrow physical realm her society had decreed was suitable for a woman of her class. She would henceforth shun all direct encounters with disease, death, dirt, obscenity, and deformity while dealing obsessively with all of these on paper. She would live a life of irreproachable respectability. It was a tragic parody of the Victorian ideal of pure, ethereal, private, protected womanhood, untouched by the material world, which Nightingale herself had denounced with almost unparalleled vigor in *Suggestions for Thought*. Small wonder that Florence Nightingale in her middle years was an angry, bitter, resentful woman, convinced that no one had suffered, no one had sacrificed, no one had lost as much as she.

REFORM WAS A fundamental impulse in Victorian society, and Florence Nightingale's dedication to reform and philanthropy does not make her unique. Many Victorian lives were a dizzying round of lectures, negotiations, lobbying, inspections, commissions, official dinners, business lunches, breakfast strategy sessions—in other words, meetings, with all the letters, reports, articles, essays, and minutes associated with them. Florence Nightingale differed from her counterparts, both male and female, because she did not do meetings. Occasionally she granted inter-

views, but after 1857 most of her business was carried on by correspondence. She became that rare phenomenon, a person committed to action
in the public sphere who remained not only out of the public eye but di-
vorced from the arenas of public life. To compound the oddness of her
situation, even though she spent much of her life writing, Nightingale
was not an author, and she published only scraps of her immense textual
output.

Nightingale differed from other Victorian women philanthropists
because her most important work was fundamentally political in nature—parliamentary lobbying, educating the public, and implementing
an enlightened public policy—even though politics at this time was a
largely male game. Private philanthropy was always a large part of
Nightingale's life, and it became more so after 1872, but it was not her
preferred sphere. During the years of her greatest influence and efficacy,
Nightingale was an outsider leading a team of male outsiders and
middle-level male insiders, negotiating with top-level insiders, and seeking to influence the conduct of the all-male Establishment.

Since even by the standards of her day Florence Nightingale was an
anomaly, it is difficult to get the measure of her achievement and assign
her a historical ranking. Was she or was she not, in Lytton Strachey's
phrase, a Great Victorian? Palmerston, Gladstone, Disraeli, and Shaftesbury made more important contributions to human history than Florence Nightingale did, but they also had far greater opportunities to do
so. General historians who favor the study of large databases, major
trends, and *mentalités* have no interest in individual heroes, much less
legends like Florence Nightingale. Historians of the army and of medicine have reduced her to the status of footnote at best, asserting that all
the things she worked for so frantically would have been achieved without her. Historians of women have found it hard to find a good slot for
Florence Nightingale, who refused to work for suffrage, wanted to be a
nurse, not a doctor, and was often vitriolic in her comments on women
of her own class. Why did Nightingale have to be so neurotic, so dys-
functional? Why could she not simply have embraced her fame and been
happy in the limelight?

Answering the question of Florence Nightingale's place in history is
made more complicated by the size and inaccessibility of the written
record that Nightingale left. To a terrifying degree, she reduced herself

to black marks on a white page. Thus, to know what she achieved—indeed, to know her—we need to read what she wrote. But most of her writing has remained unpublished, much of it in private collections, much of it handwritten and difficult to decipher. Palmerston, Gladstone, Disraeli, Shaftesbury, and the rest were prodigious writers who left an immense trove of documentation, but they were not creatures of the pen as Nightingale was. They spent their lives in company. They chaired meetings, conferred with allies, dined at the club, entertained constituents, made speeches, horse-traded at the House of Commons, hunted, fished, sailed, chopped wood, acted in plays, dandled babies on their knees, bailed children out of scrapes, chatted to tenants, and, at the end of the day, climbed contentedly into bed, usually with their wives. All of these men were important not just for what they wrote but also for what they did and for what they physically were, rubbing up against other human beings in love and lust and conflict. They left behind them a million memories in thousands of hearts. Florence Nightingale meanwhile ate alone and slept alone except for her cats. In her last fifty-two years she rarely went out. For at least two decades she never left her bedroom. She spent an inordinate portion of her ninety years lying down. She ate, drank, read, wrote, and prayed. She conversed mainly with her maid. She struggled, with terrifying success, to eliminate the body, to reduce her physical presence to text.

And all the while she documented every step of her dark and secret path, and the papers piled up. Though at several points in her life she destroyed some of her papers, she kept a great number. Though she begged friends to burn her letters or return them to her, some, like Henry Manning, refused. In the third codicil of her will, she finally decided not to order her executors to burn her papers but left the matter to their discretion, and so many of the papers she left have come into the public domain. The Nightingale collection is one of the largest in the British Library, and there are other significant holdings in private and public collections. Small caches of documents exist all over the world.

Florence Nightingale after the Crimean War lived a hidden life and acted anonymously, but in the end she decided to give the unknown future reader a chance to know her as no one who knew her could know her. Today, as her published and unpublished writings become available in electronic databases, we can see what she wrote to Herbert, to Mohl, to Bracebridge, to her mother, to her sister, to her lawyer, in the same year and over forty years. We can read what in her life no one else saw—her private notes. Her mind was a large, rich, wild, volcanic territory to which she has given us charts, projections, soundings, diagrams, surveys, reports. Florence Nightingale offered us the opportunity to criticize or admire her, praise her or blame her, love her or hate her, understand her more comprehensively than her companions in the flesh could. It is an almost intolerable burden.[13]

Chapter 21

FAMILY MATTERS

A workaholic who can barely get out of bed. A political lobbyist who avoids meeting people. An ascetic who lives in Mayfair. A recluse with contacts all over the world. A control freak who struggles to leave it all up to God. Florence Nightingale in the long last section of her life was a living oxymoron, and that she managed to achieve so much is a measure of her extraordinary capacity. But long-term invalidism is expensive in money and labor. People with no income who fall seriously ill either die, stagger out of bed to get on with life as best they can, or are cared for by their nearest and dearest. Nightingale probably would not have seen her fortieth birthday, much less enjoyed four decades of productive work as an internationally acclaimed expert in public health, without the wise, warmhearted, and unstinting support of her extended family.

Able, energetic, adoring allies flocked to Nightingale after the Crimean War, eager to serve as her legs, hands, eyes, and ears in the world because they recognized in her a superb tactician and policy analyst with an unparalleled capacity for work. But these men—and they were really almost all men at the outset—were practical men of business as well as idealists, and they also took Nightingale as their leader because she was so evidently a part of the political Establishment. Through her kinship network, Nightingale had been able to set up outstanding channels of communication with the government and civil service, notably the Queen and Prince Albert, Lord Palmerston, and Sidney Herbert, and with the leaders of British philanthropy, notably Lord Shaftesbury. Her membership in England's elite group was signaled by the fact that for forty-five years she lived and maintained her organizational headquarters in the City of Westminster, a forty-minute walk from the Abbey, Big Ben, and Buckingham Palace. No one was more aware than Nightingale herself that once she fell ill and was unable to get about the country or even the city, physical proximity to the Houses of Parliament and to the government offices at Whitehall was essential to her work. As she wrote to Sutherland: "Had I lived anywhere but handy"—that, is close to the Houses of Parliament—"would Mr. Herbert have used me?" Hence the Nightingale group's efficacy was made possible because people with clout were willing to find out what Florence Nightingale had to say because her house was in Mayfair and her hospitality impeccable.

But Florence Nightingale had no money of her own, and her earning capacity plummeted after the chronic brucellosis set in. Unlike her associate Harriet Martineau, she could not support herself and others through her work. Nightingale was able to live and work independently at 35 (later 10) South Street, just off Park Lane, because her father was willing to divert a considerable part of his income to her. Such paternal generosity was unusual. Victorian patriarchs, however wealthy, however loving, expected unmarried daughters to wait on them and had no incentive to be generous with money. Furthermore, the rest of the family, after some grumbling and backbiting from Fanny and Parthe, not only acquiesced to WEN's liberality but worked to make the philanthropico-political enterprise a success. Maintaining Florence became a clan project for three generations. Given the fact that she never married and had neither children nor nieces and nephews, this is a remarkable tribute to the extended family surrounding the four Nightingales.

WILLIAM EDWARD NIGHTINGALE did not receive a great deal in return for his generosity. The years 1857 to perhaps 1865 were among the most important and productive in Florence Nightingale's life, but they were also the years when she went into violent palpitations and felt unbearable pain at the mere idea that her parents and sister might try to see her. For months on end, they received not even a penciled note from her and her door was quite literally shut to them. But if Florence abandoned her family for some eight years, they did not abandon her. For two years she had been a hero, and now that she was helpless and dependent the family rallied around to do what was needed. Had Florence Nightingale remained healthy, it is unclear to what extent her father would have supported her work financially, but once she fell ill, once her life seemed to hang from a thread, her father could refuse her nothing. She had Harley Street specialists, an apartment in the Burlington Hotel, a rented house in Hampstead, and regular visits to the Malvern spa. When in 1861 Florence met a series of losses and professional setbacks, her family set her up in a home on South Street that gave her as much pleasure and comfort as she would permit herself, while also facilitating her work.

When Florence Nightingale had her first major breakdown in 1857, she had the luxury not only of Malvern and Hampstead but of a choice of caretaker. Hearing that her niece was mortally ill and had run away from her mother and sister, Aunt Mai rushed to Flo's rescue. Mai closed up her own home at Combe, sent her husband, Sam, and two younger daughters (unmarried at this point) to live with the Nightingales and any other friend who would take pity on them, and took up her station by her niece's bed.

The nursing duties Mai had undertaken were extremely taxing. Florence spent her days working like a fiend on her papers, entertaining visits from a stream of collaborators, and lying on the sofa virtually catatonic, yet unable to sleep or eat. She was a paradoxical mix of aggression and vulnerability, activity and passivity. One of Mai's most important duties was to mount guard over Flo, keeping away anyone whom she didn't specifically agree to see. This meant, above all, her parents and sister. Tact was one of Mai Smith's long suits, and she certainly needed it now. She wrote long, torturous letters to her brother and sister-in-law at Embley. She gave details of Flo's condition and justified her decisions. She sought to allay the Nightingales' extreme anxiety while at the same time precluding any attempt they might make to march into Flo's bedroom unannounced and assert parental control.

For many months, Flo and Mai lived in a fine fervor of commitment to each other and to the cause of army medical service reform. In the little enclosed world of the sickroom, the nearness of death lent exaltation to the business of everyday life, especially as the program of reform to which Florence believed she was giving her life moved forward at a giddy pace. Florence made her will, disposed of her belongings, and wrote emotional last letters to family and friends. She gave instructions that all her letters should be destroyed.[1]

But Florence did not die, and gradually the strain of the situation told upon Mai Smith. Unsurprisingly, her family—above all her husband, Sam—was unhappy to see her leave home for a second time in two years and once again become completely wrapped up in Florence. After two years, and no end in sight to Florence's need for her aunt's exclusive care, Sam Smith had had enough. He was convinced that not only his daughters' welfare and his own domestic comfort but his wife's health were being sacrificed on the altar of Florence's illness. And so Sam told Mai that if she continued to live with Florence, he would no longer come to see her. Forced to choose, in effect, between Florence and her own family, Mai Smith decided that she must return home. She had now devoted some three and a half years of her life almost entirely to her niece; she had given Florence all she had to give, and perhaps it was, in fact, too much for the good of them both.

Florence was outraged, incredulous, cut to the quick. This was betrayal of the blackest dye. Far from thanking Mai for all she had done, understanding the pressures she was under, and wishing her well, Florence was angry and unforgiving. The two women parted in bitterness.

In the coming years, family affairs inevitably brought Flo and Mai together again at Embley, but the rift was hard to breach. Toward the end of Mai Smith's life, after Sam's death in 1880, she and Florence began once again to exchange long letters, taking up the great questions that had absorbed them when Florence was still a girl—the fight of good against evil, free will and providence, woman's duty to God and man. At the end, there was a meeting of spirit, though not of body. When Mai died in 1889, her daughters, not Florence, were with her.

WHEN SAM SMITH delivered the ultimatum to his wife to leave Florence, he was acting not only for himself but for his daughter Blanche. Florence had managed to absorb the love and attention of not one but two key members of the Smith family—her aunt Mai and her cousin-in-law Arthur Hugh Clough.

Blanche Smith, Sam and Mai's eldest daughter, had married the im-

poverished poet Arthur Hugh Clough, somewhat against her parents'
wishes but with the enthusiastic support of her cousin Florence. The
Clough marriage took place in the summer of 1856, just before Florence
sailed off to Turkey, and Arthur was at the dock to wave her farewell. He
surely longed to go with her on the great adventure. Over the next years
Blanche and Arthur had three children in quick succession—little
Arthur, Florence, and Blanche Athena. When Florence returned from
the war, Arthur quickly took his place by her side as one of the soldiers in
the battle for reform, and after her collapse in autumn 1857, Clough became as indispensable to her as his mother-in-law, Mai Smith. He had
an excellent, trained mind, when it came to documentation he was an
expert, and she treasured his advice. Florence, Mai, and Clough worked
until all hours of the day and night, driven by high ideals and deep
affection.

Arthur Hugh Clough had an ill-paying job in school administration,
and when Florence asked him to become the secretary to the Nightingale Fund, he was grateful, as the salary was welcome. However, to his
two paying positions Arthur added his absorbing duties as Florence's
general factotum, and so he had little time for his family. The fact that
Clough could go up and see Florence Nightingale quite regularly while
no one else got past the front door grated on the rest of the clan, including Blanche, who had, after all, known Cousin Flo all her life. Arthur
and Mai were wafted around the country with Florence in a cloud of affluence and adulation, with Crimean veterans lining up to carry Florence
and her belongings from train to carriage. Meanwhile Blanche was left
to care for three small children on little money.

Arthur Hugh Clough's health was poor, and somewhere in his
youthful travels he had contracted malaria. After three years of working
three jobs, keeping stride with the relentlessly overachieving Florence,
breathing the polluted air of Victorian London, and finding a neglected
and reproachful family when he came home, Clough became seriously
ill. Florence, by her own account, was the one who decided that Clough
must imperatively leave England to try to regain his health, and who lent
him five hundred pounds for a journey to Italy. Clough left Florence
Nightingale and his family with bitter reluctance. He seems to have
known he was dying, and the lonely death in a foreign land of the poet
Keats a generation earlier surely haunted him. Italy did Arthur no good,

and Blanche and Arthur's sister were summoned in haste to the city of
Florence to be with him at the end.

The death of Arthur Hugh Clough followed shortly on the deaths
of four other important Nightingale friends and allies—Alexis Soyer,
Thomas Alexander, Prince Albert, and Sidney Herbert. As chairman to
the royal commission on the army and of all four subcommissions, Herbert had always been the key player in Nightingale's plan of reform.
When in 1860 the Queen made Herbert Secretary for War, it seemed
possible that all the institutional roadblocks set up by the War Office bureaucracy to impede reform would be finally swept away. But Herbert
had long been a sick man, and the War Office finished him off—he died
of kidney disease.

All the dead men were dear to Nightingale, and Herbert and Clough
were the men she loved most in the world. Their deaths also appeared to
ring the knell of all her professional hopes. She was the one supposed to
die. They were to carry on the great work, and advance the divine plan.
Florence Nightingale went into a despair that was close to madness.
Since she could never allow herself to doubt God's beneficent plan, she
struck out against those who came her way, and put her feelings down
on paper. Women became the chief target of her wrath, to judge from a
monstrous, fascinating letter she wrote to her old friend Mary Clarke
Mohl. Clarkey had at last managed to bring out her book on Madame
Récamier, which included a paean of praise to the cultural influence of
women. Florence emphatically did not agree.

> You say "women are more sympathetic than men." Now if I were
> to write a book out of my experience, I should begin, *Women have
> no sympathy.* Yours is the tradition—mine is the conviction of ex-
> perience. I have never found one woman who has altered her life
> by one iota for me or my opinions. Now, look at my experience
> with men. A Statesman [Sidney Herbert], past middle age, ab-
> sorbed in politics for a quarter of a century, out of *sympathy* for me,
> remodels his whole life and policy—learns a science of the driest,
> the most technical, the most difficult, that of administration . . . by
> writing dry regulations in a London room, by my sofa, with me.
> This is what I call real sympathy. Another (Alexander whom I made
> Director [of the Army Medical Board]) does very nearly the same

thing. He is dead too. Clough, a poet born if there ever was one, takes to nursing administration in the same way, for me. I only mention three, whose whole lives were re-modelled by sympathy for me. But I could mention others—Farr, McNeill, Tulloch, Storks, Martin, who in a lesser degree have altered their work by my opinions. And, most wonderful of all—a man born without a soul, like Undine—Sutherland. All these elderly men. Now just look at the degree in which women have sympathy—as far as my experience is concerned. And my experience of women is almost as large as Europe. And it is intimate too. I have lived and slept in the same bed with English Countesses and Prussian Bauerinnen, with a closeness of intimacy no one ever had before. No Roman Catholic Supérieure has ever had the charge of women of the most different creeds that I have had. No woman has excited "passions" among women more than I have. Yet I leave no school behind me. My doctrines have taken no hold among women . . . I have lived with a sister 30 years, with an aunt four or five, with a cousin two or three. Not one has altered one hour of her existence for me . . . Hilary [Bonham-Carter] is the type of want of sympathy. Because she is the most unselfish, and because she has a "passion" for me. Yet I have not influenced her one inch. Nay, rather all these women have influenced me . . . People often say to me, you don't know what a wife and mother feels. No, I say, I don't and I am very glad I don't. And *they* don't know what *I* feel . . . But I would mount three widows' caps on my head, "for a sign." And I would cry. This is for Sidney Herbert, I am his real widow. This is for Arthur Clough, I am his true widow . . . And this, the biggest widow's cap of all, is for the loss of all sympathy on the part of my nearest and dearest. (For that my aunt [Mai] was. We were like two lovers).[2]

After Arthur Hugh Clough's death, relations between Florence Nightingale and her cousin Blanche were at first distant, even frosty. However, with time, the ties of affection and shared commitments proved stronger than resentment. Florence's ardent championing of Clough as a great poet and heroic man could not but please Arthur's devoted widow and sister. Florence showed great admiration for Anne Jemima Clough's work to advance the cause of higher education for women and rejoiced when she became the first president of Newnham, the second women's college at Cambridge University. Above all, Florence, who had always loved children and been a great favorite with them, worked on establishing a good relationship with the three Clough children from the time they were born. When young Arthur, for example, was having troubles with love, perhaps surprisingly he confided his feelings to Aunt Florence, and she responded with tact and humor. Arthur Clough Jr. was one of the trustees under Nightingale's will, and he and his sisters received a sizable legacy from her.

WHEN MAI SMITH left for good, Florence still did not need to call in her mother and sister to look after her. Hilary Bonham-Carter was waiting in the wings, eager to take over her aunt Mai's duties.

Unfortunately, as a housekeeper, as an assistant, Hilary proved to be all goodwill and no efficiency. When the leaking cistern in the attic Nightingale had long complained about actually fell through the floor onto her bed, flooding the room and ruining the furnishings, Hilary, along with WEN and Uncle Sam, received a tongue-lashing from the furious invalid. Then there was the vexed issue of the statue. Florence Nightingale hated to have any portraits made and had persistently refused to sit for artists or sculptors. However, as a special favor, she agreed to allow Hilary to model a small standing figure of her. Unfortunately, Hilary could not get the sculpture right. She destroyed the head of her first attempt and agonized over the second while her reluctant sitter fumed. When Hilary's statuette was finally presented at the Royal Academy show in 1862, the Nightingale family all hated it.[3]

At the end of 1861 Florence asked Hilary to move out. She made the request as tactfully as possible. It would be a terrible wrench, almost like losing a limb, Florence said, but Hilary must now be free to pursue her own interests and live her own life. Florence would cope; in fact she had found a housekeeper who was paragon of efficiency, even if she did have a liking for drink. Not deceived, Hilary went away desolate. In February 1862, Mary Clarke Mohl, who for years had been Hilary's champion, wrote to Florence urging her to take Hilary back. "My Dearest, if she is useful to you as a limb, why should you amputate her? . . . She loves you better than anyone else, and it would be balm to her poor worn out spirit if she thought she was useful to you. . . . I agree with you, she ought to do for herself, but I am not sure her nature can bear it."[4]

Hilary continued to come over to do secretarial work for Florence, but soon her presence became as insupportable as Parthe's. Florence could not bear the sound of Hilary's step on the stairs and felt ill at the very idea that her cousin might dare to enter her room uninvited, as we see from this nasty little undated note: "You cannot think that I could consent to your coming & wasting all your afternoons here when *never* except by previous concert can I see you in the afternoon. Indeed it is a great aggravation to me to hear of your writing letters downstairs as I do continually. If you must spend your life letter-writing let it not be here. The utmost I think right to require is that you come once a week, if you will be so good & that always by previous concert. But never that you come to 'inquire' when it just only upsets me. Ever yours FN."[5] After 1862, Florence did not see her cousin. Hilary, Flo complained to Clarkey, was quite incapable of making an appointment and coming on time.

Hilary drifted from one relative to another, and then her health began to give grave cause for concern. One day, in the pouring rain, she arrived at Florence's door, but she could not get permission to go up. In May 1865, Hilary was diagnosed with cancer, and her last months were torture. Perhaps worse, the terrible pain fractured Hilary's faith in God. She reached out in her despair to her cousin Barbara Leigh Smith Bodichon, a wise and worldly person on the outskirts of the family, who could be trusted not to meet religious doubt with shock and horror. Barbara wrote back that she too struggled to preserve her faith in God. She got along through ritual and routine, by taking pleasure in friendship and putting on a bright gown when life was black. The most important thing her father taught her, wrote Barbara to Hilary, is never to stop working to make this world a better place. It is a beautiful letter. I hope it helped.[6]

Hilary Bonham-Carter died in September 1865, age forty-three. Her youngest sister, Elinor Dicey, whom she had cared for so lovingly as a child, was Hilary's nurse and companion through the final months. William Edward Nightingale probably felt the death of his niece Hilary more grievously than did her mother, Joanna. Hilary's father, John Bonham-Carter, had been WEN's best friend, and he too had died young. In recent years Hilary had been more of a daughter to WEN than his own. They had walked out together, attended art shows, talked books and politics. Sometimes she had come to look after him when he was sick. He would miss her terribly.

Florence was alerted to the fact that Hilary was fighting with death by their mutual friend Benjamin Jowett. She kept in close touch on events but made no effort to go and see her. In a September 15 letter to her father, Florence, inarticulate with grief, wrote of Hilary as the "golden bowl . . . the purest gold—*and the most unworked gold*—I have ever known," and in bitter self-reproach called herself "God's wild beast."[7] To Clarkey, whose grief was at least as great as her own, and who was all too likely to rail against a Providence that had seen fit to try a gentle, loving soul so cruelly, Florence deflected her impotent rage toward Hilary's family. As Florence saw it, Hilary had been slowly murdered by her relatives. She had laid herself as an offering on the altar of family, but her sacrifice was worthless. It had been made not to God but to the "dirty and disgusting" fetish of women's traditional duties to their parents. "Hilary's [sacrifice] really seemed to me to partake of a delusion. Because no one could say stronger things than she has to me, not only against her mother, but to the effect that she was quite aware she was positively a bad influence in her mother's way. And so she was . . . I shall never cease to think of you and M. Mohl as Hilary's *only* friends . . . I shall never speak of her more, I have done . . . How I hate well meaning people."[8]

IN 1861, following the deaths of Herbert, Clough, and the rest, Florence seemed once again to be at death's door, and Queen Victoria, herself recently widowed and in the deepest mourning, offered Miss Nightingale a grace-and-favour apartment in one of the royal residences in London. The first news of this offer seems to have come to the Verneys, Florence's sister and brother-in-law, and Parthe at once decided that Flo should be moved into Kensington Palace. When Florence heard of this plan, she was furious. She fired off a letter of protest to her father, who once more found himself unhappily mediating between his two daughters. "The proposition made, as I learn from the B [Board] of Trade," wrote Florence to WEN, "was to find me an apartment *which would suit me* in one of the R [Royal] residences. Without the slightest communicat[io]n with me, the Verneys pitch upon Kensington . . .

Where should I have been now in any part of my life's work had I followed any part of her [i.e., Parthe's] life's advice? It would not appear to me so extraordinary had they disposed of me in marriage as their disposing of me in my habitation . . . The 'Sanitarians' tho' this is a secondary matter, persist in saying that Kensington Palace is very unhealthy . . . Remember that Sir H bought me a horse at the very time he was afraid that my ever riding again on horseback was just as possible as that a man's leg which had been cut off should grow again. Ever dear Pa. Your loving child F."[9] The Verneys did Florence a great service here. By treating her like a poor helpless invalid and trying to take charge of her life, they made her mad as a hornet and revived her will to live.

For several more years, poor Mrs. Sutherland, the wife of that much maligned and persecuted sanitarian Dr. John Sutherland, scurried about London finding suitable places for Miss Nightingale to rent. In 1862, moving into a rented house at 4 Cleveland Row, Florence had the gall to tell her mother that she longed for death to find herself "setting up for the first time a fashionable old maid's house in a fashionable quarter (tho' grateful to Papa's liberality)."[10] At last in 1865, WEN, who had always refused to buy his wife a house in town, bought one for his younger daughter. It was not just any house. WEN acquired from his friend the Duke of Westminster, one of Florence's devoted admirers, the leasehold on a house just off Park Lane in Mayfair. The house was a good investment of capital, and 35 (later 10) South Street was also pretty much Florence's dream house, though of course she never said that. After all, her sister, Parthe, had for some years been living on the same street, at number 32.

The back of number 35 looked onto a large private garden, and from her front windows Florence had a view of Hyde Park. Thus she was able to report in her letters not only on the bird population, a matter of passionate interest to her, but also on the processions and demonstrations frequently staged in her neighborhood. Having a home entirely of her own, one that she could organize to her satisfaction, was for a woman of such formidable domestic energies as Florence Nightingale a pleasure in itself. The large, spare, sunny, curtainless rooms on the second floor, full of books and papers and engravings, soon became like a hermit crab's shell to her.

Anyone who visits South Street today will understand that Florence

Nightingale had one of the most exclusive addresses in the world, even if in her day there was a rowdy public house just across the street. The Nightingale sisters say little about the cachet of living just off Park Lane, but that does not mean that they did not feel it more and more as the years went on and London sprawled in all directions.

William Edward Nightingale's generosity toward Florence was a matter of choice, not of obligation, and it involved sacrifice. He was a man of the canny Midlands business class, and fiscal prudence was in his blood; opening his purse so wide to one daughter did not come easily. In the last ten years of his life, when Florence emerged to play a central role in the family once again, WEN began to niggle her about money, cavil over expenses, and challenge the occasional bill. He was an old man now, his eyesight was pretty much gone, and he felt accountable to his sister, Mai, his brother-in-law, Sam, and his nephew, Shore Smith. When her father grumbled or made an accounting error, Florence, perhaps the best accountant in a family of good accountants, wrote directly to her uncle Sam to sort things out and keep relations between Nightingales and Smiths as cordial as possible.

WEN's liberality was a measure not just of his love for Florence but of his admiration for what she achieved and of his profound commitment to the campaigns she was leading. His support was not limited to money. He remained one of her most important correspondents on matters religious, political, and philosophical, and seemed content now to play the role of student to her master. Perhaps no one in the world ever understood Florence Nightingale better than her father. When in 1861 the death of Sidney Herbert reduced her to the blackest despair, he knew what to write. "My hand & heart misgive at the thought of approaching within the shadow of such grief as yours. Perhaps it is better to magnify it not to try to soften," WEN wrote. And then, simply and with utmost tact, he reminded Florence that though she had much to mourn, she also had much to celebrate, far more, after all, than most women. She and Herbert had together accomplished so much. And Florence's father ended his letter with a mention of the cats, playing around him on the window seat at Lea Hurst. If he could not reach Flo in her black misery, perhaps the cats might.

William Edward Nightingale was a man who delighted in the exchange of ideas, but he was uncomfortable with the display of emotion.

Florence once remarked that even when she was a little girl she never remembered her father petting her. For thirty years his sister, Mai, and sister-in-law Julia, who loved him very much, had been saying that WEN was a lonely man, a man made for solitude and chosen intimacy, obliged to live a life of bustle and squabble. Florence Nightingale, who also commented several times on her father's deep unhappiness, knew that he was unhappy in part because of her and the family feuding she had occasioned as a young woman. Though he said little about it, WEN was the one who most depended on Florence's company. She was the person who most delighted him, and as he sank into blindness and frailty WEN missed having his daughter by his side every day, as other, less generous and loving men did. Letters, the occasional London visit, and seeing Florence at Embley in the summers were not enough.

In early January 1874, sometime after 3:30 a.m. when his valet awoke and gave him some broth, WEN got out of bed to find his watch and suffered a fatal stroke. His wife, his elder daughter, Parthe, his niece Blanche, and Blanche's children were all in the house, but he did not call out to them. His manner of death was in striking contrast to the long months of painful leavetaking that his mother and aunt had known at the end and that his only sister, Mai, was to replicate in her turn. "I do not think his death awful for *him*," wrote Florence to her sister. "His was the purest mind and I think the most single heart I have ever known. It is his New Year; he was quite ready to part with his life. He always wished to go out of the world quietly—it was a part of his single-minded character to do so—he was as shy as a bird. For us it is sad and dreary to have no last word or farewell, but he would have had it just so, if he could, I believe."[11]

FANNY NIGHTINGALE, perhaps surprisingly, seems to have taken Florence's withdrawal from normal family life in 1857 more calmly and matter-of-factly than WEN or Parthe. Fanny had left her anger and her need to dominate behind. She tired easily now, and seemed both more withdrawn and more placid. Fanny accepted that her younger daughter was infinitely precious and infinitely vulnerable, that henceforward work would take precedence over family in Flo's life, and that her own role would be that of Flo's chief domestic liaison with the outside world. On the whole, Fanny did exactly what Florence asked and refrained from asking for what her daughter was not ready to give.

All the same, it must have hurt Florence's mother to know quite particularly from Parthe and Harry Verney that a flow of nurses, politicians, and Indian sanitarians went in and out of Flo's house all day long while she herself received letters like the following, written on July 28, 1865: "Dearest Mum—I hardly know what to say to your coming tomorrow. Even ten minutes' talk with those I love best secures me a night of agony and a week of feverish exhaustion. I must make some great change or I shall not be able to go on with the work at all. But, if you would come up, so as to be here about 4:00, and just come in and kiss me, that would be a great delight. But there must be no talk, specially not about anything agitating nor about my going this year into No. 35, or anything of that business, nor about maids."[12]

Fanny wrote regularly and at length to Florence, giving her news of family, friends, and neighbors. Florence in her usually brief replies says over and again how much she loves to get her mother's weekly letters and appreciates the fact that Fanny never demands an answer. Letters were not Fanny's only task. With what seems to me immense good nature, Fanny set about satisfying Florence's whims and tickling her palate. Every week, boxes of stuff—grapes, strawberries, asparagus, flowers, rabbit pies, sausages, whole-meal Derbyshire rolls called "wuts," flannel nightdresses, custom-made shawls, and veritable copses of seasonal greenery—were dispatched to Flo in London from Embley and Lea Hurst by her mother.

Florence prided herself on paying out of her personal income for both the contents of the weekly boxes and their transport, and Fanny had servants to do most of the real work. All the same, keeping track of all the requests, sending on all the gifts that came for Flo from other well-wishers, and above all thinking up things Flo would really like when she was feeling low took time and involved much aggravation. Flo was so immensely fussy. Could the nightgown necklines be cut lower in future? Did Fanny mind that she had given away all the grapes, asparagus, and vintage port to Burton, an old servant long a-dying, who claimed she could stomach nothing else? How had the partridges promised her turned into grouse? The following is typical of Florence's letters to her mother: "12 December 1864 . . . I take this opportunity to thank for the magnificent supplies of game, etc., and to beg for Christmas greenery in

LARGE quantities for my hospitals. As Christmas Day is on a Sunday, I suppose people will dress up on Christmas Eve, so that if you would send me please the greenery *on the 23rd.* If you will send me mince pies or any other Christmas fooleries, you know I have plenty of poor people, *not* sick."[13]

Cats formed one of the main subjects of correspondence between Florence and Fanny Nightingale. Julius Mohl at one point brought back from Persia a real Persian cat, and somehow from this animal arose a whole line of vastly admired felines. Fanny received one or more of these beasts from her dear friend Mary Clarke Mohl, and over the years there was a constant traffic of pampered pussies between England, France, and Germany. Purebred Persians with extravagantly long hair were what everyone wanted, but, given the promiscuous ways of cats, many of the litters turned out to be mongrels who found homes with less distinguished admirers.

Florence Nightingale had a succession of Persian cats—Mr. Bismark, Muff, Darius, Ataxerxes, Tom, Barts, and others. They were a chief joy in her life, and a source of constant anxiety and labor for her domestic staff. The cats were valuable, inclined to roam, and a temptation to thieves. They had delicate appetites and ate specially prepared food in china plates on folded newspaper in their mistress's room. Their litter boxes, filled with the sand and sod imported weekly in the boxes from the country, had to be changed every day. When one precious cat and her kittens died in agony at the hands of a fashionable but ignorant veterinarian, Nightingale lodged a furious letter of protest with the authorities. She often sat at her work with a cat wrapped around her shoulders, and once recalled the comfort she got in one of her saddest years when her cat would lick the tears from her eyes.

Another of Fanny's duties to her younger daughter was to offer some weeks of pure country air and good food to any of Florence's allies who deserved to be entertained, or nursing favorites who were under the weather. When it came to her protégés, Florence Nightingale was brazen in her demands, as we can see in this letter of February 1863 begging Fanny to invite Miss Mary Jones to Embley for two weeks of R&R: "To be let alone, to feel perfectly at her ease, to have entire rest of body and mind is what she wants. A drive in an open carriage occasionally is all she is fit for and to be sent to bed at 9.00 o'clock. She is often unable to go up and down stairs . . . Hers is such a valuable life. I know Webb [Fanny's personal maid] would wait upon her kindly and take her meals to her *cut up*."[14] Poor Webb!

By the mid-1860s, Florence Nightingale was once again prepared to look her family members in the face, at least occasionally and one on one, and she spent some weeks of every summer with her parents, at Embley or Lea Hurst. When Fanny came up to see Flo in her rooms, mother and daughter at last had the chance to talk at length of the past and lay down the heavy baggage of old grievances. This new understanding did not come too soon, as Florence began to notice that things were not well with her mother. Fanny was losing track of things, she found it hard to make simple decisions, and awareness of her confusion made her distressed. If you sat down quietly by her side, Florence reported carefully to her father and sister, Fanny would be calm and talk collectedly and be her old self, but trying to speak to her when she was walking about or when there were a lot of people was not only useless but upsetting. On May 13, 1868, Florence penned an anguished note: "Dearest Mum—It has been a dreadful disappointment not to hear from you today or yesterday, and not even to have the weekly flowers or things from you. It is the first birthday I have ever had without hearing from my dearest Mum. Indeed I may say that, except one Tuesday, I have heard from you every Tuesday. I have been so terrified—I don't think I ever was so frightened in all my life. But I have just received Watson's telegraph, for which God be thanked. I can write no more. Ever dearest Mum your loving child. F."[15]

Florence was to get only a few more letters and parcels from her dearest mum. Fanny Nightingale's descent into senility was rapid, and Florence's reintegration into semi-normal family life was precipitated by her mother's problems. WEN had for decades been a distant and detached husband who left domestic matters strictly to his wife. Now, almost blind, he was neither willing nor able to undertake the care of his wife. Parthe and Fanny had always been close. Parthe was happy to receive her mother as a regular visitor in London or at Claydon, and she liked to be consulted. But Parthe had never been the practical one; besides, she had a husband and two households to manage, and she was embarked on a successful career as a writer. She traveled a good deal, for pleasure, for health, and to do field research. Above all, Parthe was often terribly ill. She was simply not up to taking primary responsibility for her mother.

Nursing was Florence Nightingale's great specialty. No one could do for Fanny what she could do. With deep apprehension and intense indignation, Florence stepped into the breach. Parthe, Mai, Shore and his delightful Irish wife, Louisa, and Aunt Julia would all take turns to look after Fanny, but Florence would have chief responsibility for her mother's welfare. This made her furiously unhappy and resentful, and she vented her feelings in letters to friends—but which dutiful child with a difficult aging parent has not?

By 1872, Florence was spending most of the year with her mother, working and sleeping in the room next to her, keeping her calm, and desperately trying to ensure that when she herself returned to London to do essential business Fanny was not neglected by the staff. The situation became acute when Mai Smith discovered that Webb, Fanny's trusted maid, was secretly abusing her. If no family member was around, Webb would lock Mrs. Nightingale up alone in her bedroom, sometimes for twelve hours at a time. Florence was faced with the knotty problem of discreetly sacking the elderly and sorely overtaxed Webb without making her revengeful, finding a new maid and a companion who would divide Webb's duties, and getting her mother used to being cared for by someone else. March 7, 1872, proved a disastrous day. Florence was in the room next door to Fanny, but the new staff did not call her when Fanny woke up in the early afternoon. She apparently wet the bed and became extremely upset. Florence wrote to Parthe: "For seven years, no one has given my mother the po [chamberpot] but Webb and me . . . Nothing would have induced my mother to ask Miss Pringle or Harriet for the po. And it seems hard that the very day after the person who has never left her for an hour for fifteen years is gone, this should happen."[16]

The weight on Florence's shoulders increased immensely when WEN died suddenly in early 1874 and the Nightingale entail came into effect. Embley and Lea Hurst now belonged to Mai and Sam Smith. Fanny was capable of understanding that her husband was dead but not why she herself was obliged to give up her home and so many of her oldest possessions. The Smiths were loving and kind to Fanny, but the fact was that Mai and Sam had for decades wished to make their home at Embley, and their children wanted Fanny to move out as soon as decently possible. It was a difficult and tense time for all concerned, and though the Nightingale sisters had always understood the legal situation, they were inevitably bitter, as we see from this brief but typically hyperbolic note Florence wrote to Parthe in May 1874: "My Dear P, Though this day robs me of the last vestige of an earthly home (and instead of people providing a home for one so worn out and helpless as I, we have now to provide a home for dear, dearest mother). Yet I do not forget what this day must be to you in speeding her departure from the home of fifty years. I cannot speak of it. *Please return me* THIS *letter* from Claydon with your answer. I will not write now of what I feel. Indeed I cannot. God bless dear mother and you and the Coltmans [cousin Bertha Smith and her husband William] for taking care of her."[17]

Fanny Smith was ninety-three when she died in 1880, and the strain of her last six years was great, especially on Florence. Money was not the main problem. It seems that the Shore part of William Edward Nightingale's fortune, the part that was not subject to the Nightingale entail and which had been settled on Fanny and her children at the time of her marriage, had been well invested and had grown over the years. Florence, under the terms of her father's will, received an extra five hundred pounds in annual income and was given life possession of 10 South Street. Parthe received a comparably large inheritance, though hers was put in trust according to the terms of her marriage settlement. Fanny could afford a decent household staff, travel about the country in comfort, and rent Lea Hurst from her sister-in-law in the summer. Fanny spent months at Claydon with Parthe, she went to Embley when Mai invited her, and when in London she always stayed in the home of Shore and Louisa. The Smith children—Rosalind, Benjamin, Louis, and Thyra (later known as Barbara)—were Fanny's delight. However, the Verneys and the Shore Smiths were now fairly openly in conflict. Florence had to be extremely careful with her mother's accounts and make it clear to her sister and brother-in-law that, for example, when the Shore Smiths stayed at Lea Hurst with Fanny, it was Florence, not Fanny, who paid for their expenses.

In her last years, Fanny ceased to recognize her daughters, though she always knew Shore by name. He was the darling of her heart, her son in all but name. Florence spent hours with Fanny, talking of the past, bringing in old friends, reading old, beloved books to her, especially the Bible, singing hymns, reciting poetry. Fanny's soul, it seemed to Florence, shone brighter as her mind dimmed, and she was amazed by her mother's serenity, her capacity for pleasure, and the sweetness of her temper. Fanny Nightingale died at Shore's London home, holding his hand and surrounded by his family. Her death, Shore and Louisa said, was a calm and beautiful experience. Fanny seemed to see heaven opening up and waved her arm in welcome. At the end Fanny's face brightened, and she folded her hands, closed her eyes, and fell asleep. Her body in death looked like that of a young woman, and though the coffin, filled with white spring flowers, remained open from Sunday until Thursday, there was no perceptible change. The Smith children were allowed to go in and out of the room to kiss their great-aunt. It was a death worthy of Dickens or Gaskell.

Every detail of what occurred was reported to Florence and Parthenope by their cousin and was duly passed on to mourning friends and relatives. Neither sister attended the funeral, when Fanny was laid to rest by WEN's side. Parthe and Flo contented themselves with mulling over the inscription that would adorn Fanny's side of the four-sided Nightingale memorial in East Hallow churchyard. Florence had various suggestions, including one that spelled out the part played at the time of Fanny's death by their cousin Shore Smith, but this was unacceptable to Parthe. Finally Florence plumped for this: "Frances, for 56 years wife of William Edward Nightingale and daughter of William Smith, MP for Norwich, died 2 February 1880. God is love. 1 John 4:16." This seemed to match the simplicity of WEN's inscription: "William Edward Nightingale of Embley in this county and Lea Hurst Derbyshire, died Jan. 5 1874 in his 80th year. And in Thy light shall we see light. Ps. 36:9." In the end, however, written into the stone were these words: "Devoted to the memory of Frances Nightingale, wife of William Edward Nightingale, died Feb. 1st 1880. God is love. 1 John 4:16. Bless the Lord O my soul and forget not all His benefits. Ps. 112:2. By F. Parthe Verney and Florence Nightingale." Parthe did not choose to emphasize the fact that her mother was older than her father, and she wanted her name and

Flo's, not her grandfather Smith's, memorialized. It is thus thanks to Parthe that the complete name of Florence Nightingale does appear on the family monument, on her mother's side. On her own side, at her request, there are only the initials "F.N."[18]

IT WILL BE PLAIN to my readers by now that Parthenope Nightingale, unlike her sister, did finally marry. Indeed, the most important change in the lives of the Smith-Shore-Nightingale subset of the clan was the marriage in June 1858 of Parthenope Nightingale to Sir Harry Verney of Claydon House in Buckinghamshire.[19] Verney was a fifty-six-year-old widower, very tall and reputed in his youth to be so handsome that people stopped in the street to gawk at him. He had begun his life as Harry Calvert and was one of several sons of the fiercely Christian General Sir Harry Calvert. Young Harry first went into the Life Guards and then spent some years traveling in South America and India until ill health forced him to return home. In 1826 he inherited the Claydon property and in 1832 he went into Parliament as member for Buckinghamshire, the county seat that had been associated with the Verney family for generations. The Verney family can be traced back to the fifteenth century, and the direct line ended in 1810 with the death of the unmarried Mary Verney, Baroness Fermanagh.[20]

When the newly minted Sir Harry Verney took possession of Claydon, he found the property neglected and encumbered with debt, and he worked tirelessly to improve the farms and raise the living standards of his tenants. He and his first wife, Elizabeth Hope Verney, had four children, Emily, Edmund, George, and Frederick. According to Baroness Bunsen, who knew the Verneys well, the family led a simple, almost spartan life but enjoyed a wealth of affection, culture, faith, and benefaction.[21] Lady Verney seemed more like the children's sister than their mother, so young and merry was she. But in 1856 Elizabeth Verney died, leaving her husband and children desolate. Before her death, Lady Verney reportedly told her husband that she wished their daughter Emily to make the acquaintance of Florence Nightingale.

Thus, when Florence Nightingale returned to England from Turkey and began her great army reform campaign, Sir Harry Verney, M.P., was one of the many men who came to call, and begged to be allowed to help. Florence, initially, had little use for him—she described him to Sidney Herbert as a "pompous princess"—but he persisted in his attempts to get to know her and her family better. Soon he was invited to spend Christmas at Embley. Then he proposed marriage to Parthenope and was gladly accepted. Historians of the Verney family insist that there is no archival evidence or tradition in the family that Sir Harry Verney first proposed to Florence Nightingale and was refused. All the same, there seems little doubt that Sir Harry Verney fell in love not so much with Parthenope as with the Nightingale connection. In a letter to his eldest son, Edmund, Harry Verney described Parthe, his bride-to-be, with less than rapture, as "in her fortieth year, with the appearance of a lady but without the beauty of her sister Florence."[22]

Both Fanny and WEN were delighted with the match. Sir Harry's combination of courtly manners and religious piety was most congenial to Fanny Nightingale. Verney's liberal political views were very much to the taste of WEN. Florence was too absorbed in royal commissions and her own ill health to take much notice of the fact of her sister's marriage. The sight of middle-aged spinsters succumbing to the delights of cake and rice had always struck Florence as a little ludicrous, and she had yet to see Harry Verney as an important addition to the family circle. However, Florence told friends she was pleased that her sister was pleased.

Parthenope Verney was too sensible to reject an eligible man just because he was interested in her sister. Life for Parthe had ever been thus. Though Sir Harry was some seventeen years her senior, he was a strong, active, virile man, and to be mistress of Claydon, a beautiful old manor house where family portraits were stacked unidentified in outhouses and the attics were piled high with family records dating back four centuries, was a dream come true. Parthe longed for a child and mourned when she was unable to bring a baby to term, but she rejoiced to be mother to four delightful young people.

The people least pleased by the Verney marriage were the Sam Smiths and their children. Sam and his son, Shore, were well aware that the four Nightingales were able to live such an affluent life because WEN had command of two sources of income—the Shore money, originating in his natal family, invested in coal pits, mills, shares and such, and the Nightingale money, invested in land, notably the Lea Hurst and Embley estates, entailed upon Mai Smith and her son, Shore. By the terms of

WEN and Fanny's marriage settlement, the Shore money would come
to Fanny and her children. If Parthenope and Florence, both of whom
seemed likely to die young, were to die unmarried and without children,
their share in the Shore money would most probably go to their Smith
double cousins, Blanche, Shore, Bertha, and Beatrice.

The arrival of Harry Verney on the scene upset the whole Smith
scenario, and the Verney debts carried much more weight with the
Nightingale aunts, uncles, and cousins than the Verney charm. It appears
from Frances Parthenope Verney's will that at the time of her marriage
she signed a settlement that placed her eventual legacy from her parents
in trust, with the trustees chosen from her own family. Even after her father's death, Parthe had little authority over her fortune and was thus unable to pay off the Verney debts or finance any improvident raise in the
Verney lifestyle. Unsurprisingly, as Parthenope came to understand her
husband's difficult financial situation and to feel part of the Verney family, these restrictions became more irksome and a constant source of fric-
tion with members of her own extended family.

AS LADY VERNEY, Parthenope blossomed. Family life became ever
more absorbing as the new generation of stepgrandchildren made its appearance. The Verneys took a London house at 32 South Street, and their
home became a center for liberal politics just as the house at 6 Park Street
(Queen Anne's Gate) had been for Parthe's Smith grandparents. When
WEN was persuaded in 1865 to buy the leasehold of number 35 for Florence, South Street became a mecca for reform politicians and social scientists from all over the world. Both houses were hives of activity, though
the interaction of mistress with guests could not have been more different. Florence rarely left her own room, but her house was usually full of
colleagues, assistants, and guests, and she prided herself on providing excellent food and service. Sometimes the overflow guests were sent over
to Parthe, but since Florence had no faith in her sister's housekeeping,
she supplied bedlinens that had been washed, starched, and aired to her
own high standards. Parthe loved to see people, kept her social calendar
as full as possible, and ran a small salon where Sir Harry's parliamentary
and philanthropic colleagues mingled with family members and old

friends like Monckton Milnes. It was like the old days at Embley, and Parthe loved it. If Florence believed that her sister just talked about doing things while she herself actually got them done, she at least tried to keep her thoughts to herself and preserve the family truce.

One of the things about Florence and her *modus reformandi* that irked her female relatives was the way she drew husbands into her orbit and squeezed the breath out of them. Poor doomed Arthur Hugh Clough, the delicate poetic soul married to her cousin Blanche, was the most evident case in point, but by 1860 Florence had begun to absorb more and more of the time and energy of another cousin-in-law, army engineer and sanitation expert Douglas Galton, Marianne's husband. Marianne was now fully reconciled to her Nightingale relatives, but it is unclear that she ever scheduled an appointment with Flo. When Marianne and Douglas's baby son died, Florence was too wrapped up in her own misery over Herbert and Clough to respond appropriately. She insensitively referred to the dead child as "Galton's baby" and wondered why people had more sympathy for Marianne's loss than her own. On the other hand, when fragile toddler Gwendolyn Galton was brought over for a ceremonial visit to South Street, Florence left an indelible picture of her as a tiny, precious package that needed to be sent back for more serviceable wrapping. Happily, Gwendolyn survived and in later life she too would have fond relations with her aunt Florence. Cousin Henry Bonham-Carter was another family man who was ready to run over whenever Flo crooked her little finger, though he did insist on going home to dinner. Henry was a rather unsuccessful lawyer who took over from Clough as secretary to the Nightingale Fund, supervised Florence's legal affairs, and was trustee under her will. Henry Bonham-Carter and his wife, Sibella, had twelve children, and their family received the largest slice of Florence's estate.

But after Clough's death in 1861, no male relative was more useful and more willing to serve than Sir Harry Verney. He became Florence Nightingale's messenger, representative, and parliamentary liaison, and he was the one person who could occasionally persuade her to take a drive in the park. From time to time, Harry would write a note begging Flo to give Parthe a few minutes—it was her birthday, she had been so very unwell—and Flo would graciously agree, though stipulating the exact hour and length of the proposed meeting. Unsurprisingly, there were times when Parthe felt Flo saw more of her husband than she did, and resented the way Florence exposed him to fatigue and excessive travel.

Between 1857 and 1880, when their mother died, relations between Parthe and Flo were often fraught. Each sister knew exactly what to do to enrage and upset the other. To the world at large, no one was a fiercer supporter of her sister's reform projects than Parthe, but in private Parthe felt obliged at times to take her sister to task or report what she heard about town, as in this early note: "There is one thing I want to say tho' I'm afraid you don't quite like outsiders giving opinions upon what they don't understand. I feel nervous whether people will not say that you are entering into what does not concern you when you open the whole question of army reform, & whether this will not weaken what you say about Hospital reform in their eyes, if they say you have gone out of your sphere." When Florence went into deep mourning over the death of her nursing protégée Agnes Jones and memorialized her as "Una and the Lion" for *Good Words* magazine, Parthe could not resist saying that, just perhaps, Agnes had not been quite perfect. "I am grieved that you have lost your friend Miss Jones. I hope from what you say that she has done great work but her wrecking of the nursing at King's College which they do not seem to have recovered from in all these years must have been a sore blow & a great discouragement & it is very beautiful of you to have forgotten it altogether."[23]

But there were moments when their physical woes brought the sisters together, and when Florence better than anyone could cheer Parthe up. In May 1861, both Flo and Parthe were seriously ill. Both, it seems, were attended by a Dr. Williams, as we learn from this seriocomic letter in response to a sad letter from Parthe that Flo dictated from her bed to Hilary Bonham-Carter:

> My dear, I did not know that you had been 'a case of poisoning by belladonna' 'atop of a state of rheumatic fever for a month' . . . When you are [better?] we will compare sensations. As for mine I did not know that any pain could make me groan & here was I groaning for 12 hours aloud, on Monday night—& I've had to send for Williams two nights—Of course, Williams does *not* acknowledge this to the world because he sanctioned tho' he did not

originate the treatment by Mr. Brown Legrand [?] Which was blistering the spine with Belladonna—which is now nothing but one raw place from top to bottom—the general rash was all that appeared to the vulgar eye so I suppose it is that of wh. you heard—Had Hilary been in town I should have sent for Mrs. Roberts [her Crimean friend and ally], who is the only doctor who does good and no harm, but now I am glad I did not. Neither experience nor theory have ever enabled me to comprehend the doctrine that a patient is better for having another disease a top of the original one, but the reverse—I mean to put into the 'Lancet' 'Case of poisoning by Belladonna' & then Brown Legrand will see it & say: 'Singular case' 'but not well reported.' Thank you very much for the 'sparagus—Williams won't let me have a bit of fruit or vegetables now, but don't let that stop the supplies. I've always plenty of folk to give to.[24]

There were also times when the two sisters could exchange a mildly ribald joke. "I had a letter from Major Powys Keck's niece," wrote Flo to Parthe on August 22, 1862, "asking me to help a young lady who has had *a 'passion' for 'soldiers'* all her life and wants to *'get her bread by it.'* In profane English, how would you construe this?"[25]

For all its tensions and spats, which anyone who has family living nearby will consider normal, the South Street alliance, with its strange combination of propinquity and distance, its constant exchange of notes, books, magazine articles, gifts, and guests, worked successfully. Parthe could rely on her sister in emergencies but was mainly required to maintain independence, which was good for her. Harry Verney, who had enormous energy, could get away from home and his ailing wife when he wanted, had all the business he could possibly handle, and felt useful and stimulated. Florence had the luxury of receiving the support of her kin largely on her own terms.

One reason Parthenope and Florence on the whole got on pretty well was that Parthe had become too busy on her own account to obsess about Flo. As Florence moved back into the shadows, Parthenope took the limelight, not just as the wife of a public man but as a successful published author. During her teens and twenties, Parthenope Nightingale had tried her best to make a writer of her sister, but all in vain. In her mid-forties, she surprised herself and the world by taking up her pen and writing novels, stories, sociological essays, literary reviews, and finally an extensively researched volume on the Verney family during the English Civil War.

Parthenope started out with two novels, *Stone Hill* and *Lettice Lisle*. These were published anonymously, but after some years she was assured enough to write first "Lady Verney" and finally "Frances Parthenope Verney" on the title pages of her works. She published with reputable houses (Smith Elder, Longmans) and in distinguished journals of a liberal-radical bent (*Contemporary Review, Cornhill, Frasier's, Nineteenth Century*). A collection of her essays called *Peasant Properties* was brought out in two volumes by Longman's in 1885. Another collection, *Essays and Tales*, with a touching memorial to the newly dead author, appeared in 1891, re-edited by her stepdaughter-in-law Margaret Verney.

Parthenope Verney had an easy, elegant style, she understood plot, and she argued more logically than her sister. Her point of view is often quirky: for example, she dismisses Henry James's recently published *Portrait of a Lady* as a typical example of the American obsession with hob-nobbing with the English aristocracy and wearing high-fashion clothes. But as a social commentator and amateur political anthropologist, Parthenope Verney had real talent. She was extremely well read, she understood about fieldwork, and she had the skills to get ordinary people, in France and Germany as well as England, to talk about their lives.

Her first published work, the novel *Stone Edge,* is a remarkably unsentimental and feminist book that owes as much to Balzac as to George Eliot and Gaskell. The novel, named after an old farm, is set in the wilds of Derbyshire just before the end of the eighteenth century. This was exactly the time, before Verney's own birth, when the Arkwright mills were revolutionizing the old rural society. Much of *Stone Edge* is written in Derbyshire dialect, and Verney gives fascinating descriptions of two old Derbyshire customs—the dressing of the wells, and the annual no-holds-barred village football game, in which the numerous players risk serious injury and even death. As she presents it, preindustrial Derbyshire was a place of great natural beauty and quaint customs but also a place where illiteracy, prejudice, and domestic tyranny were endemic. Verney thus uses her novel to argue that industrialization tended to free women from domestic tyranny, a radical idea for her time.

The last and most difficult project Parthenope Verney undertook was a history of the Verney family during the English Civil War, based upon the immense set of papers that had been preserved at Claydon House. By the time she began this she was crippled with rheumatism and unable to walk. At first she was able to write with a special pen, but in her last years she was unable to hold anything or even to turn a page, and the sheer quantity of documentation weighed heavily on her mind. She was assisted by Margaret Verney, wife of Sir Harry's oldest son and a notable amateur historian in her own right, who completed the first and wrote the second two volumes.

In her old age Parthenope Verney was not an easy person to live with. She and Sir Harry fell out with both his eldest and youngest sons, Edmund and Frederick, who favored radical measures like Home Rule for Ireland and the disestablishment of the Church of England. Florence was on the side of the young Verneys, but she was a model of tact and played the role of peacemaker. As with her mother, Florence grew fonder of her sister as Parthenope grew old. She was enthusiastic about Parthe's books, ordered them by the dozens as gifts for friends and libraries, and managed to desist from giving her sister literary advice. In her last years, Parthenope Verney was not only paralyzed with arthritis but eaten by cancer and racked by coughing. For years she was unable to sleep and relied massively on opiates to kill the pain, but she kept working as long as she could, to her sister's amazement and disapproval. There was now something heroic about Parthe, and Florence was closely involved in her sister's care, finding nurses and giving advice on things like the best treatment of bedsores, an old specialty of hers. She was an immense support not only to Sir Harry but to Margaret Verney, upon whom so much of Parthenope's care devolved, and came often to Claydon. When Parthe was in London, she was carried over to her sister's house every Sunday afternoon so that the two could spend time reading, joking, and talking of the old times. "I learn at your courage," wrote Florence to her dearest Pop in February, 1889, "but it is indeed a privilege . . . to watch and see and know the last years of such a life . . . Hail to thee, happy soul, the soul of sweetness and faith. Would I were with you, but God is with you, the Almighty Strength and Wisdom. Now we feel him."[26]

Parthenope Nightingale Verney, age seventy-one, died at Claydon on May 12, Florence's birthday. "My thoughts and prayers are yours," wrote Florence to her brother-in-law on hearing the news, "but Christ is closer still. I write by post. Her suffering was over sooner than she expected. Can we grudge it her? Though we shall miss her until we see her again."[27]

After Parthe's death, Florence and Sir Harry Verney became even closer than before. He relied upon her, and she was often at Claydon, even coming down to the garden to sit with him and allowing some photographs to be taken. Her health in these years was better than it had been when she was forty, and she could even walk about. Florence delighted in the company of Sir Harry's sons and daughters-in-law, whose views and characters were remarkably consonant with her own. The tribe of grandchildren was another great attraction.

The first Verney child to be close to Florence was Emily, the only daughter. Emily followed the advice of her beloved mother and made Miss Nightingale her mentor and inspiration. She was anxious to go into the field of education, became involved with the Red Cross during the Franco-Prussian War, and then went out to work in Malta in 1871, a notoriously unhealthy place at the time. Tragically, Emily Verney quickly fell ill in Malta, was sent home, and died within months, at the age of twenty-nine. The whole family was heartbroken, and for Florence it was another burden of sorrow. Now at last, young, able, idealistic young women like Agnes Jones and Emily Verney were following in her footsteps, and they died while she lived on. From that time, Florence Nightingale had a wreath of flowers placed on Emily Verney's grave each year on the anniversary of her death.

Margaret Verney, the wife of Sir Harry's eldest son, Edmund, was a loving and devoted daughter-in-law to Parthenope, but her really close relationship was with Florence. Margaret Hay Williams—whose younger sister Maude married Sir Harry's youngest son, Fred—was a Welshwoman of great sweetness, resolution, intelligence, and culture, as well as great Christian faith. Like Parthe and Flo, Margaret had been the daughter of a man whose estate was ruled by an entail. Margaret's pregnancies were difficult, and Florence Nightingale followed each of them with deep anxiety, cheering as, after several miscarriages, Margaret delivered three daughters in a row—Ellin, Lettice, and Ruth Florence, Miss Nightingale's goddaughter—and finally Harry, the much-longed-for heir to the Claydon estate. Florence called her "Blessed Margaret."

Edmund Verney, Margaret's husband, did not have an easy life. He shot himself in the foot just after his marriage and was obliged to have it amputated. Sir Harry insisted on retaining the family seat in Parliament, and so it took years of hard, fruitless campaigning before Edmund at last entered Parliament. In 1889, when Parthenope was in her tormented final year, a new kind of tragedy shook the Verney family. Edmund was convicted of procuring a minor for immoral purposes and served a year in Brixton prison. His crime was not a heinous one. He persuaded a nineteen-year-old woman to go to Paris with him. When she refused to have sex with him, he did not force himself upon her but paid her fare home, at which point she presumably reported him to the police. It transpired that, under the name of Mr. Wilson, he had seduced other young women.

Edmund Verney paid a terrible price. He lost his parliamentary seat, and the stain on his name made all public affairs more difficult for the rest of his life. For a man of high ideals, devoted to public service, it was a sad fate, but perhaps the worst burden was the shame and suffering inflicted on his family. Sir Harry was filled with anger and reproach, but he was persuaded by the rest of the family to forgive Edmund. Margaret stood by her husband through the whole sordid affair, visiting him in prison and welcoming him home. Florence too never faltered in her conviction that Edmund was a good and loving man who had simply made a mistake and was ready to atone. She used all her influence with Sir Harry to bring father and son together again.

Florence's own family was less than delighted by her increasing closeness to the Verneys. The Smiths, Coltmans, Lushingtons, and Bonham-Carters feared that not only Parthe's but Florence's share of the Shore money would go to the Verneys. They need not have worried. In her will, Florence Nightingale distributed her property, which was valued at some thirty-six thousand pounds, as fairly as she could among her blood relatives, and named male blood relatives as her executors and trustees. To the Verney children she left only a few personal mementos, and for the grandchildren perhaps twenty pounds each, the equivalent of the welcome old "ten-pun" note she would press on them in the past as a Christmas present.

When Sir Harry died in 1894, Florence stayed on for some months at Claydon, sending a constant flow of messages to the young Verneys—

about the squirrels, about the birds (whose swift decline in numbers she was horrified to report), and about the tenants (all of whom she knew by name and whose housing problems she recited in detail). From this point on, however, Florence remained in her London home, paying no more visits.

FLORENCE NIGHTINGALE in her last years was a serene, affectionate, considerate woman. All the people who had been closest to her, even those who were much younger, like her cousin Shore, died. But though she grieved, she had learned to let God decide her fate, and enjoyed life as it came. Professionally, until at least 1900, she kept in touch with people near and far—sanitary enthusiasts, hospital architects, nurses, Indian politicians. She never ceased to care for the lives of the people in the villages around Lea Hurst. That was really her house, just as Embley was Parthe's, and though Shore inherited Lea Hurst he never cared about it. As far as her income would allow, Florence took on the role played by her father, keeping in close touch through the Bratbys, two former servants, near Lea. "Dear Bratby," she wrote on December 29, 1886, "I send for Mrs. Broomhead a soft invalid gown, a flannel for drawers and singlets. Lyddy Price an 'active' gown; Mrs. Holmes (who gives away the milk) a cloth gown. Please give to each of these who have gowns 2/6 for lining etc. or whatever it was we gave before . . . All my kindest regards and hopes that the things, which all come from Wales and, I am told, are the best of their kind, will prove comfortable and good."[28]

Florence Nightingale had a happy and secure old age not because she was good with money, though she was, but because she was good with people. Many old people far richer than she, and with children and grandchildren, end their lives in misery and neglect. In her final years, Nightingale was at the mercy of her domestic staff, but she was not abused. She paid her staff well, she treated them with understanding and humanity, and they adored her. She had an able and devoted companion, and it was an excellent young woman doctor who signed her death certificate.

Until 1905, when she suffered the same fate as her mother, Florence remained a key part of the family network. Children had always been her delight, and as the years went by, she took the trouble to make friends with not just the children of her cousins but the children of those children. She was genuinely interested in their lives, she knew their tastes and interests, and she kept up with their achievements and their difficulties, sending hundreds of notes and remembering birthdays with little gifts. When the young people came to see her, she made them feel special, and in return they cared about her welfare and remembered her with deep affection and admiration after her death. Independent, she made few demands upon them, and even as they appreciated the Great Victorian in her and enjoyed having a legend in the family, they relished her frankness, her fun, her wit, her openness to ideas, her lack of cant.

To her first cousin once removed Rosalind Smith Nash, an earnest, learned, delicate young mother who was both a vegetarian and an ardent supporter of the cooperative movement, Florence Nightingale wrote on November 8, 1887: "Dearest—I send you two 'vegetables' in their shells. We shall have some more fresh ones tomorrow. A new potato is, I assure you, *not* a vegetable. It is a mare's egg, laid by her, you know, in a 'mare's nest.' No vegetarian would eat it. I send you some Egyptian lentils. I have them every night for supper, done in milk, which I am not very fond of. The delicious thing is lentil soup, as made every day by an Arab cook in Egypt, over a handful of fire not large enough to roast a mosquito . . . Ever your loving Aunt Florence."[29]

NOTES

CHAPTER 1: ENTAILS AND ABOLITIONISTS

1. Noel Annan's famous essay "The Intellectual Aristocracy" is reprinted in his collection of essays called *The Dons*, published in 1999 by the University of Chicago Press.
2. Virginia Woolf, quoted by Hermione Lee in *Virginia Woolf* (New York: Knopf, 1997), p. 51.
3. The superb book *Darwin, His Daughter, and Human Evolution* (London: Fourth Estate Limited, 2001; New York: Riverhead Books, 2002) is one small but telling example of the continuing productivity of the clan. Its author, Randal Keynes, is a great-great-grandson of Charles Darwin, the great-nephew of artist Gwen Raverat, who wrote the classic memoir *Period Piece*, and also the great-nephew of John Maynard Keynes.
4. The Bonham-Carters remained practicing Unitarians for a generation at least after the Nightingales, and Benjamin Smith also appears to have brought up his Leigh Smith children more as Unitarians than anything else.
5. "No one can approach to an understanding of the English institutions, or of others, which, being the growth of many centuries, exercise a wide sway over mixed populations, unless he divide them into two classes. In such constitutions there are two parts . . . First, those which excite and preserve the reverence of the population—the *dignified* parts, if I may so call them; and next, the *efficient* parts—those by which it, in fact, works and rules." Walter Bagehot, *The English Constitution* (London: C. A. Watts, 1964), p. 120. Bagehot, a banker and for some years the editor of *The Economist*, was himself a member of the "efficient classes." His name is familiar to us today as the byline of *The Economist*'s English editorial page.
6. Longfellow's famous poem eulogizing Miss Nightingale is called "Santa Filomela."
7. Jane Austen nails the commonness of the name Smith in *Persuasion* where the snobbish elder sisters of Anne Elliot are aghast to find she prefers to visit her sick school friend Mrs. Smith rather than attend a reception at the mighty Dalrymples.
8. It is probably impossible to discover the precise terms of the Nightingale entail or when it began. Not until the late nineteenth century was a national registry for real-

property transactions established. Since by definition entailed property could not be bequeathed by the current landholder, no account of the entail appears in either WEN's or Mai Smith's wills. See *A History of the Land Law* by A. W. B. Simpson (Oxford: Clarendon Press, 1961/1986).

9. Unpublished manuscript on William Smith by his descendant Lady Barbara Stephen, Smith Collection, Cambridge University Library (henceforth CUL), Add. 7621/71, Chapter IX, p. 6.

10. Most of the information given here on Peter Nightingale and his ancestors comes from a useful little book about Florence Nightingale and Derbyshire by local historian Norman Keen, *Florence Nightingale* (Ripley, Derbyshire: Footprint Press, 1982). Mr. Keen was born in the Nightingale Memorial Hospital in Derby and subsequently became the headmaster of Lea County Primary School. His book is worth looking up for anyone planning a pilgrimage to Lea.

11. This building still stands today, and is now a farm. See Keen.

12. For most of the American Civil War, British public opinion was massively pro-South.

13. The deleterious effects of lead poisoning, especially on young children, are now so canvassed as to need no more emphasis from me. Some critics have sought to attribute the neuroticism of Florence and Parthenope Nightingale to the effects of lead poisoning in youth, but this seems a stretch. Their great-aunt Elizabeth Evans spent most of her life in Cromford and in her early eighties was still eminently sane and able to walk over to Lea Hurst for a visit and back—some six strenuous miles.

14. As Jenny Uglow makes clear in *The Lunar Men* (New York: Farrar, Straus and Giroux, 2002), Derbyshire in the mid- to late eighteenth century was already a tourist mecca for a small subclass of Englishmen like the Darwins, Wedgwoods, and Edgeworths, who were fascinated by the new industrial development. Derbyshire offered the vigorous, monied merchants and their families a special combination of walks in hilly countryside and tours of manufactures, mines, canals, etc.

15. To take one remarkable document that was first published in 1828, Robert Blincoe described the eleven years he worked as a child and teenager in the Derbyshire mills. Blincoe was a London orphan who was at the age of ten sold by the authorities of his parish to indentured work in Derbyshire. There, hundreds of barely clothed, chronically undernourished boys and girls worked from five in the morning to late at night seven days a week, eating their oat bread lunch as best they could while continuing to work. At night, they were imprisoned in stone barracks where no fire was ever lighted. Subjected to savage beatings and sadistic punishments, especially if they sought outside help or ran away, many died, more were deformed, some went mad. *The Dark Satanic Mills: Child Apprentices in Derbyshire Spinning Factories,* edited by Edmund and Ruth Frow (Manchester: Manchester Free Press, 1980).

16. Martineau, quoted by James Pope-Hennessy, *Monckton Milnes* (London: Constable, 1949–1951), 1:188. The most famous account of a woman's life in the Massachusetts mills in the nineteenth century is probably Lucy Larcom's *A New England Girlhood*. Originally published in 1889, Larcom's book was reissued in 1986 by Northeastern University Press with a foreword by eminent historian Nancy Cott. Larcom writes of how hard it was to spend her days cooped up in the mill at Lowell where she was obliged to find work, but she also has chapters entitled "Mill-Girls' Magazines" and "Reading and Studying."

17. Lady Stephen's ms., Chapter IV.

18. Claydon, Bundle 390. Florence Nightingale told Lady Margaret Verney that she remembered her grandfather Shore well, but this seems impossible since he died when she was just over two years of age.

19. Edward Cook, *The Life of Florence Nightingale* (London: Macmillan, 1914), 1:14.

20. "Private reflection," British Library, Add. 43402, f. 79.

21. In 1847, WEN did absorb some financial losses but was not nearly as badly affected as his businessman brother-in-law Octavius Smith.

22. This section on the Smiths is based mainly on "The Papers of William Smith M.P. and the Smith Family, 1678–1951," which were given to the Cambridge University Library in 1961 by three of William Smith's descendants, Mr. Victor Bonham-Carter, Miss Katherine Duff, and Mr. Philip Leigh Smith. The collection includes the typescript of an unfinished biography of William Smith written around 1940 by another descendant, Lady Barbara Stephen, together with her extensive research notes, transcriptions, etc. (CUL, Add. MS. 7621/70, 71, 72). Margaret Thyra Barbara Smith Stephen was the second daughter and fourth child of William Shore Smith (later Nightingale). She was an excellent writer and indefatigable researcher, and I, like all subsequent biographers and historians, owe her an immense debt. Richard W. Davis was instrumental in tracking down and bringing together the Smith papers for consultation by the general public. In 1971 Davis published his excellent historical study *Dissent in Politics, 1780–1830: The Political Life of William Smith M.P.* (London: Epworth Press). In 1998 Pam Hirsch moved on to the next generation of Smiths and, not incidentally, of political reform in her biography *Barbara Leigh Smith Bodichon, 1827–1891: Feminist, Artist and Rebel* (London: Pimlico, Random House, 1999). The *Dictionary of National Biography* has entries on William and his eldest son, Benjamin. Let me here express my gratitude to Jennifer Bobrowski, who has been working for years on the eighteenth-century Smith family and generously gave me the benefit of her scholarship and insight.

23. *William Smith—A Letter to William Wilberforce, Esq. M.P. on the Proposed Abolition of the Slave Trade, Under the Consideration of Parliament* (London, 1807); Davis, p. 27.

24. A good example of Victorian revisionist history is the section devoted to William Smith by Sir James Stephen in his celebrated eulogy of William Wilberforce and the Clapham Sect in volume 2 of his *Essays in Ecclesiastical Biography* (London: Longman, Brown, Green & Longmans, 1850). Stephen was a pillar of the Victorian establishment determined to gild the laurels of his Clapham forebears. His account of Smith is brief, vague, and selective. Ah yes, William Smith too lived in Clapham, Stephen tells us, a capital fellow—never sick in his life!—and undoubtedly a loyal lieutenant to Wilberforce and the other Clapham Saints. Wilberforce and Clarkson had "almost brotherly love" for Smith, Stephen writes, and "of all their fellow labourers there was none who was more devoted to their cause, or than whom they more entirely trusted" (2:543–44).

25. Both Lady Stephen and Davis cover in detail the minefields Smith had to negotiate during the French Revolution and the wars with France that followed. William St. Clair in his magisterial study *The Godwins and Shelleys* (New York: Norton, 1989) is eloquent on the jingoism that prevailed in Britain after 1789, and the persecutions of members of the Godwin circle.

26. Richard Price, a friend of Joseph Priestley and a notable scientist in his own right, will be familiar to students of American history. He published a pamphlet called "Observations on Civil Liberty and the Justice and Policy of War with America," which sold sixty thousand copies in a year, and is said to have encouraged the Americans to declare their independence. Price was similarly enthusiastic about the French Revolution, moving a motion at a dinner given by the Unitarian Lord Stanhope to congratulate the National Assembly in Paris and rejoice in the new liberty and justice in France. Price's speech had disastrous consequences since it led to the defeat of the parliamentary motion to repeal the Test and Corporation Acts, which had been within a few votes of success. The reform movement was set back thirty years. See Lady Stephen, Chapter II, p. 22; also Davis.

27. Lady Stephen, Chapter I, p. 2; also Davis.

28. Davis, p. 3.

29. CUL, Add. MS. 7621/9, 10.

30. See Davis, p. 95.

31. Davis shows clearly that it was not so much the specific acts of persecution that made life difficult for Dissenters under the Test and Corporation Acts, but the disabling fear that some provision of the acts could be invoked by an opponent to gain advantage or out of revenge. Thus, Patty Smith in her reminiscences notes that the town and country houses of Dissenter William Hutton were burned down in the riots of 1791. Patty comments: "WH was not only a dissenter—he had been President of the Court of Requests—had attended it 19 years & above one hundred cases had passed through his hands, those who had lost their cases revenged themselves." CUL, Add. MS. 7621/9.

32. Lady Stephen, Chapter I, p. 1.

33. Ibid., p. 14.

34. CUL, Add. MS. 7621/1/12.

35. Lady Stephen, Chapter II, p. 1.

36. Sudbury apparently was still notoriously corrupt in 1835, after the first Reform Bill, if we credit the lively account Charles Dickens wrote in *Pickwick Papers* of the election in that borough, which he called "Eatanswill."

37. St. Clair, p. 147.

38. Davis, Chapter 8.

39. We may compare the Smiths with John Gladstone, William Ewart Gladstone's father. A Presbyterian Scot who converted to the Church of England on becoming an English landowner, John Gladstone's large fortune came from trading sugar, tobacco, and cotton. After buying himself a seat in Parliament, Gladstone devoted himself to defending the rights of West Indian slave owners. See *Gladstone: A Biography* by Roy Jenkins (New York: Random House, 1995), p. 4.

40. For my account of Wilberforce and the Clapham sect, I am chiefly indebted to the brilliant book *Fathers of the Victorians: The Age of Wilberforce* by Ford K. Brown (Cambridge: Cambridge University Press, 1961) and to James Stephen's classic essay.

41. James Stephen's presentation of Wilberforce is opaque. He writes of Wilberforce's odd charm, of the eloquence that could never be transferred to writing, of the man's whimsicality and surprising turns of humor. These traits set Wilberforce apart from somber men like the Thorntons and made him a friend even to people who hated his ideas

and opposed his goals. All this emphasis on how weird Wilberforce was in person came to make much more sense for me when I discovered that he was one of the many high-functioning opiomanes of the late eighteenth century. Wilberforce openly admitted that when he had to give a speech in the Commons he gained inspiration from laudanum, a substance then cheap, freely available, and used by all classes of society. See Richard Davenport-Hines, *The Pursuit of Oblivion: A Global History of Narcotics, 1500–2000* (London: Weidenfeld & Nicolson, 2001).

42. James Stephen, Virginia Woolf's great-grandfather, was married to William Wilberforce's sister. Their son, also James, married Jane Venn, the daughter of John Venn, rector of Clapham. The second James Stephen (Sir James) wrote the essay on the Clapham Saints.

CHAPTER 2: ONE BIG HAPPY FAMILY

1. Personal communication from Jennifer Bobrowski.
2. William Smith named his eldest child Martha after his dead mother, his eldest son Benjamin after his uncle on the Isle of Wight, and his second son Adams, which was his mother's family name. Benjamin Smith in his turn would call his first family of illegitimate children the Leigh Smiths, sardonically reviving the name of his patrician ancestress Elizabeth Leigh.
3. CUL, Add. MS. 7621/9.
4. I rely here on Lady Stephen's summaries of Frances Smith's diaries.
5. Lady Stephen, Chapter V, p. 20.
6. Ibid., Chapter I, p. 38.
7. Patty Smith's reminiscences, CUL, Add. MS. 7621/9.
8. For a detailed account of Sunday schools in the late eighteenth century see Ford K. Brown.
9. CUL, Add. MS. 7621/9, Patty Smith reminiscence of April 1784.
10. Davis, p. 99.
11. Octavius Smith, William and Frances's fourth son and eighth child, fell in love with Scotland, and in 1845 he purchased a property called Achranich in Morvern at the head of Loch Aline, and in 1859 the neighboring estate of Ardtornish. Octavius's son Valentine Smith built a magnificent house called Ardtornish Farm, and his sister Gertrude and her husband, Alexander Sellar, occupied the nearby Ardtornish House. Even after the advent of the railroads, Achranich was hard to get to, and visits there became part of the family legend for William Smith's numerous great-grandchildren. Bonham-Carter Papers, Hampshire Record Office.
12. This may be the place to explain to younger readers that the English pound was once made up of twenty shillings, and a shilling of twelve pence. A guinea was one pound and one shilling.
13. Smith also owned a number of canvases by Cuyp, Hobbema, Ruysdael, Carlo Dolce, Guido Reni, Sassoferrato, Rubens, Van Dyck, Claude, and Poussin, some seventy paintings in all, as well as many drawings, etchings, and maps. He was generous in loaning paintings to the British Institute, where aspiring artists could copy them. For the catalogues of sales in which William Smith bought or sold pictures, see CUL, Add. MS. 7621/20–27. See also Lady Stephen, Chapter V.

14. CUL, Add. MS. 7621/9.

15. Ibid. Sarah Siddons was a member of the famous theatrical family the Kembles. Her niece Fanny followed her on the stage, and her niece Adelaide became a noted diva. See Chapter 7.

16. CUL, Add. MS. 7621/12.

17. William Smith was obliged to sell off the contents of his library in June 1822, and the catalogue of the sale—annotated, I think, in Smith's hand—was lovingly kept by the family. We thus have a fairly complete list of what books Smith owned and what his children, notably his daughters, had the chance of reading in their youth. The collection of 1074 items fetched one thousand, six hundred and ninety three pounds and ten shillings. CUL, Add. MS. 7621/20-27.

18. Quoted by Lady Stephen, Chapter VI.

19. Ibid, Chapter X.

20. Lady Stephen quoting Frances Smith, Chapter X, pp. 8–9.

21. As Ellen Moers has explained in her now classic study, reading Madame de Staël, notably her novel *Corinne* (1807), was a defining experience for almost every great nineteenth-century woman writer. See *Literary Women* (Garden City, NY: Doubleday, 1976).

22. For a superb overview of the generation of English scholars that included Erasmus Darwin and Joseph Priestley, see Jenny Uglow, *The Lunar Men*.

23. Like Wordsworth, the Misses Seward and Ponsonby were visited by anyone who was anyone who came through the area. There is an excellent account of the Ladies of Llangollen in Lilian Faderman's *Surpassing the Love of Men* (New York: William Morrow, 1981), pp. 120–26.

24. Lady Stephen, Chapter IX.

25. Ibid.

26. CUL, Add. MS. 7621/9. Patty Smith's diary entries are difficult and disappointing. They cover only her life as a teenager and young woman, and she included almost nothing about her personal or inner life.

27. William Smith's affection and concern about his daughter's failing health, self-absorption, increasing withdrawal from the family circle, long hours spent in the saddle, and peculiar eating habits are expressed in an undated letter he wrote when Patty was probably in her mid-twenties. Lady Stephen, Chapter V.

28. See E. M. Forster, *Marianne Thornton: A Domestic Biography, 1797–1887* (1956; repr., London: André Deutsch, 2000).

29. CUL, Add. MS. 7621. Many of Julia Smith's handwritten reminiscences are singed around the edges, so we can count ourselves lucky they survived.

30. CUL, Add. MS. 7621/12.

31. CUL, Add. MS. 7621.

32. John Opie painted William Smith and his wife, Mrs. Henrietta Monckton Milnes, and Mary Wollstonecraft, this last now a famous portrait.

33. In *Intellectual Women and Victorian Patriarchy: Harriet Martineau, Elizabeth Barrett Browning, George Eliot* (Ithaca: Cornell University Press, 1987), Deirdre David says that women did not read Wollstonecraft in the generations after her death. My feeling is that the key women such as Martineau and Barrett Browning did read Wollstonecraft but did not cite her because she had become a case study for the

supposed degeneracy and misfortune that awaited the woman of ideas. George Eliot, who read everything, dared to review some works by Wollstonecraft, but George Eliot herself became shunned by society for living with a man not her husband. Victorian revisionism exacted a particularly vicious toll on Mary Godwin Shelley. As Miranda Seymour shows in *Mary Shelley* (New York: Grove Press, 2000), to survive as a writer and as a mother after Percy's death, Mary Shelley had to savagely bowdlerize her own past and her mother's in order to comply with the wishes of her prudish in-laws and later of that caricature of a Victorian who was her son.

34. The quotation (MS. 8992, f. 56) is from the collection of documents relating to Florence Nightingale from the Verney family archives at Claydon House in Buckinghamshire that was copied soon after the Second World War and housed at the Wellcome Library for the History and Understanding of Medicine. The Wellcome Library copies (cited in these notes as Wellcome/Claydon), numbered by folio and placed in folders, have been easily accessible to scholars. The Claydon originals (cited in these notes as Claydon), usually unnumbered and sorted into bundles, have been difficult to access since the archives were open only on the first Monday of most months, by appointment. No list exists to provide cross-referencing between the now-aging copies and the originals.

35. Frederic Smith, who went out to India as a young man, also had four children, but his wife seems to have been unacceptable to his family so he passes out of the story.

Chapter 3: Wen and Fanny, Ben and Anne, Sam and Mai

1. See Victor Bonham-Carter's history of his family, *In A Liberal Tradition* (London: Constable, 1860).

2. The Claydon documents indicate this. Davis notes that William Smith was in communication on agricultural policy with Sir James Sinclair, presumably a relative of Fanny's James.

3. These attitudes come through clearly in the March 16, 1816, letter Frances Coape Smith wrote to Fanny in Brighton, telling her forthrightly that the Caithnesses were adamantly opposed to the marriage. "They saw, and what parent could avoid seeing, that for JS to marry was highly improper," wrote Mrs. Smith to her daughter. Claydon, Bundle 18.

4. See the letter of Lord Caithness to William Smith, where James is referred to as young and improvident and deficient in the skills needed for an aide de camp. Claydon, Bundle 18.

5. All the quotations from family letters written at the time of WEN and Fanny's wedding are taken from documents in the Claydon collection, Bundle 12.

6. Claydon, Bundle 214/f. 1.

7. I am extremely grateful to Susan Randon, archivist at Claydon, who put this fascinating document in front of me on my first visit to the house.

8. To quote a famous example, some ten years earlier, the teenage Mary Godwin lost several infants when she came to Italy with her lover, Percy Bysshe Shelley, and his friend Byron.

9. See *Mother Nature: Maternal Instincts and How They Shape the Human Species* by Sarah Blaffer Hyrdy (New York: Ballantine, 1999), pp. 350–62. Wet nurses were

called "angel makers" since the mortality of their charges was so high, especially in institutions.

10. The Villa Columbaia still exists, at via Santa Maria a Marignolle 2. It is now a school (Beata Maria de Mattias) and a convent (Adoratrici del Sangue de Cristo). *Collected Works of Florence Nightingale,* ed. Lynn McDonald (Waterloo Ontario: Wilfred Lauerer University Press, 2001) (henceforth CWFN), 1:15.

11. Readers of Dante will remember that outside the first circle of the Inferno is limbo, inhabited principally by virtuous men like Virgil who lived before Christ's act of atonement, and by babies who died before the sacrament of baptism could be administered. However personally blameless, these babes were still not admissible to heaven as they had not been absolved of original sin. Conversely, a mother whose child died soon after christening had at least the certainty that he or she had gone straight to God. Even in my generation in England it was common to perform the christening even if the mother had not recovered enough from childbirth to attend.

12. Ida B. O'Malley, *Florence Nightingale: 1820–1856: A Study of Her Life Down to the End of the Crimean War* (London: Thornton Butterworth, 1931).

13. Florence Nightingale was very interested in breast-feeding, as in all forms of nursing, and in the "Cassandra" fragment she cuttingly refers to affluent mothers whose maternal instincts take the form of driving out to secure a wet nurse for their daughter's child. Perhaps Florence did not know of the nursing problems that her mother had with Parthe, especially since her aunts seem to have given up breast-feeding their own babies by the time Florence was old enough to observe the situation.

14. This account of William Smith's bankruptcy and the family doings following that event is based on Claydon, Bundles 4, 12, and 18.

15. Davis, pp. 189–90.

16. Roy Jenkins in his biography of Gladstone says to multiply nineteenth-century pounds sterling by fifty to get an estimate of currency values today. This seems a remarkably large transfer of capital.

17. Claydon, Bundle 390. This quotation is from a set of letters between the Nightingales and the Shores that was once in the Claydon collection but is now apparently lost. All that remains is the extracts and paraphrases made of the letters by Lady Margaret Verney, who read them and discussed them with Florence Nightingale. Lynn McDonald uncovered the astonishing news that Mai Shore had once sought to marry Ben Smith. I quote at length from Lady Verney's reminiscences since the astonishing information that Benjamin Smith was once engaged to Mai Shore has been lost since the nineteenth century.

18. Frances Smith to Fanny Nightingale, November, 1821, Claydon, Bundle 214.

19. In this account of Benjamin Smith and his two common-law marriages, I rely on Hirsch, op. cit., and Sheila H. Herstein, *Barbara Leigh Smith Bodichon: A Mid-Victorian Feminist* (New Haven: Yale University Press, 1985).

20. Hirsch, p. 10.

21. CUL, Add. MS. 7621/11.

22. Hirsch, p. 97.

23. O'Malley, p. 16, quoting (in her translation) from "La Vie de Florence Rossignol" and from Florence Nightingale's childhood diary. Both these documents have disappeared since O'Malley read them in the late 1920s.

24. CWFN, I: 837, paraphrasing Jowett's notes, now in the Balliol College Archives, I H 43 1880 f. 52.
25. Claydon, Bundle 390.

CHAPTER 4: LEA HURST AND EMBLEY

1. The material in this chapter is based on the massive collection of Florence Nightingale's papers in the British Library (henceforth BL) and in the Claydon collection. The biographies by Cook, O'Malley, and Cecil Woodham-Smith, *Florence Nightingale: 1820–1910* (London: Constable, 1950), referred to hereafter as Woodham-Smith, are not only invaluable guides to interpretation but key sources as well because these writers were able to read, cite, and paraphrase important documentation that has since disappeared.

2. Florence Nightingale once casually remarked that Lea Hurst was hardly a large house since it had only fifteen bedrooms. This has been cited as evidence of her snobbery and detachment from ordinary life. No one was more aware than Nightingale of how much nicer Lea Hurst was than the ordinary Holloway cottage, but in comparison with many of the homes in which she stayed in during her youth—Waverley, Wilton, Broadlands, even Embley after its enlargement in the late 1830s—Lea Hurst was modest. Indeed, even today the original Lea Hurst structure would be too small for a gentrifying British soccer idol or rock star.

3. Description first quoted by Cook, 1:8.

4. Thanks to Jennifer Bobroski for this information, gleaned from the Claydon documents.

5. Even though Elizabeth Gaskell was accustomed to the north of England, when she visited Haworth, the Yorkshire home of her friend Charlotte Brontë, she had the same adverse reaction to the local folk as Fanny had initially in Lea-Holloway. As Juliet Barker has explained, Elizabeth Gaskell in her biography of Charlotte Brontë over-dramatized the social isolation of the Brontë sisters and exaggerated the brutality and lack of culture of the people they lived among. See Juliet Barker, *Brontës* (New York: St. Martin's Press, 1995).

6. Mr. and Mrs. Sydney Shore were at the Nightingales' wedding, and in one of her early letters, Florence recounts a visit to Lydia Shore and her three sisters, WEN's cousins.

7. Wellcome/Claydon, MS. 8991, f. 61.

8. Quoted Cook, 1:9.

9. Both Embley and Claydon are situated in some of the most beautiful and unspoiled rural areas of England. When I first visited them, I was astonished to feel so close to the world of the Nightingales.

10. Claydon, Bundle 390.

11. According to Jenny Uglow, the seven remarkable Tollett (or, according to some spellers, Tollet) sisters were one of the main connections between the Nightingales and the Wedgwoods and the Darwins. Charles Darwin thought highly enough of Georgina Tollett to send her part of the manuscript of *On the Origin of Species* for editorial comment (Uglow, *Elizabeth Gaskell: A Habit of Stories* [New York: Farrar, Straus & Giroux, 1993], p. 360). Fanny Nightingale was perhaps even closer to Fanny Allen,

another Darwin and Wedgwood cousin, and herself a remarkable woman.

12. Apart from the large number of letters to various correspondents from Florence Nightingale, we also have hundreds of letters from Mai, Fanny, WEN, Parthenope, Benjamin Smith, Samuel Smith, Julia Smith, Patty Smith, Joanna Bonham-Carter, Anne Nicholson, Frances Coape Smith, Maria Coape, as well as friends from which to piece together an account of the clan's life in the 1820s and 1830s.

13. Hampshire Record Office, Bonham-Carter Papers.

14. Claydon, Bundle 390.

15. Wellcome/Claydon, MS. 9031, f. 30.

16. When Florence was staying with the Bonham-Carters in February 1830, she wrote to her father about the fights that had broken out between the small band of cousins, led by Jack Bonham-Carter, and their uncle Adams Smith. After Adams, whom the children nicknamed Gog, complained to John Bonham-Carter about their wild behavior, the children lodged a counter-complaint with "5 formal accusations viz. 1. Breaking 2 carts. 2. Hurting Hilary's hand. 3. Accusing us of doing it. 4. Beating my legs. and 5. Hurting me." (Martha Vicinus and Bea Nergaard, eds., "Ever Yours, Florence Nightingale": Selected Letters (Cambridge, Mass.: Harvard University Press, 1990).

17. Wellcome/Claydon, MS. 9031, f. 21.

CHAPTER 5: A PRIVILEGED VICTORIAN CHILDHOOD

1. CWFN, I:90.

2. Making an accurate count of the Nightingale sisters' cousins is less easy than it seems, and the standard biographers of Florence Nightingale trace only those branches of the family with which Nightingale had contact as a child, omitting the children of both Benjamin and Frederic. Even for the Nicholsons and Bonham-Carters there are still unresolved issues. In her family tree, Barbara M. Dossey (Florence Nightingale: Mystic, Visionary and Healer, Springhouse, PA: Springhouse, 2000) lists the eldest Nicholson child as Samuel, born in 1815, and McDonald in her genealogy (CWFN, 1, p. 850) says that there were six Nicholson children but lists only five. I have found no mention of a cousin Samuel Nicholson in the letters, so I presume he died in infancy. Neither Dossey nor McDonald gives Marianne Nicholson's birth date, so we do not know whether she was the same age as Parthe or Flo or older than both. In the case of the Bonham-Carters, things are made complicated by the fact that there were two male children named Hugh, one born in 1830 who died as an infant, and another born in 1832 who lived until 1896, married, and had two children.

3. Ben's other illegitimate family, the three Bentley Smiths and their mother, Jane Buss, lived in Fulham, then another London suburb, in comfort but not luxury, several steps down the social ladder from all the rest. See Hirsch, p. 96.

4. O'Malley, summarizing from the lost "La Vie de Florence Rossignol," p. 20.

5. The family took the name Bonham-Carter only after the death of Thomas (Bonny) Carter. As late as 1855, Florence Nightingale is still referring to the "Carters" in her family letters.

6. This letter and several others of Florence's youthful epistles are reproduced from the

originals in the Claydon collection in Barbara Dossey's gloriously illustrated book *Florence Nightingale: Mystic, Visionary, and Healer.*

7. CWFN, 1:219.

8. Cook, 1:10–11.

9. Cook, 1:10. Florence Nightingale's youthful flower catalogue appears to be lost.

10. CWFN, 1:112–13.

11. See Cook, 1:13–14. Sarah A. Tooley has a particularly lengthy version of this incident. I quote a section to give the flavor of biography written during Miss Nightingale's lifetime: "Kneeling down on the mud floor she caressed the suffering dog with her little hand, and spoke soothing words to it until the faithful brown eyes seemed to have less pain in them and were lifted to her face in pathetic gratitude. That look of the shepherd's dog which touched her heart on the lonely hillside Florence Nightingale was destined to see repeated in the eyes of suffering men as she bent over them in the hospital at Scutari." *Life of Florence Nightingale* (London: Cassell, 1910, p. 27).

12. CWFN, 1:280–81.

13. Dossey, p. 12. The italics reflect Nightingale's own underlinings.

14. O'Malley, p. 22. Again, this copybook seems to have been lost.

15. As a little girl the future actress Fanny Kemble also excelled in summarizing sermons, a useful exercise for a future writer but very hard for the less talented child.

16. CWFN, 1:105. Maria Brent died soon after this letter was written, after a long illness. The Nightingales seem to have been contributing to her support.

17. Wellcome/Claydon, MS. 9045, f. 3.

18. Ibid., MS. 9031, f. 2, Mai Smith to Fanny Nightingale.

19. CWFN, 1:428.

20. Charles and Emma Darwin, both of whom were brought up in the Unitarian persuasion, treated the governess they hired for their daughters in the same way as the Nightingales treated Miss Christie. Miss Catherine Thorley was recommended to the Darwins by the Tolletts of Byerley Hall. Mr. Thorley, Catherine's father, had been the Tolletts' solicitor, but after his death the family was forced to sell up and move to London, and three of the daughters became governesses. Catherine Thorley botanized with Charles Darwin, and he cites her work in *The Origin of Species.* See Randal Keynes, p. 128.

21. The Martineaus were friends and coreligionists of the Smiths, and they had a school at Tynemouth. Julia Smith was a friend of the Martineau sisters, and Florence Nightingale's cousin Hilary Bonham-Carter spent some time at the Martineau school. See the Bonham-Carter papers, Hampshire Record Office. The Byerley sisters ran an important girls' school that was attended at different times by Elizabeth Gaskell, the daughters of James Martineau, Eliza Priestley (American granddaughter of Joseph Priestley, mother of Bessie Parkes Belloc, grandmother of Hilaire Belloc), Bella Leigh Smith, Jessie Boucherett (the feminist reformer), and Effie Gray (the wife of Ruskin). As we shall see, Florence Nightingale's parents also considered enrolling her in the Byerley school when she was about ten. The Byerley children—five sons and eight daughters—were the great-nieces and -nephews of Josiah Wedgwood, the great pottery tycoon, and Josiah gave each of them two hundred pounds, with which the girls were able to start their school. See Uglow, *Elizabeth Gaskell,* pp. 34–35.

22. All accounts of Florence Nightingale's childhood are based on O'Malley, who gives by

far the most extensive account. O'Malley calls the governess Florence's "best friend," "dear Miss Christie." O'Malley bases her portrait of Christie largely on Florence's early journals, letters, and autobiography, an apparently impeccable source that has since vanished. O'Malley tries very hard not to ruffle any family feathers, but I notice that when she actually quotes or closely paraphrases Florence's papers, the details point more to conflict between governess and pupil than affection. In any case, "La Vie de Florence Rossignol" was a school exercise completed under the direct supervision of her governess, so little Flo's freedom to comment on Miss Christie was limited.

23. "From the Lebenslanf" or autobiographical sketch Nightingale wrote in 1851. CWFN, 1:90.

24. Claydon, Bundle 277. I have taken the liberty of adding some punctuation marks to Lady Verney's hurried notes to make her meaning clearer.

25. Claydon, Bundle 114, my own transcription. Slightly different transcriptions are included in Dossey, p. 14, and in CWFN, I: 109. The words are scribbled on two sides of a small sheet apparently torn from a notebook. Neither Susan Ranson, the Claydon archivist, nor I could identify the handwriting.

26. CWFN, 1:461.

27. To judge by the large childish printing and the extremely rudimentary human figures, this little annotated drawing was done by Florence when she was about five. Claydon, Bundle 223.

28. Cook, 1:12; Woodham-Smith, p. 7. Both biographers appear to be summarizing a lost autobiographical fragment, and it is unclear to which precise period in her youth Nightingale is referring, and whether her feelings of not fitting in date from before or after Miss Christie's plan to reform her. If Florence indeed described herself as a monster, this is significant, as she had probably read Mary Shelley's *Frankenstein*. Recent critics have argued that Frankenstein's monster is in many ways a displaced expression of the teenage female author's own feelings of anger, deformity, and estrangement.

29. Woodham-Smith was the first biographer to comment on Florence's crushes. "Her childhood was a series of passions—for her governess Miss Christie, for WEN's younger sister Mary, 'Aunt Mai,' for a beautiful older cousin. When Miss Christie left, when Aunt Mai married, when the beautiful cousin got tired of her devotion, the violence of her feelings made her physically ill" (p. 8).

30. Cook, 1:11.

31. I discuss Florence Nightingale's dreaming in some detail in Chapter 12.

32. In a letter to her grandmother Shore, probably written after the arrival of Miss Christie at Embley in 1827, Florence says that both her parents, Aunt Mai, Uncle Sam, and Miss Johnson (the former governess of her mother's cousins the Cure girls) are away and that she is in the care of Aunt Julia. "Aunt Julia is very kind . . . Aunt Julia did not tell me to say she was very kind," Florence notes. To me this implies that someone was now telling her what to say about the adults who cared for her. Wellcome/Claydon, MS. 8991, f. 1.

33. Woodham-Smith, p. 7.

34. O'Malley, pp. 24–25. She says in a note that this little book "is preserved at Lea Hurst," but it too seems to have been omitted from the Nightingale papers deposited at the British Library.

35. *"Maman, faut-il que je prends deux promenades, et si longs car j'ai été si fatigué aujour-*

d'hui et si froid." Her governess would no doubt have pointed out to Flo that this sentence has two major grammatical mistakes (*prends* for *prenne,* and *fatigué* for *fatiguée*), and one incorrect expression (*froid* used as an adjective). Even at age nine, Florence Nightingale had excellent command of grammar and was highly sensitized to the correct inflections of verbs and adjective endings. Thus, the number of errors in the sentence is a measure of how upset she is.

36. Florence signs a July 20, 1830, letter to her mother "your affectionate child β" with a very flowery beta. I suspect that the name "Bo" was some small cousin's pronunciation of "Flo," and that it signals the transformation of Florence into the stellar baby-sitter of the family. See Chapter 6.

37. Wellcome/Claydon, MS. 8991, f. 41.

38. Ibid, f. 55.

39. Cook, 1:11.

40. Benjamin Smith gave his Leigh Smith children an extraordinarily liberal education, great personal freedom, and, at their majority, a small independent private income, for boys and girls alike. Bessie Parkes Belloc, Barbara's closest friend in childhood and youth, remembered how amazed she had been to see Benjamin bend down and retie one of his daughter's shoelaces. See Herstein, pp. 9–16.

41. See Georgina Battiscombe, *Shaftesbury: The Great Reformer, 1801–1885* (Boston: Houghton Mifflin, 1975), p. 25.

CHAPTER 6: IN FATHER'S LIBRARY

1. Wellcome/Claydon, MS. 8991, f. 66 and f. 88.

2. Cook, 1:30.

3. O'Malley, p. 35.

4. Cook, 1:30.

5. Florence's interest in breast-feeding is shown in another letter to her grandmother where she reports on a Mrs. Coltman who is too sick even to see her newborn son "who is being suckled [by] another person." CWFN, 1:410. This letter should probably be dated 1832, not 1828, since Florence refers to "Aunt Mary and Baby and Blanche." In Florence's mind, "Baby" (i.e. Shore) now takes precedence over "Blanche."

6. Wellcome/Claydon, MS. 8991, f. 81.

7. I owe this insight to Sarah Blaffer Hyrdy's *Maternal Instinct.*

8. Florence Nightingale says in a letter to her grandmother Shore that Mai calls her baby "the thing," remarking "Is not that very disrespectful?" CWFN, 1:411.

9. BL, Add. 45794, f. 21.

10. CWFN, 1:90.

11. The Nightingale parents apparently had no thought of sending Parthe to school, probably because they agreed the two girls should be kept separate, and Parthe was too fragile for school.

12. O'Malley, p. 27.

13. Wellcome/Claydon, MS. 9405, f. 4.

14. Ibid. f. 6. These three letters to the Nightingale parents have been pulled from a more extensive correspondence from Miss Taylor in the Claydon collection, much of it ad-

dressed to Parthenope. The letters do not have year dates. I would tend to place them in 1834, when WEN was seeking to become M.P. for Andover.

15. An excellent Germanist and theologian, Miss Hennell is most notable for having passed on to her dear friend Mary Ann Evans the unenviable assignment of translating into English Strauss's *Leben Jesu,* with its long sections of Latin, Greek, and Hebrew. See Gordon Haight, *George Eliot: A Biography,* (Oxford: Oxford University Press, 1968). pp. 46–47 and passim.

16. Summarizing early letters from Florence Nightingale to Hilary Bonham-Carter that appear not to be extant, O'Malley writes: "For some time Flo had not been quite sure what she felt about Aunt Julia. When they were all at Ryde the year before, she had not begun by loving her much; but every day the love had got a little stronger . . . Hilary had always wanted her to love Aunt Julia, who was her own admired model and friend." (p. 35).

17. Mary Keele, ed., *Florence Nightingale in Rome: Letters Written by Florence Nightingale in Rome in the Winter of 1847–1848* (Philadelphia: American Philosophical Society, 1981), p. 146.

18. In letters written as an adult to her father, Florence Nightingale translates German, which leads me to assume that he was not well up in that language.

19. BL, Add. 45791/ff. 270–72.

20. A Compendium of Useful Facts, BL, Add. 45848.

21. Wellcome/Claydon, MS. 8991, ff. 86 and 88.

22. Woodham-Smith, p. 11, who describes this piece by WEN as a "characteristic letter—involved, vague and curiously reminiscent of a soliloquy in a poetic drama."

23. Ibid., p. 12.

24. Woodham-Smith, whose biography of Florence Nightingale has most influenced opinion over the last fifty years, is harsh in her condemnation of Parthenope Nightingale. She implies that bad relations between the sisters went back to their girlhood. "Flo dominated. Flo led and Parthe followed, but Parthe followed resentfully. She was possessive toward Flo. She adored Flo, wanted Flo's entire devotion, could not bear Flo to have another friend, but she was bitterly envious of Flo." Woodham-Smith, p. 10. There is obviously some truth in this, but it is also essentially a portrait of Parthe as painted by the adult Florence in her bitterest and most resentful moments.

25. This illness is dramatically described in the series of a dozen or so letters that Fanny Nightingale wrote to WEN and which she begged him to keep. Claydon, Bundle 218.

26. This period in early 1837 is covered in a series of family letters, Wellcome/Claydon, MS. 8991, ff. 80–94.

27. Cook (1:15) says that in a private note written in 1867 Florence Nightingale first recorded that on February 7, 1837, "God called me to His service." Woodham-Smith says that in another note from 1874 Nightingale recorded hearing voices four times—in 1837, 1852, 1854, and 1861. Woodham-Smith is quite clear that Nightingale had what Catholics term an "audition," that is, hearing a voice outside oneself speak. O'Malley, on the other hand, says that though Nightingale referred many times in her private papers to her 1837 call, "no record survives of the form in which it reached her" (p. 43).

CHAPTER 7: DOING EUROPE IN STYLE

1. For Parthe's letter, see Wellcome/Claydon, MS. 8991, f. 73. Florence's letter to her mother is quoted by Dossey, pp. 31–32.

2. The carriage must have worked well since the Bonham-Carter ladies borrowed it when they undertook a lengthy European tour some years later. Benjamin Smith also had a large customized carriage to take his Leigh Smith children when they went abroad.

3. O'Malley, p. 44n. The Claydon collection contains extensive material written by Parthe, WEN, and Fanny during this European tour, as well as letters from Florence. Florence's diary, however, from which O'Malley happily makes extensive quotations and paraphrases, appears to be lost.

4. Claydon, Bundle 66.

5. According to Elizabeth Abbot, "until the late eighteenth century, Italian opera and castrati were indistinguishable concepts, and 70 percent of male opera singers were castrati." By the beginning of the nineteenth century, women were permitted to perform on the stage in Italy and "opera no longer demanded gelding, though the Vatican chapel and other Roman choirs continued to employ castrati especially maimed for the purpose. The last known castrato was Alessandro Moreschi, who made recordings as late as 1903 and performed in the Sistine chapel until 1913." *A History of Celibacy* (New York: Scribner, 1999), p. 333.

6. In *Daniel Deronda* (1876), George Eliot's heroine Gwendolyn Harleth believes she has talent as a singer but is soon disabused when she meets Herr Klesmer, a German-Jewish pianist whom George Eliot may have modeled on Lizst. Before the First World War, the teenage Agatha Miller was an accomplished musician and nourished hopes of making a career as a concert singer. Chronic shyness ended those hopes and Miss Miller, soon to become Mrs. Christie, had to satisfy her ambitions by writing detective stories. See my *Agatha Christie: The Woman and Her Mysteries* (New York: Free Press, 1990).

7. Younger sister to the famous actress Fanny Kemble, daughter of Charles Kemble, and niece of Sarah Siddons, Adelaide Kemble enjoyed a brief but exalted career in opera during exactly the period when Florence, Parthenope, and their cousin Marianne Nicholson were most opera-mad. Both Adelaide and Fanny Kemble were haunted by fear of the price they would have to pay for the fame, adulation, and wealth that came with success on the stage. Victorian society increasingly defined women as modest, self-sacrificing, private beings, and this role was hard to play in life for an actress who not only earned her own living but also enacted the great passions on stage for an audience composed largely of men. Fanny Kemble failed to resolve this problem satisfactorily, but in her late twenties Adelaide Kemble married the rich, distinguished, and devoted Edward Sartoris. From then on, Mrs. Sartoris moved in the upper reaches of Victorian society, singing only in private homes to please friends like William Thackeray and Henry James. See Blainey.

8. CWFN, 1:90.

9. Cook, 1:17.

10. For my information on Mary Clarke Mohl, I have relied chiefly on Margaret Lesser's valuable book *Clarkey: A Portrait in Letters of Mary Clarke Mohl* (Oxford: Oxford University Press, 1984). Also on M. C. M. Simpson, *Letters and Recollections of Julius and*

Mary Mohl (London: Kegan, Paul, Trench & Co., 1889) and on Mary Clarke Mohl's own book *Madame Récamier, with a Sketch of the History of Society in France* (London: Chapman and Hall, 1862). Mary Charlotte Muir Simpson's book includes some reminiscences by Parthenope Verney, but nothing from Florence Nightingale, who refused to collaborate with people writing memoirs of people she had known.

11. According to Mary Keele, the Clarkes' apartment house on the rue du Bac was still numbered 112 in 1848, but is referred to as 120 subsequently. Keele, p. 11.

12. In her book, Mary Clarke Mohl explains how Englishmen will do anything for their womenfolk except listen to them and treat them as rational, informed, interesting beings.

13. On February 2, 1839, Florence wrote to her grandmother Shore: "There is a most extraordinary actress here at the great French theatre who promises to be as fine as a Mrs. Siddons, she is only seventeen, her name is Mademoiselle Rachel." Wellcome/Claydon, MS. 8991, f. 99a. In *Villette,* Charlotte Brontë offers perhaps the greatest description of the effect Rachel had on her audience in her most famous role, Jean Racine's Phèdre. See Rachel M. Brownstein, *Tragic Muse: Rachel of the Comédie-Française* (Durham: Duke University Press, 1995).

14. Simpson, p. 4.

15. Quoted by Woodham-Smith, pp. 26–27, no reference given.

16. Ibid.

17. Simpson, p. 90.

18. Ibid., p. 18.

19. My account of the relationship between Mary Clarke and Claude Fauriel is based on Lesser's book, where sections of Mary's letters to her lover or would-be lover are reproduced for the first time.

20. She once wrote to him from England: "Oh if only I could feel your arms about me, I think I should be satisfied for ever so long! I try not to think of it, I desire it too much. I feel as dry as a plant that has not been watered." Lesser, p. 36.

21. Simpson, p. 35.

22. In *Literary Women: The Great Writers,* Ellen Moers brilliantly captures the impact of reading Sand on Elizabeth Barrett Browning, Margaret Fuller, Julia Ward Howe, Charlotte Brontë, George Eliot, and Emily Dickinson, to name only a few, all of whom read her in French.

23. After the death of Mary Clarke Mohl, the letters from Florence Nightingale that the Mohls had kept were returned to her (Cook, 1:vi). Cook and Woodham-Smith saw these letters, and Woodham-Smith took notes and made extracts from them when researching her book. According to Margaret Lesser (p. viii), these extracts remain in the possession of Woodham-Smith's family and are "especially valuable, since nearly all the originals have been destroyed." The remaining original letters between Mary and Florence are in the British Library.

24. Lesser, quoting Mary Clarke's letters to Claude Fauriel, p. 59 and p. 73.

CHAPTER 8: COMING OUT

1. According to Cecil Woodham-Smith, this carpet came into the collection of the Victoria and Albert Museum. (Woodham-Smith, p. 35).

2. In an attractive contemporary drawing by Hilary Bonham-Carter, Fanny Nightingale is shown in a similar gown and a superb cap; Fanny looks chic while her daughters look mousy.

3. Sarah Tooley claimed in her 1910 biography that Florence Nightingale was an expert needlewoman who "mastered the finest and most complicated crochet patterns, sewed delicate embroideries, and achieved almost invisible hems on muslin frills" (p. 39).

4. Woodham-Smith (p. 32) describes finding a package containing the hair of both Flo and Parthe, cut in 1839, and showing a marked difference.

5. Ibid., p. 64.

6. Cook, 1:38–39.

7. BL, Add. 45846, f. 63.

8. Florence wrote to her grandmother Shore on May 10, 1839: "I believe Mama & I are going to the Queen's birthday drawing-room on the 19th. I was presented at the last Drawing-room and was not nearly so much frightened as I expected. Mr. Parker [M.P. and one of WEN's closest friends] went with us greatly to our satisfaction. The queen looked flushed & tired but the whole sight was very pretty." Wellcome/Claydon, MS. 8991, f. 102.

9. O'Malley, p. 34.

10. Ibid., p. 26.

11. I owe this point to Woodham-Smith, who is the biographer most interested in the relation of Florence Nightingale to the Nicholsons: "Marianne's capacity to love was reserved for her family. She adored her brothers and sisters. All the Nicholsons adored each other and stood by one another through thick and thin, and of all her family the one Marianne loved best was her brother Henry" (p. 33).

12. George Eliot portrays such a woman in Gwendolyn Harleth, the heroine of *Daniel Deronda*—before she finds herself trapped in the sadistic Grandcourt's web.

13. Cook, 1:26.

14. I do not think that Florence Nightingale attended the wedding of Victoria and Albert. In her letter to her sister, she is simply giving a graphic narration of what she had been told along the grapevine by friends who were there.

15. The first Lord Ashburton was the head of the immensely rich English banking family, the Barings. His first wife was an equally rich heiress from Pennsylvania, and through her family connections the Barings extended their financial empire into the United States. Florence Nightingale never visited Boston, but her family had many friends there through the Unitarian network.

16. Cook, 1:37. I quote this passage at length both because it is so lively and because, according to Woodham-Smith, Nightingale recorded in her diary that she had become so taken up with a daydream that she had been unable to make conversation with the Ashburtons.

17. "With the phantom companion of their fancy . . . they [women like herself] talk, in fancy, of that which interests them most; they seek a companion for their every thought, the companion they find not in reality they seek in fantasy . . . they see themselves engaged with him in stirring events, circumstances which call out the interest wanting to them." *"Cassandra" and Other Selections from "Suggestions for Thought,"* edited by Mary Poovey (New York: New York University Press, 1992), p. 206.

18. O'Malley, p. 176.

19. Florence Nightingale was already proposing a little mathematical puzzle to Henry Nicholson when she was eight. See CWFN, 1:462.

20. No one seems to know exactly when Marianne Nicholson was born.

21. See Alison Winter's superb discussion of Martineau's *Life in the Sickroom* in *Mesmerized: Powers of Mind in Victorian Britain* (Chicago: University of Chicago Press, 1998), pp. 218–21.

22. The letters from home bearing the sad news that John Bonham-Carter had died were delayed by floods and snow, and the Nightingales learned of the death only in Florence. WEN was especially hard hit, as Carter had been one of his closest friends. See Wellcome/Claydon Collection, MS. 8991, f. 96, Florence Nightingale to Grandmother Shore, March 3, 1838.

23. Many of the letters exchanged by Hilary Bonham-Carter and Florence Nightingale that are quoted by Cook and O'Malley are, unfortunately, not in the British Library collection.

24. O'Malley, pp. 60–61, and the Bonham-Carter papers.

25. These entries form part of a bundle of sections from various journals kept by Hilary Bonham-Carter, which are now in the Bonham-Carter collection in the Hampshire Record Office (94M72/F528). The fact that the pages are detached indicate that someone has gone through the original document and performed some kind of triage.

26. The almost total lack of Christian faith and biblical knowledge among the lower ranks of society, particularly the industrial proletariat, was exhaustively documented and a matter of deep concern to the upper classes in the early decades of Victoria's reign.

27. O'Malley, apparently quoting a letter circa 1840 from Hilary Bonham-Carter to Florence Nightingale, p. 73.

28. Bonheur was born in 1822 like Hilary Bonham-Carter, Hosmer in 1830. Berthe Morisot (b. 1841) and Mary Cassatt (b. 1844) are part of the next generation.

29. The letters Florence wrote at this time are in the Claydon collection. Many have been included in CWFN, vol. 1.

30. Cook, vol. 1, p. 27.

CHAPTER 9: PROBLEMS WITH THE NICHOLSONS

1. Elizabeth Gaskell, who lived in Manchester and whose Unitarian minister husband was close to the starving, embittered workers, offers us a moving portrait of those times in her great novels *Mary Barton* and *North and South*.

2. Patty Smith says this in a letter to Fanny. Wellcome/Claydon, MS. 9038, f. 22.

3. Ibid., f. 19.

4. See Amanda Foreman, *Georgiana, Duchess of Devonshire* (New York: Random House, 1998) and J. Lees-Milne, *The Bachelor Duke: William Spencer Cavendish, Sixth Duke of Devonshire, 1790–1858* (London: John Murray, 1991).

5. The two men met in 1826 when the young Paxton was working as a gardener at the Horticultural Gardens near the duke's house at Chiswick. The duke hired Joseph as a gardener at Chatsworth. The two men traveled all over the world together, collaborated on many projects, and were constant companions, though Paxton was married and had eight children. When the duke died, "the main spring of [Paxton's] life was snapped." Violet Markham, *Paxton and the Bachelor Duke* (London: Hodder and

Stoughton, 1935, p. 303). Markham was Paxton's granddaughter.

6. Wellcome/Claydon, MS. 8991, f. 97.

7. O'Malley, pp. 84–85.

8. "Occasionally an eminent banker or merchant invested a large portion of his accu-
   mulations in land, and in the purchase of parliamentary influence, and was in time
   duly admitted to the sanctuary . . . But the manufacturers, the railway kings, the
   colossal contractors, the discoverers of nuggets, had not yet found their place in society and the senate. There were then, perhaps, more great houses open than at the
   present day, but there were very few little ones." Disraeli, writing in 1881, quoted by
   Elizabeth Lee, *Wives of the Prime Ministers 1844–1906* (London: Nisbet, 1918), p.
   111.

9. Broadlands is now regularly opened to the public and is popular with the British public largely through its recent connection to the Mountbatten family.

10. For this section on Lord Palmerston I have relied chiefly on Jasper Ridley's biography,
    Lord Palmerston (London: Constable, 1970).

11. For the life of the seventh Earl of Shaftesbury, see Battiscombe.

12. *The Water-Babies* (1863), the most lasting of the novels of the Christian Socialist
    Charles Kingsley, centers on the life and death of a small chimney sweep.

13. Wellcome/Claydon, MS. 8991, f. 89a.

14. As she wrote to Mary Clarke in 1847, on a visit to Oxford with her father to attend a
    meeting of the British Association: "Here we are in the midst of loveliness and learn-
    ing; for never anything so beautiful as this place is looking now, my dearest, have I
    seen abroad or at home, with its flowering acacias in the midst of its streets of palaces.
    I saunter about the churchyards and gardens by myself before breakfast, and wish I
    were a college man." Cook, 1:65.

15. The Nightingales were some of the people in England (Harriet Beecher Stowe in the
    United States was another) who stoutly defended Lady Noel Byron in her various run-
    ins with those advancing the cult of Lord Byron in the decades following his death.
    The name "Noel Byron" came to Byron's widow as the result of a large legacy from
    her relatives the Noels. The surname Noel pops up often in the Nightingale corre-
    spondence. Florence Nightingale was very affected by the news of Ada Byron's death
    and went to view her body when it was taken to Newlands Abbey, the Byron family
    estate. Ada Byron probably died of cancer, but rumors about her fatal disease ran wild
    among Lady Byron's friends. Florence wrote: "I thought of the words 'conceived in
    sin,' & what an account that man, her father, has to render from whose excesses her
    dreadful sufferings must date." Wellcome/Claydon, MS. 8993, ff. 116–18.

16. When his daughter Elizabeth wanted lessons in advanced Greek prosody Mr. Robert
    Barrett took the prudent course of hiring a gentleman who was not only elderly but
    blind. In his 1993 play *Arcadia,* Tom Stoppard shows the delicately erotic relation-
    ship between a young female math prodigy and her male tutor. Ada Byron, aged six-
    teen, tried to run away with her statistics tutor.

17. According to O'Malley, Florence saw her grandmother on her deathbed and marveled
    that her beauty had seemed to grow with age and sorrow. Florence noted the small,
    plump hands and tapering fingers, now closed and still. See O'Malley, p. 72.

18. CWFN, 1:115.

19. Wellcome/Claydon, MS. 8991, f. 19.

20. Cook, 1:33.

21. Henry Reeve was later one of Florence Nightingale's allies, notably when she was preparing to go out to Turkey. See Cook, 1:157.

22. Wellcome/Claydon, MS. 9038, f. 58.

23. The chronology of events in the Nightingales' lives during the early 1840s is difficult to establish and will remain so until all the documentation at Claydon has been thoroughly reexamined. Biographers have assigned different dates to such important events as the beginning of Florence's friendship with Hannah Nicholson and refusal of Henry Nicholson's proposal. The dating I offer here is carefully considered but should still be regarded as provisional.

24. Florence promised to tutor him in mathematics, and in November of 1843 William came to work with her privately at Embley. Florence wrote to her mother to keep the tutoring strictly to herself, as Mr. Nicholson was sure that William's life at Sandhurst would be a misery if it were known he was being taught by a woman. Unfortunately, Parthe could not resist extolling her sister's pedagogic excellencies in a letter to Aunt Mai, letting the cat out of the bag. The Nicholsons were furious, and to Florence's intense chagrin, a flurry of angry, explanatory, and apologetic letters ensued.

25. BL, Add. 45794, f. 2. I would date this letter to 1842 or 1843, not 1844.

26. Ibid., f. 10.

27. The current British Library collection of Florence Nightingale's drafts of letters to Hannah Nicholson seems to be identical to the one seen by biographers before the Second World War.

28. BL, Add. 45794, f. 20.

29. Ibid. ff. 38–40.

30. The letters written from Henry Reeve's house are in Wellcome/Claydon, MS. 8992, ff. 36–56.

31. The documents relating to Florence's quarrel with Marianne have been lost. I quote sections from the long passages quoted by O'Malley (pp. 104–5) and Woodham-Smith (p. 53).

32. O'Malley, p. 124.

33. Woodham-Smith, p. 33. To recapitulate the evidence, no letters exchanged between Florence Nightingale and Marianne Nicholson during the period of their great friendship have ever been reported. Presumably the two women destroyed them early on. The letters Nightingale wrote to Hilary Bonham-Carter about her split with Marianne were seen by O'Malley, probably by Cook, and perhaps by Woodham-Smith, but have since been lost. Her diary from this period is also lost.

34. See McDonald, Appendix B, "The Rise and Fall of Florence Nightingale's Reputation," CWFN, I: 843–47.

35. Cook, 2: 14. For a longer extract from this letter, see Chapter 21, p. 440–41.

36. It is possible that the enlightened Unitarian community on both sides of the Atlantic was among the first to entertain modern suspicions about the wisdom of allowing young people of the same sex to sleep together. Certainly, Samuel Gridley Howe astonished his women teacher colleagues at the Perkins school when he forbade any teacher, student, friend, or relative to share a bed with Laura Bridgman after she turned fifteen. Sharing a bed was normal among New England women at this time, and to force deaf and blind Laura to sleep alone seemed especially harsh, given how

much all her relationships depended on touch. Historian Elizabeth Gitter surmises that whereas Howe himself had passionate friendships with men like Charles Sumner (Longfellow wrote that Sumner "was quite in love with Howe"), he felt that Laura would be unable to withstand the temptations posed by the homosocial intimacies which society then accepted. "Howe feared that cuddling with another girl might be too stimulating for a female of Laura's defective character. Perhaps he imagined that physical closeness could awaken lascivious desires, encourage masturbation, or arouse hysterical passions in such a vulnerable young girl." (Elizabeth Gitter, *The Imprisoned Guest: Samuel Howe and Laura Bridgman, the Original Deaf-Blind Girl* [New York: Farrar, Straus & Giroux, 2001], pp. 191–92.

Chapter 10: Mrs. Nightingale Says No

1. Wellcome/Claydon, MS. 8992, f. 96.
2. Mère Angélique Arnauld was the abbess at Port-Royal des Champs, one of the great cultural centers of France in the early seventeenth century. Jean Racine was a pupil of the abbey and Blaise Pascal retired there before his death. Florence Nightingale studied Port-Royal carefully and regarded the women there, notably the Arnauld sisters, as among the handful of significant women intellectuals and spiritual authorities the world had known. The influence upon Florence Nightingale of French theology and spiritual practice—not only the Jansenists but the Quietists and Madame Guyon—merits further study.
3. O'Malley, p. 108.
4. Ibid., p. 109. Parthenope Nightingale was astonished and upset when she read what Florence had said about Gale. O'Malley found the word "Illusory" written apparently in Parthe's handwriting over the sentence where Florence referred to Gale's lack of faith. When Parthenope wrote to Hilary about Gale's death, her grief took a more conventional turn. She felt that Gale's suffering was now over, she was in heaven and from there her spirit would look tenderly down on her darlings, and await their coming. Parthe was especially aware that, with Gale dead, a part of her own childhood was gone too. "No one to call me 'dear Pop' again and recount our baby days with such unfailing interest . . . She had such a memory and such a boundless affection."
5. O'Malley, p. 87.
6. Ibid., p. 93n.
7. Letter of 1846, unsigned but with envelope, BL, Add. 45794, ff. 110–16. Anna Jameson (1794–1860) was a close friend of Julia Smith, well educated but of little means, who was forced for some years to work as a governess. After a disastrous marriage, she became a successful writer. When Elizabeth Barrett eloped to Italy with Robert Browning, Jameson accompanied her.
8. Woodham-Smith, p. 56.
9. Nightingale's idea of a Protestant lay sisterhood devoted to the care of the sick based on the Catholic nursing orders was not unique. There were several attempts along these lines. See Anne Summers's superb book, *Angels and Citizens: British Women as Military Nurses, 1854–1914* (London: Routledge, 1988), pp. 15–23.
10. Cook, 1: 44–45. Also Woodham-Smith, p. 56. I quote this letter at length as it is not included in the first volume of CWFN. Nightingale's entry from the missing diary

was even more extreme. She begged God to let her die, even though her personal theology led her to believe that there would be a new life after death where she would have to bear the burdens of today's failures.

11. By 1851, during her second visit to the Kaiserswerth Institute, Nightingale understood why her mother had not wanted her to go into an English hospital. CWFN, I: 91.

12. Florence Nightingale to Mary Clarke Mohl, BL, Add. 43397, f. 292.

13. Wellcome/Claydon, MS. 9038, f. 50.

14. Noel Annan devotes an interesting section to the naturalists William Buckland and his son Frank in the second chapter of *The Dons*. The bear was called Tiglath-Pileser, Tig for short, and he was part of the extraordinary domestic menagerie kept by the Bucklands. Annan says the bear "led a full social existence" until expelled from college by the dean.

15. Wellcome/Claydon, MS. 8992, f. 114. This letter is addressed to "My Dear," and in my view was written to Parthenope Nightingale, not to Hilary Bonham-Carter, as assumed by Vicinus and Nergaard, p. 27.

16. The interesting little book *Death at the Priory: Sex, Love, and Murder in Victorian England* by James Ruddick (New York: Atlantic Books, 2001) tells the story of Florence Campbell Ricardo, a young married woman, sexually at odds with her husband, who came to the Great Malvern clinic and engaged in a passionate love affair with the elderly Gully. When Mrs. Ricardo went on trial for murdering her husband and word of her affair with her doctor came out, Gully's successful medical practice was ruined. Ruddick, following earlier historians, paints the hydropathic clinics as havens for women anxious to escape the demands of their domestic lives.

17. Wellcome/Claydon, MS. 8993, f. 2.

18. Ibid., MS. 8992, f. 65.

19. CWFN, 1:219. A good example of the evolving intellectual relationship between Florence and WEN is one wonderful letter in the British Library collection where Florence vigorously combats her father's tendency toward fatalism and inaction. She takes an anti-Malthusian tack, arguing that even if it is true that God helps those who help themselves and that charity often does more harm than good, this does not mean we should all sit on our hands and refuse to help those less privileged. Yes, schools are usually bad, and Sunday schools are positively bad, but would you, Florence asks her father, wish *not* to have had the best education money can buy? Would you wish to begin science and technology and mathematics with no teacher, from ground zero? Do we not all usefully build on the foundation made by those before us? See BL, Add. 45790, ff. 111–15.

20. CWFN, 1:228–29.

21. Ibid., p. 221.

22. See *Florence Nightingale in Rome*, p. 20. Julia Smith volunteered to take over her niece's patients at the Spinal Institute while Florence was in Italy.

23. The Ragged School at Field Lane in Saffron Hill, for example, was in the 1840s a "place of filth and disease and every kind of vice, the inhabitants of which were . . . a separate race who found the shortest route to prison or the gallows." Dickens based Fagin's district in *Oliver Twist* on Saffron Hill. See Peter Ackroyd, *Dickens* (New York: Harper, 1992), p. 405.

24. BL, Add. 43402, f. 180.
25. News about the Leigh Smith family must have been leaking through to Flo and Parthe as they approached their thirtieth birthdays. As Barbara, the eldest and most vibrant and social of the Leigh Smiths, moved into her twenties she and her Nightingale cousins had an increasing number of acquaintances and friends in common in London. The Parkeses, for example, were good friends of both the Bonham-Carters and the Leigh Smiths. Elizabeth Gaskell knew both the Nightingales and Barbara Leigh Smith, and savored the gossip about their relationship. Mary Ann Evans, before she became George Eliot, was a good friend to Barbara Leigh Smith, and was introduced to Florence Nightingale as well as to Hilary Bonham-Carter, whom she found stuck-up.
26. O'Malley, p. 119.
27. Edward Cook was the first of Florence Nightingale's biographers to note the extent and variety of her private notes, that is to say, writings where she addressed largely herself. As I keep noting, many of the papers seen by the early biographers seem no longer to be extant, and it is now difficult to ascertain what Nightingale was, in some sense, inviting posterity to read. It is certain that she kept and bequeathed private notes where she is harshly critical of her parents and sister. Some of the most damning of these documents that have been extensively quoted (for example, in Vicinus and Nergaard's 1990 collection of letters) are dated 1851 or 1856 and yet are written on notepaper that bears the South Street address. Since Florence did not move to South Street until November 1865, she presumably copied these from some earlier versions.

CHAPTER 11: FLORENCE NIGHTINGALE IS TEMPTED

1. Wellcome/Claydon, MS. 9038, f. 69.
2. In the mid-nineteenth century in Great Britain, there was an imbalance between the male and female populations, with about 115 women for 100 men.
3. BL, Add. 45794, f. 86.
4. CWFN, 1:302.
5. Cook quotes this marvelous letter *in extenso,* 1:47–49.
6. My discussion of celibacy is based on Elizabeth Abbott, *A History of Celibacy* (New York: Scribner, 1999).
7. BL, Add. 43397, f. 295. Elizabeth Grey, a friend of the Nightingales nicknamed "Pots and Pans" by Florence, was the author of two books on Etruscan art and history. See *Florence Nightingale in Rome,* p. 98n.
8. In her book on celibacy across the centuries, Elizabeth Abbott gives strong evidence that, even though women are assumed in most cultures to be essentially carnal and more libidinous than men, those monastic women who have freely chosen the religious life have generally found it easier to conform to the rules of celibacy than monastic or eremitic males.
9. BL, Add. 43397.
10. A draft has luckily been retained in the collection of Nightingale's letters to Mary Clarke Mohl, BL, Add. 43397, ff. 296–300.
11. See O'Malley, pp. 133–34, particularly for Parthenope Nightingale's absorption in

her sister's preparations. Hilary Bonham-Carter wrote a sweet note to Parthe, commiserating with her on not going to Italy with Flo. See Wellcome/Claydon, MS. 9045, f. 16.

12. Letter to Julius Mohl, November 21, 1869.

13. Wellcome/Claydon, MS. 9038, f. 50.

14. *Florence Nightingale in Rome*, p. 56.

15. Ibid., p. 110.

16. On another occasion, Florence and Selina visited the Ludovisi gallery and were much struck by a little-known head of the goddess Juno. Florence commented to her sister: "All other Goddesses have been to me beautiful women—nothing the least divine, like Jupiter Capitolinus and the Apollo, so I always thought *we* should be *men* in the next stage—as there could not be made an ideal of a woman—but now I have seen a Goddess." Here Florence echoes what Plato says in the *Timaeus*. A man who led a less than meritorious life would next be reborn as a woman, and so on down the stages of being. A virtuous woman would be reborn as a man.

17. Ibid., pp. 117–118. In his play *The Cenci*, Percy Bysshe Shelley portrays the father as an historical version of the Marquis de Sade's male protagonists. English young ladies were not encouraged to read the notorious atheist and libertine Shelley, and yet in her reactions to the Reni portrait, Florence Nightingale shows a clear sense of Shelley's presentation of Beatrice as the ultimate tragic heroine, a victim of incest who stands condemned of patricide, not just by a male court and a male Pope but by a male God who cannot countenance any attack on patriarchal power. *The Cenci* was not performed onstage until some decades after Shelley's death and was known only to a small and select coterie, but I would bet Richard Monckton Milnes had a copy.

18. In 1859 Charles Bracebridge made himself a laughing stock among the English intelligentsia by persisting in the claim that Joseph Liggins of Nuneaton was the author of the anonymously published bestseller *Adam Bede*. See Haight, *George Eliot*, pp. 284–85.

19. O'Malley, p. 125.

20. Cook, 1:34. Ithuriel can be found in Milton's *Paradise Lost*, Book IV.

21. Florence Nightingale to Hilary Bonham-Carter, April 26, 1846, BL, Add. 45794, f. 103.

22. *Florence Nightingale in Rome*, pp. 115–16.

23. Wellcome/Claydon, MS. 9045, f. 19.

24. Wilton is one of the country house jewels of the south-west of England, and I recommend a visit. The Wilton collection includes a number of mementos of Florence Nightingale's visits there.

25. Lady Caroline was one of the three granddaughters of the Irish playwright Sheridan and not only one of the great beauties of her generation but a published author and a renowned wit. Meredith left a fictional portrait of her, and a fanciful account of her relationship with Sidney Herbert, in his novel *Diana of the Crossways*. Sidney Herbert's biographer, Lord Stansgate, meticulously avoids any mention of Lady Caroline, presenting his hero as a veritable Galahad of purity, until his marriage to his cousin, the demure and delightful Miss À Court.

26. Woodham-Smith, p. 322.

27. Elizabeth Herbert converted to Roman Catholicism after her husband's death.

28. *Florence Nightingale in Rome*, p. 142.

29. The account I give here is a shortened form of the lengthy paraphrase that Iva O'Malley fortunately gave of Florence's vanished diary notes. O'Malley, pp. 139–44.

30. CWFN, 1:91.

31. The family of Henrietta Monckton Milnes's mother came from Antigua. Her grandmother was Kitty Da Silva, identified as a "Portuguese Jewess" by Pope-Hennessy who ascribes the "florid streak" in Monckton Milnes to this great-grandmother. Even after the Second World War such casual anti-Semitic prejudice was not uncommon among British writers.

32. Pope-Hennessy, 1:103.

33. Ibid., 1:17.

34. Ibid., 1:14.

35. Ibid., 1:32–33.

36. Ibid., 1:57.

37. Gladstone argued for Byron and Milnes for Shelley, whom the elegant Oxonian debaters claimed never to have heard of. Gladstone of course won.

38. Quoted by Pope-Hennessy, 1:3, from *The Education of Henry Adams*.

39. In 1856, Lord Palmerston offered Robert Pemberton Milnes a baronetcy, but he refused it, saying he could not in conscience support a liberal government. His son Richard was apoplectic.

40. Pope-Hennessy, 1:305.

41. CWFN, 1:91.

42. Ibid.

43. Cook, 1:100. This famous and important document appears to be lost.

44. Woodham-Smith, p. 77. I retain the exact punctuation of this published text since it is not clear if the elision marks are transcribed from the original document or show pieces of text Woodham-Smith herself omitted.

45. Ibid., p. 87.

46. In 1890 Sir Thomas Wemyss Reid wrote a suitably expurgated two-volume official biography of Baron Houghton, but the Sadeian side to Richard Monckton Milnes began to emerge in the entry devoted to him in *The Dictionary of National Biography*. This concludes with delicate ambiguity: "In society, where he found his chief occupation and success . . . he was always amusing. But he was eminently the dilettante . . . He had many fine tastes and some coarse ones."

47. Pope-Hennessy, 2:132, summarizing Praz and Lafourcade.

48. Ibid., 1:128.

49. Ibid., 1:165.

50. The Goncourt brothers met Hankey in 1862 and, with their habitual stylistic restraint, described him in their diary as "a madman, a monster, one of those men who hover on the edge of the abyss." Through him they claimed to glimpse the "dread aspect of a bored aristocracy of wealth . . . libertines who find their pleasure only in the suffering of women."

51. Pope-Hennessy, 2:133.

CHAPTER 12: DE PROFUNDIS CLAMAVI DOMINE

1. In this account of Florence Nightingale's travels in Egypt, I have used a hybrid set of conventional European place names that corresponds neither to accepted Victorian spelling nor to the current transliterations of Arabic words. Thus I retain Cairo and Alexandria, even though these names no longer appear on a good modern atlas map, and I am aware that Nubia no longer exists as a cartographic entity. I have also chosen recent American spellings for well-known sites such as Abu Simbel, which Nightingale calls Ipsamboul. A large selection of Nightingale's Egyptian letters, based on the 1854 text, was reissued in a beautifully illustrated edition by the British travel historian Anthony Sattin: *Letters from Egypt: A Journey on the Nile, 1849–1850* (London: Barrie & Jenkins, 1987). In my view, no other single work offers a better introduction to Florence Nightingale and the depth and diversity of her worldview. Fortunately, this book is still in print, as is the other key book, Michael D. Calabria's *Florence Nightingale in Egypt and Greece: Her Diary and "Visions"* (Albany: State University of New York Press, 1997).

2. See the letter from Monckton Milnes to WEN, Wellcome/Claydon, MS. 9038, f. 61.

3. Calabria, p. 50.

4. When Florence returned from Greece, Mariette continued to be her maid, and it is not clear why Trout, not Mariette, was chosen, or obliged, to accompany her mistress abroad this time.

5. Calabria is excellent on the importance of *Shirley* to Nightingale.

6. Cook, 1:94.

7. *Letters from Egypt*, p. 47. The pennant is now exhibited at the Florence Nightingale Museum.

8. Ibid., p. 178.

9. Ibid., p. 181.

10. Ibid., p. 26.

11. Circassia was an area of Russia on the Black Sea.

12. *Letters from Egypt*, p. 208.

13. Calabria, p. 58.

14. It is unclear which account of her life Nightingale is referring to here, but I would suggest that it could be the "Cassandra" fragment, and that she is remorseful for things like the dialogue she imagined for the death scene of her unnamed alter ego. On the last page of "Cassandra," the female friends attending the dying woman say to her: "But . . . so much talent! So many gifts! Such good which you might have done!" She replies: "The world will be put back some little time by my death . . . you see I estimate my powers at least as highly as you can." Mary Poovey, ed. *Florence Nightingale: "Cassandra" and Other Selections from "Suggestions for Thought"* (New York: New York University Press, 1993).

15. BL, Add. 45790, ff. 1–91.

16. Calabria, p. 66. The letter Nightingale wrote about this visit to the cave of the Eumenides gives a wholly different impression. She describes riding out on horseback with Sigma on a beautiful evening, and records a meditation she had at the famous site, hallowed by the Oresteian trilogy, which was perhaps her most beloved work of literature after the Bible. Both the diary and the letters reflect sides of Nightingale's complex mind.

17. See Chapter 5.

18. Both Cook and O'Malley agree that sections of the first draft of *Suggestions for Thought* were begun in Egypt. The name "Cassandra" is immediately evocative of the *Oresteia*. The allusion to the "Thebaïd" would have come naturally to Nightingale since she had just been walking in the Theban desert and had been studying the lives and works of the early Egyptian fathers of the Church.

19. This fragment was first published in 1928 by Ray Strachey in *The Cause,* and since then "Cassandra" has been part of the feminist canon. Certain passages are famous, such as this image of force-feeding: "What is it to be read aloud to? . . . It is like lying on one's back, with one's hands tied and having liquid poured down one's throat." (*"Cassandra" and "Suggestions for Thought,"* p. 213). Or this, where FN compares herself to an old toy: "My people were like children playing on the shore of the eighteenth century. I was their hobbyhorse, their plaything, and they drove me to and fro, dear souls! never weary of the play themselves, till I, who had grown to women's estate, lay down exhausted, my mind closed to hope, my heart to strength." Ibid., p. 232.

20. Ibid., p. 206.

21. Blaise Pascal's famous "Thought" ("le silence éternel de ces espaces infinis m'effraie") is apt here. Nightingale was greatly influenced by Pascal and Port-Royal.

22. Calabria, Dossey, and McDonald have stressed Nightingale's mysticism. They concentrate on her visions and her voices, accept that the "dreams" were imagined philanthropic adventures, and in my view fail to confront the problem of why Nightingale herself for so many years regarded "dreaming" as a sin. The best authorities I have been able to bring to bear on her dreams are William James in *The Varieties of Religious Experience* and the post-Freudian revisionist accounts of the life and writings of Daniel Paul Schreber.

23. BL, Add. 45846. The same sequence occurred in Germany. "June 29, Four long days of slavery . . . I cannot write a letter & do nothing. [July 1] I lay in bed at night & called upon God to save me. My Lord spoke to me & I was comforted."

24. After she died, Athena was stuffed, and today she forms part of the collection at Lea Hurst.

25. This is not strictly true. She wrote one memorable description of the islands near Patras to Parthe on April 20. BL, Add. 45791, ff. 270–72.

26. Calabria, pp. 67–68.

27. Ibid., p. 69.

28. CWFN I: p. 91.

CHAPTER 13: BREAKING FREE

1. *Letters from Egypt,* p. 205.

2. BL, Add. 43402, f. 180. The second part of the sentence I have quoted has been crossed out on the note and the word "fainted" is substituted.

3. Wellcome/Claydon, MS. 9038, f. 67. Apparently Nightingale's Kaiserswerth pamphlet is an extremely rare bibliographic item.

4. "Seest thou thy father and mother. They have lived together more than all thy life and they understand each other not a bit more than they did the first time they came together. The planes of their orbits never cross." A private note written by Nightingale, quoted by Woodham-Smith, p. 96.

5. Ibid., p. 97.

6. "*Cassandra*" and "*Suggestions for Thought,*" p. 138.

7. Woodham-Smith painted the most vivid picture of the disagreements of Fanny and Florence Nightingale in the early 1850s but the less sensational view taken by Cook and O'Malley seems to me more correct.

8. Letter of Mai Smith to Fanny Nightingale, probably written in 1852. Wellcome/Claydon, MS. 9045, f. 20.

9. Undated document CWFN, I: 94-97. Florence Nightingale also did "characters" around this same time of Marianne Nicholson and Selina Bracebridge.

10. CWFN, 1:96.

11. Expressions used by WEN in a letter to Parthenope, quoted by Woodham-Smith, p. 84.

12. CWFN, 1:94.

13. Woodham-Smith (p. 84) notes that Parthenope Nightingale had taken to calling herself "Miss Pop," and sending friends "wee" presents of water lilies and colored leaves.

14. "[Parthe] has never had a difficulty, except with me," wrote Florence in a private note. "She is a child playing in God's garden & delighting in the happiness of all His works, knowing nothing of life but the English drawing room, nothing of struggle in her own unselfish nature—nothing of want of power in her own Element. And I, what a murderer I am to disturb this happiness . . . What am I that I am not in harmony with all this, that their life is not good enough for me? Oh God, what am I?" "*Ever Yours, Florence Nightingale*, p. 47.

15. CWFN, 1:97.

16. Ibid., 1:70.

17. Only with the publication of later volumes of the *Complete Works of Florence Nightingale,* notably volume 5, *Society and Politics* and volume 8, *Suggestions for Thought,* will it be possible to chart in any detail what people, events, and books were influencing Nightingale in the late 1840s and early 1850s. Given the extraordinary narrowing of her life that occurred after 1858, this is in my view a critically important and largely neglected period in her life. The influence on her of socialists like Fourier and Owen and Christian socialists like Maurice and Kingsley especially needs to be explored in depth.

18. Florence Nightingale was acquainted with Mrs. Caroline Chisholm, who ran a society dedicated to funding and organizing the emigration of "fallen women" who wished to make a new life for themselves abroad. On one of her visits to the London slums, Nightingale came upon a destitute Irish woman whose fourteen-year-old daughter was on the brink of a life of prostitution. Nightingale did everything she could to dissuade the girl, and at last made a personal appeal to Henry Manning to find a place for the girl in one of the Catholic institutions. So Nightingale did see something of the seamy underside of Victorian society and she did not feel that helping prostitutes sullied her own reputation. On the other hand, as she showed on the boat back from Egypt, she would have nothing to do with women of her own class who chose to live immoral lives.

19. Engineer-industrialist Robert Owen (1771–1858) in his early years demonstrated that industries could be run humanely and profitably. Later his essays and books and even his failed experiments in communal living were very influential. Owen was

revered by WEN and his sister, Mai Smith, and Owen's work, especially *A New View of Society, or Essays on the Principle of Formation of the Human Character* (1813), was the subject of hot debate among friends like Harriet Martineau, Richard Monckton Milnes, Elizabeth Gaskell, Charles Kingsley, and Lord Shaftesbury. Owen rejected all known religions and insisted that men became evil by the force of circumstance. Children who were reared with adequate means in a loving, humane way would lead moral lives. Robert Owen was one of the fathers of British socialism and unionism, and his son Robert Dale Owen was instrumental in bringing a married women's property bill, a free school system, and liberal divorce laws to the state of Indiana.

20. "The first (and only) statistical analysis of England's faithful which was published in 1854, disclosed that on 30 March, 1851 5,292,5551 people attended the Church of England; 383,630 worshipped at a Roman Catholic church; and 4,536,264 people in the main Protestant dissenting churches. Since the total population of England and Wales, according to the 1851 Census, was 17,927,609, the compiler of the religious census, Horace Mann, concluded that over five and a quarter million people who ought to have attended some place of worship on the Sabbath, did not. The majority of the non-attendants, he asserted, were poor or working class." Poovey, in "*Cassandra,*" p. xiii. Florence Nightingale made a detailed analysis of the 1851 census in her personal journal, noting, among other things, that 312,00 women worked in cotton mills, 124,000 in woolen mills, 41,000 in flax, 44,000 in silk. One in five inhabitants of London was a felon. Of the London population of 2,450,000, only 750,000 attended Sunday worship, and of these only 100,000 took communion; 1,700,000 Londoners never attended any form of worship. See BL, Add. 43402, ff. 96–97.

21. In 1858, Gerard Smith, another son of Octavius and Jane Smith, somehow wandered onto a railway line and was run over by a train. See CWFN, 1:526.

22. BL, Add. 45790, f. 124.

23. CWFN, 1:495.

24. Several of the charming letters Florence wrote to her cousin Shore during his teenage years are included in volume 1 of CWFN.

25. Wellcome/Claydon, MS. 9038, f. 34, undated, probably 1845, since Shore Smith was born in 1831.

26. Florence Nightingale to Shore: "I would read law if thou wert to put on a chancery wig." BL, Add. 45794, f. 135.

27. Sir Francis Palgrave is perhaps best known as the editor of that once canonic poetry collection *The Golden Treasury,* which included a few poems by his friend Clough.

28. Woodham-Smith, p. 97.

29. Clough was offered the position of examiner at the Education Ministry with an annual income of three hundred pounds and twenty-five pounds more each year, up to six hundred (letter from Florence Nightingale to Fanny Nightingale, Wellcome/Claydon, MS. 8993, f. 53). His close friend and fellow poet Mathew Arnold made a living in this kind of job for many years.

30. Wellcome/Claydon, MS. 8993, f. 46.

31. From Gilbert and Sullivan's operetta *Patience.*

32. CWFN, 1:92.

33. Woodham-Smith, p. 89.

34. CWFN, 1:127.

35. Ibid., 1:304.

36. In 1897 Nightingale wrote: "The nursing there was nil, the hygiene horrible. The hospital was certainly the worst part of Kaiserswerth. But never have I met with a higher tone, a purer devotion than there. There was no neglect." Woodham-Smith, p. 91.

37. CWFN, 1:129–30.

38. BL, Add. 43402, f. 66.

39. *Suggestions for Thought* was first issued in three volumes by Eyre and Spottiswoode as a private printing in 1860. Much of it was first written between 1850 and 1852, but Nightingale enlarged and revised the manuscript after her return from the Crimea. FN sent copies of the printed work to six readers, who included her own father, her uncle Samuel Smith, her old flame Richard Monckton Milnes, and her friends and colleagues Sir John McNeill, the Oxford classicist Benjamin Jowett, and the philosopher John Stuart Mill.

40. *"Cassandra" and "Suggestions for Thought,"* p. 130 to the end. In certain respects, *Suggestions for Thought* was a work of revenge and self-vindication designed to hurt those who loved her. I do not find it surprising that the work was never published in Nightingale's lifetime. What is surprising is that Mai, Hilary, and Selina all read sections of it and were enthusiastic. Nightingale was apparently speaking for them, too. See Cook, I: 120–21.

41. Shane Leslie, "Forgotten Passages in the Life of Florence Nightingale," *Dublin Review,* October 1917, p. 185. Nightingale wrote in similar terms to the Anglican cleric Arthur Manning: "The Church of England has for men bishoprics, archbishoprics, and a little work . . . For women, she has what? I had no taste for theological discoveries. I would have given her my head, my hand, my heart. She would not have them. She did not know what to do with them. She told me to go back and do crochet in my mother's drawing-room; or, if I were tired of that, to marry and look well at the head of my husband's table. You may go to the Sunday School if you like it, she said. But she gave me no training even for that." Quoted by Woodham-Smith, p. 98.

42. This is famously the regime imposed, later in the century, upon the heroine of that feminist classic *The Yellow Wallpaper* and in real life upon its author, Charlotte Perkins Gilmore.

43. The best single history of hysteria is still Ilza Veith's classic *Hysteria: The History of a Disease* (Chicago: University of Chicago Press, 1965). Also useful are Nina Auerbach, *Woman and the Demon: The Life of a Victorian Myth* (Cambridge: Harvard University Press, 1982); Charles Bernheimer and Claire Kahane, eds., *In Dora's Case: Freud-Hysteria-Feminism* (New York: Columbia University Press, 1985); and Elaine Showalter, *The Female Malady: Women, Madness, and English Culture 1830–1980* (New York: Pantheon, 1986).

44. Wellcome/Claydon, MS. 8993, f. 112. All the letters Florence wrote home while she was escorting her sister back to Lea Hurst are given in CWFN, 1:130–36.

45. Woodham-Smith, pp. 103–4.

46. O'Malley, pp. 199–200.

CHAPTER 14: MANAGING HARLEY STREET

1. CWFN, 1:136–37.

2. Ibid., 1:313–14.

3. The life of Octavia Hill, a contemporary of Nightingale's and a well-known philan-thropist, illustrates this point very well. Hill came from a family of Unitarian tradi-tion dedicated to public service, but she and her many sisters were very poor. Octavia was only able to begin running training workshops for poor women and reforming the housing stock in London when she received the financial backing of John Ruskin.

4. Woodham-Smith, p. 106.

5. Cook, 1:128. The British Library collection has a large amount of documentation from this period in Nightingale's life.

6. CWFN, 1:415–16.

7. Wellcome/Claydon, MS. 9031, f. 107. Nightingale makes no reference here to her mother's relationship with Mrs. Shore. This seems to me indirect confirmation that the two did not get on though everyone maintained a polite fiction that they did. Parthe, who could have got to know her grandmother Shore had she wished, pre-sumably sided with her mother.

8. O'Malley, p. 201.

9. Woodham-Smith, p. 112.

10. Wellcome/Claydon, MS. 9039, f. 9. Florence gave an account of the Marianne Galton incident in a letter to Hilary Bonham-Carter written just after her grandmother's death. See CWFN, 1:446.

11. These notes are in the British Library collection.

12. My consultant on infectious diseases assures me that it is in fact impossible to con-tract true measles twice in an eighteen-month period.

13. Florence Nightingale's amusing letter to Mary Clarke Mohl narrating this event is quoted in full in Cook, 1:131–32.

14. Nightingale's year as superintendent at 1 Upper Harley Street is very well docu-mented. There is an extensive correspondence, mainly with her father and with Madame Mohl, now in the British Library collection. Around 1969, Sir Harry Verney published Florence's own handwritten reports to the committee, which he had re-cently discovered among his mother's papers. This delightful and informative little book is *Florence Nightingale at Harley Street: Her Reports to the Governors of her Nurs-ing Home 1853–1854* (London: Dent, 1970).

15. Woodham-Smith, p. 118.

16. Cook, 1:134–35.

17. Woodham-Smith, p. 123. Patients apparently wrote Nightingale adoring letters, and a woman she had met in Germany turned up in London, begging to work by her side.

18. Sir Harry Verney, pp. 15–16.

19. Woodham-Smith, pp. 135–36.

20. Elizabeth Gaskell informed Catherine Winkworth in the beginning of October that Florence Nightingale "is thinking (don't name it because she has not named it to the committee of her present institution) of becoming the Matron of one of the great London Hospitals." John A. Chapple and Arthur Pollard, eds., *The Letters of Mrs. Gaskell* (Manchester: Manchester University Press, 1966), p. 305.

21. BL, Add. 45790, ff. 158–59.
22. Mary Seacole gives a detailed account of the many cholera outbreaks she had witnessed in several countries. Seacole, who calls herself a "doctoress," was credited with saving lives where formally trained doctors either failed or refused to intervene. Seacole actually performed a secret autopsy of a small child victim to try to find out what she could about the disease's effects. However, the treatments she enumerates (mustard plasters, emetics, calomel, mercury painted onto the most prominent blood vessels, frequent doses of sugar of lead) are unpersuasive. See *The Wonderful Adventures of Mrs. Seacole in Many Lands* (Oxford: Oxford University Press, 1966).
23. *The Letters of Mrs. Gaskell*, p. 305.
24. Ibid., pp. 318–19.
25. BL, Add. 45790, ff. 149, 160.
26. Ibid., ff. 158–59.
27. *Letters of Mrs. Gaskell*, p. 306.
28. Ibid., p. 307. All the early biographies of Nightingale attribute the famous remark about her as the ugly duckling to Mrs. Fanny Nightingale, but Chapple and Pollard insist in their edition "Miss [sic] Nightingale," and according to their appendix, they consulted the manuscript of this letter.
29. Ibid., p. 319.
30. By the dates given in Chapple and Pollard's edition, Athena died on the evening of October 19. Mrs. Gaskell's letter to Parthe reporting this fact was written the next day. Florence left for Turkey on October 21.
31. *Letters of Mrs. Gaskell*, pp. 321–22.

CHAPTER 15: BRITAIN GOES TO WAR

1. In this and subsequent chapters, my account of the Crimean War—or more precisely the British engagement in the Crimean War, since French, Russian, and Turkish historians have very different stories to tell—is based on the following works of general history: Trevor Royle, *Crimea: The Great Crimean War, 1854–1856* (New York: St. Martin's Press, 2000); Andrew Lambert and Stephen Badsey, eds., *The Crimean War: The War Correspondents* (Dover, New Hampshire: Alan Sutton Publishing, 1994); Cecil Woodham-Smith, *The Reason Why: The Story of the Fatal Charge of the Light Brigade* (London: Penguin Books, 1958); Mark Adkin, *The Charge: The Real Reason Why the Light Brigade Was Lost* (London: Pimlico, 1996); Alexander Kinglake, *The Invasion of the Crimea: Its Origin and an Account of Its Progress Down to the Death of Lord Raglan* (New York: Harper & Sons, 1881); Christopher Hibbert, *The Destruction of Lord Raglan: A Tragedy of the Crimean War* (Harmondsworth, Middlesex: Penguin Books, 1963); Kingsley Martin, *The Triumph of Lord Palmerston* (London: Hutchinson, 1963); John Shepherd, *The Crimean Doctors: A History of the British Medical Services in the Crimean War*, 2 vols. (Liverpool: Liverpool University Press, 1991). Of the many firsthand accounts of the war, I have relied chiefly upon Mary Seacole, *The Wonderful Adventures of Mary Seacole in Many Lands* (Oxford: Oxford University Press, 1999); Frances Isabella Duberly, *Journal Kept During the Russian War: From the Departure of the Army from England in April 1854, to the Fall of Sebastopol* (London: Longman, 1856) [available through Elibron Classics, www.elibron.com]; Anthony

Sterling, *The Highland Brigade in the Crimea: Founded on Letters Written During the Years 1854, 1855, and 1856* (London: Remington, 1895; Minneapolis: Absinthe Press, 1995); Alexis Soyer, *A Culinary Campaign,* (London: Routledge, 1857; Lewes, East Sussex: Southover Press, 1995); Elizabeth Davis, *The Autobiography of Elizabeth Davis: A Balaclava Nurse,* ed. Jane Williams, 2 vols. (London: Hurst and Blackett, 1857); Margaret Goodman, *Experiences of an English Sister of Mercy* (London: Smith & Elder, 1862); Sidney Godolphin Osborne, *Scutari and Its Hospitals* (London: Dickinson, 1855); Sarah Anne Terrot, *Nurse Sarah Anne,* ed. Robert Richardson (London: John Murray, 1977); Alexander Tulloch, *The Crimean Commission and the Chelsea Board* (London: Harrison, 1857); Alicia Blackwood, *A Narrative of Personal Experiences and Impressions during a Residence on the Bosphorus Throughout the Crimean War* (London: Hatchard, 1881); Frances M. Taylor, *Eastern Hospitals and English Nurses: The Narrative of Twelve Months' Experience in the Hospitals of Koulali and Scutari (by a Lady Volunteer)* (London: Hurst & Blackett, 1856). Last but not least, let me cite and give full homage to *Florence Nightingale: Letters from the Crimea, 1854–1856,* ed. Sue M. Goldie (Manchester: Manchester University Press, 1997). For anyone seeking to understand Florence Nightingale's work in the Crimea, this is the indispensable work. It is also the crowning achievement of Sue M. Goldie, a great scholar and historian who has devoted decades of her life to Nightingale studies.

2. Lambert and Badsey (pp. 5–6), summarizing the current historical consensus, point out that the four points that the Tsar refused to accept in early 1854 were exactly the same points he accepted in the spring of 1856. They argue that the so-called Crimean War was important because the British navy racked up overwhelming victories in the Baltic as well as the Black Sea and the Sea of Azov. These victories could have been won without sending a single redcoat soldier to the Crimean Peninsula.

3. This was short for Sublime Porte. In official British diplomatic communication the Porte was referred to as "she" and "her," which encapsulates the common English perception that the Turks were corrupt and effeminate.

4. Lord Stratford de Redcliffe, the Great Elchi in Constantinople, traveled with twenty-five servants and seventy tons of plate, i.e., silver and gold tableware. *The Reason Why,* p. 160.

5. Tsar Nicholas I refused to accord the title of Napoleon III to the new French autocrat.

6. Kingsley Martin's fascinating book, written soon after the calamity of the First World War, tries to establish just how public opinion is formed, and how a whole nation can be persuaded to embark on adventures that will prove tragically misguided.

7. Martin, p. 83.

8. Ibid., p. 84.

9. Opposition to the declaration of war came mainly from the small but vocal Manchester School, led in the Commons by Cobden and Bright. Some members of this group were Quakers. See Martin, pp. 59–60, and Royle, pp. 117–18.

10. Martin, p. 72.

11. Quoted in Hibbert, p. 48.

12. The journal of the Crimean campaign kept by Frances Isabella Duberly, first issued in 1856 and still available, is a fascinating document. Duberly was probably in love with her husband, but it seems clear that she accompanied him to war in part be-

cause she intended to write a book. Duberly was highly educated (she quotes Greek, Latin, Italian, and German authors in the original), a lover of nature and landscape, and deeply musical. Duberly took for granted her right to be with the army—at her own risk—and accepted every kind of service with thanks but also a sense of entitlement. However, she clearly raised army morale, and she wrote a wonderful book. One can forgive many things in a woman who personally sews a huge waterproof canvas coat to withstand the winter—for her horse. Duberly's eye was sharp and her mind clear. Her closeness to the top commanders makes her reluctant condemnation of the allied military strategy all the more forceful. Like Florence Nightingale, Duberly considers Lord Raglan a charming and lovable man but a very poor general. After the fall of Sebastopol—which was almost entirely a French victory, achieved at enormous cost—she traveled back to the sea along the "good even road" the English had finally got around to constructing, and mused on the failings of her nation: "After all, Englishmen are not so helpless, so hopeless, and so foolish, as they tried hard last year to make themselves out to be. I think they rested so entirely on the prestige that attached itself to the name of a British soldier, that they thought the very stars would come out of their courses to sustain the luster of their name. Alas! Their name was very literally dragged through the mud during the miry winter months" (p. 305).

13. Quoted in Woodham-Smith, p. 157.

14. See Hugh Small, *Florence Nightingale: Avenging Angel* (London: Constable, 1999), p. 109.

15. *The Reason Why,* p. 62.

16. Russell on March 31, quoting from an 1829 report. All references to the *Times* coverage are from *The Crimean War: The War Correspondents.*

17. For information on cholera I am indebted to my son Dr. Christopher Gill, a consultant in infectious disease and assistant professor of public health at Boston University School of Public Health. My husband, D. Michael Gill (1940–1990), was the first to establish the basic biochemistry of cholera toxin.

18. Hibbert, p. 54, quoting Frederick Robinson's *Diary of the Crimean War.*

19. In her novel *Master Georgie* (New York: Carroll & Gray, 1998), Beryl Bainbridge gives a terse, dramatic account of life at Varna, which documentation from the period thoroughly supports.

20. Adkin, p. 53.

21. Estimates varied from 45,000 to 140,000. Hibbert, p. 57.

22. By the summer of 1855, the telegraph cable had been laid as far as the Crimean Peninsula.

23. Seacole, p. 162.

24. Adkin, p. 62.

25. Menchikov had been castrated in 1829 by a Turkish cannonball. His pathological hatred of the Turks did not improve his military judgment.

26. Hibbert gives two good maps of the complicated geography of the Chersonese Peninsula, on which the city of Sevastopol stood, and it was from his book that I finally understood that the city not only stood on a major waterway—the Sevastopol Roadstead—but was divided north and south by the Man-of-War Harbor, into which the River Tchernaya debouched. However, no one has given a more detailed and

informed visual representation of the area about Sevastopol than Mark Adkin, to whom all future historians should be grateful.

27. Duberly, pp. 144–45.

28. *The Crimean War: The War Correspondents,* pp. 120–21.

29. Ibid., pp. 88–89. Duberly (p. 163) notes that on January 27, 1855, 250 sick men were sent off to Scutari; 130 on the 28th; 295 on the 29th. If these numbers, which did not include men who had died in the Crimea, continued for a year, an army equivalent in numbers to the one that had set out for Turkey from Great Britain would have been on the sick list.

30. *Letters from the Crimea,* pp. 17–18. "A work-house sick-ward" provided, by general consent, the worst possible medical care in England.

31. Ibid., p. 18. In their selection of newspaper articles written during the Crimean war, Lambert and Badsey choose not to reprint the section of Russsell's October 9 report after Balaclava, cited by Goldie, which remarks adversely on the army's provision for handling the wounded. Instead they include the first report filed by Chenery from Constantinople where he echoed the rosy and self-congratulatory official briefing he received about conditions in the wards. Once Chenery saw the hospitals with his own eyes, his reports changed dramatically, as my quotations have shown. Having excised the most damaging reports on the medical scene both at Scutari and in the Crimea, Lambert and Badsey proceed to dismiss Nightingale's work as unimportant or even futile. They conclude: "How much impact Florence Nightingale and her nurses had [on the mortality figures] is doubtful. Historians have been rather less kind to her than she was to herself, seeing her as a self-publicist with little understanding of the harshness and cruelty of warfare, who through her connections with London society, took the credit for improvements in transport, supplies, and the care of the sick which had already been put in hand" (p. 86).

32. See, for example, the letter she wrote to her sister on June 6, 1856. "Now don't give in to the weak wishy-washy sentiment which is here talked about poor Sevastopol, poor Russia. What was Sevastopol there for? For aggression—for aggressive fanaticism. Not for the purposes of defence. I can feel for the poor wretches who have suffered and died. But what did they die for? To make Russia the tyrant of the world." *Letters from the Crimea,* p. 270.

33. Ibid., p. 21.

34. Testimony of Lord Newcastle before the 1855 Roebuck commission of inquiry on the war, cited in *Letters from the Crimea,* p. 22.

35. Ibid., p. 24.

36. Ibid., p. 28.

37. Cook, 1:166.

38. Ibid., 1:155.

39. Mary Seacole, by her own account, did not arrive in London from Jamaica until after Florence Nightingale and her party had left for Turkey. Seacole recounts how she waited for hours for an interview with "Mrs. H.," presumably Elizabeth Herbert who was recruiting nurses to go out to Turkey under the leadership of Mary Stanley. Seacole, who for most of her narrative carefully avoids accusing the British of prejudice against her as a woman of mixed race, writes, when she has been turned away by Mrs. H.: "Did these ladies shrink from accepting my aid because my blood flowed beneath

a somewhat duskier skin than theirs?" Trevor Royle is inaccurate to state that Seacole's "perseverance [in wanting to go out to the Crimea] is all the more remarkable given the fact that Florence Nightingale rejected her offer to serve in the Scutari hospital" (Royle, p. 257).

40. In *The Friendship of Florence Nightingale and Mary Clare Moore* (Philadelphia: University of Pennsylvania Press, 1999), editor Mary C. Sullivan, RSM, has expertly edited the letters exchanged by the two women, given an insightful account of their long and loving relationship, and told the story of the Sisters of Mercy at the Bermondsey Convent up to and including their heroic service in the Crimean War. Sullivan's work is an important corrective to *The Sisters of Mercy in the Crimea* by Evelyn Bolster, RSM (Cork: Mercier Press, 1964), which is based in turn on *Memories of the Crimea* (London: Burns & Oates, 1904) by Sister Mary Aloysius Doyle, who went out to the Crimea in Reverend Mother Frances Bridgeman's party.

41. According to Woodham-Smith, the average nurse in London earned between seven and ten shillings a week, whereas the Scutari nurses were promised free board and lodging, free uniforms, first class travel, and between twelve and fourteen shillings at the beginning, sixteen to eighteen after three months' service, and eighteen to twenty shillings after a year. *Florence Nightingale,* p. 142.

42. O'Malley, p. 222.

43. *Letters from the Crimea,* p. 36.

44. Woodham-Smith, p. 147.

45. Ibid., p. 148.

46. *Letters from the Crimea,* p. 33.

47. Sarah Anne Terrot gives a detailed account of the sufferings of the women aboard the *Vectis.*

48. Ibid.

49. Woodham-Smith, p. 149. Sarah Anne Terrot says that Napier had his first meeting with Florence Nightingale in the Barrack Hospital. Whether on board the *Vectis* or in the tower at the Barrack Hospital, the provision of a sofa for Nightingale to recline upon is interesting.

50. Woodham-Smith, p. 149.

CHAPTER 16: STEEPED UP TO OUR NECKS IN BLOOD

1. Hibbert, p. 43.

2. *Letters from the Crimea,* p. 47. An araba was a rough Turkish cart.

3. One of the things Florence Nightingale held against Lord Stratford was that he was too preoccupied with defending his reputation as a diplomat to secure convenient locations for the sick and wounded troops. All the British hospitals were scattered on the Asian side of the Bosphorus, far away from the markets of Constantinople.

4. Lady Alicia Blackwood came out to Scutari with her clergyman husband to do what they could in the hospitals. He served as chaplain and she as one of Florence Nightingale's most valuable volunteer helpers. Lady Alicia, an accomplished artist, also left an interesting pictorial record of Scutari. Her account of life there during the Crimean War was published in 1881.

5. For most of Nightingale's time at Scutari, the commandant was Lord William Paulet,

a charming and sensitive man of exquisite politeness. Unfortunately, as far as possible Paulet avoided inspections of the hospitals under his command, as he found conditions there too distressing. In this his response mirrored that of Lord Stratford and of Lady Stratford, who went onto the wards at the Barrack Hospital only once when Sister Elizabeth Wheeler dragged her there. Paulet was succeeded in September 1855 by the energetic and responsive General Storks.

6. *Letters from the Crimea,* p. 37.

7. Counting and identifying the estimated 229 women who nursed during the Crimean War is surprisingly difficult, and gets more so as the war progresses. Barbara Dossey, citing the work of Irene Sabelberg Palmer, gives the best account of them, in table form (pp. 174–76).

8. O'Malley, p. 236.

9. On November 5, 1854, Lord Stratford wrote to the British government effusively welcoming the nurses whose arrival in Constantinople was imminent and expressing confidence that the women would make a big difference in the hospitals, "notwithstanding the reluctance of the Faculty to admit nurses of the softer sex." O'Malley, p. 288.

10. *Nurse Sarah Anne,* pp. 84–85.

11. Dr. Cumming, member of the first ("Newcastle") government commission at Scutari, was senior to Menzies, and for some weeks the jockeying for position between the two made decision-making even more fragmented at a time when the strains on the hospitals were increasing by the day. In the end Cumming took over from Menzies and was pretty much as ineffective.

12. One doctor did tell the truth and was duly punished. On July 5, 1855, an anonymous letter from a Crimean medical officer was published in *The Times,* describing exactly the administrative nightmare Florence Nightingale had reported in her private letters, and concluding that "as long as the army medical system continues the preposterous rotten thing it is, so long must you look for results similar or worse than those I have described." The letter was by R. Hall Bakewell, M.R.C.S., L.S.A., and he was rapidly court-martialed and summarily dismissed from the service on the charge that he had attacked the Medical Department, and that the situation at Scutari was in fact excellent. See *Letters from the Crimea,* p. 150. Nightingale was outraged that a junior officer like Bakewell was punished for telling the truth while senior men like Hall and Smith received knighthoods for lying.

13. In a letter of November 14 to Dr. Bowman, Nightingale described with admiration a series of amputation cases at the General Hospital. She ends her account thus: "The next case is a poor fellow where the ball went in at the side of the head, put out one eye, made a hole in his tongue, and came out in the neck. The wound was doing very nicely when he was seized with agonizing pain and died suddenly, without convulsion or paralysis. At the P[ost] M[ortem], an abscess in the anterior part of the head was found as big as my fist—yet the man kept his reasoning facilities till the last. And nature had thrown out a false coat all round it" (*Letters from the Crimea,* p. 38). Observations like this mark Nightingale as a born clinician and surgeon. When copying her sister's letters for circulation to other friends, Parthenope excised these passages.

14. It was quite astonishing for me to learn from the memoirs by Duberley, Seacole, and

Soyer how many gourmet meals with fine wines were eaten by parties of officers even during the first year of the Crimean War.

15. One thing that did rouse the men to protest at the worst of the crisis was to see the orderlies stripping a dead man of his shirt and his blanket before carrying him off to be buried in the communal grave. British officers and men all seem to have preferred to suffer pain than to have their genitals exposed.

16. Florence ends her November 25 letter to Sidney Herbert: "All the above is written in obedience to your PRIVATE instructions. Do not let me appear as a Govt. spy here which would destroy all my usefulness." *Letters from the Crimea*, p. 40.

17. Ibid., p. 37.

18. For Florence Nightingale's feeling of being a mother to the dead and wounded soldiers, see, for example, the letter she wrote on November 23, 1856, to Lady Canning: "Oh my poor men, who died so patiently—I feel I have been a bad mother to you, coming home & leaving you in your Crimean graves—unless truth to your cause can help teach the lesson which your deaths were meant to teach us." *Letters from the Crimea*, p. 287. In her memoirs of Balaclava, Mary Seacole also refers over and over again to the maternal love and solicitude she felt for the British soldiers, and she rejoiced in her nickname of "Mother Seacole." Florence Nightingale used the expression "identifying her fate with the heroic dead" in a letter to her sister on March 8, 1855.

19. *Letters from the Crimea*, p. 37.

20. Ibid., p. 175.

21. Osborne, p. 41.

22. *Nurse Sarah Anne*, pp. 113–15.

23. Ibid., pp. 91–92.

24. *Letters from the Crimea*, p. 65, n. 18.

25. O'Malley, p. 245, citing Nightingale's report to the Roebuck committee in 1855 (p. xxvii) and the correspondence between Dr. Hall and the adjutant general.

26. Duberly, pp. 143–44.

27. Osborne, p. 2; Royle, pp. 250–51.

28. Royle, p. 253.

29. Osborne, p. 3.

30. Ibid., p. 27.

31. "Copy of Manuscript Found at 10 South Street" [January 1860], attributed to Robert Robinson, BL, Add. 45797. In response to laudatory reports by men like Robinson, Nightingale's critics have cited negative remarks made about her and her work by such senior officers as Lieutenant Colonel Sir Anthony Sterling and General Sir John Burgoyne. However, neither of these gentlemen visited the Scutari hospitals when Nightingale was there, and they probably did not meet her when she came to Balaclava. Sterling and Burgoyne were convinced that a woman who was not related to a soldier had no place in an army hospital, and that even wives were usually a nuisance.

32. *Letters From the Crimea*, p. 39. Goldie points out that Florence was not the only person in Turkey telling the British government that the whole system of purveying the army was a disaster and in urgent need of reform. Lord Stratford was saying this loud and clear in his letters to the Foreign Secretary.

33. Florence Nightingale to Sidney Herbert, January 8, 1855: "The extraordinary circumstance of a whole army having been ordered to abandon its kits, as was done when we landed the man before Alma, has been overlooked entirely in all our system." *Letters From the Crimea,* p. 71.

34. Florence never lost her belief in wine as medicine, and it is amusing to find her in later years sending quantities of her best port to sustain her beloved friend Mother Mary Clare Moore and the other sisters who were poorly at the Bermondsey convent.

35. See *Nurse Sarah Anne,* p. 43.

36. Exactly how Nightingale financed her purveying is not entirely clear. Certainly, the money from the *Times* fund was channeled largely through her office, and she also had smaller sums of money from private donors that probably were replenished as the war continued. She also used all her private income. However, the correspondence with Herbert shows that most of the money she used came somehow out of government funds, and that as soon as Panmure replaced Herbert he tried to regularize the purveying system and stop her from drawing on the government's purse.

37. Taylor, *Eastern Hospitals and English Nurses,* vol. 1, p. 68. Note Frances Taylor's careful distinction between ladies, nuns, and nurses. I shall be dealing with these distinctions in the next chapter.

38. One of the recurring themes of Mary Seacole's account of her life at Balaclava is her unavailing attempt to keep thieves at bay. Seacole and her male business partner lost a high proportion of everything they bought on site or imported, either to local predators or to French army scavengers. She writes amusingly of the French Zouaves, who filled the baggy trousers of their famous uniforms with the most astonishing collections of foodstuffs.

39. Nightingale's letters of January 8 and 28 offer the reform blueprints. See *Letters from the Crimea,* pp. 70–81. To those who argue that the changes at Scutari were already in train when Nightingale arrived in Turkey and would have occurred without her intervention, it should be noted that the government's three-man Hospitals Commission of two doctors and one lawyer who arrived in Turkey just after she did made no practical difference. It is true that the members of this commission were not given authority to override the officers in the field, but then neither was Nightingale, and this did not stop her doing something.

40. *Letters from the Crimea,* p. 52. Nightingale had promised Sidney Herbert to send him not only regular official reports but also letters, supposedly intended for his eyes only but which could be passed along to select associates. This system of double communication with the authorities at home was standard among officers from Lord Raglan down.

41. Ibid., p. 52.

42. Cook, 1: 213, quoting Queen Victoria's letter to the Duke of Cambridge.

43. *Letters from the Crimea,* p. 59.

44. Trevor Royle writes that at Scutari Nightingale's "stubbornness—allied to an occasionally shrill and self-righteous belief in her own abilities—came to her aid" (p. 248) and later dismisses her as a "bossy-boots" (p. 255).

45. *Nurse Sarah Anne,* p. 117.

46. Osborne, p. 26.

47. O'Malley, p. 235.
48. Florence Nightingale was not the only person at Scutari who wrote letters on behalf of the men or who conveyed the news of men's deaths to families in Britain. This was one of the primary functions of the chaplains of the various faiths, and the sisters did a good deal of writing too. Nonetheless, the care and effort Nightingale devoted to this task was, according to contemporary observers, unusual and exemplary.
49. O'Malley, p. 248.
50. Ibid., telling a story told to her by a woman who got it from the soldier himself (p. 351).
51. Woodham-Smith, p. 207.

CHAPTER 17: WOMAN TROUBLE

1. Opponents like Sir John Hall in Nightingale's own lifetime and recent critics like F. B. Smith have sought to sap her reputation as a national heroine by pointing out how many Crimean nurses heartily disliked and enthusiastically rebelled against her. Mary Stanley, Elizabeth Davies (or Davis), and Frances Bridgeman of Kinsale especially have been the poster girls for anti-Nightingale sentiment.
2. Cook, 1:246, quoting one of Florence's private notes.
3. Nightingale recognized that, had circumstances permitted, her friend and colleague the Reverend Mother Mary Clare Moore might well have been a more effective leader to the whole group of nurses than herself. Florence wrote to Moore from Balaclava in late April, 1856, when the Reverend Mother was forced by ill health to repatriate: "I do not presume to express praise or gratitude to you, Revd. Mother, because it would look as if I thought you had done the work not unto God but unto me. You were far above me in fitness for the General Superintendency, both in worldly talent of administration, & far more in the spiritual qualifications which God values in a superior. My being placed over you in our unenviable reign in the East was my misfortune & not my fault." Sullivan, p. 72.
4. As Nightingale remarked to Sidney Herbert in January 1855, the events at Scutari "are only a symptom of what is going on in the Krimea [sic]. We are only the *pulse* which marks the state of the army." *Letters from the Crimea*, p. 80.
5. Nightingale wrote to her mother on February 5, 1855: "I have often thought in early life (how little I then expected Scutari) that I should throw my body in the breach, that I should bridge the chasm to reform—that there must be an Originator, a Promulgator, an Executor for each Reformation . . . I remember thinking, So perish those who pioneer the way for Mankind. But they may perish, but I shall endure. I shall not break my heart of disappointment, though even mine own familiar friend turns against me. No, dearest Mother, I shall do nothing, the originator never does, but greater things than these shall others do—the Army shall be reformed, the Army Medical Board, the Military Hospitals—those three sinks of jobbery & official vice—& I have done all I hoped by representing these things." *Letters from the Crimea*, pp. 86–87. The treacherous friend Nightingale refers to is presumably Mary Stanley.
6. Ibid., p. 115.
7. The Reverend Mother Frances Bridgeman of Kinsale lodged a series of charges against the Reverend Mother Mary Clare Moore with Archbishop Culler. These charges in-

clude (1) that Moore's Bermondsey nuns at Scutari had done menial work (2) that they had on occasion gone off to distant parts of the hospitals with orderlies (3) that they had cut off their trains. Claydon, Bundle 110.

8. Sarah Anne Terrot was an angel of mercy to the sick, but in her diary she makes no mention of the nurses working and living by her side as either colleagues or friends.

9. According to Cook, one morning six of Florence Nightingale's best nurses turned up with six sergeants and corporals to announce that they wished to be married. Cook, 1:247.

10. Elizabeth Davis was obviously an exception.

11. Nightingale related this anecdote to Sidney Herbert in her letter of January 28, 1855. *Letters from the Crimea,* p. 80.

12. The other women included in this picture are Mrs. Bracebridge, Mother Mary Clare Moore, and Miss Margaret Tebbutt.

13. Goldie establishes that everyone at Scutari testified that the Bermondsey nuns performed in the most exemplary and selfless way. The admiring letters written to Dr. Hall by Dr. G. S. Beatson in mid-November and by the Reverend Thomas Cooney in early December refer to the Bermondsey nuns who came out with Nightingale, not the Irish nuns who came out with Mary Stanley. The only people who did not like the Bermondsey nuns were, in fact, the "Irish" nuns, their Mother Superior, and their priest, Father Ronan.

14. Hearing that Nightingale's critics were calling her the new Pope for the Roman Catholic nuns at Scutari, Sister Mary Gonzaga of Bermondsey started to refer to her jokingly as "Your Holiness." Nightingale continued the joke by calling Gonzaga "My Cardinal." See O'Malley, p. 288.

15. *Letters from the Crimea,* p. 81.

16. Osborne, p. 26. *Punch,* the popular magazine of humor, similarly defended Nightingale with a piece of doggerel that ended: "Let bigots call thee as they will / What Christ preached, doest thou." O'Malley, p. 288.

17. *Letters from the Crimea,* pp. 51–52.

18. In regard to the Stanley party affair, I have followed the line indicated by Goldie and O'Malley, who both are at their best in discussing this affair. With her customary judiciousness Goldie summarizes: "A great deal of controversy has since surrounded Florence Nightingale's reception, or rather refusal, of [the Stanley] party, and certainly it was a tactical blunder on her part, leading to untold difficulties in both the short and the long term which on occasion threatened to destroy her mission, and which, had she been more conciliating, might have been avoided" (p. 49).

19. O'Malley, p. 273. It is interesting to note that Liz Herbert as well as Florence Nightingale used the pet name Sigma for Selina Bracebridge. Mrs. Herbert did not know that Florence Nightingale had been keeping copies of her letters ever since adolescence.

20. O'Malley, p. 251.

21. Nightingale reported this information about what Mary Stanley had said about her on the boat out to Turkey in a letter to her aunt Mai written in the fall of 1855. She probably heard it from a member of the Stanley party she became friendly with in the Crimea. See *Letters from the Crimea,* p. 170.

22. One of the things that makes the Nightingale-Stanley dispute so fascinating is that during her time in Turkey, Mary Stanley was in regular correspondence not only with Elizabeth Herbert, Florence's friend, but with Parthenope Nightingale, Florence's

sister. Florence, Mary, Parthenope, Elizabeth, and Selina were all part of a close-knit female network characterized by a mixture of intimacy and backbiting, confidence and treachery that will be familiar to most women. They all negotiated it expertly and, on the whole, pleasurably, except Florence.

23. Lady Alicia Blackwood gives an amusing account of Miss Stanley's inability to so much as mention the word "flea" even though in Scutari society it had become customary to greet friends with the salutation "How are your fleas today?" See Blackwood, p. 259.

24. Nightingale variously spells this place as "Koulali," "Koulalee," and "Kullali."

25. See Shepherd, vol. 2, for a discussion of the appointment of John Meyer to head the hospital at Smyrna.

26. O'Malley, p. 268.

27. *Letters from the Crimea*, p. 260.

28. Mary Stanley's term of service in Turkey is given a worshipful write-up by Alexander Kinglake, who was a friend of her brother: "But of the ministering power that a gentle lady can wield, and of the blessings her very step brings when even she ventured no more than to 'nurse'—simply 'nurse'—the poor sufferers, Miss Stanley with the Sister that followed her, became a gracious example. Impelled by a ceaseless desire to assuage human sufferings, and gifted with indomitable energies never taught to do battle for self, Miss Stanley had accepted the destiny which—in language half precept, half prophecy—a loving mother foreshadowed as the one that her 'Mary' must face; and devoted herself heart and soul to a life of beneficent toil." (*The Invasion of the Crimea* vol. 4, p. 281.) The encomium continues for another two pages, though Kinglake shows a glimmer of realism when he notes: "What number of lives were saved—saved even in that pest-stricken hospital of Kullali—by a long gentle watchfulness, when Science almost despaired, no statistics, of course, can show." Clearly Miss Stanley's family was as determined as Miss Nightingale's to promote their "angel," while Miss Stanley herself had no intention of providing statistics that might discredit her. How very different from Florence Nightingale!

29. That Mary Stanley was received into the Church of Rome before she left Constantinople is attested to by all the Roman Catholic authorities. Mother Mary Aloysius refers to it in her *Reminiscences,* and Henry Manning in his April 14 letter to Mary Stanley appears to reply to a question from her as to whether she should make her conversion public or not: "I see no obligation to publish the fact from Constantinople at the moment. The moment for declaration will be when you meet your family" (O'Malley, p. 289). Given the need to get her influential family solidly on her side in her quarrel with Florence Nightingale, and given the overwhelmingly anti-papist sentiment in English society on all levels, Mary Stanley found it politic to conceal her conversion for as long as possible. Certainly Mary's brother bitterly attacked Mr. Sabin for what he had told Lady Stratford about Mary, presumably because he believed that Sabin was wrong. Kinglake makes no mention of Miss Stanley's Catholicism in his eulogy of her as ministering angel.

30. O'Malley, p. 328.

31. Ibid., p. 355. The enigma of Miss Stanley continued to haunt Florence, especially after the Salisbury affair (see Chapter 19). On October 28, 1855, she wrote to her family from Balaclava: "I cannot tell you *how* much to distrust Miss Stanley. I have never

known it till now. She is false to the very backbone. Her treachery began *before* she arrived at Constantinople. I have always defended her, pitied her, allowed for her *till lately.* Now I tell you, distrust her, you will find out some day why, there is not a villain in a French play more false than she. I can hardly believe it with the proof of it in black and white before my eyes." *Letters from the Crimea,* p. 170.

CHAPTER 18: SPRING AT LAST

1. W. H. Russell's report for *The Times* of January 22, 1855; *The War Correspondents,* p. 160.
2. Ibid., p. 161.
3. Ibid.
4. O'Malley, p. 281.
5. From Florence Nightingale's written report submitted to a royal commission appointed to inquire into the regulations affecting the sanitary state of the army, which appeared as Appendix LXXII in the commission's 1858 report, and in the pamphlet "Mortality of the British Army, at Home and Abroad, and during the Russian War, as compared with the Civil Population in England."
6. *Letters from the Crimea,* p. 83.
7. Ibid., p. 93.
8. Florence Nightingale to Sidney Herbert, February 12, 1855. *Letters from the Crimea,* p. 91.
9. Ibid., p. 107.
10. Ibid., p. 96. Nightingale's idea of a medical school never got off the ground, as the medical officers at Scutari had no interest in medical research. When they were first presented with new operating tables, they sawed off the legs for firewood. See *The Crimean Doctors,* 2:417.
11. *Letters from the Crimea,* p. 102.
12. My account of McNeill and Tulloch is based on that of Hugh Small, *Florence Nightingale, Avenging Angel,* and on *The Crimean Doctors,* vol. 1.
13. Shaftesbury headed up the ill-fated Poor Law Commission with Edwin Chadwick, the great apostle of public health in England during the first half of the nineteenth century. A self-righteous and irascible man who professed contempt for the whole medical profession, Chadwick made a host of private enemies. Furthermore, the enormous expense of realizing his plans to clean up cemeteries, slaughterhouses, and infirmaries, tear down the slums, and establish sewer and water systems scared the purse-conscious national and local authorities to death. When the Poor Law Commission was dissolved and Chadwick was disgraced, *The Times* jauntily voiced its satisfaction: "We prefer to take our chance with cholera and the rest, than to be bullied into health." Lord Palmerston defended Chadwick in the Commons and to the cabinet. See the introduction by M. W. Flinn to Chadwick's *Report on the Sanitary Condition of the Labouring Population of Gt. Britain* (Edinburgh: Edinburgh University Press, 1965).
14. The most notorious attempt to whitewash the army's record during the Crimean War, both on the battlefield and in the hospitals, was the Chelsea Board, appointed almost openly to deny the multiple errors of omission and commission cited by McNeill and Tulloch. Their report, unlike Sutherland's, appeared before the end of the war and aroused a furor since it named names.

15. Small, p. 47.
16. Mary Seacole and Fanny Duberley document the high jinks of spring and summer from opposite ends of the social spectrum.
17. BL, Add. 45797, p. 86.
18. Soyer, pp. 86–87
19. *Letters from the Crimea,* pp. 134–135.

Chapter 19: In the Crimea

1. Soyer, pp. 153–54.
2. BL, Add. 45790, f. 169.
3. *Letters from the Crimea,* p. 130.
4. Ibid.
5. If indeed Nightingale's illness was brucellosis (see Chapter 20), she would have contracted it from some milk product, presumably before leaving Constantinople. However, on the boat, which was full of convalescents, whom she continued to look after, as well as in the various Crimean hospitals she inspected, she could have contracted a number of diseases from a number of vectors. Two days before her collapse, she made Alexis Soyer anxious by spending a long time with a man ill of typhus in a small, close, stinking hut. Soyer, usually imperturbable, also offered in his memoir a stirring account of beating the rats off at night from his berth on board the ship in Balaclava harbor, so Nightingale's berth on the *Robert Lowe* was obviously no luxury suite.
6. O'Malley, p. 308.
7. *Letters from the Crimea,* p. 174. Spartan mothers are said to have told their sons to return from war either with their shields (i.e., victorious) or on them (i.e., dead).
8. Ibid., p. 132. In one of her private notes written soon after the war, Nightingale compared Lord Raglan to Ophelia, "devoted, unselfish . . . but floating along & being dragged down, along with his troops" (BL, Add. 43402, f. 170). Comparing the commander in chief of the British army to Shakespeare's victim girl is a wonderful example of how Nightingale casually crossed gender boundaries.
9. Soyer in his memoir avoids any accusations against Hall et al. On October 19, 1855, Nightingale wrote to her aunt Mai: "It is quite true that Drs. Hall & Hadley sent for a List of Vessels going home & chose one, the Jura, which was NOT going to stop at Scutari *because* it was *not* going to stop at Scutari—& put me on board of her for England (when I was ill here before). And that Mr. Bracebridge & Lord Ward took me out, at the risk of my life—to save my going to England though unconscious at the time that it was intended" (*Letters from the Crimea,* p. 166). Presumably someone in the Crimea told Nightingale this news, which may have been true or gossip.
10. *Letters from the Crimea,* p. 131.
11. Florence Nightingale to her sister, July 9; *Letters from the Crimea,* p. 133.
12. Letter from Elizabeth Gaskell to Parthenope Nightingale, July 21, 1855; *Letters of Mrs. Gaskell,* p. 359.
13. BL, Add. 45790, f. 179.
14. *Letters from the Crimea,* p. 165.
15. Claydon, Bundle 110.
16. The best information about Miss Clough comes from Sir Ronald Roxburgh, "Miss

Nightingale and Miss Clough: Letters from the Crimea," *Victorian Studies,* September 1969, pp. 71–89. Roxburgh's ancestor Mary Roxburgh was Miss Clough's best friend in England and to her she sent some thirty letters. Sir Ronald presents Martha Clough as a tragic heroine whose sweet nature and feminine frailty were no match for the steely Miss Nightingale.

17. *Letters from the Crimea,* p. 140.

18. Jane Shaw Stewart was a woman very like Florence Nightingale in her sense of religious mission and in her taste for asceticism. She did extraordinary service in the Crimea, but Nightingale thought her a little mad.

19. O'Malley (pp. 321–28) gives the most complete account of the Salisbury affair, though she refers to Charlotte Salisbury as "Miss X."

20. Florence wrote to her cousin Shore on January 20, 1856: "My Dearest Friend, Our paths have taken us so wide apart in life that I can only say, in answer to what your mother told me, that I have always felt that we were each of us striving to do the work for which God has made us . . . that I have never placed, or wished to place, my selfish gratification in merely seeing you or seeing you help *me,* in comparison with the much higher gratification, to me, of seeing you do the work you liked . . . if we ever meet again, we shall meet again in this most perfect love & confidence. I have never wished for your laying aside your own work to help mine." CWFN, 1:507.

21. In the winter of 1855–56, an outbreak of cholera raged at Scutari, killing Florence's great allies Dr. McGregor and Nurse Drake, among others. Sam Smith was in despair, convinced that his wife, Mai, was going to die.

22. Cook, I: 305–6. Lord Stanley was introduced to Florence Nightingale only after the war, but then he became one of her most important supporters. When Lord Stanley was appointed viceroy of India, Nightingale was able to direct her army health initiatives to the subcontinent.

23. *Letters from the Crimea,* p. 138.

24. Ibid., p. 139.

25. Ibid., p. 144.

26. Ibid., p. 155.

27. This is the version Florence Nightingale wrote to Colonel Lefroy on March 6, 1856. See *Letters from the Crimea,* p. 221.

28. *Letters from the Crimea,* p. 138. Queen Victoria sent newspapers and magazines for the soldiers' reading rooms, but these were purloined by the officers. Florence Nightingale was outraged and made official protests, but these were ignored. Claydon, Bundle 110.

29. Cook, I: 280–81.

30. By December 1855, Lady Cranworth had replaced Lady Canning as the person in London chiefly charged with selecting and sending out women to nurse in Turkey and the Crimea, and Florence informed Lady Cranworth of how various nurses and ladies had turned out. With a calculated barb probably aimed at the Mary Stanley faction in London, she noted to Lady Cranworth of the Koulali nursing staff: "As *Lady-Sisters,* it is supposed, *may do anything!* i.e. marry gentlemen who stay in their houses, & themselves stay in the houses of unmarried gentlemen, I thought it prudent to let a few of the Koulali Ladies go home, whom I felt I could not reduce to my merciless working rules. They will soon reappear here as the wives of their respective husbands.

Please do not betray me in this piece of diplomacy—meant only for yourself." *Letters from the Crimea*, p. 181.

31. In July a ship containing a party of three wounded officers and ninety-eight wounded men, most of them severe amputees, destined for England, had been forced to stop at Scutari when its crew deserted. Three men had been brought over to the base hospitals and were given immediate medical assistance, but two had rapidly died. Nightingale, who had watched Mrs. Richards, her best nurse, vainly attempt to clean one of the men's wounds, had been horrified by the condition of these patients, who just days before had been in the care of the hospital at Balaclava.

32. In her October 18 letter to General Richard Airey, Nightingale makes detailed recommendations about establishing water closets and baths at the Castle Hospital, using either filtered rainwater collected in rum puncheons or water obtained by drilling. This letter is just a list of practical suggestions to keep the men warm and amused during the coming winter. See *Letters from the Crimea*, p. 164.

33. This account of Nightingale's journey to Balaclava in 1855 is based on Robert Robinson's 1860 narrative, BL, Add. 45797, ff. 82–101.

34. *Letters from the Crimea*, p. 165.

35. Ibid., pp. 178–79.

36. Woodham-Smith, p. 236; O'Malley, p. 339.

37. Cook, I: 270–71.

38. O'Malley, p. 340.

39. Peter was a Russian boy abandoned by his parents, taken as a servant by an English officer, and grossly abused. Ordered to carry a large can of hot water, he let it slip off his head and was horribly scalded. Nightingale took him into her household and protected him from his former master of whom he was terrified. Claydon, Bundle 110. When Nightingale returned to Britain, Peter went too.

40. O'Malley, p. 345.

41. Cook, I: 295–96.

42. O'Malley, p. 346.

43. Ibid., p. 350. To her sister after the war, Nightingale called Lady Stratford "that foolish, flirting wife." Claydon, Bundle 110.

44. *Letters from the Crimea*, p. 208.

45. Goldie gives a superb account of Nightingale's bureaucratic battle over a secret report highly critical of her nurses that Fitzgerald submitted to the War Office. She publishes the key documents from all the parties concerned.

46. Tulloch was so outraged by the decision of the Chelsea Board that he published a book at his own expense giving the key statistical information on mortality and morbidity during the Crimean War that Panmure had suppressed. Subsequently, in no small part thanks to Florence Nightingale, Tulloch was given a knighthood.

47. From the letter to Colonel Lefroy. *Letters from the Crimea*, pp. 222–23.

48. On March 16, as she was about to depart for Balaclava, Nightingale assured Colonel Lefroy that she would not "molest the 'Brickbats' [i.e., Bridgeman's party of nuns]. Above all, I am afraid of their resigning & making martyrs of themselves, which is their grand object. I shall interfere in no way whatever." *Letters from the Crimea*, p. 231.

49. In *Florence Nightingale: Letters from the Crimea*, Sue M. Goldie argues persuasively

that in her dealings with Hall, Florence was needlessly haughty and in fact tried improperly in certain small instances to encroach on the medical officers' prerogatives. My feeling is that Florence, tired and overwrought, had not yet learned to play the bureaucratic game as well as Sir John, but that while she was willing to call a truce, Hall, Fitzgerald, and Bridgeman were not.

50. *Letters from the Crimea,* p. 253. Goldie gives a typically thoughtful and well-documented presentation of this whole affair.

51. For Bridgeman's account, see *Letters from the Crimea,* p. 254. Sergeant McDonald's most urgent wish was to be buried in a proper grave, with the proper service, and he left money to pay for the coffin and the minister. When McDonald died, however, Fitzgerald went to the extraordinary lengths of spiriting his body out of the morgue and dumping it in the communal grave. When Nightingale found this out from the man's distraught brother, she had the body dug up and properly buried. When McDonald's brother was arrested for impertinence, the commander in chief and the chaplains were furious and secured his release. Claydon, Bundle 110.

52. This is just a small part of the long letter Florence Nightingale wrote to Sidney Herbert from the Crimea on April 3, 1856.

53. Nightingale in her letter to Herbert acknowledges that whereas Sir John McNeill in his reports writes calmly as an historian, she writes as "the officer in the heat of battle providing for his men's safety." *Letters from the Crimea,* p. 249.

54. Ibid., pp. 260–61.

55. O'Malley, p. 386. What happened to the little terrier given to Nightingale by Sidney Herbert is not clear.

56. Claydon, Bundle 110.

57. Cook, 1:303.

CHAPTER 20: LIVING TO FIGHT THEIR CAUSE

1. Cook, 1:328.

2. Ibid., 1:309.

3. My analysis here rests on Walter Bagehot's famous assertion that the success of British democracy depended on the effective interaction of the "symbolic powers" of the monarch and aristocracy and of the "efficient" powers of the new middle class. See the introduction.

4. "A Contribution to the Sanitary History of the British Army During the Late War with Russia," 1859, Wellcome Institute Copy, M:WB100 1859 N68c.

5. Florence Nightingale's work in the training of nurses and in the development of nursing as a profession for women has been studied extensively and well over the last fifty years. I would cite for special mention the work of Monica Baly, Sue Goldie, Anne Summers, and Barbara Dossey, but the bibliography on this issue is both huge and distinguished. Ian McEwan's novel *Atonement* (2001) offers a compelling portrait of the Nightingale nurse and her training at the beginning of the Second World War.

6. These acts had been passed in an attempt to curb the spread of syphilis and other venereal diseases, especially in the armed forces. The acts allowed the police to detain any woman on the suspicion of being a prostitute, to subject any prostitute to exam-

ination, and to detain her for "treatment," whether or not she was willing. The campaign to repeal the Contagious Diseases Acts was spearheaded by Josephine Butler.

7. Lynn McDonald has compiled a detailed list of Florence Nightingale's charitable donations, giving the full archival reference for each item. See CWFN, 1:742–54.

8. "I must be alone, quite alone," wrote Florence to her sister when she collapsed and went to Malvern in August 1857. "I have not been alone for 4 years, I who required more time alone than anybody, who could not live without solitude & silence, have never had one moment to myself since I went to Harley Street. I don't call writing being alone. It is by far the greatest sacrifice I have made." Woodham-Smith, p. 299.

9. Cook, 1:368–69.

10. BL, Add. 45847.

11. D. A. B. Young, "Florence Nightingale's Fever," *British Medical Journal,* 1995; 311: 1697–1700 (23 December).

12. Letter to the *British Medical Journal* 1996; 312:1040 (20 April).

13. The challenge to modern scholarship is great, and it has still to be fully met. For an overview of Florence Nightingale's life and achievement, and especially for an assessment of the years 1857–98, we still rely to an astonishing degree on Edward Cook's magisterial two-volume biography, published in 1914, never reissued, available only in specialist libraries. In five or perhaps ten years, it will finally be possible for scholars, historians, and critics to get the measure of Florence Nightingale. By then, the remaining volumes of the *Collected Works of Florence Nightingale,* dedicated to her work in politics, public health policy in Britain and India, hospital reform, feminism, the Crimean War, and War Office reform, will be in print. Lynn McDonald, the general editor of the *Collected Works* project, plans to eventually make the whole corpus of Nightingale's published and unpublished writing available electronically as manuscript text and edited text. The idea of going online and subjecting this vast corpus to the full resources of modern scholarship is a giddying prospect. Furthermore, the materials at Claydon, a huge, largely unexplored trove of information on Nightingale's family, may at last be fully catalogued and, it is to be hoped, made easily accessible.

CHAPTER 21: FAMILY MATTERS

1. Thus she wrote to Cardinal Henry Manning, with whom she had long been at odds over the Mary Stanley affair: "My object in reminding you of my existence is a well-founded horror lest after my death my letters should be collected & published. Will you be so good as to burn all mine that you can find or know of? . . . I have alas met with so much treachery in my poor life that any carelessness on the part of those who I know to be friendly to me might easily be turned to bad account. 'Nunc dimittis' [Now lettest thou thy servant depart in peace] is now the only prayer I can make as regards myself" (BL, Add. 47597). Manning did not oblige.

2. I quote this letter at length, as it is not included in the correspondence with Mary Clarke Mohl currently in the British Library collection. I give selections from the passages from this letter from Florence Nightingale to Mary Clarke Mohl of December 13, 1861, that are quoted by Cook, 2:13–16, and by Woodham-Smith, pp. 384–87. Cook includes parts of the letter when Nightingale reacts more temperately to her

friend's recently published book on Madame Récamier, and he omits her criticisms of individual family members.

3. There is one sculpted head of Florence Nightingale by Sir John Steell, based on two fairly brief sessions he had with her in April 1859. See Woodham-Smith, p. 362.

4. Woodham-Smith, p. 435.

5. BL, Add. 45794, f. 171.

6. This letter is included in Hirsch, pp. 213–14.

7. BL, Add. 45790, f. 178.

8. Woodham-Smith, p. 437.

9. BL, Add. 45790, ff. 202–4.

10. Ibid., f. 258.

11. CWFN, 1:273.

12. Ibid., 1:177.

13. Ibid., 1:173.

14. Ibid., 1:160–61.

15. Ibid., 1:192.

16. Ibid., 1:201–2.

17. Ibid., 1:205.

18. The deaths of Florence's parents are carefully covered in CWFN, vol. 1.

19. I have based this account of Florence Nightingale and the Verney family on the British Library collection, a thoughtful selection of which is included in the first volume of CWFN. I am also indebted to Lynn MacDonald's invaluable biographical material and notes in that volume.

20. According to Susan Ranson, the archivist at Claydon, Mary, the last of the Verneys, left Claydon to her stepsister Catherine Calvert Wright. She was also childless and chose her cousin General Calvert to inherit the estate on condition that he took the name of Verney. General Calvert died before Catherine Wright, so his son Harry was the first of the Calverts to take the name Verney.

21. See *Life and Letters of Baroness Bunsen,* Augustus C. Hare, ed., (New York: Routledge, 1889), vol. I, pp. 509–12. The Claydon portraits of Elizabeth Hope Verney show a radiantly beautiful woman.

22. Woodham-Smith, p. 305.

23. BL, Add. 45791, f. 353.

24. Ibid., 45791, f. 334.

25. Ibid., 45791, f. 336.

26. CWFN, 1:395.

27. Ibid., p. 403.

28. Ibid., 1:780.

29. Cook, 2:390. Rosalind Nash never forgot her aunt Florence. She was to be the chief custodian of the Nightingale papers in the first half of the twentieth century and the most zealous guardian of the Nightingale legend.

ACKNOWLEDGMENTS

The British Library has a large collection of the private papers that, according to the terms of her final will, Florence Nightingale left to the care of her trustees. The second-most-important repository of papers relating to Florence Nightingale and her family is at Claydon House. Other key collections relating to the Nightingale family are to be found in the Hampshire Record Office (repository for the Bonham-Carter family papers), the Wellcome Institute for the History of Medicine (authorized copies of some selected documents in the Claydon collection and other original documentation relating to Florence Nightingale), and the Cambridge University Library (repository for the Smith family papers). My thanks are due to the professional staff at all these institutions, especially to Dr. Anne Summers of the British Library, who is herself an acknowledged expert on Florence Nightingale's work.

Jane A. Cunningham and Melanie Blake at the Courtauld Institute helped me with my research on the artists in the family and were helpful about illustrations. I would like to thank Alex Attewell, the director of the Florence Nightingale Museum at St. Thomas' Hospital, and Dr. Susan Laurence, the curator, for their information and encouragement. I am especially indebted to Susan Ranson, the archivist at Claydon. Few archivists have to cope with such difficult working conditions, but Mrs. Ranson not only responded to my requests with care and grace, but also guided my research at one or two key points. It was Susan Ranson who introduced me to Jennifer Bobrowski, who, in collaboration with Hazel Lake, is working on a study of the Smith family during the Parndon years. Jennifer has been making her way steadily through the Claydon "Bundles" for more than five years, and she has generously passed on to me some of her unrivaled knowledge of the documentation referring to Frances Smith Nightingale and her family. Let me also thank Dr. Jill Sutherland of Newnham College, Cambridge, for help with my research into the Clough family.

For a few months Jenny Gottschalk served as my research assistant, finding me books and articles here in the United States and then dedicating part of her English vacation to exploring collections on my behalf. Jenny had one of the precious Claydon Mondays and even managed to use her laptop there. Later, my niece Bethan Wakeling did sterling work for me at the British Library and the Wellcome Institute. What a pleasure it was to share my work for a time with such eager, sharp young minds.

By some extraordinary stroke of good luck, I met Lynn McDonald on my first research trip to England. As the general editor of the *Collected Works of Florence Nightingale* and the motive force behind the magnificent project to find, transcribe, and publish every extant page that Florence Nightingale wrote, Lynn McDonald has taken on the mantle of Monica Brady and Sue Goldie as doyenne of Nightingale studies. Lynn has been unfailingly generous with information and advice, and I am extremely grateful to her.

While in England doing research, I have relied heavily on the help and support of family and friends who proved to be providentially close to important collections. In Cambridge, Anne Lonsdale put me up at the President's Lodge at New Hall, my old college, and fed me several comradely meals. Margot Gill did lots of research in preparation for chauffeuring me expertly around the various sites associated with the Nightingales in Hampshire. My sister, Rose Wakeling, and her husband, Martin, did the same for me in Derbyshire. The Wakelings even found time, at an extremely busy point in their lives, to read early chapters of this book that were not so much half baked as raw.

Judge Kenneth Laurence and attorneys Neil Moynahan and Bonnie Moynahan all put on their legal historian caps in regard to the Nightingale entail. Psychologist Dr. Francesca von Broembsen helped me frame my discussion of Florence Nightingale's dreaming. These are friends I know I can count on to share their expertise. In matters medical, I have relied on my son, Dr. Christopher John Gill, who was always ready to discuss cholera or measles or lead poisoning and e-mail me the latest medical literature. His help was especially important when I was working on the Crimean chapters. Catherine Gill and Tobias McElheny read the first part of the book at an early stage and managed to be both enthusiastic and constructively critical.

Stuart Esten has been my in-house technical-support provider throughout the two years of writing this book. Since I cannot type, suffer from advanced technophobia, and will read ketchup labels before computer manuals, it is no easy business keeping me on-line. Thanks to Stuart, I have never lost a day of work or a page of text.

My agent Jill Kneerim was largely responsible for getting this book project launched. The proposal for the book was written in close consultation with Jill's associate Brettne Bloom. Jill and Brettne had a vision for the book as well as the skills and experience to get that vision accepted and lately they have been the leaders of my cheering section. Let me add that I would never have got past the circular file at Jill Kneerim's agency had it not been for the urgent recommendation of her friend Merloyd Lawrence. Merloyd was my editor on the Mary Baker Eddy book, and I value her counsel.

As with my first two books, I have been lucky in my *Nightingales* editors. Rowena Webb in London has been a model of calm, enthusiastic cooperation. The warm welcome I got on my visits to the offices of Hodder and Stoughton made me realize how much *Nightingales* forms a bridge between my British and my American selves. Elisabeth Kallick Dyssegaard, my editor at Ballantine Books, is an intense Scandinavian intellectual masquerading as a cool, laid-back New Yorker. The modern personification of the Protestant work ethic, Elisabeth has sweated through countless drafts of this book, always on schedule, always in touch, always positive, always demanding one more draft. By the end she felt able to give her ironic sensibility free rein and showed a disconcerting ability to read my mind. In Rowena and Elisabeth I have found surrogate daughters, and I have loved it.

When I contracted to finish this book in two years, I confess I did not think I could actually do it. Writing has been rather a lonely, fraught business, and I would not have got through it without the loving support of my husband, Stuart, my children, Christopher and Catherine, my daughter-in-law, Noriko, my sister, Rose, my brother, Harry, and last but not least my three granddaughters. Talking books with Bronwyn, admiring Fiona's birds and butterflies, holding one-sided conversations with baby Delia on our weekly excursions, and getting, at last, an answer back ("I don't want to do that, Grandma!")—all this sustained me as I read and fretted and wrote about the Nightingale family.

ABOUT THE AUTHOR

Gillian Gill was born in Cardiff, Great Britain. She received her Ph.D. in modern French literature from Cambridge University. Gill has taught French, women's studies, and literary theory at Northeastern, Wellesley, Yale and Harvard. She is the author of *Agatha Christie: The Woman and Her Mysteries* and *Mary Baker Eddy*. She lives in a suburb of Boston.

PICTURE ACKNOWLEDGMENTS

INDEX

Page numbers in *italics* refer to illustrations.

Aberdeen, Lord, 198, 298, 313, 315, 325, 364

abolitionism, 15, 20–23, 39, 40, 45, 79, 176, 194, 208

Adams, Henry, 228

agriculture, 8

Airey, Richard, 308

Albert, Prince of England, 121, 158–61, 171, 175, 298, 303, 401, 415–16, 435, 482n.14; death of, 440, 444

Alexander, Thomas, 440

Alexandria, 233, 234, 242–43, 254

Alford, Lady Marian, 238

Allen, Fanny, 474n.11

Alma, Battle of the, 338, 384

Ampère, Jean-Jacques, 147, 149

amputation, 269; at Scutari, 329–31, 333, 349, 372, 502n.13

Andover, 135, 136

anesthesia, 191

Anglicanism, 16, 19, 21, 30, 58, 75, 133, 254, 360; sisters, 355, 356, 360, 364

antiseptic practices, 191

Apostles, 223

Aristotle, 125, 235

Arkwright, Richard, 6, 72

Arnold, Matthew, 266

art, 154, 165, 212–13; William Smith's collection of, 32–33, 59, 60, 86, 470n.13; women artists, 165–66, 483n.28

Ashburton, Lady, 81, 160, 482nn.15, 16

Ashley, Francis, 113

Athena (owl), 250–51, *251*, 268, 295–96, 317, 373–74, 389, 492n.24, 497n.30

Athens, 233, 243–51

Austen, Jane, 46; *Emma,* 50; *Persuasion,* 49, 466n.7; *Pride and Prejudice,* 3, 4, 47; *Sense and Sensibility,* 50

Australia, 178, 181

Babbage, Charles, 78, 124

Bagehot, Walter, 2, 512n.3

Bakewell, R. Hall, 502n.12

Balaclava, 309, 322, 331, 335, 344, 348, 355, 370, 372, 376, 383, 385–88, 391, 398–412, 503n.31, 504n.38, 512n.31; battle of, 309–11, *311,* 312, 314; Castle Hospital, 409, 510n.32; Florence in, 398–412; General Hospital, 399–401, 405, 407–12; religious tensions among nurses, 398, 408–9

Baldwin, Mary, 244

Baly, Dr. Monica, 429

Balzac, Honoré de, 460

Barbauld, Anna, 14, 40, 43
Barrett, Jerry, "Florence Nightingale
    Receiving the Wounded at Scutari," 359
Barrett Browning, Elizabeth, 20, 121, 227,
    261, 429, 471n.33, 484n.16, 486n.7
Beale, Frances, 120
bedsores, 350, 408
Belgioioso, Princess, 40
Bentham, Jeremy, 14
Berlin, 251, 252
Bermondsey Convent, 318–19, 500n.40,
    503n.34, 505n.7, 506n.13
Bible, 128, 272, 491n.16
Biddone, J. M., 131, 132
Black Sea, 299, 303, 304, 308, 323, 398,
    399
Blackwell, Elizabeth, 78, 161, 261
Blackwood, Lady Alicia, 325, 501n.4,
    506n.23
Blake, William, 7
Blessington, Lady, 225
bloodletting, 131, 191, 214, 339
Bodichon, Barbara Leigh Smith, 39,
    43–44, 64, 68, 83, 89–90, 120, 200,
    443, 478n.40, 487n.25, 488n.25
Bonham Carter, Alfred, 164
Bonham Carter, Alice, 164
Bonham Carter, Bonny, 89, 90, 96,
    475n.5; death of, 96–97, 117
Bonham Carter, Fanny, 164
Bonham Carter, Henry, 164, 457
Bonham Carter, Hilary, 26, 82, 84, 89,
    146, 163–67, 206, 441, 442–44, 458,
    476n.21, 479n.16, 481n.2, 488n.25;
    death of, 443–44; Florence and, 89–91,
    111, 115, 151, 164–67, 182, 184–85,
    193, 279, 353, 442–44; spinsterhood
    of, 166–67; spiritual and artistic
    aspirations, 164–66, 442
Bonham Carter, Hugh, 164, 264, 265,
    475n.2
Bonham Carter, Jack, 89, 90, 111, 166,
    221, 475n.16
Bonham Carter, Joanna Smith, 26, 36, 37,
    45, 46–47, 50, 57, 64, 65, 74, 77,
    83–84, 88, 89, 111, 138, 163–67, 209,
    443
Bonham Carter, John, 13, 46–47, 89, 121,
    475n.16; death of, 84, 164, 166, 443,
    483n.22

Bonham Carter, Laura Nicholson, 89, 221
Bonham Carter, Sibella, 457
Bonham Carter, William, 200
Bonheur, Rosa, 166, 438n.28
Boswell, James, 20
bowels, Victorian obsession with, 102
Bowman, Dr. William, 326, 330, 331
Boxer, Admiral, 347
Bracebridge, Charles, 211, 213–16,
    233–43, 252–54, 316, 359, 400, 426,
    489n.18; Crimean War and, 316–17,
    325, 341, 344, 365, 385, 387–88, 390,
    400; Nightingale Fund and, 403
Bracebridge, Selina, 182, 202, 211, 280,
    506n.19; Crimean War and, 316–18,
    325, 326, 359, 362, 365, 389, 390,
    393, 395; Florence and, 211–16, 221,
    233–53, 314, 316, 322, 353, 359, 365,
    389, 390
Bridgeman, Mother, 366, 367, 398, 399,
    405, 407–9, 505nn.1, 7, 511n.48
Bridgman, Laura, 194, 485n.36
British army, 300, 301–6; buying
    promotions in, 302, 302; cavalry, 303,
    308, 309, 310, 322; Crimean War,
    297–413, 497–513; health care,
    312–13, 322–413, 416–20, 497–513;
    health care reform, 355, 374–84,
    416–20, 424, 454, 503n.32; in India,
    419; inefficiency and disarray, 301–3,
    306, 312, 328–31, 334, 342–47; officer
    class inequities and grievances, 301–2;
    peacetime mortality rate, 418; royal
    commission on, 406–9, 416–20,
    508n.5; Sanitary Commission and,
    374–84, 406; sanitation issues, 324–25,
    331, 334–36, 339–41, 347, 349,
    374–84, 406–9, 418; Scutari hospitals,
    322–413, 497–513; transportation,
    305–6, 308, 310, 312, 314, 324, 370,
    372, 399, 409–10
British Association for the Advancement of
    Science, 124–25, 197, 256, 271,
    484n.14
British Library, Nightingale papers in, 433
British navy, 300, 498n.2
Broadlands, 173, 176, 474n.2, 484n.9
Brontë, Charlotte, 98, 99, 121, 225, 296,
    474n.5; Jane Eyre, 46; Shirley, 237;
    Villette, 481n.13

Brontë, Emily, 50, 98, 99, 121; *Wuthering Heights*, 10–11, 50, 73
Brown, Charles, 227
Brown, General Sir George, 306, 308
Browning, Robert, 20, 226, 486n.7
brucellosis, 424, 428–29, 509n.5
Brunel, Isambard Kingdom, 378
Buckingham Palace, 171
Buckland, Frank, 197
Bunsen, Christian, 159, 170–71, 193, 237
Bunsen, Frances Waddington, 159, 170–71, 454
Burdett-Coutts, Angela, 201
Burney, Fanny, 46
Burton, Sir Richard, 231, 232
Buss, Dorothea, 120
Buss, Jane, 68, 475n.3
Byron, George Gordon, 68, 156, 178, 224, 225, 472n.8, 484n.15, 490n.37

Cairo, 233, 234, 238, 240–43
Caithness, Earl of, 47, 49, 472n.3
Calvert, Sir Harry, 454
Cambridge, Duke of, 306, 401
Campbell, Colin, 391–92
cancer, 288, 443
Canning, Lady, 280, 289, 318, 510n.30
Cardigan, Lord, 302, 303, 310, 335, 338, 406, 416
Carlyle, Thomas, 78, 225
castration, 140, 230, 480n.5
Catholic Emancipation Act (1829), 13
Catholicism, 133, 194, 206–7, 218–20, 254, 271–72, 277, 285, 430; nurses, 318–20, 326, 355, 356, 358–69, 398, 408–9, 486n.9, 505–7
celibacy, 206–8, 488n.8
Cenci, Beatrice, 213, 489n.17
Chadwick, Edwin, 190, 335, 376, 508n.13
Charge of the Light Brigade, 384, 406
Chartist movement, 169, 261
Chateaubriand, Monsieur de, 144, 145, 148, 149
Chatsworth, 171, 172, 173
Chaucer, Geoffrey, 5, 53
Chelsea Board, 406–9, 508n.14, 511n.46
Chenery, Thomas, 312–13, 330, 336, 344, 500n.31
Chisholm, Mrs. Caroline, 493n.18

cholera, 252, 290–91, 292, 496n.22, 499n.17; at Scutari, 304–7, 335, 348, 384, 402, 510n.21; transmission of, 304
Chopin, Frédéric, 150
Christie, Miss Sarah, 95–96, 98–109, 112–14, 115, 121–22, 249, 476n.22, 477nn.22, 28
Church of England, 9, 16, 19, 272, 319, 360, 461, 495n.41
Clapham, 18–19, 25, 34, 38, 42
Clapham Saints, 22, 468n.24
Clarendon, Lord, 298, 300
Clark, Sir James, 372, 373, 374
Clarke, Charles, 146, 147
Clarke, James, 159
Clarke, Mrs., 326, 328
Clarkson, William, 39
Claydon House, 454, 455, 461–64, 472n.34, 474n.9, 514n.20
Clive, Caroline Archer, 208
Clough, Anne Jemima, 441–42
Clough, Arthur, Jr., 439, 442
Clough, Arthur Hugh, 265–67, 320, 420, 423, 438–42, 457, 494n.29; death of, 440, 441, 457; Florence and, 438–42
Clough, Blanche Athena, 439, 442
Clough, Blanche Smith, 84, 85, 107, 109, 115, 117, 119, 262, 264, 438–42, 447, 456, 457; marriage of, 266–67, 438–42
Clough, Florence, 439, 442
Clough, Martha, 391–92, 394, 409, 509n.16
Coape, Joanna, 24
Coape, Maria, 24, 25, 27, 28, 140
Cobden, William, 225–26
Colbran, Isabella, 140
Coleridge, Samuel Taylor, 14, 39, 162
Coltman, Bertha Smith, 85, 115, 118, 119, 264, 266, 437, 452, 456
Coltman, William, 452
Columba, Madre Santa, 219–21, 363
Comédie-Française, 145–46
Constantinople, 303, 309, 314, 322, 323, 324, 336, 341, 344, 373, 380, 501n.3, 502n.9
Contagious Disease Acts, 422
Convent of the Sisters of Charity, Paris, 285
Cook, Edward, 488n.27, 513n.13
Corn Laws, 169

cotton mills, 6–8, 11, 467n.15
Cowper, William, 31
coxcombs, 420
Cranworth, Lady, 318, 413, 510n.30
Crew, Lord, 229
Crimean fever, 335
Crimean War, 129, 138, 223, 297–413,
    497–513; Balaclava, 309–11, *311*, 312,
    314, 322, 331, 335, 344, 348, 385–88,
    398–412, 503n.31, 504n.38, 510n.31;
    British inefficiency and disarray, 312,
    328–31, 334, 342–47; British press on,
    300, 307–14, 317–18, 330, 336–37,
    345, 362, 365, 370, 378, 380, 381,
    400, 500n.31; casualties, 333, 334, 335,
    336, 371, 381; disease and pestilence,
    304–7, 310–13, 324, 327, 329,
    333–36, 339–41, 347, 371, 374–84,
    399, 406–9, 418, 510n.21, 512n.6; end
    of, 405–9; Florence's plans to go to,
    313–22; hospital conditions, 261, 309,
    312–13, 324–37, 416–20, 497–513;
    postwar army inquiries and reforms,
    405–9, 416–20, 508n.5; Sanitary
    Commission, 374–84, 406; sanitation
    issues, 304–5, 324–25, 331, 334–36,
    339–41, 347, 349, 374–84, 406–9,
    418; Scutari hospitals, 261, 312–13,
    322–413, 416–20, 497–513;
    Sevastopol, 305–9, 314, 348, 386–87,
    398, 499nn.12, 26
Cromford, 6, 7, 8, 11, 71, 72, 170, 262,
    276–77
Cruickshanks, Dr., 359
Cumming, Dr., 364, 365, 366, 367, 374,
    509n.11
Cure, Mrs., 37

d'Agoult, Marie, 150
Dante, 125, 162, 473n.11
Darwin, Charles, 14, 22, 38, 198,
    474n.11, 476n.20
Darwin, Erasmus, 14, 38
Darwin family, 14, 37, 38, 79, 467n.14,
    474n.11
Davies, Emily, 120
Dawson, George, 206
Delane, John Thadeus, 300, 307
Derbyshire, 2, 4, 5–9, 11, 53, 71, 73, 74,
    86, 92, 162, 448, 460, 467nn.14, 15

de Staël, Germaine, 144, 146, 148,
    471n.21; *Delphine*, 38
Devonshire, Duchess of, 174
Devonshire, Duke of, 78, 171–73, 174,
    415
dialects, English, 53, 93, 460
Dicey, Elinor Bonham Carter, 164, 443
Dickens, Charles, 7, 72, 190, 196, 201;
    Bleak House, 201; *Nicholas Nickleby*,
    113; *Pickwick Papers*, 469n.36
disease, 33, 55, 89, 118–19, 129, 132,
    252, 288, 290–91, 496n.22;
    contamination and, 334–36, 339–41,
    384; Crimean War and, 304–7,
    310–13, 324, 327, 329, 333–36,
    339–41, 347, 371, 374–84, 399,
    406–9, 418, 510n.21, 512n.6;
    Florence's sanitation practices for,
    334–36, 339–41, 374–84, 406–9, 418
Disraeli, Benjamin, 34, 81, 172–73, 205,
    225, 230, 432, 433; *Tancred*, 225
Dissenters, 9, 10, 12–14, 16, 18, 19,
    21–23, 37, 38, 46, 47, 55, 74–75,
    98–99, 103, 161, 222, 266, 469n.31
Donizetti, Gaetano, 141; *Lucrezia Borgia*,
    140
Dresden, 251, 252
Duberly, Frances, 310, 336, 498n.12
Duberly, Captain Henry, 301
dysentery, 302, 312, 324, 329, 334, 335,
    347, 383

Eden, Emily, 172
education, 33–37, 44, 119, 120, 200;
    governesses, 98–109, 112; of
    Nightingale sisters, 93–112, 119–30;
    Unitarian tradition of, 98–99, 121; for
    women, 120–21, 200–202
Egypt, 105, 139, 294, 491n.18; Florence
    in, 233–43, 245, 250, 251
Eliot, George, 39, 77, 121, 261, 425, 460,
    472n.33, 479n.15, 488n.25; *Adam
    Bede*, 8; *Daniel Deronda*, 480n.6,
    482n.12
Embley Park, 4, 11, 76, 77–79, 80, 81,
    83–86, *88*, 91, 102, 118, 132, 153,
    169–70, 173, 176, 200, 448, 450, 455,
    464, 474nn.2, 9; inherited by Mai and
    Sam Smith, 86, 451–52; renovation of,
    86, 136, 137, 153, 167–69

Emerson, Ralph Waldo, 8, 225, 266
English Civil War, 301, 460, 461
Enlightenment, 21, 41, 174
entail, Nightingale, 2–4, 58, 69, 80,
    85–86, 451–52, 466n.8
Evangelicalism, 19, 22, 79, 318, 319
Evans, Alice, 428–29
Evans, Anne Nightingale, 2, 4, 5
Evans, Elizabeth (aunt Evans), 10, 71, 75,
    76, 83, 106, 170, 262–63, 467n.13;
    death of, 276, 280

Fair Oak, 77, 90, 111
Farr, William, 190, 196, 420
Fauriel, Claude, 145, 149, 151
feminism, 14, 43–45, 120, 208, 248, 432
Ferucci, Madame, 144
Fitzgerald, David, 405, 407–11, 511nn.45,
    51
Fliedner, Theodor, 252, 253, 269
Florence, 57–59, 142
flu epidemics, 118–19, 129, 132–33
Forester, Lady Maria, 313
Forster, E. M., 41
Fowler, Dr., 195, 196, 272
Fox, Charles James, 20, 37–38, 65
France, 13, 21, 28, 54, 214, 279, 285,
    421, 486n.2; Crimean War, 297–99,
    302, 304–13, 344, 370, 373, 376,
    504n.38; Nightingale family in,
    137–40, 144–52; Revolution, 13, 14,
    147, 468n.25
Franco-Prussian War, 421, 464
French language, 93–94, 125
frostbite, 347, 370, 371, 372, 408
Fry, Elizabeth, 208
Fryston, 229–31

Gale, Francis, 55, 88, 96, 106, 117, 137,
    142, 486n.4; death of, 192–93;
    Florence and, 118, 192
Galton, Douglas, 267, 283, 284, 457
Galton, Sir Francis, 38
Galton, Gwendolyn, 457
Galton, Marianne Nicholson, 81, 89, 153,
    155, 206, 267, 475n.2, 482n.11;
    Florence and, 90, 115, 139, 157–58,
    161, 167, 179–86, 193, 263, 283–84,
    457, 485n.33
Galway, Lord, 226

gangrene, 383
Garibaldi, Giuseppe, 422
Gaskell, Elizabeth, 72–73, 78, 79, 148,
    225, 290, 292, 460, 474n.5, 476n.21,
    483n.1, 488n.25, 496n.20; Florence
    and, 292–96, 389–90
Gavin, Dr. Hector, 374, 377
Geneva, 143–44, 172
Genlis, Madame de, 139
Genoa, 140–42
George IV, King of England, 65, 174
Germany, 7, 105, 123, 138, 160, 221,
    224, 421; Kaiserswerth Institute, 193,
    221, 222, 251–53, 267–70
germ theory, 334
Gilmore, Charlotte Perkins, 495n.42
Gladstone, John, 469n.39
Gladstone, William, Ewart, 225, 226, 423,
    432, 433, 469n.39, 490n.37
Godwin, William, 14, 38, 43, 68
Gordon, George, 421–22
governesses, 98–109, 112, 287
Granville, Lady, 172
Great Britain, 169; abolitionism, 20–23;
    art, 32–33; Chartist movement, 169;
    colonialism, 301, 419, 420; Crimean
    War, 297–413, 497–513; government,
    12–14, 16, 19–23, 135, 169, 174–76,
    299–303, 384, 419; health care,
    190–92; Hungry Forties, 169–70;
    industrialization, 6–8, 74, 169–70, 303,
    460; land ownership, 78, 169; political
    system, 176, 298–301; postwar army
    reforms, 405–9, 416–20, 508n.5;
    unemployment and famine, 169–70. See
    also British army; specific cities and
    counties; Victorian era
Greece, 105, 126, 224; Florence in,
    243–51
Greek language, 34, 120, 128, 237
Grisi, Giulia, 140

Hall, Dr. John, 315, 347, 377, 386, 388,
    398–402, 405–11, 416, 417–18,
    505n.1, 509n.9, 511n.49
Hallam, Arthur, 223
Halsey, Thomas, 17
Handel, George Frederick, 140
Hankey, Frederick, 231
Hanum, Engeli, 243

Hawes, Benjamin, 355, 378, 394, 405, 406, 407
Hawthorne, Nathaniel, 225
health care, 190–92; army, 261, 312–13, 322–413, 416–20, 497–513; army reforms, 355, 374–84, 416–20, 424, 454, 503n.32; Crimean War, 261, 312–13, 322–413, 416–20, 497–513; poor conditions and treatment, 191–92, 277, 286, 289–90, 312–13, 324–36, 421; public, 190–92, 278, 421. *See also* disease; hospitals; public health
Hennell, Sarah Sophia, 123–24, 479n.15
Herbert, Elizabeth À Court, 216–18, 267, 280, 283, 289, 313, 318, 362–64, 489n.27, 500n.39, 506nn.19, 22
Herbert, Sidney, 161, 201, 216–17, *217*, 218, 267, 489n.25, 504n.40; army health care reform effort, 417, 419; Crimean War and, 313–16, 319, 321, 328, 344–47, 360–62, 372, 383, 390, 406, 410, 417; death of, 440, 446; Florence and, 216–18, 221, 261, 278, 289, 313–16, 360–63, 384, 401, 410, 417, 430, 435, 440
Heyer, Georgette, 48
Hill, Frances, 243–44, 414
Hill, John Henry, 243–44
Hill, Octavia, 495n.3
Hobbes, Thomas, 125
Holland, Lord, 31
Holloway, 71, 74
Homer, 128, 235
homosexuality, 186–89, 223–24, 230–32
Hooker, Sir W. J., 197
Hosmer, Harriet, 166
hospitals, 190–92; Catholic, 272, 277, 318; Crimean War, 261, 309, 312–13, 322–413, 416–20, 497–513; disease and sanitation principles, 324, 327, 329, 333–36, 339–41, 374–84, 399, 406–9, 418; Florence's work in, 190–96, 252–53, 261, 278–79, 282–96, 313–413, 497–513; reforms, 190–92, 278, 337, 355, 375, 416–21; poor conditions in, 191, 277, 286, 289–90, 312–13, 324–26, 421; Scutari conditions, 312–13, 324–27, 416–20. *See also specific hospitals*

House of Commons, 12–14, 20–23, 31, 47, 74, 77, 135–36, 224, 226, 338, 433
House of Lords, 226
Howe, Julia Ward, 78, 193–94, 208
Howe, Samuel Gridley, 193–94, 485n.36
Hughes, Thomas, 425
hysteria, 272–73, 288, 495n.43

illiteracy, 200
India, 60, 375; British army in, 419; British rule, 300, 419, 420; Florence's interest in, 419–20, 421
industrialization, 6–8, 74, 169–70, 303, 460
infant mortality, 73
Institution for Ill Gentlewomen, 280, 282–91
Irby, Paulina, 414, 422
Ireland, 175, 272, 461; potato famine, 338, 378
Isle of Wight, 77, 225
Italy, 29, 54–58, 73, 138, 299, 311, 439; Florence's visit to Rome, 211–21; Nightingale family in, 54–58, 140–43; Risorgimento movement, 142–43

James, Henry, 460, 480n.7
Jameson, Anna, 120, 194, 486n.7
Jews, 16
Joan of Arc, 133, 207
John of the Cross, 133–34
Jones, Agnes, 458, 462
Jowett, Benjamin, 70, 128, 422, 444, 495n.39

Kaiserswerth Institute, 193, 221, 222, 251–53, 267–70, 384n.11, 492n.3, 494n.36
Keats, John, 227, 231, 439
Kemble, Adelaide, 140, 480n.7
Kemble, Fanny, 476n.15, 480n.7
Kensington Palace, 444–45
Kinglake, A. W., 223
King of Clubs, 31, 159
Kings College Hospital, 289
Kingsley, Charles, 261, 301, 484n.12
Kipling, Rudyard, 113
Kontaxiki, Elizabeth, 244
Koulali, 366–67, 378, 398, 510n.30

Lafayette, Marquis de, 148

Lafourcade, Georges, 230
Lamarckism, 38
Lamartine, Alphonse de, 225
Lamb, William, 31, 159
Land Service Corps, 370
Land Transport Corps, 399, 410
languages, 34, 53, 93–94, 120, 125–28,
    479n.18
Latin, 34, 94, 120, 125
Lawfield, Mrs., 320
Lea Hall, 2, 5, 6, 71, 73
Lea Hurst, 4, 7, 8, 11, 71–72, 72, 73–75,
    77, 80, 86, 92, 106, 109, 117, 118,
    136, 162, 163, 169, 182, 200, 251,
    292–96, 413, 415, 448, 450, 452, 455,
    464, 474n.2; architecture, 71, 72–73;
    cold conditions, 73
Lea mill, 6–8
leeches, 131, 191, 214, 339
Lefroy, Colonel John, 405–6, 416
Le Havre, 137, 139
Leicestershire, 76–77
Leigh Smith, Benjamin, 64, 68, 83, 89–90
lesbianism, 38, 45, 186–89
lice, 333–34, 347, 376, 382, 383
Limited Service Act, 303
Lind, Jenny, 196
Linnaean Society, 31
Locke, John, 14, 97, 125
London, 5, 15, 18, 31, 51, 52, 53, 74, 77,
    80–81, 91, 135, 182, 225, 299, 318;
    Florence's debutante season, 153–69;
    Florence's move to, 285–96; Florence's
    South Street house in, 436, 437,
    445–46, 452, 456, 459
Longden, Anne, 64–68; death of, 67–68, 89
Longden, Dolly, 64, 67, 68
Longfellow, Henry Wadsworth, 466n.6
Louis XVI, King of France, 28
Lovelace, Ada Byron, 14, 78, 79, 155–56,
    178, 484nn.15, 16
Lucan, Lord, 302, 308, 310, 406
Lushington, Beatrice Smith, 85, 115, 118,
    264, 266, 280, 437, 456

Macaulay, Tom, 191
Macaulay, George Babington, 78, 79
Macdonald, John Cameron, 336–37, 341,
    344

MacGrigor, Alexander, 380, 384
madhouses, 191
Malibran, María, 140, 141
Malta fever, 428
Mathus, Thomas, 29–30, 31, 79
Manning, Henry, 261, 271, 272, 320,
    363, 493n.18, 513n.1
Marseilles, 320, 321, 379
Martineau, Harriet, 8, 79, 120, 163, 225,
    419, 423, 425, 471n.33, 476n.21;
    Eastern Life Past and Present, 237
Martineau, James, 163
Martineau, Rachel, 163
masturbation, 249
mathematics, 126, 178, 196, 265,
    482n.19, 485n.24
Maule, Colonel Lauderdale, 391
Maurice, F. C., 261
McAuley, Catherine, 318
McDonald, Sergeant, 408, 511n.51
McNeill, Sir John, 374–75, 376, 386,
    387, 406, 416, 495n.39, 508n.14,
    512n.53
McNeill-Tulloch Commission, 374–84,
    406
Melbourne, Lady, 174
Melbourne, Lord, 31, 159, 174, 217
Menchikov, Prince, 308, 309, 499n.25
Menzies, Dr. Duncan, 315, 316, 324, 328,
    330, 336–37, 344, 347, 502n.11
Mérimée, Prosper, 148
Meyer, Dr. John, 364–65, 366
Michelangelo, 212–13
middle class, 1–2, 169–70, 176, 191, 270,
    299, 512n.3
Middlesex Hospital, 290
Midlands, 2, 5, 8, 11, 27, 53, 75
Mill, James, 121
Mill, John Stuart, 121, 422, 495n.39
Millbank distillery, 59
Milnes, Amicia, 229
Milnes, Annabel, 229, 232
Milnes, Florence, 229
Milnes, Harriette, 226
Milnes, Henrietta Monckton, 222, 226,
    471n.32, 489n.31
Milnes, Richard Monckton, 8, 33, 197,
    201, 212, 221–32, 298, 401, 457,
    490nn.31, 37, 46, 495n.39; childhood

and education, 222–24; Florence and, 221–22, 227–33, 245, 252, 256, 320; homosexuality of, 223–24, 230–32; political career, 224–26
Milnes, Robert Offley Ashburton, 229
Milnes, Robert Pemberton, 222, 224, 226, 229, 490n.39
Milnes family, 33, 38, 222–26
Mohl, Anna, 279
Mohl, Julius, 145, 149, 151, 209–10, 221, 237, 279, 285, 449
Mohl, Mary Clarke (Clarkey), 40, 144–52, 157, 161, 163, 167, 171, 172, 187, 202, 207, 214, 221, 275, 279, 283, 285, 317, 353, 423, 440, 442, 444, 481nn.12, 19, 23, 513n.2; marriage of, 209–10; salon of, 147–52, 225
Moore, Reverend Mother Mary Clare, 326, 359, 360, 390, 500n.40, 503n.34, 505nn.3, 7
Morton, Ann, 403
Mozart, Wolfang Amadeus, 140
Mulready, William, 165, 166
Muncaster, Lord, 28, 32
Musset, Alfred de, 150

Naples, 55–57
Napoleon Bonaparte, 26, 45, 234, 299, 302, 379
Napoleon III, 226, 298
Napoleonic Wars, 45, 298, 299, 300, 302
Nash, Rosalind Smith, 465, 514n.29
Newcastle, Lord, 315, 328, 362
Nice, 139–40
Nicholson, Anne Smith, 26, 33, 36, 45, 46, 52, 57, 65, 69, 74, 77, 83–84, 89, 157, 162–63, 179–80, 184, 209
Nicholson, George, 46, 52, 89, 121
Nicholson, Hannah, 119, 181–83, 220, 284, 485n.23
Nicholson, Henry, 89, 206, 482n.11, 485nn.23, 24; death of, 263; Florence and, 90, 161–63, 178–80, 184–85, 263
Nicholson, Lothian, 284
Nicholson, William, 119, 181
Nightingale, Fanny Smith, 2, 3, 11, 12, 26, 27, 46, 69, 481n.2; birth of, 46; childhood, 28–37, 46, 105; conservatism of, 44–45, 178; Continental tour (1837–39), 86,

136–52; Crimean War and, 316, 334, 358, 390, 402, 405; death of, 452–54; dependence on Florence, and resentment of her work, 195–96, 202–5, 253, 254–57, 283, 294–95; education of, 33–37; at Embley Park, 77–78, 81–86; Florence's reclusive years and, 424, 431, 436, 447–54, 458–59; ill health of, 81–82, 450–54; Lea Hurst disliked by, 73–75, 80, 106; marital disputes, 81–82, 255, 283; marriage and family life, 49–58, 61, 71–86, 106, 131–32, 136, 169, 255–56, 450; old age and senility, 86, 450–54; as a parent, 55–58, 73, 76, 87–88, 95–114, 125, 131, 136, 157, 162, 195–96, 235, 455; personality of, 46, 47, 48, 51, 79, 103, 105; pregnancies and childbirths, 55–59; relationship with daughter Florence, 45, 76, 97–114, 178, 181–82, 195–204, 211, 255–57, 260–75, 291, 353, 428, 431, 447–54, 492n.7; relationship with daughter Parthe, 113, 131, 255, 257, 268, 273–74, 450–51; relationship with her mother-in-law, 50–54, 75–76, 496n.7; James Sinclair and, 47–51; Mai Smith and, 84–86, 109–10, 118, 255; social climbing of, 78–80, 98, 105, 135–36, 153–54, 157, 161, 169–77, 203, 234, 255–56; travel, 54–58, 73; wedding of, 50–54, 75
Nightingale, Florence, 2; animals loved by, 91–93, 107, 250–51, 317, 389, 449; army reform campaign, 355, 374–84, 416–20, 424, 454, 503n.32; attitude of moral superiority and religious enlightenment, 339, 353, 356, 361, 420–21; in Balaclava, 398–412; birth of, 58–59; Hilary Bonham Carter and, 89–91, 111, 115, 151, 164–67, 182, 184–85, 193, 279, 353, 442–44; Bracebridges and, 211–16, 221, 233–44, 251–53, 254, 268, 314, 316, 322, 353, 359, 365, 387–89, 390, 400, 402, 426; breaking free from her family, 114, 130, 183–84, 204, 254–75, 285, 295; brucellosis of, 424, 428–29, 436, 509n.5; "Cassandra" fragment, 44, 161, 246–48, 473n.13, 491nn.14, 18, 19; Catholicism and, 218–20, 254, 271–72,

285, 430; cats of, 449; celibacy of, 187–89, 206–9; character of, 97, 101–6, 157, 177, 187, 256–59, 350, 422; childhood, 8, 58, 69, 73–86, *86*, 87–114, 245–46; children loved by, 209, 457, 464–65; Miss Christie and, 98–109, 112–15, 121–22, 249, 476*n*.22, 477*nn*.22, 28; Clarkey and, 144–52, 167, 209–10, 279, 285, 353, 440; "Compendium of Useful Facts," 126; Continental tour (1837–39), 86, 136–52; cousins of, 89–91, 96, 111, 115, 116–19, 157–58, 161–67, 179–86, 283–84, 394–95, 457, 475*n*.2; Crimean fever of, 387–90, 428; crushes on older girls, 104, 105, 249, 477*n*.29; dealings with other Scutari nurses, 353–69, 372–73, 505*n*.1; death of, 351, 422; death of her parents, 447, 451–54; debutante season, 153–69; depression of (1850), 105, 240, 244–53; "dreaming" habit of, 104–5, 139, 245–49, 294, 492*n*.22; dying soldiers comforted by, 350–52, 503*n*.18, 504*n*.48; education of, 93–112, 119–30, 178, 477*n*.35; in Egypt and Greece, 233–51; estate of, 463; fame and influence, 414–22, 432, 435; family dependence on, and resentment of her work, 195–96, 202–5, 221, 253, 254–77, 283, 294–95; family legend about, 293, 294; finances of, 283, 350, 436, 452; Sidney Herbert and, 216–18, 221, 261, 267, 268, 278, 289, 313–16, 360–63, 384, 401, 410, 417, 435, 430, 440; homeless boys brought back from war zone, 403, 413, *415;* hospital work, 190–96, 252–53, 261, 278–79, 282–96, 313–43, 497–513; illnesses of, 89, 114, 155, 181, 184, 271, 285, 387–90, 423–31, 436–37, 458, 462; as Institute for Ill Gentlewomen superintendent, 280, 282–91; intellectual self-confidence of, 101–4, 128–30; interest in medicine, 92–93, 502*n*.13; invalidism of, 423–49; aunt Julia and, 44, 98, 115, 123, 194, 353; as Kaiserswerth nursing intern, 193, 221, 222, 251–53, 267–70, 486*n*.11, 494*n*.36; as Lady with the Lamp, *382,*

384, 414; last years, 464–65; at Lea Hurst, 71–75, 92; lesbian accusation, 186–89; aunt Mai and, 69–70, 84, 89, 92, 98, 104, 106, 109–19, 123, 177–78, 261, 262–67, 275, 276, 280, 353, 395, 403–4, 425, 437–39, 442; men and, 161–63, 180, 184–85, 188, 209, 221–32, 457; Richard Monckton Milnes and, 221–22, 227–33, 245, 252, 256, 320; move to Harley Street, 261, 285–86; musical interests, 26, 140–42; mysticism and visions, 133–34, 207–8, 249–50, 479*n*.27, 492*n*.22; myth of, 317–18, 348, 381, 384; name of, 58; Hannah Nicholson and, 181–83; Henry Nicholson and, 90, 161–63, 178, 179–80, 184–85, 263; Marianne Nicholson and, 90, 115, 139, 157–58, 161, 167, 179–86, 193, 263, 283–84, 457, 485*n*.33; nonconformism of, 45, 80, 97–106; *Notes Affecting the Health, Efficiency, and Hospital Administration of the British Army,* 417; *Notes on Nursing,* 340, 419; nurse and caretaker role, 117–19, 131–33, 180–84, 190–96, 200–204, 267–96, 313–413, 497–513; as nurse in Crimean War, 313–413, 497–513; as opera lover, 140–42; Order of Merit given to, 422; owls of, 250–51, *251,* 268, 295–96, 317, 373–74, 389, 492*n*.24, 497*n*.30; Palmerstons and, 173–77; Parthe's "character" of, 275; penmanship, 94–95, 111; philanthropy of, 431–32; physical appearance, 154–57, 292–93, 385–86, 395; plans to go to Crimea, 313–22; political views of, 174–77, 432; postwar life of, 414–65; power and ambition of, 177, 187, 244, 256–57, 339, 347, 384, 414; press on, 317–18, 380–81, 384; pro-Kaiserswerth pamphlet, 253, 254–55, 492*n*.3; as a recluse, 422–49, 456, 464; "reformed" as a young girl, 97–109; relationship with her father, 11–12, 92, 106, 107, 114, 121–32, 135, 199, 203, 211, 233–35, 255–56, 267, 271, 283–84, 291, 390, 431, 436–37, 445–47, 487*n*.19; relationship with her mother, 45, 76, 97–114, 178, 181–82, 195–204, 211, 255–57, 260–75, 291,

353, 428, 431, 447–54, 492n.7; relationships with nurses and other women, 353–54, *354*, 355–69, 391–95, 408–13, 505–7; relationship with sister Parthe, 100–103, 111–14, 115–33, 163, 179, 183, 197, 257–75, 291, 294–96, 353, 428, 445, 457–61, 479n.24; religious faith of, 133–34, 152, 182, 189, 192, 206–8, 218–20, 249–50, 254, 261, 267, 271–72, 286, 291–92, 351, 360, 423, 495n.41; return home from Turkey, 412–15; rivalry with Parthe, 129–31, 155, 163, 216, 234–35, 258–60, 274–75, 458; in Rome, 211–21; royal commission on the army and, 406–9, 416–20, 508n.5; Salisbury affair, 392–94; as a sanitarian, 334–36, 339–41, 349, 374–84, 406–9, 418; Sanitary Commission and, 374–84, 406; at Scutari, 296, 322–413, 414, 497–513; Scutari improvements, 337–52, 377, 381–84, 396–98; Scutari tensions and disputes, 330–32, 340–47, 353–69, 372–73, 505–7; sexuality of, 105, 186–89, 206–9, 231–32, 248–49, 430; Shaftesburys and, 174–77; Shore Smith and, 116–19, 264–67, 394–95; social success, 153–67, 170–77, 255–56, 261, 464–65; social views and reform efforts, 8–9, 22, 90, 103–6, 118, 133–34, 140, 157, 176–77, 190–204, 251–53, 261–62, 270–71, 355–57, 416–20, 431, 493n.17; solitary nature of, 354, 430–34, 512n.8; South Street house of, 436, 437, 445–46, 452, 456, 459; spinsterhood of, 187, 189, 206–9; Stanley debacle, 361–69, 386, 390, 394, 398, 506nn.13, 18, 21, 22, 507nn.28–31, 513n.1; *Suggestions for Thought*, 114, 246, 256, 260, 251–62, 270, 431, 491n.18, 495nn.39, 40; as a teacher, 200–202, 261; teenage years, 115–34, 135–52; travel diaries and letters, 137–39, 143, 236, 237–38, 245, 250; travels, 105, 136–53, 197–99, 211–21, 233–53, 261, 279, 322; in Turkey and the Crimea, 187, 261, 297, 322–413, 414, 497–513; "La Vie de Florence Rossignol," 91, 94, 108; views on marriage and motherhood, 80, 114,

161, 166–68, 206–9, 270–71, 356–57, 473n.13; writings of, 81, 94, 100–101, 114, 126, 137–39, 198, 204, 237–38, 246–48, 253, 254, 261, 340, 417, 419, 425–27, 432–34, 488n.27, 491n.14

Nightingale, Peter, 55, 75

Nightingale, Peter (Mad Peter), 2, 4, 5–6, 71, 75

Nightingale, William Edward (WEN), 2, 29, 31, 45, 65, 483n.22, 493n.19; Hilary Bonham Carter and, 443–44; childhood of, 3–4, 9; Clarkey and, 144, 151; Continental tour (1837–39), 86, 136–52; Crimean War and, 313, 334, 390, 402; death of, 86, 447, 451, 453–54; death of his mother, 281; dependence on Florence, and resentment of her work, 195–96, 202–5, 254; Duke of Devonshire and, 171–72; education of, 53, 124; education of his daughters, 121–30; at Embley Park, 77–78, 81–86, 153, 167–69; eye problems, 252, 255, 267, 271; financial affairs, 9–12, 49–50, 72, 78–80, 86, 170, 446, 455, 468n.21; Florence's reclusive years and, 431, 436–37, 442, 445–47; inheritance of, 3–5, 9–11, 58, 69–70, 80, 451–52, 455; at Lea Hurst, 71–75, 77, 80, 106, 109; library of, 125–30; marital disputes, 81–82, 255, 283; marriage and family life, 49–58, 61, 71–86, 106, 114, 131–32, 169, 255–56, 267–68, 450; as a parent, *86*, 87, 92, 97, 106, 121–31, 162, 195–96, 233–35, 255, 259, 274, 443, 446–47, 455; personality of, 50, 51, 53, 79, 82, 446–47; political interests and ambitions, 135–36, 173; relationship with daughter Florence, 11–12, 92, 106, 107, 114, 135, 199, 203, 211, 233–35, 255–56, 267, 271, 283–84, 291, 390, 431, 436–37, 445–47, 487n.19; relationship with daughter Parthe, 130; travel, 54–58, 136–52; wedding of, 50–54, 75

Nightingale Fund, 395, 401–3, 421, 457

Nile River, 233, 236, 238–40, 245

Noel Byron, Lady, 79, 178, 484n.15

Nonconformism, 9, 25

Northampton, Marquis de, 238
Norton, Lady Caroline, 217, 218, 225

O'Brien, Stafford Augustus, 223
opera, 140–42, 480nn.5–7
opiates, 191, 340, 461
Opie, Amelia, 14, 40, 43
Opie, John, 43, 154, 471n.32
Osborne, Sidney Godolphin, 324,
    330–33, 336–38, 344, 361
Owen, Robert, 261, 493n.19
Oxford Movement, 218

Paget, Sir James, 419
Paine, Tom, 14, 34
Palgrave, Francis, 266, 494n.27
Palmerston, Lady, 159–60, 172–77, 225,
    228, 229, 289
Palmerston, Lord, 77, 81, 159–60,
    172–77, 190, 225, 230, 243, 278, 432,
    433, 435, 490n.39; Crimean War and,
    298–99, 301, 313, 346, 348, 374, 375;
    Nightingale family and, 173–77;
    political career, 174–76
Panmure, Lord, 376, 378, 391, 394, 396,
    405–6, 416, 417, 504n.36, 511n.46
Papists, 319
Paris, 144–52, 225, 279, 285; salons,
    147–52
Parkes, Bessie, 43
Parkyns, Mansfield, 227
Parliament, 12–14, 20–23, 47, 74, 77, 79,
    135–36, 222, 224, 226, 299, 338, 384,
    419, 433, 436, 463
Parndon, 29–30, 32, 37, 39, 45, 51,
    59–60, 105
Pasta, Giuditta, 140, 146
Pasteur, Louis, 334
Paulet, Lord William, 374, 377, 501n.5
Paxton, Sir Joseph, 171, 172, 483n.5
Peel, Robert, 230
Pembroke, Earl of, 217
Peninsular War, 302
Percy, Jocelyne, 364–65, 366
Perkins School for the Blind, 194,
    485n.36
Pickering, George, 427–28
Piozzi, Hester Thrale, 28, 29
Pitt, William, 21, 22, 177
Pius IX, Pope, 214, 218

Plato, 125, 128, 187, 207, 235, 243, 422,
    430, 489n.16; Republic, 128
Pompadour, Madame de, 147
Ponsonby, Sarah, 38, 471n.23
Poor Laws Commission, 190, 508n.13
Poovey, Mary, 187
Pope-Hennessy, James, 221, 222, 223,
    230–31
pornography, 230–32
Potocki, Count, 227
Presbyterianism, 16, 19, 75
press, British, 299, 300; on Crimean War,
    300, 307–14, 317–18, 330, 336–37,
    345, 362, 365, 370, 378, 380, 381,
    400, 500n.31; on Florence, 317–18,
    380–81, 384
Price, Richard, 14, 469n.26
Priestley, Joseph, 14, 38, 469n.26
prostitution, 261, 290, 493n.18, 512n.6
public health, 176, 177, 190–92;
    international, 176, 200; reforms,
    190–92, 278, 337, 355, 375, 421;
    sanitation practices, 334–35, 339–41,
    374–84, 418. See also health care;
    hospitals
purges, 191, 340

Quakers, 21, 79, 208

Rachel, 145–46, 481n.13
Ragged Schools, 201, 261, 487n.23
Raglan, Lord, 302, 306–11, 315, 324,
    386, 388, 499n.12, 504n.40; death of,
    388
Rational Christians, 1, 14
Rawlinson, Mr. Robert, 374, 375, 377,
    416
Récamier, Juliette, 145, 147–48, 149, 440
Red Cross, 421, 462
Reeve, Henry, 180, 300, 317, 484n.21
Reeve, Hope Richardson, 180
reform, 7–8, 20, 22, 120, 174–77,
    190–91, 200, 208, 261, 431; army
    health care system, 355, 374–84,
    416–20, 424, 454, 503n.32; public
    health, 190–92, 278, 337, 355, 375,
    421; Sanitary Commission in the
    Crimea, 374–84, 406
Reform Act (1832), 18, 19, 469n.36
Reform Club, 378

Reid, Elizabeth, 200
Rembrandt van Rijn, 32, 33
Reni, Guido, 213, 470n.13, 489n.17
Renkioi, 378
Reynolds, Sir Joshua, 32–33
Ricardo, David, 143
Richardson, Helen, 180, 183–84
Richardson, Samuel, 46
Roberts, Elizabeth, 358–59, 367, 385,
    387–90, 399, 404, 408, 411, 413
Robinson, Robert, 338–39, 359, 379, 385,
    387, 399, 400, 403, 409
Roebuck committee, 374
Romantic movement, 41
Rome, 29, 211, 363; Florence in, 211–21
Rossetti, Christina, 121, 227
Rossetti, Dante Gabriel, 226, 227, 266
Rousseau, Jean-Jacques, 14, 17, 34, 178
Royal Academy, 33, 442
Royal Commission on the Sanitary State of
    the Army, 406–9, 416–20, 508n.5
Royal Society, 31, 124
Royle, Trevor, 347
Rubens, Peter Paul, 32, 33, 470n.13
Ruskin, Effie, 232, 296
Ruskin, John, 232, 495n.3
Russell, William, 304, 307–112, 370
Russia, 217; Crimean War, 297–313,
    498nn.2, 5
Russo-Turkish campaign (1828–29), 304

Sade, Marquis de, 230–31, 490n.46
Saint-Arnaud, 306, 309
St. John's House, 318, 319
Salisbury, Charlotte, 391, 392–94, 405,
    507n.31
Salisbury Infirmary, 195–96
Sand, George, 150–51, 187, 225,
    481n.22; Gabriel, 150
Sanitary Commission, 374–84, 406
Saxe-Coburgs, 121, 158–61, 171
science, 38, 120, 124–25, 191, 192,
    196–97
Scotland, 27, 31–32, 273, 470n.11
Scott, Walter, 46, 123
Scutari, 295, 296, 304, 309, 311, 322–413,
    414, 497–513; Barrack Hospital,
    322–52, 354–84, 389, 391, 398, 403,
    501nn.5, 49; bathing, 331, 382; "camp
    followers," 325; casualties, 333, 334,

335, 336, 371, 381, 418; closing of, 412;
    decline in mortality, 381, 383; disease
    and pestilence, 324, 327, 329, 333–36,
    339–41, 347, 371, 374–84, 399, 406–9,
    418, 510n.21, 512n.6; first aid and
    triage, 332; Florence's improvements in,
    337–52, 377, 381–84, 396–98;
    Florence's plans to go to, 313–22; food,
    326, 331, 341–43, 345, 376, 380,
    382–83, 396; frostbite, 347, 370, 371,
    372, 408; General Hospital, 323, 324,
    329, 332, 336, 337, 349, 359, 372, 377,
    378, 381, 502n.13; hostility of army
    medical personnel, 328–32, 340–47,
    372, 383; inebriation problems, 328,
    393; laundry, 325, 331, 334, 338, 341,
    382; nurses' quarters, 326–27; nurse
    tensions and insubordination, 316, 319,
    353–69, 505–7; orderlies, 349–50, 383,
    502n.15; poor conditions, 312–13,
    324–37, 416–20; recruiting nurses for,
    318–20; religious tensions among nurses,
    318–20, 355–69, 372–73, 398, 408–9,
    505–7; remittance scheme, 397–98;
    Sanitary and McNeill commissions,
    374–84, 406; sanitation issues, 324–25,
    331, 334–36, 339–41, 347, 349,
    374–84, 418; social classes of nurses,
    355–61; Stanley debacle, 361–69, 386,
    390, 394, 398, 506nn.13, 18, 21, 22,
    507nn.28–31, 513n.1; supply shortages
    and disappearances, 344–48, 374,
    393–94, 504n.38; surgery, 329–31, 333,
    349, 350, 372, 373, 502n.13; water,
    327–28, 384; wounds, 333, 341, 350,
    383
Seacole, Mary, 307, 496n.22, 500n.39,
    503n.18, 504n.38
Sellonites, 318, 319, 324
Sensi, Felicetta, 219
Sevastopol, 305–9, 314, 348, 376,
    386–87, 398, 499nn.12, 26
Sévigné, Madame de, 139
Seward, Anna, 38, 471n.23
Shaftesbury, Lady, 173, 174, 175
Shaftesbury, Lord, 22, 81, 173, 174–77,
    201, 261, 278, 432, 433, 435, 508n.13;
    Crimean War and, 374, 378; reform
    efforts, 175–77, 190, 374
Shakespeare, William, 180, 509n.8

Shaw Stewart, Jane, 387, 400, 401, 411, 509n.18
Sheffield, 9–10, 51
Shelley, Mary Godwin, 68, 113, 472nn.8, 33; *Frankenstein*, 477n.28
Shelley, Percy Bysshe, 68, 225, 472n.8, 490n.37; *The Cenci*, 489n.17
Shore, Mary Evans (Grandmother Shore), 2, 4–5, 10, 50–54, 61–63, 75–76, 83, 84, 106, 107, 170, 192, 262–63, 276, 280–82, 484n.17; death of, 280–82; relationship with daughter-in-law Fanny, 50–54, 496n.7
Shore, William, 5, 9–10, 50–54, 61, 62, 64, 169–70; death of, 62
Siddons, Sarah, 33, 471n.15
Sieveking, Amalie, 252
Sinclair, James, 47–51, 80
Sinope, 297, 299
Sismondi, Jean-Charles-Léonard de, 143–44
Sisters of Mercy, 318
slavery, 6, 13, 15, 20; trade, 20–23, 40. *See also* abolitionism
smallpox, 33
Smedley, John, 6, 7
Smith, Adam, 14, 143
Smith, Andrew, 406, 418
Smith, Benjamin, 15, 17, 25, 26, 28, 33–35, 37, 40, 42–45, 47, 50, 61–68, 70, 74, 83, 89–91, 98, 121, 168, 265, 470n.2, 473n.17; business and wealth, 59–61, 64, 67, 68, 69, 200; illegitimate children of, 64, 66–68, 70, 83, 89–90, 121, 470n.2, 475n.3, 478n.40, 480n.2, 487n.25; Anne Longden as common-law wife of, 64–68, 80; as a parent, 68, 89–90; Mai Shore affair, 61–63, 64, 70, 75
Smith, Edith, 179
Smith, Elizabeth, 15
Smith, Frances Coape, 3–4, 14, 19, 24–45, 52, 61, 65, 256; death of, 179; marriage and family life, 24–45; old age, 61, 179; as a parent, 33–39, 40, 48, 50–52, 61, 97
Smith, Frank, 428
Smith, Fred, 89, 91, 178–79
Smith, Frederic (Fritz), 26, 52, 60, 83, 472n.35

Smith, Jane Cooke, 61, 178–79
Smith, Joan, 83–84, 89, 209
Smith, Joseph, 15, 17
Smith, Julia, 19, 26, 30, 34, 41–44, 45, 47, 51–54, 59–61, 68, 69, 74, 83, 84, 90, 113, 120, 138, 166, 179, 200, 378, 451, 477n.32, 479n.16, 487n.22; childhood of, 34–37, 42–43; Florence and, 44, 98, 115, 123, 194, 353; sketches by, 86; as a spinster, 61, 151, 208
Smith, Louisa, 451, 452, 453
Smith, Mai Shore, 3, 4, 5, 9, 51–52, 61–64, 68–70, 72, 75, 84–86, 451, 473n.17, 477n.29, 493n.19; Embley Park and, 86, 451–52; Florence and, 69–70, 84, 89, 92, 98, 104, 106, 109–19, 123, 177–78, 261–67, 275, 276, 280, 353, 395, 403–4, 425, 437–39, 442; inheritance of, 69–70, 85–86, 170, 276, 451–52, 454–55; marriage and family life, 68–70, 76, 84–86, 89, 109, 114, 116–19; Fanny Nightingale and, 84–86, 109–10, 118, 255; at Scutari, 359, 395, 403–5, 413; Benjamin Smith affair, 61–63, 64, 70, 75
Smith, Martha (Patty), 26, 27, 30, 43, 44, 45, 48, 59, 60, 61, 65, 83, 113, 138, 144, 233, 278, 469n.31, 470n.2, 471nn.26, 27; childhood of, 30, 33–45; decline into hypochondria and depression, 40, 47, 205; as a spinster, 61, 151, 208
Smith, Martha Adams, 17
Smith, Octavius, 25, 26, 34, 45, 60–61, 69, 74, 83–84, 89, 91, 111, 168, 178–79, 265, 468n.21, 470n.11, 494n.21
Smith, Sam, 3, 4, 26, 34, 45, 61, 68–70, 75, 84–86, 121, 168, 264–66, 283, 314, 320–21, 395–97, 407, 426, 437, 438, 495n.39; financial affairs, 84–86, 170, 266, 454–55; inheritance of, 69–70, 85–86, 170, 276, 451–52, 454–55; marriage and family life, 68–70, 76, 84–86, 89, 109, 116–19
Smith, Samuel, 15
Smith, Samuel II, 15, 17, 18–19, 24, 25
Smith, Shore, 76, 84, 85, 86, 115–19,

200, 451–56; birth of, 116; childhood
of, 116–19, 264; death of, 464;
Florence and, 116–19, 264–67, 394–95
Smith, William, 3, 12–23, 24–45, 47, 61,
64, 71, 74, 468nn.22–25, 470nn.2, 11,
13, 471nn.17, 27, 32, 472nn.2, 4;
antislavery campaign, 20–23, 45; art
collection of, 32–33, 59, 60, 86,
470n.13; childhood of, 17–18; death of,
23, 61; financial problems, 32, 47, 49,
50, 59–61, 80, 170; marriage and
family life, 24–45; as a parent, 33–39,
48–49, 64–65, 69; political life, 12–14,
19–23, 31–32, 135–36, 159, 177
Smith, William (of Antigua), 15, 17
Smith, William Adams (Adams), 26,
34–36, 59–60, 64, 74, 83, 470n.2,
475n.16
Smyrna, 366, 378
Snow, Dr. John, 290, 335
Somerville, Mary, 178
Soyer, Alexis, 378–80, 383, 385, 388–89,
395, 440, 509nn.5, 9
Spain, 139
spinsterhood, 61, 187, 206–9
Stafford, Augustus, 324, 330, 331,
337–38, 416
Stanley, Lord, 423, 510n.22
Stanley, Mary, 361–69, 386, 390, 394,
398, 500n.39, 505n.1, 506nn.18, 21,
22, 507nn.28–31, 510n.30, 513n.1
Stanton, Elizabeth Cady, 208
statistics, medical, 376, 417–18, 420,
494n.20
steamships, 303, 307, 310, 322, 388, 389
Steell, Sir John, 513n.3
Sterling, Colonel Anthony, 347, 503n.31
Stewart, Dugald, 128
Storks, General, 394, 397, 501n.5
Stovin, Sir Frederick, 167
Stowe, Harriet Beecher, 208
Strachey, Lytton, 186–87, 362, 432
Stratford de Redcliffe, Lady, 347, 364,
365–67, 404–5, 511n.43
Stratford de Redcliffe, Lord, 315, 323,
337, 344, 364, 365, 498n.4, 501n.3,
502n.9
Sudbury, 19–20, 469n.36
Sugar Loaf, 15–16, 18, 21
Sussex, Duke of, 172

Sutherland, Duke and Duchess of, 378
Sutherland, John, 374–78, 384, 386, 416,
420, 423, 441, 445, 508n.14
Swanton, Louise, 148–49
Swinburne, Algernon, 230, 231, 232
Switzerland, 54, 138; Nightingale family
in, 143–44
syphilis, 512n.5

T. G., 378–79, 380, 385
Tapton, 10, 11, 62, 69, 71–72, 75, 76, 91,
170, 262, 276, 280
Taylor, Emily, 122–23
Taylor, Frances Margaret, 343–44
telegraph, electric, 307, 499n.22
Ten Hour Work Day Bill, 22, 175–77
Tennyson, Alfred, Lord, 223, 225, 226
Teresa of Avila, St., 133, 203, 415
Terrot, Sarah Anne, 324–28, 333, 342,
347, 348, 356, 372, 501nn.47, 49,
505n.8
textile mill system, 6–8, 467n.15
Thackeray, William, 148, 425, 480n.7;
Vanity Fair, 50
Therapia, 389
Thoreau, Henry David, 225
Thornton, Henry, 18, 19
Thornton, Marianne, 40–41
Thornton family, 18, 38, 40
Times, 300, 304, 308, 308, 311–14, 320,
321, 336–37, 345, 365, 370, 378, 400,
503n.36
Tocqueville, Alexis de, 148, 225
Tollett, Ellen, 397
Tollett family, 91, 474n.11, 476n.20
Tory party, 135, 159, 169, 173, 218, 226,
298, 299
Tractarians, 319
Transcendentalism, 266
Travers, Joseph, 59
Trinity College, Cambridge, 34, 223, 224,
265, 267
Trollope, Anthony, 148, 425
Trollope, Frances, 148
Trout, 236–40, 252, 491n.4
Tulloch, Col. Alexander, 374–76, 386,
406, 416, 508n.14, 511n.46
Turgenev, Ivan, 148
Turkey, 297; Crimean War and, 296,
297–413, 497–513. See also Scutari

Turner, Eleanor Clarke, 146
Turner, Frewen, 146
typhus, 304, 383, 509n.5

Unitarian Act of 1812, 13
Unitarianism, 1, 14, 16, 18, 19, 21–23,
  30, 38, 48–50, 75, 79, 98–99, 133,
  162, 194, 218, 292, 466n.4, 485n.36;
  education and, 98–99, 121
United States, 6, 7, 8, 15–16, 65–67, 194,
  482n.15; Civil War, 421, 467n.12;
  Revolution, 13, 16

Varna, 304–7, 499n.19
Varna fever, 304, 335
Verney, Edmund, 454, 455, 461–63
Verney, Elizabeth Hope, 454, 514n.21
Verney, Emily, 454, 462
Verney, Frederick, 454, 461, 462
Verney, George, 454, 462
Verney, Sir Harry, 155, 454–62, 496n.14;
  death of, 463; financial affairs, 456;
  Florence and, 455, 457–58, 462, 463;
  marriage to Parthe, 454–58, 463
Verney, Margaret, 10, 63, 70, 125, 461,
  462, 463
Verney, Parthenope Nightingale, 2, 11, 44,
  49, 493nn.13, 14, 506n.22; arthritis,
  257, 461; birth of, 55–57; character of,
  56, 105, 159, 203, 257–58, 294;
  childhood of, 55–58, 73–74, 77–80,
  86, 87–114, 486n.4; Continental tour
  (1837–39), 136–52; Crimean War and,
  316–17, 334, 358, 386, 389, 390, 397,
  402; death of, 430, 461–62; death of
  her mother, 453–54; dependence on
  Florence, and resentment of her work,
  195–96, 202–5, 221, 254–77, 283,
  294–95; drawings by, 72, 88, 115, 138,
  251, 415; education of, 93–112,
  119–30, 478n.11; at Embley Park,
  77–78; Florence's "character" of,
  257–58; Florence's reclusive years and,
  424, 431, 436; "hysteria" of, 257–60,
  268, 272–74; ill health of, 55–57, 73,
  97, 131–32, 163, 221, 257–60,
  267–68, 271–74, 430, 451, 458, 461;
  lack of male interest in, 205, 259;
  marriage of, 454–58, 463; physical
  appearance, 154–57, 259, 455;
  relationship with her father, 130;
  relationship with Florence, 100–103,
  111–14, 115–33, 163, 179, 183, 197,
  257–75, 291, 294–96, 353, 428, 445,
  457–61, 479n.24; relationship with her
  mother, 113, 131, 255, 257, 268,
  273–74, 450–51; rivalry with Florence,
  129–31, 155, 163, 216, 234–35,
  258–60, 274–75, 458; social climbing
  of, 105, 159, 163, 203, 259; Stone Edge,
  460; teenage years, 115–34, 135–52; as
  a writer, 430, 459–61
Viardot, Pauline García, 140
Vicinus, Martha, 187
Victoria, Queen of England, 120–21,
  158–61, 171, 174, 175, 272, 273, 298,
  299, 482nn.8, 14, 483n.26; Crimean
  War and, 345–46, 397, 415, 510n.28;
  Florence and, 346, 347, 401, 415–16,
  435, 444–45; marriage of, 121,
  158–61
Victorian era, 8, 118, 158–61, 174, 334;
  bowel obsession, 102; childrearing
  practices, 56–58, 97–114, 118;
  education, 119–20, 200–202; female
  friendships and shared beds, 149,
  187–88; health care, 190–92;
  sexuality, 38, 45, 186–89, 223–24,
  230–32, 249; society, 8, 44–45, 84,
  82, 103, 149, 166, 173–77, 191, 208,
  270, 299, 480n.7, 483n.26, 493n.18;
  women and marriage, 208, 244, 249,
  270–73
Voltaire, 14

Wales, 27, 38, 60
Walker, Hannah, 64, 67
Walker, Thomas, 10
Wallachia, 297
War Office, 346, 416, 440, 511n.45;
  reforms, 337, 405–9, 416–20
Waterloo, 298, 299, 300, 302
Waverley Abbey, 77, 84, 162–63, 179–84,
  262, 263, 474n.2
Weare, Miss, 399, 409
Webb, 450, 451
Wedgwood, Josiah, 14, 38, 476n.21
Wedgwood, Richard, 38

Wedgwood family, 14, 37, 38, 79, 467n.14, 474n.11
Weld, Angelina Grimké, 208
Wellington, Duke of, 78, 299, 302, 303
West Indies, 15, 20, 21
wet nurses, 56–58, 117, 472n.9, 473n.13, 478n.5
Wheeler, Elizabeth, 356, 501n.5
Whig party, 31, 159, 173, 218, 298, 419
White, William, 164, 157
Whitman, Walt, 225, 231
Wilberforce, William, 21–23, 30, 38, 40, 79, 176, 177, 468n.24, 469n.41, 470nn.41, 42
Wilde, Oscar, 187, 223, 230
Williams, Helen Maria, 14, 43
Williams, Margaret Hay, 462
Wilton, 217, 221, 474n.2, 489n.24
Windsor Castle, 175
wine, 328, 342, 393, 503n.34
Wollstonecraft, Mary, 14, 34, 43, 44, 68, 471n.33, 474nn.33, 34; Florence and, 44–45
women, 8–9; artists, 165–66, 483n.28; education for, 120–21, 191, 200–202; feminism, 14, 43–45, 120, 208, 248, 432; health care for, 191, 286–89; in health care profession, 191–92, 277–78, 353–69; hysteria in, 272–73, 288; marriage and motherhood, 208–9, 270; nurses at Scutari, 353–69; in work force, 8–9, 208, 278, 355
Woodham-Smith, Cecil, 186, 187, 218, 266, 479n.24, 481n.23
Wordsworth, William, 39, 97, 162, 471n.23
Woronzov, Countess Catherine, 217, 314
Wreford, Mr., 344, 400, 416

Young, D. A. B., 428

Zoffany, John, 154